THE MIDDLE EAST

THE MIDDLE EAST

A Political and Economic Survey

FIFTH EDITION

Edited by
PETER MANSFIELD

Oxford New York Toronto Melbourne
OXFORD UNIVERSITY PRESS
1980

Oxford University Press, Walton Street, Oxford, OX2 6DP
OXFORD LONDON GLASGOW
NEW YORK TORONTO MELBOURNE WELLINGTON
KUALA LUMPUR SINGAPORE JAKARTA HONG KONG TORONTO
DELHI BOMBAY CALCUTTA MADRAS KARACHI
NAIROBI DAR ES SALAAM CAPE TOWN

First three editions
edited by
SIR READER BULLARD
1950, 1954, 1958
Fourth Edition 1973
Fifth Edition 1980

British Library Cataloguing in Publication Data

The Middle East. — New ed.
1. Near East — Social conditions
I. Title II. Mansfield, Peter
309.1'56 HN656.A8 79-23699

ISBN 0-19-215851-1

Printed in Great Britain by Lowe & Brydone (Printers) Ltd.,
Thetford, Norfolk.

CONTENTS

PREFACE TO FIFTH EDITION

Since the publication of the Fourth Edition of the *Survey* early in 1973 the Middle East has been profoundly affected by several major events: the October 1973 War, the quadrupling of oil prices in the same year, President Sadat's peace initiative of 1977 leading to the Camp David agreements of 1978 and the Treaty of Washington of 1979, and finally by the Iranian Revolution. The Soviet Union has suffered a severe setback in Egypt while the US has for the first time undertaken a direct role in the search for a Middle East peace settlement although it cannot be assumed that Soviet involvement in the Middle East will be less than that of the US in the future. The energy crisis has accentuated the interest of the whole world in the Middle East region.

For reasons of space the Turkey section has been omitted from this Edition. This is to be regretted although it is true that at present Turkish affairs are only marginally related to those of the Middle East.

The Editor would like to acknowledge the invaluable assistance of the Economist Intelligence Unit whose Quarterly Economic Reports have provided much of the material for the updating of the economic sections and for the statistical tables. He would also like to thank Dr. Derek Hopwood of the Middle East Centre at St. Antony's College, Oxford, for his help in revising the Reading List.

NOTE ON TRANSLITERATION

In general the transliteration of previous editions has been retained and no attempt has been made to introduce a scientific system. Wherever possible, and sometimes at variance with earlier editions (cp. Esfahan/Isfahan), the most familiar Anglo-American spelling of certain proper names has been used, e.g. Nasser, Kassem, etc.

CURRENCY EXCHANGE RATES

Early October 1979

Bahrain	Bahraini dinar	£ = BD 0·83488	$ = BD 0·37975
Egypt	Egyptian pound	£ = £E 1·5045	$ = £E 0·69745
Iran	Iranian rial	n.a.	n.a.
Iraq	Iraqi dinar	£ = ID 0·6490	$ = ID 0.2958
Israel	Israeli pound	£ = £I 63·30	$ = £I 27·10
Jordan	Jordanian dinar	£ = JD 0·644	$ = JD 0·2935
Kuwait	Kuwaiti dinar	£ = KD 0·60679	$ = KD 0·27600
Lebanon	Lebanese pound	£ = £Leb 7·200	$ = £Leb 3·2850
Oman	Saidi rial	£ = RS 0·76	$ = RS 0·3457
Qatar	Qatar rial	£ = QR 8·231	$ = QR 3·744
Saudi Arabia	Saudi rial	£ = SR 7·3650	$ = SR 3·3500
Sudan	Sudanese pound	£ = £S 1·096	$ = £S 0·50
Syria	Syrian pound	£ = £Syr 8·6121	$ = £Syr 3·9256
UAE	UAE dirham	£ = Dh 8·3323	$ = Dh 3·7900
Yemen (Aden)	South Yemen dinar	£ = SYD 0·75079	$ = SYD 0·3415
Yemen (Sanaa)	Yemeni rial	£ = YR 10·025	$ = YR 4·56

CONVERSION FACTORS

1 metric ton= 0.984206 long tons
1 barrel (petroleum)= 35 Imperial gallons
≑1/7th ton
1 hectare= 2.471 acres
1 feddan = 1.038 acres
(Egypt and the Sudan)

List of Abbreviations*

AIOC	Anglo-Iranian Oil Co.
Aramco	Arabian American Oil Co.
BP	The British Petroleum Co.
Bapco	Bahrain Petroleum Co.
BPC	Basrah Petroleum Co.
FAO	Food and Agriculture Organization
Hurewitz	J. C. Hurewitz, *Diplomacy in the Near and Middle East: a Documentary Record, 1535–1956*. New York, 1956.
IBRD	International Bank for Reconstruction and Development.
ICA	International Co-operation Administration.
IDA	International Development Association.
IMF	International Monetary Fund.
IPC	Iraq Petroleum Co.
KOC	Kuwait Oil Co.
NIOC	National Iranian Oil Co.
OAPEC	Organization of Arab Petroleum Exporting Countries.
OPEC	Organization of Petroleum Exporting Countries.
QPC	Qatar Petroleum Co.
SDR	Special Drawing Right.
Tapline	Trans-Arabian Pipeline Co.
UNEF	U.N. Emergency Force.
UNRWA	U.N. Relief and Works Agency for Palestine Refugees.

* Excluding commonly used abbreviations for U.N. agencies.

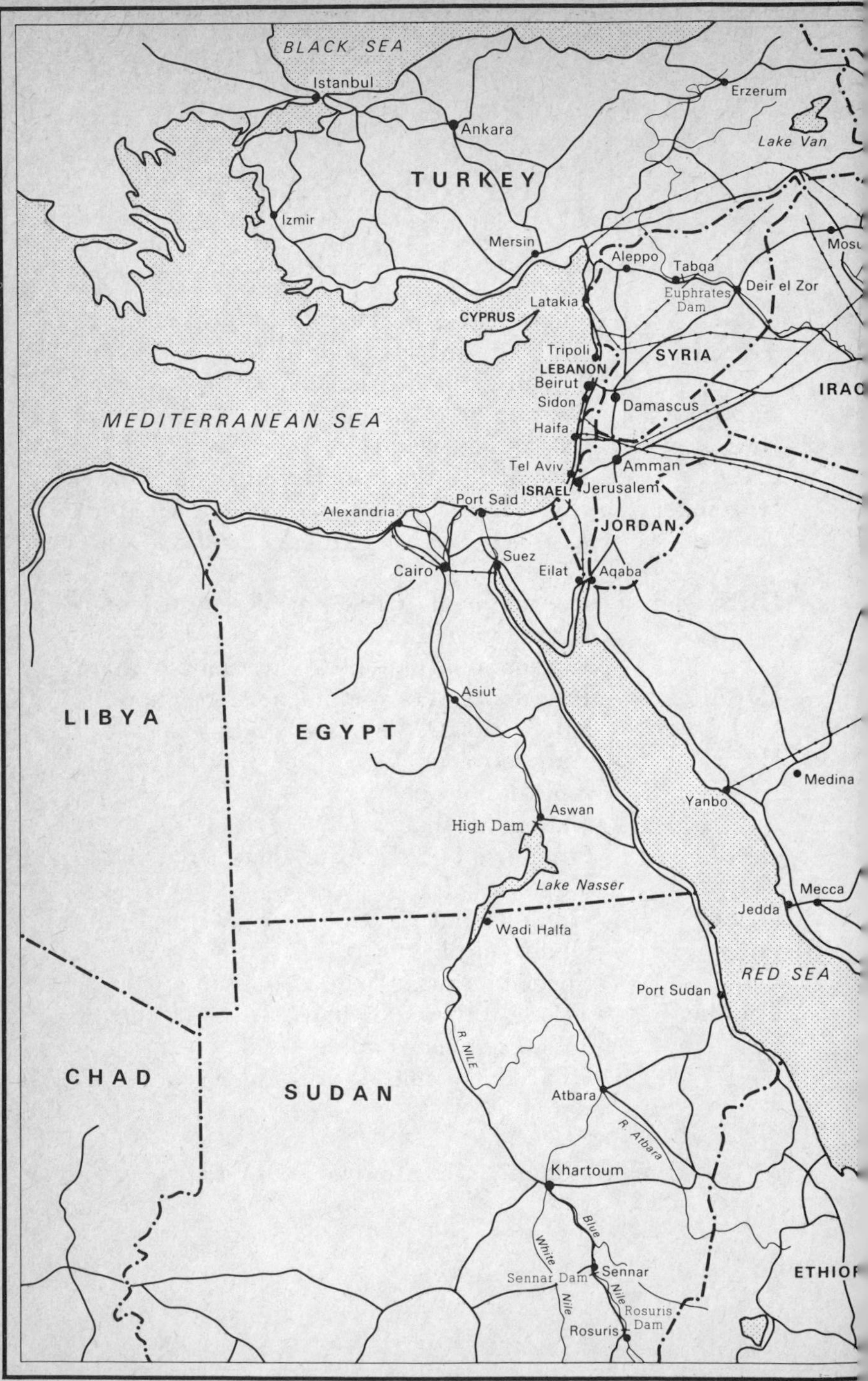
BLACK SEA
Istanbul
Ankara
Erzerum
Lake Van
TURKEY
Izmir
Mersin
Mosu
Aleppo
Tabqa
Euphrates Dam
Deir el Zor
Latakia
CYPRUS
Tripoli
LEBANON
SYRIA
Beirut
Sidon
Damascus
IRAC
MEDITERRANEAN SEA
Haifa
Tel Aviv
Amman
ISRAEL
Jerusalem
Port Said
Alexandria
JORDAN
Suez
Cairo
Eilat
Aqaba
Asiut
LIBYA
EGYPT
Medina
Yanbo
Aswan
High Dam
Lake Nasser
Mecca
Jedda
Wadi Halfa
RED SEA
Port Sudan
R. NILE
CHAD
SUDAN
Atbara
R. Atbara
Khartoum
Blue
White
Sennar
Sennar Dam
Nile
Nile
Rosuris Dam
Rosuris
ETHIOI

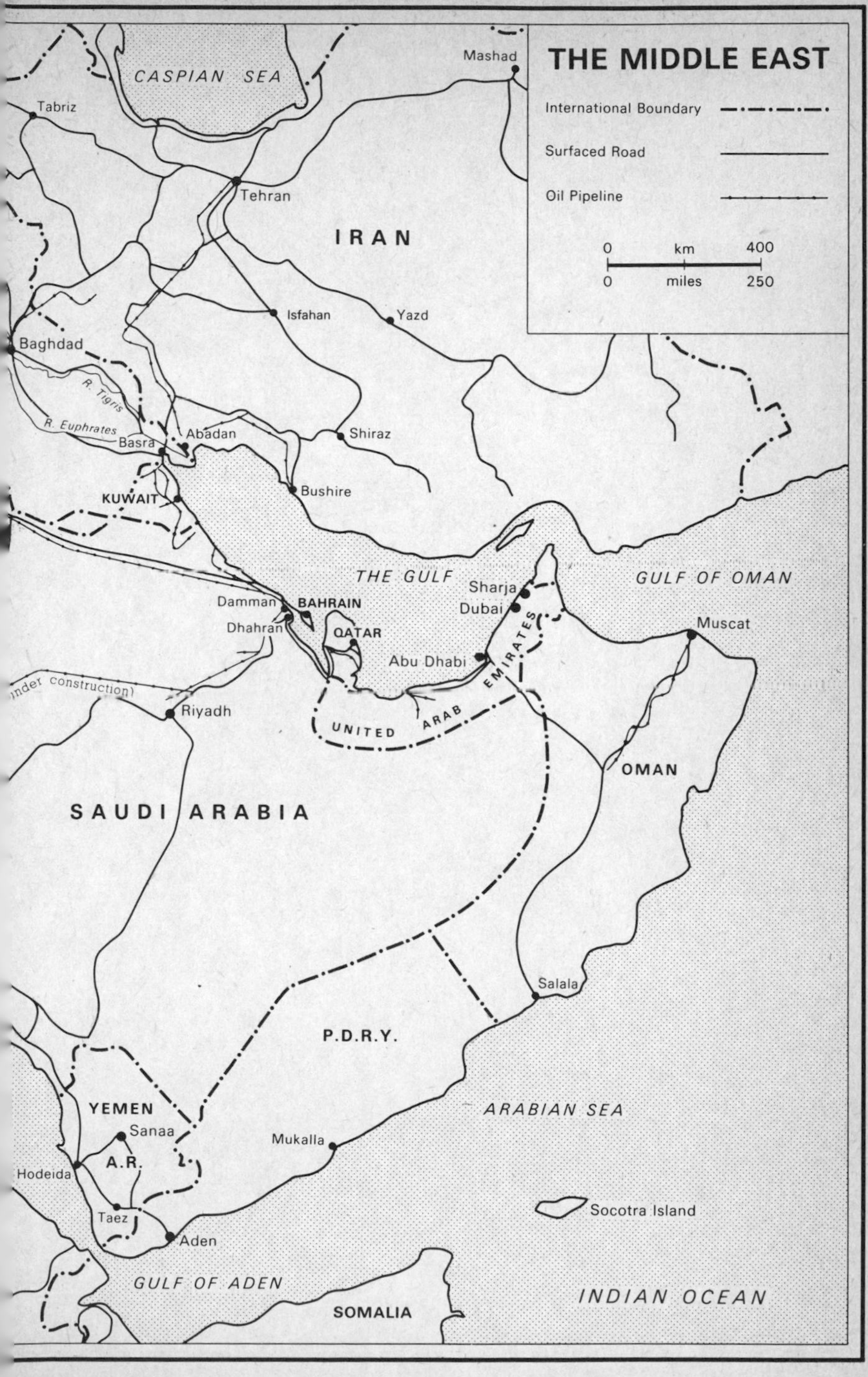
THE MIDDLE EAST
International Boundary
Surfaced Road
Oil Pipeline
0 km 400
0 miles 250
CASPIAN SEA
Mashad
Tabriz
Tehran
IRAN
Isfahan
Yazd
Baghdad
R. Tigris
R. Euphrates
Basra
Abadan
Shiraz
KUWAIT
Bushire
THE GULF
GULF OF OMAN
Sharja
Dubai
Damman
BAHRAIN
Dhahran
QATAR
Abu Dhabi
Muscat
UNITED ARAB EMIRATES
under construction)
Riyadh
OMAN
SAUDI ARABIA
Salala
P.D.R.Y.
YEMEN
Sanaa
A.R.
ARABIAN SEA
Mukalla
Hodeida
Taez
Aden
Socotra Island
GULF OF ADEN
INDIAN OCEAN
SOMALIA

I

A. INTRODUCTION

THE REGION DEFINED

Before the First World War it was customary to distinguish between the Near East, comprising Greece, Bulgaria, Turkey, the Levant, and Egypt; and the Middle East: Arabia, Mesopotamia, the Persian Gulf, Iran, and Afghanistan. It then gradually became the practice to use the term 'Middle East' to cover both those areas, less Greece and Bulgaria on the west and Afghanistan on the east, but adding the Sudan and sometimes Libya, and even other North African states. Libya, with Morocco, Algeria, and Tunisia, is dealt with in another volume.[1] The states and territories dealt with in the present survey are: the Arabian Peninsula (comprising Saudi Arabia, the Yemen Republic, the People's Democratic Republic of Yemen, Kuwait, Bahrain, Qatar, the United Arab Emirates, and Oman), Egypt, Iraq, Israel, the Hashimite Kingdom of Jordan, Lebanon, Iran, the Sudan and Syria. Their combined area is about 3,425,000 square miles.

Geography, Climate, and Vegetation[2]

Thus defined, the Middle East consists structurally of (1) a geologically ancient and stable platform underlying north-east Africa and the Arabian Peninsula, rifted to form the Gulf of Aden; (2) a more recent and highly disturbed system of folded mountains extending from the Balkans through Turkey and Iran; (3) an intermediate zone comprising the Jabal Akhdhar of Cyrenaica, Israel, Lebanon, Syria, Iraq, and the highlands of Oman.

Climatically the whole of the Middle East (except for two small regions, one in the extreme north and the other in the extreme south) has a strongly marked Mediterranean rhythm

[1] *North West Africa*, ed. Wilfred Knapp (London, 1977).

[2] This section is based on W.B. Fisher, *The Middle East: a Physical, Social, and Regional Geography* (London, 1950), pt. I, p. 432.

of summer drought and winter rain. The cause of the latter is the inflow of maritime air from the west, which is excluded during the summer by higher pressures in the western Mediterranean. The regions with the highest winter rainfall are those which combine a length of westward-facing coastline with elevated uplands, for example, Lebanon and Israel, western Asia Minor, the Jabal Akhdhar of Cyrenaica. Where these features are absent, as in Egypt and northern Sudan and the greater part of the Arabian Peninsula, winter rainfall is scanty or completely lacking in some years, and desert conditions obtain. Asia Minor, Armenia, and much of Iran are exposed to extremely low winter temperatures owing to their proximity to the Eurasian land mass; farther south, the seas have a temperate effect, but severe cold may be experienced in the Arabian interior. In summer the most intense heat occurs in lower Iraq and the interior of Arabia, but living conditions are worst on the coasts of the Gulf and the Red Sea owing to their high degree of humidity, which also affects the Mediterranean coast. The regions outside the scope of the Mediterranean climatic rhythm are the Black Sea coast of Turkey, which receives rain throughout the year; the southern Sudan and south-west Arabia (the Yemen), where a substantial summer rainfall alternates with a dry winter; and Dhufar, in Oman, which is affected by the monsoon.

In the wetter parts of the Mediterranean coastland and on the lower flanks of the neighbouring mountain ranges – in western Asia Minor, western Syria, Lebanon, Israel, and Cyprus – there is the characteristic Mediterranean cultivation of cereals, vines, olives, and fruit trees. Farther east, where the rainfall is less and the seasonal variation of temperature greater, are steppes where grass is luxuriant in the short spring but largely disappears during the long dry summer – the home of pastoral nomadism. Sheep and goats give place to the hardier camel as the steppe passes into the true desert of Sinai, Egypt, and large parts of the Arabian Peninsula; but the alluvial lowlands of the great rivers provide a striking contrast, with their intensive irrigated cultivation and the groves of date-palms. The slopes of the higher mountains were covered in prehistoric times with woodland, but have been largely deforested during the past 5,000 years. The uplands of south-western

Arabia have a vegetation reminiscent of that of the African region on the opposite side of the Red Sea.

Resources

The Middle East supports 100–120 million people. It is estimated that out of the total area of some 3,425,000 square miles, only about 5 or 6 per cent is at present under cultivation, although the cultivable area is capable of considerable expansion. The Middle East consists, in fact, of considerable expanses of virtually unpopulated land, interspersed with a few areas of relatively dense – and in one area, Egypt, of extremely dense – population. The finding of petroleum, of which immense reserves have been discovered in the region within the last sixty years, is having an increasing effect on the standard of living; it has already secured the region a prominent place in world interest.

Other important minerals which are now being extracted in the region include iron, phosphates, and, to a lesser extent, copper, manganese, coal, and salt. There are also large areas of the Egyptian, Syrian, and Arabian Deserts which have yet to be intensively surveyed and may well prove to be rich in minerals. Large deposits of titanium, an important structural metal element, were discovered in Egypt's Eastern Desert in 1971.

In the long term much of the region's economic future depends upon the full development of all the agricultural and hydro-electric resources provided by the two great river systems of the Nile and Tigris-Euphrates. For the latter it is partly a question of restoring and surpassing the high productivity of agriculture of classical Mesopotamia. The historical evidence of Yemen's former prosperity is also proof of that country's potential. The extent of underground water resources in the Egyptian and Arabian Deserts has yet to be fully determined but considerable new reclamation in both areas may be possible. (Egypt's New Valley scheme to extend the five main oases of the Western Desert to form a single stretch of cultivated land roughly parallel to the Nile Valley is the most important project of this kind which is being undertaken at present.) Of all Middle Eastern countries Sudan is probably the one with the greatest untapped agricultural resources.

International Importance

From at least the foundation of the Roman Empire the position of the Middle East, lying as it does across the main arteries of transport between Europe and Southern and Eastern Asia, has been of very great significance commercially. Constant efforts have been made by countries both within and without the Middle East to control and thereby to profit by, or to prevent others from profiting by, the commerce which passes through the area.

At the end of the fifteenth century the discovery of the route round the Cape of Good Hope somewhat reduced the importance of the area to commerce. Its position was largely restored, and in some respects enhanced, with the opening of the Suez Canal in 1869.

The discovery of immense reserves of oil in the states around the Gulf in the first half of the twentieth century and their accelerated development in the second half enhanced the commercial importance of the whole area. Despite the discovery of other important sources of oil (e.g. Alaska, Nigeria, the North Sea, and Mexico) and the development of alternative sources of energy (such as nuclear power) the demand for Middle East oil has steadily increased and pipelines to the Mediterranean coast from the oil fields as well as the Suez Canal have had to be utilized to the limit of their capacity to meet existing demand. This situation seems likely to continue. The reduction in the importance of the Suez Canal as an oil route resulting from the building of supertankers to sail around the Cape of Good Hope has been partly offset by the new Suez-Alexandria pipeline and the current expansion of the Canal. For the foreseeable future Middle East oil will be the principal source of supply for Western Europe states and Western Europe will be the principal market for Middle East oil.

While the Cold War was at its height in the decade following the Second World War, the Western Powers continued to attach great importance to the Middle East as a site for strategic bases within range of the southern borders of the Soviet Union. This importance was greatly reduced as the Cold War receded and nationalist sentiment in the Middle East states brought about by 1971 the liquidation of all Western military bases in the area except for those in Turkey and Cyprus. With the final withdrawal of the French and British military presence from the area only the United States and the Soviet Union among the Great Powers retained a direct strategic interest which was enhanced by their indirect involvement in the Arab-Israeli struggle in which the United States supported Israel and the Soviet Union the Arabs. In the 1970s the huge increase in the importance of the Middle East oil industry to the world economy gave the region significance of a new dimension. For the two superpowers it became a matter of vital interest, even while pursuing the aims of *détente*, to prevent the other from dominating the oil-producing regions.

HISTORY AND POLITICS

The Middle East, which in recent times has appeared as a meeting-ground between the civilizations of the West and the East, was to its inhabitants for many millennia the civilized world itself. Of the surviving world religions three, Judaism, Christianity, and Islam, have their geographical sources in the Middle East. Moreover, the technical and scientific mastery acquired by the West is the outcome of a development intiated in the Middle East some three or four thousand years ago. Mathematics and the sciences as known today have grown directly from the work of Greek thinkers, who themselves drew on Egyptian and Babylonian traditions, and whose work was carried on and transmitted by the Arabs.

The predominant language of the region is Arabic, a Semitic language which has invaded and enriched the widely-spoken Persian and Turkish languages. The predominant religion is Islam, but there are various Christian communities, which now as in the past play a part in the public life of the Middle East out of proportion to their numbers: these are mostly descended from Christians who adopted the faith in the early centuries of Christianity and are not modern converts, unless from one Christian sect to another.[3]

[3]For an account of the foundation of Islam, and of sects and minorities, see below, pp. 43–50.

The Arab Conquests

The early history of Islam is that of the Arab conquests. Mohammed, the prophet of Islam, himself united the Hejaz and laid the foundation for the unification of Arabia. After his death, in AD 632, the Arab-speaking Moslems poured in successive waves into the empires of Iran and Byzantium. They swept over Iran into Central Asia and India, over Syria, Egypt, North Africa, and Spain, and finally into France, where in 732 they were defeated by the Franks under Charles Martel, near Poitiers.

On the death of Mohammed a group of his followers elected a successor (*khalifa*, hence Caliph), who ruled from Medina. Factions soon appeared, however, and of the first four Caliphs (632–61) only the first died a natural death: the others, who included Ali, the Prophet's male next of kin, were all murdered. In 661 a member of the Mecca family of Umayya secured the Caliphate and so became the first of the Umayyad dynasty which ruled from Syria till 750. Meanwhile, however, a Shii[4] minority had given their support to Hussein, the son of Ali. Hussein was killed in a rising at Karbala in 680, but sporadic movements of revolt by the Shiis continued.

The Umayyads were overthrown and replaced by a new dynasty, the Abbasids (750–1258), who established themselves in Iraq and in 762 founded Baghdad as their new capital. Under the Abbasids, the most famous of whom was Harun al-Rashid (786–809), the Moslem Empire achieved great prosperity and cultural brilliance, and in that empire the Iranians played an important part. Before 850 however the Abbasid Caliphs had lost their personal power to semi-independent provincial governors, often Turkish mercenaries converted to Islam, and remained no more than titular lords of the Empire. Towards the middle of the eleventh century Iran was overrun by Seljuq Turks, converts to Islam from Central Asia, who entered Baghdad in 1055 and eventually established an empire extending from India to the Aegean. In the tenth century rival caliphates were proclaimed by the Fatimid dynasty, ruling in Egypt and North Africa (and at times Syria), and by the survivors of the Umayyad dynasty, ruling in Spain. It is to be remembered that Moslem rule lasted in parts of

[4]See below, p. 46.

Spain until 1492, a period of some 750 years, and for about half that time it extended to the greater part of the Peninsula; and that for a considerable period Moslem Spain was one of the two most highly civilized countries of Europe, the other being Byzantium.

The Turks

Through the Arabic language and the Islamic religion the Arabs gave a homogeneous basis to the vast area of their conquests. It was left to a Central Asiatic people, the Turks, to build a unified political system on this basis. The Turks entered the Islamic world as, successively, slaves, mercenaries, condottieri, and adventurers, and eventually they became its rulers. The Mongol invasion which put an end to the Abbasid Caliphate in Baghdad (1258) broke up the Seljuq Sultanate in Asia Minor; but from its ruins the Turkish dynasty of Osmanli (Ottoman) Turks emerged in north-west Asia Minor and gradually extended its influence into the Balkans. Ottoman expansion was crowned by the capture of Constantinople in 1453, which brought to an end the Roman Empire of the East. By the Ottoman annexation of the Mameluke[5] Sultanate of Egypt, Palestine, and Syria, virtually the whole of Sunni Islam (except India) came to be united against Iran, which had itself been reunited about 1500 under a Shii dynasty, the Safavids. For 200 years the Ottoman and Iranian Empires contended for the possession of Iraq, the population of which was mixed Sunni and Shii, and which finally fell to the Ottoman Empire.

The Crusades

The struggle between Christian Europe and Islam falls naturally into two periods. The first, which lasted 1,000 years, ending with the Turkish defeat by John Sobieski of Poland at Vienna in 1683, was on the whole favourable to Islam. At the end of the period Islam emerged in full control of the eastern Mediterranean, south-eastern Europe, and North Africa, although it was ousted from Sicily in 1090 and from Spain in 1492. In the second period, from 1683 onwards, Islam was

[5] *mamluk*, a slave. The 'Mamelukes' of Egypt were a slave corps from which the Sultans themselves came to be elected.

gradually forced to retreat, and from 1815 to modern times its countries have been to a greater or lesser extent dominated by the West.

Western Christendom had been menaced by Islam from the time of its first expansion, but with the turning of the tide in Spain and Sicily in the course of the eleventh century and the rise of the Seljuqs in the Levant, the West was free to embark upon the first of the Crusades, which were designed to secure an 'open door' to the Holy Land. The attempt failed, in spite of the establishment of Latin principalities in Syria and Palestine, the most important of which was the Kingdom of Jerusalem (1100–87); final defeat came in 1291. Nevertheless the Crusades created new commercial relations between East and West; they also reinforced the knowledge of Islamic arts and sciences (such as it was) already acquired in Christendom through Italy, Sicily, and Spain.

The Ottoman Empire

Ottoman rule was a military-religious autocracy of the Islamic pattern centred on a Sultan-Caliph[6] whose office was hereditary in the house of Osman (Othman). The non-Moslem subjects of the Empire, predominantly Christian, were organized in *millets* or religious minority communities, each of which had internal autonomy under an ecclesiastical functionary with temporal powers in matters of personal status and enjoyed a considerable individual and communal freedom. This however was offset by the periodical levy of Christian youths for service as *janissaries* (*yeny chery*, or new troops), which were for long the shock troops of the Ottoman army. Some of these conscripts manned the Sultan's court, and the most promising were trained to run the administration. During the Ottoman Empire's period of decay it became tyrannical, arbitrary, and inefficient, while the janissaries became increasingly rebellious. The massacre of the janissaries in 1826 by Sultan Mahmud II (1808–39) enabled him to pursue the modernization of the army envisaged by Selim III (1789–1807), and gained a century's respite for the Empire. At its zenith the

[6]The title of Caliph began to be used by the Ottoman Sultans in the eighteenth century. It became in the nineteenth century a device for persuading the Powers that the Sultan's spiritual status was analogous to that of Pope or Patriarch, so that he could claim the spiritual allegiance of Moslems outside the Ottoman dominions.

Ottoman Empire ranked with the greatest of Western Powers. France quickly entered into relations with the Sublime Porte,[7] as the Ottoman Government was called, and in 1535 obtained from the Sultan the first formal Capitulations.[8] In 1553 an English traveller to Aleppo obtained from the Sultan a 'safe-conduct or privilege' granting him the same privileges as those enjoyed by the French and the Venetians. This led to the founding of the Levant Company in 1581. The English merchants were seeking to eliminate the middlemen and to reach the sources of supply of oriental wares. They tried two routes through Russia and a third through Syria and the Gulf, but finally adopted as the cheapest the long sea route round the Cape. They had first to deal with the Portuguese, who, although officially at peace with England, were trying to establish in the East by force of arms a monopoly of trade such as the Spaniards claimed in the West. The pretended monopoly was destroyed when the newly-founded East India Company, at the request of the Shah of Iran, helped the Iranians to eject the Portuguese from the island of Hormuz, in the Gulf. In the wars with Holland and France the Gulf was frequently the scene of hostilities which in the end resulted in British predominance. The British had also to contend with the Arab pirates, whose power was only broken, by the British and British-Indian navies, in the nineteenth century.

As a trade route, and as a line of defence for India and British communications with the East, the Gulf was long of great importance to Britain. To forestall an attempt by Napoleon to establish himself in the Gulf, at the time when he was in occupation of Egypt, the British in 1798 concluded a treaty with the Ruler of Muscat. From 1820, however, they concluded with other rulers in the Gulf a long series of treaties designed to maintain local security as well as to guard against unfriendly intrusion by any other Power.[9] On the other side of Arabia Aden, near the entrance to the Red Sea, was occupied by a British expedition in 1839.[10]

[7] A mistranslation of the Turkish, which means rather 'High Gate' (of administration and justice).

[8] Capitulations were originally unilateral charters modelled on those granted by the Byzantines, Crusaders, and Mamelukes to the Italian city-states.

[9] See below, pp. 164–90 [10] See below, p. 151

The occupation of Egypt by the French, in 1798, may be regarded as one phase of the Eastern Question: the problem of filling up the vacuum created by the gradual recession of the Ottoman Empire from the frontiers it reached at the height of its expansion. Pressure by Austria on the Ottoman Empire had begun at the end of the sixteenth century; about a century later began attempts by Russia to increase her influence at the expense of the Porte, either by annexation of territory, or by securing control of the Straits, or by acquiring a right to intervene in the internal affairs of the Empire. This policy was illustrated when the forces of Mohammed Ali, the rebellious Pasha of Egypt, approached Constantinople, and Russia, in exchange for protection by Russian troops, extracted from the Sultan the Treaty of Hunkiar Iskelessi, which not only gave Russia a right to interfere in Turkish affairs, but contained a secret clause giving Russia the right to secure the closing of the Dardanelles if she should ever be at war. This treaty, and a second advance by Mohammed Ali's forces on Constantinople, brought about negotiations between the Powers which left Egypt an autonomous territory, and by this and other signs showed how far the power of the Porte had declined. Greece had already obtained her independence, in 1832, thanks to the destruction of the Turkish and Egyptian fleets by those of Britain, France, and Russia. This process continued, and by 1914 all the Christian territories of the Balkans, as well as the island of Crete, had been freed from Ottoman sovereignty.

During the greater part of the nineteenth century Britain pursued consistently a policy which had first been propounded by William Pitt in about 1791: to preserve the Ottoman Empire lest, if it disintegrated, parts should fall into more dangerous, specifically Russian, hands. Hence the British (and French) defence of Turkey against Russia in the Crimean War; hence, too, British policy at the Congress of Berlin, where with the aid of Bismarck the Tsar was induced to grant Turkey better terms than those of the Treaty of St. Stefano. British support of the Sultan at this time was illustrated somewhat ambiguously when Britain obtained from the Sultan the right to occupy the island of Cyprus in return for an undertaking to defend Asia Minor against further aggression. Nevertheless,

British opposition to Russian pressure in the nineteenth century was the main factor in the preservation of the integrity of Turkey and Iran.

The pendulum of power which had swung from the Middle East over Spain in the eighth century, and later over the Balkans and Hungary and Austria, had now, as Western states became stronger, swung back across the Middle East and over much of Asia, even as far as Japan, where the United States and European Powers secured capitulatory rights for their nationals in the 1850s. In the Ottoman Empire the Capitulations enjoyed by most foreigners, in the courts and in matters of direct taxation, had by now developed to such an extent as to place them in a position much more favourable than that of Ottoman nationals. This was the more burdensome to the Porte in that during the nineteenth century the deteriorating finances of the Empire put it increasingly in debt to foreign interests. The Porte could not increase customs dues without the permission of the Powers, which was given grudgingly after being withheld sometimes for years. The Powers even set up, in 1881, the Ottoman Public Debt Administration, on which Turkey had one member (without a vote), to collect and distribute direct to foreign bondholders the proceeds of taxation on tobacco and certain other articles. In Iran the Capitulations, though less elaborate, were nevertheless onerous. It was in Egypt, however, that they had attained their widest extension, and after the occupation in 1882 the British authorities found them obstructing at every turn the task of restoring the finances and improving the administration. It was during the last half century or so before 1914 that the West established in the Middle East certain great enterprises, e.g. the Baghdad Railway, the Suez Canal, and the oil industry in Iran, for which the East had not the capital, the skill, or the experience. These enterprises, however impressive and useful, were to come to be regarded with suspicion and dislike by the local populations and governments as alleged instruments of foreign economic and even political influence.

Towards the end of the nineteenth century Germany came forward as the Sultan's only friend. The Ottoman Empire had lost the Crimea and parts of the Caucasus to Russia, Cyprus and Egypt to Britain, Algeria and Tunisia to France, and Bosnia and Herzegovina to Austria: only Germany of the great European Powers had acquired no Ottoman territory. Germany now embarked upon the training of the Turkish army, and the construction of the railway eastwards from Constantinople which was afterwards known as the Baghdad Railway. Moreover, when the Armenian massacres of 1894–5 aroused general hostility towards Turkey, the German Emperor went out of his way to declare himself the Sultan's friend. When the German railway company secured an extension of its concession, providing for a branch to the Persian Gulf, the British Government became alive to this threat to its interests in the Gulf. It was the looming peril from Germany which induced Britain to join with Russia, crippled by the war with Japan and by internal revolution, in the 1907 agreement about Iran (and Afghanistan and Tibet), and to ally herself with Russia in the First World War. Nevertheless Britain was not intransigent, and by the time war began in 1914, she had arrived at agreements with Germany on all the main points of dispute in the Middle East, particularly the Baghdad Railway, Tigris navigation, and oil concessions.

At the turn of the century the pendulum of power began to swing back from the Far East. In 1899 Japan established herself as a Great Power, and threw off the Capitulations which had been imposed on her less than half a century before; in 1905 the Japanese inflicted on the Russians a victory which sent a thrill of excitement and hope throughout many parts of Asia, since not for a very long time had a European been defeated by an Asian Power. It is believed with some reason that the example of the resurgence of Japan helped to bring about the Iranian and Turkish revolutions in the period 1905–8.

Arab Nationalism

Although the Turkish Constitution of 1878 remained in force only for two years and was followed by thirty years of severe despotism, it left a ferment in the Empire. The Arabs may have been influenced to some extent by Midhat Pasha, one of the authors of the Constitution, who was for several years Governor-General of Baghdad and was later for a short time Governor-General of Syria. Syria and Lebanon were simmering with political ideas which had grown out of a literary movement encouraged by the American and French missions and their printing presses. In Egypt the Arabi movement of 1882, misunderstood abroad and repugnant to the Khedive and the Sultan, found its chief support in the Egyptian agricultural class; it demanded internal reform but it also attacked the subservience of the Turkish-speaking ruling caste to foreign influence. Mustafa Kamil, who led a movement for constitutional reform in the 1890s, was more fortunate than Arabi. At that time the British-inspired regime in Egypt offered a haven to reformers in the Ottoman Empire, whether Egyptian or refugees from Syria or Turkey. Cromer even encouraged the reformist party, Hizb al-Umma, which was inspired by the Egyptian religious reformer Mohammed Abduh. The almost complete freedom of the Egyptian press provided a field for discussion of which good use was made.

Pan-Islamism and Pan-Arabism

The pan-Islamic policy of Sultan Abdul Hamid (1878-1909) was partly designed to attract the Arab element in the Empire. A rival doctrine, of Islamic revival under Arab leadership and an Arab Caliphate, was preached by a Syrian, Abdul Rahman Kawakibi (1849-1903), whose books, published in Cairo, were secretly circulated among Arab nationalists in Syria. But by studied displays of piety, by using Arabs at court, and particularly by the building of the Hejaz Railway, which was advertised and voluntarily subscribed for as a great act of piety to assist the pilgrim to Mecca – whereby its true military importance was disguised – the Sultan-Caliph won considerable support.

The Revolution of 1908

The Arabs of the Ottoman Empire welcomed the Young Turk revolution with enthusiasm, hoping for a regime in which they would have an equal place with the Turks. It became clear, however, that the Turks were outnumbered by the Arabs and other non-Turkish elements combined, and having created the Empire and been for centuries the ruling race, and moreover having been the authors of the 1908 revolution, the Turks had no intention of allowing themselves to be voted down. Arab requests for decentralization and for some concession to the Arabic language and to Arab sentiment were pared down to a derisory level, and the future seemed dark for Arab national hopes in an Empire inspired on the one hand by pan-Turanianism, which regarded every Turkish-speaking area outside the Empire as *terra irredenta,* and on the other by Ottomanism, looking to 'the fusion of the different races into a single Ottoman democracy with Turkish for its distinctive language'.[11] Early in 1914, therefore, the Amir Abdullah, the second son of the Sharif Hussein of Mecca, approached the British High Commissioner in Cairo to find out what attitude the British would adopt if the Ottoman Arabs revolted against the Sultan. Given the traditional British policy of preserving the Ottoman Empire lest worse should befall, the reply could only be discouraging.

The First World War[12]

When the war in Europe began, on 2 August 1914, Turkey was at first neutral, but a secret alliance with Germany was signed that day. On 29 October Turkish warships bombarded Russian Black Sea ports; Russia declared war on Turkey on 4 November, Britain the following day. By the time the Turks signed the Mudros armistice on 30 October 1918 the Arab provinces of the Empire had been almost completely cleared of Turkish troops by the British forces in Palestine and Mesopotamia (Iraq).

The Arab Revolt

The entry of Turkey into the war on the German side induced the British Government to re-open the talks with the Sharif of Mecca.[13] It had become important for Britain to secure his support, in order to reinforce war operations in the Arab countries and also because the Sultan-Caliph had proclaimed a *jihad* (a holy war) and was trying to induce the Sharif to support it. There ensued an exchange of letters between the Sharif Hussein and the British High Commissioner in Egypt,

[11] G. Antonius, *The Arab Awakening* (London, 1938), p. 102.

[12] C.R.M.F. Cruttwell, *A History of the Great War, 1914–18* (Oxford, 1934).

[13] See above p. 14.

Sir Henry McMahon. The correspondence ended in January 1916, and on 5 June the Arab revolt began. In November Hussein proclaimed himself King of the Arab Lands: Britain and France, however, recognized him only as King of the Hejaz.

Loyalties in the Arabian Peninsula were divided. The Amir Ibn Rashid of Hail sided with the Turks, as did the Imam of the Yemen. The Ruler of Nejd, Abdul Aziz ibn Saud, threw off the overlordship of the Sultan which he had been compelled to accept in 1914, and in December 1914 he signed a treaty with the British Government which gave Britain a large measure of control over his foreign policy, but acknowledged the independence and territorial integrity of Nejd and granted him a monthly subsidy. Ibn Saud made a contribution towards the Arab cause by keeping Ibn Rashid busy from time to time.[14] He might perhaps have given some assistance in the Hejaz campaign, but for King Hussein's persistence in treating him as an insignificant subordinate.

The Arab revolt immobilized some 30,000 Turkish troops along the railway from Amman to Medina, and included valuable guerrilla operations on the right flank of the British army in Palestine. These operations would not have been possible without the help of the British navy on the Hejaz coast, and the participation of numerous British personnel among whom T.E. Lawrence holds a high place. The Arab forces are sometimes stated by Arab writers to have 'captured' Damascus, but Damascus fell because of the total rout of the Turkish armies, and the first Allied troops to enter the city were a body of Australian cavalry.

Partition and Mandates

At the end of the war the Arabs expected the fulfilment of promises made or understood to have been made to them by Britain. These consisted of various statements and declarations (one of them in conjunction with France) during the war,[15] and of the so-called McMahon correspondence. Unfortunately the correspondence is not perfectly clear as to the area of Arab independence. The Arabs maintained that it included

[14] H. St. J.B. Philby, *Arabian Jubilee* (London, 1952), ch. 4.

[15] Antonius, *Arab Awakening*, pp. 433–5.

Palestine; the British Government and its principal negotiators, that it did not. There are various indications that Hussein and his son, the Amir Faisal, were aware that the British Government always intended to keep a hold over Palestine, but it would have been difficult to deduce the mandate system from the McMahon correspondence, still more the National Home for the Jewish people. In fact the British themselves did not in 1915 foresee such developments: they were trying to safeguard in a general way the vital interests of Britain, particularly in regard to India, Egypt, and British communications with the East, and also those of their French and Russian allies, who were not parties to the negotiations.

French and Russian interests were dealt with specifically in the 'Sykes-Picot' Agreement (1916)[16] which conflicted with the McMahon correspondence in regard to the area and degree of Arab independence. Under its terms Russia was to have, besides Constantinople and a strip of territory on each side of the Bosphorus, the greater part of the four Turkish provinces adjacent to the Russian frontier. Russia laid no claim to any Arab territory, and recognized the claims of France and Britain in regard to them. As between themselves Britain and France agreed that there should be:

(1) an international zone in Palestine (much smaller than the eventual area of mandated Palestine);
(2) a British zone of Basra and Baghdad;
(3) a French zone of Syria (and Cilicia);
(4) an independent Arab state or federation, between the British and French French zones, divided into British and French spheres of influence.

The text of the Balfour Declaration (2 November 1917) reads as follows:

> His Majesty's Government view with favour the establishment in Palestine of a National Home for the Jewish people, and will use their best endeavours to facilitate the achievement of this object, it being clearly understood that nothing shall be done which may prejudice the civil and religious rights of existing non-Jewish communities in Palestine, or the rights and political status enjoyed by Jews in any other country.[17]

The motives behind the Balfour Declaration were various: messianic, humanitarian, strategic. Many people in Britain, far

[16] Hurewitz, ii. 18. [17] Ibid., p. 26.

more in the United States, believed that to promote a Jewish return to Palestine was to help to fulfil prophecies in the Old Testament. There was widespread sympathy for the Jews, scattered in many countries, often suffering from misgovernment or worse, yet preserving through all a memory of a former home in Palestine. Finally, the policy of the National Home might work in favour of the retention of Palestine by Britain as a point in her defensive system, and might moreover win sympathy for the Allied cause among world Jewry, particularly in Russia, where the influence of the Jews, now that the Tsarist regime had fallen, might help to counteract the drift towards a separate peace with Germany. But however strong these considerations may have appeared in Britain, they were never to have any weight with the Arabs.

After the Turkish defeat in Syria the whole area was occupied by British troops with a small French force on the coast and the army of King Hussein in the interior. In Palestine there was a British military administration, in the coastal region north of Palestine a French provisional government, and in the four cities of Aleppo, Homs, Hama, and Damascus, and east of Jordan, an Arab administration under the Amir Faisal, to whom a number of British and French officers were attached. On 30 January 1919 the Peace Conference decided that the Arab provinces of the Ottoman Empire should be wholly separated from Turkey, and announced the adoption for some of them of the mandate system, a kind of trusteeship, as a bridge to complete independence. Britain and France disagreed over the boundaries of the mandated territories. An investigation into the wishes of the population which was to have been international dwindled, through French opposition, into an inquiry by two Americans, and the 'King-Crane' Report which they presented to the President of the United States was ignored at the time, and was only published, and then unofficially, in December 1922.[18] It was opposed to a French mandate for Syria and questioned the wisdom of the Balfour Declaration.

In September 1919 an agreement was reached between Britain and France whereby British troops were withdrawn

[18] Ibid., p. 66.

from Syria (excluding Palestine) and from Cilicia, and replaced by Arab troops in the interior of Syria and by French troops on the coast and in Cilicia. On 20 March 1920 a congress of Syrian notables at Damascus offered the crown of Syria and Palestine to Faisal, who accepted it. This action was repudiated by the British and French Governments, who subsequently, at the conference of San Remo (24 April 1920), received mandates: the French for Syria and Lebanon, the British for Palestine, with Transjordan, with the obligation to carry out the policy of the Balfour Declaration. This award was repudiated by Faisal. Subsequently the French Commander-in-Chief advanced into Syria and occupied Damascus. Faisal departed into exile, but later became King of Iraq.

The mandates for 'Palestine' and 'Syria and Lebanon',[19] were formally approved by the Council of the League of Nations in July 1922 and became effective in September 1923.[20] In 1924 the United States gave its concurrence to the mandates. Article 2 of the mandate for Palestine laid on the Mandatory the responsibility for placing the country under such political, administrative, and economic conditions as would secure the establishment of a Jewish National Home without prejudice to the rights and position of the rest of the population. Transjordan was added to the mandated territory, but the Mandatory was permitted to exclude it, and in fact did exclude it, from the area of Jewish settlement. In 1922 Transjordan was constituted a semi-autonomous Arab principality under the Amir Abdullah, subject under mandate to the British High Commissioner in Jerusalem.[21]

The Arabs of the Middle East recognized neither the Sykes-Picot Agreement nor the Balfour Declaration. The former became known to the world in December 1917,[22] when the Bolsheviks, having discovered it in the Tsarist archives, published it and, in so far as it affected Russia, repudiated it. The

[19] *League of Nations Official Journal*, August 1922, pp. 1007–12 and 1013–17.

[20] For the arrangements for Iraq see below, p. 325.

[21] Proclaimed 25 May 1923.

[22] Elie Kedourie argues that the Sharif Hussein must have been aware of the Sykes–Picot negotiations and have had a shrewd idea of Anglo-French intentions towards the Arab territories (*England and the Middle East* (London, 1956), ch. 2).

agreement was modified in December 1918 by an arrangement between Lloyd George and Clemenceau, in which Mosul and Palestine were included in the British sphere of influence.

With the final disintegration of the Ottoman Empire, Western penetration became Western domination, and Arab nationalism, which had allied itself with Britain against the Turks, became the formula for resistance to Western (in particular British and French) economic and political power. It covered also the realization that the adoption of Western techniques and social innovations was a condition of successful resistance. As the dominant foreign Powers were no longer Moslem but Christian, it was inevitable, too, that the Islamic tendencies in Arab nationalism should assert themselves more strongly; yet it embraced, under the name of Arabs, all those whose mother-tongue was Arabic: Moslem fundamentalists and reformers, Orthodox, Coptic, and Catholic Christians, free-thinkers, and the illiterate masses of peasants just beginning to be aware of the possibility of social reform.

The End of the Caliphate

On 1 November 1922 a law was passed by the Great National Assembly which marked the overthrow of Ottoman rule by the Turkish nationalists under Mustafa Kemal. This law deprived the Caliph of all secular authority in the new Turkish state. The last Ottoman Sultan-Caliph was deposed and expelled and the dynasty came to an end; a relative was elected Caliph, but he became a rallying point for the opposition to Mustafa Kemal, and on 3 March 1924 the Caliphate itself was abolished by the National Assembly and the Caliph expelled from Turkey. Though these acts were strongly challenged at the time, particularly by Indian Moslems, the Caliphate has not been revived. The assumption by King Hussein of the Hejaz of the title of Caliph was not recognized except in the Hejaz, Transjordan, and Iraq, and lapsed some months later when Hussein abdicated after his kingdom had been attacked by Ibn Saud. In May 1926 a Caliphate Congress, attended by delegates from 13 Moslem countries (not including Turkey) was held in Cairo, but was inconclusive. Since then the Caliphate has scarcely been an issue in Moslem politics.

Regional Relations

The internal relations of the Middle East took some time to recover from the disruption of the war and the dissolution of the Ottoman Empire. Memories of the Arab revolt and of Turkish excesses against Arabs were for long a barrier to Turco-Arab understanding. The first step towards improved relations was taken in 1935, when negotiations begun on the initiative of Iraq resulted in a four-Power pact of *bon voisinage,* signed on 8 July 1937 by Turkey, Iraq, Iran, and Afghanistan. This Middle Eastern or 'Saadabad' Pact had in fact little influence before the Second World War, and has had none since. The pact was preceded by agreements settling boundary disputes between Turkey and Iran (23 January 1937) and Iraq and Iran (4 July 1937). Turkey had previously, on 9 February 1934, signed a Balkan pact with Greece, Rumania, and Yugoslavia.[23]

The Arab world itself was split by the quarrel between the families of Hashim and Saud. Ex-King Hussein died in 1931; the reign of his successor, his son Ali, had come to an end on the capture of Jedda by Ibn Saud in 1925. The Hashimis, however, were still represented by Hussein's sons: Faisal in Iraq and Abdullah in Transjordan. A further source of discord were the towns of Aqaba and Maan, annexed by Britain to Transjordan though claimed by Ibn Saud for the Hejaz. It was Ibn Saud who first tried to improve relations with his neighbours, by signing a treaty of friendship and *bon voisinage* with Transjordan (27 July 1933); a treaty of Arab brotherhood and alliance with Iraq (2 April 1937); and a treaty of friendship with Egypt (7 May 1936).[24]

Turco-Arab relations were also complicated by the question of the *sanjaq* of Alexandretta (Hatay), which formed part of French mandated territory. It was regarded as Arab by the Arabs, but was claimed by Turkey because of its partly Turkish population and its strategic and economic importance. On 29 May 1937 an agreement was reached at Geneva by which the *sanjaq* was transformed into the autonomous Republic of Hatay jointly guaranteed by France and Turkey.[25] Just before

[23] For text see RIIA, *Documents on International Affairs, 1934,* p. 298.

[24] For the text of these treaties see ibid. *1937*, pp. 517 ff.

[25] Ibid. p. 490.

the outbreak of the Second World War, and as a prelude to the Treaty of Mutual Assistance of 19 October 1939 between Britain, France, and Turkey,[26] the territory was incorporated in the Turkish Republic by the Franco-Turkish agreement of 21 June 1939. This transaction over their heads was deeply resented by the Syrians.

Arab Unity

Although from 1920 the re-unification of the Arab world under an independent political regime was to be a main objective of Arab nationalism (an idea which was given expression at more than one pan-Arab Congress), nevertheless the separate development of each territory created in time political loyalties which accentuated the tendencies to disunity already present. Egypt, detached from the Ottoman Empire in the nineteenth century, had developed, first under Mohammed Ali and then under British occupation, a national consciousness which tended to conflict with pan-Arabism. This detachment had also put Egypt socially and politically far in advance of the rest of the Arab world. Again, the earlier modernization and relative wealth of Egypt gave her a leading position in Arab affairs, and the superior publishing facilities of Cairo made it the centre of Arab influence through books and newspapers, and, later, films and radio.

Saudi-Hashimite rivalry was a factor in Arab politics, and the greater dependence of the Hashimi family on Britain usually induced the nationalists of Egypt and Syria to side with Saudi Arabia. In external relations, however, dislike and fear of Zionism tended to bind all the Arab states together. The first formal recognition of a community of Arab states was seen in the participation of the Arab Governments in the Palestine Conference in London in 1939.

Great-Power Rivalry between the Wars

The Straits. The interests of the Powers in the Straits were regulated first by the Convention signed at Lausanne, on the same day as the treaty of 24 July 1923, by Turkey, Britain, France, Italy, Japan, Bulgaria, Greece, Rumania, and the

[26] Hurewitz, ii. 226.

Soviet Union,[27] providing for full freedom of passage for commercial vessels of all nations both in peace and in war and, subject to certain conditions, for warships of all Powers in peacetime, as well as in a war in which Turkey was neutral; and for the demilitarization of the European and Asiatic shores of the Bosphorus and Dardanelles and of the islands. This instrument was replaced on 20 July 1936 by the Montreux Convention, to which the Soviet Union and Yugoslavia, but not Italy, were signatories, and which maintained the principle of freedom of navigation for merchant vessels through the Straits but by a protocol abrogated the demilitarization of the Straits and allowed Turkey to refortify them. The Soviet Union was further given the right to send any number of warships of any size through the Straits in time of peace without Turkish permission being obtained, while the non-littoral Powers were limited to sending light surface vessels into the Black Sea. In time of war, if Turkey were neutral, belligerent warships were not to pass except to execute obligations under the League Covenant or under a mutual assistance agreement within its framework; if Turkey were belligerent or threatened, the passage of warships was left to Turkish discretion.

Progress towards Independence. The Capitulations disappeared between the wars. Turkey got rid of them by the Treaty of Lausanne of 1923, Iran in 1926, Egypt in 1937. The Turkish Government used its independence to expropriate, on terms favourable to itself, all foreign railway, mining, and other concerns. The Arab territories placed under mandate were dissatisfied with a political status inferior to that of less advanced countries such as Yemen and Hejaz. Nevertheless, except in Palestine, where there was an exceptional regime under international supervision, all the mandated territories made political progress between the wars, and one of them, Iraq, in 1932 attained independence. Egypt too, which when the First World War ended was a British protectorate, became independent, in 1936.

Britain. Britain emerged from the post-war settlements in a predominant position in the Middle East. Nevertheless in more than one area there were dangerous stresses. The British

[27] The Soviet Union, however, signed under protest and subsequently refused to ratify.

Declaration about Egypt in 1922 followed several years of acrimonious dispute and serious outbreaks of violence, and the agreement of 1936 would have been less popular but for Mussolini's open designs on Egypt. In Iraq the mandate ended in 1932, but the arrangement by which Britain retained two air bases provided the extreme nationalists with a grievance, and, like other Arabs, the Iraqis, however friendly towards Britain, detested the Zionist policy.

Throughout the inter-war period the Palestine problem caused unceasing anxiety and conflict.[28] There were outbreaks of violence on the part of the Arabs, from 1920 onwards; there were many inquiries and reports and White Papers. In 1937 a Royal Commission recommended the partition of Palestine between Arabs and Jews; in 1938 a Partition Commission found the proposal to be impracticable. Throughout the period, and especially after Nazi brutality had begun to drive the Jews out of Germany, the Mandatory had difficulty every year about the number of Jewish immigrants to be admitted: the Jews asking for a higher quota, and the Arabs demanding that not merely illegal immigration, which was considerable, but all immigration by Jews should be stopped. Finally there was the British White Paper of 1939, providing for the cessation of Jewish immigration, except with Arab consent, when 75,000 more Jews should have been admitted, for a ten-year scheme of preparation for self-government, and for restrictions on the acquisition of land by Jews. This White Paper was rejected by the Arabs, though they were to look back upon it later as a Magna Carta, while the Jews in Palestine and elsewhere attacked it violently. It had critics in Britain; it failed to secure the approval of the Mandates Commission of the League of Nations; and in the United States the voice of Zionism drowned all other opinions on the Palestine problem.

The Totalitarian States. One consequence of British predominance was a tendency for the Middle East nationalists to look to rival Powers for support. Fascist Italy was active in propaganda and political intrigue in Middle East countries,

[28] George Kirk, *A Short History of the Middle East* (London, 1955), pp. 146–59; Sir Reader Bullard, *Britain and the Middle East* (London, 1952), pp. 94–107.

but was handicapped by Arab memories of the ruthless suppression of the Senussi in Cyrenaica. Another and perhaps fatal setback to Italian aims was a speech by Mussolini on 18 March 1934 in which he referred to Italy's 'historic objectives' in the Middle East. Again, one effect of the conquest of Ethiopia in 1935–6 was to make all parties in Egypt anxious to sign the long-delayed treaty with Britain. A more formidable Power in which the Arabs began to see a counterweight to Britain and France was Nazi Germany. Hitler's anti-Jewish policy enabled Germany to pose as the sole champion of the Arabs against Anglo-Jewish imperialism, but at the same time increased Jewish pressure on Palestine through the enforced emigration of Jews from Germany. By 1939 extensive anti-British activities were being conducted from German and Italian missions and consulates in the Middle East. Italian activities concentrated chiefly on Egypt and the Red Sea coast of Arabia, particularly the Yemen, and they did not entirely cease after the signature of the Anglo-Italian Agreement of 16 April 1938, 'regarding questions of mutual concern' in the Middle East. German activities were directed upon Turkey, Iraq, and Iran.

France. By the end of the First World War French financial and cultural interests in the Middle East had long been considerable, and French was the language of polite society in Egypt and in other parts of the Levant. France's traditional political interests were now given concrete form by the mandate over Syria and Lebanon, but this was resisted, except by some of the Christians, from the first. In 1936 the French Government initialled agreements with the two states on something like the lines of the Anglo-Iraqi Treaty of 1930, but political changes in France prevented their ratification.

The United States. Until the First World War the interests of the United States in the Middle East were mainly philanthropical, with commercial interests developing slowly.[29] So remote did the United States feel from Middle East politics, that although she went to war with Germany and her European allies in 1917, she remained at peace with Turkey. When,

[29] The leading American educational institutions today are: Robert College, Istanbul (opened in 1863); the Women's College of Istanbul (1890); the American University of Beirut (1866); and the American University in Cairo (1919).

however, the Ottoman Empire broke up, the United States, in spite of her refusal to accept a mandate over Armenia and her attempt to retire into her traditional isolation, was gradually drawn into Middle East affairs: by the Zionist question; by oil; and finally by the requirements of defence.

When the Balfour Declaration was issued by the British Government in November 1917, neither the President of the United States nor the State Department made any official comment. President Wilson seems to have conveyed his approval beforehand, through Colonel House, and in any case the exigencies of internal politics drew the President into public approval of the Declaration as early as August 1918.[30] Zionist interests in the United States, Protestant as well as Jewish, maintained pressure on the administration, and helped to create general hostility to the British White Paper of 1939.

American oil companies at first had some difficulty in securing participation in the oil resources of the Middle East, owing to the exclusive rights that were held, through treaties and in other ways, by Britain. Indeed, in almost every case governmental negotiations on a high level were needed before a commercial project could be realized. In the name of the 'open door' the United States refused to recognize the written promise of the oil of Baghdad and Mosul which the Grand Vizier had made in writing to the Turkish Petroleum Company (Anglo-German) in 1914, and after prolonged pressure secured for American interests a 23¾ per cent share in what became the Iraq Petroleum Company. Between 1930 and 1934 oil concessions were secured by American companies, in Bahrain, in Kuwait (in equal shares with the AIOC, now British Petroleum), and in Saudi Arabia.

The Soviet Union. As a continental Power, Russia's first concern in the Middle East has been with the two neighbouring states of Turkey and Iran. From 1917 to 1921 the Bolsheviks followed a 'liberation' policy in that area and exploited the revolutionary appeal with some success among its down-trodden peoples. Then, after the withdrawal of the Soviet armies, the policy from 1921 onwards became one of non-intervention and support of the national independence of

[30] Frank E. Manuel, *The Realities of American-Palestine Relations* (Washington, D.C., 1949).

Middle East countries against the 'imperialist penetration' of Britain and the West.

There was a steady growth of Soviet trade with these countries, particularly with Iran. An important factor for Soviet-Middle East relations was the economic and social development of the Soviet national republics to the north and east of the region. The policy of cultural emancipation in the new Soviet republics, with their racial and religious affinities with national minorities in the Middle East States, was also used as an instrument of Soviet foreign policy. It had to contend with the distrust of neighbouring communities for anything Russian, and in particular for the Soviet system, and also with the evidence of the political subjection of the republics to the Soviet State. On the other hand Russia's rapid industrial development might well serve as a magnet to areas beginning to resent their backward condition. Whatever the cause, Communist parties began to form in Arab countries, for example in Egypt as early as 1920, in Syria and Iraq in the 1930s.[31]

Soviet relations with the inner ring of Middle East states remained more vague. The Soviet Union, one of the first Powers to recognize Ibn Saud (16 February 1926), concluded a treaty with the Yemen on 1 November 1928. The Soviet missions in both countries, which were under the Soviet representative in Jedda, were closed in 1938. Neither Egypt nor Iraq would admit the Soviet Union to diplomatic relations, even when, after 1922 and 1932 respectively, they were free to do so, and Lebanon and Syria were limited by the French mandate for the whole of the inter-war period. In regard to Turkey, the Soviet Union refused to ratify the Convention about the Straits which was signed at Lausanne in 1923, and secured much better terms in the Montreux Convention of 1936.[32] In Iran, after the failure of the Soviet republic in Gilan, the Russians behaved on the whole with discretion, though it was found that among the thousands of Iranians who were ejected from the Soviet Union in the 1930s on the ground of refusal to take Soviet citizenship there were a considerable number of Soviet agents. On the whole, until 1939

[31] W.Z. Laqueur, *Communism and Nationalism in the Middle East* (London, 1956).
[32] See above, p. 18.

the Russians were content not to push their interests too hard in the Middle East but to wait upon events.

The Second World War

It was with relief that the British learned that no attempt would be made by the Palestine Arabs to embarrass them while they were at war with Germany. They were thus able to build up the organization based on Cairo that was to serve them so well. Internal opposition was dealt with early. German assistance for the abortive *coup d'état* of Rashid Ali in Iraq in May 1941 was small and arrived too late. The Vichy regime in Syria was defeated by British and Free French forces, and replaced in July 1941 by a regime dependent on General de Gaulle. In August 1941 British and Russian forces entered Iran, where strong Axis influence had aroused the deep anxiety of the Allied Governments. This opened the supply line to Russia, which was worked largely by American non-combatant troops operating under the British command in Baghdad. Finally, British pressure on King Farouk in February 1942 brought into power the helpful government of Nahas.

The task of denying the Middle East to the Axis Powers and of creating there a base for a counter-offensive against southern Europe was given high priority in Allied strategy; the actual defence of the area was a British responsibility. After the internal threats to the Allies had been removed, the Middle East for about a year was in danger from German forces which in the summer of 1942 were established in Egypt on the west and in the Caucasus on the north. Until after the victories of el Alamein and Stalingrad there was little to persuade the Middle East that the Allies might win the war.

Even after the ending of Axis resistance in North Africa the Middle East retained much of its importance. Among the war activities centred on Cairo were those of the Middle East Supply Centre established by the British Government in 1941 and made into a joint Anglo-American supply agency in the following year. The task of the Centre was to ensure that the civil population of the Middle East was provided with essential supplies and at the same time to limit their imports in order to economize in sea and land transport and in port space. To this end local food production had to be greatly increased, and many short-term measures – changes in method, encouragement of local industries, introduction of fertilizers and agricultural machinery – were put into operation.[33]

Formation of the Arab League

In a speech delivered in May 1941 Anthony Eden said that the British Government would give full support to any scheme that commanded general approval among Arabs for strengthening the cultural, economic, and political ties between the Arab countries. Syrian and Lebanese independence, promised by the Free French and confirmed by the British on their entry into Syria in June 1941, was formally recognized by the British Government on 27 October (Syria) and 26 December (Lebanon) 1941. In December 1942 Nuri al-Said, Prime Minister of Iraq, brought forward a scheme for the unification of Syria, Lebanon, Palestine, and Transjordan, with 'semi-autonomy' for the Jews in Palestine, as a first step towards Arab unity. This proposal was not pursued, but a general Arab Conference met in Alexandria in September-October 1944 which was attended by representatives of the Governments of Egypt, Iraq, Lebanon, Syria, Transjordan, Saudi Arabia, and Yemen, and by an observer on behalf of the Arabs of Palestine. The proceedings resulted in the foundation of the Arab League, and in the signature on 22 March 1945 of the Pact of the League.[34] The League set up a Council with its seat in Cairo and with provisions for various commissions: economic, cultural, etc. The real bond of unity at that time was opposition to the growing Jewish Home in Palestine and fear of its continued expansion, and the defeat of the Arab States in the Palestine War discredited the League and mutual recriminations weakened it from the inside. The Inter-Arab Joint Defence Alliance, which was concluded in the period 1950–52, led to no practical results at the time, and differences as to its interpretation were to exacerbate subsequent disputes about the Baghdad Pact. Attempts by members of the League to establish closer relations between themselves met with little

[33] See 'Economic Problems: The Middle East Supply Centre' by Guy Hunter in G. Kirk, *The Middle East in the War* (RIIA, *Survey of International Affairs, 1939–46*), pp. 169–93.

[34] Hurewitz, ii. 245–9.

success. King Abdullah strove to bring about the union of Jordan with Syria, but although many Syrians wished for union, there was no general desire in Syria to come under a monarchy, particularly a monarchy alleged to be under British control. After Abdullah's death Jordan for a time tended towards closer relations with Iraq, chiefly because of her financial difficulties. At one moment Syria made overtures for some form of union with Iraq, but withdrew almost at once. Not only vested and other local interests stood in the way of union; the attitude of third states often constituted an obstacle. Egypt, as pretender to headship of the Arab world, looked with suspicion on any combination in which she had no part, while Saudi Arabia opposed any move that might strengthen the rival Hashimite dynasties in Baghdad and Amman.

The National Home and its Consequences

By the end of the Second World War it had become plain that the *status quo* could not continue in Palestine. During and after the war the eyes of thousands of Jews who had suffered from Nazi persecution were turned towards Palestine, not only as containing the Jewish National Home but as their only place of refuge, and their fellow Jews, eager to help them, were in revolt against British restrictions on immigration. Jewish demands enjoyed strong support in the United States, where both candidates for the Presidential election in 1944 supported the Zionist 'Biltmore' Programme, demanding that Palestine should become a Jewish state, and that unlimited Jewish immigration, under the control of the Jewish Agency, should be allowed. Terroristic acts against the mandatory authorities in Palestine, begun on a small scale by the Stern Gang in 1940, by the end of the war had reached serious proportions, while President Truman made repeated requests to the British Government to admit into Palestine forthwith 100,000 of the homeless Jews of Europe. The British Government tried unsuccessfully to reach agreement with the United States Government, with the Arabs, and with the Jews, and in February 1947 it referred the problem to the United Nations, to whom it gave warning on 26 September that if no settlement acceptable to both Jews and Arabs could be found it would plan for the early withdrawal of British forces and British administration from Palestine. A United Nations plan for partition of the territory was approved by the Assembly on 29 November, but the Arab States refused to accept it. On 14 May 1948 the British mandate was abandoned and the last of the British troops withdrew from Palestine. On the same day the State of Israel was proclaimed: it was recognized immediately by the United States, followed closely by the Soviet Union. On 15 May the forces of Egypt, Jordan, and Iraq began to invade Palestine. In spite of the efforts of the United Nations fighting did not finally stop until January 1949, while the signature of armistice arrangements between Israel on the one hand and Egypt, Jordan, Syria, and Lebanon on the other, was not completed until July. No peace treaty has followed. In 1950 a tripartite Declaration was issued by Britain, France, and the United States, expressing readiness to supply the Arab States and Israel with arms for internal security and self-defence and to take action, 'both within and outside the United Nations', to prevent the violation by force of any Middle East frontier or armistice line. In November 1950 the Arab League decided to continue the war-time blockage of Israel, on the ground that an armistice did not constitute a state of peace.

The failure to resolve this conflict has been the root cause of the chronic violence and instability which are regarded as characteristic of the Middle East. It is the principal reason for the growth of anti-Western feeling in the Arab countries as two Western powers – Britain and the United States – were held to be chiefly responsible for the creation of Israel.

Middle East Defence and the West

What came to be called the Truman Doctrine was first set forth in Truman's address to Congress on 12 March 1947, in which he asked for authority to furnish aid to Greece and Turkey (which Britain could no longer give) to assist them to maintain their integrity and independence. This policy, in which Iran was soon included, can be explained by reference to the attitude of the Soviet Government as shown by the secret Soviet-German negotiations of 1940 (revealed by captured German documents), when the Soviet Union demanded, as part of the price of adherence to the Axis, bases near the

Straits, and recognition of a wedge of territory from the Caucasus towards the Persian Gulf as the centre of Soviet aspirations; by the Soviet demand for bases near Istanbul, addressed to the Allies at Potsdam and then to Turkey; by the support of the 'autonomy' movements in Azarbaijan and Kurdestan; and by the retention of Soviet troops in Iran for more than two months after the treaty date, in order to obtain oil rights from the Iranian Government. These facts remained although the Soviet Union was now operating more discreetly, through her diplomatic missions established in 1943 in Egypt and in 1944 in Iraq, Syria, and Lebanon, and through the Russian Orthodox Church in the Middle East whose properties she had taken over after the Second World War.

The Doctrine provided support for the 'northern tier', but behind that lay the mass of Arab countries thinking of defence as defence against Zionism. Such unity of feeling as there was seemed to be strong only against Israel, whose victory over the Arab States dealt it a severe blow. No Arab state could claim the leadership: Egypt, the strongest and the most advanced, had done particularly badly in the war against Israel. Nevertheless the nationalism which had begun at the turn of the century was growing, fed from inside by the French episodes in Syria in 1943 and 1945 and by problems such as Israeli and British relations with Egypt, and encouraged from outside by the attainment of independence by India and other former British territories. The demonstrations in Iraq against the abortive Treaty of Portsmouth in January 1948 owed something to local grievances against the Iraqi Government, but much more to nationalism. The time was propitious for fresh advances towards independence, and Britain concluded two agreeements with Egypt: on self-government and self-determination for the Sudan (12 February 1953), and on the Suez Canal base (19 October 1954). In the Sudan the momentum was so great that the possibility of union with Egypt was evenutally rejected for complete independence.

The Baghdad Pact

In the early 1950s the Western countries had not abandoned hope of including the Middle East in an anti-Soviet defence system. Already in 1951, the Wafd Government had rejected a proposal that Egypt should join with Britain, France, the United States, and Turkey in a Middle East Defence Organization. By 1953 the US Secretary of State J.F. Dulles had decided that such an organization was not immediately feasible, but he believed that he had detected in the northern tier of states a greater awareness of danger. It was therefore with American encouragement that the Turkey-Pakistan agreement of 1954 was concluded, and the United States then entered into two agreements: with Iraq for military assistance (21 April 1954) and with Pakistan for mutual assistance (19 May 1954). Nasser, the new leader of republican Egypt, was strongly opposed to any Arab country joining such a pact because he believed that a Western alliance meant the perpetuation of Western influence. However, his efforts to dissuade Nuri Said, the veteran pro-Western and anti-Communist leader of Iraq from joining were in vain. Iraq signed with Turkey on 24 February 1955 an agreement which came to be called the Baghdad Pact. It received on 5 April the adherence of Britain, happy to be able to exchange the treaty of 1930 with Iraq for an arrangement for the reactivation of bases in time of war similar to that embodied in the 1954 agreement with Egypt. Pakistan joined on 23 November, Iran on 3 November. Through Turkey the Baghdad Pact had a link with NATO, through Pakistan with SEATO.

From then on the Arab states were bitterly divided, but the weight of articulate Arab opinion was on Nasser's side. A conservative minority in Syria and King Hussein of Jordan would have favoured joining the Baghdad Pact but they were prevented by a wave of popular hostility supported by increasingly effective Egyptian propaganda. In Saudi Arabia the royal family was opposed to the Baghdad Pact because it feared any increase in the power of its Hashimite enemies reigning in Iraq and Jordan.

The Growth of Arab Neutralism

The dispute between Nasser and his allies in the Arab world on the one hand and the Baghdad Pact countries and their Western allies on the other rapidly grew more serious. Nasser had strong popular support for his policies but Egypt's military weakness had been exposed, on 28 February 1955, by a sudden and heavy bout of fighting with Israel at Gaza. Nasser was aware that Israel was receiving secret arms supplies from France. He still hoped to obtain new arms from Britain and the United States but having failed he turned to the Soviet Union which proved more responsive, and in September 1955 he announced a large-scale purchase of Soviet arms through Czechoslovakia.

Nasser's neutralism (which for him meant cutting Egypt's former ties with the West) gained a new dimension with the Bandung Conference in April 1955 and was further strengthened by his close relations with Premier Nehru of India and President Tito of Yugoslavia. At the same time his relations with the West rapidly worsened and by July 1956 he had become both the West's *bête noire* and the hero of the Arab masses. The Suez affair of July-October 1956, which followed the West's abrupt withdrawal of aid for the Nile High Dam and Nasser's reaction in nationalizing the Suez Canal Company, increased Nasser's hold on Arab opinion but temporarily divided the Western Powers as the United States opposed the Anglo-French-Israeli action against Egypt. United States pressure helped to secure an Anglo-French withdrawal from the Suez Canal area and an Israeli withdrawal from Sinai and Gaza.

Britain and France's collusion with Israel in the Suez affair served to destroy much of what remained of these two countries' direct political influence in the Arab world. Nasser's diplomatic triumph added to his popularity with the Arab masses which reached its climax with the declaration of the Syrian-Egyptian union in February 1958. In July 1958 the anti-Western trend swept away Nuri Said and the Iraqi monarchy and destroyed the last possibility of including a major Arab state in the West's defence system.

The United States *rapprochement* with Egypt over the Suez affair was short-lived as the United States Government became alarmed at growing Soviet influence in the Middle East and the Nasserist threat to conservative pro-Western elements in the Arab world. The United States response took the form of a message to Congress from President Eisenhower on 5 January 1957 embodying what came to be called the

Eisenhower Doctrine. After stressing the economic and strategic importance of the Middle East area to the West, the message called for joint action by President and Congress to authorize action in regard to the Middle East nations designed to assist the development of economic strength for the maintenance of national independence; to undertake upon request programmes of military assistance and co-operation; and to secure and protect the territorial integrity and political independence of such nations requesting such aid against overt aggression from any nation 'controlled by international Communism'.

From 1947 onwards the United States had become increasingly involved in Middle East affairs and this trend continued. In 1957 it gave assistance to King Hussein of Jordan in his struggle with his own left-wing opposition, under the terms of the Eisenhower Doctrine, and in July 1958 landed troops in Lebanon during this country's muted civil war when the Iraqi Revolution raised fears that all remaining pro-Western elements in the Middle East might be swept away. But the United States' relations with the Arab countries were generally unsatisfactory. Initially, and especially while Mr. Dulles was the US Secretary of State, this was partly due to United States distaste for Arab neutralism in the Cold War; but the primary underlying cause has been the United States' enthusiastic diplomatic support for Israel backed by large-scale military and economic aid. Periods of improved relations between the United States and Egypt, founded on a United States belief, in Nasser's lifetime, that Egypt could be a moderating and anti-Communist influence in the Middle East, always proved to be short-lived. Pro-US Arab regimes (such as Lebanon, Jordan, and Saudi Arabia) found it increasingly difficult and dangerous to show their sympathies. Some Arab governments, such as the Syrian and Iraqi, expressed the view after the 1967 war that there was no possibility of any future compromise with the United States since it would always side with Israel. Others, however, including the Egyptian, still hoped that the United States would adopt a more 'even-handed' policy between Arabs and Israelis and based their policies on the assumption that no Middle East settlement was possible without United States participation.

For similar but opposite reasons the Soviet Union made

immense political gains in the Middle East after 1950. Stalin's successors, having abandoned the idea of trying to work through the weak and divided Arab Communist parties, based their policy on close co-operation with nationalist and non-aligned Arab governments – especially the Egyptian and Syrian. Apart from the building of the High Dam, it had a large and growing economic stake in the Arab countries through its aid for industrialization and the economic infrastructure and it became the principal supplier of arms to Egypt, Syria, Iraq, and Sudan. The Soviet Union has unarguably established itself as a Middle East Power (like Russia in the nineteenth century) and no political settlement in the area is conceivable without its involvement. These gains have just as clearly brought disadvantages. The Arab states' failure to inflict a military defeat on Israel has caused a growing Soviet involvement in their defence which carries with it the danger of a military confrontation with the United States. Also the possibility of ideological friction with Arab Moslem states remains wherever Arab Communists are capable of making a bid for power (as in Iraq in 1958–9 or Sudan in 1971). Soviet relations with the northern tier states, especially Iran, improved considerably after the early 1960s.

Following the collapse of the Baghdad Pact in 1958, Britain's military role in the Middle East was restricted to its membership of the Pact's successor the Central Treaty Organization (CENTO) (which increasingly concentrated on its nonmilitary aspects of communications and economic co-operation), and the military bases in Aden and the Gulf. With the abandonment of these in 1968 and 1971 respectively, British interests in the area, although considerable, were largely economic and commercial and it's political influence was negligible.

With the ending of the Algerian War in 1962, France's bad relations with the Arab countries steadily improved and its former close alliance with Israel simultaneously deteriorated. France remained Israel's principal arms supplier until the 1967 war but President de Gaulle's arms embargo, maintained by his successors, and French criticism of Israel's continued occupation of Arab territory, both improved France's image in the Arab world and jeopardized Franco-Israeli relations. While there has been no question of France recovering its former political influence in the Levant, it has gained clear commercial advantages in the Arab countries and traditional French cultural influence in the area has been intensified.

Arab Disunity

The high hopes of Arab nationalists which were raised by Nasser's early successes and the creation of the Syrian-Egyptian union were soon disappointed. Rivalry between Kassem of Iraq and Nasser, between Baathists and Nasserists, and subsequently between Iraqi and Syrian Baathists meant that even the Arab 'progressive' camp was divided. Egypt's support for the Yemeni republicans against the royalists in 1962–7 sharpened the differences between conservatives and radicals and carried the struggle into the Arabian Peninsula. Nasser's efforts from January 1964 onwards to soften the divisions and create a unified Arab front against Israel's plans to divert the waters of the River Jordan to the Negev were only superficially successful. The Unified Arab Command which the Arab Heads of State set up at their summit meetings in 1964 proved worthless because of political mistrust, and the Palestine Liberation Organization they created under the leadership of Ahmad Shukairy was an act of inter-Arab political compromise which cost the Arabs dearly in terms of world opinion. Conservative–radical differences reached their height in 1966 with the efforts of King Faisal of Saudi Arabia to create an informal alliance or Islamic Front against Arab socialism.

The results of the 1967 Arab-Israeli War did something to reduce the inter-Arab conflict. A compromise was reached over Yemen and three Arab monarchies – Saudi Arabia, Kuwait, and Libya – joined to provide aid for Egypt but the creation of a common military strategy, which alone could enable the Arab countries to match Israel's military power, remained unattainable. In particular, Jordan's bad relations with both Syria and Iraq prevented the establishment of a solid northern front against Israel.

The formation of the Syrian–Egyptian–Libyan federation in September 1971 raised few optimistic hopes among Arabs and there were obvious difficulties in creating a sound and permanent federal structure to the union although previous unsuccessful experiments in Arab unity provided the means for avoiding past errors. The Arab League, which remained a loose association of states without any strong central authority, still provided the only framework for comprehensive Arab action. Its subsidiary agencies perform an important function in promoting inter-Arab cultural, technical, and economic co-operation.

The Palestinian Movement

Organized Palestinian Arab guerrilla activity, mainly based in Syria, had existed before 1967 but the June war gave the movement a wholly new impetus. Following the disastrous failure of the Arab armies, the Palestinian Arabs came to the conclusion that they must rely on their own efforts to liberate their lost territory. They received strong emotional sympathy and material support from Arab governments and individuals and they were rapidly successful in promoting and canalizing the Palestinian national consciousness which had remained partially dormant since 1949. The name Palestinian came to be used all over the world. The publication of their aims as a 'democratic, secular state in which Moslems, Jews and Christians could live together with equal status' gained them fresh support in many parts of the world. But their political success was not matched by their military achievements. Although their leadership lacked neither courage nor ability the extreme difficulty of the terrain and the lack of co-operation of the inhabitants of the occupied territories prevented them from posing a serious military threat to Israel. (Israeli casualties on the Suez front with Egypt in the years 1967–70 were considerably higher than in Jordan.) Moreover, the political success of the Palestinian organizations alarmed the governments of Jordan and Lebanon where the guerrillas began to act with unjustified over-confidence as a 'State within a State'. At the same time they failed to overcome their own disunity. The guerrillas were united in their broad aims and in their opposition to the UN Security Council Resolution 242 of 22 November 1967 calling for an Arab-Israeli territorial settlement, but a series of attempts between 1968 and 1970 to adopt a common military strategy and a united attitude towards the Arab regimes for all the various Palestinian organizations were only very partially successful. In particular the Maoist Popular

Front for the Liberation of Palestine of Dr. George Habash refused to accept the leadership of the larger and more moderate al-Fatah organization headed by Yasir Arafat.

This disunity had fatal consequences for the guerrillas in the civil war with the Jordanian Army in September 1970, and the subsequent operations ended with the virtual liquidation of the movement in Jordan during the following year. In 1971 the Palestinian movement was in a seriously weakened position. Iraq, which had given them the strongest moral support, failed to back it with practical action. Syria maintained its own guerrilla force, al-Saiqa, under strict military control, and guerrilla operations against Israel were confined to the Lebanese border. In the occupied territories active resistance to the Israelis was confined to Gaza as the Arabs of the West Bank appeared to have resigned themselves, with reluctance and bitterness, to an indefinite Israeli occupation. There was little enthusiasm for an autonomous Palestinian State on the West Bank either from Israelis or Arabs, and following the events in Jordan of 1970–71 few Palestinians were anxious for a return to Hashimite rule.

Despite the apparent failure of the Palestinian resistance movement in the military field, it remained abundantly clear that there was no simple solution to the basic problem of the Middle East which left the Palestinians out of account. If there was no prospect of their obtaining all that their leaders demanded, they were in a position to ensure that there could be no lasting peace in the area without at least some satisfaction for the aspirations of the Palestinian Arabs.

The 1973 War

Sufficient Arab unity was restored to give the fourth Arab-Israeli war a markedly different outcome from its predecessors. In their co-ordinated surprise-attack on two fronts, Egypt and Syria were initially successful. Egypt crossed the Suez Canal to destroy the Bar-Lev defence line and establish a bridgehead in Sinai. Although the Israeli forces soon rallied to throw back the Syrians and later to cross the Suez Canal the performances of the Arab and Israeli armies were much more evenly matched than in previous wars. In particular the use of Soviet surface-to-air missiles deprived the Israelis of their unchallenged command of the air, which had been decisive in 1967. The Soviet Union and the USA intervened by supplying massive quantities of arms to Arabs and Israelis respectively and then imposed a cease-fire through the UN Security Council.

The relative success of Arab arms had an important effect on the morale of the Arab states, especially Egypt. It became easier for Egypt to contemplate negotiations with Israel that would not be a national humiliation. Of even greater international consequence was the use of the oil weapon by the Arab oil-producing states led by Saudi Arabia in the form of a slowdown in oil exports and an embargo on countries supporting Israel. This move, which had previously been dismissed as unlikely by many Western oil experts, profoundly altered the balance of forces in the region. The Arab reduction in oil output at a time of world-wide energy shortage caused many industrialized countries to introduce restrictions on fuel consumption. The use of the oil weapon caused many governments to modify their attitudes in favour of the Arabs. The EEC countries and Japan made foreign policy declarations on the Middle East which were generally satisfactory to the Arabs although they rejected Libya's demand that they should break relations with Israel and supply the Arabs with arms.

The effect on US policy, although less immediately apparent, was of the greatest significance. One of President Sadat's major objectives in launching the 1973 war was to cause US policy in the Middle East to be more evenly balanced between Arabs and Israelis. In this he was successful. Egypt restored relations with the USA and the US Secretary of State Dr. Henry Kissinger, with whom the Egyptian President established a friendly working relationship, acted as mediator in the negotiation of a First Egyptian-Israeli Disengagement Agreement in Sinai (January 1974), a Syrian-Israeli Disengagement Agreement (April 1974), and a Second Egyptian-Israeli Disengagement Agreement (September 1975).

However, this new relationship between the US and the Arab states placed a severe strain on their unity which had been briefly restored during the 1973 war. Certain Arab states, such as Iraq, Libya, and Algeria, were convinced that the US was still fully committed to Israel and rejected any political solution based on UN Resolution 242. Syria took a position between that of the Rejection Front and Egypt. It was suspicious of both US and Egyptian intentions but was prepared for a political solution. Syria roundly condemned the September 1975 Israeli-Egyptian Agreement which it believed had effectively removed Egypt from the Arab front with Israel. Syria moved closer to Jordan, which shared its fears about Egypt.

For the Palestinian Movement the results of the October War were paradoxical. Because of the shift of world power in favour of the Arabs the Palestinian cause had gained. In 1973 and 1974 the PLO won increasing international recognition. At their summit meeting at Rabat in October 1974 the Arab states accepted the PLO as the sole legitimate representative of the Palestinian people. In November the PLO Chairman Yasir Arafat was invited to address the UN General Assembly with the honours accorded to a head of state. Only Israel and the US continued to refuse any recognition to the PLO. On the other hand, the Palestinians, who had played no part in the decision to go to war in 1973, had to accept that world recognition of the justice of their claims depended heavily on Arab diplomacy; and the key Arab states, notably Egypt, wanted peace. The Palestinian Movement became divided between those who adopted the rejectionist position in varying degrees and those who were prepared to accept the idea of a small independent Palestinian state to include the West Bank and Gaza. Yasir Arafat and the PLO leadership were generally successful in preventing this division from appearing publicly but this was at the cost of failing to adopt any clear programme of political action. The PLO Executive did not transform itself into a transitional government because this would have required a statement of political objectives that would have split the Movement.

Arab divisions were clearly reflected in the Lebanese civil war of 1975–76 of which one of the primary causes was the increased presence of Palestinian guerrillas in Lebanon since the Jordanian civil war of 1970–71. The Lebanese conflict could not be ended until Saudi and Kuwaiti mediation brought about an Arab summit meeting in November 1976, at which Syria agreed to withdraw its opposition to Egypt's Sinai 2 agreement with Israel and Egypt, and most of the other Arab states accepted the presence of the Syrian army in Lebanon as the majority element of an Arab League Deterrent Force.

The Egyptian Peace Initiative

From November 1976 onwards the US Government discussed with Israel and the governments of the Arab front-line states the possibility of convening a Middle East peace conference at Geneva or elsewhere but the objective was constantly frustrated because of the Arab demand that the PLO should represent the Palestinians which was rejected by Israel with American support. The accession to power in Israel in June of a government led by Mr. Begin and dominated by the right-wing Likud caused increased pessimism about peace prospects. In November 1977 President Sadat transformed the situation by announcing his readiness to visit Jerusalem for direct talks with the Israeli Government.

Although President Sadat insisted that the core of the Middle East problem remained that of the Palestinians and that Egypt had no intention of concluding a separate peace with Israel, the majority of Arab states, whom he had not consulted, concluded that this was his objective. Syria, Algeria, Libya, the PDRY, and the PLO formed themselves into a self-styled Front of Steadfastness in opposition to President Sadat.

Israeli-Egyptian negotiations reached an impasse in the spring and summer until the deadlock was broken through the initiative of President Carter who invited President Sadat and Mr. Begin to a tripartite summit meeting at Camp David in the USA in September 1978. This resulted in two agreements: a Framework for the Conclusion of a Peace Treaty between Egypt and Israel, and the Framework of Peace in the Middle East, which referred to the legitimate rights of the Palestinian people and stated that they would participate in the determination of their own future.

With varying degrees of intensity the great majority of Arab states denounced the Camp David agreements. They took special exception to the absence of any formal link between the two agreements and to Article 6 of the draft treaty worked out in subsequent negotiations between Israeli and Egyptian negotiators which gave precedence to the Israeli-Egyptian agreement over Egypt's previous commitments to the other Arab states. The Arab states saw this as proof of their contention that Egypt was aiming for a separate peace. At a meeting called by Iraq in Baghdad in November 1978 the heads of state or representatives of 21 members of the Arab League signed a joint communiqué condemning the Camp David agreements as harmful to the Palestinian people's rights, although the moderate Arab governments successfully prevented the adoption of concrete sanctions against Egypt, at least until the conclusion of any bilateral Israeli-Egyptian agreement. When Egypt signed the Treaty of Washington with Israel on 26 March 1979 the other members of the Arab League, except Sudan, Oman, and Somatra, responded by imposing sanctions against Egypt and removing the headquarters of the Arab League from Cairo to Tunis.

The United States and the Soviet Union

The United States had some causes for satisfaction from developments in the Middle East in the 1970s, at least in the earlier part of the decade. Following President Sadat's expulsion of the Soviet military advisers from Egypt in 1973, his regime moved steadily away from the Soviet camp towards a close alignment with the United States. Saudi Arabia, the United States' closest ally in the Arab world and staunchly anti-Soviet, gained steadily in power and influence during the decade while even American relations with Syria improved for a time following the 1973 war. However, the corollary of this new American relationship with major Arab states and the adoption of a policy which professed to be evenly balanced between Arabs and Isralies, was increased American responsibility for achieving a Middle East peace settlement which culminated in the direct involvement of the US Government as a party to the Camp David agreement between Egypt and Israel in 1978. Moreover, while the United States had gained in influence over certain key Arab states the reverse was also true. By the mid-1970s it could be said that Saudi Arabia, as the largest oil exporter of the non-communist world and a major influence over the international monetary system, carried as much weight in Washington as Israel.

The fragility of improvement in the United States' position in the Middle East was exposed in 1978. Whereas the Soviet Union had suffered a severe setback in Egypt and declining influence in Iraq and Syria, it made important gains on the periphery of the region: with Soviet and Cuban support the Ethiopian regime scored victories over the Arab-backed Somali and Eritrean nationalists. The quasi-Marxist regime in the PDRY provided a link for the communist forces in Africa, and moved closer to the Soviet camp following a coup in October 1978. A left-wing regime took power in Afghanistan. Finally, in a shift of the greatest importance, the regime of the Shah of Iran, the most powerful American surrogate in the region on which the United States relied for the security of the oil-producing Gulf region, collapsed during 1978. The consequences were far-reaching. Already alarmed by Soviet advances in the region and the apparent failure of the US to respond, Saudi Arabia began seriously to question its American alliance. Pro-American Egypt seemed increasingly isolated.

In general, the Soviet Union benefited from the United States' setbacks just as the reverse had occurred in 1972 and 1976. However, there were some factors causing the Soviet Union to act with caution. The vital importance of the Gulf region to the West meant that the acquisition of a Soviet hegemony in the area could provoke a confrontation between the two superpowers. While there were few grounds for expecting that the regime which replaced that of the Shah would be pro-Soviet rather than fiercely Iranian nationalist, this only added to the likelihood of increasing Iranian-Arab rivalry in the Gulf region. This was a potential cause of instability in the Middle East which seemed to rival that of the Arab-Israeli dispute in the 1970s.

FAITHS, SECTS, AND MINORITIES

Islam and the Arabs

Islam, an Arabic word originally meaning 'submission' (to the will of God), is used in two senses: first, the religion of those who believe in the mission of Mohammed as the final revelation of God's will to humanity, and in the Koran as the Word of

God vouchsafed to mankind through Mohammed; and second, the social, cultural, legal, and political system that has grown up around that religion.

Mohammed, who died in AD 632, was an Arab of the family of Hashim, belonging to Quraish, the tribe which occupied Mecca, then a centre of the caravan trade and also of pilgrimage to the Kaaba, the palladium containing a meteoric black stone, long an object of pagan worship and still revered by Moslems at the present day. According to tradition, Mohammed received his first revelation when he was about forty years of age. The Meccans, fearing the loss of the profitable pagan cult centred on their shrine, opposed the new prophet and persecuted his followers, and in AD 622 Mohammed accepted an invitation from the people of Yathrib, thereafter known as al-Madina, 'the City', to settle among them as arbitrator and leader. The Moslem era is reckoned from the beginning of the Arab lunar year in which this migration *(Hijra)* took place. In Medina the Prophet established the first Moslem state which, under his successors the Caliphs (Arabic *khalifa*, deputy) grew into a vast empire.

The chief sources of Islamic doctrine and law are: (1) the Koran, the collected revelations of God to Mohammed, believed by Moslems to be the literal word of God; and (2) the *Sunna*, or practice of the Prophet, who is believed to have been divinely inspired in all his deeds and sayings. These latter were therefore handed down by oral tradition (*Hadith*), and later collected and given an authority second only to that of the Koran. From these two sources, supplemented in the course of time from other sources, by means of 'Reasoning by Analogy' *(Qiyas)* and Consensus (*Ijma*) a complete rule of life and a complex social and legal system were evolved. The Holy Law (*Sharia*) deals with constitutional, civil and criminal matters as well as with cult, ritual, and belief, and is in strict Moslem theory the only legally valid code. It has, however, from early times suffered the competition of customary and state-made law, and is today displaced from many fields of jurisdiction by secular codes of European type.

The Islamic faith is a strict monotheism. Moslems recognize the divine origin of the Old and New Testaments, and are bidden to tolerate Jews and Christians, as possessors of a divine revelation, albeit an incomplete one. Both are believed to have falsified their scriptures, which are superseded by the Koran, the final revelation granted to the last and greatest of the prophets. Pagans and polytheists must be given the choice of Islam, slavery, or the sword.

Islam has no priesthood, but the *ulema*[35] are the authorized interpreters of the Koran and of its application to everyday life. The body of *ulema* supply the *muftis*, who are officially charged to give *fatwas*, or rulings on problems of doctrine and law, and the *qadis*,[36] or judges, who administer the *Sharia*. Islam has a body of observances of which the five most important are called 'the pillars of Islam'. These are: the profession of faith, contained in the formula 'There is no god but God and Mohammed is His Prophet'; prayer, consisting chiefly of the five daily ritual prayers which the believer must perform, wherever he finds himself, facing in the direction of Mecca, and prayers in the mosque on Fridays (the Moslem day of public worship)[37] and festivals; alms; fasting, obligatory for all believers during the whole month of Ramadan, from daybreak until sunset, and comprising total abstinence from food, drink, perfumes, tobacco, and conjugal relations (exemptions are provided in case of illness, travel, holy war, etc.); and pilgrimage, the ceremonial visit to the holy places of Mecca (where the pre-Islamic shrine of the Kaaba remains the sacred centre of Islam) performed on a certain (*Hijra*) date every year, and expected of all believers who can afford it at least once in their lives. Among the tenets of Islam are circumcision, abstention from alcohol, a ban on certain kinds of meat such as pork, and on gambling and usury. An important part is played in all Moslem countries by the system of *waqfs* (Arabic pl. *awqaf*), or endowments for pious purposes, the administration of which is sometimes in the hands of special ministries.

[35] Arabic *'ulemā*, plur. of *'ālim*, learned. In Turkey they are called *Hoja*, in Iran and India *mulla* (maula), or master.

[36] The title *qadi* is used differently in Yemen.

[37] It is only in modern times, and under Christian influence, that Friday has become a weekly day of rest.

Sects

The sects of Islam originated in the disputes over the succession to the Prophet after his death. They subsequently acquired a rather greater significance, which however in modern times they appear to be losing in many areas. The main division is between the Sunnis and the Shiis. The Sunnis are the followers of the *Sunna* – the practice of the Prophet, and they recognize the orthodox Caliphs. They form the great majority of Moslems in almost all countries. They are divided into four legal schools, recognized as equally orthodox: Hanafi, Shafii, Hanbali, Maliki. The Shafii school predominates in the Arabic-speaking countries of the Middle East, except for Upper Egypt and the Sudan, which are Maliki, and Saudi Arabia, which is Hanbali. The Hanafi school is strongest among the Turks, but also has many followers in Syria and Iraq.

Within Sunni Islam there are many forms of faith which, though not condemned as heretical, are aberrant and regarded with suspicion by the *ulema.* Such are the Sufi fraternities (*tariqa*), professing a more mystical and intuitive kind of religion, often associated with the worship of local saints and other local superstitions and customs. At the opposite extreme are the puritanical and fundamentalist Wahhabis, followers of the eighteenth-century Nejdi teacher Mohammed ibn Abdul Wahhab. Wahhabism is the state religion of Saudi Arabia.

The Shiis take their name from the party of Ali (*Shiat Ali*)– those who believed that on the death of Mohammed he should have been succeeded by his son-in-law and cousin Ali. Subdivided into numerous sub-sects, they have in common a belief that the succession was reserved to the direct descendants of Mohammed through his daughter Fatima and her husband Ali. The successor, or Imam, who was also the infallible interpreter of Islam, was generally nominated by the previous Imam from among his sons.

The many Shii sects may be broadly divided into two groups, moderate and extreme. The moderate sects are:

(*a*) The Twelvers (Ithna asharis or Imamis), by far the largest and most important Shii group, who believe that there were twelve Imams – Ali, Hasan, Hussein, and nine in line of descent from Hussein – of whom the twelfth, Mohammed, born in 873, disappeared mysteriously. The believe that the Imam is only 'hidden' and will reappear as the Mahdi (the rightly guided) to establish the golden age. Imamism is today the state religion of Iran. It has a considerable following in Iraq, and a smaller one in parts of Syria and Lebanon, where its adherents are known as Matawila.

(*b*) The Zaidis, the most moderate, who admit the election of Imams and take their name from a grandson of Hussein whom they recognized as Imam. Their doctrine differs very little from that of the Sunnis. Zaidism is the state religion of Yemen.

The extremist sects are:

(*a*) The Ismailis, who take their name from Ismail, a son of the sixth Imam. The Ismailis are subdivided into several groups and have their main centres at the present day in India. In the Middle East they are represented by minorities in the Yemen, in central Syria, and in eastern and north-eastern Iran. The Iranian and some of the Syrian Ismailis belong to that branch of the sect that is headed by the Aga Khan, and known in India as Khojas.

(*b*) The Druzes, another occult sect, who are an offshoot of the Ismailis, from whom they parted company in the early eleventh century, when they accepted the Fatimid Caliph Hakim as the final incarnation of the Deity. They are to be found only in parts of Syria, Lebanon, and Israel.

(*c*) The Alawis (also called Nusayris), who carry the Shii tendency to its ultimate extreme and believe that Ali was an incarnation of God Himself. They are to be found in the coastal highlands of northern Syria, and also in the adjoining Turkish provinces.

(*d*) The Ahl i-haqq, who profess similar doctrines and are to be found in western Iran and eastern Turkey.

Two other groups which belong neither to Sunni nor to Shii Islam are:

(*a*) The Kharijites (*khawarij* = seceders), in early days an important sect in Islam, surviving today only in the Ibadi communities of Algeria and Zanzibar, and in Oman, where Ibadism is the state religion.

(*b*) The Yazidis, described by their neighbours as devil-worshippers. Their religion is rather a denial of the existence of evil; it seems to be an amalgam containing pagan, Zoroastrian, Manichaean, Jewish, Christian, Moslem, Sabaean, and Shamanistic elements. They are to be found in north-eastern Syria, in the Jabal Sinjar area of Iraq, and in the Caucasus.

The 'Legacy of Islam'[38]

The first Arab rulers made extensive use of Iranian, Syrian, Christian, and Jewish engineers, technicians, and doctors, and from Abbasid times began consciously to encourage learning and the arts. The Caliph al-Mansur (754–75), who founded Baghdad, employed large numbers of astronomers, engineers, and scholars. A need was soon felt for the translation into Arabic of Greek and other scientific and philosophic works. Many of these translations were made not from the originals but from Syriac versions. A pioneer in this development was the great patron of scholarship and science, the Caliph al-Mamun (813–33), who also founded the Arab university system. The encouragement of science and learning came to be a regular part of the functions of a Caliph, and distinguished scholars were attached to the courts of different Moslem rulers of Africa and Spain as well as in the East. By its union of Hellenic with Iranian and Indian scientific traditions, and by the transmission of Hellenic thought, Islam performed what is often regarded as its most important service to the world, though there are hardly any sciences to which it did not also make important original contributions. During the pre-Renaissance period in Europe it was to Arabic sources that Europeans turned in their attempts to rediscover the scientific heritage of Greece and Rome; and the improvement which the Arabs were able to introduce into mathematics by the use of a simplified system of notation of Indian origin was of critical importance in European intellectual development.

Islamic medicine was also of great significance. Some leading names were Hussein ibn Ishaq (809–77), the great Baghdad translator, who was also a physician; al-Khwarizmi (d.

[38] Joseph Schacht with C. E. Bosworth, eds., *The Legacy of Islam* (2nd edn., Oxford, 1974).

c. 840), the astronomer and mathematician; al-Razi (Rhazes: *c.* 865–925), an Iranian, 'the greatest physician of the Islamic world and one of the great physicians of all time';[39] Ibn al-Haitham (Alhazen: *c.* 965), the physicist, whose work on optics was of the first importance; al-Kindi (b. *c.* 850) who made contributions to philosophy and a number of sciences; al-Battani (Albategnius: *c.* 900), the astronomer who made most impression on Europe; al-Farabi (d. *c.* 951), the Turkish philosopher, who also wrote a treatise 'On music'; Omar Khayyam (d. 1123), the Iranian mathematician and poet; Ibn Rushd (Averroës; d. 1198), 'among the very greatest of Aristotelian philosophers'; and Moses Maimonides (1135–1204), the Jewish physician and philosopher at the court of Saladin.

Minorities in the Islamic World[40]

The emergence of nationalism in the Islamic world had an adverse effect on the conditions of minorities. The use of minorities by great powers, particularly Russia, as an instrument of policy, and the corresponding tendency of such minorities to seek outside assistance against oppression or their communal enemies at home caused the 'atrocities'[41] which have aroused world opinion from time to time.

The victims of these persecutions sometimes achieved national independence themselves.[42] In other cases they found themselves in one of the new nation-states, no longer persecuted perhaps, but precariously situated, and deprived of the communal autonomy and immunities which the Christians and Jews had enjoyed under the *millet* system. Still worse, they might be split up among different states.

A minority is identified either by language, as in the case of the Kurds, or by religion, as in the case of the Copts and the Druze, or by both together, as in the case of the Armenians. While linguistic minorities have tended to become national in character, religious minorities have on the whole tended to

[39] Ibid.

[40] See A.H. Hourani, *Minorities in the Arab World* (London, 1947).

[41] e.g. the 'Bulgarian atrocities' of 1876 and the 'American atrocities' of 1894 and 1915 in Turkey; or the Assyrian massacre of 1933 in Iraq.

[42] Greece, 1832; Rumania (autonomous principality), 1862; Serbia, 1878; Bulgaria (partial self-government), 1878; Montenegro, 1878.

become nationally assimilated to their chief linguistic group. In both cases, however, contrary tendencies have also been at work. The most difficult minorities have been those which had a special language, a special national church, and a past history of greatness, like the Armenians or the Jews. Here the new nationalism merely stimulated a sense of nationality which was already present.

Armenians

The Armenians are the descendants of a people who, from the sixth century BC until the First World War, had had a continuous national existence in what is today eastern Turkey and part of Soviet Transcaucasia, which together make up the Arminiyya of the Abbasid geographers. (Of the area, estimated at 115,000 square miles, about one tenth remains Armenian today, as a Soviet republic.) The Armenian language is an independent member of the Indo-European family, and is written in a script invented in AD 404. The Armenians are the oldest Christian nation; they have their own Church (correctly known as the Armenian Apostolic, and not Armenian Orthodox or Armenian Gregorian). The head of the Church is known as the Catholicos. Since the fifteenth century there have been two Armenian Catholicoses; today one resides in Echmiadzin, Soviet Armenia, and the other in Antilias, Lebanon. In ancient and medieval times Armenia had a long tradition of self-government. Sometimes the nation achieved actual independence, as under the Bagratid monarchy (886–1045), which was recognized and initially courted by both the Byzantine emperor and the Abbasid caliph.

After the collapse of the Bagratids under Byzantine and Seljuk pressure, the Armenians set up a new homeland in Cicilia, in the north-east corner of the Mediterranean. Here they established a kingdom which lasted for almost three hundred years, until it fell to the Mamelukes in 1375. A number of Armenians embraced the Catholic faith when their ruling family married into the Lusignans.

The Ottoman sultan recognized the Armenians as a separate community in 1461, when the Armenian patriarchate of Constantinople was established. Armenia itself was not conquered by the Ottomans until the first half of the following century, after which Kurds were introduced into the country to guard the frontier with Shiite Persia.

In the nineteenth century Russia replaced Persia as the empire hostile to Ottoman Turkey whose border with her ran through the middle of Armenia. The new power brought to Armenians stability and the possibility of improving their lot. From 1828 to 1840 the Tsar created an *Armyanskaya oblast* (Armenian district) out of the former Persian khanates of Erevan and Nakhichevan, and regulated by means of statutes (*polozhenye*) the affairs of the Armenian Church, giving it a wide measure of autonomy.

Meanwhile, in Ottoman Armenia, the situation deteriorated: the mostly agricultural Armenians were at a perpetual disadvantage to their Kurdish neighbours, since as Christians they were unable to bear arms. Also the level of Ottoman administration was low. The promised 'reforms' always turned out to be illusory, at least in the provinces, and so Armenian political societies emerged. In 1894 there was a rising in Sasun, which Sultan Abdul Hamid crushed with extreme ferocity; and in the following year there was a series of government-inspired massacres throughout Anatolia and Turkish Armenia. Tens, perhaps hundreds, of thousands of Armenians were slain. Many Armenians fled, some as far as California. (The community at Fresno dates from these events.)

Ten years later, in the year of the first Russian revolution, the Tsar himself attempted to suppress the Armenians, whose revolutionary politics had made them suspect. Through the agency of the Azarbaijani Tatars he attempted to kill them in manner of Abdul Hamid. But, except in Baku (where the oil-fields were also set alight) and Nakhichevan, he was largely unsuccessful, since the Armenians had learnt the techniques of self-defence.

With the promulgation of the Ottoman constitution in 1908 – a revolution in which Armenians played a significant part – their position in the Turkish empire improved; but by 1912 even the most ardent Armenian supporters of the Committee of Union and Progress had become disillusioned, mainly because the CUP refused to discuss the return of lands taken from Armenians in the massacres of 1894–6. The influence of pan-Turkism in the CUP was a sinister development for

Armenia as a whole, since the CUP developed close ties with chauvinist circles in Baku.

On the outbreak of the First World War Ottoman Armenians saw little to fear, but on 24 April 1915 over 250 of their leading figures in the imperial capital were taken into the Anatolian interior and murdered. There followed mass killings of Armenians of all classes throughout the Armenian plateau and Cicilia; many were driven into the deserts and left to die so as not to waste bullets. Reasonable estimates of those killed put the number at 1¼–1½ million.

After the Russian Revolution eastern (Russian) Armenia was able to proclaim its independence, which was strengthened with the conclusion of the Great War. Despite high hopes of the Paris Peace Conference nothing except uncertain quantities of food was delivered to Armenia; the delay in producing the Turkish treaty (the Treaty of Sèvres) meant that by the time it was signed it could not be implemented. The rise of the Turkish Nationalist movement, and the establishment of a new Turkish army out of the Ottoman 15th Army Corps led to an assault on Armenia in September 1920 and the collapse of the republic of Armenia: Turkey took all the land up to the Arpa Chai (as well as the region of Surmalu, on the plain of Ararat, which was not part of Mustafa Kemal's maximalist 'National Pact'). The government in the Armenian capital, Erevan, handed over power peacefully to the Bolsheviks on 2 December. (However Communists today hold that Bolshevik rule began with an uprising on 29 November.)

Western (Turkish) Armenia was no more; and the French, keen for concessions from the new Nationalist Turkey, withdrew in 1921 from Cilicia which they had been occupying since November 1919. The remnants of Armenians fled, mostly to Syria and Lebanon. Armenians were not strangers to the Arab world: for centuries an Armenian community had clustered around their patriarchate in Jerusalem, and the first and last governors of the independent Mt. Lebanon, Daud Pasha (1861–8) and Ohannes Pasha Kuyumjian (1912–15), were both Catholic Armenians. In Lebanon, Armenians were offered citizenship in 1924; they gained their first deputy in parliament in 1934 (currently they are allotted five), and their first government minister in 1958.

Throughout the Middle East, and indeed everywhere outside Soviet Armenia and Turkey, Armenian political life is dominated by three parties, known in their Western Armenian forms as the *Hunchags* (consistently socialist, founded in 1887, today supporting Armenia on most issues), the *Tashnags* (the Armenian Revolutionary Federation, founded in 1890, basically nationalist with a socialist tinge, often critical of Soviet Armenia), and the *Ramgavars* (democratic liberals, founded in 1921, a party which attracts liberal intellectuals and conservative merchants, which supports Soviet Armenia as being the alternative to obliteration, and which opposes political adventurism).

Soviet Armenia acts as an ambiguous lodestone to Armenians throughout the world. Since 1956 the Soviet authorities have built it up as a land of prosperity and cultural development. Although religion *per se* is criticized, the Armenian Church is unofficially well respected, and the part it played in the struggles against the Ottomans and the Romanovs acknowledged. A number of Armenians from the Middle East, Europe and America have settled in Armenia, aware that this is the only way they can be sure that their families will remain Armenian. (An estimated 105,000 settled in 1945–7, when there was a strong likelihood that Armenia would regain Kars and Ardahan).

If one takes into account their natural preoccupation with Soviet Aremnia, dispersed Aremnians have, as a refugee community, identified quite strongly with their countries of refuge. (And the Arabs for their part have shown remarkable absorptive capacity in accepting a non-Moslem, non-Arabic-speaking people.) Armenians do however go to great lengths to preserve their own identity and culture. What they feel as the cruel injustice that they suffered at the hands of the Turks still rankles within nearly all of them, and hostility to Turkey seems to grow, rather than to diminish, with passing years.

Assyrians

The Assyrians are Nestorian Christians speaking a form of Syriac. At the outbreak of the First World War they were living in three main groups: in the Hakkiari highlands of south-eastern Turkey, the plains to the west of Lake Urmiya in north-west Iran, and the lowlands to the south of the Hakkiari district, now part of Iraq. 'In their mountain-home they lived as shepherds, feudally organized under their *maliks* with their Patriarch, the Mar Shimun, as their temporal as well as spiritual ruler.'[43] During the war the Hakkiari Assyrians revolted under Russian instigation against the Turks. They were expelled and joined the Urmiya Assyrians and the Russians. After the collapse of Russia they fled, and the British military authorities disarmed them and sent them to the refugee camp at Baquba near Baghdad. In 1919 there were 25,000 of them there. The frontier settlement of 1925 assigned almost the whole of the Hakkiari highlands to Turkey, so that it was impossible for the majority of them to return home. A great deal was done to resettle them in Iraq, and many were recruited by the British (during the mandatory period) into the Assyrian Levies to guard aerodromes and police the tribes – tasks which did not increase their popularity. A section of them led by the Mar Shimun were intransigent and petitioned to leave Iraq or to be granted autonomy there. After Iraq had become an independent member of the League and accepted as a member an obligation to protect her minorities, a clash occurred on 4 August 1933 between Iraqi troops and some Assyrians who had crossed the Tigris into Syria and then tried to return under arms. The Assyrians were repulsed and the Iraqi army then organized a massacre of unarmed Assyrians at Simel. About 600 were killed here and in other places, and sixty Assyrian villages were looted. Their spirit broken, about 6,000 Assyrians crossed over into Syria, where they have since been settled, while those who remained in Iraq have not been involved in further incidents.[44]

Kurds

A people with an ancient history, of mountain origin, speaking an Indo-European group of dialects (Kurdish) related to Persian, the Kurds inhabit an arc stretching from Kermanshah in Iran across the north-eastern corners of Iraq and Syria, to Kars and Erzerum in Turkey, just crossing the western frontier of

[43]Hourani, *Minorities in the Arab World,* p. 99.

[44]RIIA, *Survey of International Affairs, 1934,* pp. 135–74. Large numbers of Assyrians from Syria were again recruited into British levies during the Second World War.

Soviet Armenia, and from there south-west as far as Birjik. Many are now plain-dwellers and townsmen, which has favoured the growth of nationalism in a group of communities which are still fundamentally tribal and disunited. The Kurds are mostly Sunni Moslems. Estimates of Kurdish population are exceptionally difficult to establish. The Minority Rights Report on the Kurds of 1975 gave estimates of their distribution as follows: Turkey 3.2 million – 8 million, Iran 1.8 million – 5 million, Iraq 1.55 million – 2.5 million, Syria 320,000 – 600,000.

The Treaty of Sèvres of 1920 between the Allies of the First World War recognized an independent Kurdish state of Kurdistan but this was cancelled by the Treaty of Lausanne of 1923. The Kurdish minorities have been in frequent conflict with the authorities, particularly in Turkey, Iraq, and Iran. During the period of Soviet-sponsored Azarbaijan autonomy in 1945–6, an independent Kurdish Republic was set up at Mahabad of which Zaki Mohammed was elected President on 22 January 1946. After the Iranian reoccupation of Azarbaijan, Zaki Mohammed was arrested, sentenced to death, and hanged on 31 March 1947. In Iraq there were Kurdish uprisings against the Government in 1922–3, 1931–2, 1944–5 and almost continuously throughout the 1960s following the return from exile in the Soviet Union of the Kurdish Democratic Party leader Mustafa Barzani. Fighting ended following the Iraqi Government's agreement with Barzani and his followers in March 1970 which provided for a four-year transitional period leading to the establishment of an autonomous Kurdish region within the Iraqi state. Kurdish-Arab relations improved for a time until March 1974, on the fourth anniversary of the agreement, when Barzani and his followers rejected the Baghdad government's formal offer of autonomy as hypocritical and inadequate and rose once again in rebellion. The fighting was bitter, with heavy casualties on both sides. The Kurdish nationalists received support from Iran which also provided a refuge for their guerrilla forces across the border. In March 1975, however, Iraq and Iran reached an agreement to settle their various differences; Iran withdrew its support, the rebellion collapsed and Barzani went into exile. The Iraqi government went ahead with the establishment of the Kurdish

Autonomous Region in the Kurdish majority areas although Kurdish nationalist sources charged that Kurdish villages were being forcibly moved to the south to alter the structure of the population. In 1977–8 there was some revival of Kurdish nationalist activity although on a smaller scale, and it seemed unlikely that the Kurdish problem had been finally solved in Iraq. In Iran the Khomeini Revolution of 1978–9 gave rise to the revival of demands for regional autonomy among Iranian Kurds.

Christian Communities:[45] *A. The Greek Orthodox and Western Churches*

The Orthodox Eastern Church is a group of autocephalous churches using the Byzantine rite. It comprises the four original Eastern Patriarchates, out of which it grew historically, and a number of national branches. Its adherents in the Middle East are nearly all Arab or Greek. The Eastern Patriarchates, which finally broke with the Western Church in AD 1054,[46] are Constantinople, Alexandria, Antioch, and Jerusalem. In addition there are the Church of Cyprus and the Church of Mount Sinai, consisting of little more than the monastery of St. Catherine.

The Oecumenical Patriarch at Constantinople enjoyed in Ottoman times almost the same exalted position as he had under the Byzantine Emperors. Modern Turkey has been persuaded to allow the Patriarchate to continue, though it is of much diminished importance. But it still has jurisdiction over the Greeks who have remained as Turkish subjects in Constantinople. In Greece the Church has been autocephalous since 1850.

The Patriarch of Alexandria, resident in Cairo, has a following of about 100,000 Arabs and Greeks. The Patriarchate of Antioch, with its seat now at Damascus and some 300,000 members, is 'almost wholly Arab'[47] in hierarchy, laity, and liturgy. In the Patriarchate of Jerusalem, with 30,000 members,

[45] Hourani, *Minorities in the Arab World.*

[46] They were excommunicated by Pope Leo IX. There was a brief period of reunion in the fifteenth century.

[47] Hourani, *Minorities in the Arab World.*

'the upper clergy are Greek, the lower clergy and most of the laity Arab'.[48]

Roman Catholics, Anglicans, and Protestants. The Roman Catholics are subdivided into Roman Catholic and Uniate Churches. Roman Catholics of the Latin rite are ordinary members of the Church of Rome. They have a Roman Catholic (Latin) Patriarch in Jerusalem and Apostolic Delegates or Nuncios in Beirut, Cairo, and Baghdad. The Uniate Churches are those which have been allowed to retain their own Oriental rites and customs. They enjoy autonomy under their own elected Patriarchs. Those in the Middle East are:

1. The Greek Catholic Church (ex-Greek Orthodox). Greek liturgy; Patriarch of Alexandria, resident in Cairo.
2. The Syrian Catholic Church (ex-Syrian Orthodox). Syriac liturgy; Patriarch of Antioch, resident in Beirut.
3. The Armenian Catholic Church (ex-Armenian Orthodox). Armenian liturgy; Patriarch of Constantinople, resident near Beirut.
4. The Chaldean Catholic Church (ex-Nestorian). Syriac liturgy; Patriarch of Babylon, resident in Mosul.
5. The Coptic Catholic Church (ex-Coptic Orthodox). Arabic liturgy; it has a Patriarch of Alexandria resident in Cairo.
6. The Maronite Church (ex-Monothelete).[49] Syriac liturgy; Patriarch of Antioch, resident in Lebanon.

The Anglican Church, besides ministering to the British communities distributed throughout the Middle East, has a few thousand non-European baptized members, for whom it maintains colleges and schools.

The Protestants are converts made by English, Scottish, American, and other Protestant missions during the nineteenth and twentieth centuries. Though few in numbers, they have produced some leading intellectuals, notably through the medium of the American University at Beirut.

[48] Ibid.

[49] A modification of Monophysitism abandoned by the Maronites in the twelfth century.

Christian Communities: B. The Oriental Churches

The Monophysites emphasized the single nature of Christ and rejected the Council of Chalcedon. Monophysite Churches in the Middle East are:

1. The Coptic Church in Egypt (of which the Ethiopian Church is a branch) has its own Patriarch of Alexandria (now resident in Cairo) and has a liturgy in Coptic and Arabic.

2. The Syrian 'Orthodox' Church (Jacobite Church), organized under a Patriarch of Antioch (resident in Homs), which has a Syriac liturgy.

The Armenians, accounted Monophysites, disclaim Monophysitism and should perhaps be listed with the Greek Orthodox. The Armenian Apostolic ('Gregorian') Church, the national Church of the Armenians, dates from the fourth century. It has three Patriarchs, the most exalted of whom is the Catholicos of Echmiadzin in Soviet Armenia, and an Armenian liturgy.

The Nestorians emphasize the dual nature of Christ. The Nestorian Church is headed by a Patriarch, the Mar Shimun, and has a Syriac liturgy. It grew up in the fifth century in Syria, Mesopotamia, and Persia and sent missions across Asia as far as China. It was largely destroyed by the Mongol invasions of the fourteenth century and today the Assyrians are all that remain.

The Sabaeans ('Baptists'), also called the Mandaeans and the 'Christians of St. John'; their religion combines elements of various origins and periods.

SOME ARAB POLITICAL MOVEMENTS

The Syrian Social Nationalist Party (al-Hizb al-Suri al-Qawmi or *Parti Populaire Syrien)*

The SSNP has been described as 'the first organized party in the Arab East to have a definite national doctrine and a well structured ideology'.[50] It was founded in 1932 by Antoun Saadeh, the son of a Lebanese Greek Orthodox emigrant to Latin America who returned to the Near East in 1929.

[50] Labib Zuwiyya Yamak, *The Syrian Social Nationalist Party: an Ideological Analysis* (Harvard Middle Eastern Monographs), 1966.

The first of his eight principles which he published in his book *Nushu' al-umma* (Beirut, 1938) states that 'Syria is for the Syrians, and the Syrians are a complete nation'. They were not Arabs but the people whose natural home had been Syria since prehistoric times.

In exalting the Syrian nation he preached the absolute need for social unity: 'Through national unity, the conflict of loyalties and negative attitudes will disappear and will be replaced by a single healthy national loyalty which will ensure the revival of the nation.'[51] Thus he identified society with the nation, which he placed above everything.

Saadeh also proposed five principles of reform which he regarded as an integral part of his doctrine. They were: (1) separation of Church and State; (2) prevention of the clergy from interfering in political and judicial matters; (3) removal of the barriers between the various sects and confessions; (4) abolition of feudalism, i.e. the organization of the national economy on the basis of production, the protection of the rights of labour, and the interests of the nation and the State; and (5) formation of a strong army which would be effective in determining the destiny of the nation and the State.

These were practical ideas which appealed to many Arab intellectuals from the 1930s onwards even if they rejected Saadeh's exaltation of Syrian, as opposed to Arab, nationalism. His anti-sectarianism was especially attractive to the religious and racial minorities – Christians, Druzes, Kurds, and Alawis – who became a majority in the party hierarchy.

Saadeh possessed all the natural qualities of leadership, and the idea of absolute obedience to a single leader *(al-zaim)* became enshrined in the party's principles.

Not unnaturally, while the SSNP attracted some enthusiastic and even fanatical adherents it was deeply repugnant to many of the inhabitants of geographical Syria. Lebanese separatists and Arab nationalists rejected it for opposite reasons, the French authorities found it subversive. Others disliked its anti-democratic fascist tendencies and still others its secularism. The history of the party was troubled and violent.

In the 1930s, the party was in constant trouble with both the French and the Lebanese authorities, and Saadeh was

[51] *The Principles of the Syrian Social Nationalist Party* (Beirut, 1949), pp. 28–9.

twice imprisoned. In 1939 Saadeh was caught by the outbreak of war in South America and was unable to return to the Middle East until 1947.

In June 1949 there was a serious armed clash in Beirut between the SSNP and members of the right-wing Lebanese nationalist Katayib Party. Saadeh eventually fled to Syria where he was at first warmly received by the leader of Syria's first post-independence military coup, Husni al-Zaim. But Lebanese diplomatic pressure combined with anti-SSNP elements inside Syria persuaded him to agree to Saadeh's extradition to Lebanon where he was tried and sentenced by a secret military tribunal and executed the following day.

Armed resistance by the SSNP militia, which Saadeh had ordered on the strength of Zaim's initial support, ceased after his execution. The party had suffered a catastrophe; it was leaderless and demoralized but it did not collapse completely. In the November 1949 elections nine SSNP members were elected to the Syrian National Assembly. The party headquarters under the new President, George Abdul Masih, moved to Damascus. However, the party never made real headway against the combined strength of the Syrian traditional forces and rising power of the left – Baath socialists and communists. After the assassination of Colonel Malki in 1954 by a sergeant in the SSNP the party was ruthlessly suppressed in Syria.

The party managed to survive this new disaster. In Lebanon its recovery was more lasting than in Syria. In 1951 three members assassinated Riyadh al-Sulh in Jordan and in 1952 the SSNP was an important element in the bloodless coup which overthrew Bishara al-Khoury and brought Camille Chamoun to power.

The party was still officially illegal in Lebanon but it enjoyed Chamoun's protection. It had its own newspapers and a disciplined organization. During the muted civil war in the summer of 1958 it gave Chamoun effective armed support for which it was rewarded by official recognition.

But the SSNP with its rigid dogma was unhappy in the post-1958 Lebanon of President Chehab, with his policy of national reconciliation. While the party was detested by the pan-Arab nationalists and the left it was still suspect to its temporary allies the Lebanese nationalists on the right. It had virtually no support in the army which was overwhelmingly loyal to President Chehab. In the 1960 elections it was heavily defeated. Shortly afterwards Dr. Abdullah Saadeh (no relative of the founder) was elected president of the party. Since he was more flexible than his predecessors and aware that if the party was to thrive it must come to terms with both Lebanese and Arab nationalism the SSNP might have improved its prospects. Instead Saadeh allowed himself to be persuaded to endorse an attempt to overthrow the Lebanese Government by force on 31 December 1961. Since it was opposed by every other political group in Lebanon the gesture was hopeless and futile. Mass arrests of party members were followed by long and laborious trials. The eight death sentences were later commuted to life imprisonment.

Since the party has survived more than one apparently final disaster, it cannot now be pronounced extinct. It would not be licensed by any conceivable regime in Syria, but it is able to remain above ground in Lebanon. In the Lebanese civil war of 1975–6 the party, with its armed militia, inclined towards the Moslem/leftist side against the Christian separatists.

The Moslem Brotherhood and Islamic Revivalism

The Moslem Brotherhood has been called by one distinguished Arab writer 'the greatest of modern Islamic Movements',[52] although it never succeeded in spreading beyond the frontiers of the eastern Arab states.

The Brotherhood was founded in Ismailia in 1928 by a 22-year-old elementary school teacher named Hassan al-Banna, the son of a respected orthodox Islamic scholar. 'At its inception the Brotherhood was in essence a religious revival movement – a "revitalization movement" in the terminology of modern anthropologists. It soon developed into a politico-religious action society, and eventually, as it gained political influence, it became more political than religious.'[53]

Banna was small, vital, eloquent, and intelligent, with outstanding qualities of leadership. Initially his movement was

[52] Ishak Musa Hussaini, *The Moslem Brethren* (Beirut, 1956).

[53] Christina Phelps Harris, *Nationalism and Revolution in Egypt* (London, 1964).

concerned with protecting Islam against the forces of immorality and secularism encouraged by Western influence. In a sense he was a successor to Islamic reformers such as Jamal el-din al-Afghani or Rashid Rida, but Banna simplified their arguments to a simple demand for a return to the laws of the Koran and the Tradition.

In the early years Banna appealed most to the poor and uneducated but in 1934 he moved his headquarters to Cairo and began to attract supporters from all classes including students, teachers, civil servants, and army officers. Already in the 1930s Banna had expanded his programme from religious revival to demands that the entire political, legal, and administrative system should be based on the Koran. But despite Banna's vigorous assertion that Islam could provide everything needed for the social order without recourse to alien Western systems such as Communism or Fascism, he had no clearly thought out political programme. The Brotherhood published many books but at this stage they had no consistent theoretical basis. What Banna did concentrate upon was the disciplining and organization of the movement into a formidable political force. He overrode the objections of some of his followers and became increasingly authoritarian. He changed his title from General Guide to Supreme Guide.

The Brotherhood was organized in a network of branches whose activities included social welfare, education, and physical training. There were youth groups which were given paramilitary training. In 1936 Banna denounced the Wafdist Government's treaty with Britain and in the following year gave active assistance to the Arab rebellion in Palestine. Intervention in Palestine helped the movement to spread outside Egypt. The first branch was founded in Damascus in 1937, followed by others in Lebanon, Palestine, Sudan, and Iraq.

In 1948 many of the Brotherhood volunteered to fight with the Arab armies in Palestine where they showed courage and gained valuable guerrilla experience. In Egypt the political atmosphere was sharply deteriorating. The already unpopular regime, beset by scandal and accusations of corruption, was blamed for the disasters of the war. Terrorism and assassination, for which the Moslem Brotherhood bore much of the responsibility, were on the increase. In December 1948 the Prime

Minister, Noqrashi Pasha, made use of wartime martial law to strike back by proclaiming the Brotherhood dissolved and closing its branches. On 28 December, Noqrashi was murdered, almost certainly by the Brotherhood, and two months later Banna himself was assassinated – probably by King Farouk's counter-terrorist forces.

After this shattering blow the movement remained largely quiescent until the lifting of martial law in 1950 when it was declared legal provided it refrained from political activity. But on the election in 1951 of a new Supreme Guide, a well-educated ex-magistrate named Hassan al-Hudaybi, the movement began to reorganize and to give itself a more consistent ideological position. Rapidly the Brotherhood recovered its spirits, denouncing the Government for the continued restrictions on its liberty and resuming its paramilitary activities. As Egypt sank into near-anarchy the Brotherhood saw its opportunity. Although the shares of responsibility for the burning of Cairo on 26 January 1952 have never been allocated, the Moslem Brotherhood undoubtedly played an important role.

The Brotherhood had reason to hope that when the monarchical regime collapsed it would take a leading role in the new Government if not control it entirely. But when the Free Officers carried out their coup in July 1952 they did not consider handing over power to the Brotherhood. In general they were favourably disposed towards the movement. But when the Brotherhood asked the new Revolutionary Command Council to create an Islamic state with an Islamic constitution, it declined. When the RCC refused, the movement silently resolved to go into opposition. It issued its own reform programme and when this was ignored by the RCC (although many of the Brotherhood's social and economic ideas coincided closely with its own) it turned to organizing a subversive movement within the police, armed forces, and labour unions.

But behind the scenes Colonel Nasser, who was only just emerging as the real leader of the Free Officers, began to show his great ability as a political tactician. Making skilful use of divisions within the Brotherhood, he broke up its cells in the police and army. The RCC dissolved the Brotherhood as a political movement and arrested several leaders, including the Supreme Guide. The Brotherhood temporarily recovered as a result of the Nasser-Neguib crisis in February in which Neguib at first came out on top. Neguib had never been a sympathizer but he was prepared to be used by any potential opponents of Nasser and the RCC majority.

During this summer Nasser was engaged in prolonged negotiations with Britain for an agreement on evacuation. In order to show that he could ensure security in the Canal Zone he arrested and dispersed the Communists and Brotherhood guerrilla groups in the area. Hudaybi at once toured the Arab states denouncing Nasser as a 'traitor to the national cause'. The Brotherhood also attacked the draft Anglo-Egyptian treaty as a sell-out. Nasser replied by repriving the Egyptian Brotherhood's leaders in Syria of their nationality.

When on 26 October 1954 a simple-minded member of the Brotherhood tried unsuccessfully to murder Nasser at a rally in Alexandria the Government was fully prepared. Police and army broke up all the Brotherhood's cells, confiscated their arms, and arrested more than 4,000 people. The would-be assassin and three terrorists were executed together with two members of the Supreme Guidance Council. Hudaybi himself was sentenced to life imprisonment.

In 1954 the movement seemed to have few prospects. A strong branch remained in Syria as an outspoken opponent of Nasser's Egypt. But in the 1950s it was swimming against the powerful current of triumphant Nasserism which was sweeping the Arab countries. In Egypt itself Nasser's political control was virtually complete and for years the Brethren shared political prison camps with Communists. When Syria was united with Egypt in 1958 the Syrian Brethren had to go underground also. They had a brief opportunity to reassert themselves after the secession in 1961 but had little sympathy from the Baathists who took control of Syria in 1963 – still less from the neo-Baathists in 1966.

President Nasser's announcement in August 1965 that a widespread Moslem Brotherhood conspiracy had been uncovered in Egypt therefore caused some surprise. Some 2,000 people were arrested and about 400 stood trial on charges of planning to assassinate the President and sabotage all major government installations. It seems likely that the seriousness of the physical threat posed by the Brotherhood to the regime in 1965 was exaggerated; on the other hand the fact that prominent members included a number of university lecturers, scientists, and engineers was alarming for the regime.

Those of the Egyptian Brotherhood who escaped were able to find refuge in the Sudan, where the Moslem Brothers had a flourishing organization in political alliance with the Umma Party, and to Saudi Arabia. But although the Saudi regime was sympathetic and held the suppression of the Brotherhood as proof of Egypt's irreligion, it did not consider it necessary to encourage the growth of a branch of the movement in Saudi Arabia, the home of Wahhabism and Islamic puritanism.

The Brotherhood emerged again as a strong political force in Egypt under President Sadat. The Brothers who remained in prison were released in 1971 and although they were not licensed as a political party when a limited party system was restored in 1976, they were tolerated and permitted to publish their own newspaper *al-Da'wa* (the *Call*). The Sadat regime saw the Brotherhood as an anti-communist force and Saudi Arabia provided support from outside. However, the regime was not tolerant towards extreme radical Islamic revivalist groups which were suspected of terrorism and believed to have Libyan support, such as the al-Takfir wal-Higra (Repentance and Flight from Sin) group responsible for the kidnapping and murder of a prominent religious figure in July 1977.

The movement of Islamic renaissance was very evident in Egypt from 1977 onwards. It was not confined to members of the Brotherhood but manifested itself in parliament with demands for the institution of pure *sharia* law in Egypt. Islamic revivalist candidates were dominant in university student elections in 1978. In Egypt and elsewhere in the Middle East such elements received strong inspiration and encouragement from the Khomeini movement in Iran. There were indications that the Sadat regime was beginning to regard the Brotherhood and its allies as a threat when, contrary to government policy, they welcomed the overthrow of the Shah of Iran.

Nasserism

Nasserism cannot be regarded as an organized political movement, still less as a political party. Gamal Abdul Nasser himself denied its existence, yet the term is used to describe something which most people can identify. In its time it has influenced the lives of almost every Arab and for several years it was infinitely more powerful than any political movement in the Middle East.

As the leader of the Egyptian Free Officers, Nasser was essentially a pragmatist with little interest in ideology. His energies were concentrated on the twin problems of ridding Egypt of the British and purging its corrupt monarchical parliamentary regime. The Free Officers had drafted an agrarian reform programme which was implemented soon after they came to power but its purpose was less to solve Egypt's agrarian problems than to break the political power of the big landowners. For similar reasons Nasser opposed the restitution of Egyptian political parties. He was convinced that the parliamentary system had prevented Egypt from obtaining 'independence with dignity' but he had no plan for anything to replace it. He created out of his own mind a single political organization – the Liberation Rally – which was succeeded by the National Union and, in 1962, the Arab Socialist Union.

But it was not the political ideas of the Free Officers which constituted the appeal of Nasserism to the Arab world. In the first years after 1952 Nasser was regarded with suspicion in many nationalist quarters. The change in his standing in the Arab nationalist movement came in 1954 with his determined opposition to the Baghdad Pact, his adoption of non-alignment, and his defiance of the West with his recognition of Communist China and the Czech arms deal. To the Arab man in the street Nasser was a new Saladin who, having shown he could successfully defy Western opinion, would lead the Arabs to unity, independence, and the recovery of Palestine. The Suez War, in which Nasser triumphantly survived a determined Western attempt to overthrow him, swelled the Nasserist tide which reached its crest in 1958–9 with the union of Syria and Egypt and the downfall of the Iraqi Hashimites.

It would be hard to exaggerate Nasser's influence in these years. In every Arab state – but especially Jordan, Lebanon, Syria, and Iraq – there were hundreds of thousands who were prepared to place complete trust in him. Nasserism was backed by money, numerous agents, and an increasingly potent propaganda machine. But if it had not satisfied the emotional aspirations of millions of Arabs it would never have been so successful. At the same time its weaknesses as a political movement soon became apparent. Outside Egypt, Arab regimes which feared the rising tide of radical nationalism were able to appeal to local pride and interests and to make capital out of the fact that because Nasserism was Cairo-based its triumph would mean Egyptian domination.

The first counter-attack came with King Hussein's ousting of the pro-Nasser Nabulsi Government in 1957. This was followed by Kassem's adoption of anti-Egyptian policy within a few weeks of the Iraqi Revolution in 1958 and Syria's secession in 1961. Nasser was aware that in all three countries a mass of the people – perhaps a majority – still supported him.

In face of this dilemma, the approach he adopted was to declare that Arab unity must wait until the Arab states had progressive rather than 'reactionary, secessionist' regimes or, as he was to put it in 1961–2, there must be 'unity of aims' before 'unity of ranks'. At the same time he claimed that the bonds between him and the Arab people were stronger than ever.

In May 1962 Nasser presented his National Charter to the Egyptians. It showed the influence of Marxism and Yugoslav revisionism but it also confirmed that Nasser remained first and foremost an Egyptian nationalist in the tradition of Arabi and Zaghlul. Starting from the assumption that Egyptian parliamentary democracy before the Revolution was a sham, the Charter states: 'Political democracy cannot be separated from social democracy. No citizen can be regarded as free to vote unless he is given the following three guarantees: (*a*) he should be free from exploitation in all its forms; (*b*) he should enjoy an equal opportunity with his fellow citizens to enjoy a fair share of the national wealth; (*c*) his mind should be free from all anxiety likely to undermine his future security.' In other words, true democracy can only be achieved through socialism and the welfare state. The Charter lays down that the entire economic infrastructure (roads, railways, ports, etc.), the majority of heavy, medium, and mining industries, the import trade, banks, and insurance companies should all be in the public sector.

In the Charter and elsewhere, Nasser emphasized where his political and economic ideas differ substantially from Marxism. He rejects the atheistic state, the dictatorship of the proletariat, and the inevitability of the class struggle.

In the first part of the Charter Nasser refers to the Arab Revolution which would reach its objectives of Freedom, Socialism, and Unity. Freedom has come to mean 'freedom of the country and of the citizen' and socialism has become both a means and an end 'namely, sufficiency and justice'. He emphasizes that the Arab Revolution is now facing new circumstances demanding appropriate solutions. 'The Arab revolutionary experiment cannot afford to copy what others have achieved.' After listing these new circumstances the Charter says: 'The great part of the responsibility for this pioneering revolutionary action devolves upon the popular revolutionary leadership in the UAR since natural and historical factors have given the UAR the responsibility of being the "nucleus state" in this endeavour to secure freedom, unity, and socialism for the Arab Nation.' From this point onwards, the Charter concentrates upon Egypt's revolutionary struggle and its problems.

In the 1950s, when Nasserism was as its apogee in the Arab world, Nasser does not seem to have given much thought to how the Arab states should be governed if they achieved union under his leadership.

The first experiment – the Syrian-Egyptian union of 1958–61 – was a failure. Nasser regarded the Syrian Baathists' demands for immediate union as ill-considered and hasty, but once he had agreed he insisted on a centralized system of government and the uniform application in both regions of the UAR of all social and economic measures with little regard for their different circumstances. The Syrian Baathists, who had expected to control Syria under Nasser's umbrella, were ousted and the majority of them ceased to support the union. This left no indigenous Syrian political forces with the will to hold the union together and hostile elements carried out the secession in 1961 with little difficulty.

The fact that Nasserism, in the sense of Egypt's politico-economic system, was not necessarily applicable to other Arab states became even more apparent with the Egyptian intervention in Yemen in 1962. Before long the Egyptians found themselves virtually administering a medieval tribalized society in which the basic concepts of the National Charter had little meaning.

When the Baathists seized power in both Iraq and Syria in 1963 and proposed a union of these countries with Egypt, Nasser, although sceptical about the outcome, was unable to reject such an offer of Arab unity.[54] When the union was stillborn he bitterly attacked the Baathists but he had few illusions that the Nasserists in either Syria or Iraq were capable of ousting them and even when the Iraqi Baathists were replaced by a more sympathetic regime in November 1963 he remained cool towards proposals for Iraqi-Egyptian political union. He seems to have concluded that only a common military front against Israel was worth considering and it was for this reason that he called the first Arab summit meeting in January 1964 which set up a United Arab Command (UAC). However, the united military front was undermined by political differences and the UAC had ceased to function effectively when the June 1967 war broke out.

After the defeat of 1967, Nasserism could no longer be identified with the modern Arab nationalist movement as it had been ten years earlier. Abdul Nasser himself might still be the most outstanding figure in the Arab world, but henceforth no non-Egyptian Arabs could believe that he was capable of solving their problems for them. The Saladin image had been destroyed. Yet Nasserism had had a profound effect not only on all the eastern Arab states but further afield in Africa, Asia, and even Latin America. It had proved that a military coup in a developing country could mean much more than a colonel occupying the Presidential Palace. The example of Egypt's social and economic revolution was noted throughout the Third World and in many cases the threat of Nasserism was enough to frighten corrupt and extravagant rulers into making concessions to their people. Yet there has been little attempt in other Middle Eastern countries to imitate Nasser's methods of government which were both personal and peculiar to Egypt.

[54] See Kerr, M., *The Arab Cold War: Gamal 'Abd Al-Nasir and his Rivals 1959–1970* (New York, 1971).

It was probably inevitable that President Sadat, who regarded himself as a loyal and enthusiastic Nasserist in the early years of the 1952 Revolution,[55] should have tended to dissociate himself when he stepped out of Nasser's shadow to establish his own distinctive style of government.[56] What began as a declared policy of remedying the defects of the Nasserist system, developed into one of full-scale 'De-Nasserization'. After the widespread food riots in January 1977, when many of the crowd shouted Nasser's name, Sadat himself declared that Nasserism had died in 1967 and that those who called themselves Nasserists were impostors.

Nevertheless the term Nasserist has not disappeared in the Arab countries. In Egypt a movement still exists which, although lacking any organizational structure, describes itself as neo-Nasserist. Even in Baathist Syria – and to a lesser extent in Iraq – there are active Nasserists, while in Lebanon there is a Nasserist Union of Working Peoples Forces and an Independent Nasserist Movement with its own militia – the Murabitoun – who played a major role in the civil war. President Qaddafi of Libya would describe himself as a Nasserist although he has developed his own political system.

These Nasserists of the present day would subscribe in general terms to Nasser's principles of Arab Socialism, but the essence of their ideology is their view of Nasser as the symbol of an independent and united Arab nation, unaligned with any of the great powers.

The Baath

The Arab Baath Socialist Party can claim to be the only Arab political movement that has successfully transcended the frontiers of the Arab states. Although the Moslem Brotherhood and the SSNP spread into more than one Arab country, the one was Islamic more than Arab while the other specifically rejected Arabism. Nasserism, which in its heyday was infinitely more powerful than the Baath has ever been, was never an organized political movement.

The Baath Socialist Party was formed by the union at the

[55] See Sadat, A., *Revolt on the Nile* (London, 1957).
[56] See Sadat, A., *In Search of Identity* (London, 1978).

end of 1952 of the Baath ('resurrection') party in Syria and Akram Hourani's Socialist Party. The alliance arose out of common opposition to the Shishakli dictatorship and the Syrian right-wing parties.

The founders of the Baath were two Syrians, Michel Aflaq and Salah Bitar, who met as students in Paris in the early 1930s. Both of them flirted with Communism but became disillusioned as they reached the conclusion that the policies of the Soviet-based Communist movement were unsuited to the special problems of the Arab people. While teaching in a Damascus secondary school they began to hold political meetings and write pamphlets until they abandoned teaching in 1942 to devote themselves to full-time political work. The founding of the Baath Party dates from 1944 although it only emerged as an officially constituted political movement after the departure of the French in 1946.

Aflaq was more the party philosopher and Bitar the organizer. Aflaq, a withdrawn ascetic, has been called the 'Gandhi of Arab nationalism'. His writings, which are romantic and idealistic in tone, are far from lucid. Yet his personality and ideas, which he expounded at private meetings, attracted ardent disciples. These ideas, which owed something to Marxism and to romantic German nineteenth-century nationalism, he gave a specifically Arab character. He summarized the three Arab objectives as 'Freedom, Unity, and Socialism'. (The Baath could claim that these were ultimately adopted by all progressive Arab movements – including Nasserism.) He injected all three terms with his own somewhat mystical idealism summarized in his central slogan 'One Arab nation with an eternal mission.' Freedom meant political, cultural, and religious liberty as well as liberation from colonial rule. Unity meant not only the political unification of the Arab peoples but their regeneration through the release of the 'hidden vitality' which is the true source of nationalism (hence the name Baath). Socialism, which comes last in the Baath trinity, is less a set of socio-economic principles than a rather vague means of national moral improvement. Neither Aflaq nor Bitar ever showed much interest in the adoption of specific socialist measures. All they said was that socialism was a means of abolishing poverty, ignorance, and disease, and achieving progress towards an advanced industrial society capable of dealing on equal terms with other nations.

Running through all Aflaq's writings and statements is a belief in the need of revolution in the Arab world, but revolution in the sense of a total and organic change of mind and attitude involved in what he called 'the awakening of the Arab spirit at a decisive stage in human history'. He constantly emphasizes the need for love. 'Nationalism is love before everything else' because the renaissance will not take place until the Arab people show selfless unquestioning love for each other and their nation. In this context, although a Christian himself, he emphasizes the importance of Islam in its close connection with the spirit of the Arab nation.

From 1949 the Baath began to win seats in the Syrian parliament. It had benefited from its alliance with Hourani and its improved organization but also from the widespread disillusion among the younger generation with the older political parties. These still had a majority in parliament but the Baath, which remained in opposition until 1956, was stronger than it appeared. It was actively gaining support among army officers and it was benefiting from the general anti-Western radical current in the Arab world. In 1956 they entered a Coalition Government with the key posts of Economics and Foreign Affairs.

In Abdul Nasser's first years in power the Baath regarded him with suspicion as a regionalist and compromiser with the West. But with his increasingly successful defiance of the West the party cast away its doubts and called for union with Egypt. The feeling was strengthened by the Suez crisis and its consequences.

The year 1957 was a crest in the Baath party's fortunes. In Jordan the party had been legalized in 1954, although it had been active for several years before and had attracted a substantial youthful following on both East and West Banks. In 1956 a Baathist, Abdullah Rimawi, became Deputy Premier in the Nabulsi Government and although this was overthrown by King Hussein's counter-coup in the following year, the Baathist organization, with Syrian and Egyptian support, survived in Jordan. In Iraq also the regional branch of the Baath was growing in strength and importance to become one of the major forces behind the overthrow of the monarchy in the following year.

However, the left-wing trend in Syria was also benefiting the Communists. It is not certain how far the Syrian Baathists believed a Communist takeover was possible. What is certain is that in leading their unwilling coalition partners into the union with Egypt in 1958 they thought that Nasser would guarantee their control of Syria. More than this they believed that they would be able to propagate their ideas throughout the union and provide Nasser with the philosophy that they thought he lacked.

But this was not Nasser's intention (although he seems to have at least partly regretted it later). He appointed Baathists to high office in the UAR Government but allowed them no privileged position within the National Union. The consequence was that the Baathists were heavily defeated in the National Union elections in 1959 by independents and right-wingers.

The Baath's position rapidly deteriorated. In September, Nasser dismissed the Baathist Minister of National Guidance in the Syrian region and in December all remaining Baathists in the UAR central and regional governments, including Hourani and Bitar, resigned.

From then until Syria's secession in September 1961 Nasser ruled Syria through the Baathists' former ally the head of the intelligence service, Colonel Sarraj, and Field-Marshal Amer, whom he sent as his proconsul to Damascus. But the Baathists remained in disgruntled retirement.

The secession placed the Baath in a cruel dilemma. It was not enough to blame the break on Nasser's authoritarian rule. The act of secession went against everything the Baath had stood for. The Baath organization consisted of a National Command for the whole Arab nation and Regional Commands which theoretically existed in each Arab country. The National Command was now divided. Although communications between the different branches were now very difficult the party structure had survived the dissolution of the organization in Syria and the National Command continued to hold secret meetings in Lebanon. The Syrian regional command said that the secession should be accepted but the majority of the

Lebanese, Iraqi, and Jordanian Baathists condemned it and demanded immediate reunion. Eventually the National Command proposed that the Party work for a new union on a federal basis.

In Iraq, as in Jordan, the Baath were now in opposition again as hopes raised by the 1958 Revolution were rapidly disappointed.

The Party was in disarray in 1961 but once again events were moving in its favour. The Baath's opportunity in Iraq came in February 1963. Kassem was arrested and executed; the Baath formed the majority of the Government although Abdul Salam Aref, a non-Baathist, became President. One month later the Damascus Government had also been toppled.

The two coups were warmly welcomed by Egypt. The way seemed to be open for a union between three progressive Arab countries subscribing to the slogan 'Freedom, Unity, and Socialism'. Discussions began immediately and continued intermittently until a formal agreement was announced on 17 April 1963. In fact the union was doomed before it came into existence.

Nasser was aware that he still had a wide following among the Syrian people. But the Baathists, with the help of a determined strongman, General Hafez, held on to the reins of power, suppressed opposition, and dismissed all anti-Baathist officers.

The two Baathist regimes in Iraq and Syria grew closer together in common defence against Nasser. In September they concluded an economic agreement and when the Iraqis renewed military operations against the Kurds the Syrians sent a battalion of troops. In October the Sixth National Convention of the Baath, the most important in the party's history, was held in Damascus following regional conferences in Iraq and Syria. But the alliance was short-lived. Although the Syrian Baathists were widely regarded as weaker it was the Iraqi Baathists who were first overthrown.

In its nine months in power in Iraq, the Baath had made itself exceedingly unpopular. Imprisonment and torture were widely used against all opponents of the Baath – Communist and Nasserist. There was also a strong element of resentment among the Iraqi people that Iraq should be placed in a subordinate position to Syria, the headquarters of the Baathist movement.

The Baath's overthrow left the Syrian regime in a weakened and dispirited state, but it survived its external and internal troubles because its opponents remained divided and leaderless. It overcame a merchants' strike, backed by religious elements, which started in Hama and spread to the rest of the country. However, the Government was forced to make concessions to the middle classes and to mark time on its socialization measures. In December 1965 the left-wing of the party was ousted and Bitar took office with a programme of moderation and *rapprochement* with Egypt. In consequence, in February 1966 it too was overthrown by a group of left-wing neo-Baathists led by Colonel Salah Jedid, a former chief of staff. The old Baathist leaders either were imprisoned or escaped into exile. The Baath was now in power in only one Arab country and there it had repudiated its own founder (rather as if a Communist Government should denounce Marx and Lenin).

Contrary to the expectations of many, the neo-Baathists remained in control of Syria after the 1967 war without relaxing in any way the defiant extremism of their policies. They boycotted the Arab summit at Khartoum in August 1967 and rejected any efforts to reach a political solution with Israel. At home they strengthened State control of the economy; the private sector came virtually to a standstill.

When President Abdul Rahman Aref of Iraq was ousted in July 1968 and replaced by a regime in which moderate 'orthodox' Baathists were dominant, the Syrian Government did not welcome the event. Obviously it strengthened the hand of moderate Syrian Baathist exiles in Lebanon. However, the Baathist revival in Baghdad did show the survival power of Baathists' ideas despite the extreme unpopularity of some of their actions when they were in power.

The return of the Baath to power in Iraq inaugurated a decade of tension and hostility between the rival Baathist regimes in Baghdad and Damascus, with only brief periods of relative amity (as when Syria supported Iraq's oil nationalization measures in 1972). In December 1970 Hafez Assad in Syria imposed his authority over the doctrinaire civilian wing of the party led by Salah Jedid and instituted a more broadly based regime which shared a limited amount of power with other groups such as communists, nationalists, Nasserists, etc. But this did not lead to any collaboration between the Syrian and Iraqi Baathist organizations. While Salah Bitar withdrew from the Baath into retirement, Michel Aflaq gave his support to the more 'orthodox' Iraqi Baathists and became an honoured guest in Baghdad where he made frequent political statements. The Syrian Baathists were obliged to refer to other founding members of the Baath such as Zaki Azouzi and Sidki Ismail for statements of party ideology.

Of the two parties the Iraqi, under its ideologist and Secretary-General Saddam Hussein, is the more tightly organized. Although, as in Syria, the Baath in Iraq has formed a Progressive Pan-Arab Nationalist Front with other elements – the Communists, the Kurdish Democratic Party, the Revolutionary Kurdish Party, and pan-Arab nationalists and other independent Iraqi nationalists – the Baath has remained dominant in every aspect of Iraqi life – youth and women's organizations, trade unions, etc., and above all in the armed forces where no non-Baathist political activity is allowed.

The Palestine Liberation Organization

The Palestine Liberation Organization was set up by the Arab heads of state at their summit conference held in Cairo in January 1964. It was headed by Ahmad Shuqairy, a Palestinian lawyer who had been Saudi Arabia's representative at the UN and subsequently a member of the Political Committee of the Arab League to represent the Palestinian refugees at the UN. The PLO, which was intended to represent the Palestinian community, consisted of the National Congress or quasi-parliament, the PLO Executive Committee, and the Palestine Liberation Army (PLA).

The National Congress had 422 popularly elected delegates (although certain groups refused to take part), and held its first meeting in Jerusalem in May 1964. The Congress elected the Executive Committee. It was to meet at the request of the Executive to consider matters affecting the Palestinian community, and its decisions then became binding on the Executive. The Executive Committee, with ten members and a chairman (Shuqairy) was intended to act as a cabinet. However, the demands of the new Executive that the PLO should have the right to function as a supra-national authority among the refugees in every state, with the right to levy taxes on them and freedom to draft the refugees into the PLA, were refused by the Arab states who insisted that the PLA should be composed of recruits contributed by member states of the Arab League.

The fact that a Palestinian quasi-government would not be given any freedom of action by the Arab states had already been recognized by certain militant national groups of which the two most important were al-Fatah (Harakat al-Tahrir al-Filastiniya), founded by Yasir Arafat and others in 1956, and the Arab Nationalist Movement established in Beirut in 1950 by George Habash and Naif Hawatmeh. At first these groups gave their support to the Nasser regime in Egypt in the belief that this was the best hope of recovering Palestine for the Arabs; but by 1964, discouraged by the failure of the Arab states to act even to prevent Israel from diverting the Jordan River to Israel, they decided to act on their own by launching guerrilla attacks against Israel.

The defeat of the Arab armies in June 1967 and the discrediting of the PLO leadership sponsored by the Arab states enabled the militant Palestinians to gain control of the PLO in 1968–9. Yasir Arafat became Chairman of the PLO Executive in February 1969. Henceforth the guerrilla organizations, of which al-Fatah is the largest, were dominant in the Central Council which includes the Executive Committee and the additional non-permanent member from each of the guerrilla groups. The Central Council acts as a link between the Palestine National Council (replacing the Congress) and the Executive and meets occasionally to clarify policy between meetings of the PNC.

The PNC had 155 members in 1974 but the numbers have been increased at subsequent meetings to reach 301 at the 14th session of the Council, held in Damascus in January 1979. The Council includes representatives from Jordan, the West Bank, the Gulf states, and other countries.

The military organizations of the PLO now consist of the Palestine Liberation Army made up of several brigades stationed mainly in Syria and equipped by the Syrian army. The Palestine

Armed Struggle Command, established in 1969, acts as a police and security organization and also co-ordinates the activities of the various guerrilla groups.

The principal guerrilla organizations are as follows:

1. Groups represented on the PLO Executive
   - Al-Fatah.
   - Popular Democratic Front for the Liberation of Palestine; Marxist; split from the PFLP in 1968.
   - Saiqa (Vanguard); Syrian Baathist; established in 1967.
   - Palestine National Front; established in 1971 inside the Occupied Territories; led by members of the banned Jordanian Communist Party.
2. Groups outside the PLO Executive
   - Popular Front for the Liberation of Palestine (PFLP); Marxist; grew out of the Arab Nationalist Movement; joined PLO in 1971 but withdrew from the Executive in 1974.
   - Popular Front for the Liberation of Palestine – General Command; joined PFLP when it was established but left in 1968.
   - Arab Liberation Front; Iraqi Baathist; established in 1969.
   - Popular Struggle Front; nationalist; established in 1967.
   - Popular Revolutionary Front for the Liberation of Palestine; Marxist; split from PFLP in 1972.

ECONOMIC AND SOCIAL

Many elements of similarity still run through the economic and social life of the Middle East. Because of the dominance of the desert and the seasonal concentration of water, there has evolved a three-fold agricultural pattern of irrigation, dry farming, and nomadic pastoralism. In Ottoman times most of the region was subjected to the same economic and commercial politics.

Many of these basic similarities remain despite the strong

forces of social and economic change which accompanied the political awakening at the end of the nineteenth century. In some parts of the Middle East this awakening was long delayed. Yemen and Oman were isolated and virtually immune to the forces of change until recent years. Today there is no part of the region which is insulated from change.

Two factors, which are interrelated, have accelerated the changes and established the pattern they have taken. One is the rapid increase in the output and profits of the Middle East oil industry and the other is the strong nationalist tide which has caused the Middle Eastern states to seek to match their political sovereignty with economic power and independence through industrialization and the development of their resources.

The immense increase in oil revenues has enabled some of the Middle Eastern oil-producing states with small populations, such as Kuwait, Qatar, and Abu Dhabi, to transform themselves socially and economically in less than a generation despite their lack of other resources. Through the oil industry Saudi Arabia has achieved power and political influence out of all proportion to its natural capabilities. By an accident of nature, oil has been discovered in the more sparsely inhabited countries in the region. Of the major oil producers covered by this *Survey*, only Iraq and Iran have large enough populations to ensure the absorption of all their oil revenues. Much of the oil wealth has spread and is spreading to other parts of the Middle East through two related processes: first through private investment by the oil states, public investment (through such institutions as the Kuwait Fund for Arab Economic Development, the Abu Dhabi Arab Development Fund, the Islamic Development Fund based in Jedda, and the Arab League's Arab Fund for Social and Economic Development), or direct subsidies such as those paid to Egypt, Syria, and Jordan by Saudi Arabia and other Gulf states. Also the Arab oil states with small populations have provided employment for hundreds of thousands of skilled and unskilled workers from other parts of the Middle East – Egypt, Jordan, Syria, Lebanon, Yemen. The remittances sent back by these workers now form a major element in the national incomes of their home countries.

In the period following World War II economic nationalism, like political nationalism, in the Middle East, usually meant reducing dependence on the West. The process was first seen clearly in Egypt in 1956 in the take-over of the still considerable French and British interests, which was followed shortly afterwards by the 'Egyptianization' of the whole economy. Syria, Iraq, and Sudan later followed Egypt's example. In each case the trend resulted in closer economic ties with the Soviet Union and Eastern European states. In the 1970s these ties with the communist states were sharply reduced in Egypt and Sudan, and to a lesser extent in Syria and Iraq (with the important exception of arms supplies). But this resumption of economic relations with the non-communist industrialized countries did not imply a reversal of the national trend or a return to the previous *status quo.* In every case Middle East producers acted to take over control of the oil operation in their territory from foreign oil companies. This trend received an additional impetus with the Islamic Revolution in Iran in 1979, which was at least partly directed against Western control of the Iranian economy.

The impulse for Arab political unity has been reflected in the economic field but has been hampered by the same types of obstacles. An Economic Unity Agreement was signed in 1962 by Jordan, Egypt, Morocco, Kuwait, and Syria and later adhered to by Yemen, Iraq, and Sudan. The aims were similar to those of the EEC: the abolition of internal tariffs and the complete freedom of movement of labour and capital. Another agreement establishing an Arab Common Market was signed in 1965 by Egypt, Jordan, Iraq, Kuwait, and Syria. Yemen and Sudan have since adhered to this agreement but the Kuwait National Assembly voted against ratification. The ACM should more properly be termed a free-trade area since it has never adopted a common external tariff. Progress has been slower on removing internal trade restrictions but most agricultural and some industrial tariffs have been decreased or eliminated. But the ACM cannot be regarded as the prime factor in Arab economic integration. Although Jordan's successful expansion of agricultural exports to Kuwait has been credited to the ACM, Lebanon, which never joined, has been even more successful in this respect. Similarly, the increasing trend towards the spread of Arab oil revenues to all the Arab states has not depended on any formal economic union.

Further steps towards the goal of complete freedom of movement of labour and capital between the Arab states depend heavily on the provision of the necessary political framework. The Arab Gulf states and Saudi Arabia, while remaining dependent on manpower from the other Arab states, are certain to continue restricting the inflow of Arab labour and its period of residence. On the other hand, there is a strong probability that the economic integration of the Gulf states themselves will continue in the direction of a common passport, common currency and freedom of movement of capital, etc. Similarly, the moves towards political integration of Egypt and Sudan and Syria and Iraq, if pursued, will have important economic effects. (For example, the former bad political relations between the rival Baathist regimes in Iraq and Syria was the reason for the closure of the pipeline carrying Iraqi oil across Syrian territory). One regional development of the greatest importance in the 1970s has been the realization that Sudan's great agricultural potential could make it the major supplier of food to the Arab world. Large scale investment of Arab oil funds in Sudanese agriculture is already in progress.

Agriculture

Agriculture and pastoralism are still the basic economic activities and the major employers of the population in most Middle Eastern countries. The chief exceptions are Kuwait and the other small desert oil-producing states, Israel in which industry is now the major sector, and Lebanon whose economy is dominated by trade and services. Nomadic pastoralism is gradually declining with the spread of irrigation and the efforts of governments to settle nomads on the land.

In general, the harsh environment has hindered cultivation, which is restricted to small areas imprisoned by vast stretches of desert and steppe. Outside the mountains annual rainfall totals are low and inconsistent. Moreover, the seasonal concentration of rainfall is restrictive; much falls in one or two months (during winter and early spring in the north), leaving the rest of the year virtually rainless. In Iraq, the rivers flood when additional water is least needed, i.e. in the spring.

Because of these climatic facts, irrigation and flood-control are of capital importance, particularly along the lower Nile and Tigris-Euphrates valleys and in the Gezira district of the Sudan. Modern methods of irrigation offer an escape from the severe droughts which frequently afflict the dry-farming areas and enable a wide range of summer crops to be grown – cotton, rice, vegetables, and others – besides the traditional winter staples of wheat and barley. Two or occasionally three crops a year can be grown on the same land. Silting greatly reduces the need for the long fallow periods characteristic of unirrigated fields. Hence irrigated zones are the most stable and intensive producers in the area.

Middle Eastern farming is still largely for local subsistence. Only in a few places like the lower Nile valley, the Lebanon, and the Shatt district of southern Iraq is there significant regional specialization. Elsewhere the overwhelming emphasis is on cereals – wheat, barley, maize, rice, millets, and others – and to a lesser extent fruit and vegetables, with commercial crops receiving much less attention.

Excluding petroleum, about 90 per cent of the Middle East's exports are agricultural. Syria and Iraq are small and fluctuating exporters of barley and wheat. Of the cash crops, cotton is exported mainly from Egypt, the Sudan and Syria, dates from Iraq and Iran, dried fruit from Iran, citrus from Israel, many kinds of fruit from Lebanon, and tobacco from Syria and Turkey. Opium in Turkey, coffee in Yemen, and silk in Lebanon are of local and limited importance. Although the olive is by far the leading fruit tree in the northern half of the region, most of the fruit is consumed locally.

Productivity is very low. Nevertheless, in spite of natural hazards, unsatisfactory land-tenure systems, fragmentation of holdings, rural indebtedness, and other drawbacks, cultivation has improved in the last twenty years.

The two major irrigation schemes in the area are the Nile High Dam in Egypt (completed in 1971) and the Euphrates Dam in Syria, but Iran, Sudan, Iraq, Jordan, Israel, Lebanon, and Saudi Arabia have also extended the irrigated area through the building of dams. The main achievements of desert reclamation have been in Egypt and Israel.

Industry

Although agriculture remains the principal activity in the area, the share of industry is increasing in the economies of nearly all Middle Eastern states. The urge towards industrialization depends heavily on the relation between population and agricultural resources. It is less in Syria, Sudan, and Iraq – where there are large areas of potentially cultivable land which are now unproductive – than in Egypt where the limits of cultivation have nearly been reached and industrialization is an urgent necessity. The Egyptian manufacturing sector has expanded rapidly over the past decade and now accounts for over 20 per cent of GNP. In Lebanon light manufacturing industry is the fastest growing sector of the economy. The desert oil-producing states, such as Kuwait and Saudi Arabia, with their limited agricultural potential, see in industrialization a means of diversification to reduce their present dependence on crude-oil production but they are handicapped by the lack of a local labour force and their small domestic markets. Israel is a unique exception to all these considerations. For political reasons it is cut off from its natural markets and sources of fuel and raw materials but it receives massive external aid. Over the past ten to fifteen years it has developed a range of technically advanced industries and can no longer be included among the developing countries.

Social Change

The most significant social development in the Middle East since the Second World War has been the increase in size, importance, and political power of the new middle class at the expense of the traditional élite of kings, tribal shaikhs, and bourgeoisie.[57] In the more advanced areas the traditional élite has lost its political power or disappeared entirely as a consequence of agrarian reform, nationalization, and revolutionary changes in the political structure. Egyptian agrarian reform in 1952 was followed by similar measures in Syria and Iraq. In Iran a parallel 'White Revolution' has been conducted from the top. Even in the more backward areas, such as Yemen or Oman, the strength of tribalism has begun to decline.

[57] See Manfred Halpern, *The Politics of Social Change in the Middle East and North Africa*, Part II (Princeton, 1963).

In spite of agrarian reform, industrialization, and the adoption of various radical and socialist measures in Middle Eastern countries, industrial and agricultural workers and peasant farmers have only begun to enter the field of politics. While it was the declared intention of the Arab Socialist Union in Egypt (which is the model for similar organizations in Sudan and Libya) and the Baath Party in Syria and Iraq that these majority elements in society should participate in the political process, none of them has yet made it possible to any significant extent. On the other hand the 'new middle class' has gained steadily in power and influence. This bears little resemblance to the property-owning entrepreneurial Western middle class of the nineteenth century; it consists mainly of salaried administrators and 'technocrats'. Because of the increase in the scope and function of the state in most Middle Eastern countries, the great majority are working directly or indirectly for the Government. The military is also a key element in this new middle class and army officers or ex-officers are playing a vital political role in the majority of Arab countries.

All the Arab states of the Middle East and Iran have been influenced to some extent by the increasing income from oil exports. Those states that are major oil exporters have naturally been most affected, but even those with small oil resources or none, such as Lebanon, Jordan, and Egypt, have been influenced substantially. A major part of Lebanon's commercial prosperity before its civil war could be ascribed to the provision of services to the Arab oil states, while the boom in the Yemen Arab Republic in the 1970s has largely been due to the injection of Saudi aid and remittances from Yemeni workers in the oil states.

In the initial stages, when the new income began to flow in the 1950s, much was wasted by the profligate spending of the ruling families on luxuries, although in some of them such as Kuwait and Bahrain, funds were diverted into social services from an early stage. It was partly because of the attacks from the Nasser regime in Egypt on the conduct of the 'oil sheikhs' that the more spendthrift ruling families of Arabia were forced to mend their ways out of a sense of self-preservation. In all these states a high and generally increasing proportion of oil revenues has been spent on health, education and the social services. Since in every case these services were either non-existent or rudimentary before the increase in oil revenues, the social effects have been profound.

In education the effect has been most striking for girls. A generation ago only a tiny minority in the Arabian states had access to education but in every case the rulers have now accepted, sometimes against strong opposition from conservative opinion, that girls should be educated.

The rise and spread of wealth has meant increased contacts between these states and the rest of the world. Physical communication has improved with the building of modern airports and hotels and the inauguration of frequent air services. Because facilities for higher education were extremely limited in the area (and, though increasing, are still inadequate for the rising numbers who receive secondary education), many of the younger generation go abroad to universities – either in the Arab world or in Europe and America. In addition it has become the habit among the people of the Arab oil states to spend the hottest months abroad, especially in European capitals.

Inevitably, the two-way flow of contact created by non Arabs (mostly Westerners and Asians) entering the oil states as business representatives or on contract work and by the local inhabitants travelling abroad has acted as a modernizing or Westernizing influence on these highly conservative societies. Many young Arabs are attracted to various aspects of Western culture and way of life, to a relatively permissive society, and to sexual liberty and equality.

But along with the Westernizing influence, a totally different trend is also discernible. In the 1970s in varying degrees throughout the Moslem populations of the Middle East there has been a reaffirmation of Islamic values. This has been reinforced by the acquisition of world power through oil wealth after centuries of domination by the Christian West. This can be seen most clearly in Saudi Arabia which happens to be the wealthiest and most influential of the oil states of the Arabian Peninsula and also the one in which a puritan Islamic tradition is strongest. Saudi ascendancy throughout Arabia and growing Saudi influence in the rest of the Arab world have had recognizable effects in supporting the growth of Islamic revival movements, as in Egypt, and in the reassertion of the Islamic *sharia* in all aspects of life, as in the United Arab Emirates. Similarly, the chief impetus of the Iranian Revolution of 1979 was the reassertion of the Iranian's people's Islamic identity against the Westernizing policies of the Shah.

Thus two contrary tendencies are at work in the Moslem countries of the Middle East: secularization and 'westernization' on the one hand, and the reaffirmation of Islamic values on the other. The outcome cannot be predicted but it may not be seen as a straightforward conflict between progressive and liberal ideas, such as the emancipation of women, and enlightened legal reform and black reaction. There is a strong social content in the Islamic revivalist movements; these have the support of many Moslem women who feel no envy for the position of women in Western society. Various reforms have been introduced in most Arab countries to strengthen the legal position of women in marriage, but it is not to be assumed that these reforms would be reversed if the full *sharia* were to be applied. The principle of girls' education, the key to female emancipation, has been accepted by all Islamic governments of the Middle East so that the trend to the wider employment of women, which has already taken place in countries such as Egypt, Syria, and Iraq, seems certain in even the most conservative societies. This does not mean that women will enter all the same professions or types of employment as men and work alongside them in these societies. The concept of the professional woman living and working independently from her family is still very remote. Social change, accelerated by the new oil wealth, is inevitable but it cannot be assumed that it will all tend towards the norms of secular Western society.

B. THE OIL INDUSTRY IN THE MIDDLE EAST

Ever since the end of the Second World War, the industrialized and industrializing countries of the world outside North and South America and the Communist countries have come increasingly to rely on the Middle East for their supplies of oil.

Output in the United States, still the largest single oil producing country in the world until 1974, has been falling at around 3 per cent per year since the beginning of the decade, and in 1977 it accounted for only some 13 per cent of the world's total compared to nearly a quarter in 1970. The USSR had outstripped it, as had Saudi Arabia. Output in Venezuela also had been declining at a rate of some 7 per cent per year over the previous five years, and the country has fallen from third to fifth place among world oil producers.[58]

By contrast the output of the Middle East rose from nearly 10 million barrels per day in 1967 to over 22 million in 1977, an annual increase of 8.3 per cent, and accounted for 36.2 per cent of total world output – 42 per cent if Arab North Africa is added. The role of the Middle East in world trade is an even more significant measure of its importance, for in 1977 the area accounted for 59 per cent of world exports (68 per cent if North Africa is included). Western Europe, in spite of rapidly increasing domestic output, primarily from the North Sea, was by far the largest importer from the Middle East, and over two-thirds of its total imports came from there (including North Africa, 79 per cent). With the rapid industrialization of Japan and the recovery of Europe after the Second World War, oil consumption in the Eastern Hemisphere grew very rapidly, averaging over 11 per cent per year in the 1950s and 1960s but declining to a little less than one-third of this in the 1970s as world economic growth slackened.

The growing dependence on the Middle East was already worrying the industrialized countries, and in particular the United States, long before the Arab–Israeli war of October 1973 and the subsequent oil 'crisis'. The importance of Middle East oil reserves was, of course, well known, for they had been discovered and developed entirely by American and European companies. These companies went abroad in search of oil very largely because it was realized that foreign sources would sooner or later be required to meet the rising demands of the industrialized world. For reasons of 'national security' governments had encouraged companies to search for and develop oil abroad, but the dependence on foreign sources which ensued

[58] Except where otherwise stated, all these figures are from British Petroleum, *Statistical Review of the World Oil Industry, 1978* (London).

seemed equally to threaten such security. The very success of the foreign companies, the revenues they generated, the 'modernization' they brought, hastened the economic and political development of the countries of the Middle East, leading them increasingly to attempt to control the companies. Eventually they could assume effective authority over their own industry. No longer did foreign 'ownership' of oil reserves abroad, 'control' by American or European companies, nor even the possibility of military intervention ensure the security of the sources of oil supplies.

Perhaps even this change of circumstance would not have worried the industrial world unduly had it not been for the unstable political condition of the area. In addition to the political tensions endemic in all developing countries struggling with disrupting economic and political change, was the severe political disaster for the Arab world of the Israeli invasion of Palestine and the expulsion of large numbers of its inhabitants. This has kept the area in constant turmoil for a quarter of a century, powerfully exacerbating indigenous conflicts and pushing increasing numbers of Arabs into extreme political positions as no overall solution seems possible in the short term. Inevitably such deep-rooted political resentment had repercussions for the operations of the oil companies and for the security of the flow of oil from the area, and in the end created a 'crisis' with far-reaching implications for the Middle East and its relations with the rest of the world.

In 1977 the largest producing countries in the Middle East were Saudi Arabia (9.2 million b.p.d.), Iran (5.7 million b.p.d.), Iraq (2.3 million b.p.d.), and Kuwait (1.8 million b.p.d.). Output in all cases was much less than capacity in view of the world recession of demand, and both Kuwait and Saudi Arabia had placed upper limits on their total production.

Of these countries, only Iran, where oil had been discovered in 1908, and Iraq, from which exports became significant after 1934, were important producers before the Second World War. In Iraq, commercial oil had been discovered in 1927 but exports did not begin until seven years later, partly because of the need to build a pipeline from land-locked Kirkuk to the see, partly because of the depression, and partly for other reasons.

Oil had also been discovered in Saudi Arabia and Kuwait before the war but its development had been held up, especially in Kuwait, and exports only became significant from the middle 1940s in Saudi Arabia and later in the decade from Kuwait. In 1977 these four countries accounted for 31 per cent of Middle East production, the rest coming from the United Arab Emirates (2 million b.p.d. of which 1.7 million were from Abu Dhabi), Qatar (445,000 b.p.d.), Oman (344,000 b.p.d.), Syria (169,000 b.p.d.), and Bahrain (57,000 b.p.d.). Production in North Africa reached 3.7 million b.p.d. (of which Algeria produced 1.2 million and Egypt 417,000 b.p.d.). Most of these smaller producers arrived on the scene in the 1960s; only Bahrain, where oil was discovered in 1932, was exporting before the Second World War. Oil was discovered in Qatar in 1939 but development there, as in Saudi Arabia and Kuwait, was hindered by the war, and exports did not begin until 1949. In other words apart from Iran and Iraq, the emergence of the Middle East as the world's greatest exporting region dates only from the middle of the century. Oil from northern Iraq reached the sea through pipelines in the 1930s, but Tapline for Saudi oil and additional Iraqi pipelines to the Mediterranean came into operation only after the war.

The Advent of Profit-Sharing

It is not surprising, therefore, that the first big change in the nature of the concessionary relationships between the governments of the crude-oil producing countries and the great international oil companies which had discovered, developed, and completely controlled their oil resources, should occur at mid-century, following closely on the immediate post-war readjustments in international affairs. The companies[59] produced the oil under concessions obtained before the war from the governments. The terms of the concessions varied, but essentially they gave the companies the right to explore, produce, transport and sell oil in return for various fees and (except in Iran) a tonnage royalty. Only in Iran was the oil produced by a single international company; in the other countries it

[59] EXXON (then Standard Oil, New Jersey), Royal Dutch Shell, British Petroleum (then Anglo-Iranian), Gulf Oil, Texaco, Standard Oil of California, Mobil Oil (then Socony Mobil), and Compagnie Française des Pétroles.

was produced by consortia of two or more international companies. The original Iranian concession dated from 1901, and after a series of abortive negotiations was cancelled in 1932/33 and re-negotiated, the new concession to run until 1993. The Iranians were to be paid a royalty and 20 per cent of the dividends distributed by the Anglo-Persian Oil Company. In 1951, after a bitter dispute, the company's properties were nationalized by the government of Musaddiq, and Iranian oil was shut down for nearly four years before a new agreement was made, this time with a consortium of foreign companies.[60] It also included the new profit-sharing arrangements that had by then become prevalent in the Middle East.

The Iraq Petroleum Company, together with its sister companies, Mosul Petroleum and Basrah Petroleum, was a non-profit-making British company owned in equal shares by Anglo-Iranian, Royal Dutch/Shell, Compagnie Française des Pétroles, and the Near East Development Corporation (composed of Standard Oil Co. (New Jersey), and Mobil Oil), with 5 per cent for the C.S. Gulbenkian interests. The Kuwait Oil Company, also British, was owned equally by Anglo-Iranian and Gulf Oil Company. Aramco, whose concession covered most of Eastern Saudi Arabia, was an American company owned by Standard Oil Co. (New Jersey), Standard Oil of California, Texaco, (30 per cent each), and Mobil (10 per cent). These same international companies were also the world's largest refiners and marketers of oil products outside Northern America, and most of the oil they produced in the Middle East went to their own subsidiaries; only a small proportion was sold to third parties in free markets.

After the war, demand for oil rose rapidly and although the revenues of the oil producing countries rose as exports increased, the governments wanted a greater share of the profits from their oil. Ibn Saud was most pressing in his demands on Aramco, and at the end of 1950 he obtained a fundamental revision of the financial arrangements with the company.

[60]The consortium is composed of British Petroleum (40 per cent), Royal Dutch/Shell (14 per cent), Mobil Oil (7 per cent), Standard Oil Co. (New Jersey) (7 per cent), Texaco (7 per cent), Gulf Oil (7 per cent), Standard Oil of California (7 per cent), Compagnie Française des Pétroles (6 per cent), and Iricon, a group of American Independents, (5 per cent).

Revenues were to be received by Saudi Arabia in the form of an income tax which, including a royalty of 12½ per cent, would equal 50 per cent of the profits attributed to crude oil. (Venezuela already had an income tax which enabled the government to obtain 50 per cent of the companies' profits). Under US tax laws Aramco could credit these income tax payments to the Saudi government against its United States tax liability and, in effect, the US Treasury lost what Saudi Arabia gained within the limits of Aramco's tax liability to the US Government. Naturally, the '50-50' arrangement spread quickly to the other countries and became standard in the Middle East, constituting the first major change in concession arrangements in the area generally.

As a result of the adoption of the income tax method of paying revenues to the governments, however, it became necessary for the companies to define what was meant by 'profits' on crude-oil production, since little crude had been sold in international trade before the war and no recognized price for crude had been established. They did this by posting a price in the Middle East at which they were prepared to sell crude to outsiders as well as to transfer it to their own refining subsidiaries, the latter being by far the most important outlets.

Traditionally the price of products had been calculated with reference to a type of basing-point system. After the war, as refineries were established in consuming countries and crude oil entered increasingly into international trade, this method of pricing was extended to crude oil. The 'system' was somewhat unsystematically, loosely, and erratically applied and became increasingly weakened after the war. But when crude-oil prices were for the first time publicly announced in the Middle East in 1950 as the result of the introduction of '50-50', they naturally reflected the previously prevailing levels; valued at these prices, crude-oil production appeared extremely profitable in relation to refining and marketing (although it must be remembered that crude is of little use unless it is refined). This distribution of profits was advantageous to the US companies since under the US tax laws profits attributed to crude-oil production attract depletion allowances and are taxed at a lower rate than profits on refining and marketing. Moreover, the higher the price of crude oil, the higher the revenues of the oil-producing countries and the higher the costs of competing oil companies without access to 'owned' or 'cost' crude.

Posted prices were intended to be, and for a time were, the prices at which Middle East crude oil actually moved to the world's refineries, as well as the prices used to value oil for tax purposes. They were not determined by impersonal 'market forces', nor could they have been, given the nature of the 'market', and were soon seen not to be so determined. In consequence, before the decade was out, the right of the companies to post prices without consulting their host governments, and thus to determine unilaterally the unit tax revenues of governments, was to be strongly challenged by the governments.

The Development of 'Surplus'

At the beginning of the 1950s the full development of Middle Eastern oil was in the early stages; in the next ten years, production was nearly to triple and to triple again in the following ten. One of the chief problems of the companies was to bring this oil into world markets in a way that would not disrupt the world price structure. Since such a large proportion of both refining and marketing was in the hands of the same international companies which also controlled Middle Eastern crude production, it could be expected that if each of the companies adjusted the production of its own crude to the growth of its own market outlets, the result would be a smooth integration of the new supplies of oil into international markets.

The difficulty was, however, that the companies had a great deal of very cheap oil to dispose of. As a result, during the 1950s effective delivered prices began to reflect the competitive pressures on the companies to find outlets for this oil. Companies at first cut prices in a concealed form (e.g. a company might itself absorb some of the freight in order to cut delivered prices) and later overtly in the form of open discounts. Thus developed the so-called 'world oil surplus' that afflicted the industry from the late fifties until the June 1967 war with Israel sharply disrupted the prevailing patterns of supply.

For a while the emerging 'surplus', that is to say the increasing availability of oil at prices below those posted by the companies, was masked by various fortuitous circumstances: the conflict between Iran and the AIOC took Iranian oil off the market for almost four years, the Korean war gave an unexpected boost to demand, the closure of the Suez Canal in 1956 and the shut-down of pumps on the Iraqi pipeline through Syria further interrupted supplies. As soon as the effects of the Suez crisis wore off, prices of oil and products in world markets began to fall in earnest. To the companies, it seems obvious that in such circumstances the prices on which they paid tax – the posted prices – should reflect this development and in consequence the posted prices were reduced in 1959 and again in 1960.

The Formation of OPEC

The producing countries reacted immediately with the formation in 1960 of the Organization of Petroleum Exporting Countries (OPEC) dedicated to the restoration of posted prices. This did not prove to be possible, but OPEC did succeed in preventing any further cuts in posted prices in spite of the fact that market prices continued to fall.

The freezing of posted prices by OPEC was the beginning of a concerted struggle by the host governments to increase their revenues from oil. The remnants of the allowances for marketing expenses that the companies had been able to claim for tax purposes were soon abolished, and in 1964 an agreement was obtained to treat royalties as an expense rather than as part of the 50 per cent 'income' tax.

In addition to these financial gains, the OPEC countries in the 1960s insisted on and obtained widespread relinquishment by the companies of the areas held under concession but not exploited. The major companies accepted the principle of relinquishment for all their concession areas, which were thereby quickly reduced from their original size. In Iraq, however, the government unilaterally expropriated in 1961 some 99.5 per cent of the IPC's concession area even though the IPC had already expressed its willingness to give up over 90 per cent of this area provided only that it be allowed to choose the parts to be retained. This the government was not prepared to permit.

The other objectives of the OPEC countries, however, met with little success during the 1960s: the introduction of an effective programme to control supply, and the acceptance of government companies as equity partners in their major oil concessions. As market prices continued to fall in response to competition in the market place, OPEC's hopes of raising tax prices became fainter and OPEC even began to fear that the existing level of tax prices might at some point be endangered. The obvious answer was to restrict the rate of supply. In 1965 a production programme was drawn up and supply quotas were allocated to member countries, but neither governments nor companies paid much attention to them and the scheme was a failure.

The End of an Era

During the 1960s four major interrelated changes occurred in the international oil industry which prepared the way for the revolution in relationships and control that was to take place in the Middle East in the years 1970–4. The first was the coming into production of new areas; the second, the entry of new companies; the third, the weakening of the traditional controls over supply; the fourth, the increased influence of host governments.

In the early 1960s oil exports were beginning from Algeria, Libya, Nigeria, and the United Arab Emirates. The output of these four countries rose from 198,000 b.p.d. in 1960 to 6.2 million in 1970, or from 2.2 per cent to 26.5 per cent of the output of the countries now in OPEC, of which Libya alone accounted for 14.2 per cent. There was thus a substantial and steady increase in oil production from new areas outside the five founder members of OPEC (Iran, Iraq, Kuwait, Saudi Arabia, and Venezuela). The combined production of these five rose from 7.9 to 15.9 million b.p.d. but, as a proportion of OPEC output, fell from 91 per cent to 68 per cent between 1960 and 1970.

Much of the new oil production was in the hands of new companies without integrated outlets for their oil, without a stake in the older areas, and therefore with no concern for the effect of the lower prices of the new supplies on the prices of oil elsewhere. The share of oil production controlled by the eight majors in the OPEC countries fell from some 92 per cent in 1960 to 82 per cent in 1970.

These three developments in the 1960s – the entry of new producing countries, that of new companies, and the increased supplies in the hands of the old-established companies – were unconnected with the activities of OPEC and indeed would have weakened OPEC's position in the subsequent years had it not been for two other equally unconnected sets of circumstances which emerged with astonishing rapidity in the first four years of the 1970s. On the one hand there was a sudden surge in demand on Middle East oil as a result of a general economic boom in the industrialized countries in the early 1970s and the growing dependence of the United States on oil imports, combined with growing inflation and currency instability, especially of the US dollar; on the other, there was an intensification of the tension between Israel and the Arabs. These developments brought the industry to a turning point, or 'crisis', in the four years 1970–73.

1970–73: The Years of Crisis

In these four years the oil-exporting countries of the Middle East brought about irreversible changes in the industry. In 1970 they shattered the profit-sharing arrangements of the past two decades. In 1971 they forced the companies to 'recognize' the negotiating power of OPEC and forced a further increase in tax prices, but they accepted a five-year agreement designed to stabilize prices. In 1972 they forced the companies to accede to the long-pressed but fiercely-resisted demand for equity participation in the companies which produced crude oil. In 1973 they not only took over complete control of pricing but made it clear that from then on they intended to exert full control over all aspects of the companies' operations in their countries.

The 1970 fiscal changes were the result of the actions of the new Libyan revolutionary government under Colonel Qaddafi, which was determined to rectify what it considered, with some justification, to have been the unequal fiscal treatment of the country by the companies relative to other major producing countries. He succeeded brilliantly owing to the dependence of Europe on his oil, his bold, uncompromising, and threatening attitudes, and the weakness of the non-integrated newcomers. The companies quickly moved to offer new terms to the producers in the Gulf, and in 1971 new price agreements were concluded in Tehran and Tripoli.

These agreements improved on the Libyan terms largely because of tough bargaining by the Saudis and the Iranians, but also because of the collective pressure of all governments through OPEC. The first and only time that OPEC formally threatened unilateral collective action against the companies was in connection with the Tehran agreement; and for the first time the companies asked to negotiate collectively with OPEC as an organization (which they had earlier refused to do), only to have their request turned down by OPEC. The greatest fear of the companies was that the two groups of countries – those delivering oil to the Gulf and those delivering to the Mediterranean – would vie with each other for better terms and engage in a game of 'leapfrog' at the companies' expense. The two groups of governments preferred to negotiate separately but the existence of the OPEC forum was a moderating influence, for without OPEC it would have been much more difficult for the companies to contain the 'leapfrogging' tendency. As a result of the agreements, the price of Arabian light crude was increased from $1.80 to $2.18 a barrel. Provision was made for inflation but not for currency devaluations. Supplemental agreements were therefore demanded later and obtained. By mid-1973, however, unexpectedly high rates of continued inflation, unexpectedly large depreciation of currencies and increasing international economic disorder had completely undermined the agreements and in September and October negotiations were taking place designed to revise the basis of pricing.

The negotiations on equity participation, led by Zaki Yamani, the Saudi Arabian Oil Minister, followed immediately on the conclusion of the price agreements. They were completed successfully in 1972 in the form of a general agreement on a framework within which each individual government would negotiate the details of its own participation, and in particular the prices at which its own oil could be bought back by the companies should the government so desire. The question of these 'buy back' prices was one of the more difficult issues in the subsequent negotiations because of the steadily rising market prices, for no government wanted to commit itself to a sales price in advance.

Each of the governments had a somewhat different policy on the question of participation. Shaikh Yamani had viewed participation as a way of neutralizing the more extreme political demands for nationalization. Iran was not interested, having already nationalized the foreign companies in 1951, but of course watched carefully the 'buy back' and other terms on which the companies obtained oil. Iraq had been in dispute with the IPC ever since the expropriation in 1962, and in 1972 the government finally came to an agreement for the nationalization of the IPC. In the end, the participation agreement was overtaken by the events of October 1973. Kuwait was the first country after Iraq to take '100 per cent participation', but only did so in 1975. At the time of writing, agreement on the Saudi take-over of Aramco had not yet been announced.

The Governments Take Control

Discussions with the companies on the revision of the Tehran and Tripoli agreements had begun in September 1973 and continued even after the outbreak of war. Negotiations broke down and on 16 October the six Gulf producers (Saudi Arabia, Iran, Kuwait, Iraq, Abu Dhabi, and Qatar) unilaterally raised the price of Arabian light crude from $3.01 to $5.12 a barrel. After the OPEC meeting in December the price was further increased to $11.65, largely on the insistence of the Shah of Iran, who noted that buyers had been prepared to bid as high as $20 a barrel when oil supplies were restricted by the Arabs in pursuance of the war with Israel.

The October War brought to a head changes which had been in process for a decade but which would have come about much more slowly in the absence of the war, and therefore with much less disruptive effect on the world economy. How much of the subsequent acceleration of inflation and deepening of recession in the industrialized world can properly be attributed to the sudden increase in oil prices is unclear, but as a result largely of the decline in industrial activity and partly of the entry of new producers (North Sea, Alaska, Mexico) the demand for Middle East oil remained stagnant between 1974 and 1977. The real price fell by nearly 30 per cent as inflation eroded the value of the dollar.

OPEC was unable to agree on increases in prices to offset inflation largely because of the unwillingness of Saudi Arabia, and later of Iran, to accept increases which might further damage the world economy and, even more serious, further weaken an already weakened dollar in which most of the very substantial financial assets of Saudi Arabia were held. Only once was there an agreed decision – for a 10 per cent increase in September 1975. On another occasion, disagreement led to different groups of countries taking different actions – in 1976 most members raised prices by 10 per cent or more, but Saudi Arabia and Abu Dhabi agreed to only 5 per cent.

Saudi Arabian light crude (34° API) was treated as the 'marker crude'. So long as it was made available at the announced prices, the prices of the 130-odd varieties of crude oil produced by the OPEC countries had sooner or later to fall roughly into line with it, after making allowances for quality differences – which affect refining yields and costs – and for differences in transport costs. Different crude oils are substitutable in refining, and refiners will tend to use the marker crude instead of any other crude for which the price differential is too great. Conversely, of course, too small a differential will divert demand from the marker crude.

The marker crude is a light crude. Light crudes are in greater demand but consitute a smaller proportion of total reserves than the heavier ones. This imbalance, leading to a more rapid depletion of light crudes than reserves would warrant, began to worry Saudi Arabia early in 1978, and the government imposed a limit of 35 per cent on the proportion of Aramco's share that it could take in light crudes. This was an important indication of the way in which the oil-exporting countries could use their new-found control to ensure the development and conservation of their oil supplies in their own interests.

This mechanism for setting prices did not require that OPEC should act as a cartel in enforcing agreed price decisions. Formal enforcement was not necessary because no member of OPEC had oil resources large enough to enable it to sustain such a volume of sales at lower prices as to affect Saudi Arabia's exports enough to induce her to lower the price of marker crude. So long as she was willing to accept reductions in her exports in order to accommodate the exports desired by other countries, there was little difficulty in maintaining the general level of oil prices. And indeed this willingness was probably one reason why the Saudis were able to get their way in OPEC without even greater manifestations of bitterness from their less well-endowed colleagues.

Although the Saudi policy had not become excessively strained by the middle of 1978 and the OPEC countries, in spite of open disagreement, were by no means in a critical position, it was nevertheless becoming increasingly clear that, in the face of continuing world recession and currency weaknesses, especially of the US dollar, the oil-exporting countries would have to work out a more coherent oil policy for, since 1974, their policy had in effect been simply to try to ride out difficulties and wait and see. They clearly hoped for a revival of industrial demand. The differences of view among them were great. For Algeria, Iraq, and Libya the only really important question had become, how to raise prices at once. Others, and especially those with very large assets such as Saudi Arabia, Kuwait, Iran, and the UAE, were forced to consider the effect on the value of their foreign assets of a further weakening of the world economy. Moreover, the weight in the world's financial system which their wealth gave them, the domestic political needs of some of them, and the desire to increase US support for the Arab cause in the Israeli conflict, led them to take a wider and more internationally responsible view than their 'radical' colleagues. Thus, in June 1978 a 'Ministerial Committee on Strategies' was established under the chairmanship of Shaikh Zaki Yamani to study and report on various aspects of long-term policy on which decisions by the oil-producing countries would be necessary: relations with consumer governments and the international companies, supply and depletion, pricing, domestic industrialization, the role of gas, access to markets, etc. At the same time another committee under the chairmanship of Shaikh Ali Khalifa al-Sabah, Oil Minister of Kuwait, was set up to consider the short-term problem of oil prices in light of the weakness of the dollar. The stage was being set for further formal discussions with the international community, perhaps even for a revival in some form of the 'North-South Dialogue' which the 1976 CIEC conference in Paris was designed to represent.

National Policies

Although all the Middle East oil-exporting countries have a common interest in OPEC there are a number of divergent cross currents resulting from the somewhat different position of different countries and groups of countries. In 1968 the Organization of Arab Petroleum Exporting Countries was formed on the initiative of Saudi Arabia, and including Libya and Kuwait as founding members. OAPEC was created as a means of pre-empting possible moves by the more 'radical' countries – Iraq and Algeria – to form an Arab oil organization which might take action damaging to the interests of the major and more conservative exporting countries. After the Libyan Revolution of 1969 OAPEC changed in character, and by 1972 it included all of the Arab oil producers. Its chief functions are to promote co-operation and development among the Arab countries, especially in matters relating to hydrocarbons. It was never intended as a rival to OPEC and it has not become one.

The governments of the major oil-exporting countries all established their own national oil companies, some of which by the end of the 1960s had made numerous sales abroad on their own account and were actively pushing both domestic and international operations. Nearly all of the new concession arrangements in the 1950s and 1960s provided for joint ventures between the national companies and the foreign companies. The Petroleum Law of 1957 in Iran gave preference to companies agreeing to take NIOC, the national company, as a partner. AGIP, a subsidiary of the Italian ENI, was the first to sign and others followed. In the 1960s Saudi Arabia took the lead in pushing joint ventures with its national company, Petromin, and in obtaining more and more favourable terms. Iraq did not make use of partnership arrangements for the development of the areas taken from the IPC (partly because of difficulties raised for foreign companies by the doubtful legality of the Iraqi expropriation), but went in for a variety of contractual and service arrangements, notably with French companies. In both Iran and Iraq new forms of agreement were pioneered by the French company, ERAP. Egypt's oil is produced under joint ventures, the most important producing area being the Morgan field in the Gulf of Suez owned jointly by Egypt's national oil company and Pan-American, a subsidiary of Standard Oil of Indiana, which began commercial production in 1967.

For a long time the major companies resisted proposals to form joint ventures with the governments of the producing countries, although Shell did make such an agreement in 1951/52 for offshore Kuwait, and some agreed to joint ventures in an abortive agreement with Iraq in 1965. But to grant equity participation in their major producing operations, let alone in their refining and marketing operations in Europe, as requested by the Oil Minister of Saudi Arabia and urged by OPEC, was completely unacceptable to them. In this respect, the OPEC countries made no headway whatsoever until after October 1973.

The only non-Arab producer of note in the Middle East is Iran, and the Shah has played a major role in OPEC. Although Iran is, and probably will remain for some time to come, OPEC's second largest producer and is often regarded as a rival to Saudi Arabia, she does not have anywhere near the weight of the Saudis in oil affairs. Her proved reserves are less than half those of Saudi Arabia (an estimated 62 billion barrels), her reserve/production ratio in 1977 of about 30 years[61] was the lowest of the major producers' in the Middle East.

Following the Revolution of the winter of 1978/79, Iranian production levelled off in March and April 1979 at 3.6 million b.p.d. or about two-thirds of previous output. Iran remained the second largest Middle East producer, but the maintenance of the lower level of production would postpone the exhaustion

[61] These and subsequent statistics of reserves and reserve/production ratios are taken from J.E. Hartshorn, *Objectives of the Petroleum Exporting Countries* (in co-operation with *Middle East Economic Survey* and Energy Economics Research Ltd., Cyprus, Middle East Petroleum and Economics Publications, 1978), p. 226. The reserve/production ratio refers to the reserves as estimated in this publication at the end of 1977 in relation to total production during 1977. It will be appreciated that reserve estimates from different sources vary widely and there are no clear criteria for choosing some over others.

of reserves by at least a decade. Perhaps of more importance for the rest of the world is the fact that exports will probably decline more rapidly than production, for Iran's own consumption is high.

Iran took the lead in insisting on the really drastic increase in oil prices at the end of 1973, and she remained a 'price hawk' in the deliberations of OPEC until the middle of 1978 when the Shah changed his policy and joined Saudi Arabia in disapproving further substantial increases in prices. At that time the Shah was faced with considerable domestic political unrest and had been under pressure from President Carter on the question of 'human rights'. His reversal of policy on oil prices was in line with the insistence of the United States that the recession of the world economy would be seriously aggravated by any further increase in the price of oil.

In Iraq, the third largest producer in the Middle East, output grew very slowly during the 1960s. Not only were successive governments continually in dispute with the IPC after the expropriation, but none seemed able to formulate a coherent oil policy in circumstances of considerable political instability. In 1967 the Aref government made arrangements with the Soviet government which laid the basis for extensive Russian assistance in the development of the country's oil fields, and in 1968 the Iraq National Oil Company was given a mandate to move ahead. In 1972 the IPC was finally nationalized, and a full settlement was reached in 1973 on terms favourable to the company. Since then there has been considerable progress both in output and in the development of the INOC. The rival Baath governments of Iraq and Syria are on bad terms and to avoid the political risks and the cost of sending oil across Syria to the Mediterranean, Iraq built additional pipelines, one which could take Kirkuk oil to the Gulf and another to take it across Turkey to the Mediterranean.

Iraq, Libya, and Algeria have formed a radical group within the Arab world and in OPEC, taking a particularly uncompromising line on the need to increase prices and to control production. Iraq has been especially shrill in its criticisms and attacks on Saudi Arabian oil policy. She tends to be secretive about her oil affairs; even production statistics, let alone price data, have frequently been withheld. Her estimated proved reserves are not far from those of the United Arab Emirates, both being between 30 and 35 billion barrels with a reserve/production ratio of slightly over 40 years, but no one would put much confidence in these estimates. She has on occasion apparently cut prices to sell the oil she wants to produce, but has firmly denied all such accusations. In oil, as in political affairs generally, her government takes extreme positions which tend to isolate it from the other countries of the Middle East.

Kuwait has adopted a very different policy from either Iran or Iraq. Her proved reserves of over 70 billion barrels in 1977 were estimated to be second only to those of Saudi Arabia and her reserve/production ratio was about 97 years, as her output was less than 1.8 million b.p.d., or nearly 500,000 b.p.d. less than that of Iraq. Kuwait must plan to live on her oil revenues more completely and for a longer time than most other countries since she has no other natural resources. She therefore puts a ceiling on production, which at the end of 1977 remained at 2 million b.p.d. Kuwait was the first country to proclaim 'allowables' – the production to be allowed in a given period.

Abu Dhabi, too, has imposed 'allowables' but unlike Kuwait, which took over its foreign concessionaire in 1975, Abu Dhabi has preferred to take only a majority interest in the foreign operating companies and continues to use the foreign partners for their expertise and other services. The oil of Abu Dhabi is a low-sulphur, high-quality product which can command a premium price. For the most part the government has accepted the Saudi leadership in OPEC.

Saudi Arabia remains the 'swing producer' of the OPEC countries – the producer whose exports will be cut back disproportionately when demand is weak and on whom calls for any very large increments of demand must fall. With the literally fabulous Ghawar field – the world's largest oil reservoir with reserves (as at present known) greater than those of the USA, including Alaska, and the North Sea combined – Saudi Arabia has proved reserves which have been estimated to lie between 110 and 250 billion barrels, giving a 1977 reserve/production ratio of anywhere between 30 and 75 years.[62] The pressure in the Ghawar field has given rise to some concern and Aramco has a very large water injection scheme designed to maintain pressure. This is apparently adequate but from time to time there are expressions of uneasiness over the technical performance of the field.

It is clear, however, that the Middle East contains enough oil to supply the world's needs at growing rates for a long time to come – if the governments of the oil-exporting countries are prepared to deplete their respective countries' chief natural resource at a rate to suit the interests of the consuming countries and not their own. Such a policy could hardly be expected of any government. Saudi Arabia, the country on which all pressures will focus, has a very small population, and few natural resources, and thus a limited capacity productively to invest her very large oil revenues. Domestic processing of oil in both refining and petrochemicals, along with the infrastructure required for the purpose, is the most obvious outlet. But in addition to the technical and managerial problems all this involves, and to the severe economic and perhaps political strains which inevitably accompany rapid change, the government must accept the responsibility, not only of being the price leader in oil, but also the manager of the chief source of supply upon which the world will apparently have to rely to meet any large increases in demand. To a country so recently and hesitantly entering into the 'modern world' to be thrust so suddenly into the centre of the world stage and with such power over a natural resource still vital to the economic life of most countries presents a challenge difficult even to imagine let alone appreciate. And there is an undeniable conflict between the interests of Saudi Arabia as a country and those of the rest of the world – at least in the short run.

Edith Penrose

[62] Ibid., Hartshorn's accepted estimate was 153 billion barrels with a reserve/production ration of 45.

II

ARABIA

1. Saudi Arabia

THE LAND AND THE PEOPLE

The Arab Kingdom of Saudi Arabia is the creation of the late 'Ibn Saud' (King Abdul Aziz ibn Abdul Rahman ibn Faisal al-Saud), although in fact he was reviving ancestral claims. In 1921 he was proclaimed and recognized officially by the British Government as Sultan of Nejd and its dependencies, including the former Sultanate of Hail. On 8 September 1926 he was proclaimed King of the Hejaz at Mecca and six years later King of Saudi Arabia, formed by the union of the Sultanate and Kingdom, with its capital at Riyadh. The new kingdom comprised 90 per cent of the entire Arabian Peninsula, its western coastline stretching from Aqaba in the north, some 1,000 miles southwards down the Red Sea to the frontiers of Yemen. Its southern and south-eastern borders, which are still mostly ill-defined, march with Yemen, Democratic Yemen, Oman, Qatar, and the United Arab Emirates on the Gulf. On the east its coast stretches along the Gulf through Hasa northwards to the partitioned zones shared with Kuwait. To the north lie Jordan and Iraq. At the time of its creation Saudi Arabia was a primitive and backward state. The population was estimated between one-and-a-half and two million: probably more than a quarter of whom were nomadic, about a half were agricultural and concerned with cultivation in a widely dispersed zone, and the remaining quarter inhabited the relatively numerous market towns and the Holy Cities. Mecca, which was the largest town probably had a population of 50,000. Administration and organization were essentially tribal, the economy was basically subsistence-orientated except for the small component of pearling in the Gulf and the income derived from services given to the Mecca-bound pilgrims.

Physical characteristics

The physical landscape of the Arabian peninsula owes much to its structural character. Briefly, a geologically ancient and relatively stable platform of crystalline rocks has been tilted so that the western edge is uplifted in the highlands which extend from Hejaz south to Aden. This western uplift was accompanied by extensive fracturing and faulting, which gives the pronounced steep scarp edge overlooking the Red Sea and also extensive volcanicity, including great basaltic flows. The south coast of the Democratic Republic of Yemen is similarly fault defined.

The platform tilts eastwards from the Red Sea to the Gulf and is largely covered by more recent sedimentary rocks which attain great thickness where the old block plunges into the great structural depression of the Gulf. In the extreme east the Oman highlands are part of the fold mountain complex of the Zagros mountains of Iran.

The oil wealth of Saudi Arabia is found along the eastern zone where, in sandstones and limestones laid down in shallow water, organic material has been transformed into petroleum hydrocarbons. Recent exploration has established that these are to be found both at relatively great depth in the Gulf itself and also in the shallower land deposits of ancient marine transgressions well inland as in the Rub al-Khali.

On this basic structure arid and semi-arid erosion processes produced during the wetter phases of the Pleistocene Ice-Ages great wadi systems that are, as in the case of the Wadi Batin, now relics in the present more arid epoch but along the lines of which lie some of the linear patterns of wells of great traditional importance. These ancient wadis generally trend south-west to north-east, cutting through the opposing, structurally controlled series of scarps, one of which, the Jabal Tuwaiq, dominates the surrounding plateaux for hundreds of miles.

In the north, eroded sandstones alternate with sand desert basins in the Great Nafud. In the south far greater sand seas dominate the 400,000 square miles of the Rub al-Khali. Central Nejd is a diversity of hills and basins which, where shallow groundwater permits, support oasis settlement.

Only along a narrow zone in the south-western highlands of Saudi Arabia, the Assarah region, does precipitation permit rainfed and irrigation-assisted agriculture and support regionally extensive communities of sedentary cultivators. Elsewhere sub-surface hydrology is all-important since rainfall is minimal and evaporation extremely high; only in the Esh Sham region south of Palmyra does winter precipitation support even relatively stable pastoralism. The traditional centres of life have therefore been oases and well complexes as at Mecca and Medina in the west, Riyadh in Nejd and al-Hasa in the east. The Saudi Arabian coastlands along the Red Sea are dissected and waterless while those on the Gulf are characterized by lagoons, mangrove swamp, and *sabkha,* the better favoured coastal locations all having been pre-empted by the independent emirates, now sovereign States of Kuwait, Bahrain, and the United Arab Emirates.

The People

A census conducted in September 1974 gave an official Saudi population of 7,012,642 although this is generally thought to be too high and some informed observers still maintain the real figure is lower than 4 million. According to the census, 73.1 per cent of the population is settled and 26.9 migratory. Previously, a rough estimate had made only about two-thirds of the population settled. The settlement of nomadic people is certain to increase during the coming years as the economy develops. There are estimated to be 1–2 million non-Saudis in the Kingdom: mainly Yemenis, Omanis, and other Arabs, but also now including Pakistanis, Malaysians, South Koreans, and other Asians, as well as a few thousand Americans and Europeans. The main cities are Riyadh, the administrative capital (666,840), Jedda, the main business centre (561,104), Mecca, the religious capital (366,801), Taif (204,857), Medina (198,186), Dammam (127,844). All figures are estimates from the 1974 census.

The people are nearly all Sunni Arabs, and most of them are Wahhabis. There are no native Christians or Jews, but several thousand Christians (US, Europeans, and Arab) are employed in the oil industry. Non-Moslems are forbidden within the sacred areas that surround Mecca and Medina; foreign diplomatic missions have been located in Jedda, but the decision was taken in 1977 to move them to Riyadh, the capital.

THE RELIGIOUS BACKGROUND

The Holy Places and the Pilgrimage

Until recently the possession by Saudi Arabia of the Holy Places of Islam was the central political fact and the main source of wealth in the kingdom. The custodianship of the Holy Places remains a most important element in the political status of Saudi Arabia and even today spending by pilgrims provides the third largest revenue item in the kingdom's balance of payments. During the month of the hajj in 1971 almost 400,000 foreign pilgrims as well as more than 700,000 Saudis are believed to have visited the Holy Places.

Mecca had been a Holy City before the time of Mohammed, a centre of a religious blend of animism together with ritual worship of the sun, moon, and other deities and part-mythical heroes. The Kaaba, a square building in the courtyard of the main mosque – the Haram – was traditionally reputed to have been built by Adam and rebuilt by Abraham and Ishmael, who inserted into one of its corners the famous Black Stone; a present, the tradition continues, from the Archangel Gabriel. The same tradition names the nearby well of Zam-Zam as the well to which Hagar and Ishmael were guided by God to find water. They both have traditional graves near the Kaaba itself, while Eve's grave was believed to be located at Jedda. (The visiting of such graves is discouraged by the Wahhabis.) The tradition of pilgrimage to Mecca was taken over by the Koran, and is enjoined on Moslems as a sacred duty. The date of the pilgrimage is fixed for the tenth day of the twelfth month of every Moslem year, the climax named the Feast of Sacrifice.

The ritual of the pilgrimage is strict. Once within the sacred area, which starts sixteen miles west of Mecca, all pilgrims must wear the pilgrim's garb – the '*ihram*'. On reaching Mecca the first duty of every pilgrim is prayer at the Kaaba, followed by a procession seven times round the building, after which each kisses the Black Stone. A drink of water is then taken at the well of Zam-Zam. The Feast of Sacrifice itself is celebrated in the plain of Muna, and the following morning each pilgrim stones the three pillars where the Devil is supposed to have been chased away by stones thrown by Abraham, Hagar, and Ishmael. The sacrifice follows. Each family slays its goat or sheep with traditional ritual, and the rest of the day is passed in eating and thanksgiving. Every true believer who accomplishes the pilgrimage is entitled thereafter to call himself 'hajj' and, if he wishes, to wear a green cloth folded round his headdress.

The organization of the reception and handling of the yearly pilgrimage has become a very considerable responsibility in that no longer is it possible or desirable to allow the numbers of pilgrims to find their own transport, food, sleeping accommodation, and transport facilities. On arrival at Jedda, which is still the main point of entry for most foreign pilgrims, the individual pilgrim must produce vaccination certificates, or be vaccinated on the spot; any sickness is dealt with in the hospital outside Jedda, a hospital of 3,000 beds built exclusively for the hajj. Transport is now supplied to carry the pilgrims between Jedda and Mecca as a decreasing number do the whole journey on foot, and further transport facilities have to be arranged for the journeys to Medina and once more back to Jedda. Accommodation must be arranged at Mecca, Medina, and Jedda, in each case capable of holding some 100,000 people; the supply of food and potable water is an equally vast operation. Since the State has been able to rely in the main on oil revenues, the fee which traditionally was paid by pilgrims has been abolished. The organization of the hajj now results in costs being incurred by the Saudi Arabian Government which far outweigh the indirect profit made from sales of commodities and services to the pilgrims. There is the further matter that the custodianship involves the State in very considerable expenditure on maintenance and improvement of many of the buildings.

HISTORY AND POLITICAL ORGANIZATION

History

The present ruler of Saudi Arabia is King Khaled, a direct descendant through his father's lineage of the founder of the house of Saud. Ibn Saud died in 1953 and was succeeded by the former Crown Prince Saud. Prince Faisal, his younger brother, who presided over the Council of Ministers, was called on to take over the Government between 1958 and 1960. In 1963 Faisal once more became *de facto* ruler, as King Saud's health deteriorated and his control of affairs became increasingly of concern to the Royal Family and the Ulema. In 1964, following traditional procedure and in response to persuasion, Faisal replaced his brother on the throne. In March 1975 King Faisal was assassinated by an unbalanced nephew and was succeeded by his brother, Crown Prince Khaled.

The royal house of Saudi Arabia has ruled in Nejd since the eighteenth century. The founder of the house of Saud in Nejd, Saud ibn Mohammed ibn Muqrin, died in 1747, and was succeeded by his eldest son, Mohammed ibn Saud, who offered asylum to the religious reformer Mohammed ibn Abdul Wahhab (1703–91), the founder of the Wahhabi movement. The latter had been driven out of his own country by local opposition to his new creed, which preached the purification of Islam. All worship other than of God was false worship; the cult of saints, their invocation in prayer, the veneration of their tombs, and other similar practices implied unbelief in God; and among its precepts for the stricter observance of Islam were obligatory attendance at public prayers and a ban on smoking. Wahhabi mosques are built with the minimum of architectural adornment.

From 1746, except for short intervals of peace, Nejd was at war for the next century and a half. Slowly the Wahhabi rule spread throughout Nejd and later into Hasa province on the Gulf, though its spread was generally resisted. In 1801, to avenge an attack by Iraqi tribesmen on a pilgrim caravan the Wahhabis had agreed to protect, they invaded Iraq, sacked Karbala (the Shii Holy City), massacred its inhabitants, and desecrated the tomb of Hussein. Two years later they captured Taif and Mecca in the Hejaz, destroyed several shrines, and stripped the Kaaba of its ornaments. By 1806, Yanbo, Medina, Mecca, and Jedda were in Wahhabi hands.

These victories and their religious repercussions had an immediate effect in Egypt, where Mohammed Ali had just begun to consolidate his personal supremacy. With the approval of the Ottoman Sultan an Egyptian expeditionary force was organized, and in 1811 it invaded Arabia. The campaign lasted eight years and ended in the complete defeat of the Wahhabis and the fall of Riyadh, the capital of Nejd. This victory restored the Sultan's control over Mecca and Medina, the Holy Cities of Islam, and up to 1840 Turkish and Egyptian influence on the Hejaz and Nejd was unchallenged; the ruler of Nejd was forced to accept Ottoman suzerainty.

Meanwhile, north of Nejd the Rashidi family of Hail had succeeded in establishing itself as a powerful rival of the Saudi family, and for many years was almost unbroken between the two. Fortunes fluctuated, but in 1891 the head of the Saud family, Abdul Rahman was forced to flee the country with his young son Abdul Aziz and took refuge in Kuwait, where they and their followers remained as refugees until 1902, when Abdul Aziz with a few followers recaptured Riyadh by a brilliant surprise attack. Rashidi power in Hail declined and, with the danger of attack from the north thus removed, Abdul Aziz, who was recognized as leader even in the lifetime of his father, was free to contemplate the recovery of the Wahhabi territorial losses of the past hundred years. In 1913, his army suddenly occupied the Turkish province of Hasa, on the Gulf.

During the First World War, on 26 December 1915, Ibn Saud signed a treaty with the British Government and received British recognition of the independence and territorial integrity of Nejd and a subsidy of £5,000 monthly; but the growing power of King Hussein of the Hejaz inevitably brought the two neighbours into conflict, which ended in a disastrous Hejaz defeat at Turaba in 1919. Ibn Saud then advanced against Hail, where the last Rashidi ruler surrendered in November 1921. Following an abortive attack on Transjordan in 1922, he agreed to refrain from aggression against Iraq, Kuwait, and the Hejaz, and to co-operate with Britain in furthering peaceful conditions and economic interests in Arab countries. In 1924, after the subsidy had ceased, a Wahhabi force raided the Hejaz, where King Hussein abdicated in favour of his son Ali. In December 1925 Jedda, Medina, and Yanbo were overrun by the Wahhabi armies and Ali abdicated and withdrew to Iraq, where he died in 1934. Ibn Saud was proclaimed as King of Hejaz at Mecca on 8 January 1926. British recognition followed in the Treaty of Jedda, signed on 20 May 1927.

Meanwhile Asir to the south of Hejaz, which had been ruled

by a branch of the Idrisi family of North Africa, had also come under Ibn Saud's domination. He had acquired the mountain districts in 1920, and in 1925, during a civil war between two Idrisi rivals in which the King of the Yemen had supported one pretender, the other accepted what amounted to a protectorate from Ibn Saud; on his death Asir was annexed to Nejd. In 1934 hostilities broke out between Yemen and Saudi Arabia. Saudi forces were quickly victorious and the settlement which followed led to amicable relations for the next thirty years. On Saudi Arabia's northern borders, suspicion of the Hashimite kingdoms of Transjordan (later Jordan) and Iraq ruled over by the sons of the ill-fated Hussein of Hejaz remained strong. Ibn Saud also remained deeply suspicious of British actions in Palestine but as the prospects of oil revenue appeared during the late 1930s and as the need and opportunities for pursuing remarkably successful policies of internal consolidation became more apparent so also did the Saudi Government's freedom of international manoeuvre grow more limited.

Following the Second World War and the creation of Israel in 1948 Saudi Arabia pursued a more vigorous but yet cautious foreign policy utilizing in particular its growing economic power and status. A founder-member of the Arab League, Saudi Arabia joined with Egypt and Syria in opposing Abdullah of Jordan and Nuri al-Said of Iraq in their Greater Syria ambitions, this policy continuing in Saudi opposition to the Baghdad Pact. The assassination of King Abdullah in 1951 and the overthrow of the Egyptian monarchy in 1952 did not in themselves alter Saudi attitudes except that suspicion of Hashimite intentions decreased and the traditional policy of friendship with Egypt was not as easy to maintain. Ibn Saud's personal control of government up to the time of his death in 1953 not only coloured his attitude to his northern neighbours but also towards those in the south-west bordering the Buraimi group of oases. The discovery of oil only emphasized the traditional claims made in this region by the rulers of Abu Dhabi, Oman, and Saudi Arabia; and the continued British championing of the cause of the smaller states somewhat strained Ibn Saud's friendship with Britain. In 1949, after three years of dispute with the British Government (which by treaty automatically acted for Abu Dhabi and by invitation also for Oman), Saudi claims to the whole region were put forward very strongly and Saudi forces occupied one of the oasis villages. In 1954 the forces withdrew but neutral arbitration proceedings broke down within a year; the Shaikh of Abu Dhabi and Sultan of Muscat and Oman thereupon resumed control of the whole area approximately up to the lines expressed in a Sauds claim map of 1935. Since that time the *status quo* has remained in being but the full Saudi claims remain on record.

The reign of King Saud was a period of greater difficulty for Saudi Arabia. Oil-derived wealth under Ibn Saud had already led to some degree of public extravagance and of the personal enrichment of the Royal Family and Court at variance with strict Wahhabi tradition, but the personal status and strength of the creator of the Kingdom prevented internal strains and tensions from becoming too great. Similarly with administration, where only a life-time of exercising authority and the unchallengeable respect he commanded enabled Ibn Saud to rule a rapidly changing and modernizing State with little except traditional tribal machinery. King Saud inherited none of these advantages. He was faced by an accelerating pace of change at home and increasingly delicate situations abroad, and, as ultimately was recognized by the Royal Family and their advisers, he did not possess the ability to meet the various and heavy demands made on a ruler in such a situation.

Within Saudi Arabia the unity created by Ibn Saud appeared less strong as divisive forces reappeared. In a theocratic state, the Ulema, the learned Islamic judiciary which interprets and administers the *sharia*, the divine law of Islam, was a body whose strength Ibn Saud appreciated and utilized. As Riyadh, the centre of government, became more and more associated not only with personal wealth and laxity but also with the graft and corruption which accompanied the growth of disorganized administrative machinery and the inflow of advisers and administrators many of whom were blatantly self-seeking, so members of the Ulema were alienated. Regionalism, always a danger to a weak central Government, grew as the Hejaz began to lose respect for the once conquering Nejd and also as the Hasawis of the east contrasted the efficiency and prosperity resulting from the activities of Aramco and the provincial Government of al-Hasa, with the increasingly infirm character of the Riyadh Government. All this was doubly dangerous because the results of early investment in education produced a growing number of young people who were beginning to think for themselves, and who provided fertile soil for the concepts of Arab socialism and nationalism propagated by immigrant teachers and administrators. Moreover, the flood of Egyptian radio propaganda, included a strong element of anti-Riyadh sentiment. Prince Faisal, who had conducted foreign affairs for his father, remained President of the Council of Ministers, a nominated body largely drawn from the Royal Family, but King Saud pursued the system of largely personal rule drawing support increasingly from a group of favourites. Dissension was met by increased expenditure on internal security and the taking of more power by the provincial governors.

Externally, circumstances were even more confused and policy equally vacillating. Friendship with Egypt was maintained after Nasser's rise to power even though the new brand of Egyptian Arab Socialism was anathema to Saudi ruling circles. In 1955 Saud joined Egypt and Syria in a joint command system aimed at the Baghdad Pact group; in 1956 he publicly supported Egypt's seizure of the Suez Canal; and after the Suez venture he broke off relations with Britain – these were not restored until 1964.

In January 1957 Saudi Arabia joined with Egypt and Syria in undertaking to pay Jordan for at least ten years £12.5 million annually to replace the British subsidy. But King Saud was already apprehensive about the rapid rise of radical revolutionary Arab nationalism led by Abdul Nasser and about the increasing Soviet influence in the Middle East. In April, during the disturbances in Jordan, he sent troops there, as much to forestall any Syrian attempt to take over the country as to guard against an attack by Israel. He settled his differences with the Hashimites in order to create a common monarchical front against the revolutionary republics. The United States responded by showing its approval of King Saud's anti-Communism and the State Department seems to have considered the possibility of buttressing Saud as a rival to Nasser's leadership of the Arabs.

Saud and his advisers still tried to avoid an open clash with Nasser. He worded his acceptance of the Eisenhower Doctrine so that it should appear as approval without full acceptance. But a crisis was reached in February 1958 when the Syrian Colonel Abdul Hamid Sarraj publicly accused Saud of attempting to have President Nasser assassinated on the eve of the formation of the United Arab Republic of Egypt and Syria. The princes, shaikhs, and Ulema who represented public opinion in Saudi Arabia combined to force the King to hand over full powers in domestic and foreign affairs to his younger brother Prince Faisal who at that time was regarded as relatively pro-Egyptian. Saud's forays in foreign policy and his wild extravagance had made Saudi Arabia something of a laughing-stock in the Arab world.

Faisal initiated a period of economy and restraint to restore Saudi Arabia's chaotic finances. But although Saudi Arabia's image abroad was improved, financial austerity was unpopular at home – especially among the tribesmen who had received regular subsidies from Saud. Saudi 'progressive' intellectuals saw their opportunity and formed an undeclared alliance with Saud on the understanding that if they helped him recover his powers a constitution providing for some form of representative government would be introduced. Saud did recover his authority in December 1960 when Faisal resigned as Prime Minister, but constitutional government did not follow and the small group of progressives went into jail or exile.

Saud's new period of rule was only brief. The republican coup in Yemen in September 1962 was a direct threat to the Saudi monarchy. Saudi Arabia at once began helping the Yemeni royalists but Saud's position was precarious. In October he reshuffled his Government and announced a reform programme which included the abolition of slavery. The loyalty of the regular Saudi forces was far from certain and two of the small band of trained Saudi pilots defected with their planes to Egypt. In failing health, Saud was obliged to return power to Faisal who by the end of 1963 had once again become the effective ruler of Saudi Arabia.

Austere in his private life, astute and experienced in international diplomacy, Faisal was a much more real threat to President Nasser's position than his brother had been. He made no concessions to those Saudis who wanted a more liberal regime but he earned their respect. At the same time he encouraged steady progress in social and economic development. In his previous period of power he had tried to avoid any heavy involvement in Arab politics in order to concentrate on domestic affairs. This time he embarked on a vigorous diplomatic offensive in favour of the conservative Arab monarchies and against the radical republics. He was helped by Egypt's increasing difficulties in Yemen where he was able to continue supplying the Yemeni royalists with money and arms without involving his own forces.

In November 1964 Saud was formally deposed by a majority of the princes and the council of religious leaders and Faisal became king. Saudi-Egyptian relations were generally worsening although there was some brief improvement after August 1965 when President Nasser flew to Jedda to conclude the so-called Jedda agreement for peace in Yemen. But while the abortive Haradh peace conference which arose out of this agreement was in progress, King Faisal paid a state visit to Iran where in a speech to the Iranian Majlis he proposed closer collaboration between Moslem states against alien and atheist influences. Cairo's press and radio at once began to denounce what it called Faisal's Islamic Pact.

During 1966 King Faisal made a series of diplomatic visits mainly to Moslem states such as Turkey, Pakistan, and Sudan. He was advised in Riyadh by a group of anti-Egyptian Arab emigré politicians. His public speeches were consistently anti-Communist with the implication that Egypt, and to a lesser extent Syria too, was responsible for the growing Soviet power and influence in the Arab world. Saudi Arabia was diplomatically strong but militarily weak and in 1966 the Government began a major rearmament programme which included a £300 million deal with British firms to provide an air-defence network. Egyptian Yemeni-based planes had on several occasions bombed with impunity Saudi border towns which the Egyptians alleged were being used as bases by the Yemeni royalists.

King Faisal's challenge to President Nasser was genuine and

powerful as he was the acknowledged leader of anti-Nasser elements. But his diplomatic achievements were limited because, except for Iran and Jordan, the key states in his potential Islamic front – Pakistan, Turkey, and Sudan – declined to commit themselves to an anti-Egyptian policy, and his proposal for a summit meeting of Moslem Heads of State in Saudi Arabia came to nothing.

The 1967 Arab-Israeli war transformed the situation. In the short term it brought several advantages to King Faisal. The Egyptian army was badly beaten and President Nasser's prestige shaken. At the Khartoum Arab summit meeting in August he took the lead in proposing that, in return for a general agreement, the pumping of oil supplies to the United Kingdom and United States cut off during the war should be resumed, and that the three leading Arab oil states, Kuwait, Libya, and Saudi Arabia, should provide Jordan and Egypt with an income to compensate for the losses of the war. Egypt was thus placed in a position of accepting Saudi charity. At the same time, President Nasser was finally obliged to agree to withdraw all his troops from Yemen – a cardinal aim of Saudi policy.

The disadvantages to Saudi Arabia of the Arab defeat, though less obvious, were equally genuine. King Hussein, his foremost ally among Arab leaders, was now in such a weak position that he could not afford to join Faisal in opposing radical elements in the Arab world. The war had if anything pushed the Arabs further to the left and although Britain fairly rapidly mended its bridges with the Arab world the United States remained deeply unpopular for its continued diplomatic support for Israel. The Russians, on the other hand, were championing the Arab cause and King Faisal's extreme anti-Communism aroused little response. Even in South Arabia events did not develop as King Faisal might have hoped. The withdrawal of Egyptian troops did not lead to the expected collapse of the Yemeni republican regime and the NLF takeover in South Yemen meant that another revolutionary republican regime had been installed on the Arabian Peninsula – something King Faisal had striven to prevent. His efforts to establish a form of protectorate over the Hadhramaut states failed when the rulers returning from a visit to Saudi Arabia found their territory in the hands of the National Liberation Front (NLF).

Following the 1967 war, Saudi foreign diplomacy was very much less active and the King no longer attempted to take any strong lead in the Arab world. He refused to agree to the holding of a further Arab summit meeting on the ground that this should await the outcome of the mission of Dr. Gunnar Jarring, the UN Special Envoy. King Faisal pursued his efforts to achieve a *rapprochement* between Iran and the Arab states—a matter which had become more urgent with Britain's decision to withdraw all its forces from the Gulf by 1971. His relations with Egypt and other socialist Arab states were correct but cool. When an Arab summit was finally held in Rabat in December 1969, its failure was due at least partially to Saudi Arabia's refusal to increase its financial support for the Arab nations directly confronting Israel by the amount these countries desired. The Saudi Government as well as private individuals continued to give considerable financial assistance to the Palestine guerrilla organization al-Fatah; King Faisal showed his preference for al-Fatah rather than its Marxist rivals such as the Popular Front for the Liberation of Palestine.

The Saudi Government refused to recognize the revolutionary Government of South Yemen on the ground that it threatened Saudi Arabia's security. On the other hand, it finally recognized the Government of Yemen in July 1970 following the compromise settlement of the Yemeni civil war. The Saudi regime was alarmed at the spread of left-wing influences in the Arabian Peninsula. In June and September 1969 there were attempted coups against the regime by Baathist and Arab nationalist elements in the armed forces and civil service and again in March 1970 several prominent civilians were arrested.

Although Saudi Arabia's influence in the Arab world and beyond was growing in the 1960s as a result of King Faisal's firm but cautious leadership and increasing oil revenues, it was transformed as a result of the October 1973 war in which Saudi Arabia played a crucial although non-military role. In backing Egypt and Syria's military action by leading the other Arab oil-producing states in the use of the oil weapon by reducing production and embargoing supplies to the US and Netherlands, Saudi Arabia abandoned its normally cautious policies to an extent that many Western experts had predicted it would never do.

Partly as a consequence of the war, Saudi oil revenues rose from $2,744.6 million in 1972 to $22,573.5 million in 1974, and by the following year the Kingdom's financial reserves were second only in the world to those of West Germany. As the owner of the largest proven oil reserves (over one-third of the non-communist's world's total) and with huge spare capacity of oil production, Saudi Arabia is the dominant member of OPEC with a decisive influence on world oil prices. These factors have combined to give Saudi Arabia something of the status of a world power, despite the Kingdom's lack of military strength.

Saudi foreign policy has remained pro-Western with special favour towards the USA and a strong preoccupation with the threat of communism. King Faisal resisted pressure by other oil exporters during 1974 to introduce further rises in oil prices because he feared such increases would seriously weaken the economies of Western industrialized countries and the Saudi leaders continued to exercise a moderating influence within OPEC in the late 1970s. It has opposed proposals in OPEC to switch financial reserves from US dollars to some other currency. In economic matters Saudi Arabia maintains a vigorous faith in capitalist private enterprise, although tempered by Islamic principles. It shows a strong preference for Western technology, especially that of the US and in June 1974 signed a wide-ranging economic, technological and industrial co-operation agreement with the USA. At the same time, the Saudi leaders have been anxious that the USA should not take their pro-Westernism for granted and, with their customary caution, have indicated to Washington that they expect a response in the form of more pro-Arab and less pro-Israeli policies.

King Faisal's death in March 1975 caused no fundamental change in Saudi domestic or foreign policies. The Kingdom has pursued its role as a mediator in the Arab world even more vigorously. While it has strengthened its ties with the Arab oil states it has also patched up its quarrel with its radical neighbours Iraq and settled a border dispute. In 1976 it even established diplomatic relations with the PDRY. In 1976 also, Saudi Arabia played a leading role in the Arab summit meetings at Riyadh and Cairo which made possible the formation of the Syrian-dominated Arab Deterrent Force in Lebanon. When President Sadat's peace initiative to Israel of December 1977 again split the Arab world, Saudi Arabia's prime concern was to restore Arab unity.

In Africa and Asia, Saudi Arabia showed its desire to help and support Islamic causes and pro-Western regimes and to oppose the spread of Soviet influence and Marxist ideas, One special focus of Saudi concern was the Red Sea area where it aimed to secure an anti-Soviet entente with Sudan, Somalia, the YAR and Egypt. However, when Egypt proceeded to sign a bilateral peace treaty with Israel in March 1979, Saudi Arabia showed its extreme disapproval by breaking with Cairo and joining the other Arab states in the imposition of sanctions on Egypt.

Constitution and Government

Saudi Arabia has no constitution except the Koran. Its law is the *sharia* supplemented by various decrees. While the last ten years have seen the growth of Cabinet Government and the development of a modern type of ministry, budgeting, etc., the reins of power remain in the hands of the King who is also Prime Minister. The King's brother Fahd is Crown Prince and First Deputy Prime Minister; King Khaled has delegated to him full powers to manage the affairs of the country. All the key posts in the Cabinet are held by members of the royal family. The capital is Riyadh but the King and most of the Government reside and work in Taif during the summer months. Foreign embassies are in Jedda but are to be moved to Riyadh by the early 1980s. There are no political parties or franchise although the formation of a consultative council has been considered.

The administrative areas are the Hejaz, Nejd, the Eastern Province (al-Hasa), Asir, and Najran. There are General Municipal Councils – each with an Administrative Committee – for the towns of Mecca, Medina, and Jedda. In the rest of the country there are district councils, tribal councils and village councils.

Economic and Social Survey

Saudi wealth began to flow in large quantities in the early 1950s and led to heavy spending by a Royal Family about 5,000 strong. By 1956–8, though revenues were rising, the country was plunged into a balance of payments crisis. Devaluation and a monetary stabilization programme devised by the Saudi Arabian Monetary Agency (SAMA), headed by a Pakistani (Anwar Ali), succeeded in remedying the situation.

The change of target from luxury expenditure at home and real estate purchases abroad to domestic development projects began when the IBRD was asked to make a survey in May 1960. A Supreme Planning Board embarked on infrastructure projects, and in particular on the building of a road network, but the first planning body which aimed to co-ordinate the efforts of individual ministries and to establish priorities between their needs was King Faisal's Central Planning Bureau set up by the Cabinet in 1969. In 1969 a Five-Year Plan for the period 1970/71 to 1975/76 was announced with the broad aim of maintaining the rate of economic growth, developing and creating fresh opportunities for the country's human resources, and diversifying and broadening the base of the economy.

The vast increase in revenues caused by the quintupling of oil prices in the 1973–5 period made possible the launching of a development plan on a wholly different scale. The Second Development Plan for 1975–1980 calls for an expenditure of $142 billion over the period – a level of investment nine times higher than that proposed for the previous development plan. The plan has the following goals: to secure the defence and internal security of the Kingdom; to maintain a high rate of economic growth; to reduce expenditure on oil; to develop human resources; to improve the standard of living and develop the physical infrastructure. Major items in the Plan include defence ($22.2 billion); education and manpower training ($21.1 billion); external aid, emergency funds, and food subsidies ($18 billion). The Plan envisages that GDP will more than double between 1974/75 and 1979/80 from 148,800 million rials to 318,624.6 million rials (in November 1978, $1=3.24 rials).

The Oil Industry

The transformation of Saudi Arabia within three decades has been made possible by the discovery and exploitation of oil on a vast scale.

The first oil concession was granted in 1933 and the first exports took place in 1938. The Second World War resulted in the virtual shutting down of the first oil-fields but from 1946 onwards production soared dramatically. In 1968 revenue from oil totalled $926 million and production reached 1,114.1 million barrels, making Saudi Arabia the largest Middle East producer and the fourth largest producer in the world. The rate of increase slowed down somewhat during 1969 and both Libya (much nearer European markets) and Iran (which put great pressure on producing companies) overhauled Saudi Arabia in tonnage raised. Nevertheless the kingdom possesses the largest national proven oil resources in the world, capable without further exploration of supporting present extraction rates for a further century. Extending from the Neutral Zone from which oil receipts are shared with Kuwait, offshore as at Safaniya and near Bahrain, and onshore as at Abu Hadriya and the giant Ghawar field, a series of oilfields stretch south into the Rub al-Khali and border the territories of Abu Dhabi and the State of Oman. The extent and wealth of these fields increases with each exploratory survey. Aramco, the consortium of Standard Oil California (30 per cent), Standard Oil New Jersey (30 per cent), Texaco (30 per cent), and Mobil (10 per cent), still produces over 90 per cent of the crude petroleum. The remainder comes from the Getty onshore concession and the AOC Japanese offshore concession in the Neutral Zone.

In December 1972 Saudi Arabia signed the General Agreement on Participation under which the government acquired an initial 25 per cent stake in Aramco's assets in Saudi Arabia and those of the other oil companies operating on its territory. This agreement provided for a staged increase in the government stake until it held a 51 per cent interest by 1982. But during 1973 Saudi Arabia pressed for an immediate majority holding in the company. In June 1974 an interim agreement was concluded with the company under which the government's 25 per cent share in Aramco was raised to 60 per cent retroactive to 1974. Negotiations for a 100 per cent take-over were still in progress in 1978.

The Saudi oil and mineral corporation Petromin, set up in 1962, is attached to the Ministry of Petroleum and Mineral Resources and empowered to implement and administer public projects for petroleum and minerals, import raw materials if necessary, conduct all types of oil operations, and co-operate with private companies in these fields. The domestic distribution of all oil products is also in its hands but Petromin's first responsibility has been to establish a stake in the exploitation of the country's oil resources. Because of the scale of the industrial projects planned, a new Ministry of Industry and Electricity was created in October 1975 to take over from Petromin all responsibilities outside the production, refining and marketing of oil and gas.

Saudi crude oil is channelled to market in a variety of ways. Some is refined at Aramco's refinery at Ras Tanura and about 10 per cent of total output is piped to the Bahrain refinery. Tapline, the Aramco-controlled pipeline link with the Mediterranean coast, has a capacity of 500,000 barrels per day.

Total Saudi oil output in 1971 averaged 4.77 million barrels per day (b.p.d.) rising to over 6 million b.p.d. when production was interrupted by the Arab oil restrictions imposed after the October Middle East war. Output fell back from the end of 1974 and averaged only 6.97 million b.p.d. in 1975 but recovered again in 1976 to reach over 9 million b.p.d. in 1977.

The question of Saudi Arabia's maximum sustainable productive capacity has been the subject of dispute. Earlier estimates by the CIA of 16 million b.p.d. are now generally regarded as too high and a long-term production level of 12 million b.p.d., with a maximum productive capacity of about 14 million b.p.d., is more widely accepted. The implications are of immense importance. For Saudi Arabia it would mean that reserves and revenues would survive well into the next century but for oil consumers it means that they cannot rely on Saudi Arabia to meet their increasing needs for more than a decade and a world economic recovery could bring the crisis forward to the early 1980s.

Agriculture

Saudi economic policy has increasingly turned towards the utilization of oil revenues for the diversification of the economy as a whole. Agriculture, the mainstay of the traditional pre-oil period, was estimated to employ between 50 per cent and 60 per cent of the population, but according to official estimates this proportion has declined from 40.4 per cent of the national labour force in 1970 to 28.0 per cent in 1975. Cultivation until recently has been dependent on the application of traditional technology in arid and semi-arid environments; for this reason it has been tied either to the relatively pluvious highlands of the western ranges in Asir and parts of the Hejaz or to the dispersed zones where ground-water can be easily extracted. Wherever simple irrigation has not been possible nomadic pastoralism is dominant. Considerable investment has been made in hydrological and agricultural potential surveys organized on a national basis in eight regions. These have revealed that the centre and east of the country overlie an aquifer containing a reservoir of sweet fossil water at least 29,000 years old. Estimates of how long these resources will last vary from 30 to 100 years.

Of the total land area of 225.3 million hectares, FAO estimates show 373,000 hectares under arable and perennial crops and 1.7 million hectares classified as forested. Soil and water surveys have shown that, subject to the availability of water, the cropped area could be more than doubled; that the potential for a big increase is in nearly all areas under cultivation; that most of the cultivated areas could be increased by improved water utilization; and that large areas of good quality water exist in the Wadi Dawasir, Wadi Miyah and Qasim.

A policy of economic diversification and of resource development has led to a vast expansion in agricultural development. In 1971 more than 300 million rials were allocated for the completion of various projects of which the major were: the Faisal Resettlement Project which has involved the establishment of a 4,000 hectare irrigation scheme on virgin land at Haradh – this primarily for settlement of about 5,000 bedouin; a completely new irrigation and drainage system for the ancient irrigated area of southern al-Hasa, this covering some 20,000 hectares and involving almost 100,000 inhabitants, and including a major and successful sand stabilization protection scheme; the Wadi Jizan water storage dam and land reclamation scheme in the southern Tihama on the Red Sea littoral. A large number of other projects ranging from fisheries to plant protection are also in hand.

On the other hand, agriculture's share of the development budget has progressively decreased from 6 per cent in 1973/74 to 4 per cent in 1974/75 and 2.3 per cent in 1975/76. The estimates of the Second Development Plan are that by 1980 domestic wheat production will meet half the Kingdom's needs, compared with a very small proportion in 1975. Meat production should amount to 68 per cent of local needs (compared with 59 per cent in 1975), poultry production 87 per cent (compared with 22 per cent in 1975), and egg production 50 per cent (compared with 27 per cent in 1975). Milk production is expected to rise from 185,000 tons a year to 280,000 tons.

However, there remain substantial obstacles both to the improvement of output in existing agricultural communities and to the settling of bedouin on the land. For the first it is essential that improved agricultural techniques should be demonstrated to the farmers and at present only Aramco has the personnel to do this. There is a serious danger that the extension of irrigation will lead to soil salination. Planned attempts to settle bedouin have yet to prove successful anywhere in Arabia as the bedouin usually prefer to take the houses offered to them and let the land to established cultivators. The agricultural training centre which is being organized with UN assistance in Riyadh is therefore of the greatest importance for the future.

Mining and Other Industries

There are as yet no mineral industries apart from oil and some output of salt, gypsum, and limestone; but there are good prospects for minerals, especially phosphates of which substantial deposits have been discovered near the Jordanian border, iron ore along the Red Sea coast, a rich concentration of heavy metals on the Red Sea floor, and copper in the Jabal Sayid area. The 1972 mining law (revised in 1973) offers important incentives to foreign mining companies and French, British, Canadian, and Swedish companies are surveying the prospects for copper, lead, zinc, phosphates, and gold. Uranium has also been discovered.

The new Ministry of Industry and Electricity established in 1975 has launched a 50.7 billion rial plan for hydrocarbon-based industries to be implemented by 1985. Natural gas at present being flared in the eastern oilfields will be used for power and feedstock. The industrial centre in the east is to be at Jubail, and in the west, Yanbo. Oil and gas pipelines will cross the country from the east to supply Yanbo's industries. A 10 billion rial Saudi Arabian Basic Industries Corporation has been set up to take responsibility for all heavy industry other than oil refining.

Traditional cottage industries are weaving and mat-making; there are also small-scale enterprises catering for domestic needs (such as tanning, soap-making, pottery, furniture, and household articles). It is government policy to encourage the development of industry; a General Investment Fund, set up in 1971, is designed to finance government and semi-permanent sponsored projects. Foreign capital is guaranteed the same privileges as Saudi capital, and any project in which it is invested is exempt from income and company taxation for five years after the beginning of production, provided there is at least a 25 per cent Saudi investment. An Industrial Research and Development Centre report on industries which can profitably be developed includes foods and beverages, textiles, furniture, paper and rubber products and chemicals.

In March 1974 the Council of Ministers endorsed a new industrial policy for Saudi Arabia aimed at accelerating the country's development. This provides a wide range of incentives – loans, tax exemptions, provision of infrastructure and industrial zones – to encourage the Saudi Arabian private sector to carry out industrial projects, and foreign capital and technical expertise to participate. Foreign investors are guaranteed freedom of movement of capital in and out of the country. The siting of new factories is a crucial element in government planning and is aimed to open up new industrial areas in the Kingdom. In addition to existing 'industrial estates' at

Jedda, Riyadh, and Dammam, new ones are under construction at Mecca, Hofuf, Qasim, and other smaller cities. But the centre-piece of Saudi industrialization, described as 'the biggest simple industrial project in history', is the building of two new industrial cities at Jubail (projected population 300,000) and Yanbo (projected population 150,000), at a total estimated cost of $70 billion.

Transport and Communications

Nearly a quarter of total investments in the Second Development Plan has been allocated to infrastructure and communications. Road building has been given priority in planning. About 7,000 miles of surfaced roads have been built and there are about 3,000 miles of rural roads. A further 9,000 miles of surfaced roads and 6,000 miles of secondary roads are to be built by the end of the Plan. The massive increase in imports of the early 1970s caused serious congestion of the country's ports. Jedda, Yanbo and Jizzan on the Red Sea, and Dammam and Jubail on the Gulf, are all undergoing major expansion and improvements. A Ports Corporation was set up in August 1976 to take over the administration of the ports. The chief international airports are Jedda, Dhahran and Riyadh, but there are 22 airports altogether. Both Jedda and Riyadh have been considerably improved in recent years but new airports are being built for both cities at a total cost of $3 billion.

The telephone and telegraphic network is being expanded rapidly and the number of telephones is to increase from 93,600 to 487,000 in the 1975–80 Plan with additional capacity to 667,000 lines. Jedda has telex, and systems are being installed in Riyadh and Dammam.

Banking and Finance

Notes are issued by the Saudi Arabian Monetary Agency (SAMA) which is, in effect, the central bank. The rial was linked to the SDR on 15 March, 1975. The rial is freely convertible and there are no restrictions on the operation of bank accounts by residents or non-residents in any currency or on any remittance of currency or bullion into or out of the Kingdom.

As a capital market Saudi Arabia is at least ten years behind Kuwait. Until the sudden increase in the money supply caused by the upsurge of oil revenues in the early 1970s, SAMA discouraged the commercial banks from placing money abroad and the almost total lack of telecommunications with the outside world prevented any regular dealing with international money markets.

This situation is now rapidly changing. By the end of 1975 there were 12 commercial banks in Saudi Arabia with 79 branches. Two were domestic banks with between two-thirds and three-quarters of the total balance sheet. The government requires majority Saudi participation in Saudi branches of foreign banks.

The Saudi Industrial Development Fund (SIDF) was set up in 1974 with an initial capital of 500 million rials (later increased to 3 billion rials) to encourage the private sector to establish or expand local industry. Long-term loans (interest-free in conformity with Islamic principle) are advanced for up to 50 per cent of the total cost of the project. Another source of medium- and long-term finance for industry is the Saudi Investment Banking Corporation set up in July 1976 with a capital of 30 million rials of which 35 per cent was subscribed by foreign banks, 29 per cent by Saudi Arabian institutions, and 36 per cent by the Saudi Arabian public. The Real Estate Development Fund was established in 1974 to encourage private and commercial housing construction. It grants interest-free loans of up to 300,000 rials for the building of owner-occupied homes and up to 15 million rials for housing compounds.

Aid

Before the 1973 war Saudi Arabia only gave limited assistance to a few states with which it had close links. Of a total of about $200 million, nearly $150 million went in annual subsidies to Egypt and Jordan to compensate for their losses in the 1967 war.

Since 1973 the Saudi Arabian aid programme has been massively increased. SAMA estimates foreign aid totalled $10,960 million in 1972–5 or about 10.6 per cent of GDP. In 1976 aid was officially put at $5.5 billion. A Saudi Development Fund was established in 1974 to finance projects in developing countries. Saudi Arabia was also the prime mover behind the establishment of the Islamic Development Bank and has subscribed 200 million 'Islamic dinars' of the banks' capital of one billion Islamic dinars (about $1,150 million). Saudi Arabia has also been a major contributor to the Arab Bank for Economic Development in Africa, the Asian Development Bank and the IBRD. It was the principal contributor to the IMF's 'oil facility', designed to help members badly hit by the oil prices over their balance of payments problems.

Since 1973 Saudi Arabia's support for the economies of Egypt, Jordan, Syria, and the YAR, as well as for the PLO, has been crucial. Saudi Arabia is also the principal source of funds for Arab arms purchases although it is never prepared to finance the acquisition of Soviet weapons. Saudi Arabian aid, like that of any major power, serves both political and philanthropic purposes. Saudi Arabia is prepared to consider assistance for any institution or organization which seems to further the cause of Islam and Arabism, and opposes the spread of communism.

Social and Economic Policies

High expenditure on all social services has been a marked feature of Saudi Arabia in recent years. Education is free at all stages, and at the stage of higher studies, particularly in technical studies and for teachers' training, the student is paid to study. The Ministry of Education budget increased from 114.6 million rials in 1960 to 389 million rials in 1969, and over the same period the number of boys in primary and special education rose from 96,000 to 254,000 while the number in intermediate and secondary boys' schools rose from 4,280 to 39,501.

The pace of expansion accelerated in the mid-1970s and the Ministry of Education budget increased fivefold. The aim is to have 1.3 million Saudis in school in 1980 compared with 760,000 in 1974/75. By 1980 all Saudi boys will receive primary education from the age of six or seven. Some 95 per cent of the boys aged 12 will go on to intermediate schools, and 60 per cent of those in intermediate schools will go on to general teacher training or vocational schools at the secondary level.

Girls' education started only in 1960, but by 1974/75 there were 250,000 girls receiving primary education with a planned increase to 350,000 by 1980. The aim is to increase the number of Saudis at teacher training colleges from 9,000 to 20,000 by 1980 and to expand the numbers at vocational schools to train young people for roles in industry and agriculture. In the same period the numbers of women receiving higher education will increase from 15,600 to 53,300 through a big expansion at Riyadh University, King Abdul Aziz University at Jedda, the University of Petroleum and Minerals at Dhahran, and girls' colleges at Riyadh and Jedda, as well as the Islamic universities of Medina and Mecca.

There has been a comparable expansion in medical services. The King Faisal Medical City in Riyadh is a specialist hospital with the most modern equipment. In 1975 the Kingdom had 62 hospitals, 215 clinics, and 373 health centres, and during the Second Development Plan the number of hospital beds is being increased from 4,000 to 11,400, the number of clinics from 215 to 452, and of doctors from 1,900 to 4,200. At present the health service depends heavily on expatriate doctors and nurses but they are gradually being replaced by qualified nationals. A College of Medicine is being formed at Riyadh University.

The social philosophy of the present leaders is strong and coherent. Their aim is to create a powerful and technically modern financial and economic power without sacrificing Islamic social and religious values. This has the immense advantage that Saudi citizens do not feel that their cultural heritage is being destroyed in the course of hasty westernization for purposes of national ambition. Young Saudis rarely suffer from a sense of loss of identity and wounded pride, such as has created a strong counter-reaction in some comparable societies. It helps to explain why so many young Saudis who receive their higher education abroad seem able to adapt themselves again to Saudi social mores on their return.

Yet undeniably the unique experiment in reconciling an ultra-conservative social philosophy with an advanced twentieth-century capitalist system creates severe strains and anomalies. One obvious example is that of girls' education. This was accepted in principle in 1960, against some strong traditionalist opposition, and has since been rapidly expanded. Yet Saudi women are still kept in social seclusion. They may not drive a car or hire a taxi, or travel abroad except in the company of a male relative. They may not work except as teachers or in the medical services (and then for women only). This is in spite of the fact that the lack of trained manpower remains one of the main obstacles to rapid development, and the reason for the great emphasis on the expansion of education.

This lack of manpower has profound social effects. Because the growth rate of the Saudi economy has so far depended heavily on the money available to hire expertise and labour from abroad, the average Saudi has little inclination for sustained work (especially as a technician or manual labourer). The high drop-out rate of the educational system is due to the fact that any Saudi can obtain undemanding and adequately paid work as soon as he has reached the intermediate level. There is no immediate prospect of Saudi Arabians becoming a minority in their own country as has happened in Kuwait and some of the other smaller oil-producing states, but there is a large and growing minority of non-Saudis (perhaps one third of the population) who are sustaining the economy but inevitably in some aspects are second-class members of the community.

It is this social phenomenon which casts the greatest doubts over Saudi Arabia's future. The economic problems created by the enormous and sudden increase of wealth in a very underdeveloped economy – bottlenecks, inflation (especially in land values), and increasing disparity of wealth between the labourer or salaried worker and the self-employed businessman or merchant – can be and are being dealt with by economic measures. Towards the end of 1976 a clear government decision was taken to cut government spending (which has risen from $5.3 billion in 1973/74 to $10 billion in 1974/76). Some of the more grandiose industrial projects were postponed or cancelled and as a result the merchant community was obliged to trim its formerly high profit margins. The housing shortage was eased with the help of the new Real Estate Fund. Altogether the rate of inflation, although still between 20 and 30 per cent, was reduced in 1977/78.

2. Yemen Arab Republic

THE LAND AND THE PEOPLE

Yemen (now the Yemen Arab Republic – YAR) lies at the extreme south-western corner of Arabia. It has an estimated size of 74,000 square miles, comprising two well-defined climatic and topographical zones – the highlands inland, and the Tihama (the coastal strip along the Red Sea). Its frontiers march with Saudi Arabia on the north (Asir) and east (Najran). The western boundary is the Red Sea from a point opposite the Farasan Islands to Shaikh Said Peninsula, opposite Perim Island. On the south, Yemen is bounded by the People's Democratic Republic of Yemen but the frontier remains uncertain. The climate of the highlands is considered the best in all Arabia. Summer conditions are temperate and winter temperatures cool, with some frost. The rainfall is usually heavy, varying from 32 inches in the extreme south-west (monsoon region) to 16 inches at Sanaa, but periods of lighter rain and even droughts are not infrequent. On the coast the climate is hot and damp, and there is little rainfall. The people of the highlands, who are Shiis of the Zaidi sect,[1] constitute about 40 per cent of the total; the remaining 60 per cent are nearly all Sunnis of the Shafii sect.[2] They live in Tihama and along the Aden frontier. The population was 5.24 million at the February 1974 census (4.52 million plus under-enumerated and uncovered areas) which, together with 1.23 million working abroad, gives an estimated total of about 6.5 million. About 120,000 live in Sanaa, the capital, about 90,000 in Hodeida, the Red Sea port, and about 80,000 in Taez.

History

No country in the world – except Tibet until 1951 – has succeeded in keeping itself so isolated as Yemen. Until quite recently few strangers had ever penetrated its fastnesses.

In classical times Yemen, with the Hadhramaut, formed the south-eastern area of Arabia Felix, which also included southern Hejaz and the remainder of the peninsula south of Arabia Deserta. The best-known of the southern Arabian kingdoms was Saba (or Sheba or Sabu). It had a recorded

[1] See above, p. 47 [2] See above, p. 46

history from 950 to 115 BC, but no authentic evidence has yet been found of a 'Queen of Sheba'. The Sabaeans earned great profits from the incense trade; but their prosperity slowly dwindled in competition with the Indian trade routes through Iraq and Syria, and with the Roman exploitation of commercial navigation from the Gulf and the East through the Red Sea to Egypt and Europe.

The Sabaean religion of those days was pagan, and monuments of pagan cults are still to be found near Sanaa. In the fourth century Christian missionaries settled in the country. There was also a blend of Judaism owing, it is believed, to Jewish immigration after the fall of Jerusalem in AD 70. From the sixth to the second century BC Arabia Felix was ruled by the Himyarite dynasty, from whom the modern Imams claim descent. Some of these rulers embraced Judaism, others were Christian. In AD 525 the Christian Ethiopians of Axum invaded and overthrew the Himyarite kingdom. Ethiopian rule in its turn was overthrown in AD 575 by an Iranian invasion; but within another hundred years the country had made a nominal submission to Islam, and although Christianity and Judaism and even paganism still survived, the Sunnis of the Shafii rite had established their powers in the Tihama, while the Zaidis, a moderate branch of the Shia, held the highlands.

In the ninth century the Zaidi Imam Yahya al-Hadi ila'l Haqq founded the Rassid dynasty of the Yemen. It survived, with some interruptions of power, until 1962. Its name comes from al-Qasim al-Rassi, who was a direct descendant of Mohammed through Hassan, a son of Fatima and Ali.

In 1517 Yemen was conquered by the Ottoman Sultan Selim I, but for the next two centuries Ottoman authority there and throughout the coastal regions of Arabia was in turn wooed and contested by various European nations seeking, after the discovery of the Cape route to India, for openings for their commercial fleets. The Turks maintained themselves on the coast, however precariously; and the European penetration was sporadic and never established with any permanence inland.

At the opening of the nineteenth century the Yemen was entered, but not subdued or converted, by the Wahhabis. After the Egyptian victory of 1818 Ibrahim Pasha descended on the Tihama, which had been overrun by Wahhabi forces. The Wahhabis were expelled, and the Zaidi Imam restored to nominal authority in return for a subsidy to the Sultan in Constantinople, who placed Egyptian garrisons in Hodeida and Moka, the main ports. The Egyptians withdrew in 1840, but Turkish suzerainty remained. Turkish policy alternated between appeasement and ruthless suppression, until in 1911 a full-scale revolt, headed by the Imam Yahya (1904–48), compelled the Turks to intervene in strength. Sanaa fell, and the campaign ended with a treaty which confirmed Turkish suzerainty and divided administrative control between the Imam in the highlands and the Turks in the Tihama. Meanwhile to the north, during the Italo-Turkish war, the Asiri tribes, under the leadership of Sayyid Mohammed ibn Ali al-Idrisi, had risen against the Turks, and with Italian help succeeded in estabishing a degree of independence, which they consolidated during the First World War by overrunning much of the northern Tihama. When war began in 1914 the Turkish army of occupation, numbering some 14,000 men, marched southwards against the British in Aden, while British war vessels bombarded Yemeni ports in the interests of the Idrisi invaders from Asir. These operations were continued intermittently during the next four years; but with the Mudros Amistice in October 1918 the Yemen became free of Turkish suzerainty. The Imam lost no time in asserting his authority over the Shafii-occupied areas of the south and west which the Turks had kept under their administrative control.

The Imam Yahya became ruler of an independent and unified Yemen. As both Imam and King he was the temporal and spiritual head of his people. He was chosen as Imam, or head of the Zaidis, from among the Sayyids or descendants of Ali, of whom there are some thousands in Yemen, all enjoying special privileges.

Yahya was faced with the formidable task of creating a governmental structure for the country. Although he persuaded some of the former Ottoman officials to remain to assist him, his methods were highly autocratic. He established a system of extreme personal rule in which every item of government business depended on his decisions. His son the Imam Ahmad (1948–62) maintained the system during his reign.

Yahya and Ahmad both accepted the continuing strength of tribal loyalties in Yemen. They made little attempt to supersede tribalism with a regular army loyal to the throne but endeavoured to manipulate tribal alliances to ensure that the balance of tribal power was on their side. As Yahya extended his control over all his territory he resorted increasingly to an ancient Yemeni tradition: the taking of hostages. One or more of the relations of the heads of important tribes would be held in a prison school maintained by the Imam. Both Imams were fairly successful in this policy. Yahya and Ahmad also tried as far as possible to keep Yemen isolated and insulated from foreign influences which would undermine their own autocratic power as well as the Yemenis' traditional religious way of life. Again they were fairly successful but at the cost of keeping Yemen in a state of medieval backwardness which provoked increasing criticism from those Yemenis who were aware how the outside world was changing and who demanded reforms.

In accordance with his isolationist policy, Imam Yahya kept his relations with foreign powers to an absolute minimum. However, he was concerned to establish his claim to all the territories that had once been ruled by his ancestors and which could be said to form a 'Greater Yemen', i.e. in addition to the internationally recognized Yemeni Kingdom, Asir on the Red Sea (now part of Saudi Arabia) and the territories which now form the People's Democratic Republic of Yemen. His claim to Asir brought him into conflict first with Britain and then with Saudi Arabia. In 1919 British troops occupied Hodeida in support of the Idrisi ruler of Asir who had fought against the Turks in the First World War. The British troops withdrew and in 1920 Ibn Saud (then Sultan of Nejd) sent his son Faisal to annex the highland areas of northern Asir. On the death of Mohammed al-Idrisi in 1925 a small-scale civil war broke out between two rival Idrisi claimants, with the Saudis and the Imam supporting opposing sides. Yahya seized the opportunity to occupy the Tihama coastal plain including Hodeida but Wahhabi military superiority forced him to accept what amounted to Ibn Saud's protectorate over the rest of Asir. In 1932 the Idrisi ruler rebelled against Ibn Saud and was defeated. Yahya supported his claims and in 1934 war broke out between Saudi Arabia and Yemen. The Yemeni forces were quickly routed and a treaty of peace was signed in Taif on 20 May 1934. The Saudis annexed the disputed Asir and Najran areas but otherwise imposed only minor frontier adjustments. Ibn Saud's moderation, which was due to foreign pressure, made Yahya his friend for life.

Immediately after the First World War Imam Yahya sent his troops to occupy several frontier areas which Britain regarded as part of the Western Aden Protectorate. Attempts at negotiation failed until 1934 when a forty-year Anglo-Yemeni treaty of peace and friendship was signed in Sanaa which accepted for the time being as Yemen's southern boundary a line slightly more favourable to the Yemen than the one agreed between Britain and Turkey in 1914.

To strengthen his hand with Britain, Yahya had turned to Italy which had begun to take an interest in Yemen as early as 1877. An Italo-Yemeni treaty of amity and commerce was signed on 4 September and this was followed by a secret agreement signed on 1 June 1927.

Yemen remained neutral in the Second World War but after the defeat of Rommel yielded to British requests to intern Axis nationals in its territory. It participated rather hesitantly in the talks leading to the creation of the Arab League but soon ratified its covenant.

In February 1948 the Imam Yahya, over eighty and partly paralysed, was assassinated and Abdullah al-Wazir, his personal adviser, was proclaimed Imam. Abdullah al-Wazir promised to rule as a constitutional monarch but his rule lasted barely a month. Crown Prince Ahmad, who secured some tribal support, defeated him, and had him and other leaders of the revolt executed.

The Imam Ahmad, a formidable character, tinged with sadism, made no fundamental changes in his father's system of government. He was slightly more willing than Yahya to call upon the assistance of foreigners but the circumstances of his accession made him deeply suspicious of his own people.

The social and economic backwardness of Yemen was even more striking at the end of his reign than at the beginning.

As soon as Imam Ahmad had consolidated his position at home he took up his father's claim to the Aden Protectorate and there was a series of border incidents. This anti-British campaign led Imam Ahmad to seek outside support despite his ingrained xenophobia. Yemen had Arab League support for its claim to the island of Kamaran and to the whole of the Aden Protectorate as part of the ancestral territories of Yemen. In the late 1950s Abdul Nasser had become the most important figure in Arab politics and his star was rising. When Egypt and Syria joined to form the United Arab Republic in February 1958 Imam Ahmad cabled President Nasser asking for Yemen to be allowed to join the new federation. Egypt, Syria, and Yemen then formed a somewhat tenuous and ill-defined union known as the United Arab States.

Imam Ahmad turned also to the Soviet bloc for support, and in 1955 he signed a friendship pact with the Soviet Union. In 1956 Yemen recognized Communist China, which offered technical and economic aid and later undertook the building of a metalled road from Hodeida to Sanaa.

Imam Ahmad was aware of the danger to his conservative regime of the import of revolutionary socialist ideas. He attempted to balance Soviet influence by developing relations with the USA and in 1959 he allowed a US aid (ICA) mission to be established in the country. He also kept to a minimum the number of Egyptian officials and technicians who were loaned to Yemen under the United Arab States agreement.

As under Imam Yahya, opposition to Imam Ahmad was of two kinds: (*a*) progressive reformers who wanted to bring Yemen into the twentieth century; and (*b*) conservative traditionalists who resented the virtual monopoly of government by the Hamideddin family.

In the late 1950s a number of Yemeni exiles in Aden and Cairo formed opposition groups of Free Yemenis.

While Yemen was theoretically federated to the UAR, the Imam's regime was protected from the powerful attacks of Cairo's propaganda machine. But in September 1961 Syria seceded from the UAR and Imam Ahmad, who was delighted to see Arab revolutionary socialism in decline, condemned Nasserist ideology and policies in a poem which was broadcast on Sanaa Radio. In December 1961 President Nasser declared the United Arab States dissolved and Radio Cairo at once opened a strong campaign against the Imam and his regime.

Throughout the first half of 1962 violent opposition increased but Imam Ahmad succeeded in containing it until his death on 18 September. Mohammed al-Badr succeeded him and announced a general amnesty for political prisoners and other conciliatory measures. But the UAR Government and the Free Yemenis in Cairo remained sceptical in their attitude towards him while Yemeni conservatives, alarmed by al-Badr's liberal tendencies, exerted their influence to make him adopt more traditional attitudes.

Civil War

On 26 September 1962, eight days after Imam Ahmad's death, Brigadier Abdullah Al-Sallal, who had al-Badr's confidence and had been made Commander of the Royal Guards on his succession, seized Sanaa and declared a Republic. The coup was only partially successful because although the revolutionaries controlled the main towns and roads al-Badr escaped to loyal tribes in the north and raised the flag of royalist counter-revolution.

Sallal at once formed a Revolutionary Command Council and announced the establishment of the Yemeni Arab Republic which was promptly recognized by Egypt, Syria, Iraq, and the Soviet bloc. But al-Badr's uncle, Prince Hassan, returned from New York where he was Yemeni UN representative, and a concerted movement began, to restore the monarchy with the aid of royalist tribes, Saudi Arabia, and Jordan. Sallal appealed to President Nasser for assistance, which promptly arrived in the form of a large expeditionary force.

This marked the beginning of royalist-republican civil war which lasted with varying intensity for over seven years and affected principally the northern and eastern parts of the country. Whenever the royalists made military gains the Egyptians increased their commitment, until by 1964 they had an estimated 40,000 troops in Yemen. This was enough to ensure that the principal towns and roads would remain in republican hands but it increased the natural xenophobia of the Zaidi tribes, some of whom rallied to the royalist cause after initially supporting the republic. In December 1962 the US Government (followed by fifty nations but not the UK) recognized the Yemeni Republic which was then seated at the UN. But US hopes that the Republic would be secure enough for Egypt to withdraw its troops were not fulfilled. US and UN attempts at mediation between Egypt and Saudi Arabia were unsuccessful and both countries maintained support for opposing sides in the civil war.

The Egyptians had superior equipment and command of the air but they were hampered by a lack of experience in guerrilla warfare in which the Yemeni tribesmen excelled. The lack of roads in most of the country made it difficult to supply their forward outposts. The royalists, on the other hand, were assisted by foreign mercenary officers (mostly British and French) and the Egyptians were unable to prevent the infiltration of supplies of money and arms from Saudi Arabia and Beihan State in the Aden Protectorate. Finally, the Egyptians encountered extreme difficulty in building up the regular Yemeni republican forces from among the unmartial urban Yemenis; generous subsidies to the fighting tribesmen were not enough to ensure their continued loyalty to the republic, and the Egyptians could always be outbid by the superior financial resources of Saudi Arabia.

Political stability consistently eluded the republic. The difficulty was in forming a government which could reconcile Yemeni national pride with the reality of the republic's heavy dependence on Egypt.

A cease-fire called in November 1964 after a conference of royalist and republican representatives in the presence of Egyptian and Saudi Arabian observers at Erkawhit in east Sudan failed to hold. A government formed in April 1965 by Ahmad Naaman, a moderate Shafii political leader, decided to make peace overtures to the royalists. But Naaman was not supported by President Sallal or the Egyptians and in June he was forced to resign by Sallal who took over the premiership with a group of hard-line army officers. The highly unfavourable political situation in the republic, combined with a new series of royalist military successes in the spring and summer of 1965, were factors which induced President Nasser to go to Saudi Arabia to conclude what became known as the Saudi-Egyptian Jedda agreement on Yemen. This provided for an immediate cease-fire, the formation of a royalist-republican provisional government to be followed one year later by a national plebiscite by which time all Egyptian troops would be withdrawn.

As part of the agreement a royalist-republican conference was held at Harad in north Yemen in November to decide on the form of the transitional government. This broke down over royalist refusal of republican claims that the Imamate had already been permanently abolished and replaced by the republic. Meanwhile the cold war within the Arab world intensified. While the Harad Conference was still in progress King Faisal launched his idea on a visit to Iran of a grouping of Islamic nations. Egypt regarded this as a plan to form an anti-Nasser front and reacted accordingly. President Nasser's conviction that Britain was supporting the Yemeni royalists was strengthened by a British agreement to supply Saudi Arabia with large quantities of arms including an air-defence system. However, the British Government's announcement in February 1966 that it intended to withdraw all its forces from South Arabia by the time it achieved independence was a powerful boost for Egypt. Faced with renewed royalist harassment after the inevitable breakdown of the cease-fire President Nasser and his military advisers decided in the spring of 1966 to withdraw all Egyptian forces from the north and east of the country to the 'triangle' based on Hodeida, Taez, and Sanaa. While this left about half the country in royalist hands it ensured the defence of the main centres of population and greatly reduced the cost of maintaining the Egyptian force in Yemen.

President Sallal, with the aid of a handful of fairly ruthless lieutenants, succeeded in improving the security situation in the republic but there was still no prospect of the Egyptian troops' being able to withdraw.

The situation was transformed by the 1967 Arab-Israeli war. Yemen took no part in the war but one of its consequences was that President Nasser decided to withdraw all his troops from Yemen. At the Khartoum Arab summit conference (29 August–1 September) he reached an agreement with King Faisal, through Sudanese mediation, to withdraw in return for a Saudi undertaking to halt all aid to the royalists. Egyptian troops had all left by the end of the year (at about the time when British troops had all withdrawn from South Arabia).

On 5 November 1967 Sallal was overthrown while he was on a visit to Iraq, in a bloodless high-command coup that brought to power a group of moderate republicans with Qadi Iriani as Chief of State and Mohsin al-Aini as Premier. Hopes that this would make it possible to end the civil war were dashed when the royalists launched an all-out assault on Sanaa which nearly succeeded. But the republicans rallied their forces and with emergency assistance from Syria, Algeria, and the USSR succeeded in lifting the siege, although the main Sanaa-Taez road remained cut by the royalists. In May a serious rift appeared in the royalist ranks with opposition to the ex-Imam led by his cousin Prince Mohammed ibn Hussein. The republicans were also divided between conservatives and young radicals as well as between Zaidis and Shafiis. In August 1968 there was serious fighting with heavy casualties between republican forces but General Amri as Commander-in-Chief succeeded in ending the strife and on 15 September formed a new government with seven Shafiis and nine Zaidis.

During 1969 the position improved for the republicans as King Faisal cut off his aid to the royalists although he still refused recognition of the Yemeni Republic.

On 5 February 1970 a new republican government was formed by Mohsin al-Aini and on 21 March he went to Jedda at the head of a Yemeni delegation to the Saudi-sponsored Islamic foreign ministers' conference. On 23 May a party of prominent royalists headed by Ahmad al-Shami, a former royalist foreign minister, arrived in Sanaa. He was appointed an additional member of the three-man Republican Council. In July al-Aini returned to Saudi Arabia which then recognized the Sanaa regime and was followed by France, Britain, and Iran. The civil war had ended with a compromise although it was the moderate republicans who held the majority of posts in the Government.

The Republic

In December 1970 the country's first permanent constitution provided for the establishment of a Consultative Council of 159 members – some appointed by the President, the rest elected by general franchise – which would be the country's supreme legislative authority. Elections, in which political parties were banned, were held in March 1971. The YAR is divided into six provinces (*liwas*) which are in turn divided into districts and sub-districts. The *liwas*, which are named after the chief towns, are: Sanaa, Ibb, Taez, Hodeida, Hajja and Saada.

There are three main political groups in the country: the tribal chiefs (Mashayikh) supported by their tribes, the conservative Ulema, and the younger generation of the towns who include a variety of Baathists, Nasserists, communists, etc. Of these the first grouping has the support of Saudi Arabia and deplores any move towards union with southern Yemen while it remains under the extreme PDRY regime. The youth, on the other hand, deplores excessive Saudi influence and looks more to union with the south. Tension between these two trends has made the establishment of a strong central government extremely difficult. The failure of the Presidency Council led by the moderate Abdul Rahman Iriani to cope with the country's political and economic difficulties led to a military coup in June 1974 headed by Colonel Ibrahim al-Hamdi who suspended the Consultative Council and introduced a new provisional constitution in which he headed a military Command Council. Colonel Hamdi had considerable success in unifying the country under a more centralized administration, despite the opposition of powerful leaders who were jealous of their traditional authority, until he and his brother were assassinated in October 1977 shortly before he was due to visit the PDRY. The succession was ensured by the establishment of a three-man presidential council headed by the previous Vice-President Colonel Ahmad Ghashmi and the civilian premier. Colonel Ghashmi proceeded to change the constitutional system, abolishing both the Command Council and the Consultative Council which he replaced with a Constituent People's Assembly. In February 1978 the 99-member Assembly elected Colonel Ghashmi

President for a five-year term with the power to appoint two Vice-Presidents. When President Ghashmi was in turn assassinated in June 1978 when a bomb carried by a special envoy from the PDRY President exploded, the system he had created survived to provide a smooth transition of power. The Constituent Assembly elected as President Major Ali Saleh, a former close associate of President Ghashmi and a member of the powerful Hashed confederation of tribes.

Whatever their attitude towards the PDRY regime, all YAR politicians are united in the view that the two halves of Yemen form a single country. The YAR has tens of thousands of exiles from the south, including some members of the YAR government. Political relations between the two regimes have always been difficult since independence.

In 1972, after a series of border skirmishes, an agreement was signed in Tripoli to form a single state.

Eight committees, formed to work out details of unification, were to have completed their work by June 1973 but there have been constant delays. After the assassination of President Ghashmi, relations again deteriorated, leading to a brief but fierce border war in March 1979. This was ended through Syrian-Iraqi-Jordanian mediation and followed by a new agreement on a plan to unite the two countries, although the prospects for its implementation remained remote.

Relations with the YAR's powerful and wealthy northern neighbour are of comparable importance. Saudi aid and political influence have increased substantially since Colonel Hamdi took power in 1974 and the remittances from the hundreds of thousands of Yemeni workers in Saudi Arabia are a major factor in the economy. Yet no YAR leader can afford to allow himself to appear as a satellite of the Saudi regime.

ECONOMIC AND SOCIAL SURVEY

Agriculture has always been the mainstay of the Yemeni economy and almost all products are consumed locally. The only exceptions are coffee and hides which form a very small proportion of the total. Although there is enough rainfall in the hills for dry farming – mainly millet and sorghum – most of the cultivated lands are irrigated. Yemen is known to have begun to lose its pastures from the time when the great Marib Dam broke down some time between AD 542 and 570. The great forests which existed in classical times have also largely disappeared. The traditional crops are: millet and sorghum (production of one million tons or more); wheat (75,000 tons); maize (80,000 tons); barley (180,000 tons or more); and oats (mainly along the coast.) Green vegetables are also grown – especially around Sanaa and Taez – and because of the climatic conditions a variety of fruits which range from dates, bananas, papayas, and mangoes on the tropical Tihama plain, to citrus, apples, pomegranates, grapes, apricots, and others above 200 m. The famous Yemeni 'moka' coffee is the principal export crop; Yemen is the only country in the world where coffee is grown on irrigated land. Coffee exports between 1952 and 1962 ranged from 4,000 to 5,500 tons but in some areas coffee cultivation has given way to the planting of *qat*, a shrub of which the leaves are chewed as a narcotic by most of the population. *Qat* has been a more profitable cash crop than coffee, and efforts to control its export to Aden and South Yemen have never been very successful. According to FAO estimates there were 3.1 million sheep and one million cattle in 1974; many camels, mules and donkeys are used for transport purposes.

Cotton has long been grown in Yemen in the Tihama but on a very small scale until 1951 when the industry began to expand. From a production of 800 tons from 80 hectares in 1952/53 it rose to 3,200 tons from 2,500 hectares in 1961/62, and about 5,000 tons in 1976.

Share-cropping is practised in the large properties which form a substantial proportion of the cultivated area. Techniques are primitive and productivity low although there is still abundant evidence of the existence of the fine agricultural system which has steadily declined over the centuries.

The civil war and its aftermath have changed the YAR from a net exporter of agricultural produce into an importer, mainly of cereals. The development of agriculture has therefore become one of the country's top priorities. It is estimated that about 15 per cent of the YAR's total area or 3 million hectares is cultivable and that only about half of this is cultivated at present. The wider use of fertilizers and pesticides has been encouraged. A $42.4 million five-year plan for water projects was launched in 1977. Two of the biggest schemes – irrigation and rural development – are in the Tihama coastal area. A large-scale livestock development scheme includes the establishment of a national Livestock Development Corporation.

Minerals

The only known minerals are rock salt, copper, and a little coal. Attempts to find oil have so far been unsuccessful although Deutsche Shell has a concession north of Hodeida. In 1973 a national oil company – Yemen Petroleum – was set up to distribute and market petroleum products, and a state Minerals Resources Corporation to formulate petroleum and minerals policy.

Industry

A few light industries have been built since 1962 with the help of Yemeni emigrant, Arab, and foreign capital, but they remain on a small scale. They include the production of textiles, building materials, household goods, foodstuffs, beverages, cigarettes and pharmaceuticals. The largest factory in the country is a Chinese-built textile mill in Sanaa. The Soviet Union has built a cement factory, an aluminium smelter at Taez, and a fish-canning factory at Hodeida. Industrial estates are being set up at Sanaa, Hodeida, and Taez, and future plans include several more food-processing industries.

Transport and Communications

Lack of roads has probably been the greatest single obstacle to Yemen's economic development. In 1962 the only metalled road in the country (apart from a few miles in Taez) was the Chinese-built Hodeida-Sanaa road.

Since then a road between Taez and Sanaa has been built by the USA and surfaced with West German aid, the Russians have built a road from Taez to Hodeida, and the Chinese have completed a highway from Sanaa to Saada in the north. IDA and Kuwait have helped finance the building of a road between

Taez and Turba, and the Chinese a road between Amran and Hajjah. Other major new roads include one from Sanaa to Marib in the east (UAE financed), one from Damman to Raddafal-Baida (Saudi financed), and an important new surfaced road from Taez to Aden.

The main port at Hodeida has been improved and expanded by the USSR, while Moka harbour has been improved. However, the import boom has created severe bottlenecks and the YAR makes some use of Aden. Hodeida is to be further expanded and the ancient salt port of Salif to be revived to take over a major role.

Sanaa and Taez have international airports and both are to be expanded with Saudi and Iraqi aid. International communications have been improved by the opening of an earth satellite station near Sanaa in 1976.

Currency and Banking

The Yemeni rial (now divided into 100 fils) was introduced in 1964. A Central Bank was established in 1970, replacing the Yemeni Currency Board which had performed its functions. The Yemen Bank for Reconstruction and Development, founded in 1962, is a shareholder in most jointly owned projects and provides facilities financing trade and development. Since the introduction of a new banking law in 1970 several foreign banks have established themselves in the country.

Education and Health

In 1962 the educational system in Yemen was rudimentary and affected only a small proportion of the population. There were no schools for girls of whom only a few of the privileged learned to read the Koran at home. Accurate statistics are not available but according to secret Education Ministry documents at the end of 1958[3] there were 38,653 boys in 688 primary schools, 468 in 4 intermediate schools, 228 boys in the single secondary school, and 1,766 in the 16 advanced secondary schools. There were about 500 boys studying abroad.

[3]See Mohammed Said el-Attar, *Le Sous-développement économique et social du Yemen* (Algiers, 1964), pp. 90–92.

The republican regime had a strong desire to expand education as rapidly as possible but it was handicapped by the prolonged unrest in many parts of the country. The total number of pupils in primary schools rose from 61,325 (including 1,780 girls) in 1963 to 72,107 (including 6,003 girls) in 1970. In Taez, which was relatively undisturbed by the civil war, the number rose from 7,000 to 29,000 during this period. The number of pupils in intermediate and secondary schools rose from 730 in 1963 to 4,057 in 1970.

By 1973 there were 1,525 schools, including eight secondary and 16 specialized or training colleges, with 166,000 pupils and 4,700 teachers. The new university founded in 1970 is linked to Ain Shams University, Egypt.

Despite the healthy climate of the high plateaux on which three-quarters of the population live, the almost complete lack of medical facilities, malnutrition, and addiction to *qat* have kept drastically low health standards in Yemen. In 1962 there were three hospitals in the country with a total of about 1,500 beds and twenty doctors. The most common diseases were tuberculosis in the mountain areas and malaria and amoebic dysentery in the Red Sea plain.

By 1973 there were 31 hospitals with 3,878 beds and about 200 doctors. Many more educational and health services are being created with help from Arab, Western, and Communist countries.

Development and the Future

Economic and social development has started from very low levels but with the help of foreign (especially Saudi) aid and remittances from Yemenis working abroad the country has been experiencing an economic upsurge. In 1979 it was regarded by many foreign exporting firms as the fastest-growing market in Arabia.

The economic system lays emphasis on private enterprise. An investment law, covering national and foreign capital, was introduced in November 1970 and revised in 1975. This guarantees freedom of investment, repatriation of capital and profits, and certain exemptions from Customs duties and tax to investors whom it is desired to encourage. There has been rising domestic demand. Almost half the total imports are of severe inflation but the value of exports actually decreased even in money terms between 1974 and 1976, partly owing to a poor performance by coffee growers but partly because of foodstuffs. The mass emigration of young men between the ages of 15 and 45 has denuded large areas of the YAR of its working population. This has created an acute shortage of both skilled and unskilled labour in the towns and pushed up wages to levels that are sometimes as high as in Saudi Arabia or the other oil states. The large visible trade deficit is met by budgetary aid (since 1975 Saudi Arabia has covered budget deficits over $100 million), foreign loans, and transfers from Yemenis working abroad (estimated at $677 million in 1976). This enormous inflow of funds adds to inflation. Some of it is invested in housing or light industry but most is spent on consumer goods and makes no contribution to production.

In Yemen's first development plan, for 1973/74 to 1975/76, about 75 per cent of expenditure was to come from foreign sources. In the new five-year plan for 1977–81 some 85 per cent of estimated $3,630 million expenditure must come from outside, chiefly in the form of loans from Arab countries.

3. The People's Democratic Republic of Yemen

THE LAND AND THE PEOPLE

The People's Democratic Republic of Yemen (or the People's Republic of Southern Yemen as it was then called) came into existence on 30 November 1967, incorporating the Aden Colony and both the western and eastern administrative regions of the Aden Protectorate. It forms a triangle of territory based on the western half of the Arabian Peninsula's southern coast, reaching from Bab al-Mandeb, at the entrance to the Red Sea, to the frontier of the State of Oman. It is bounded on the north by Saudi Arabia and the west by Yemen, and occupies about 112,000 square miles.

The republic also possesses those islands which were protected or governed by the British from Aden. They are: Kamaran Island, one of a group which lies off the Salif peninsula of Yemen about 200 miles north of Bab al-Mandeb;

Perim, which is in the Bab al-Mandeb; and Socotra, the largest island in an archipelago lying about 220 miles off Qishn near the eastern end of the republic's Arabian coast. The Kuria Muria islands off the coast of the State of Oman are claimed by the republican Government but were transferred to Oman by the British in the 1967 settlement on the grounds that they were only nominally the responsibility of the Governor of Aden, were in practice administered by the British Resident, Persian Gulf, and formerly belonged to the Sultanate.

The area of the former Colony of Aden is the most notable urban complex. The high, rocky and volcanic structure of the peninsula falls sharply into the sea around the harbour, and the original town, Crater, lies in an extinct volcano of the eastern promontory where the enclosing ridge opens to the Arabian Sea. The modern harbour and town, Steamer Point, are about five miles away and between them and Crater the original village of Ma'alla has been developed as an industrial and residental area. The eastern promontory is joined to the mainland by the isthmus of Khormaksar on which stands the airport and the former British military town. The town of Shaikh Othman on the mainland has some cultivation and from it a road sweeps south-west round the bay to the western promontory and the oil refinery and township of Little Aden.

The western region of the republic is divided into the littoral belt varying between 4 and 40 miles in depth; the maritime range, between 1,000 and 2,000 feet above sea-level; the intra-montane plains, over 3,000 feet high; and the highland plateau, ranging from 5,000 to 8,000 feet, which falls away steeply into the Rub al-Khali desert plateau at about 2,500 feet. The eastern region (formerly the Wahidi Sultanates of Balhaf and Bir Ali, the Qaiti State of Shihr and Mukalla, the Kathiri State of Saiyun, and the Mahra Sultanate of Qishn and Socotra) is notable for the fertile Hadhramaut valley. Its wide upper and middle reaches run almost parallel with the coast about 125 miles inland, but at its lower eastern end it turns sharply to the south and becomes a narrow gorge through the hills as it descends to the sea. For the rest, the territory is desert and barren mountains intersected by wadis, some of which are fertile enough for cultivation. There are some comparatively large towns, notably Mukalla and Saiyun.

Climate

The maritime plains are damp and hot in summer and are subject to sandstorms and high winds. From October to March they are cool – sometimes cold – at night and are much less humid. There is little rain in the littoral and maritime hills and cultivation depends mainly on irrigation from seasonal water-courses and channels. The Aden promontories share the climate of the plains modified sometimes by the closely sheltering hills and at others by the surrounding seas; the climate is not unhealthy but the humidity makes it oppressive at times, notably in May, June, and September.

Population

There are no accurate figures for the population of the republic but it is estimated there are about 1,700,000 inhabitants. Almost the entire population consists of Arabs who are the direct descendants of the pagan peoples who were part of the ancient Minaean, Sabaean, and Himyarite kingdoms which flourished in succession between about 1400 BC to AD 500. The most important town is Aden, the capital (population 250,000), which is divided into several townships – Crater, Khormaksar, Ma'alla, Steamer Point, Madinet al-Shaab (formerly al-Ittihad), Shaikh Othman, and Little Aden. Mukalla in the east has a population of 50,000.

Religion

The population is predominantly Moslem of the Orthodox Shafii sect, as are the lowland Arabs of the Yemen Arab Republic. The Yemenis in Aden Port, however, include some of the unorthodox Zaidi Moslems who came from the Yemen highlands.

HISTORY

Democratic Yemen was part of the tribal empire of the Minaean people whose origins are lost in antiquity but who are known to have had kings in the fourteenth century BC and to have ruled over an area roughly corresponding to the territories of the Yemen Republic and Democratic Yemen. The wealth of this kingdom derived from frankincense which was found nowhere else in the ancient world and was transported by camel caravan or by ship to the sacrificial fires of Egypt, Babylon, Iran, and Greece. The caravan trains formed in time the Incense Route, perhaps the most famous of its kind in history, which had its starting point at Husn al-Ghurab, a tiny island 200 miles east of Aden.

The Minaeans were succeeded by the Sabaeans and then the Himyarites, all of whom had their royal capitals in the region of Sanaa in Yemen. The decline of Himyarite power began in the first century AD, in the main because the Arab transport monopoly was broken by the development of sea routes through the Persian Gulf and Mesopotamia. At this time Judaism and Christianity penetrated the region and in 356 the first church was built in Aden. The Christian emperor of Abyssinia overthrew the last Himyarite ruler, Dhu Naawas, a Jew, in 525 AD. Fifty years later the kingdom was conquered by the Iranians and within another century South Arabia was conquered by the Islamic Caliphate.

During the later period of Himyarite rule the tribes of South Yemen became more and more independent of the central power and during Abyssinian, Iranian, and Caliphate periods they were to all intents and purposes independent, living in a state of anarchy modified only by tribal custom and a primitive form of religious law. The tidal conflicts of Islam touched it slightly but it almost disappeared from history for a thousand years. Aden had a flourishing trade and magnificent fortifications in Roman times but was in considerable decay when Europe, in the form of the Portuguese fleet, first attacked it in the sixteenth century: and when the British conquered it in 1839 it was no more than a fishing village with 500 inhabitants.

At this time Democratic Yemen was nominally part of the Ottoman Empire. The British annexation in 1839 inaugurated 130 years of British rule in Aden and increasing influence in tribal hinterland, interrupted only briefly by Turkish reoccupation during the First World War.

The Aden Settlement was attached to the Bombay Presidency which had despatched the expedition to conquer it and in 1932 it became a Chief Commissioner's province under the central Government of India. The leaders of the Adeni community, fearing that they might one day be annexed to an independent India, persuaded the British Government in 1937 to make the Settlement a Colony administered from London by the Colonial Office.

Treaties of Protection

In the latter half of the nineteenth century the Turks were actively trying to subdue the Yemen and laying claim to the whole of South Arabia. The tribes surrounding Aden were anxious to prevent their subjection either to the Turks or to the unorthodox Zaidi Imams of Yemen and nine of them therefore accepted British Protection, although without formal treaty, and became known as the Nine Cantons. In 1886 the British Government signed a formal treaty of protection with the Mahra Sultan of Qishn and Socotra and in the following year the Sultan of Lahej accepted protection in return for a monthly stipend. In 1954, when the last was signed, there were 31 treaties of this sort, by which Britain undertook to protect each Ruler and his heirs forever and the Ruler promised not to have dealings with other powers or to cede any of his territory to any country other than Britain.

Meanwhile the British took control of the main islands off South Arabia. The Kuria Muria islands were ceded by the Sultan of Muscat and Oman in 1854 and became part of the Aden Settlement, as did the island of Perim which was occupied in 1857. The island of Socotra came under British protection when the Mahra Sultan signed the treaty of 1876. The British ousted the Turks from Kamaran Island and the Lighthouse Islands in 1915 and made the Governor of Aden responsible for their security and administration.

The land frontiers of the Aden Protectorate were never satisfactorily defined. For years before the First World War the British Government sought to demarcate the frontier with Yemen by agreement with the Turks and in 1914 signed a convention with the Porte establishing what became known as the Violet Line. The Aden Government thereafter based itself on this line but when Yemen became independent after the war, the ruler, Imam Yahya (1903–48), rejected the convention and his forces overran substantial protectorate areas between

1920 and 1926. In 1928 the British began to use aircraft to fulfil their promise of protection, on which the Imam had brought discredit, and their success (and the Imam's defeat at the hands of the Saudi bedouin forces of King Abdul Aziz ibn Saud) forced the Imam to accept a new agreement in 1934 which established the Violet Line as the *de facto* frontier without, however, either side renouncing its claims. An uneasy truce was maintained on the basis of this agreement until 1943.

The aggressiveness of Yahya's policy compelled the British to pay more attention to the protectorate areas which they had hitherto been content to leave in their natural state of tribal anarchy. They formed and trained Tribal Guards in each tribal area, created a security force of Government Guards under British and Arab officers and then in 1934 recruited a tribal force called the Aden Protectorate Levies which was the army of the western protectorate region.

Advisory Treaties

Because British policy was concerned primarily to protect Aden which had acquired great importance as a bunkering port for trade and naval vessels, the Aden Government policy was concerned almost entirely with the protected area surrounding it, neglecting the larger eastern region. There the abiding enmity between Qaiti and Kathiri Sultans and tribal and family feuds had reduced the region to anarchy and even the great Hadhramaut valley was known only to a few intrepid travellers. During 1936 and 1937 Harold Ingrams conducted an ill-defined mission in the eastern protectorate on behalf of the Aden Governor and persuaded the tribes and rulers to sign a truce which became known as Ingram's Peace.

In 1938 the Qaiti Sultan signed a new treaty with the British Government under which he accepted a Resident Adviser, the first being Ingrams. This was the first of a series of advisory treaties by which Britain was able to establish its influence over the entire eastern area of protection. The Aden Government subsequently extended the system to the western region and by 1954 thirteen advisory treaties had been signed. Although they did not constitute direct rule they led Britain more and more to control the ruler, either by removing anyone who disobeyed advice or supporting an obedient ruler against the will of his family.

Federation

In 1948 Imam Yahya of Yemen was assassinated and the reign of his son Ahmad opened with extreme bitterness towards Britain because the plot against his father had been hatched by the Free Yemeni movement in Aden. Although the Aden Governor and Imam Ahmad negotiated an ineffectual *modus vivendi* for demarcating the frontier in 1950, the latter disputed the Sanaa Agreement of 1934 and claimed the right to rule both the Protectorate area and Aden.

This worried western protectorate rulers who assembled in Aden in 1955 to consider a plan of federation drafted by the British. They failed to agree but the Imam decided to forestall further federal plans by mounting an offensive in 1957 against the frontier state of Beihan. Six of the western protectorate rulers thereupon federated as the Arab Amirates of the south on 11 February 1959, and were joined later by most of the other western rulers.

The colony of Aden was given a Legislative Council without elected members in 1947, and in 1955 this was changed to permit a minority of elected members. There was increasing pressure from the trades unions and embryo political parties for more self-government and in 1959 elections were permitted to give elected Adenis a small majority on the Council. The formation of the Arab Amirates made it obvious that a federation could not exist without Aden and that Aden could not remain a colony and be denied further constitutional advance if it joined. Overcoming strong objections from the Adenis, who feared the feudal power of the tribal rulers, the Aden Government rail-roaded a Council vote in favour of the merger in September 1962 and the Federation of South Arabia came into existence in January 1963.

The Struggle for Independence

A *coup d'état* in Yemen which overthrew the Imam and established a republic, and the entry of Egyptian troops to support the republic, strengthened resistance to the merger in Aden, led by the People's Socialist Party (PSP), the political wing of the Aden TUC. Behind the scenes the National Liberation Front (NLF) supplied with arms from Yemen was preparing militant resistance. The campaign opened in October 1963 and in December an attempt was made at Aden airport to assassinate the Governor in which one of his senior staff was fatally wounded. A State of Emergency was declared and 57 members of the PSP arrested.

Aden was at this time an important British military base. It was intended that the new federal State would be granted independence in 1968, by which time the retention of the base would be negotiated and the States of the eastern protectorate region brought in, but as good order crumbled the British troops were needed more and more to maintain security in Aden and up-country. On 25 September 1965, the High Commissioner (the former Governor) suspended the Aden constitution and imposed direct rule in the colony because some Adeni ministers would not co-operate in the suppression of terrorism, which was daily increasing.

The federal rulers and the few moderates in Aden who supported the federation did so in the firm conviction that the British base would remain to guarantee security but in February 1966 a new British Defence White Paper stated that the base would be withdrawn by 31 December 1968 and there would be no defence treaty with the South Arabian Federation. This further encouraged the militants who now included the Front for the Liberation of South Yemen (FLOSY), which was led by the PSP and the NLF; the NLF and FLOSY competed in violence against the British and those who collaborated with them, and against each other. A new draft constitution prepared by two British specialists at the request of the federal Government, and the intervention of a UN mission at the request of the British Government, failed to halt disorder.

The British called from retirement a distinguished ambassador, Sir Humphrey Trevelyan, to be High Commissioner and on his arrival in May 1967, he stated that Britain would continue to base itself on the federal Government but invited *all* leaders to help him to broaden it. He announced that British troops would be withdrawn by 9 January 1968, when South Arabia would be given independence.

As the British troops withdrew from the tribal areas in June 1968, the NLF progressively took over; in August the federal Government collapsed; and in October the NLF took control of the eastern protectorate States, none of which had joined the federation. The federal army (formed of the former Protectorate Levies and still partly officered by British) remained largely intact and it asked the High Commissioner to negotiate with the NLF and FLOSY. They agreed on 1 November to form a joint delegation to negotiate with the British, and it was announced in London that British troops would withdraw by the end of the month. This forthright declaration precipitated the final struggle between FLOSY and the NLF in Aden which ended in victory for the NLF when the army supported it. It was therefore an NLF delegation which negotiated the take-over from Britain at a conference in Geneva, and the Republic of South Yemen came into existence at midnight on 30 November with Qahtan al-Shaabi, leader of the NLF, as President.

Independence

Apart from the President, who was forty-seven, the government consisted of young men in their thirties whose attitudes covered the political spectrum all the way from Chinese Communism to Nasser-type Arab socialism. The President declared the new Government's policy to be socialism at home, non-alignment abroad, Arab unity, the liberation of Palestine, support for national revolutionary movements, and 'the reunification of the Arab peoples of North and South Yemen'. This 'progressive' policy was in conflict with the penury of the State which required maximum financial support from all quarters, including rich but traditional Arab states, and there quickly developed a dispute between the left-wing ideologists and those pragmatists in the Government who put the economic problem first. This soon manifested itself in the eastern region where pro-Chinese Communist elements of the NLF began to act independently of the central Government. In June 1969 President Qahtan al-Shaabi was ousted from power in a move to the left. He was replaced by a five-man Presidential Council headed by Salem Rubayyi Ali. Mohammed Ali Haitham, whom President Qahtan had recently dismissed from the post of Minister of Interior, became Prime Minister in the new Government. Abd al-Fattah Ismail took the key post of Secretary-General of the National Front.

A constitution published in August 1970 declared the state to be Islamic with sovereignty to be invested in an elected Supreme Council of 101 members.

President Rubayyi Ali and Abd al-Fattah Ismail combined to take the country further to the left. In November 1969 thirty-six companies, mostly British, were nationalized. They included banks, shipping, trading, and insurance companies. Most of the import trade was brought under public control. In 1970 an Agrarian Reform Law was passed and in the following three years state control was extended to the salt industry, buses, advertising, printing, hotels, soft drinks, cinemas, and, finally, private buildings. In 1971 Haitham, widely regarded as a moderate, was replaced by Ali Nasser Mohammed.

Despite the apparent unity of the regime there was a division between the President and Ismail. While the latter was a committed Marxist-Leninist, determined to impose a full Marxist ideology on the state, President Rubayyi Ali was more of a pragmatist who was prepared to consider compromise with moderate elements in the Arab world. In October 1975 Ismail consolidated left-wing power by merging the other tolerated parties with the NLF into a single United National Front of Progressive Organizations. To counterbalance the army, which Ismail regarded as conservative, Ismail formed a Cuban-trained People's Militia.

When in 1976 and 1977 President Rubayyi Ali made several moves to improve relations with the conservative Arab oil states he was opposed by Ismail and his supporters who prevented them from proceeding very far. In May 1978 President Rubayyi Ali was faced with a complete Marxist take-over in the form of Ismail's new Vanguard party. As he tried to rally his own supporters, matters came to a head following the murder on June 24 of President Ghashmi of the YAR. Although the bomb which killed President Ghashmi was being carried by an envoy of President Rubayyi Ali it may have been planted in order to discredit him (or possibly have been the work of North Yemeni opponents of President Ghashmi). It provoked a violent struggle in Aden in which Ismail and his supporters were victorious. President Rubayyi Ali was tried and executed with two of his supporters for crimes against the state. The victors of the coup formed a new Vanguard party, the Yemen Socialist Party, with a strong pro-Moscow line. Under the revised constitution, the offices of Chairman of the YSP, Chairman of the Supreme People's Council, and head of state, are held by Ismail.

In the first decade of the PDRY's independence there has been severe internal repression and a strong concentration on security. In 1968 the People's State Security Court was established to deal with a wide range of offences punishable by death and in 1974 a Ministry of State Security was created. Also in 1974 a Homeland Preservation Law urged caution in dealing with foreigners and Yemeni leaders have constantly demanded vigilance against imperialist and reactionary forces. The PDRY's isolation in the Arab world, the hostility of three neighbouring regimes (Saudi Arabia, Oman, and the YAR), and the existence of several hundred political exiles, some of whom are working actively against the regime, have increased the sense of insecurity. Estimates of the number of political prisoners vary but they are substantial and many individuals have disappeared.

Foreign Relations

At independence the PDRY claimed from Britain the £60 million that had been promised to the Federation of South Arabia but with the expulsion of British officers, relations deteriorated and in the end only a minimal sum was paid. Since then the PDRY has only enjoyed good relations with the communist states and has received very little aid from any other source. It has, on the other hand, been successful in remaining on good terms with both the USSR and China. The only exceptions among the Arab states were Kuwait, the only Gulf state to recognize the PDRY at independence, and to a lesser extent Iraq and Libya. In 1978 the PDRY associated itself with the 'front of steadfastness' of Arab states opposed to President Sadat's peace initiative but this did not bring any financial support.

Saudi Arabia refused to recognize the independent republic and there was serious border fighting between the two countries in 1969. Even the establishment of diplomatic ties in 1976 brought no material improvement, because of the PDRY's support for the Marxist regime in Ethiopia, fighting against Somalis and Eritreans supported by most of the Arab states. The PDRY acted as a staging-post for Cuban troops helping Ethiopia. Relations with Oman were also bad because of the PDRY's support for the Dhofari rebels of the Popular Front for the Liberation of Oman, which was based in Aden. Even when the revolt collapsed in 1975 there was no real improvement.

Relations with the YAR vary between uneasiness and open hostility, but are always intense because of the feeling shared in the north that the two states form a single whole and the presence of so many PDRY exiles in the YAR. The serious border conflict in 1972 ended with the Tripoli agreement to form a single state called the Yemen Republic. This has not been achieved, although joint political committees have continued to meet and PDRY leaders, like those in the north, have regularly declared themselves in favour of union. The assassination of President Ghashmi of the YAR, followed by the overthrow and execution of President Rubayyi Ali, caused renewed tension. A meeting of the Arab League, called by the YAR and dominated by Saudi Arabia and Egypt, decided to freeze political and economic ties with the PDRY.

A further brief border war with the YAR in March 1979 was ended through Arab mediation and was followed by a new agreement to unite the two countries, although there was little prospect of this being implemented.

Administration

The republic is divided into six governorates which, broadly speaking, are arranged numerically from west to east. These are: 1st, Aden and the nearby villages of Dar Saad and Imran, and the islands of Perim, Kamaran, Socotra, and Kuria Muria; 2nd Lahej, Subbeyha, Haushabi, Alawi, Radfan, Shaib, Halmain, and Muflahi; 3rd, Upper and Lower Yafa, Fadhli, Audhali, Dathina, and Lower Awlaqi; 4th, Beihan, Upper Aulaqi, Wahidi, and the north-western Hadhramaut; 5th, Hadhramaut except the north-western area; 6th, Mahra, bordering Oman.

ECONOMIC AND SOCIAL SURVEY

Aden Port achieved relative prosperity as a colony, and in the final few years before independence was enriched by income of various sorts totalling about £11 million a year from the British military base, but even in this condition of artificially expanded wealth there was little it could do for the protectorate hinterland where only one per cent of the land is cultivable and yet 75 per cent of the population lives by agriculture.

The civil disorders of 1967 reduced the port trade but the closing of the Suez Canal as a result of the Arab-Israeli war of June that year was a disaster.

The total withdrawal of British forces in the last half of 1967 greatly accentuated the economic depression by putting 25,000 people out of work. The general reduction in the purchasing power of the people progressively hit the small indigenous consumers, thus increasing the unemployment.

The newly independent State had to face the fact that the economy was hardly viable. Outside Aden the harsh terrain provides few opportunities for development on a scale that would be worth while. The inadequacy of the road network was due to the fact that the area offers too little in the way of commodities to justify the vast cost of building roads through difficult and insecure terrain. The British could never visualize a State rich enough to maintain an adequate road network even if the money was available to build it. The new regime therefore concentrated on raising funds to build the vital road from Aden to Mukalla, linking the western and eastern parts of the country. A Chinese undertaking to provide £18 million to build the road was the main item in a bulk offer of £21 million aid.

Agriculture and Fisheries

Agriculture is the main occupation of most people outside Aden city but arable land is only 1.4 per cent of the total land area and of this barely 30 per cent is cultivated. Production is hampered by alternating droughts and disastrous floods. In the fertile areas (the mountain valleys of the former Western Protectorate and wadis of the Eastern), a highly developed water conservation system permits crops of sorghum, wheat (15,000 tons of which was exported in 1974), tobacco, barley, millet, sesame, and cotton (5,000 tons in 1974, most of which was exported); and the western area is self-supporting in fruit in most seasons. Dates are grown extensively in the Hadhramaut and Wadi Hajr.

With aid from Communist, Arab, and UN sources irrigation is being developed in certain areas such as Hadhramaut and Wadi Turan, and finance and technical aid is provided for the use of new farming methods. The Abyan scheme, covering 32,000 hectares, closely resembles the Sudan Gezira scheme and involves extensive irrigation and controlled production, mainly of cotton and sorghum. Lahej is also an important irrigation area. According to FAO estimates, there were 99,000 cattle and 230,000 sheep in the country in 1974.

Under agrarian reform laws of 1968 and 1970 land ownership was limited to 20 feddans of irrigated land and 40 feddans of grazing land. Land belonging to the former Federal rulers and to anyone leaving the country without permission was distributed to peasants for co-operative cultivation. In addition there are some 30 state farms.

Before independence very little was done to develop the abundant fisheries of the Gulf of Aden. The fishing fleet has been modernized, partly with Soviet assistance, and Arab funds have financed a multi-purpose fisheries project in the Mukalla area. Fish production rose to about 134,000 tons in 1974 and now accounts for about 36 per cent of exports. A Fisheries Board was established in 1970 and fishing now has priority in development.

Industry

Modern industry is on a small scale apart from the former BP refinery at Little Aden (160,000 b.p.d. capacity) which was sold to the Yemen National Oil Company in 1977. BP now operates the refinery under contract and modernization is being undertaken with Arab aid. Local marketing of oil products was nationalized in 1969 and a company for oil storage and export has been founded by the Yemen National Oil Company and the Kuwait National Petroleum Company.

Apart from the refinery, salt extraction, soap production, and mineral water are the three most important industries.

There are also small factories for aluminium utensils, cigarettes, clothing, perfume, vegetable oils, metal implements, matches, paint, shoes, building materials and textiles. Most factories operate well below capacity because of the narrowness of the local market.

Minerals

The Government has hopes of discovering mineral deposits in the hinterland with UAE aid, and a British firm is carrying out mineral surveys in the Mukalla area. The search for oil has centred chiefly on the Hadhramaut but has so far been fruitless. Soviet Technoexport, a Czech agency, and the Italian Agip retain concessions in the area.

Transport and Communications

Road-building has priority in development. In addition to the 190 mile Aden to Mukalla road another is being constructed from Mukalla to the Wadi Hadhramaut. The building of an important highway from Aden to Taez in the YAR is being held up by political difficulties.

Aden has long been an important cable communications centre. The Aden branch of the British Cable and Wireless Limited, the last major British company operating in Aden, was nationalized in April 1978.

Aden Port, the largest harbour between Suez and India, used to provide the area's main form of revenue and employment. It was one of the world's major bunkering stations (accounting for about one third of exports), and as a free port it was a great commercial centre, with numerous foreign banks, insurance companies, foreign shipping agencies etc. The closure of the Canal in 1967 and the removal of the British base, followed by the imposition of import duties in 1970 (although a small 'free zone' was retained), destroyed this basis for Aden's prosperity. The reopening of the Suez Canal in 1975 brought some improvement but the results have been disappointing. Improvement schemes with UN and Arab aid, including a small Japanese floating dock, are under way. An improvement in relations with the YAR and the completion of the Aden-Taez highway offer the best prospects for the revival of Aden Port at the present time.

Currency, Banking, and Finance

The unit of currency is the dinar, originally at par with sterling. At the end of October 1978 £1 = 0.722 dinars. The PDRY became a member of the IMF and IBRD in 1969.

Apart from the central bank, the Bank of Yemen, which replaced the Yemen Currency Authority in 1972, the only bank in the PDRY is the National Bank of Yemen, a commercial bank representing an amalgamation of eight nationalized foreign banks.

The loss of revenues from Aden Port and the removal of the British base have meant that the PDRY has had to rely heavily on foreign aid for economic survival as well as for development. For political reasons, the main donors have been the USSR, China, East Germany, and North Korea, and Libya, Iraq, and Kuwait among the Arab countries. The government has still been forced to adopt a very austere economic policy to keep the budget deficit in control, with sharp salary cuts in the civil service, and higher taxes and duties.

Since the decline of Aden's entrepôt trade more than half the country's exports and a high proportion of imports have since been accounted for by the oil refinery. Other exports are mainly fish, ginned cotton, hides and skins, and cotton fabrics. Exports have been declining while imports have been difficult to control, but in 1976–7 the government had some success in stabilizing the balance of payments.

Education and Health

At the time of independence the educational system was founded on that of the former Aden Colony, where the Government maintained 18 schools and subsidized 24 others, and provided free education for children born in the Colony. It also maintained Aden College for academic secondary education, a technical institute, and two teacher training colleges. The colony provided education for girls and a Girls' College was opened at Khormaksar in 1956. The level of education varied in the States outside the Colony, depending on their wealth, degree of development, and the enlightenment of their rulers, but those children who did qualify from the former protectorate and federal areas could continue their higher education in Aden.

In 1971 there were 403 primary schools and intermediate schools, and twelve secondary schools and teacher training colleges, with about 168,000 pupils. Since then there has been a great drive to increase education (which includes Marxist teaching), especially for girls.

In September a university was established with faculties of education, agriculture, economics, commerce, and medicine. A faculty of geology is to be provided by the Russians.

At the time of independence there was one hospital bed for every 1,500 people and one doctor for every 30,500. At the latest UN estimate, at the end of 1973, there were 32 hospitals with a total of about 2,340 beds.

Development and the Future

As long as the present regime remains in power the PDRY will be socialist with no significant private sector and the bulk of foreign aid coming from the communist states. The three-year development plan of 1971–4 was drawn up with Soviet assistance. Of the £40.7 million expenditure envisaged (of which half was to be provided by loans and grants), the largest investment was in transport.

A new five-year plan for 1974–9 envisaged investment of 92 million dinars, also heavily dependent on foreign aid. Priority is given to fishing, agriculture, animal breeding, industrial development, and minerals, including oil. In 1979 a further five-year plan for 1979–83 was launched with allocations of 410 million dinars. An indication of the PDRY's pro-Moscow trend was that it joined Comecon.

4. Kuwait

The Amirate of Kuwait is set in the desert country which lies in the north-western corner of the Gulf around the Bay of Kuwait. Kuwait city occupies one of the rare firm coastal features lying between extensive areas of shoal, mudflat and coral reef although the city is rapidly expanding south eastwards towards Mina al-Ahmadi, the oil port on the Gulf proper.

Inland a few small oases lie in the waterless undulating desert which rises in altitude to the west. Medium depth aquifers of slightly brackish as well as sweet water have allowed small-scale traditional oasis agriculture, but the economy of Kuwait is almost entirely dependent on the exploitation of vast on-shore and offshore oil deposits, export of which commenced in 1946 and which has overwhelmed the traditionally dominant marine trade. To the south lies the Partitioned Zone, jointly administered with Saudi Arabia and completely negative save for oil. To the north and east lie scattered islands of the marshland complex of extreme south Iraq.

In the 7,400 square miles of territory lives a population estimated in 1976 at 1,055,000, almost ten times larger than that of 1934 and most of which is concentrated in the city of Kuwait and in the industrial zone to the south which contains the centres of Ahmadi, Fahaheel, and Shuaiba. According to the 1976 census about 48 per cent of the population had Kuwaiti nationality. The rest are mainly Arabs, especially Jordanians and Palestinians, Egyptians, Syrians, Lebanese, and Iraqis, with substantial Indo-Pakistani and Iranian minorities.

RECENT HISTORY

Early in the eighteenth century members of the Anaiza tribe occupied the site of the present town and developed marine and trading interests which dominated the life of Kuwait until recently. By 1760 a fleet of more than 800 dhows was based on the port which grew even faster after the East India Company established its head of Gulf base at Kuwait following the Iranian occupation of Basra in 1776. Even so the population remained at between 10,000 and 12,000 until the end of the nineteenth century.

In 1756 a member of one of the leading Anaiza families, the Sabah, was chosen as first Amir of Kuwait and his line has ruled continuously ever since. Shaikh Mubarak the Great, 1896–1915, was first to assert the independence of the Amirate, at a time when Britain was concerned about German negotiations with Turkey for the southern part of the Berlin-Baghdad railway and its extension to the south, and when

Russian attempts to secure a naval supply station at the head of the Gulf were also giving some anxiety to Britain. In 1899 Britain acceded to Shaikh Mubarak's request for support and protection, and the treaty was further extended to include recognition as an independent State under British protection. Turco-British negotiations over the status of Kuwait started in 1909 and the establishment of a British Political Agency in 1914 were landmarks in the history of the new State. In accordance with the 1899 treaty, Kuwait's foreign relations were conducted by Britain through its Political Agent. By 1910, as a result of the increased trade which was associated with growing world interest in the region the population had increased to about 35,000, the first stage in a rapid period of growth.

In the period of post-1919 settlements the most crucial was the 1922/3 conference to settle the Kuwaiti-Saudi Arabian frontiers in which the interests of the newly established State of Iraq, under British mandate, were also concerned. Two neutral zones were established, one to the west between Iraq and Saudi Arabia and one to the south, adjoining the coast, which thenceforward were jointly administered by Kuwait and Saudi Arabia. During the 1920s and 1930s Shaikh Salim and Shaikh Ahmad ensured that economic growth in Mesopotamia and the oilfields of Iraq and Iran subscribed to the mercantile wealth of Kuwait whose population increased to about 75,000 by 1934. During the same period oil exploration commenced. Politically, relations with Saudi Arabia improved from the nadir of the Saudi blockade of Kuwait in 1919 although the land frontier remained closed for almost twenty years afterwards. Fears of Iraqi expansionism, however, have never been completely eliminated and the growth of dependence on the supply of fresh water from the Shatt al-Arab near Basra, a traffic which lasted from 1925 to 1951, made Kuwait conscious of vulnerability.

The first oil concession was granted in 1934 for a period of 74 years to the Kuwait Oil Company, representing the Gulf Oil Corporation and the D'Arcy Exploration Company (a subsidiary then of Anglo-Iranian, now of British Petroleum). The first well was drilled north of the city of Kuwait at Bahra in 1936 but not until 1938 was oil found at Burgan, 25 miles south of the city. The Second World War prevented the full exploitation of what appeared a rich field and the wells were plugged until 1946 when production effectively started. Between 1946 and 1961 KOC drilled an average of 26 wells a year and KOC production rose in 1961 to over 81 million tons.

Throughout the 1950s the town of Kuwait was being dramatically transformed with the aid of its steadily increasing oil income from a small and somnolent mud-walled trading and fishing port into a modern city. Shaikh Abdullah, who succeeded as Ruler in 1950, was a social and religious conservative but he favoured the spread of education (for girls as well as boys) and rapid economic development. Under his rule Kuwait became a comprehensive welfare state not only for the native Kuwaitis but also for the immigrant Arabs, Iranians, and Indians who exceeded them in numbers. Political power remained in the hands of the ruling family but it was divided both traditionally between the Jabir and Salim branches of the Sabah family and on a basis of personality. The Deputy Ruler Abdullah Mubarak, who favoured an old-fashioned type of shaikhly rule, was contrasted with the younger Shaikh Jabir al-Ahmad who was regarded as a 'progressive'.

In June 1961 Kuwait and Britain terminated the 1899 agreement and Kuwait became an independent State. In July it joined the Arab League and in 1963, after the USSR had withdrawn its objection, the United Nations. In June 1961 General Kassem, the ruler of Iraq, renewed Iraq's claim to Kuwait in strong terms. British troops landed at the request of the Ruler but these were replaced in September by an Arab League force of UAR, Jordanian, Saudi, and Sudanese troops. It was doubtful whether General Kassem seriously contemplated an outright military invasion of Kuwait; its survival as an independent State in any case depended more on the fact that this was the desire of all the other Arab states (except Iraq) than on British military support.

In December 1961 Kuwait took a major step away from traditional forms of government with the selection of 20 members of a Constituent Assembly who joined with the ministers in drafting a permanent Constitution. This was published in November 1962. In January 1963 a 50-member

National Assembly was elected and Crown Prince Salim became Prime Minister at the head of a new Government.

In the new Assembly a small group of radical nationalist deputies succeeded in acquiring influence out of all proportion to their numbers and as a result Kuwait never openly sided with the camp of the conservative Arab kings in opposition to the revolutionary republics. Kuwait's influence and importance in the Arab world were greatly strengthened by the creation at the end of 1961 of the Kuwait Fund for Arab Development which provided loans on easy terms for viable development projects in the Arab states. Kuwait's great wealth and consequent independence has enabled it at times to adopt a radical Arab nationalist stand on certain foreign policy issues. But the national interest remained paramount for both the Government and the majority of the National Assembly, and Kuwait carefully maintained its neutrality between the conservative and radical camps in the Arab world while adopting firm measures at home to prevent non-Kuwaiti Arab immigrants from acquiring undue influence in the State. These measures, which included the expulsion of a group of 'subversive' non-Kuwaitis, were unsuccessfully opposed by the Arab nationalist deputies in the National Assembly.

In November 1965 the much respected Shaikh Abdullah died and was succeeded by the 51-year-old Shaikh Sabah Salim. Shaikh Jabir, the Minister of Finance, became Prime Minister and Crown Prince. In the June 1967 war Kuwait expressed its support for the other Arab states and sent a small contingent of troops to Egypt; it also cut off the supply of oil to the US and Britain. In Khartoum in August 1967 the Ruler agreed to make the largest single contribution of £55 million a year to aid Jordan and Egypt.

Following Britain's announcement of the withdrawal of all its forces from the Gulf area by 1971, the Anglo-Kuwaiti defence agreement concluded after Kuwait's independence was cancelled in May 1968 by mutual agreement. Kuwait took a leading part in negotiations concerning the Iranian claim to Bahrain, the clarification of sovereignty rights over various Gulf islands, and, together with Saudi Arabia, in promoting the development of a viable federation of Arab States in the region which was to become the United Arab Emirates.

In 1968 Kuwait became a founder member, together with Libya and Saudi Arabia, of the Organization of Arab Petroleum Exporting Countries (OAPEC), expressing the need of states whose economies are dominated by the export of oil, particularly to the West, to be free from political pressures.

In 1969 the Kuwait Government became seriously alarmed at the sharp increase in the non-Kuwaiti population, estimated at 200,000 since the 1967 war, many of them unemployed. As a consequence new restrictions were imposed in March. The National Assembly elections held in January 1971 were widely regarded as having been entirely free. The composition of the Assembly remained basically conservative but the radicals considerably increased their representation.

The radicals combined with a variety of elements in the Assembly who might be described as nationalists to form an opposition which successfully obstructed the government on a number of issues, always upholding Kuwait's national interests against the oil companies and other foreign concerns. The radicals were weakened as a result of the 1975 elections but the new parliament proved even more critical and obstructive. In August 1976 the government resigned, charging the National Assembly with having made its task impossible. The Ruler dissolved the Assembly and suspended certain key articles in the constitution. New curbs were imposed on Kuwait's relatively free press and subsequently various papers were suspended for violating the press law. On 31 December 1977 the Ruler Shaikh Sabah Salim died and was replaced by the Crown Prince Shaikh Jabir. The new Ruler's cousin Shaikh Saad Abdullah Salim became Crown Prince and Prime Minister.

Stability and internal security in Kuwait were strongly affected by political tensions among the non-Kuwaiti population, especially the Palestinians, whose numbers greatly increased after the 1967 war. These tensions were further exacerbated by the Lebanese civil war and the divisions in the Arab world which followed President Sadat of Egypt's peace initiative in 1977–8.

In foreign policy Kuwait has consistently tried to maintain an independent, neutral, and mediatory role in the Arab world. This has sometimes proved difficult in view of Kuwait's small size and vulnerability, and the rival influences of its two Arab neighbours – conservative Saudi Arabia and Baathist Iraq. In 1977, relations with Iraq improved as a result of the settlement of border disputes, but fears of a revival of Iraqi claims to Kuwait have not wholly disappeared.

THE ECONOMY

Kuwait's GNP *per capita* ranks with those of the USA and Abu Dhabi as among the highest in the world in spite of its having virtually no commercially viable agriculture, of being dependent on desalination plant for fresh water, and of having limited manufacturing activity. Oil is the dominant factor in the country's economy, and revenue from its production and sale – some £5,000 million – accounts for about 95 per cent of total budget revenue.

Production in Kuwait state proper has always been by the Kuwait Oil Company (KOC) which for many years was owned by BP and Gulf Oil on a 50–50 basis. In 1974 the government took 60 per cent participation in KOC and in 1975 this was increased to 100 per cent which means that the government has increasing quantities of oil available for direct sales. In the Kuwaiti-Saudi Partitioned Zone (formerly Neutral Zone), Kuwait's interests are represented by the American Aminoil in the onshore fields and the Japanese Arabian Oil Company in the offshore fields.

The Kuwait National Petroleum Company was established in 1960 with 60 per cent state and 40 per cent private ownership, and is now 100 per cent state-owned. KNPC's venture into exploration with the Spanish Hispanoil was unsuccessful. The company is responsible for internal distribution and operates a major export refinery at Shuaiba. Kuwait has the second largest refining operation in the Middle East after Iran. KNPC is responsible for marketing the products of the KOC refinery and has started to create an oil product tanker fleet. It is the owner of the Kuwait Aviation Fuelling Company (formerly BP), and has taken over ship bunkering from KOC.

Natural gas is the basis of much of Kuwait's current development. The proportion that is flared off has been steadily reduced and output of liquid petroleum gas will greatly increase when the present Kuwait Oil Company Gas Project is completed. However, production will be lower than originally intended because the natural gas is associated gas, which means that it is directly related to crude oil output, and this has been reduced from about 3 million b.p.d. to 2 million b.p.d. in order to conserve the country's reserves.

The main traditional industry was shipbuilding but the government has actively encouraged new industries as a means of diversifying the economy. A 1965 law protects local industries, and in the Shuaiba Industrial Area the government has created an infrastructure which includes power, water, and a port. Success in this policy has been restrained by the small size of the local market and the Kuwaiti preference for investment in trade and real estate, and increasingly in foreign securities. However, state development and the oil industry stimulated some large-scale local contracting companies at an earlier stage and other private industries including light engineering, printing, tile-manufacture, furniture, and soft drinks, and a variety of others are projected. The largest industries remain state-owned or part of the joint state-private sector which has been important in Kuwait's development. This includes fisheries, livestock, and food supplies, as well as service industries – hotels, transport, banking, real estate, and insurance.

Agriculture is necessarily very limited but there has been some significant experimental state agricultural development since 1953, and a fair proportion of eggs, poultry, vegetables, and milk are now produced locally while shrimp-fishing has become an important export industry.

Finance and Banking

Since the departure of the British Bank of the Middle East, the only foreign bank ever permitted to operate in Kuwait, all commercial banks have been wholly Kuwaiti owned. These are limited to some six banks – mostly private, although the State has a share in two. There are also two state or semi-state banking institutions – the Savings and Credit Bank, and the Industrial Bank of Kuwait, inaugurated in 1974 as the government's means of stimulating private and joint-sector industry. There are also some 25 insurance companies.

Despite some government restraint on the banking sector to improve liquidity and curb speculation in order to combat inflation, Kuwait has developed into a major international investment centre – substantially in advance of Saudi Arabia, Qatar, and the UAE, although these are now catching up. In Kuwait the way was paved by two joint-sector investment companies, the Kuwait Investment Company (KIC), and the Kuwait Foreign Trading Contracting and Investment Company; but there is now a whole range of investment institutions which participate in innumerable bond issues. One of the KIC's achievements was the underwriting and placing of six World Bank bond issues entirely on the Kuwait market.

Direct Kuwaiti investment is also substantial and increasing through such companies as Gulf International which has a substantial holding in the British conglomerate Lonhro and large investments in Sudan. The investment of the Kuwait government's own reserves is handled through a department of the Ministry of Finance. In early years this was mainly kept in liquid funds but more recently it has been used to build up assets in property and portfolio shareholdings. Kuwait's total investment income in the late 1970s is estimated to exceed one billion dollars.

Aid

Kuwait was the pioneer in the spreading of oil wealth among the Arab states – with the foundation in 1961 of the Kuwait Fund for Arab Economic Development – to provide government-to-government loans on easy terms within the Arab world. Since then its capital has been increased to KD 1,000 million and its operations have been extended to all developing countries. KFAED is run on World Bank lines and makes a careful appraisal of all projects before lending.

Kuwait was instrumental in helping to launch the Arab Fund for Economic and Social Development and takes part in a number of other multilateral aid and development agencies. Since 1967 it has provided large amounts of direct aid to the Arab front-line states with Israel, and has also helped the less favoured states of the Arabian Peninsula through the General Authority for Southern Arabia and the Gulf States.

Social Services

Over the past 20 years Kuwait's oil wealth has been used to develop one of the most advanced systems of social services in the world. Health services are free; in 1974 there were 11 hospitals and sanatoria with 3,896 beds, and 417 clinics; and the expansion programme in 1977 provided for six new hospitals with 2,500 more beds. Education is also free, with some exceptions, and the number of pupils and students exceeds 200,000. One remarkable characteristic of Kuwaiti education is that the proportion of girls in school (45 per cent) is almost exactly equal to the female proportion of the population. The University of Kuwait, founded in 1964, has some 4,500 students of whom half are female and half non-Kuwaiti.

The Kuwaiti government also has a large-scale programme to provide free housing for low-income families.

Development and the Future

Even in times of falling sales of crude oil, as in 1978 when they were well below the average of 2 million b.p.d. imposed by the government in 1977, Kuwait's current surplus of oil revenues and investment income is estimated to exceed 5 billion dollars a year. A Planning Board (now Ministry of Planning) has existed for some years and played an important role in influencing the course of development but the state has not committed itself to detailed development plans. A substantial part of the oil revenues has always been channelled towards the creation of social and economic infrastructure and the development of industry, but this is done mainly through allocations to the ordinary budgets and other means. Today the tendency is for an increasing share of the overall current surplus to pass into private hands. The short-term economic problem is that of keeping the economy buoyant. In the early years of the oil boom massive public works absorbed the surplus revenues, but this is no longer sufficient and the government has to resort to expedients such as buying up desert land at inflated prices or intervening to support prices in the stock market.

In the longer term Kuwait is faced by the obvious problem of diversifying the economy to reduce dependence on oil if the country is not to be obliged to become a rentier state (i.e. living off its investments) when the oil runs out. It is also confronted by the difficult choice between extending Kuwaiti citizenship to some of the non-Kuwaiti Arabs who have hitherto been denied it, and becoming a continuously decreasing minority in their own country. The extraordinary social and economic development of Kuwait in the past generation would not have been possible without the non-Kuwaitis. The 1976/77 – 1980/81 five-year development plan drafted by the Ministry of Planning forecast the creation of 124,000 new jobs – only 31 per cent of which would be filled by Kuwaiti citizens.

5. Bahrain

The Shaikhdom of Bahrain comprises a small group of low-lying limestone islands located in generally shallow waters some twenty miles off-shore from Saudi Arabia and from the Qatar peninsula. From over 500 drilled wells and natural springs sweet water is obtained in quantities which have always seemed inexhaustible and which, utilized for irrigation, has provided the basis for sedentary settlement for five millennia and encouraged the growth of the port of Manama on the main island of Bahrain and of the second most important island of Muharraq.

Of the 1976 population of approximately 260,000, half are resident in Manama (the capital) and Muharraq, and about 35,000 in the new Isa Town. Both Sunni and Shii sects are represented in the population. About 15 per cent of the population is non-Bahraini (Indo-Pakistan, Omani, Iranian).

All executive and legislative power rests with the Ruler of Bahrain, Shaikh Isa ibn Sulman al-Khalifa, who is assisted by a Council of Administration composed of other members of the Ruling Family and the appointed heads of certain government departments. By various treaties, dating in the first instance from 1820, Great Britain had special responsibilities for defence and foreign affairs which were relinquished when Bahrain declared its independence in 1971.

RECENT HISTORY

In 1783 the chief family of the Utub tribe, the al-Khalifa, was instrumental in expelling the Iranians from Bahrain and became hereditary rulers. Iranian claims to sovereignty were based on their control of this region of the Gulf prior to that date. Until 1935 the history of Bahrain was closely associated with entrepôt trade and pearling, and it is as a mercantile centre victualled by spring-watered agriculture that Bahrain developed. During the nineteenth century this fundamental characteristic involved Bahrain in the changing geopolitical scene in a new way. The British desire to maintain a free and fluid position in the Gulf ran counter to Ottoman and Iranian political claims and to German politico-economic ambitions; in 1861 Britain supported the independent sovereignty of Bahrain in return for anti-piracy and anti-slavery agreements. Further treaties in 1880 and 1892 resulted in the British Government assuming all responsibility for external affairs. Bahrain became the seat of the British Resident in the Gulf and of the Chief and Full Courts for the Gulf. Following the discovery of oil Bahrain became the first of the Gulf States to experience the difficulties of socio-economic change, particularly since 1948. In 1956 the first non-traditional administrative councils were established and in 1957 the powers of the Bahrain judiciary were extended to their present limits. Education and welfare services date from the 1920s, the earliest in the Gulf. These did not prevent Bahrain from being the scene of socio-political trouble, notably in 1956 when anti-British sentiment inflamed by the Suez affair exacerbated internal (but externally-encouraged) unrest, the outward manifestations usually taking the form of strikes in the oil industry.

No organized political opposition was tolerated by the Ruling Family and there was no move during the 1960s towards a more democratic form of government. However, serious political unrest was largely stifled by the island's prosperity during this decade as the educated Bahrainis who were the potential source of opposition to the regime devoted themselves to commercial enterprise. Nevertheless, the withdrawal of British protection was a matter of serious concern to the Ruling Family. Baathist and other radical elements were active in parts of the Gulf area and the Marxist opposition elements in Oman were regarded as a threat by all the shaikhly rulers. Bahrain took part in the negotiations for a federation of Arab Gulf states between 1968 and 1971 but finally opted for full independence because the other Rulers would not agree to allow Bahrain the preponderant position which Bahrainis felt that their population and degree of development should allow them.

In contrast to the effect of the British withdrawal, Bahrain's sense of security was greatly enhanced by Iran's abandonment of its long-standing claim to the island. Following an enquiry by a UN Under-Secretary General in 1970, Iran accepted his verdict that the great majority of the population wanted Bahrain to be a sovereign Arab state. A Constituent Assembly elected in 1972 devised a new constitution providing for a 44-member National Assembly in which 30 members were elected and 14 were members of the government. The Ruler retained considerable powers under the constitution. In August 1975 he dissolved the Assembly and temporarily suspended the constitution after his brother the Prime Minister resigned saying that parliament had consistently thwarted his legislation and development programme.

The Economy

Bahrain has been an oil exporter for longer than any other Arab state. Shipments by the Bahrain Petroleum Company – Bapco – (Caltex Group) began in 1934 and the refining of local crude oil in 1936. However, Bahrain is a very small producer compared with its neighbours and output has been slowly declining in the 1970s. Reserves are small and the search for new fields has been disappointing. The Bapco 260,000 b.p.d. refinery also processes large quantities of Saudi oil and is a major source of income. Bahrain is also becoming an increasingly important exporter of non-associated natural gas.

A major development has been the construction of an aluminium smelter (total investment now $228 million) by Aluminium Bahrain (ALBA) which is now 77.9 per cent owned by the Bahraini state. Related ancillary industries have been developed on the basis of recent technological advances in the use of aluminium in 'atomized' and plate form as protective covering.

The traditional industries are boatbuilding, fishing, and weaving and to these have been added a range of light industries and services. Two large-scale projects of the 1970s have been the construction with OAPEC funds of a huge dry-dock and ship repair yard. The government's intention is to make Bahrain the services and communications centre for the Gulf. The excellent existing facilities will be enhanced by the construction of a 15-mile Saudi-financed causeway to link Bahrain with the Saudi mainland.

The Bahrain Monetary Agency, which assumed the full powers and duties of a central bank in 1975, has been reluctant to licence more than the 18 commercial banks which existed in 1977 for local operations; but in October 1975, in order to establish Bahrain as an alternative financial centre to Beirut, it decided to allow the establishing of 'offshore banking units' (OBUs) which, in return for an annual licence fee, can be operated internationally provided they do not compete for local business.

Bahrain is traditionally an entrepôt centre, re-exporting chiefly to Saudi Arabia although this has recently been affected by development of Saudi ports and strong competition from Dabai. In 1977, customs duties amounted to 26.0 million Bahraini Dinars out of total revenues of BD 235.5 million. Imports (especially of machinery and transport equipment) have risen very sharply from BD 175.9 million in 1974 to BD 232.9 million 1975 and BD 387.6 million in 1976. (At end-1978, $1 = BD 0.383).

After declining as a proportion of total revenues for some years, oil income rose again after the 1973 price increases to reach BD 150 million in 1977. Nevertheless, Bahrain's future depends on diversification, and in this respect the island has distinct advantages over most of its neighbours.

Four decades of oil production has enabled Bahrain to act as a pioneer in the fields of education and social services, and it now has a developed and varied system which is constantly being expanded. Educational facilities include the Gulf Technical Institute, and Saudi Arabia is financing a further technical complex.

6. Qatar

The Shaikhdom of Qatar comprises the peninsula of that name lying midway along the western coast of the Gulf. It has an area of about 4,000 square miles, with a population (in 1978) of just over 200,000, of whom more than half were foreigners, including foreign Arabs. From a shallow coastline the land rises to a low monotonous plateau. The only natural water supply is from wells. Its only land frontier, with Saudi Arabia and Abu Dhabi, has never been demarcated.

Economic development is concentrated in the capital Doha where nearly all the population lives. Executive and legislative power is in the hands of the ruling al-Thani family.

From 1868 Qatar was an independent shaikhdom in treaty relationship with Britain which undertook its military defence and the conduct of its external affairs. With Britain's final withdrawal from the Gulf in 1971 and the breakdown of negotiations for the creation of a federation with Bahrain and the Trucial Coast states, Qatar decided to opt for complete independence.

RECENT HISTORY

An agreement with Britain of 3 November 1916 had provisions similar to those with other Trucial shaikhs, and included a clause making the grant of pearling concessions or other monopolies dependent on British consent. Relations are close with Saudi Arabia, whose rulers are also Wahhabis, and with Dubai, with which the al-Thani family is linked by friendship and marriage, but relations with the neighbouring island of Bahrain have not been good since Qatar seized in 1937 the ruined village of Zubara, on the Qatar Peninsula, which is claimed to be the ancestral home of the Ruling Family of Bahrain. Qatar's refusal to join a federation of Arab Gulf Shaikhdoms which seemed likely to be dominated by Bahrain was the principal reason for its opting for complete independence. The size of its population allows Qatar to attain the normally accepted minimum qualifications for membership of the United Nations.

Shaikh Ahmad ibn Ali al-Thani, who succeeded his father, Shaikh Ali ibn Abdullah ibn Qasim al-Thani on his abdication in 1960, was ousted in a bloodless coup in February 1972 by his cousin Shaikh Khalifa ibn Hamad al-Thani, Deputy Ruler and Prime Minister, who endeavoured to create a more dynamic and efficient administration.

Under his leadership, Qatar has taken a much more active role in regional and international politics. Shortly after his accession, Shaikh Khalifa formed a 30-member Advisory Council.

THE ECONOMY

At one time pearl fishing and nomadic herding provided a primitive population with the bare means of subsistence, and the decline of the pearling industry from about 1930 reduced it to even greater poverty. The discovery of oil transformed the situation entirely. Doha has been rebuilt and social services provided for the entire population.

The first oil concession in the area was obtained in 1935 by Petroleum Development (Qatar), later renamed the Qatar Petroleum Company (QPC). Oil was struck in 1939 in the Dokhan structure but drilling was interrupted until 1948 by the war. Production began in 1950 with 1.6 million tons and then rose steadily to about 8 million tons (about 130,000 b.p.d.) in the 1960s and 222,000 b.p.d. in 1977. Reserves are modest and new exploration has been unsuccessful. A pipeline connects QPC's producing field with the terminal at Umm Said on the east coast.

The 'continental shelf' offshore area, east of Qatar and outside the three-mile limit, was conceded for development in 1952 to Shell Overseas Exploration Ltd. Two fields were discovered and production began in 1965. Another field was discovered in 1970. Both QPC and Shell Company of Qatar were subject to 25 per cent state take-over in 1973, 60 per cent in 1974, and 100 per cent in 1976, through the Qatar Petroleum Producing Authority, a wholly owned subsidiary and controlling arm of the Qatar General Petroleum Corporation, the organization which holds the state share in all oil, gas, and petrochemical enterprises in Qatar and abroad. Other exploration concessions are held by US, Canadian, and German companies.

Under the present Ruler, Qatar has concentrated on the vigorous development of the infrastructure and the diversification of the economy. A natural gas liquefaction plant with a large export capacity was brought into production by QPC in 1975 and is now owned by QGPC. A similar project is under way on an adjacent site. Residual dry gas goes as feedstock to a fertilizer plant exporting ammonia and urea and as fuel to the state electricity department and cement plant. Of two other major projects, a steel mill came into operation in 1978 and a petrochemical complex was due to start production in 1980. The development of the fishing industry and the establishment of light industries are also planned.

Although there is no surface water, wells have permitted a remarkable development of agriculture. About 2,000 hectares are now under cultivation and the state is now effectively self-sufficient in vegetables.

With revenues exceeding $2,000 million a year, Qatar has at present a large surplus on current account. However, the government's immensely ambitious capital spending programme, combined with the depressed state of the oil market in 1977 (which led to an 11 per cent fall in output against that of 1976), caused the government to cut its capital development budget in 1978. Qatar is expected to be the first of the Gulf members of OPEC to encounter balance of payments problems.

Qatar has 108 schools and a school population of about 40,000 of whom nearly 50 per cent are female. A university was nearing completion in 1978. There is a free health service and medical services are under constant expansion.

7. The United Arab Emirates

The United Arab Emirates (formerly the Trucial States) consist of seven sovereign States, Abu Dhabi, Ajman, Dubai, Fujaira, Ras al-Khaima, Sharja, and Umm al-Qaiwain. Their territories lie on the southern shores of the Gulf, extending eastwards to the Gulf of Oman.

In addition to the following, further information is given, individually, for Abu Dhabi and Dubai (pp. 185ff. and 188 ff.).

The Emirates' coast, extending between Qatar and the rocky headlands of the Ras Musandum headland (in the State of Oman) is characterized by shallow seas, a fringe of sand bars, coral reefs and islands, and by stretches of *sabkha,* saline/alkaline mudflats. Wherever groundwater seepage has allowed human settlement on relatively firm sandspits, bars, and islands then small marine-based communities have become established. At Dubai, Ras al-Khaima and Sharja, the presence of creeks encouraged greater than average growth based on Gulf and long-distance trade. Inland lies a zone of inhospitable sand desert which grades into an arid gravel and silt outwash belt at the foot of the Omani mountains. Where this belt opens onto the coast at Ras al-Khaima settlement extends inland from the sea. Where water from the highlands percolates at shallow depths into this belt then oasis agriculture, on a large scale in the Buraimi complex, has been established. The spinal mountains themselves are inhospitably rugged except for small upland valleys and basins where surface water derived from higher rainfall supports grazing and crops. On the east coast rugged headlands alternate with small embayments in which communities subsist on fishing and garden-oases. Khawr Fakkan, the only true port, has grown around one of the few safe harbourages. Aridity is general, and on the coasts high summer temperatures and humidity make the climate very oppressive. Drier air and greater temperature ranges characterize the interior.

Approximately half the population may be described as urban and is concentrated on the Gulf coast. The 1975 census gave the following population totals for the States and the chief towns: Abu Dhabi 235,662; Ajman 21,566; Dubai 206,861; Fujaira 26,498; Ras al-Khaima 57,282; Sharja 81,188; Umm al-Qaiwain 16,879. The urban populations of the four largest States have all grown significantly since 1968. In the interior, apart from al-Ain in Abu Dhabi, the population lives in oasis villages of up to about 1,000 inhabitants. Of the total UAE population of 655,000 well over half were immigrants – mainly Indo-Pakistanis and other Arabs. A further census on 31 December 1977 gave a total population of 862,000 of whom 71 per cent were male.

RECENT HISTORY

The British presence in the Trucial Region until 1971 derived from the quasi-official status of East India Company agents in the Gulf during the early eighteenth century. From 1770 onwards the Royal Navy became increasingly active in the protection of maritime trade, and expeditionary forces were landed in Ras al-Khaima, where Qasimi power was strong, several times in the early nineteenth century. Treaties signed in the 1820s binding the Rulers to refrain from piracy, developed into annual truces negotiated through the Gulf Political Residency and the Resident's Agency established at Sharja in 1823. Suppression of the slave trade was the purpose of other British diplomatic interventions while local and dynastic disputes, though not eliminated, became less frequent. In 1892 various factors which included apprehension of Turkish and Iranian infiltration, alarm at French activity, and concern at the growing influence of Russia in Iran, caused the British Government to conclude the so-called Exclusive Agreements with the Rulers of the Trucial States. In them the Rulers agreed never to cede any part of their territory except to the British Government, not to enter into agreements with any government other than the British, and not to admit foreign representatives without British consent. A similar treaty was signed with Qatar in 1916 which carried a definite assurance of British protection (as had been done to Bahrain in 1861). No such assurance was ever given to the Trucial States although there was an implicit obligation on the British Government to protect them in return for the very considerable concessions the Rulers made, and no British Government ever attempted to argue that there was not. Fujaira, which had formerly been part of Sharja, became independent in the early years of this century, and was admitted, at her Ruler's insistent request, to the Trucial system in 1952. Each State had full sovereignty save for the limitations of British treaty responsibilities for external affairs. From 1960 a Trucial States Council on which all Rulers were represented met regularly to discuss problems of mutual interest and to co-ordinate various activities. Its executive arm was the Development Office financed principally by the Ruler of Abu Dhabi and the UK Government.

From 1892 onwards the Rulers conducted all their external affairs through the British Government, and local Political Officers were finally superseded by a Political Agent in 1953. Since the British Government's main aim was to maintain internal security, a central military force capable of intervening in inter-State disputes was established in 1953, the Trucial Oman Scouts which, with both Arab and British officers, were able to maintain stability effectively. The base for the British military forces was in Sharja. The expansion of Imperial Airways led to an airstrip being established in 1932 and in 1940 it became an RAF base. After 1945 Sharja became the main air-staging base for the Gulf and following the British withdrawal from Aden there was in addition an army build-up. This considerable base was abandoned as part of the British withdrawal from the Gulf in 1971.

By the 1970s Britain had maintained stability in the area for nearly a century but at the same time it had helped to create a political problem of the first magnitude. In recognizing and making treaties with these tiny States and defining their boundaries, Britain effectively froze them in their nineteenth-century condition. Without the British presence they would almost certainly have been swallowed by a neighbouring power such as Saudi Arabia. As it was, when the inevitable time came for the quasi-imperial British presence to be withdrawn, the Trucial States were clearly unsuited for independence while the very fact of the British presence had enabled the Rulers to postpone consideration of uniting to form a larger federation. At the same time, Britain's power to intervene in their internal affairs was limited. 'While the obligations Britain has incurred towards the littoral principalities are, in many cases, those of a colonial rather than a protecting power, she does not possess the legal attributes, particularly that of political sovereignty, which would enable her to discharge those obligations effectively.'[4] Britain might have done more to urge the Rulers to form a federation but it is doubtful whether such efforts would have succeeded.

Following the announcement by Britain in early 1968 that its forces would be withdrawn from the area by late 1971 various discussions concerning federation took place between the seven Trucial States, Bahrain, and Qatar. Difficulties

[4] J.B. Kelly, *St. Antony's Papers, 1958.*

arose principally because of the disparities in size, wealth, sophistication, and oil expectations between the nine states, which exacerbated the differences stemming from local tribal loyalties. Qatar and Bahrain finally opted for separate independence.

At a meeting of the Rulers of the seven Trucial States held in Dubai on 10–18 July 1971 it was announced that six of them – Abu Dhabi, Ajman, Dubai, Fujaira, Sharja and Umm al-Qaiwain – had agreed to form a federation. Membership of the federation was left open to Ras al-Khaima, Bahrain, and Qatar. Ras al-Khaima, the only Trucial State to reject the federation, did so because it was refused veto powers. It changed its mind and accepted in 1972.

THE FEDERAL CONSTITUTION

On the establishment of the UAE, Shaikh Zaid, Ruler of Abu Dhabi, became the federation's first President, and Shaikh Rashid, Ruler of Dubai, the Vice-President, with a five-year term of office which has since been continued. There is a Supreme Council, comprising the severn rulers, and a federal cabinet consisting of a Prime Minister and 21 other ministers. Abu Dhabi provides eight ministers, including the deputy Prime Minister, and Dubai four ministers and the Prime Minister. The legislature is a National Assembly of some 40 members of which eight represent Abu Dhabi, eight Dubai, six Sharja, and six Ras al-Khaima.

Despite some internal tensions the federation has survived and there is a growing trend towards planning and action as a single nation. The main impulse towards federation has come from Shaikh Zaid of Abu Dhabi, the UAE's chief paymaster and statesman, who favours a closely knit federation. Dubai, Abu Dhabi's traditional rival, has shown less enthusiasm, especially in the question of the unification of the military forces of all the member states, which Shaikh Zaid regards as essential. In other spheres, such as a common currency, the abolition of inter-state customs, and immigration control, the federation is well advanced and the unification of foreign affairs, justice, and the social services has made some progress.

THE FEDERAL ECONOMY

The new federal currency used by all members of the UAE is the UAE dirham, issued in 1973. The UAE Currency Board, founded in 1973 with many of the powers of a central bank, is responsible for the licensing and control of banking. A liberal policy led to a rapid proliferation of local and foreign banks, but since 1975 the licensing of foreign banks has been limited and local banks have been more strictly controlled.

The UAE's first federal budget totalled only 200 million dirhams but has risen astronomically to 10.5 billion dirhams in 1978 (about $2.7 billion). It is almost entirely financed by Abu Dhabi and the bulk of development expenditure goes to the five smaller states. Since October 1972 trade between one Emirate and another has been free of duty. Non-oil UAE exports are very small (mainly scrap, dates, and dried fish), but re-exports, which almost all pass through Dubai, are important.

ABU DHABI

The Emirate of Abu Dhabi extends along the shoal southern coast of the Gulf between the states of Qatar and Dubai and into the mainly sand desert interior of the Empty Quarter. Until recently the only areas at all attractive to human settlement were some of the two hundred islands, including that of Abu Dhabi itself, on which small fishing and trading communities existed, the oasis complexes of Liwa, near the Saudi Arabian frontier, and Buraimi, on the edge of the Oman mountain ranges and the border of the State of Oman. Abu Dhabi is now connected by a causeway with the mainland. Das Island is the headquarters of the offshore oil-extracting companies. Sir Bani Yas Island, possessing deep waters, is an oil port facing the Dhanna oil terminal of the inland Murban oilfield. The indigenous population still sets store by tribal groupings which consist of the Bani Yas, the al-Manasir, al-Dhawahir and al-Awamer tribes. The rulers of the Emirate are members of the al-Nihyan family of the Al Bu Falah branch.

Recent History

By the end of the eighteenth century the land-based tribal group of the Bani Yas under Shaikh Isa ibn Nihyan had made the island of Abu Dhabi with its wells of potable water their main centre, while the al-Dhawahir tribe remained in the Buraimi region. The Emirate since then has remained in the al-Nihyan line. Shaikh Zaid ibn Khalifa (Zaid the Great) during the latter half of the nineteenth century established sovereignty over what is approximately its present territory, in particular establishing a *modus vivendi* with the State of Oman. This left al-Buraimi proper in the Sultanate and brought al-Ain, Qattara, and Hili into the Emirate.

Between 1909 and 1928 the Emirate was ruled by Zaid the Great's sons on a provincial basis and for the period between 1928 and 1960, under Shaikh Shakbut ibn Sultan, the Emirate remained little changed. Abu Dhabi, a low-grade fishing port, was the residence of the Ruler, while al-Ain with its *falaj*-based traditional agriculture was administered and developed by the Ruler's brother Shaikh Zaid. Border disputes between Abu Dhabi, Dubai, Oman and Saudi Arabia were not infrequent and British intervention was regularly necessary. In 1966 Shaikh Shakbut, overwhelmed by the problems of oil affluence, was deposed by family agreement (with British encouragement) and succeeded by Shaikh Zaid the present ruler. Since 1966 the history of Abu Dhabi has been marked by increasingly successful domestic policies of social and economic development, pacific and generous dealings with its Trucial neighbours, and a growing international stature in the Arab world and beyond.

Economy

Before the discovery of oil in 1960 the economy of Abu Dhabi was extremely poor. The difficult coast prevented all but the most limited marine activity, including pearl fishing, while inland subsistence agriculture at al-Ain and Liwa was the only alternative to desert nomadism.

The two main oil-producing companies are the Abu Dhabi Marine Areas operating the offshore fields, and the Abu Dhabi Petroleum Company in the onshore areas. Both of these are 60 per cent owned by the government through the Abu Dhabi National Oil Company (Adnoc). Production was running at about 1.5 million b.p.d. in 1976 and 1.7 million b.p.d. in 1977, but fell to 1.45 million b.p.d. in 1978.

Adnoc, which was established in 1971, is the major factor in Abu Dhabi's development. It is building up a tanker fleet and has a 51 per cent interest (with British, French, Japanese, and US companies) in the Abu Dhabi Gas Liquefaction Company which has built a plant on Das Island to produce liquefied natural gas and petroleum gas. A further giant project to establish a plant at Ruweis using onshore gas was the subject of prolonged negotiations with Adnoc's foreign partners until Adnoc decided in April 1977 to go it alone, providing the necessary $1.1 billion from its own resources.

Following the rises in oil prices, revenues increased more than eight-fold from 2,156 million dirham in 1972 to dh. 18,401 million in 1976. In the 1978–80 development plan, some 79 per cent of the total outlay will be public investment. The government's priority is still the build-up of Abu Dhabi's infrastructure and urban modernization; 49 per cent of development investment is for services and 21 per cent for public facilities. However, some 38 per cent is allocated to industry and, in addition to the gas liquefaction plant, a large fertilizer plant, a petrochemical complex, a refinery, and a steel plant are projected.

Unlike Dubai, Abu Dhabi has neither the tradition of large-scale marine trade nor the physical suitability for it; but it does possess agricultural potential in the al-Ain oasis, and the Arid Lands Research Centre on Sadiyat Island near Abu Dhabi City has had striking success in the controlled environment production of fresh foods.

Aid

Abu Dhabi's generous aid policy has given the country an international status out of proportion to its size. This, combined with the fact that Abu Dhabi virtually finances the UAE federal budget single-handed, has required periods of financial restraint. The Abu Dhabi Fund for Arab Economic Development now has a capital of dh. 2,000 million (about $500 million). It gives assistance to economically viable projects in Arab, and other Asian, African, and Islamic states. Abu Dhabi also contributes to various multilateral development agencies as well as providing bilateral aid.

DUBAI

The Emirate of Dubai is a compact territory almost entirely composed of sand desert and with a *sabkha*-fringed coast broken by Dubai creek which provides safe anchorage for vessels of up to 10 feet draught. From the nucleus of old Dubai, situated on a spit-head at the mouth of the creek, the town has now expanded along the sides of the creek and south along the coast. A new deep-water port, constructed near old Dubai, ensures that the present commercial supremacy in the southern Gulf will not be adversely affected by technical problems. The Ruler of Dubai exercises direct rule in the state. Because of the importance of Dubai Town, the most important administrative body in the state is the Dubai Municipal Council, originally founded in 1957, and given a Charter and corporate existence in 1961. The Council, of thirty appointed members, represents different sections of the community. Its decisions must be ratified by the Ruler, but with his consent the Council makes Local Orders, has power to make contracts and own land, and administers this most important element in the state through specialized committees and paid officials. A Lands Committee has responsibility for land registration and transactions and is an entity independent of the Municipality. It has always been the Ruler's policy to restrain bureaucracy and establish liberal regulations to encourage domestic and foreign private enterprise.

Recent History

Dubai shaikhdom was established by the secession in the early nineteenth century of a section of the Al Bu Falasah branch of the Bani Yas from the Abu Dhabi tribal complex. This assertion of independence was essentially a statement of the trading orientation of the people inhabiting the shores of Dubai creek but remained disputed into the late 1950s, and conflicts with Abu Dhabi and Sharja were not infrequent. Shaikh Rashid, Regent between 1939 and 1958 and now Ruler, has directed his state continuously along the path of commercial and trade development and Dubai has had a forty-year history of consistent, single-minded progress which has made it the leading City State in the region.

Economy

The economy of Dubai until very recently was almost entirely based on international trade and trade of such a type that normal economic mensuration at all levels becomes largely meaningless. During 1970, officially listed imports of £86 million were eight times larger than exports and re-exports. Customs dues levied on most imported goods at $4\frac{5}{8}$ per cent produced a revenue to the state of almost £3 million, the single largest item, and the value of imports rose by an average of 100 per cent every two years between 1962 and 1969. Not included in the normal customs statistics is the trade in gold although trade in bullion is perfectly legal. Dubai merchants annually purchase between £50 and £70 million of gold each year, most of which is smuggled into India (and Pakistan) at premiums of 10–30 per cent. The direct effect of this trade on Dubai income is significant but not quantifiable; indirectly it has contributed towards making Dubai the financial and trading centre of the southern Gulf.

Oil was first discovered in the Fatah offshore field in 1966 and production started in 1968 by the Dubai Petroleum Company.

Since then oil revenues, estimated in 1976 at dh. 5.2 billion from a production of 317,000 b.p.d., have combined with the continuing self-generating economic activity to provide the means for more ambitious development plans. These have included the construction of the new Port Rashid, with a handling capacity of 3 million tons a year, a new international airport, and bridges and a tunnel traversing Dubai creek. Further plans include a major industrial zone at Jebel Ali which will include an aluminium smelter, a cement plant, a gas liquefaction plant, and an iron and steel mill. Jebel Ali will also have its own huge 74-berth port and international airport.

Dubai's liberal policies have made the city a major financial centre. In addition to local banks there are scores of Arab and foreign banks, merchant banks, finance houses and insurance companies. The gold trade has declined in importance but Dubai remains the principal port and entrepôt centre of the Lower Gulf. Despite port development elsewhere, Dubai has remained an important centre for the UAE as well as an entrepôt for goods passing to Iran, Oman, and Saudi Arabia. Imports tripled between 1972 and 1976.

OTHER UAE STATES

The discovery of oil in 1972 in an offshore field in which Sharja has a 35 per cent share (Iran 50 per cent, Umm al-Qaiwain 15 per cent) gave Sharja revenues of some $36 million in 1976. The state's Ruler, Shaikh Sultan al-Qasimi, has ambitious plans to restore Sharja's position in the Gulf which was lost to Dubai, and to develop the state as a transport and financial centre with associated recreational facilities. The development of the sea, land, and air transport systems was already well advanced by 1978, and some 50 local and foreign banks were operating in the Emirate. Several new luxury hotels had been opened. However, in view of current developments in neighbouring Dubai, there is a danger of excess capacity in all these areas.

Ras al-Khaima has more water than the other states and some 6,000 hectares are under irrigated cultivation. The Ruler, Shaikh Saqr Bin Mohammed al-Qasimi, and his family, have not waited for the imminent oil revenues to begin the development of infrastructure and industry in the Emirate.

Sharja, Ras al-Khaima, Ajman, Umm al-Qaiwain and Fujaira all receive federal funds for development, but Ras al-Khaima in particular has protested that these are insufficient and that it has to raise loans from elsewhere.

8. Oman

The State (or Sultanate) of Oman extends over a territory of some 82,000 square miles of south-east Arabia. Trucial Oman, separated from the main area of the Sultanate, occupies the rugged highlands of the Ras Musandum peninsula. The remainder of the Sultanate extends for some 200 miles along the south Arabian coast to the borders of South Yemen, and stretches inland to the Rub al-Khali, the Empty Quarter.

Until recently the economy of the Sultanate was based simply upon pastoral nomadism, agriculture, and traditional trading in the Gulf and the Indian Ocean. In this traditional economy was reflected the regional diversity of generally rather limited resources.

On the Batina littoral small coastal plains support a series of equally small settlements dependent both on irrigation agriculture (in which date production is dominant) and fishing. Muscat, the capital city, owes its eminence to its long history as a safe harbour on a difficult coast and to the participation of its inhabitants in the millennia-old coastal sea-traffic. South of Muscat the littoral becomes increasingly inhospitable, cliffs and small embayments giving way to desertic lagoon and *sabkha*-fringed coastlands. Only in the southern province of Dhufar around Salala does sedentary agriculture reappear in the coastal lowland. Here water from the surrounding ranges of Jabal Qara, which receive monsoon rains, provides the basis for the largest concentration of farming population in the whole of the Sultanate. Population estimates vary widely. A 1975 estimate of 766,000 was increased in 1977 to an official estimate of 1.5 million. It is mainly concentrated in the Batina coastal plain, the Hajjar valleys around the capital and in Dhufar. The hinterland population is almost entirely Arab but in the Muscat-Matrah area there are substantial minorities of Indians, Pakistanis, and Baluchis, providing skilled workers and professionals.

In the interior, predominantly gravel desert capable of supporting only a very small population of bedouin tribesmen merges with the emptiness of the Rub al-Khali. West of Muscat however, between the desert and the sea, the land rises to the rugged Jabal Akhdhar ranges where precipitation is far higher than the otherwise normal annual total of some three or four inches. Still largely unknown outside the State of Oman this highland region has immemorially supported village farming populations on seasonally good pasture, rain-fed cereals, and a great range of other crops. This region, even more than the Batina coast lowlands and Dhufar, is orientated towards local and tribal subsistence rather than to the outside world.

The predominantly hostile environment of the Sultanate has impressed itself on the life of the people. Nomadism, traditionally dominant over most of the territory, is not normally associated with socio-economic stability, and the areas which do have sedentary settlements have been cut off from each other by the negative nature of the intervening wastelands and by the absence of sufficient wealth to overcome the natural difficulties.

Muscat and Dhufar, as with the port-towns of the Gulf, traditionally existed in the two worlds of the sea and the desert. Maritime influences were foreign for the most part until the eighteenth century. The mariners of the ancient world and of medieval Islam were succeeded by the Portuguese who established a naval and trading station at Muscat in 1508. In 1650 they were expelled by the local Arabs, whose regime grew in strength until by 1730 it had acquired the Portuguese possessions in East Africa, including Mombasa and Zanzibar. After a brief interlude of Iranian rule and a time of internal confusion, the Al Bu Said dynasty succeeded to these possessions and guided Muscat to the zenith of its power. The realm was divided (1861) among sons, Zanzibar and the East African possessions forming one Sultanate, Muscat and Oman the other. The present Sultan, Qabus ibn Said, is the fourteenth of his dynasty.

The majority of the inhabitants of Oman are adherents of the Ibadhi sect of Islam whose leader has normally (though not necessarily) been an elected Imam. The present dynasty was founded in 1744 by Imam Ahmad ibn Said who, himself an Ibadhi, expelled the Iranians from the territory. Two groups of tribes, the Ghafiris and the Hinawis, who inhabited an interior undemarcated by frontier lines, never completely accepted the authority of Imam Ahmad.

Imam Ahmad was succeeded on his death in 1783 by his son Said who, a year later, as a result of tribal pressure was supplanted as temporal leader by his own son Hamad, but who retained the religious functions of the Imamate.

Imam Ahmad ibn Said, himself a merchant and shipowner, had been responsible for the resurgence of Arab power on the coast. His grandson Hamad as secular ruler established his capital at the port of Muscat and henceforth the interior tribal centres such as Rostaq and Nizwa became secondary centres of power. Hamad and his successors adopted the title of Sayyid or Lord to distinguish themselves from Imam Said who retained his office until his death in 1821. The title Sultan was added at a later date by visiting Europeans. During the nineteenth century the differences between the dynastic rulers and the tribal factions became more and more associated with differences between the ocean-orientated coast and the desert and mountain interior. The struggle between the Sultanate and the Ghafiri and Hinawi was exacerbated by the intervention of the desert Wahhabis from what is now Saudi Arabia and the position was further complicated by dissension among the Ibadhis themselves. Wahhabi raids were to some extent controlled by British intervention from Egypt, intervention designed to minimize conflict in a region of growing importance to the Empire. Because the Pax Britannica involved the area in the problems of suppressing the slave trade and because it encouraged sea-trading, it tended to emphasize the secular aspects of Muscat rule; and as a result the Sultanate became even more alien and suspect to conservative religious zealots and even more vulnerable to ambitious tribal leaders. In 1895 Muscat was attacked and sacked by a temporary coalition of hostile interests. The true climax of conflict however was not reached until 1913 when the Ghafiri and Hinawi sank their differences for long enough to elect Salim ibn Rashid to the Imamate which effectively had been vacant since 1821.

A series of confused conflicts led to varying swings of fortune but the Sultanate retained control at Muscat and gradually events moved towards negotiation. Through the good offices of the British Political Agent in Muscat a number of tribal shaikhs and the Sultan's representatives met at Sib and an Agreement was signed in September 1920. The general authority of the Sultan in the territory of Oman was recognized in a variety of ways, particularly in external matters and in dealings with foreign administrations concerning law and questions of status. The Government of the Sultan of Oman has consistently maintained the view that the Agreement of Sib recognized the Imamate as autonomous only in the sphere of local and essentially socio-religious administration, and for some thirty years, during which the first oil concession was awarded, a reasonable *modus vivendi* existed between the Sultan and the shaikhs of the interior.

In the 1950s trouble arose over the classic problem of establishing formal frontier lines in relatively remote areas where tribal loyalties are dominant, and now sovereign states were involved as well as clan groupings – Saudi Arabia, Oman, and the Trucial States with their special relationship with Britain. The second factor was that of oil. Exploration during the early 1950s rapidly extended into the interior and by 1954 arrangements were being made with local tribes such as the Duru for geological operations. The area concerned lay one hundred and fifty miles west of Muscat and relatively near to Nizwa, the headquarters of Imam Ghalib ibn Ali elected in 1954 by a group of shaikhs mainly of the Hinawi. Maintaining that he and not the Sultan held sway in the interior region, Ghalib challenged the validity of the oil concession, sent levies into Duru territory and applied for membership and recognition by the Arab League. The Sultan successfully ejected Ghalib's forces from Ibri, the principal Duru town. Another operation, in conjunction with the ruler of Abu Dhabi, led to the re-occupation of the part of the Buraimi Oasis complex which had been seized by a Saudi Arabian raiding party. In 1957 the Imam Ghalib and his brother Talib re-emerged in central Oman with a band of followers to renew their challenge to the Sultan with the diplomatic and financial support of several Arab states including Saudi Arabia and Egypt. The Sultan for the first time formally requested British treaty aid, and the Trucial Oman Scouts and a few hundred British troops with air support assisted the Sultan's forces in suppressing the rebellion. However, the Arab states continued to challenge what they regarded as the British colonial presence in Oman and called for the elimination of British domination in any form.

The situation was radically transformed by the discovery of oil in commercial quantities and the first exports in June 1967. In January 1968, as State revenues began to increase, the Sultan made a statement in which preliminary investment plans were announced publicly for the first time, and it was proposed to create a Development Council with budgetary, planning, and implementation responsibilities. But Sultan Said ibn Taimur was in favour of keeping social and economic change to a snail's pace. Three years after oil revenues began rising the Sultanate, with an estimated population of between 750,000 and a million still had only three primary schools with about 100 pupils. There was one hospital at Matrah (belonging to an American Protestant mission) and a score of dispensaries in various parts of the country in the charge of a handful of doctors, dealing with a population ridden with a variety of endemic diseases such as malaria, leprosy, tuberculosis, and trachoma. Infant mortality was among the highest in the world (80 per cent according to one estimate).

The Sultan's rule was autocratic and authoritarian in the extreme. He personally issued all visas which were kept severely restricted. Government officials and all women were only allowed to leave the country with special permission. He forbade the inhabitants of the interior to visit the coastal areas and vice versa. The only surfaced road was the few miles between Muscat and Matrah. Dancing, smoking, and the playing of musical instruments were all forbidden. Three hours after dusk the gates of Muscat were closed and no one could leave or enter until dawn.

Said ibn Taimur was gifted, intelligent, and of considerable personal charm, but the extreme reactionary nature of his rule stimulated opposition and alarmed his fellow rulers of Arabia, who saw that it encouraged subversion. Apart from the continuing sporadic insurrection of the followers of the ex-Imam Ghalib, a Dhufar Liberation Movement started in 1965 in the southernmost province and became increasingly radical with active Chinese support. The Sultan, however, remained almost continuously in Salala on the coast of Dhufar, relying for protection on his army, the Sultan's Armed Forces (SAF), which was commanded by British officers on secondment with a number of Pakistani NCOs.

Said ibn Taimur was overthrown on 23 July 1970 in a palace coup led by his only son Qabus ibn Said who since his return from being educated in England had been kept virtually under house arrest by his father. Amid great public rejoicing Sultan Qabus undertook to introduce 'modern and forceful' government and announced the removal of his father's ban on smoking, dancing, and the wearing of Western dress. His uncle Tariq ibn Taimur returned from exile to head the new Government. The revolutionary opposition was divided in its attitude to the new Sultan. Some declared their loyalty but others described him as an imperialist puppet. Nearly all the

British officers and Government officials remained in the service of Sultan Qabus. The war against the Dhufar Liberation Front was pursued and military expenditure absorbed about half the oil revenues of approximately £50 million.

Sultan Qabus's succession transformed the situation. Oman's isolation ended as it became a member of the UN and the Arab League in 1971. A massive social and economic development programme was launched in which earlier tentative developments were accelerated and a wide range of new projects initiated. The rebellion of the Dhufar guerrilla movement, which now called itself the Popular Front for the Liberation of Oman (PFLO) and was supported by the Chinese and the PDRY, was a severe drain on resources. The Sultan accepted the aid of some 3,000 Iranian forces in addition to the few hundred British airmen and soldiers. By early 1976 the rebellion was virtually over although the PFLO continued to issue defiant communiqués from Aden and occasional guerrilla attacks still occurred.

The departure of the Shah of Iran in January 1979 was a cause of severe anxiety to the Omani regime. The Iranian troops were withdrawn and were partially replaced by a contingent of Egyptian commandos.

The Economy

Oil output by Petroleum Development Oman (60 per cent Oman, 34 per cent Shell, CFP 4 per cent, Partex 2 per cent) from the three interior fields of Yibal, Fahud and Natih rose rapidly to 360,000 b.p.d. in 1969, and has since remained at this level or in some years declined. Without the discovery of major new fields Oman has no prospect of expansion. New discoveries in the Dhufar province in 1977 and 1978 raised hopes of maintaining output as the northern fields decline.

On the other hand Oman is relatively rich in other materials. The best prospects are for copper, and production from mines near Sohar by a US/Canadian group is expected to reach 20,000 tons a year of refined copper in the early 1980s. The presence of large chrome deposits was confirmed in 1978 and these could turn out to be equally important. Other minerals include lead/zinc, asbestos, high quality limestone, manganese, and coal.

Since the accession of Sultan Qabus development has proceeded rapidly. The virtual absence of an economic infrastructure meant that this had to be the first priority. New seaports and airports have been built at Matrah and a system of roads (3,500 miles in 1976 compared with three miles of asphalted road in 1970) now links Muscat-Matrah with Salala in Dhufar, with the interior and with both Abu Dhabi (at Buraimi) and Fujaira in the UAE. A crash programme in education and health services increased the 900 pupils in three schools in 1970 to 55,800 pupils in 207 schools by 1975/76, and the handful of rural clinics and dispensaries to two main hospitals, 22 other hospitals or health centres, and 40 dispensaries.

High development and military expenditure exceeded oil revenues (currently about $1,400 million) in the early 1970s and the deficits were covered by drawings on deposits with banks, and foreign grants and loans. Development planning is now more cautious and places greater emphasis on income-generating projects. A co-ordinated five-year development plan for 1976–80 envisaged a 3 per cent annual growth in GNP at 1976 constant prices. The plan's most ambitious target is a 164 per cent increase in agricultural output by 1980 with increase in the cultivated area from 36,000 hectares to 120,000 hectares, with crops of dates rising from 176,000 tons to 320,000 tons, limes 14,000 tons to 24,000 tons, bananas 9,000 tons to 24,000 tons, and equivalent increases for other fruit and vegetables and livestock. A widespread rural electricifation scheme was due for completion in 1979. A few light industries already exist and several more are planned. Foreign participation in a local company cannot exceed 65 per cent but there is a five-year tax holiday if the company is regarded as a development project.

Imports, especially capital goods and consumer durables, have been increasing very rapidly. In 1977 they rose to $874 million from $723 million in 1976. Non-oil exports remain very small; and since oil exports are not expected to increase, Oman's best prospects for an improvement in its balance of payments position is a reduction in military expenditure which has been made possible by the ending of the Dhufar war.

III

EGYPT

THE LAND AND THE PEOPLE

Egypt is about the same size as Spain and France with an area of 363,000 square miles. Of these, only 13,000 square miles, consisting mainly of the Nile valley, are cultivable and inhabitable; the rest is desert.

The Nile valley consists of:

(*a*) Lower Egypt, being the Nile Delta with its apex at Cairo and its base the Mediterranean coast between Alexandria and Port Said.

(*b*) Upper Egypt, being a strip of irrigated land in the Nile valley averaging about 20 miles wide, and stretching from Cairo to the Sudan frontier at Wadi Halfa.

The area of cultivation is divided about equally between Upper and Lower Egypt.

Apart from the Nile valley, there is the Canal Zone, consisting of a narrow strip of land some 100 miles long made cultivable and inhabitable by the Sweet Water Canal, by which drinking and irrigation water is brought across the desert from the Nile. There are also the five oases – Kharga, Dakhla, Farafra, Bahriya, and Siwa.

Egypt lies between latitude 32° N. on the Mediterranean coast, and 22°N. at Wadi Halfa. In Upper Egypt there is virtually no rainfall; in the Delta there is a slight winter rainfall which gradually increases towards the Mediterranean coast. Cultivation, and indeed the possibility of any life at all, in Egypt is entirely dependent on the Nile which rises in flood between July and October. Egypt has a hot summer from May to October when the average midday temperatures are about 105 °F (40.6 °C) in Upper Egypt and 94 °F (34.4 °C) in Lower Egypt. In early summer, a south wind (*khamsin*) is frequent, accompanied by sandstorms. At other times of the year the prevailing wind is north-west. In late summer, during the Nile floods, humidity is high. The winter climate, from November to April, is temperate in both Upper and Lower Egypt. In Alexandria and along the Mediterranean coast the rainfall is heavier and the climate generally is that of the eastern Mediterranean basin.

Population

The population at the time of the last official census in 1960 was 26,080,000 (compared with 22,924,000 in 1956 and 19,021,840 in 1947).

Sample censuses gave population estimates of 30.8 million in mid-1966 and 38 million in mid-1976. Between 1960 and 1978 the average annual growth rate was about 2.4 per cent. The crude death rate has declined from 22 per thousand in 1952 to 17 per thousand in 1957 and 14.4 per thousand in 1972, while the crude birth rate has fallen from about 44 per thousand in 1946 to 34.1 in 1972.

Of the total population in 1970, 38.6 per cent lived in towns compared with 37.9 per cent in 1960. The urban population is rapidly increasing as the agricultural area fails to absorb the growing rural population which flocks to the cities in search of work. Greater Cairo's population was estimated in 1976 at 8.8 million. The trend towards urbanization will increase and the official projection is that by 1985 the total population will be nearly 54 million of which more than half will be living in the cities.

Owing to the continuation of the state of war in the Canal Zone much of the population of its cities was evacuated. This trend has now largely been reversed. Official 1976 estimation of the population of the Cairo Governate was 6.1 million (compared with 4.2 million in 1966); of the Alexandria Governate 2.4 million (1.8 million in 1966); Giza 2.36 million (571,000 in 1966); Minia 1.96 million (1.7 million in 1966); Assiut 1.58 million (1.42 million in 1966); Aswan 750,000 (521,000 in 1966); Ismailia 464,000 (345,000 in 1966); Port Said 356,000 (283,000 in 1966); Suez 395,000 (264,000 in 1966).

About 90 per cent of Egyptians are Sunni Moslems mostly of the Hanafi rite and Islam is the official religion of the State. Of the remainder the largest minority consists of about 3–4 million Copts who are racially the purest descendants of the ancient Egyptians. There are also about a quarter of a million Egyptians belonging to various other Christian communities.

HISTORY AND POLITICS

During the first 3,000 years of known Egyptian history, thirty Pharaonic dynasties followed one another, and Egyptian civilization and the colossal monuments which marked its evolution became widely known. At length disintegration and decay set in, and the Pharaohs of the last four dynasties occupied their thrones under Persian domination (525–332 BC).

In 332 BC Alexander the Great conquered the country from the Persians. He founded a Greek Empire in Egypt and for the next 300 years successive Ptolemaic kings, descended from his general Ptolemy Soter, held their Graeco-Egyptian courts in Alexandria. Their rule ended with the deaths of Cleopatra and Mark Antony in 30 BC, and Egypt became a province of the Roman Empire. When the Roman Empire was divided between East and West 400 years later, Egypt became part of the East Roman (Byzantine) Empire. In AD 640 the Arab conquest ended Byzantine domination and absorbed Egypt in the Umayyad Empire. Subsequently, after a period of semi-independence under the nominal rule of the Abbasids, Egypt became the centre of the Fatimite dynasty, which founded Cairo. Towards the end of the eleventh century AD Egypt was conquered by Salah al-Din al-Ayyubi (Saladin), and it was ruled for the next 400 years by a series of military oligarchies, known collectively as the Mamelukes. The period of Mameluke rule, which lasted until the Ottoman conquest in 1517, was notable both for military glory and for artistic achievement. (The Mamelukes finally expelled the Crusaders from Syria and it was under Mameluke rule that most of the remaining architectural glories of Cairo were created.) Under Ottoman rule the Mamelukes were reduced to the position of domestic tyrants who were, however, allowed to do much as they pleased in Egypt so long as they paid an annual tribute to Constantinople. Under the conditions of oppressive and inefficient government which prevailed, Egypt was reduced to the lowest depths of economic and cultural decay.

Mohammed Ali and His Successors

The history of modern Egypt really began with the invasion of Egypt by Bonaparte in 1798. The French were driven out in 1801 by an alliance of British and Turkish forces and a short British occupation followed. An Albanian soldier named Mohammed Ali, who came to Egypt with the Turkish forces to help in expelling the French, remained after the British defeat and withdrawal to seize supreme power in Egypt, to smash the tyranny of the Mamelukes, and to be recognized by the Sultan as Viceroy of Egypt (1805). Under the nominal suzerainty of the Sultan, Mohammed Ali added the northern part of the Sudan to Egypt by conquest, subdued the Wahhabis in Arabia, and shared his suzerain's defeat in the Greek War of Independence, losing the Egyptian fleet at the Battle of Navarino. The vassal in due course rebelled against his suzerain and, after occupying Syria, provoked European intervention by marching on Constantinople, thus threatening the integrity of the Ottoman Empire. This European intervention, in which British participation was the decisive factor, resulted in the withdrawal of Mohammed Ali's forces from Asia Minor and Syria and in his formal submission to the Sultan, who, at British instigation, confirmed him and his successors in the viceroyalty of Egypt and the Sudan (1840).

The lasting results of Mohammed Ali's rule were seen not in his international adventures but in his administration of Egypt. Egypt's contacts with the West have been continuous since Bonaparte's invasion and the fruitful development of these contacts was initially due to Mohammed Ali. He used European technical experts but avoided the mistake his successors made, of becoming either subject to European political influences or indebted to European bankers. With their technical assistance and the proceeds of cotton exports, which he was the first to develop, he executed irrigation works, introduced railways and telegraph lines, organized the machinery of government in the form of state departments, created schools for engineering, medicine, and other purposes, started industries and reorganized Egypt's armed forces. Among Mohammed Ali's notable public works are the great Nile Barrage at the apex of the delta and its corollary canals of which the Mahmudia Canal between the Nile and Alexandria is one. Besides providing drinking-water for Alexandria, it enabled goods to and from the interior to pass through Alexandria, and this, together with the reconstruction of the port, revived some of Alexandria's former glories.

Mohammed Ali died in 1849. During his 45 years of rule the cultivated area of Egypt had increased from about 3 million to about 4 million feddans. The population had grown from about 2½ million to about 4½ million, government revenue had increased from about £1 million to about £4 million per annum, and exports had risen from an average annual value of about £200,000 to over £2 million. Much of Mohammed Ali's modernization had been achieved through high taxation and a considerable use of forced labour, but when he died Egypt was still politically independent (except for the nominal suzerainty of the Sultan) and had no foreign debt. Mohammed Ali was succeeded for a few years by his grandson, Abbas, and then by Said, who gave de Lesseps the concession for the Suez Canal. (Mohammed Ali, although devoted to modernization, was opposed to the project for a Suez Canal, realizing perhaps that it would jeopardize Egypt's independence.) In 1863 Said was succeeded by Ismail, who confirmed the Suez Canal concession. As a result of wild personal extravagance and of an undiscriminating passion for modernization, Ismail within a few years pledged Egypt's credit, mostly to European bankers, to the extent of nearly £100 million. The growing realization of the commercial and strategic importance of the Suez Canal, the anxiety of the European bankers about the security of their loans, and the growth of the European population in Egypt, all tended to increase European interest in Egypt, and that led first to interference and finally to control.

Since Egypt was still a part of the Ottoman Empire, European communities in Egypt were living under the Ottoman Capitulations.[1] Increased European interests in Egypt, and

[1] See above, p. 11.

particularly European ownership of immovable property, resulted in 1875 in the creation of the Mixed Courts for the settlement of disputes between foreigners and Egyptians, and between foreigners of different nationalities.

The British Occupation

Ismail's growing indebtedness led to forcible intervention by the European Powers, particularly Britain and France who, by 1879, had virtually assumed control of Egypt's finances and in that year prevailed on the Sultan to depose Ismail, in favour of his more amenable son, Tawfiq. In 1882 a military revolt, caused by dislike of foreign interference and particularly of a reduction of the army establishment as a measure of economy, resulted in a British occupation of Egypt in order to crush the revolt, reinstate Tawfiq, and retain European influence over Egypt's heavily pledged finances. For domestic political reasons the French abstained at the last moment from taking part in this occupation.

The army revolt in Egypt coincided with a revolt in the Sudan against Egyptian rule. After the occupation the British insisted on the temporary abandonment of the Sudan; Gordon's death in Khartoum in 1885 marked the end of this process.

The British, who were now *de facto* rulers of Egypt, were compelled by the suspicions of other European Powers, who considered Egypt as being under the joint trusteeship of the Great Powers, to act primarily on behalf not of the people of Egypt but of Egypt's European creditors. They had to retain the complicated apparatus of international control and to regard as their primary task the rehabilitation of Egypt's finances for the servicing of her foreign debts.

Sir Evelyn Baring (later Lord Cromer), the first British Agent and Consul-General, was in fact ruler of Egypt from 1883 to 1907. During these years irrigation works were actively developed, the army reorganized, the Sudan reconquered; and, in general, the country brought back from bankruptcy to solvency.

Egyptian nationalism, which had first appeared during the army rebellion of 1882[2] and had been temporarily crushed

[2]See above, p. 13.

as a result of the British occupation, began to manifest itself again towards the end of Cromer's tenure of office. This nationalism was directed against both the throne and the British. (Since 1892, when Tawfiq died, the throne had been occupied by his son, Abbas Hilmi, who, unlike Tawfiq, was on bad terms with the British.)

Cromer was succeeded in 1907 by Sir Eldon Gorst, whose three years of office saw a move towards representative government, and also of nationalist terrorism in 1910 when Butrus Ghali, the Prime Minister, unpopular both for his Coptic religion and for co-operation with the British, was assassinated. In 1911 Gorst was succeeded by Lord Kitchener.

When war broke out between Britain and Turkey in November 1914, the anomalous situation of Egypt as a province of the Ottoman Empire was regularized by its being declared a British Protectorate. Abbas Hilmi, who was pro-Turkish, was deposed and succeeded by his uncle Hussein Kamil, who died in 1917 and was succeeded by his brother, Ahmad Fuad.

When the war ended in 1918, Egyptian nationalist feeling, which had been repressed by the restrictions and uncertainties of war, was now fired by Wilson's Fourteen Points and by the prospect of the liberation of the Ottoman subject peoples and burst into active life. Saad Zaghlul came forward as the leader of Egyptian nationalism. He first came into prominence a few days after the Armistice when he headed a deputation, or *wafd*, to Sir Reginald Wingate, the British High Commissioner (the title of the British representative since the declaration of the Protectorate), demanding that he and his deputation should be allowed to go to London to present Egypt's demands. The demand was refused and there followed three years of demonstrations, riots, and assassinations, tempered by negotiations during the course of which Wingate was succeeded as High Commissioner by Lord Allenby. During this period Egypt's demands crystallized in the slogan 'Complete independence for Egypt and the Sudan'. The British Government, once convinced of the need to make some concession to Egyptian nationalism, envisaged a treaty of alliance which would reserve to Britain what were then regarded as the essentials of the British position in Egypt. In November 1922 the problem was temporarily resolved on their terms by a unilateral British Declaration which conferred sovereign independence on Egypt subject to the retention of full British responsibility for (*a*) the security of the communications of the British Empire in Egypt; (*b*) the defence of Egypt against all foreign aggression and interference, direct or indirect; (*c*) the protection of foreign interests in Egypt and the protection of minorities; (*d*) the Sudan.

Politics and Anglo-Egyptian Relations, 1923–52

On the basis of this Declaration an Egyptian Constitution was promulgated in 1923 and Ahmad Fuad, who had taken the title of Sultan, now became King Fuad I of Egypt. The first elections brought Zaghlul to power as Prime Minister, but his tenure of office was brief. His encouragement of nationalist agitation caused anti-British terrorism to flare up again, the most important victim being Sir Lee Stack, Governor-General of the Sudan and Commanders-in-Chief of the Egyptian army, who was murdered in Cairo. The British Government demanded an indemnity and an apology and the withdrawal of all Egyptian forces from the Sudan, and laid down the right to increase at will the quantity of Nile water used for irrigation in the Sudan at the expense of Egypt (this clause was in fact never invoked). Zaghlul and his Government resigned.

The forces of nationalism in Egypt were now becoming diverted by a struggle for power between on the one side Zaghlul (and later his successor Nahas) and the Wafd, and on the other side the King, together with such supporters as he could detach from the Wafd. This rivalry enabled the precarious basis on which Anglo-Egyptian relations had been poised in 1922 to last until 1936.

In 1925 Allenby was succeeded as High Commissioner by Lord Lloyd; in 1927, on Zaghlul's death, Mustafa Nahas became leader of the Wafd. Between 1927 and 1930 there was a series of abortive negotiations between the British Government and successive Egyptian Governments for a treaty to place their relations on a firmer basis. In 1930 Fuad dismissed Nahas, who was then Prime Minister, and replaced him by Ismail Sidqi, who abolished the 1923 Constitution and launched Egypt on a term of autocratic government. Since this administration was reasonably competent by Egyptian standards and considerably better than the misgovernment of the Wafd, the attempt of autocracy might well have succeeded but for the insensate greed of the King and of his entourage, and for the growing international importance of Egypt as a result of Mussolini's ambitions in East Africa. These factors brought about a united front of Egyptian politicians, determined on the one hand to check the royal power and on the other to use the international situation to obtain a fuller measure of independence from Britain. A coalition Government was formed, the 1923 Constitution was restored, and negotiations were opened with Britain.

In view of Mussolini's ambitions and the growing menace of war, the British Government urgently wished to establish such relations with Egypt as to guarantee a friendly country as a base in the event of war. The Egyptian Government for its part realized that it was a choice between Britain and Italy; King Fuad's ardent Italophile sentiments worked strongly in favour of Britain.

In the 1936 Anglo-Egyptian Treaty Britain abandoned one of the four points reserved in the 1922 Declaration: the protection of foreign interests in Egypt and the protection of minorities, but retained the other three: imperial communications, defence of Egypt, and the future of the Sudan. A convention signed at Montreux in 1937, on British initiative, abolished the Capitulations and set a term to the existence of the Mixed Courts.

The rights retained by Britain under the treaty were made more palatable to Egypt by arrangements (*a*) to remove British forces from Cairo and Alexandria to the Canal Zone; (*b*) to allow virtually unrestricted immigration into the Sudan; and (*c*) to sponsor Egypt for membership of the League of Nations.

The treaty was concluded in August 1936. In April, immediately after the death of Fuad, there had been elections which returned the Wafd with a large majority. Farouk was a minor, and Nahas, at the time of the treaty and for about two years thereafter, was both Prime Minister and head of the Regency Council.

Farouk attained his majority in 1938 and the struggle between Palace and Wafd was renewed. It was interrupted by the outbreak of the Second World War: under the terms of the 1936 treaty Britain, behind the façade of the Government of the day, was now in a position to exercise almost supreme power in Egypt. It was, however, important that the governmental façade should be co-operative, and the successive Palace-inspired governments of the first two years of war became increasingly unsatisfactory in this respect by reason of the pro-Italian influence of the Palace and of the effect of the Axis victories. In February 1941 Lord Killearn, the British Ambassador (the title of the British representative after the 1936 treaty), presented an ultimatum to Farouk demanding the replacement of the Cabinet by Nahas and a Wafdist Government. This change was effected and Nahas worked in co-operation with the British until October 1944 when he was dismissed by the King. By then the tide of war had receded from the Middle East and the British Government no longer needed to interfere in Egyptian domestic politics. Moreover Nahas's increasing tendency to corruption deprived him of a claim to British support.

Elections were held in January 1945 as a result of which the new Prime Minister, Ahmad Maher, and the Saadist Party (whose leaders had split off from the Wafd in 1938) were confirmed in power. In April 1945 the new Government declared war on Germany – a step postponed until then on British advice. Probably as a result of this Ahmad Maher was assassinated. He was succeeded as Prime Minister and party leader by Mahmud Noqrashi.

Nationalist feeling soon began to demand a revision of the 1936 treaty, although it was not due for revision until 1956. The aim was the withdrawal of British forces from Egypt and the union of the Sudan with the Egyptian Crown. Under heavy pressure from the Wafd Opposition, from the press, and from the usual student demonstrators, the Egyptian Government, while maintaining a correct and even friendly attitude, endeavoured to induce the British Government to come some way towards meeting nationalist demands. The British Government was slow to respond and it was not until 1947 that British forces were withdrawn from Cairo and Alexandria to the Canal Zone area.

In February 1946 the Noqrashi Government fell, mainly

through inability to deal with student demonstrations, and was replaced by a Government formed by Ismail Sidqi. He was able to reach a provisional agreement by which the British would evacuate the Canal Zone in return for a suspension of the Egyptian demand for union between Egypt and the Sudan, the future of the Sudan being left for future negotiations. Final agreement was not reached, mainly because of intrigues against Sidqi by the Palace and by his political rivals. Sidqi resigned and Noqrashi took his place.

In the summer of 1947 Noqrashi brought Egypt's case against Britain before the Security Council of the United Nations. His presentation of the case was designed rather to appease the mounting nationalist feeling in Egypt than to convince the Security Council of the rightness of his cause. As a result, Britain and Egypt were merely adjured by the Security Council to resume direct negotiations.

Meanwhile other matters were beginning to claim the attention of politicians and people in Egypt. Ever since the formation of the Arab League, adherence to which had been Nahas's last political act in October 1944, the problem of the future of Palestine had been dominating the minds of the Arab world, in which Egypt played an important and, at least in her own opinion, the leading part. During the winter of 1947–8, when Egypt's normal unreadiness for war was accentuated by a cholera epidemic and by rising economic discontent, it gradually became apparent that Britain would be relinquishing the Palestine mandate and in effect leaving the Arabs and Jews to fight it out. With effect from May 1948 Britain formally terminated the mandate; the State of Israel was proclaimed and was recognized by the United States, followed closely by the Soviet Union. Almost simultaneously the Egyptian and other Arab armies invaded Israel, and Egypt's humiliating performance in the Palestine War, owing mainly to military unpreparedness and domestic corruption, was precariously terminated by an armistice.

The disasters of the Palestine War brought to a head domestic discontent resulting in the first place from post-war inflation, and in the second from governmental incompetence and corruption and particularly the growing corruption and profligacy of the Court, which for the first time exposed the King to widespread and barely-veiled criticism.

The principal outward expression of this discontent was the growing influence and numbers of the Moslem Brotherhood, which had started as a reactionary and obscurantist religious society in the early 1930s and had now become a fanatical, ultra-nationalist, and terrorist organization. The Brotherhood had probably been responsible for the assassination of Ahmad Maher and other statesmen and officials and certainly for the murder of Noqrashi in December 1948.

There was also a clandestine revolutionary movement within the army later known as the 'Free Officers', which had been patiently organized since the early 1940s by Captain Gamal Abdul Nasser, an instructor at the Military Academy in Cairo.

Noqrashi was succeeded by Ibrahim Abdul Hadi, who set himself ruthlessly to the task of crushing the Moslem Brotherhood as a serious threat to organized government. He succeeded in this for the moment, but he was unable even to alleviate the underlying causes of discontent. This discontent resulted in the return of the Wafd to power at elections held in January 1950. Hopes built on the Wafd's election propaganda about social reform were disappointed. It appeared that the Wafd and the Palace had ended their old feud by a 'gentleman's agreement' to live and let live, each conniving at the corruption and incompetence of the other.

This was the situation when the Korean War boom in cotton prices ended in 1951. Corrupt manipulation of the market during and after the boom by the Government and the big exporters, with the connivance of Farouk, helped to turn a natural decline of prices into a disaster causing unemployment, bankruptcies, and acute budget and balance-of-payments difficulties. The Wafd Government soon found it convenient to divert the growing discontent from itself to the British. On 15 October 1951 the 1936 treaty, as well as the Condominium agreement about the Sudan,[3] was abrogated by the unanimous vote of the Egyptian Parliament. A proposal had been made by the Western Powers to Egypt on 13 October 1951 that she should join a Middle East Defence Organization as an equal partner with Britain, France, the United States, and Turkey. This proposal was rejected by the Egyptian

[3] See below, p. 468.

Government which insisted on the immediate and unconditional withdrawal of British forces from the Canal Zone and on the union of the Sudan with Egypt.

A state of virtual guerrilla warfare broke out in the Canal Zone and the Egyptian Government succeeded, by a mixture of propaganda and intimidation, in withdrawing the whole Egyptian labour force from the Zone. With anti-British propaganda at full blast in the press and on the radio, with government-encouraged recruitment of students and roughs in 'liberation units' to fight in the Canal Zone, and with tens of thousands of unemployed workmen from the Canal Zone roaming the streets of Cairo, an explosion could hardly be long delayed. The explosion, when it came, was touched off by forcible British action at Ismailia to disarm a battalion of auxiliary police which had been indulging in hostile acts against the British. A number of auxiliary policemen were killed, and the next morning, 26 January 1952, rioting broke out in Cairo. Although these riots started as anti-British and although twelve Britons were murdered in Cairo, the violence soon turned to indiscriminate looting of the prosperous in the course of which much damage was done and many lives were lost. In the late afternoon order was restored by the army on instructions from the King after the Government had failed to cope with the situation. The following night the King dismissed the Nahas Government from power for inability to maintain order.

The 1952 Revolution

The regime was now in a state of collapse and it was an open secret that there was grave discontent in the army against the Palace.

At the beginning of July the Prime Minister attempted to appease the army by asking the King to approve the appointment of Brigadier Mohammed Neguib, a prominent critic of the regime who was brought in by the Free Officers to head their movement early in 1952, as Minister of War. Farouk refused and demanded the appointment of a relative of his instead.

On the night of 23 July 1952 the Free Officers, at the head of a few battalions of troops, seized Cairo and the administration without resistance or bloodshed, and, within a few days, dismissed the Government, secured the abdication and departure from Egypt of Farouk, established a Regency Council for Farouk's infant son, and arranged for a new government under the premiership of Ali Maher.

The Free Officers' junta was virtually the same as their executive council of 1949 consisting of Gamal Abdul Nasser, Kamal al-Din Hussein, Abdul Hakim Amer, Hassan Ibrahim, Abdul Moneim Abdul Raouf, Salah and Gamal Salem, Abdul Latif al-Baghdadi, Khalid Mohieddin, and Anwar Sadat. Zakariya Mohieddin and Hussein al-Shafei now joined to form what they decided to call the Revolutionary Command Council (RCC). Neguib was President although the fiction of a monarchical constitution was maintained for the time being by the appointment of a Regency Council.

The Free Officers knew what they wanted to destroy in Egypt – the monarchy, the power of the landlords, foreign influence, and the corruption of political life – and they had a vision of the kind of society that they wanted a truly independent Egypt to become. But they had never had time to acquire the political techniques to make the vision a reality. They had had contacts with the Moslem Brotherhood and a few of them were sympathizers; Khalid Mohieddin was a Marxist but the great majority had no political ideology or affiliation.

The Free Officers had the alternative of ruling themselves or leaving the task to the traditional political parties after eliminating the monarchy. It was soon apparent that only the first alternative would enable them to carry through the reforms they wanted. They struck out alternately at left and right. On 12 August the workers in one of Egypt's largest spinning mills seized control of the factory. Fearing this might lead to workers' uprisings throughout the country the Junta occupied the mill, arrested some 200 workers and hanged two of the leading agitators. In September the RCC introduced its first important radical measure – agrarian reform. Land holdings were reduced to 200 feddans and agricultural rents were compulsorily reduced. The measure was far from revolutionary or Marxist and the redistribution only affected 10 per cent of the cultivated area, but it significantly reduced the political power of the large landowners which was its main purpose. When Ali Maher objected to the measure he was removed from the premiership and replaced by Neguib.

The Wafd Party was a potential threat to the regime but it was easily outmanoeuvred by Nasser's tactical skill. In January 1953 all political parties were abolished and their funds confiscated. Neguib announced the formation of Egypt's new political organization, the 'National Liberation Rally' and on 10 February a Provisional Constitution was promulgated which placed supreme authority for three years in the hands of the RCC. On 18 June 1953 the Egyptian Republic was formally proclaimed and the monarchy abolished along with the titles of 'bey' and 'pasha'. The property of the ex-King and his family was confiscated and the proceeds, estimated at £70 million, were earmarked for social development. Neguib became President and Prime Minister, and Colonel Nasser Deputy Premier and Minister of the Interior. In September a Revolutionary Tribunal was set up to try prominent figures of the old regime.

A division between Neguib and the rest of the RCC soon appeared. Neguib was nearly twenty years older than their average age and conservative by temperament. He did not understand collective leadership and believed he had been chosen to lead. He clashed with the Junta on several matters of policy and tended towards the view that civilian political life should be restored.

Neguib was politically maladroit but his strength lay in his popularity with the masses, who looked on him as a father figure. When Neguib resigned on 23 February the RCC at first accepted his resignation but was obliged to reverse the decision because of pro-Neguib sympathies in the army which were stimulated for his own purposes by the Marxist Khalid Mohieddin. But although Neguib had apparently recovered his power, in the following months Nasser succeeded in consolidating his own position in the army, police, and trade unions. He also manoeuvred Neguib into a position of responsibility for a restoration of political parties which was highly unpopular with the army. On 17 April 1954 Neguib in effect capitulated. Nasser became Prime Minister and the RCC was given a new lease of life. Neguib's power was broken, he lingered on as President for six months until the revelation of his association with the Moslem Brotherhood which had attempted to assassinate Nasser enabled the RCC to remove him from the presidency.

The power of the politicians had been broken with little difficulty in the first year of the Revolution but there remained two groups which caused the RCC concern – the Moslem Brotherhood and the Communists. The former, with its organization and terrorist wing, was the more formidable. The attempt on Nasser's life on 26 October 1954 by a poor workman who accused the Brotherhood leaders of having instigated him gave Nasser the opportunity to suppress the Brotherhood's organization by closing its branches and confiscating its arms.

While heavily involved in the struggle to consolidate his regime Nasser had never lost sight of his primary goal – the withdrawal of British forces from Egypt. The first obstacle was overcome with the Anglo-Egyptian agreement on the Sudan of February 1953 – the RCC having previously reached agreement with all the Sudanese political parties on the principle of Sudanese self-determination. Although the pro-Egyptian party won the subsequent Sudanese elections the Egyptians' hopes that the Sudan would opt for union with Egypt on gaining full independence were not realized. But a Sudanese settlement left the way open for a final agreement with Britain.

On 27 July, after several weeks of hard bargaining, Heads of Agreement were initialled providing (*a*) for the evacuation of all British forces from Egypt within twenty months; (*b*) for all British bases in the Canal Zone to remain activated and to be operated and maintained by British civilian contractors for a period of seven years; (*c*) for Britain to reoccupy the Canal Zone with Egypt's agreement in the event of an armed attack by any outside power on Egypt, or any other country which was a party to the Arab Treaty of Joint Defence, or Turkey. The agreement was signed on 19 October 1954.

Nasser in Power

Two years after the Revolution, Nasser had achieved many of his aims: a British military withdrawal, the abolition of the monarchy and the former political system, and land reform and the breaking up of the big estates. But this did not mean that henceforth he would concentrate on Egypt's internal problems of social and economic development. Partly through circumstances and partly by inclination he was increasingly immersed in foreign affairs. Domestic problems were not entirely neglected. After the Revolution the regime began to build schools and rural health centres much faster than before but resources were limited – especially with the conservative financial policies pursued by the regime in its early years. The Government began to place its main hopes for rapid development on the building of a High Dam at Aswan.

Two things in particular diverted Nasser's attention from home affairs along lines which were to become established – the Israeli-Arab problem and Western efforts to set up an anti-Soviet Middle East defence organization.

At first Nasser paid little attention to the Arab-Israeli dispute in which he could rightly be described as a moderate. But in 1955 the situation at the Israeli-Egyptian armistice line became highly explosive. From the Gaza Strip under Egyptian protection Arabs were crossing singly or in small groups on raiding expeditions and the Israelis responded with their usual heavy 'punishment raids'. As the situation worsened the Egyptian army and civilians demanded retaliation. Nasser could not ignore these demands although he knew the Egyptian forces were quite unprepared for a 'second round' with Israel. His response was to allow *fedayeen* (commandos or saboteurs) to penetrate deep into Israel. This brought heavier retaliation but it achieved Nasser's main purpose of avoiding full-scale war. At the same time he began to consider the need for a full-scale rearmament of Egypt's forces.

The second main problem confronting Nasser in 1955 concerned the other most powerful independent Arab state – Iraq – and its strong-minded leader and elder statesman, Nuri Said. At this time Nasser still had little interest in ideas of Arab nationalism or Arab unity but he did feel tied to the other Arabic-speaking states by their common history (see his *The Philosophy of the Revolution*, 1954). It was therefore a disaster in Nasser's eyes that Nuri should be the chief friend and ally of the Western imperialist powers in the Middle East.

There was rivalry between Egypt and Iraq, which had historical origins, for leadership of the Arab world. But in 1954 Nasser made several attempts to reach an understanding with Nuri. The Iraqi leader wanted Iraq and as many of the independent Arab states as possible to join a Middle East defence organization which had been initiated by the US Government but for which the Eden Government of Britain had now taken over the chief responsibility. Nasser was strongly opposed because he foresaw that this would tie all the Arabs to the West through the Arab Collective Security Pact (of which Iraq was a member). Nasser still believed that Nuri would wait for the Arab League Foreign Ministers' Conference to discuss the matter and was taken by surprise when a Turkish-Iraqi agreement was announced in January 1955.

This was the nucleus of the Baghdad Pact which was the principal subject of inter-Arab divisions in 1955–8. Cairo's press and radio at once launched an offensive against the Pact and relations with Britain sharply deteriorated.

The Baghdad Pact was not the only factor that helped to turn Nasser and the RCC away from the West to a neutralist position. Daniel Solod, the Soviet Middle East expert who was appointed Ambassador to Cairo in September 1953, skilfully encouraged the trend. As the traditional sales of Egyptian cotton to England steadily declined (although British purchases from the Sudan increased) Egypt looked to Eastern Europe and China for new markets. Also at about this time Nasser established close personal relations with the Indian Premier Mr. Nehru and President Tito of Yugoslavia who both influenced Nasser's outlook. His views on Arab neutralism were strengthened by his attendance at the Bandung Conference of Afro-Asian Powers in April 1955 where he made a favourable impression and was treated with respect by senior Asian statesmen such as Nehru and Chou en-Lai.

In February 1955 Israel launched a heavy and destructive retaliatory raid on Gaza. Nasser at once began secret negotiations with the Russians for the supply of arms and on 27 September he announced the conclusion of a deal with Czechoslovakia for the supply of very large quantities of arms, including Soviet aircraft and tanks, in exchange for rice and cotton. This action was denounced by the British and US Governments but applauded by the Arab masses. The Egyptian Government, supported by Saudi Arabia and Syria, pursued its campaign against the Baghdad Pact and in December 1955 British efforts to include Jordan in the Pact were thwarted by hostile popular demonstrations. By the end of 1955 Nasser's breach with Britain was almost complete, his prestige in the Arab world rapidly mounting, and his dependence on the West diminishing at the price of increasing dependence on the Soviet bloc.

The trend continued in 1956. In May Nasser without warning recognized the Peking regime. Egypt's trade with Communist China was steadily increasing and Nasser had the additional motive of evading a possible UN embargo on Middle East arms supplies (China not being a UN member). The US reaction was strongly hostile. The Western powers had not altogether given up hope of keeping Egypt within their orbit. In 1955 the British and US governments had begun tentative discussions with Egypt to finance the High Dam at Aswan and in February 1956 a provisional agreement was announced. The offer was primarily a political move in the Cold War, for the Western powers were sceptical of Egypt's ability to provide its share. There was strong domestic opposition to any large-scale US and British aid to Egypt. Convinced that the USSR would not make good its hints that it was prepared to finance the Dam, the US Government abruptly withdrew its offer (on which the IBRD loan depended) in July 1956.

The US and Britain believed that even if he did not fall from power, Nasser would become more pliable. Instead he retaliated by announcing a week later (the fourth anniversary of the Revolution) the nationalization of the Suez Canal Company and the creation of an Egyptian Canal Authority to manage the Canal.

There followed three months of abortive negotiations in London and New York in which Britain took the lead in trying to enforce some international control of the Canal. They failed largely because the US Government refused to consider the use of military force to coerce Egypt. But the British and French governments were determined to use force – the British because they regarded Nasser as a threat to all British interests in the Middle East, and the French because they believed Egyptian support to be the principal factor behind the continuation of the Algerian Rebellion. The British, French, and Israeli Governments secretly agreed on joint action and on 29 October Israel invaded Sinai. On 30 October Britain and France issued a joint ultimatum calling on Egypt and Israel to cease fighting and withdraw their forces ten miles from the Suez Canal. Israel, whose forces were not within ten miles of the Canal, accepted the ultimatum but Nasser rejected it and ordered his troops that had been sent across the Canal into Sinai and were suffering heavy losses to return. When the ultimatum expired on 31 October British and French planes began to bomb Egyptian airfields destroying almost the entire Egyptian air force except for the planes that had been sent into Syria for safety. On 5 November an Anglo-French force, assembled in Cyprus, landed in the Port Said area and after capturing the city advanced southwards along thc linc of thc Canal.

World opinion was overwhelmingly hostile and on 4 November the UN General Assembly decided to create a UN Emergency Force (UNEF) to supervise a cease fire. Britain and France agreed to a cease-fire on 6 November. As soon as UNEF began to arrive the Anglo-French forces started to withdraw and their evacuation was completed by 23 December.

The British and French Governments had miscalculated that the Egyptians would be unable to run the Canal without British and French pilots and that the Egyptian people would turn against Nasser. Despite Egypt's military defeat and the loss of 2,000 to 3,000 men killed or taken prisoner the final result was almost a complete victory for Egypt. United Nations pressure, led by the US and the USSR (especially the former) forced the British and French to withdraw from the Canal, and later the Israelis from Sinai and Gaza, leaving Egypt in full control of the Canal and its immense quantities of British military stores. With US assistance the Canal was cleared of the ships sunk to block it by the Egyptians, and was reopened in April 1957. All British and French property in Egypt was sequestered; about 3,000 British and French nationals were expelled and many thousands more left because of loss of livelihood.

Egypt's loss and Israel's only gain was the replacement by a UNEF detachment of the Egyptian military post at Sharm al-Shaikh which controlled the entrance to the Gulf of Aqaba. The net result of the Suez War was that Nasser's popularity among the Egyptians and the Arabs rose to new heights. Egypt moved further away from the West; the Western economic boycott – which the United States chose to join, thereby dissipating most of the credit it had gained through opposing the Suez action – did not bring Egypt to its knees, because Soviet aid intervened.

Nasser had consolidated his position at home in June 1956 when a new Republican Constitution (which declared Islam to be the religion of the State, recognized Egypt as part of the Arab nation, and provided for government by a President and Council of Ministers and a single legislative chamber) was promulgated and approved by a 99 per cent affirmative vote in a referendum which also confirmed him as President for a six-year term. The Constitution also provided for a single political organization to replace all the political parties and the rather vague Liberation Rally which Nasser had founded after the Revolution. The National Union was formally established in May 1957 and played a leading role in the elections held to the National Assembly in July 1957.

The years 1956–9 marked the high tide of Nasserism in the Middle East as it seemed that he swept all before him. In February 1958 President Nasser's 'neutralist' camp was immensely strengthened by the proclamation of a complete political union between Syria and Egypt, the United Arab Republic. The climax came with the Iraqi Revolution of 14 July which at one blow destroyed the basis of remaining Western, and especially British, power and influence in the Middle East.

The United Arab Republic

To all appearances Nasser and Nasserism were triumphant. Egypt's chief rival had been destroyed, while the union with Syria had established Egyptian power in the Arab heartland. Yet the seeds of immense difficulties had been sown.

Nasser subsequently described the union with Syria as 'three and a half years of endless troubles' which absorbed three-quarters of his energies and attention. He appointed two

Syrian Vice-Presidents of the UAR, several Syrian Ministers to the Central Government, and an Executive Council for the Syrian region, but he kept most of the executive and legislative powers in his own hands. Inevitably, the Syrians regarded themselves as junior partners in the union. Some of the Egyptian officials who went to work in Syria were tactless and overbearing; some others were corrupt. The Syrian army suffered from wounded pride while the Syrian urban middle class and landowners were alarmed as Egypt began to apply socialist principles to Syria. The Government's popularity was not improved when Syria's chiefly agricultural economy suffered three consecutive years of disastrous drought. The mass of the Syrian people still regarded Nasser as their hero and leader but the middle class and intelligentsia were increasingly disaffected. In 1960 Nasser sent Field-Marshal Abdul Hakim Amer, his closest and most trusted friend, as a sort of pro-consular governor in Syria but he failed to remedy the situation.

Nor did Nasser's friendly relations with the new Iraqi regime last long. The Iraqi leader Abdul Karim Kassem purged his regime of pro-Egyptian elements and in February 1959 blamed an abortive revolt in Mosul on Nasser. As the Iraqi Communists strengthened their position *vis-à-vis* Arab nationalists, Nasser became convinced that Communism was now a mortal danger to the Arab nation. During 1959 several hundred Egyptian left-wing intellectuals were interned. His bitter attacks on Kassem and the Communists led to an open breach with the Soviet Premier Nikita Khrushchev. Nasser was taking a severe risk because Egypt was heavily dependent on Soviet economic and military aid and the Russians were about to decide whether to finance the second stage of the High Dam. Eventually the crisis receded as the Russians concluded that their relations with Nasser's Egypt were of more importance than those with the unstable and politically incompetent Iraqi Communists.

1961–67

On 28 September 1961 the disaffected elements in Syria combined forces to secede from the union. Many believed that this enormous setback would end Nasser's political career. At the least it would compel him to abandon his claim to Arab leadership and concentrate on Egypt's internal affairs. In the long run this did not happen because despite the collapse of this first experiment in Arab unity under Nasser's authority, Nasser and Egypt remained the most substantial force in the Arab world. In the shorter term, Syria's secession gave Nasser an opportunity for the first time since the Revolution to examine his political and economic ideas in depth. His first reaction to the secession was to conclude that the Syrian property-owning classes had inspired it because of their fear of Egyptian socialism and that they had been able to do this by infiltrating into the National Union. He also feared that the equivalent Egyptian classes might try to do the same. In a precautionary counter-offensive six hundred of Egypt's wealthiest families had their property sequestered by the State.

In November 1961 Nasser convened a National Congress of Popular Powers whose task was to prepare a Charter of National Action to be the basis of the country's political, social, and economic policies. The National Charter, which was drafted by Nasser and approved by the Congress without amendment, stated that previous revolutionary movements in Egypt had failed because they were weak in strategy and narrow in vision, and overlooked the need for social change. The essence of the Charter is contained in the words, 'Political democracy cannot be separated from social democracy. No citizen can be regarded as free to vote unless he is given the following three guarantees: (*a*) he should be free from exploitation in all its forms; (*b*) he should enjoy an equal opportunity with his fellow citizens to enjoy a fair share of the national wealth; (*c*) his mind should be free from all anxiety likely to undermine his future security.'

The Charter laid down the principles on which the majority of the economy should be publicly owned (see below, Economic Policy and Industrialization). Ownership of agricultural land was limited to 100 feddans per family but there was no question of land nationalization, and private ownership of buildings was maintained.

As regards the political organization of the State, the National Union was replaced by the Arab Socialist Union with its various branches at all levels from the roots in the villages, workshops, and factories up to the National Executive headed by the President. The parliamentary branch of the ASU was the National Assembly with its 350 members elected by adult suffrage in 175 constituencies. In all elected bodies of the ASU, including Parliament, half the seats had to be filled by workers and farmers (defined as anyone owning less than 25 feddans). The ASU was to have the task of drafting a new permanent constitution.

In September 1962 Nasser restored Cabinet government by creating a Council of Ministers headed by Ali Sabry, the former head of his private office.

During 1961–2 Egypt was under heavy attack from the regimes in Jordan, Syria, Saudi Arabia, Iraq, and Yemen.

Between 1961 and 1963 Egypt became increasingly involved in African affairs through its association with Morocco, Mali, Ghana, and Guinea in the 'Casablanca' group of radical African states which in 1963 established on paper a joint military command and a common market. But by the time of the first OAU Conference at Addis Ababa in May 1963 Nasser had concluded that there was nothing to be gained and much to be lost through the polarization of the African continent between radicals and moderates.

Henceforth Nasser was a moderating, almost conservative influence in the OAU. He constantly affirmed that the African states should seek the spirit of unity before adopting any constitutional form.

The Arab political scene was transformed in September 1962 by the republican rebellion in Yemen led by Brigadier Abdullah Sallal, which overthrew the Imam Badr who had just succeeded his father Imam Ahmad. In answer to Sallal's call for help Nasser sent a substantial expeditionary force. The Yemeni coup had given Nasser the chance to seize the initiative once again in the Middle East. The campaign was a severe strain on the Egyptian economy and the Egyptian forces suffered heavy losses at the hands of the Saudi-supported Yemeni royalists. Egyptian aerial bombardment of tribesmen (including the alleged use of poison gas) antagonized world opinion but the immediate effect of the Yemeni rebellion and Egypt's intervention was to place the Arab conservatives on the defensive. Because the Saudis and Jordanians assisted the Yemeni royalists, seven Saudi pilots and three Jordanians (including the Air Force Commander) defected to Cairo.

On 9 February 1963 Kassem was overthrown by Arab nationalists led by Iraqi Baathists and a month later the secessionist regime in Syria collapsed under joint pressure from Baghdad and Cairo. In both Iraq and Syria the new regimes pledged themselves in support of 'the new movement of Arab unity'. Iraq, Syria, and Egypt at once began negotiations for a close federal union.

Obstacles very soon appeared. Nasser and the Baathists were still mutually suspicious and the Iraqi and Syrian Baathists soon eliminated their non-Baathist allies from power. In Syria pro-Nasser demonstrations were rigorously suppressed and although the differences were papered over to allow a tripartite federal State to be proclaimed on 17 April this had no substance.

Egypt's relations with Syria and Iraq steadily worsened throughout the summer but in November 1963 Abdul Salam Aref who had been kept as a figurehead President by the Iraqi Baathists, seized power with the help of the army and ousted the Baath who had split between moderate and extreme wings. Relations between Cairo and Baghdad improved again but although the idea of an Iraqi-Egyptian union was revived again at President Aref's request, Nasser remained cautious.

In the winter of 1963 Nasser reached the conclusion that a serious danger threatened the Arab world. The Israelis had completed the diversion of some of the waters of the River Jordan to the Negev Desert. The Arab states had often sworn to prevent this by force and although there was little hope of their taking effective joint action in their divided state there was a serious possibility that one of them – most probably Syria – would act on its own in launching a war for which Egypt was unprepared. In a speech at Port Said on 23 December 1963 Nasser proposed that all thirteen Arab Heads of State should meet in Cairo to consider the situation. He knew it would be difficult for them to refuse and he made use of the occasion to repair his relations with President Bourguiba of Tunisia, King Hussein of Jordan, King Hassan of Morocco, and King Saud of Saudi Arabia. In effect Nasser was reverting to his earlier policy of 'unity of ranks' taking precedence over 'unity of aims'. The Arab Summit agreed to set up a Unified Arab Military Command under an Egyptian general. There was an agreement not to go to war with Israel but instead to build up the armies of Israel's neighbours and set about diverting the head waters of the River Jordan in Arab territory.

In May 1964 the Soviet Premier Nikita Khrushchev visited Egypt to inaugurate the second stage of the High Dam project. From 1956 onwards President Nasser paid frequent visits to the Soviet Union and relations were generally cordial. Although President Nasser always emphasized his independence of action there was no doubt that Egypt was placing increasing reliance on Soviet economic, military, and technical aid. In contrast, relations with the Western powers, especially the US, deteriorated fairly steadily. There had been a temporary improvement at the end of the Eisenhower Administration and under President Kennedy who was much admired in Egypt. The State Department had concluded that Egypt could still be a barrier to Communism in the Middle East and between 1958 and 1964 the US provided Egypt with over $1,000 million in aid – mostly in cheap long-term loans under the PL 480 arrangement for the sale of surplus foodstuffs. This continued even after a sharp deterioration in US-Egyptian relations as a result of Egyptian military assistance to the Congolese rebels. But although there was no complete diplomatic break until 1967 and President Nasser always made clear that he had not abandoned hope of a reconciliation with Washington, US influence on Egyptian policy was minimal. Nasser had reached the conclusion that it had been a mistake for Egypt to become so heavily dependent on US food supplies.

Except for a brief interlude after the conclusion of the Anglo-Egyptian agreement in 1954 relations between Britain and Egypt were almost uniformly bad between 1952 and 1967. In contrast, relations with France steadily improved after the ending of the Algerian War in 1962, and after 1967 it became the most popular of the Western powers in Egypt.

In July 1964 Cairo was host to the second summit conference of the OAU and in October fifty-six Heads of non-aligned States or their representatives met there. The constant flow of foreign statesmen from West, East, and the Third World into Cairo gave it the status of a major world political centre.

But Egypt's leadership of the Arab states was far from unchallenged. In July 1965 a coup in Algeria removed President Nasser's close friend Ahmad Ben Bella from power. In August

Nasser paid a sudden and unexpected visit to Saudi Arabia to conclude an agreement with King Faisal on Yemen, but this also proved abortive.

In the summer of 1965 Nasser was faced by serious trouble at home in a revived threat of the Moslem Brotherhood. Elections to a 350-member National Assembly had been held in March 1964 under the new Provisional Constitutional and Electoral Law and a start had been made in creating the pyramidal framework of the ASU as provided in the National Charter. A year later Nasser was elected for a further six-year term as President (having consistently refused to be elected for life). But the continued stagnation of Egypt's political life showed the difficulty of endowing the nation with a lively political organization within an authoritarian framework. Despite the affirmation of freedom of the spoken and written word contained in the National Charter, in practice there was little public criticism in the Government's domestic policies and none of foreign policy. It was partly as a reaction against this conformism that an illegal and extra-constitutional movement such as the Moslem Brotherhood gained support.

The summer of 1965 was also a time of exceptionally acute economic difficulties. The first Five-Year Plan had achieved a high growth rate but some of it had been too ambitious, factories were lying idle for lack of spare parts or raw materials and Egypt was losing its international credit-worthiness as it failed to pay its debts.

In 1966 the division between the 'radicals' in the Arab world (led by Egypt) and the 'conservatives' (led by Saudi Arabia) grew steadily wider. King Faisal's diplomatic efforts to create a new grouping of Islamic states was regarded by Egypt as an attempt to create an anti-Nasser front. Egypt's position in Yemen was strengthened by Britain's announcement of a complete withdrawal from the Aden base by 1968, but Egypt completely failed to assist in the formation of a stable republican regime in Yemen and the drain of its resources continued.

The Six Day War

In February 1966 a new coup in Damascus had brought to power in Syria a group of left-wing Baathists who cautiously began to improve their ties with Egypt. In November 1966, under strong Syrian pressure Nasser agreed to a highly comprehensive Egyptian-Syrian defence agreement. Shortly afterwards Israel launched a strong attack against three villages near Hebron in Jordan and after the ensuing disturbances among Palestinians on Jordan's West Bank, King Hussein bitterly criticized both Nasser and the Syrians and taunted Nasser with hiding behind the protection of the UNEF in Sinai.

Meanwhile, Nasser's relations with the Arab monarchies deteriorated (in the summer of 1966 he had caused the indefinite postponement of summit conferences on the grounds that Arab reactionaries were exploiting them for their own ends) and the United Arab Military Command had virtually ceased to exist.

Although Nasser had no affection for the Syrian regime he felt closer co-operation with Damascus was necessary. Tension with Israel rose sharply in April and May 1967 as Israeli leaders threatened Syria with retaliation if guerrilla attacks from Syrian territory continued. Nasser, who had been warned by the Russians of an impending Israeli attack on Syria, felt compelled to react and his response was an official request to the UN Secretary-General for the withdrawal of the UNEF from Sinai. When this was done and Egyptian troops were once again at Sharm al-Shaikh at the mouth of the Gulf of Aqaba Nasser announced the closure of the Straits of Tiran to Israeli shipping.

On 30 May King Hussein flew to Cairo for a last-minute reconciliation and the signing of a Jordanian-Egyptian defence agreement. Egypt now had agreements with both Syria and Jordan but there was no co-operation between these two and no semblance of a joint Arab Command.

On 5 June Israel attacked all seventeen of Egypt's military airfields, destroying most of its air force on the ground; and on 6 June Israeli forces advanced rapidly into Sinai. The seven Egyptian divisions in Sinai were defeated and put to flight and an estimated 10,000 Egyptian soldiers were killed or died of thirst in the struggle to return across the Suez Canal which Israeli forces reached in the early hours of 9 June. Acting on the basis of information from King Hussein on the morning of 6 June that Jordanian radar stations had detected approaching from the sea a large flight of aircraft which could only come from British and US carriers, Egypt broke relations with the US and expelled all US and British citizens.

The Egyptian public who had been roused to a high pitch of optimism in the days preceding the war understood that the worst had happened when Egypt followed Jordan in accepting a cease-fire on 8 June. On the next afternoon President Nasser spoke on Cairo Radio accepting full personal responsibility for the grave national setback and announced his decision to resign and hand over the Presidency to Vice-President Zakariya Mohieddin. It was understood that the First Vice-President and Deputy Commander-in-Chief of the Armed Forces Field Marshal Abdul Hakim Amer had resigned also.

Whether or not Nasser had expected it, the reaction was an overwhelming emotional demand from the Egyptian masses that he should remain in office. There was some official encouragement of the popular demonstrations but they had their own impulse. On 10 June Nasser announced his agreement to the unanimous demand of the National Assembly that he should stay on.

1967–1970

Egypt was in a desperately serious situation in June 1967. Most of its air force and much of its armour and artillery had been lost. The Suez Canal was closed and with the Israeli occupation of Sinai half of its oil production (about 9.5 million tons a year) was lost. Above all the authority of the President, the nation's trusted leader and father-figure had been irreparably damaged.

After withdrawing his resignation Nasser at once took over the premiership and the ASU and formed a 'government of reconstruction'.

Army discontent came to a head in August with a plot by dissident officers to reinstate Abdul Hakim Amer at the head of the armed forces. With the help of loyal and anti-Amer elements in the army Nasser crushed the plot without much difficulty and Amer shortly afterwards committed suicide in mysterious circumstances. The former War Minister Shams Badran and Salah Nasser, the head of military intelligence, had been associated with Amer; they and numerous other officers and a few civilians were arrested and put on trial. In a separate trial the air force commanders in June 1967 were charged with criminal negligence of duty. Although Nasser had taken the *political* responsibility for the defeat he did not accept the military responsibility; he said that he had repeatedly warned the army commanders to expect an Israeli attack and that it would take place on 5 June.

At the end of August the Sudanese Government succeeded in arranging an Arab summit meeting in Khartoum which only the Syrians refused to attend. Nasser made use of the meeting in two important respects: first he reached a kind of bargain with the conservative Arab oil states – Kuwait, Saudi Arabia, and Libya – whereby all pressure on them to continue their boycott of Britain and the US would be removed in return for a large financial payment to Egypt and Jordan 'until the traces of aggression are removed'; at the same time he reached a final agreement on the Yemen with King Faisal which meant that all Egypt's 40,000 troops were withdrawn by the end of 1967.

In October the Egyptian navy scored an important success by sinking the Israeli flagship, the destroyer *Eilat*. The Israelis responded with heavy shelling of Suez and other Canal cities and during 1968 the Egyptians were forced to evacuate most of the civilian population from the Canal Zone and move the rest of the oil refinery installations from Suez.

Although President Nasser's public speeches in Egypt were defiant and even bellicose in tone he made it clear that he would prefer what came to be known as a 'political solution' to a 'military solution' of the Middle East problem when he announced Egypt's acceptance of the 22 November 1967 British-sponsored UN Security Council resolution calling for an Israeli withdrawal from the occupied territories in return for Arab *de facto* recognition of Israel.

On 20 February 1968 a military court passed sentences of fifteen and twenty years' imprisonment on the senior air force officers on trial for their conduct during the Six Day War. During the following days there was serious rioting by workers at Helwan and students in Cairo and Alexandria. The riots reflected widespread dissatisfaction with the failure to make the fundamental changes that had been expected following the June War. Nasser responded by forming a new Government on

20 March still under his premiership but with several new civilian ministers drawn from universities and the professions. Ten days later he announced what came to be known as the 30 March programme to revitalize the revolution. Its basis was the holding of democratic elections to complete the structure of the ASU.

Sporadic fighting with Israel on the Suez Canal front took place throughout 1969 and the first half of 1970. In July 1969 Nasser said that the best strategy for the Arabs was to conduct a 'war of attrition' against Israel. The Israelis launched several commando raids deep into Egyptian territory and Egyptian forces also crossed the Canal into Sinai on several occasions. The Israeli Air Force bombarded Egyptian positions in the Canal Zone with increasing severity and claimed to have destroyed all the missile sites in the area.

President Nasser's planned visit to Moscow in September 1969 was cancelled for health reasons but he paid a secret visit in January 1970 when he was promised increased Soviet aid for Egyptian air and ground defences. The number of Soviet military advisers in Egypt was increased from 3,000 to 8,000–10,000; Egyptian defences improved their performance and succeeded in shooting down at least six Israeli planes in the summer of 1970. Nasser had still not abandoned hope that a political solution to the Middle East problem could be achieved through US pressure on Israel to withdraw occupied Arab territories. On 1 May he made what he called a 'final appeal' to President Nixon to withhold support for Israel as long as it occupied Arab lands and on 23 July he announced Egypt's acceptance of the Rogers Plan for peace in the Middle East which led to the cease-fire in the Suez Canal area on 7 August.

The much delayed Arab summit meeting held in Rabat in December 1969 was generally regarded as a failure fromEgypt's point of view but Egypt's general position in the Arab World was greatly strengthened by the support of the new revolutionary regimes in Sudan and Libya. Plans for a political federation of the three States were under discussion during 1970.

President Nasser was criticized by the Palestinian resistance organizations for his acceptance of the US peace plan but in

September he took a leading part in efforts to settle the Jordanian civil war. It was at the conclusion of these negotiations that he died suddenly of a heart attack on 28 September.

Sadat's Presidency 1970–

The disappearance of the man who had dominated the country and taken all the major policy decisions for over fifteen years inevitably left a political vacuum. In appointing Anwar Sadat as the only Vice-President in late 1969, Nasser had clearly indicated him as his successor. Under the constitution Sadat became acting President and after the unanimous approval of his candidature by the Arab Socialist Union Higher Executive and the National Assembly his election was confirmed by a national referendum on 15 October in which 90.04 per cent of the votes cast were affirmative. On 20 October Sadat appointed the former foreign minister and presidential affairs adviser Mahmud Fawzi to be Egypt's first civilian prime minister since 1952.

Collective leadership appeared to work well for a time as President Sadat broadly continued Nasser's policies, although in his own style. The removal of Nasser's dominating presence resulted in a perceptible relaxation in the atmosphere of public life. For the first time in many years 'Egypt First' as opposed to Arab nationalist policies were openly advocated in some quarters. It was announced that all the sequestered property of Egyptian nationals would be restored. Through a vigorous diplomatic campaign Egypt succeeded in repairing or improving its relations with Turkey and Iran and several European states. Plans for a tripartite Arab federation (Sudan having dropped out but been replaced by Syria) were pursued and on 17 April 1971 the three heads of state of Libya, Syria, and Egypt announced in Benghazi that it would come into existence on 1 September. This decision was the immediate cause of an open rift in the Egyptian regime. President Sadat dismissed Vice-President Ali Sabry who had led criticism of the federation plans in the ASU and two weeks later several senior ministers and officials (including the Defence and Interior Ministers) resigned en bloc in a clear challenge to President Sadat's authority. President Sadat, who was widely popular and also had the support of most of the army, responded vigorously. He replaced with his own supporters all the resigning officials who in many cases were arrested and charged with planning a coup. In direct appeals to the nation the President promised that all the police state apparatus would be destroyed, that the rule of law would be rigorously applied and that genuinely free elections for the National Assembly and ASU would be held.

Although the upheaval in Egypt was basically a struggle for power, the fact that Ali Sabry and his associates were known for their pro-Soviet sympathies indicated a possible shift to the right. Obviously concerned with the trend of events in a country in which they held such an important investment, the Russians sent a high-powered delegation led by President Podgorny to Cairo in June. The result was the signing of a fifteen-year Egyptian-Soviet treaty of friendship and co-operation. For the time being there was no alternative to Egypt's close association with the Soviet Union.

The years 1971–3 were of extreme difficulty for Sadat's presidency. While the US government showed no willingness to follow up the Rogers Plan of 1970 by enforcing an Israeli withdrawal in Sinai, the Soviet Union rejected Egypt's repeated appeals to supply the type of arms that made an Egyptian crossing of the Suez Canal a feasible alternative. The two superpowers were showing increasing interest in their own *détente*. At home the Egyptian people were in restive mood. Left-wing students, encouraged by the Palestinians, demanded action. The morale of the army, waiting paralyzed on the Suez Canal, was low. A million refugees from the Canal cities were heightening the social problems of the cities. The public as a whole wondered why it was being called to make sacrifices for a war to recover lost territory which never came, and President Sadat's repeated promises of action provoked mounting scepticism.

In July 1972 President Sadat made what appeared to be a desperate throw to restore his popularity when he ordered the withdrawal of all Soviet military advisers from Egypt. The move was popular because the Soviet presence was disliked, especially by the army, but at that stage Egypt had no real alternative to Soviet aid. The West's relations with Egypt were improving but not to the extent of providing arms.

The October War

During the winter of 1972/73 President Sadat decided that the inescapable option was to launch a war of limited objectives which would oblige both the West and the Soviet Union to reassess the situation. In preparing the ground, his objective was to secure Syria as his military ally, and Saudi Arabia as his diplomatic and financial ally. In the task of establishing a minimum of Arab unity for the war Sadat had an important advantage: because he lacked Nasser's authority and prestige, the other Arab states were less inclined to fear and dislike an Egyptian hegemony. In forging a closer relationship with Saudi Arabia, Sadat was sacrificing Egypt's alliance with Libya whose President Qaddafi held to a Nasserite dream of Arab unity.

Enjoying the unusual advantage of surprise, Egypt won a partial success in the war launched on 6 October. It crossed the Suez Canal to establish a powerful bridgehead, destroying a substantial part of Israel's planes and tanks in Sinai. The second week of the war saw a severe setback as the Israelis succeeded in making a brilliant thrust across the Suez Canal through a gap between the Egyptian Second and Third Armies and in consolidating a bridgehead on the western bank. By this time the two superpowers, who had rushed supplies to their respective clients as soon as the war started, were induced to intervene and a joint Soviet-US cease-fire resolution finally became effective on 23 October.

The Aftermath

Despite the sharp military reversal in the second week of the war, Sadat had achieved his main objectives. The proof that the Israeli army was not invincible greatly improved the Egyptian army's morale. Above all the prompt and effective use of the 'oil weapon' under Saudi leadership (in the form of a sharp reduction of production and a total boycott of the USA and the Netherlands) caused a reassessment of US policy in the Middle East. The basis of President Sadat's political strategy was his declared view that the USA holds 99 per cent of the cards in the Middle East. Immediately following the war he renewed diplomatic ties with Washington and established a close working relationship with the US Secretary of State Henry Kissinger. Through Dr. Kissinger's mediation,

Egypt reached military disengagement agreements with Israel in January 1973 and September 1975 which made possible the reopening of the Suez Canal in June 1975, the repopulation of the Canal cities and the recovery of Egypt's Sinai oil-fields.

The obverse side to these achievements was that Egypt's wartime alliance with Syria was shattered. Syria denounced the Sinai 2 disengagement agreement in the belief that Egypt had virtually opted out of the Arab front against Israel – especially as the agreement provided for US-manned early warning stations between the Egyptian and Israeli forces. Syrian and Egyptian differences were temporarily overcome through Saudi mediation in the autumn of 1976. Syria withdrew its objections to Sinai 2 while Egypt accepted Syrian intervention in Lebanon to end the civil war. But within a year Egypt's relations with Syria were worse than ever as a result of President Sadat's decision to launch his own peace initiative with Israel.

Another consequence of Egypt's *rapprochement* with the United States was the ending of the close relationship with the Soviet Union which halted military supplies early in 1973. This reversal of alliances correspond with President Sadat's strongest political instincts and was reflected in many aspects of domestic policy. The political opening to the West was matched by an economic and financial open-door policy (Arabic *infitah*) to encourage non-communist investment in Egypt (see pp. 246–8 below).

At home a number of liberalizing measures were taken to restore the authority and independence of the law courts, to dismantle the police state, and to increase political freedom. In 1976 permission was given for three *nawabir* or political platforms to be formed, representing respectively the right, left, and centre; and following elections in October, in which the centrists, supported by the Government, won a huge majority, President Sadat said the *nawabir* could now become fully-fledged political parties. But it was always made clear that liberalization would be within strict limits. The presidency retained overwhelming powers under the 1971 permanent constitution and President Sadat continued to use these in various ways to paralyse his critics – notably through his

control of the higher positions in the state-controlled press. When severe rioting broke out in all major Egyptian cities in January 1977 in protest against government economic measures aimed to reduced subsidies for essentials, President Sadat blamed the disturbances exclusively on the left. The rioters had chanted the name of Nasser, and President Sadat declared that Nasser and Nasserism had been dead since 1967. From then on he was openly critical of all aspects of the Nasserist era except for the achievements of the early years after the 1952 Revolution. He condemned the National Charter as valueless (see Anwar el-Sadat *In Search of Identity*, London, 1978).

In 1978 President Sadat showed increasing impatience with his critics inside and outside parliament. Against his wishes, the old Wafd Party had revived itself under the veteran Wafdist Fuad Seraggedin Pasha and was gathering support while the small but vocal left-wing party was publishing its own highly successful weekly paper. Sadat responded by holding a referendum in May to endorse measures to remove from politics and the media all those who entertained 'atheist ideologies' and those who had corrupted political life before 1952. The New Wafd then announced it was disbanding, and the left-wing Progressive Party, continuously harassed by the authorities, that it was suspending its activities. In July President Sadat announced his decision to form his own political party the National Democratic Union (which members of the government centrist party then joined *en masse*) and allow more political parties into the country's political system.

The Sadat Peace Initiative

President Sadat's internal policies in 1978 were subordinate to his determined efforts to achieve a Middle East peace settlement with American backing. Following the Arab summit meetings held in the autumn of 1976 which were partially and temporarily successful in restoring Arab unity Sadat's efforts were concentrated on securing a resumption of the Middle East Geneva peace conference but these always came up against the same obstacle: the refusal of the Israelis, backed by the USA, to have dealings with the Palestine Liberation Organization, which the Arabs were committed by their summit meeting at

Rabat in October 1974 (see p. 40) to recognizing as the sole legitimate representative of the Palestinian people. Finally, in November 1977, President Sadat decided to attempt to cut through the obstacles by accepting the Israeli Prime Minister's invitation to visit Jerusalem and address the Israeli Parliament. His action was not supported by any Arab countries except for Morocco, Sudan, and Oman. Of the key states, Saudi Arabia and Jordan were lukewarm and doubtful, while Syria and Iraq were extremely hostile. Despite Egypt's isolation, President Sadat persisted with his efforts, responding strongly to his critics while denying that he had any intention of reaching a bilateral peace agreement with Israel. Egyptian-Israeli political and military negotiations initiated after the Jerusalem visit lapsed during the spring and summer until both President Sadat and the Israeli Prime Minister Mr. Begin accepted the US President Carter's invitation to attend a trilateral US-Egyptian-Israeli summit at Camp David in the USA on 8 September 1978. After intensive negotiations the meeting ended with two agreements entitled 'The framework of peace in the Middle East', and 'A framework for the conclusion of a peace treaty between Egypt and Israel.' Further negotiations led to the conclusion of the Treaty of Washington on 29 March 1979, providing for a phased Israeli withdrawal over three years from all occupied Egyptian territory in return for the full normalization of Egyptian/Israeli relations. Spurning the almost unanimous Arab opposition, President Sadat's diplomacy in the ensuing months concentrated on negotiations for the establishment of a form of Palestinian autonomy in the West Bank and Gaza, as provided for in the Exchange of Letters accompanying the Treaty.

SOCIAL SURVEY

Social Welfare

At the time of the *coup d'état* national income per head of population (after rent had been deducted) was £25, one-seventh of the average for Western Europe.[4] Moreover it

[4] Doreen Warriner, *Land Reform and Development in the Middle East* (London, 1957), p. 20.

was estimated to be no more than three-fifths of what it had been in 1913, and there was every reason to expect that it would fall ever more rapidly as the population increased. Perennial irrigation had had evil as well as good effects, by providing a breeding-ground for water-borne and mosquito-borne diseases in the canals which were often the only water-supply for the villages. Malaria, which had formerly affected more than half the villagers, had been very greatly reduced by the special measures taken since the Second World War, but three-quarters of the villagers still suffered from bilharzia, and two-fifths from hookworm, with disastrous effects on their vitality. Tuberculosis claimed many victims in the country and still more in the towns, there was much preventable blindness, and the poor in the towns were subject to pellagra. Addiction to hashish was widespread. The Egyptian labourer of 1950 was generally admitted to be a much weaker man, physically, than his father had been. Government medical services, including free treatment in hospitals, mass radiography, and other preventive services already existed, and the sickness, death, and infant mortality rates were falling, but the magnitude of the problem needed action on a corresponding scale.

Since 1952 the regime has made concentrated efforts to improve health standards. The achievements have been considerable although much remains to be done. Bilharzia, which still affects two thirds of the *fellahin*, remains the greatest scourge but there has been encouraging progress in controlling other diseases. Tuberculosis is much reduced and there is good hope of eliminating malaria entirely in the near future. Eye diseases in Egyptian children have also been much reduced and free midday meals for four million schoolchildren have done much to build up their health and resistance to disease.

Although some rural health centres had been established before the Revolution, the programme has since been enormously expanded and speeded up. Experience having shown that villagers will not go more than three miles for treatment, the aim is to establish 2,500 new rural health units each serving 5,000 people within a radius of two miles. By 1970 there were 1,786 rural health units – from village dispensaries to combined centres – with a total of 8,149 beds. Every other village was therefore provided with some form of health facility. But a comprehensive national health service together with old age pensions and sickness and unemployment benefits for all citizens are inevitably distant goals for a country at Egypt's stage of development.

The provision of free medical care is only part of the problem; the attitude of the people themselves towards disease and infection has to be changed. Ignorance is mainly responsible for the infant mortality rate which has been reduced but remains high. Officially it was 105 per 1,000 in 1962 but because many births and infant deaths are never recorded it is probably higher. One of the outstanding achievements of the regime has been the provision of clean drinking water to almost the entire rural population – to 18 million (compared with only two million at the time of the Revolution). Yet this alone does not solve the problem because many *fellahin* still prefer to use Nile or canal water.

The Egyptian Public Health budget has risen from £E 10.1 million in 1951/52 to £E 31.2 million in 1963/64 and £E 38 million in 1969/70. In 1951 there were 5,200 doctors, or one for every 4,000 inhabitants; in 1964 there were 13,000, or one for every 2,000 inhabitants. However, current data on the number of medical doctors are scanty. Egypt, like many other developing countries, is losing large numbers of doctors through the brain drain. In 1970 there were over 71,000 beds in all the treatment establishments in the country, or one to every 479 inhabitants compared with one to every 600 inhabitants in 1952. Inevitably the rapid increase in the number of doctors has meant some decline in standards but no very high level of skill is required to deal with the basic needs of the mass of the population; and the Government's decision to make two years' service in the countryside compulsory for all qualified doctors after internship has been a major contribution towards tackling these needs.

Family Planning

Egypt, with its very limited cultivable area, faces a population explosion as dangerous as any in the Third World. Since there is no solution to Egypt's problem within the agricultural sector, rapid industrialization is essential but cannot provide a complete answer. It was not until ten years after the Revolution that President Nasser publicly advocated family planning. This was partly the natural reluctance of the ambitious leader of a developing nation to advocate restricting its manpower and partly acknowledgement of the strength of conservative forces in Egyptian society.

Some experimental birth-control clinics were established and in 1964 the Ministry of Social Affairs decided to establish clinics in all parts of the country. In 1966 415 new family-planning centres were established. Both the loop and the pill were used and all the common difficulties of reluctance and hostility were encountered. As expected, the response was much better in the towns than in the countryside. In 1968 it was estimated that about 350,000 women were using either loops or pills and about 80,000 using loops (excluding those – mainly in the towns – employing birth-control methods privately). In 1967 a three-year programme was launched with the aim of reaching 2,800,000 women by 1970 and the annual net increase was reduced from about 2.7 per cent in 1967 to about 2.3 per cent in 1977. Nevertheless, many Egyptians feel that the problem is so urgent that it should be tackled still more vigorously and with larger funds.

The Status of Women

The success of family planning and the effort to raise social and educational standards is intimately bound up with the status of women. This has been slowly but steadily improving in Egypt since the First World War and there has been some acceleration since the Revolution. President Nasser favoured a far more gradualist approach than Kemalist Turkey out of respect to conservative and religious opinion, but the principle was clearly stated in his National Charter that 'Woman must be regarded as equal to man and she must therefore shed the remaining shackles that impede her free movement so that she may play a constructive and profoundly important part in shaping the life of the country.'

President Sadat holds similar views, despite his closer proximity to conservative opinion. His wife Jihan has been a vigorous supporter of female emancipation.

The change has been much more apparent in the towns than

in the country. There is now a substantial number of women doctors, university teachers, and lawyers. Egypt's first woman Minister, Dr. Hikmat Abu Zeid, was appointed in 1962 and there are always a handful of elected women members of the National Assembly. The strongest single factor behind the emancipation of women has been the growing acceptance of their right to equal educational opportunities with men. The proportion of girls in primary and secondary schools rose to 40 per cent in 1978 compared with 10 per cent in 1913. In 1978 nearly 30 per cent of Egypt's university students were girls. Social segregation of the sexes remains the rule even among university students but is gradually breaking down.

Easy divorce in Islam and early marriage are both obstacles to family planning and female progress in Egypt. Reforms advocated by the Egyptian intelligentsia have made little headway both because of the strength of conservatism and because of the difficulty of enforcing any change in the law (such as the raising of the legal age of marriage for girls from sixteen to eighteen). In 1974 President Sadat improved women's marriage rights by decree.

Education

Elementary education has been free and compulsory since 1923, the year after Egypt became independent, and all branches of education have expanded since that time. The British authorities had not, however, left much foundation for the Egyptians to build upon and much still remains to be done. The total school population increased from 324,000 in 1913 to 924,000 in 1933 and 1,900,000 in 1951 although in 1953/54 only 41.8 per cent of the children aged between six and twelve were registered as attending school. The revolutionary regime increased its efforts until an average of two new schools was being opened every three days. By 1961 the total school population was 3.5 million, by 1970 it was approaching 4 million, and by 1976 nearly 6 million. Vocational schools for industry, commerce and agriculture were greatly increased in size and number. From 15,000 students in 1953 these had over 100,000 in 1965 and 377,000 in 1976.

The number of university students rose from 38,000 in 1951 to 351,522 in 1974 at eight universities. A new university was opened at Assiut in 1957 and the ancient Islamic

University of al-Azhar was partially transformed into a modern university in 1961 by the addition of science, medical, and engineering faculties. The number of foreign students studying in Egypt rose from 3,200 in 1952 to 18,845 in 1962, a demand on facilities only in part offset by an increase in the number of Egyptian students studying abroad from 1,984 to 5,575 in the same period. The Ministry of Education's budget rose from £E 40.2 million in 1951 to £E 96.5 million in 1964, and to £E 126 million, or nearly 5 per cent of GDP, in 1969/1970.

By 1965 there were school vacancies for about 80 per cent of the population attaining the age of six and the declared aim of providing primary education for the entire population was within sight. However, the figures for school enrolment do not give the whole picture. In the towns attendance at primary schools is normally about 85 per cent of the enrolment but in the country it drops to 60 per cent or lower in the summer when the children are needed to work in the cotton fields.

It has been the declared intention of the regime to end the socially harmful domination of the country's educational system by the 300 foreign schools. Since 1956 these have all been either nationalized or put under close state control and forced to adapt their curricula to conform with the state system. This and the extremely rapid expansion of the entire system has caused some decline in standards. Classes are far too large at all levels while many teachers are unqualified for their jobs. The shortage of teachers is accentuated by the export of many to other Arab countries (about 5,000 in 1964). The result is that although the illiteracy rate has undoubtedly fallen from its pre-Revolutionary level of 80 per cent it has not fallen as fast as had been hoped.

THE ECONOMY

Agriculture

Despite recent strides in industrialization, agriculture remains the largest single section of the economy, absorbing over half the labour force and contributing over 25 per cent of the national product. Egyptian agriculture itself is based entirely on the River Nile. The original form of irrigation was to confine the river between high mud banks and to break them in time of flood to cover the fields with water and silt. When the water drained off the crop was sown in the autumn and reaped in the spring, the land being left fallow until after the next Nile flood. This age-old 'basin' irrigation was supplemented from about the middle of the nineteenth century by the development of 'perennial' irrigation which involves the damming and storage of the flood water and its subsequent release during the period of low Nile so as to provide irrigation water all the year round and in particular to permit the growing of summer crops. This was developed considerably during the British occupation; the Delta Barrage was repaired and in the ten years from 1898 a dam at Aswan and various subsidiary barrages were completed until virtually the whole of the Delta and parts of Upper Egypt were converted to perennial irrigation. By 1950 the cultivated area was about 6 million feddans and the cropped area about 10 million feddans.

The building of the High Dam (see pp. 253–4 below) marks a new stage in providing permanent water storage in the gigantic Lake Nasser reservoir to even the supply of irrigation water between years of low and high flood. This has enabled the rest of Upper Egypt to be converted to perennial irrigation and eventually will increase the cultivated area by about 25 per cent.

It is officially estimated that 825,900 feddans of uncultivated land had been reclaimed between 1952 and mid–1968, including 84,700 using sub-soil water through tube wells. By 1977 about 1.3 million feddans had been reclaimed. Priority is given to the area with greatest potential which is within the Nile Delta (to the west of Mansoura), to the east in land south of Port Said, and to the west of the Delta near Alexandria. Other important reclamation schemes include the Kom Ombo Valley in Upper Egypt where the 50,000 Nubians displaced by the rising waters of Lake Nasser have been resettled and the so-called New Valley project to tap the underground water resources of the Western Desert near the five oases of Kharga, Dakhla, Farafra, Bahriyah, and Siwa.

Although Egypt's cultivated land is very limited the soil is rich and yields are among the highest in the world. The large-scale development of cotton which is still the principal feature of the Egyptian economy was made possible by perennial irrigation in the nineteenth century.

In 1972 1.55 million feddans were devoted to cotton cultivation out of a total crop area of nearly 11 million feddans. This allocation fell to 1.4 million feddans in 1977. In 1975 1.14 million feddans were given over to rice, of which Egypt is a substantial exporter (2.53 million tons produced in 1976) and 1.24 million to wheat, of which the country now has to import about 4 million tons a year. Other important crops are maize (2.78 million tons in 1975), sugar cane (7.9 million tons in 1975), and onions (570,000 tons in 1975).

Cotton remains the country's biggest cash crop and one of its main exports, although now surpassed by oil.

Yields per acre of cotton, wheat, rice, and sugar can be increased very little because they are so high already. Some economists have therefore advocated that a substantial increase in profit per acre could be achieved by switching to fruit, vegetables, meat, and dairy production. Egypt already grows most Mediterranean types of vegetables and fruits and some tropical ones (such as mangoes) as well as roses, gladioli, and other flowers. It is argued that by concentrating on these Egypt could build up an export trade to Europe and other Arab states in winter and in early spring. At the same time, mechanization and reduction of the areas under cereals and rice could dispense with many of the draught animals and eliminate the large area used for growing fodder. This intensification of Egyptian agriculture would however require heavy investment.

The most important development project for Egypt's agricultural sector in 1978 was the plan to invest $1,000 million to introduce tile drainage on three million feddans or half Egypt's cultivated land by 1982. This is aimed at large increases in crop yields by reducing salinity. Increased salination has been the most serious of the harmful effects of the High Dam.

Agrarian Reform

With the rapid expansion in the cultivated area during the nineteenth century, agricultural production outpaced the increase in population for a time. But this did not last and between 1897 and 1947 while the cultivated area increased by 14 per cent and the cropped area by 37 per cent the population doubled. Yields per acre also increased fairly steadily and it is thought that total agricultural production approximately kept pace with the increase in population.

In 1947 per capita real income of Egypt's rural population was roughly what it had been fifty years before but the distribution of income had become still more uneven. The situation was worse than this might suggest since two feddans is estimated as the absolute minimum from which a *fellah* family can make a living and in 1952 there were 2,018,000 (or 72 per cent of all proprietors) who owned less than one feddan. In addition there were about 1.5 million families (about 8 million people) who owned no land at all and lived by share-cropping or casual labour. More and more were forced to eke out a living by renting or share-cropping an additional small area and between 1939 and 1949 the proportion of land that was rented increased from 17 to 60 per cent. Net income per head of the active agricultural population was estimated at £E 34 in 1953. Because of his poverty and the cheapness of labour the *fellah* had neither the ability nor incentive to use modern techniques.

The principal aim of the first land reform of 1952 was the political one of reducing the power of the large landowners. Maximum holdings per family were reduced to 200 feddans then to 100 feddans in the second land reform of 1961 and finally to 50 feddans according to a decree of July 1969. In the redistribution of expropriated land, preference has been given to former tenants owning less than five feddans and to permanent labourers. This means that the very large estates have disappeared. Middle-sized estates have been untouched and there has been a small increase in the number of holdings of five feddans or less. The general pattern of Egyptian land ownership, with the vast majority consisting of very small properties, has not changed. When redistribution under the first and second land reforms has been completed it will have affected about one million feddans (out of 6 million) and benefited about 8 per cent of the *fellahin*.

Article 3 of the 1952 law which decreed the compulsory reduction of all agricultural rents, benefited many more – perhaps four million of the farming population – through an average net increase in income of about 50 per cent.

Some, although not all, of this benefit was lost as the

pressure of population on land made it easier for the landlords to evade the rent controls, often with the connivance of the tenants.

The Egyptian agrarian reform is regarded as one of the more successful of such attempts. There was no drastic fall of output. In the land reform areas where land has been redistributed special supervised co-operatives were established with a large measure of control over the farmers' cultivation and marketing. Output per acre in these areas has generally been well above the national average.

The Nawag Experiment

Improvement of farming methods is much more difficult to achieve outside the reform areas but at the village of Nawag in the Delta an attempt was made to persuade the villagers, while they retained ownership of their highly fragmented holdings, to group them for the purpose of cultivation into several large fields each under a single crop, as in the supervised co-operatives. The experiment was a success and in 1960 the Government took the decision to extend the supervised co-operatives gradually throughout the country. A start was made with the Governorates of Kafr al-Shaikh in the Delta and Beni-Suef in Upper Egypt. The emphasis is on persuasion rather than compulsion and the response is varied. One limiting factor is the supply of trained supervisors for the co-operatives.

Economic Policy and Industrialization

The economy inherited by the Free Officers in 1952 could only be described as stagnant. Owing to the pressure of population, real incomes per head were scarcely rising while inequalities of wealth (accentuated by the Korean War cotton boom) were increasing. Hopeless poverty, malnutrition, and disease were Egypt's hallmarks.

While agricultural productivity and rural conditions clearly needed to be improved, industrialization was the obvious priority for development. Between 1920 and 1950 industrial expansion based on the replacement of imported consumer goods by domestically-produced substitutes had been fairly rapid, but between 1950 and 1952 the rate of growth had slowed down. Highly protected Egyptian industry showed no signs of becoming internationally competitive and three decades of government-encouraged industrialization had failed to produce more than a handful of efficient industrial entrepreneurs and managers.

Initially neither Abdul Nasser nor the great majority of the Free Officers subscribed to any economic doctrine. If anything they were rightwards inclined and in the years 1952–6 economic policies were liberal and orthodox. Some of the pre-Revolutionary protectionist legislation was repealed in an effort to attract foreign investors. Deflation and austerity produced both budget and balance of payments surpluses.

By the end of 1954 it became apparent that economic expansion was essential to prevent a fall in per capita income and provide for increased expenditure on social services. A separate Development Budget was created and public expenditure was increased. But there was no attempt to adopt socialism or centralized planning. The regime's real hopes lay in the building of a High Dam (with Western assistance).

The Suez War in 1956 had several important effects on the economic scene. Domestic prices rose sharply, and there was a drastic fall in the price of the Egyptian pound abroad. This, with the economic boycott by the West and the consequent loss of exports, caused a severe strain on the balance of payments. The economy was only saved from disaster by the Communist bloc.

The response to the Anglo-French invasion was the sequestration of all British and French property. In January 1957 all foreign banks and insurance companies were ordered to Egyptianize themselves and British and French banks were sold to Egyptian banks. Together with the nationalization of the Suez Canal Company this meant that the greater part of the foreign share in the Egyptian economy had been liquidated. Much of this share was transferred to the Egyptian economy and between 1957 and 1960 several public economic organizations were created while others already in existence were expanded to look after the Government's interests and to fill the vacuum left by Egyptian private capital. The State's share in the economy was growing and the trend was certain to continue.

In 1959 the Bank Misr and the National Bank of Egypt were nationalized. The significance of this step was that for the first time it concerned Egyptian firms rather than foreign-owned companies. In June and July 1961 in a series of socialist decrees the Government took over the entire import trade and a large part of the export trade including cotton. All banks and insurance companies were nationalized and about 300 industrial and trading establishments were taken over either wholly or partly by the State.

In July 1960 a comprehensive Five-Year Plan for 1960–65 was launched to be followed by a Second Five-Year Plan with the ambitious target of doubling national income by 1970. Eighty per cent of the investment would be undertaken by the public sector.

One of the factors behind Syria's secession from the UAR in September 1961 was reaction against the application of the Socialist Decrees to Syria. President Nasser for the first time formulated his economic ideas in the National Charter of May 1962. In this he laid down that the entire economic infrastructure, the majority of heavy, medium, and mining industries should be publicly owned. All the import trade, most of the export trade, banks and insurance companies must be within the public sector.

The economic framework of the National Charter was fairly closely adhered to. Most of the remaining companies still in private hands were taken over by the State in 1963 and 1964.

Domestic trade remained largely in private hands although Government co-operative retail shops played an important role. The Government used various techniques to hold down the cost of living including rationing, subsidies, and price and rent controls. These measures combined with industrialization, increased industrial wages and the distribution of profits substantially increased the incomes of the urban working class. In 1965/66 prices began to rise more steeply but despite the disaster of 1967 the Government was able to check the rise in 1968/69.

The 1967 war caused the loss of £90 million a year in Canal revenues, about half of Egypt's oil output of approximately 9.5 million tons a year, and most of Egypt's tourist income. In addition it imposed a huge new armaments bill. Disaster was avoided because of the aid from Arab and East European states which after the Khartoum Conference in August 1967 was put on a regular basis of £95 million a year. Also discoveries of crude oil made by US independent companies, Pan-American in the Red Sea and Phillips in the Western Desert in 1966 soon more than made up for the loss of the Sinai fields.

From 1956 onwards Egypt's foreign indebtedness has increased at an alarming rate. It is estimated that between 1957 and 1965 Egypt received a total of £1,321 million in foreign loans and credit facilities (excluding military credits). In addition there were compensation payments for British, French, Belgian, Swiss, Lebanese, and other nationalized and sequestrated property.

Egypt's credit-worthiness reached its lowest point in 1966 when it actually stopped its $3.5 million monthly principal and interest payment to the IMF. After 1967 the Government made a determined effort to improve its reputation for paying its debts.

'Infitah' or the Open Door

After 1967 the government made a special effort, with some results, to revive the private sector – especially in export industries and construction. But the trend has been greatly increased under President Sadat and especially since the 1973 war. The *Infitah* or open-door policy can be seen as one aspect of political liberalization and the *rapprochement* with the West.

The starting-point of *Infitah* is Investment Law No. 43 of 1974 which guarantees foreign companies prompt remittance of capital and transfer of profits, immunity from expropriation or nationalization, and tax holidays of 5 to 15 years. It also provides complete freedom from local taxes and customs duties in the Port Said Free Zone. At the same time the stipulation of 51 per cent Egyptian participation in all companies was abolished.

This reversal in the attitude towards foreign investment has not meant the dismantling of the public sector. President Sadat has said that some 70 per cent of the economy will remain in the hands of the State and this view is broadly accepted by ministers in charge of the economy. However, greatly increased encouragement is given to the private sector which has become the most dynamic area of the economy. In 1978 it represented between 10 and 15 per cent of GNP and was increasing.

The objective of Investment Law No. 43 was to attract Arab and foreign investment into export-oriented industry. Critics of the policy claim that most of the investment that has since entered Egypt bears no relation to the country's real needs. Undoubtedly *Infitah* initially raised many expectations among the public that could not immediately be fulfilled and some aspects of the liberalization measures dangerously widened the gap between rich and poor.

If foreign investors were hesitant to enter Egypt on the scale that the authorities hoped, it was partly because of the obstacles presented by a still powerful Egyptian bureaucracy but above all because the entire economic infrastructure, after two decades of high and mounting military expenditure, had been brought to a point of near collapse. Public services such as telephone and transport required complete renewal while the exploding population of the cities created a social problem of gigantic proportions.

Egypt's huge foreign indebtedness, estimated at $8,300 million in 1977, has made the launching of any comprehensive recovery plan extremely difficult, especially as a high proportion is in short-term debts. (A further $4,000 million is owed to the Soviet Union for arms, but President Sadat has said this will not be repaid.) In 1977 the situation substantially improved with the agreement of the Gulf Organization for the Development of Egypt (GODE) – consisting of Saudi Arabia, Kuwait, the UAE and Qatar – to advance Egypt $2,000 million in concessionary aid, and of Kuwait and Saudi Arabia each to defer $2,000 million of short-term debt repayments. In 1977 a total of $5,400 million in aid enabled Egypt entirely to reschedule its debts.

Another aspect of liberalization has been the moves towards devaluation with a view to ultimate floating of the Egyptian pound. Tourist exchange rates were first introduced to curtail black market dealings. In August 1973 a parallel foreign currency market was established, equivalent to the tourist rate and effectively devaluing the Egyptian pound by half. The artificially high official exchange rate had meant that a foreign partner had to pay more for his equity shareholding than the local partner, and the only real entry foreign capital and companies had with Egypt was in banking and oil exploration. From 1973 onwards an increasing number of transactions were transferred from the official to the parallel exchange rate until all except a few key commodities imported by the State were coming in at the parallel exchange rate. Complete freeing of the pound was postponed on the grounds that Egypt would benefit from the usual boost to exports when a country devalues. Cotton, textiles, and agricultural products make up most of Egypt's exports, and these would not sell in bigger volume after devaluation. However, part of Egypt's undertakings to the IMF was to amalgamate the official and parallel exchange rates by the end of 1978 with a view to the eventual floating of the pound.

Egypt also promised the public sector deficit pegged at £E 2,300 million so that it would fall from 26 per cent in 1977 to 16 per cent in 1981. Hidden subsidies for basic commodities were reduced in 1978 by £E 150 million to a total of £E 660 million.

Criticisms of Egypt's *Infitah* policies are mainly of two kinds: first that the Egyptian economy is not at a stage of development in which it can be opened to the effects of international competition. The removal of protection has widened social gaps and benefited only a small entrepreneurial class. Such foreign investment as has entered Egypt has not been related to the country's needs. The second type of criticism is that *Infitah* has made centralized socialist planning virtually impossible. Both these criticisms have some validity; the 1978–82 development plan, providing for total public sector investment of £E 10 billion and private sector investment at £E 400 million, is little more than an uncoordinated compilation of proposals by various governmental departments. Supporters of *Infitah* can claim that its benefits will necessarily take time to appear because of the complexities of transforming an overcentralized and bureaucratic system but that a new and more dynamic economic atmosphere has already been created.

There were four main favourable factors for the Egyptian economy in 1978–79:

1. The huge increase in remittances from Egyptians working abroad who numbered over one million. These quadrupled between 1976 and 1978 to approach $1800 million. However this had to be set against the effect of the loss of so many of Egypt's best trained and qualified personnel, although the loss was not necessarily permanent as most of those working in the Arab oil states planned to return.
2. Tourism, earning about $400 million a year. The growth potential is very substantial.
3. The Suez Canal (see p. 252 below).
4. The oil industry (see below).

In contrast, the effects of the Arab boycott of Egypt in reaction to the Treaty of Washington in March 1979 were potentially serious in excluding Egypt from all Pan-Arab funds and banks, cutting off Arab aid investment and withdrawing Arab credit-guarantees. Much depended on the extent to which these losses could be replaced from other, mainly western, sources.

Oil

Until 1968 Egypt was a net importer of oil but by 1978 oil exports were making a net contribution of about $700 million to the balance of payments. Partnership arrangements between foreign companies and the Egyptian General Petroleum Corporation existed well before the open-door policy. In 1978 there were 26 international companies operating in a variety of flexible relationships with the EGPC. The main areas of production are the Gulf of Suez, the Western Desert, and Sinai where the oil fields were returned to Egypt by Israel in 1975. Total output was running at 450,000 b.p.d. in early 1978, some 27 per cent higher than in 1976, and expanding steadily. Some important gas discoveries have been made in the Delta and the Western Desert, which are used to fuel industry and power stations in Alexandria, the Delta, and Helwan. The output target of crude oil and natural gas in 1979 was 34 million tons, compared with 25 million tons in 1978.

Other Minerals

A reappraisal of Egypt's wealth in other minerals is taking place. Iron ore production at the rate of about 500,000 tons a year has hitherto come from the Aswan area but much better quality ore estimated at 120 million tons has been discovered in the Bahriyah Oasis, which has been linked to Helwan by rail and road so as to supply the Helwan iron and steel plant at a projected 3.5 million tons a year. Substantial deposits of phosphates have been discovered, in addition to those being mined near Esna and Safaya and Hamrawein. New discoveries in the Western Desert have raised estimates of reserves to about 1,500 million tons. Coal deposits estimated at 80 million tons have been found near Suez. Manganese is mined in the Eastern Desert as well as Sinai (whose mineral potential has been underestimated in the past). Chrome is being exploited in the Eastern Desert, where deposits of tantalum and molybdenum have also been found.

Power

Electricity output rose from 2.1 billion kilowatt hours in 1959 to 10.4 billion kilowatt hours in 1975. Installed capacity was 3.89 megawatts. The High Dam provides cheap hydroelectric power although the output is considerably below installed capacity of 2,100 megawatts because the Dam is primarily used for water control rather than for generating electricity. Production capacity is therefore 1,500 megawatts in summer falling to 500 megawatts in winter. A project is under way to link all the major generating stations in Lower Egypt and also to distribute power generated by the High Dam station throughout the country. However, the rural electrification scheme launched in 1971 to bring electricity to all Egypt's 4,000 villages has been proceeding slowly.

Egypt has had several offers of nuclear power. In 1961 the USSR supplied a 2 megawatt nuclear reactor for peaceful purposes and in 1974 the USA agreed to provide two reactors. A West German firm is studying the feasibility of a scheme first proposed in the early 1960s to generate five times the power of the High Dam by channelling Mediterranean water into the Qattara Depression.

Manufacturing Industry

Egyptian industrialization really started between the two world wars and production rose by 138 per cent between 1938 and 1951. But the pace has been greatly increased since the Revolution and especially from 1957 to 1958. The 1960/65 Five-Year Plan provided for an investment of £E 519 million in manufacturing industry, and the 1965–70 Plan for £E 960 million although this was later scaled down. According to official estimates, the value of industrial output rose by 11 per cent in 1976 and over 13 per cent in 1977. The share of the private sector in manufacturing industry is about 30 per cent. In general, industry has considerable potential for growth if under-used capacity can be exploited, bottlenecks eliminated, adequate finance provided, and defence requirements reduced.

The two largest industrial sectors are food-processing and textiles which each produce nearly one third of total output. Other important sectors are mining and chemicals. Much of the investment in the past twenty years has been in basic heavy industry. The largest single project is the Helwan iron and steel works. The opening of a third furnace raised annual production from 300,000 tons to 900,000 tons and the target for full capacity is 2 million tons.

An aluminium plant at Nag Hamadi came into operation in 1976 with a capacity of 70,000 tons a year which is to be raised to 166,000 tons. Efforts have recently been made to expand the vehicle assembly industry, and output in 1977 amounted to 13,000 cars, 475 buses, 2,761 tractors, and 1,700 trucks. In 1977 also the output of refrigerators amounted to 129,000, washing-machines 114,000, and television sets 138,000. In Egypt's new development plan the main concentration is to be on fertilizers, cement, oil-refining, and iron and steel.

In May 1975 Egypt, Saudi Arabia, the UAE, and Qatar agreed to set up the Arab Military Industries Organization with a capital of $1,040 million and its headquarters, in Cairo, but this was dissolved in 1979 as part of the Arab boycott of Egypt.

The Suez Canal

The Suez Canal was a major source of revenue for Egypt in the 1960s and its closure in 1967 was a disaster. When it was reopened on 5 June 1975, the pattern of world shipping had changed. Whereas before 1967 70 per cent of world tanker tonnage was made up of vessels under 60,000 tons, by 1975 80 per cent of tankers could not use the Canal. A programme for widening and deepening the Canal was started immediately and the first stage, to be completed in 1979, will permit passage of 150,000 ton tankers fully laden. A second stage, to be completed by 1982, will allow the passage of fully laden super-tankers of up to 250,000 tons, and of ones of up to 400,000 tons in ballast. A bypass section is to be built at the northern end of the Canal to enable northbound convoys to avoid Port Said. The gross income from Canal tolls in 1979 reached about $600 million of which about 70 per cent came from general cargo shipping and the remainder from oil tankers. In July 1979 tolls were increased for cargo vessels for the first time since the Canal was re-opened in 1975, but the rates for oil tankers remained unchanged since the policy was to attract oil cargo back to the Canal. The effect of the increases was to provide additional revenues of about $50 million over a full year.

Enlarging the Canal is part of a $10 billion plan to rebuild the entire Suez Canal zone. This includes the rebuilding of Suez, Ismailia and Port Said (already largely completed in 1978 with aid from the Arab oil states), the construction of three tunnels under the Canal, improved port facilities, industrial and free zone sectors, and agricultural development.

Egypt decided in 1968 to build a 200-mile oil pipeline from Suez to Alexandria bypassing the Suez Canal and the project was completed in 1977. In 1978 only about 30 per cent of the pipeline's capacity of 1.6 million b.p.d. was being used although a cut in tariffs showed good prospects of attracting new customers.

The High Dam

When the High Dam was being built during the 1960s the official estimate of the increase in national income that it would produce was as follows:

	£E (millions)
1. Increasing the present cultivated area by about one million feddans and converting 700,000 feddans in Upper Egypt from basin to perennial irrigation	63
2. Guaranteeing water requirements for crops even in years of low flood, improving drainage, and guaranteeing the cultivation of one million feddans of rice annually	56
3. Protecting the country against the dangers of high flood, and preventing seepage and the inundation of small islands and river banks.	10
4. Improving navigation conditions on the Nile	5
5. Producing electric power annually of about 10 billion k.w.h.	100
Total	234

When the Dam was completed it was subjected to some strong criticisms on ecological grounds which, although not without foundation, tended to obscure the Dam's major contribution to the Egyptian economy. Intensive studies carried out in 1976–8 showed that the Dam was saving 32 billion cubic metres of water a year which would otherwise be lost to the sea out of the Nile's total flow of 84 billion cubic metres. It is this water which is making possible the reclamation of 1.3 million feddans and the conversion of 700,000 feddans in Upper Egypt from basin to perennial irrigation. In addition it has carried out its purpose of guaranteeing Egypt's water supply in years of low flood. In 1972 the flood failed and the estimated crop loss that would have been suffered without the Lake Nasser reservoir is $600 million or over half the cost of the Dam. Large quantities of cheap electric power are being produced although, because priority is given to the water supply for irrigation, output is well below installed capacity.

The Dam's drawbacks were largely predicted and allowed for when it was planned. The loss of the Nile silt which is now retained by the Dam can be replaced by fertilizers and the establishment of a sand-brick industry to replace the former mud bricks. The loss of the Delta sardine catch has been more than compensated for by the growing Lake Nasser fishing industry. More serious was the erosion to banks and bridges caused by the faster-flowing silt-free waters which was greater than was foreseen. However, this danger has declined and to counter future threats a spill-way canal is being built from Lake Nasser at Toshka, near Abu Simbel.

Undoubtedly the weightiest criticism of the Dam is that crop yields have fallen since it was built. However, research has shown that waterlogging – the rise in the water table and the subsequent salination of the soil – owes most to inefficient farming techniques or faulty reclamation schemes. The aim is to counter this by introducing tile drainage in about half Egypt's cultivated area by 1982 (see p. 241 above).

IV

IRAN

THE LAND AND THE PEOPLE

Iran, comprising some 628,000 square miles in the western half of the Iranian plateau, is bounded on the north by the Caspian Sea and the Soviet Union, on the south by the Persian Gulf and the Gulf of Oman, on the east by the Soviet Union, Afghanistan, and Baluchistan, and on the west by Iraq and Turkey. The greatest extent of the country from north-west to south-east is some 1,400 miles, and from north to south, some 875 miles. It can be broadly divided into the following regions:

The Caspian littoral is a narrow strip of land between the Caspian sea and the Elburz mountains, containing the provinces of Gilan and Mazandaran. The rainfall, well distributed throughout the year has a maximum in early autumn, and varies from 50 to 60 inches in the west to 20 inches in the east, and rises to over 100 inches on the northern slopes of the Elburz. The natural vegetation is dense deciduous forest, but where this has been cleared fruit, rice, cotton, and other crops thrive.

The Persian Gulf and its hinterland. The climate is hot and humid; the eastern end of the coastal region comes under the influence of the south-west monsoon. In the coastal district of Baluchistan the average annual rainfall is 3–4 inches. Bushire has an average annual rainfall of about 10 inches. The average annual rainfall is 12–15 inches, with a maximum in December. The hinterland includes some of the poorest parts of Iran.

The plateau. The plateau is ringed by mountain ranges, the general trend of which is from north-west to south-east. Its elevation varies between 3,000 and 5,000 feet; numerous peaks rise to over 12,000 feet; vegetation on the plateau is generally limited, but some forest is found in Kurdestan and Luristan, and a narrow belt of oak forest in Fars. Considerable areas, notably in Azarbaijan, Kurdestan, and northern Fars, consist of hill country and mountain pastures. Considerable variations of climate are found. The seasons are regular; the atmosphere is dry and clear, and the sun powerful at all altitudes. There is a great range of temperature. The only source of rain or snow is a series of depressions swinging eastwards along the Mediterranean, which are to some extent concentrated across north Iran, giving Mashad (9 in.) higher rainfall than, for example, Kerman (5 in.). They are, however, mostly interrupted by the Armenian massif and the Caucasus in the north and the Zagros in the west, so that much of the available water is lost and the plateau within the mountains is in a rain shadow. In general the 10-inch rainfall line follows the inner foothills of the Zagros-Elburz-Kopet Dagh ring of mountains, and also marks the boundary between areas where cereals can be cultivated extensively without irrigation and areas dependent on irrigation. The summer grazing areas of the nomadic tribes also lie in or near the 10-inch line. Rain begins in November and continues intermittently to the end of March, and in the south and north-east to the end of April. Heavy snowfalls are common in winter. Most of the plateau drains into inland lakes and swamps. The only navigable river is the Karun, which flows into the Persian Gulf.

Hot and relatively low land, comprising primarily the two great salt deserts south-east of Tehran, the Dasht-i Kavir and the Dasht-i Lut, and Sistan. The climate of Sistan is one of extremes: May and June are hot, but in winter blizzards occur. The average annual rainfall is 2½ inches.

The People

Many peoples, both in ancient and modern times, have passed through or settled in Iran. Those known to history as the Medes and Persians probably came originally from the Eurasian steppe. Later migrations, notably of Semitic tribes and, from Central Asia, of Turkish tribes, changed the ethnological structure of the country. The most important of these migrations in modern times was that of the Oghuz Turks in the eleventh and twelfth centuries AD; the large Turkish admixture in the Iranian population is mainly attributable to them. Turki-speaking elements are found today among the settled and semi-settled population, especially in Azarbaijan, Gurgan, eastern Mazandaran, and the districts of Qazvin, Hamadan, and Saveh, and also in Varamin and Khwar, near Tehran.

The October 1976 census put the total population at 33,591,875 of whom some 15.7 per cent were urban residents and found mainly in the major cities of Tehran (4.5 million), Isfahan 670,000, Meshed 670,000, Tabriz 590,000, Shiraz 41,000 and Ahwaz 330,000. Population is increasing by about 2.67 per cent a year.

Some 34 per cent of the labour force is still employed in agriculture and about 20 per cent are semi-nomadic tribes but urbanization is advancing rapidly. Density over the whole country, even if the desert areas are excluded, is extremely low; it is highest in north-west Azarbaijan, the coastal regions of Gilan and Mazandaran, Khuzistan, and the Tehran area.

Among the more important tribes are: the Turki-speaking Qashqai of Fars, who start to migrate in March from their winter quarters in southern Fars to their summer quarters near the northern boundaries of Fars, west of Shahriza and Yazd-i-Khast, extending to the eastern slopes of Mt. Dinar, whence they return in September; the Kurds, found chiefly in western Azarbaijan, Kurdestan, and the Kermanshah region;[1] the Bakhtiaris, who range from north-east Khuzistan to west of Isfahan, and are divided into two main divisions, the Haft Lang and Chahar Lang; the Lurs of Luristan; the Shahsavan, a Turkish tribe ranging from the Mughan steppes to Qum and Saveh; the Guklan and Yamut Turkomans in the north-east frontier districts; and the Baluch of Iranian Baluchistan. Other tribal groups in Fars include the Khamseh, of mixed, partly Arab origin, the Mamasani, the Boir Ahmadi, and the Dushmanziari. In Khuzistan are a number of sedentary and pastoral Arab tribes speaking Arabic; in Khurasan the Hazara are supposed to be descended from colonists left by Jenghiz Khan in the Oxus valley.

Language

The Persian language is a member of the Iranian group of Indo-European languages. Old Persian was the language of the

[1] Small settlements also exist in western Mazandaran and Khurasan.

Achaemenian emperors, known through cuneiform inscriptions and Avestan texts; Middle Persian belongs to the Sasanian period, the chief sources for which are Zoroastrian literature and secular texts in Pahlavi; modern Persian is the most widely known branch of New Persian. Kurdish, Luri (spoken by the Lurs and the Bakhtiaris), Mazandarani, and Gilaki (spoken in the Caspian provinces) also belong to this group. Modern Persian is the language of the administration and is spoken by the educated classes throughout the country. It is written in the Arabic script and contains a large number of Arabic loan words. It has an extensive literature going back to the tenth century.

Religion

The Iranians are predominantly Moslem. The Ithna Ashari or Jafari rite of the Shii sect,[2] which recognizes twelve hereditary Imams, is the official religion of the country. The cities of Najaf and Karbala in Iraq, being the burial places of Ali, the first Imam, and of his son Hussein, the third Imam, respectively, are important centres of Shii pilgrimage; Meshed, the burial place of the eighth Imam, Reza, and Qum, the burial place of his daughter Fatima, are also pilgrimage centres. The Kurds, Turkomans, and Baluch are mainly Sunni. Christianity, Judaism, and Zoroastrianism are also officially recognized. The largest Christian group is formed by the Armenians, numbering some 80,000, mainly concentrated in the large towns, especially Tabriz, Tehran, and Isfahan. There are some 40,000 Jews, mainly in the large towns. About 7,000 Zoroastrians are concentrated chiefly in Yazd, Kerman, and Tehran. There are also a number of Bahais, whose religion is not officially recognized and against whom there have been sporadic outbreaks of violence in recent years, the most serious in 1955.

HISTORY AND POLITICS

Iran's existence as a national state in the modern sense goes back to the sixteenth century. The area over which successive Iranian governments ruled has varied; the frontiers of present-day Iran, compared, for example, with those of the reign of

[2] See above, p. 46.

Shah Abbas (1587–1629) or at the beginning of Fath Ali Shah Qajar's reign (1797–1834), have contracted considerably. The main losses have been to Russia in the north-west and north-east and to Afghanistan in the east. During the Middle Ages Iran did not exist as a political entity and was merely a geographical term.

The first great Iranian empire was the sixth-century BC Achaemenian Empire, which, at its height, extended from Transoxiana to North Africa, and was overthrown by Alexander in 334–330 BC. The Seleucids, the Arsacids, and the Greek principalities of Bactria then arose as succession states.

In the first half of the third century AD, with the rise of the Sasanians, there was a reaction against Hellenism. Sasanian rule was mainly notable for centralization, the re-establishment of Zoroastrianism as the state religion, and a hierarchical society of priests, warriors, the bureaucracy, and peasants and artisans. The main external problem was to hold the north-eastern frontier against pressure from the Eurasian steppe, while in the west the Sasanians were occupied in a struggle for power with the Byzantine Empire. The Sasanian Empire reached its height under Anushiravan (AD 531–79), but after his death it rapidly declined until its extinction by the Arabs in the seventh century.

Arabs, Turks, and Mongols

It was largely the incorporation of the Sasanian domains into the Arab empire of the Umayyad Caliphs (661–750), with its capital at Damascus, that eventually led to the transfer of power to Baghdad, the capital of the Abbasid Caliphs (750–1248). The majority of the Iranians became converted to Islam, until recent times the strongest single influence in Iranian cultural development. Under the Abbasid Caliphs Iranians played an increasingly important part in the life of the empire. After the reign of Harun al-Rashid (786–809) the effective authority of the Caliphs began to decline, and from the ninth to the eleventh centuries a series of semi-independent Iranian dynasties reigned in the eastern part of the empire. Pressure from the nomads of Central Asia was meanwhile renewed, and in 1040 Masud ibn Mahmud, the Ghaznavid, was defeated at the battle of Dendenqan by the Oghuz Turks, who subsequently overran the whole of the eastern Caliphate. The most prominent group among them was the Seljuqs, who established an empire extending, in its heyday, from Transoxiana to the shores of the Mediterranean. Under the Seljuqs the Iranians again played an outstanding part in administration and culture. Finally, in 1153, Sanjar, the last of the Great Seljuqs, was defeated by fresh bodies of Oghuz from Central Asia, and the Great Seljuq Empire broke up into a number of succession states, including that of the Shahs of Khwarazm.

During the period from the ninth to the twelfth centuries considerable changes took place in the social and economic structure of the country. Whereas in the early period of Arab domination the economy was predominantly a gold economy, the administration bureaucratic, and the civilization predominantly urban, by the tenth century the financial economy had broken down and the administration was becoming largely militarized. In Seljuq times these changes took firmer shape. The new structure, which, in broad outline, lasted until the nineteenth century, was not feudal in the European sense of the term. It was rather a bureaucracy of the Asiatic type. With the breakdown of the power of the central Government, the military leaders, as provincial governors, diverted the revenue from the state treasury into their own pockets, and arrogated to themselves such privileges as the former ruling class had enjoyed.

The next wave of invasion from Central Asia was that of the Mongols. The Shah of Khwarazm was defeated during the lifetime of Jenghiz Khan (d. AD 1227) and the way to Iran was opened. Its final conquest was brought about by his grandson, Hulagu, who founded the Ilkhan dynasty, which lasted for something under 100 years, breaking up into warring factions about AD 1335. Towards the end of the fourteenth century Iran was incorporated in the immense empire of Timur (d. 1405), which stretched from the Oxus-Jaxartes basin in the east to Iran and Iraq in the west, and whose capital was Samarkand. It did not outlive its founder in western Iran and Iraq, and the eastern portion disintegrated on the death of Shahrukh in AD 1447.

The Safavids

The political vacuum thus created was eventually filled by the Safavids, originally the heads of a religious order centred on Ardabil in north-west Iran. By 1508 the dominions of Ismail, the founder of the dynasty, extended from Herat to Baghdad and Diyarbekr. In the west the ultimate result of a long-drawn-out struggle with the Ottoman Empire was the establishment of a frontier running from the Caucasus southwards to the Persian Gulf. Using Shiism as a political instrument in this struggle with the Sunni Ottomans, Ismail imposed this form of Islam upon his subjects, most of whom had till then remained Sunnis; from this time onwards the Islamic world was split into two groups, Sunni and Shii.

During the rule of the Safavid dynasty, which reached its height under Shah Abbas (1587–1629), an Iranian political and commercial revival took place. Contact with Europe increased; a variety of missions was sent by European countries to the Safavid courts, and European trading stations were established on the Persian Gulf.

The Safavid dynasty virtually came to an end with the revolt of the Afghans (1721–30), who were in turn overthrown by Nadir Shah Afshar (1735–47), under whom the Iranian Empire extended, for a fleeting period, from the Indus to the Caucasus. The Afsharid dynasty was succeeded first by the Zands and then by the Qajars, the first of whom was Aqa Mohammed (1779–97). The Qajar dynasty lasted until 1925.

The Qajars

The emphasis in Iran's relations with Western countries during the eighteenth century began to change from commerce, where it had lain during the Safavid period, to strategy. By 1914 the main emphasis had been transferred to oil. The dominant feature of nineteenth-century Iranian politics was the rivalry of the Great Powers. During the Napoleonic period both France and Britain sent missions to enlist the support of the Iranian Government. Russian pressure upon Iran, which had been felt in the first half of the eighteenth century, when Gilan had for a while passed into Russian hands, meanwhile increased. Two Russo-Iranian wars ended disastrously for Iran:

by the treaties of Gulistan and Turkmanchai she lost to Russia all her territory west of the river Aras. By the latter, Iran granted extra-territorial privileges to Russian nationals, and fixed at 5 per cent *ad valorem* (though this was reciprocal) the customs duty on all Russian goods entering Iran. This became the basis for commercial agreements concluded with other European Powers and the grant to them of extra-territorial privileges. Subsequently there were losses of Iranian territory to Russia in the north-east. During the nineteenth century Anglo-Russian rivalry in Asia increased and there was a tendency on the part of the British Government to regard a Russian threat to Iran as tantamount to a Russian threat to India. This situation almost inevitably created a cleavage in Iranian internal affairs between those who looked to Russia and those who looked to Britain.

During the latter half of the nineteenth century maladministration reduced Iran to critical straits. Largely in order to replenish the exchequer rather than to modernize the country, concessions were granted by the Shah to foreign governments and foreign nationals for commercial and industrial enterprises, banks, road-building, and the like, and large sums were borrowed from abroad. Meanwhile, misgovernment, the extravagance of the Court, the grant of wide economic privileges to foreigners, and the restrictions put upon the political freedom of the country by the terms of certain of the foreign loans, aroused more and more discontent. This feeling, coupled with the stirrings of a desire for progress among the educated classes, culminated in the constitutional revolution of 1905–6, and the grant of the Constitution by Muzaffar al-Din Shah in 1906. The new regime, however, soon met with difficulties. On 31 August 1907 came the Anglo-Russian Agreement, which divided Iran into Russian and British spheres of influence and a neutral zone. Neither party was to seek political or commercial concessions in the sphere of the other. This agreement was a profound shock to Iranian opinion, which could not realize that with a war with Germany on the horizon Britain was compelled to compromise with Russia. It was also a prelude to more flagrant intervention by Russia, who seemed determined to prevent the successful working of the Constitution. Mohammed Ali Shah attempted with Russian support to overthrow the Constitution, one of his principal instruments being the Iranian Cossack Brigade, which had been formed in 1879 by Nasir al-Din Shah, and was led by Russian officers who remained on the active list of the Russian army. The Russians occupied Tabriz in April 1909 and remained there for over a year. In 1909 Mohammed Ali Shah was forced by the constitutionalists to leave the country. He returned, with Russian connivance, but was again driven out; and his son Ahmad Shah was placed on the throne. In 1911 north Iran was again occupied by Russia, who issued an ultimatum to the Iranian Government demanding the dismissal of Morgan Shuster, an American who had been engaged as Treasurer-General some nine months before. The result was a *coup d'état,* the closure of the Majlis, and Shuster's dismissal. Thereafter Russian ascendancy continued to increase until the outbreak of the First World War, when Iran became a battleground for Turkish, Russian, and British forces.[3]

Iran emerged from the war in a state of chaos, with three armed forces and an empty treasury. In 1919 the Government signed with Britain the abortive 1919 agreement, which provided for the supply of British advisers for the administration, some military officers and equipment for a single armed force, a loan, and co-operation in the development of transport. By the early 1920s Russian pressure began to relax, and on 26 February 1921 the Soviet-Iranian treaty was signed, by which the Soviet Government renounced 'the tyrannical policy' of Tsarist Russia, remitted all Iranian debts to the Tsarist Government, and abandoned extra-territorial privileges for Russian nationals. The treaty also gave up all concessions then held by the Russian Government or Russian nationals, but they secured under pressure the most valuable concession, the Caspian fisheries, which had formerly been held by Russian nationals but had lapsed. All previous treaties and conventions concluded by the Tsarist Government were declared null and void. This treaty was ratified by the Majlis, which however refused to ratify the Anglo-Iranian agreement of 1919. The latter had been much criticized, especially in the United States, as aiming at a disguised protectorate over Iran,

[3] Sir P.M. Sykes, *History of Persia* (London, 1930), vol. 2.

whereas the Russo-Iranian treaty received little study, and few even noticed the clause authorizing Russia to send troops into Iran in circumstances of which Russia would be the sole judge.

Reza Shah and Modern Iran

It was at this juncture that Reza Shah, a colonel in the Cossack Brigade, came into prominence. He led troops on Tehran and brought about the *coup d'état* of 1921, making himself first Minister of War and Commander-in-Chief, and later Prime Minister. In October 1925 the Majlis voted for the deposition of Ahmad Shah Qajar. A Constituent Assembly was then convened, and in December it voted that the throne be entrusted to Reza Khan, who took the name 'Pahlavi' for his dynasty, and to his male descendants. The early years of Reza Shah's reign were largely occupied in the establishment of law and order by a series of successful campaigns against the tribes. Some of the migratory tribes were 'settled' by him, in the sense that they were forbidden to move between summer and winter pastures, whereby they and the economy of Iran were impoverished. Compulsory military service was introduced, and the army was more than doubled in size. Communications were improved, legal reform was carried out, and the Capitulations were abolished. The finances of the country, which had been entrusted to an American economist, Dr. Millspaugh, as Administrator-General, were reorganized; but in 1927 a dispute between the Shah and Millspaugh as to expenditure on the army led to the dismissal of the American financial mission. Education was reorganized on Western lines, though with greater attention to numbers of schools and pupils than to quality; in 1936 women were compelled to discard the veil, and European costume was made obligatory for both sexes. Industrialization was encouraged. Gradually, however, the regime became increasingly totalitarian; the façade of parliament was preserved, but the people were deprived of political responsibility and had little opportunity for effective action. Meanwhile the Shah became the owner of large areas of good land, by confiscation on political charges or by methods of purchase which, however disguised, amounted in fact to expropriation.

It is still too soon to make a fair estimate of the reign of Reza Shah. In that he restored order, abolished the privileges of foreigners, and raised the status of Iran in international affairs, he deserved well of his country. On the other hand by doing everything himself he deprived a generation of Iranians of training in the art of government. He encouraged industry but neglected the main occupation, agriculture; he built the Trans-Iranian Railway without recourse to foreign loans but crushed the poorer classes by indirect taxation to pay for it. Through failure to take advice or from other causes his efforts were often misdirected, so that at the end of his reign his country had grain elevators with no grain in them, a steel works under construction in a spot economically impractical for a country without assured supplies of local iron ore, and a string of palaces in a capital lacking a proper water-supply. The latter part of his reign made his people forget the real services he had performed in the earlier years, and his abdication in 1941 was received in Iran with almost universal acclaim. Attempts which are sometimes made in Iran to represent him as a beloved monarch torn by the Allies from his sorrowing people have no support from contemporary Iranian records.

Reza Shah took up strongly the Iranian claim to Bahrain,[4] from which the Iranians were driven by the Arabs in 1783. The claim was maintained by successive Iranian governments but dropped in 1970.

The Second World War

On the outbreak of war Iran declared her neutrality. The country was in feeling pro-German, and in 1941 a vehement correspondence took place between the British and Soviet governments and the Shah about the removal of the Germans resident in Iran, the Allies regarding them as a great danger and the Shah denying this. On 26 August 1941 Britian and Russian forces entered the country, and Iranian resistance ceased after two or three days. The United States Government, appealed to by Reza Shah both before and after the invasion, emphasized in reply 'the global nature of the conflict with the Axis',

[4] See above, p. 175.

advised Iran to avoid assisting the Axis and to aid the Allies, and placed the invasion 'in its true light as one small element in the vast effort to stop Hitler's ambition of world conquest'.[5]

The immediate problem confronting the Allies, in addition to the danger which the Axis missions and nationals constituted, was to guard against the threat to British oil supplies and Allied security in general if the Germans should continue their successes in Russia and enter Iran. It was also essential to secure for the dispatch of aid to Russia a way less exposed to German attacks than the route to Murmansk and Archangel. On 16 September Reza Shah, believing, wrongly, that an advance on the capital by Russian troops was directed against him personally, abdicated in favour of his son, Mohammed Reza, then aged 23. The Iranian Government broke off relations with the German and Italian Governments and later with the Japanese Government. In September 1943 the Government declared war on Germany and thereby qualified for membership of the United Nations.

On 29 January 1942 a tripartite treaty of alliance was concluded with Britain and the Soviet Union,[6] who undertook 'to respect the territorial integrity, sovereignty, and political independence of Iran' and 'to defend Iran by all means at their command from all aggression'. The Iranian Government for its part undertook to render specified non-military assistance to its allies. These were permitted to maintain armed forces on Iranian soil, but their presence was not to constitute a military occupation, and they were to be withdrawn not later than six months after the termination of hostilities between the Allied Powers and Germany and her associates. The Allied Powers undertook not to interfere in the internal affairs of Iran, and jointly 'to use their best endeavours to safeguard the economic existence of the Iranian people against the privations and difficulties' resulting from the war.

After the German attack on the Soviet Union in June 1941 but before the Japanese attack on Pearl Harbour made the United States a belligerent, the Lend-Lease Act of 1941 'made the United States an auxiliary of Great Britain in the task of

[5] *Memoirs of Cordell Hull* (New York, 1948), ii. 1501–2.

[6] Cmd. 6335.

delivering supplies to the USSR through the Persian Corridor'.[7] In the end there were some 30,000 American troops in Iran, but they were non-combatants: they were employed in dispatching aid to Russia, and in particular in running the Trans-Iranian Railway from the Persian Gulf to Tehran instead of the British, who had handed over in May 1943. The Soviet authorities administered the railway section north of Tehran. The American troops operated throughout as part of the British forces, who were responsible for law and order, and in the execution of that task often incurred the sole odium for acts undertaken in the interests of the Allies in general. Some Americans held that United States interests required the regularization of the position of her troops by an agreement with the Iranian Government, but negotiations to that end dragged on for a long time and were never completed. However, on 1 December 1943 Roosevelt, as well as Stalin and Churchill, signed the Tehran Declaration, undertaking to continue to make available to Iran such economic assistance as might be possible, and expressing the desire for the maintenance of the independence, sovereignty, and territorial integrity of Iran.[8]

Except in the matter of aid to Russia the Allies were far from being united in Iran. In Millspaugh's opinion,[9] 'the Soviets acted strongly, with self-confidence, a consciousness of power, and a clear conception of their postwar national requirements, while the British and Americans acted timidly, without clarity of purpose, postponing issues, and compromising principles'. The country became divided in practice into two zones, roughly north and south of the latitude of Tehran. In spite of the treaty of 1942 the Soviet authorities interfered with the movement of goods and the passage of Iranian officials, police and troops between the Soviet zone and other parts of Iran. Iran's internal economy broke down. Transport was dislocated; the food situation worsened; security deteriorated; inflation became serious. In these circumstances the Iranian Government again had recourse to American advisers. A food

[7]T.H. Vail Motter, *The Persian Corridor and Aid to Russia* (Washington, Dept. of the Army, 1952), p.4.

[8]Texts of this Declaration and of the 1942 treaty are given by Arthur C. Millspaugh, *Americans in Persia* (Washington, D.C., 1946), App.

[9]Ibid. p. 157.

adviser was appointed in 1942, a military mission under General Ridley in July of the same year, and advisers to the gendarmerie, headed by Colonel Schwartzkopf, shortly afterwards. Finally in November 1942 Millspaugh was invited to return to Iran, with a financial mission. He took up his duties as Administrator-General of Finances in February 1943, and in May was granted additional powers to control imports and exports, prices and distribution, to fix rents, and to control wages in all public works and services. He met with opposition from various internal quarters, and he was regarded with suspicion by the Soviet authorities, who withheld their co-operation. For these and other reasons he attained only a limited success, and in February 1945 he resigned.

The Iranian-Soviet Dispute and the Separatist Movements

In 1943 the Royal Dutch Shell Company applied for an oil concession in south-east Iran, and in the spring of 1944 the Socony-Vacuum and Sinclair Oil Companies also submitted proposals. The applications were still awaiting a decision when early in September a Soviet official arrived in Tehran, and, after a tour in the north, asked for an oil concession. The Iranian Government then announced that applications for oil concessions must wait until the end of the war, but on 2 December 1944 the Majlis adopted a law forbidding ministers and officials even to discuss oil concessions with anyone. Fierce attacks by all the means of Soviet propaganda brought about the fall of the Iranian Prime Minister. Meanwhile the Soviet authorities prevented Iranian security forces from entering Azarbaijan and the Caspian provinces; in Azarbaijan the Tudeh party, which had changed its name to the Democrat party, with the support if not at the instigation of the Soviet authorities set up an autonomous government in December 1945.

In January 1946 the Iranian Government referred the matter to the Security Council, which decided to leave the parties to negotiate directly with each other, but to retain the question on the agenda. No agreement had been reached by 2 March 1946, the date after which, under the treaty of 1942, no Allied troops were to remain in Iran. The last British troops left on that date (the Americans had all been withdrawn by the end of 1945); but the Soviet Government announced that it would retain troops in north Iran until the situation should be clarified. It was not until 9 May that the Iranian Prime Minister could announce that the Soviet troops had left the country. On 5 April an Iranian spokesman had announced the conclusion of an oil agreement with the Soviet Government, subject to ratification by the Majlis. The agreement provided for the formation of a Soviet-Iranian Oil Company, in which the Soviet Government would hold 51 per cent of the shares for the first 25 years and 50 per cent for the next 25, the Iranian Government in each case holding the remainder. In June there were negotiations between the Democrat party in Azarbaijan and the Iranian Government.

In July 1946 a general strike occurred at Abadan, with violent rioting and bloodshed. Genuine grievances were exploited by the Tudeh Party, which used various non-economic cries, including the incitement of Iranians against their (Iranian) Arab fellow workers. The Prime Minister took some members of the Tudeh party into his Cabinet, and one of them 'discovered' a plot among the Bakhtiari and caused several leaders of the tribe to be arrested. A serious tribal revolt broke out in the south and the Prime Minister dismissed the Tudeh ministers and then sent troops into Azarbaijan, where the 'autonomy' movement collapsed, as did a linked movement in Kurdestan.

The oil company bill was not presented to the Majlis within the seven-month period prescribed by the Iranian-Soviet agreement. Electoral and other delays prevented its submission until 22 October 1947, and then it was rejected by 102 votes to two. The Majlis also passed a resolution forbidding the grant of any oil concession to any foreign government or the acceptance of any foreign government as partner. It decided that Iran should embark on a five-year prospecting programme out of her own resources and that, if oil was found, the Government might negotiate for the sale of the product to the Soviet Union. The Soviet Government accused Iran of treacherously violating her commitments and of hostile actions 'incompatible with normal relations between two states'. Soviet propaganda became increasingly menacing.

On 10 December the Prime Minister, Qavam al-Saltaneh,

was defeated on a vote of confidence – a sacrifice probably to Soviet anger. His policy, reinforced no doubt by the watchfulness of the United Nations, had secured the departure of the Soviet troops without payment of the price in oil that the Soviet Government had obviously counted on securing. In the same month a significant speech was made in the Assembly by Dr. Musaddiq. In its propaganda the Soviet Government had argued that the Iranian rejection of the oil agreement constituted unfair discrimination against the Soviet Union since the British held an oil concession in the south of Iran. Musaddiq maintained that Iranian interests demanded a policy of 'negative balance'. 'Positive balance', he said, would involve giving Russia an oil concession in the north because the British had one in the south – a suicidal policy. 'Negative balance' meant, by implication, the elimination of the British concession. From that moment the Anglo-Iranian Oil Company (AIOC) concession was doomed.

The American-Iranian Military Agreement

The American policy enunciated in 1947 which came to be called the Truman Doctrine[10] was soon extended from Greece and Turkey to Iran. On 22 December the United States submitted to the United Nations an American-Iranian agreement,[11] signed on 6 October 1947, which provided for the establishment of a United States military mission in Iran to cooperate with the Iranian Minister of War in 'enhancing the efficiency of the Iranian Army'. The agreement was to remain in force until 20 March 1949. It included a clause providing that Iranian army affairs might not be entrusted to military experts of other Powers without American consent. A Soviet note on 31 January 1948 accused the Iranian Government of lending itself to American plans for converting Iran into a military-strategic base, and demanded that it should take immediate steps 'to eliminate the existing abnormal situation', which it considered incompatible with the state of good-neighbourly relations proclaimed in the Soviet-Iranian Treaty

[10] See above, pp. 30–31

[11] *US Treaties and Other International Acts*, series no. 1666 (1948). The agreement has been extended annually for one year.

of 1921.[12] An Iranian reply of 5 February contained counter-allegations. The exchange of notes continued against a background of bitter Soviet radio propaganda. It was a year later, but perhaps not without relation to that propaganda, that the Shah was shot at and wounded by a member of the Tudeh party. The party was proscribed and a number of its leaders were arrested.

Nationalization of the Oil Industry

In 1948 negotiations with the AIOC had been opened for the conclusion of a Supplemental Agreement for a revision of the royalty terms. An agreement was initialled in July 1949, but although the revenue receivable by Iran with effect from 1948 would have been increased considerably thereby, the Oil Committee of the Majlis reported against the agreement in November 1950 and the Government withdrew it. The opposition to the agreement was led by Musaddiq and supported by the extreme nationalists and the religious elements. Long dissatisfied with the Iranian share of the oil proceeds, the opponents of the AIOC were easily able, in a country where since the Anglo-Russian Agreement of 1907 Britain had been the scapegoat, to persuade the public that the AIOC was responsible for the grievous state of the country and moreover guilty of political interference in the internal affairs of Iran. In March 1951 the Prime Minister, General Razmara, was assassinated; this murder, and the assassination of the Minister of Education a few days later, hastened the passage of bills for the nationalization of the oil industry through both houses of parliament in April 1951. In May Musaddiq became Prime Minister. He was now in a position to establish that 'negative balance' which he had recommended in 1947. He rejected the request of the AIOC to submit the dispute to arbitration in accordance with the terms of the 1933 agreement, and by October 1951 the company found its position impossible and withdrew the last of its employees from Iran. The British Government and the company severally filed petitions with the International Court, the former asking the Court to

[12] Full version of note in *Soviet News,* 3 February 1948; see also 'Persia and the USSR', *World Today*, March 1948.

declare Iran bound by the 1933 agreement to accept the company's request for arbitration, the latter asking the Court to nominate an arbitrator. The Iranian Government declined to recognize the Court's jurisdiction. Britain meanwhile referred the dispute to the Security Council, which decided on 19 October 1951 to defer consideration of the Iranian case pending the pronouncement of the International Court. The judgement was not delivered until 22 July 1952, when the Court held that it had no jurisdiction owing to the limitations imposed by the Iranian Government when it accepted the compulsory jurisdiction of the Court; it also held that the 1933 agreement, although concluded under the auspices of the League of Nations, was not a treaty, and that the British Government was not a party to the contract. The majority of seven to four in Iran's favour included the British judge.

From August 1951 to February 1953 repeated efforts were made to provide a solution. Proposals were put forward by the AIOC, by British and Americans jointly (on one occasion with a personal appeal from Truman and Churchill), and by the International Bank, but Musaddiq would listen to none of them. The oil industry which he had undertaken to make profitable to Iran brought in virtually nothing. To maintain his position he was compelled to rely more and more upon the Tudeh, and there were frequent clashes between supporters and opponents, often with fatal casualties.

In August 1952 Musaddiq was given full powers for six months, in economic, banking, judicial, administrative, military, and financial matters, and this period was subsequently extended for a second six months. He was thus free to try to effect a social revolution if he wished. One possible change, viz. the breaking up of large estates in favour of peasant proprietorship, he opposed strongly, and he stopped the Shah's land-distribution scheme.

Musaddiq pursued the disagreement with the British Government to the extent of closing down all British Consulates in Iran and finally of breaking off diplomatic relations. In home affairs he quarrelled with all the other elements of government; the Senate, the Majlis, and finally the Shah. On 13 August 1953 the Shah, in the exercise of his constitutional powers, appointed General Zahedi Prime Minister. Zahedi's attempt to establish himself as Prime Minister at first failed, and the Shah and the Queen left the country and went to Rome. On 19 August, however, Musaddiq's supporters were defeated and he was arrested and the Shah returned. Musaddiq was sentenced to three years' solitary confinement for trying to overthrow the regime and illegally dissolving the Assembly. His Minister for Foreign Affairs, Hussein Fatemi, was sentenced to death for treason and executed (November 1955).

The Post-Nationalization Era

In the reaction that followed the overthrow of Musaddiq, opposition activity and political parties of all shades were suppressed and the press subjected to strict controls. With Musaddiq under arrest, its leaders and members in prison or otherwise harassed, and its ranks in disarray, the National Front ceased to function as an organized political force and had to resort to covert activity. The Tudeh party was again proscribed and disappeared underground, but in January 1954 fifty of its members were arrested on charges of conspiring to murder the Shah. The *Fadayan i Islam* came into notice again when one of its members in November 1955 made an unsuccessful attempt on the life of the Prime Minister, Hussein Ala.

Power, especially after the retirement of Premier Zahedi in 1955 and the appointment of Ala, a staunch upholder of royal prerogatives, as his successor, tended increasingly to be concentrated in the hands of the Shah, a trend that continued under Premiers Manuchehr Eqbal (1957–60) and Jafar Sharif-Emami (1960–61). In the elections to the eighteenth Majlis in 1954 and the nineteenth Majlis in 1956 (when the term of the Majlis was extended from two to four years), care was exercised to ensure that only those with acceptable political views secured seats to the two Houses.

These measures of political control were tempered by efforts at economic development, through which it was hoped to secure a higher standard of living for the middle and lower classes. The budgetary position of the country, in spite of the resumption of oil revenues, was still serious. However, the steady growth of oil revenues continued, American aid permitted more ambitious economic planning, and in February 1956 the Second Seven-Year Plan Law was approved.

In foreign policy, the Government was induced by both political and economic considerations to identify itself closely with the Western camp. Diplomatic relations with Britain were resumed, and Ambassadors appointed, in January 1954. On 3 November 1955, Iran joined the Baghdad Pact, an act reflecting a desire for increased Western arms assistance and also for security against Communist subversion. These steps further strained relations with the Soviet Union.

The internal political atmosphere remained strained, however. Nationalist passions released during the oil nationalization struggle were not quelled by the post-Musaddiq settlement. The anti-Western feelings generated during the period rendered the Government's pro-Western orientation, symbolized by adherence to the Baghdad Pact, even more unpopular. Reformist aspirations could find no outlet in the restrictive political atmosphere. Large-scale Second Seven-Year Plan development projects, though necessary to build up Iran's infrastructure, could not yield results quickly. Besides, the sudden inflow of oil revenues and aid money led to widespread corruption. Political unrest was also fed by galloping inflation. At the instance of the International Monetary Fund and as a condition for the provision of foreign exchange, the Government in 1960 agreed to an economic stabilization programme severely restricting credits, imports, and foreign exchange spending. But initially at least this only added to economic pressures on the middle and lower classes.

The corrective measures adopted proved to be chiefly gestures rather than genuine attempts at reform. In 1959, at the Shah's initiative, two of his loyal supporters formed two political parties: the first, Melliyun, to serve as the majority party and the second, Mardom, to serve as the loyal opposition. But this conferred the trappings of democracy without the substance, and won no support.

These various political and economic dissatisfactions came to a head in the summer of 1960 during the elections to the twentieth Majlis, when it was expected that the Mardom and Melliyun parties and other acceptable candidates should divide the seats among themselves. Extra-parliamentary criticism could not be suppressed, however, and the National Front, Mozaffar Baqai's Toilers' Party, and a group of independents led by Ali Amini spearheaded a campaign attacking election rigging, corruption, the lack of civil liberties, and the economic situation. Election irregularities were so widespread and blatant that in August the Shah expressed dissatisfaction with the conduct of the vote and asked the deputies so far elected to resign, thus in effect annulling the election. Eqbal resigned as Prime Minister and Sharif-Emami, a member of the out-going Cabinet, was appointed to replace him.

The Sharif-Emami Government lasted a brief eight months. Elections were held and Majlis convened by February 1961. But widespread irregularities and arrests of opposition leaders and of students fed public unrest. In Majlis men like the National Front leader, Allahyar Saleh, who had been given seats as a gesture to opposition pressures, found a public forum from which to attack the Government. The final blow came on 2 May when a teachers' strike for higher pay led to the shooting of one of the strikers. The Sharif-Emami Government fell on 6 May.

The Amini Reforms

Ali Amini, whom the Shah appointed as Prime Minister at this critical juncture, was a wealthy aristocrat who had held a string of important government appointments. He also was believed to be a liberal and a reformer, a reputation he had enhanced as a critic of the Eqbal Government during the abortive 1960 elections, and initially at least was moderately acceptable to both the Establishment and its left-wing opposition. The new Premier moved with great energy during his first few weeks in office. Several high-ranking civil servants and retired military officers, including five generals, were arrested on charges of corruption. Amini also loosened controls on the press and permitted a far greater measure of freedom to the National Front and other left-wing groups. He brought into the Cabinet as Agriculture Minister Hassan Arsanjani, a left-wing politician committed to land reform and the break-up of the large estates. And he announced further programmes for economic retrenchment and civil service reorganization.

These measures, considered radical in the prevailing atmosphere of caution and conservatism, bespoke a degree of autonomy and independence that the Shah had not granted to any Prime Minister since Musaddiq. The Shah also acceded to a demand by Amini for the dissolution of Majlis, a body which the new Premier believed an obstruction to reform, and issued a decree to this effect on 9 May. On 14 November, the Shah conferred even greater authority on Amini by issuing a *farman* (royal decree) empowering the Prime Minister to rule by Cabinet decree until such time as Majlis was reconvened.

The measures undertaken by the new Government met with some degree of success. Amini was able to curb several years' runaway inflation and to introduce greater rationality in Government planning, to end nearly a decade of political paralysis by opening up a dialogue with the opposition, and to begin the great task of administrative reform which was to bear fruit five years later. A High Administrative Council (transformed in 1966 into a Civil Service Commission) was established to undertake the task of civil service reorganization. The ambitious Third Development Plan Law was approved. A revised land reform bill, perhaps the most important single step taken in Iran in the decade of the 1960s, was passed by the Cabinet on 9 January 1962. The work of breaking up the big estates was begun, and Arsanjani pursued the task with great vigour.

Amini's programmes were, however, frustrated by deep institutional problems, the difficult economic situation he had inherited from his predecessors, and opposition from both the right and the left. Several privileged and powerful factions reacted unfavourably to the Prime Minister's reform measures. The great landowners opposed the break-up of their estates and received support from their allies among the Moslem authorities. High-ranking civilian and military officials feared the extension of the anti-corruption drive. Politicians who had been prominent in former governments resented the closure of parliament and their exclusion from the higher circles of government by Amini's younger technocrats. The army was restrained by the arrest of some of its retired officers and by a well-founded belief that the Prime Minister intended to cut their budget in favour of other sectors of the economy.

Amini's excessive reliance on US support also left him open to charges of permitting foreign interference in Iran's internal affairs and caused serious deterioration of relations with the Soviet Union.

Much more crucial was the fact that the Prime Minister's relative independence of the Court and his energetic assertion of prime ministerial prerogatives strained relations between Amini and the Shah. Finally, many of the more sympathetic members of the public, though aware of extenuating circumstances, were genuinely disturbed by the continued suspension of parliamentary rule and contravention of the Constitution, while economic restrictions and the Premier's own excessively gloomy prognostications led to a flight of capital and further economic stagnation. The National Front, although enjoying greater freedom than at any time since Musaddiq, also failed to support the Government, insisting that parliamentary elections be held. This Amini refused to do, arguing that elections could not be free nor the incoming Majlis liberal unless reforms had first taken effect. The National Front leadership called for demonstrations on 30 Tir (21 July) to mark Musaddiq's return to power a decade earlier. The demonstrations were suppressed, National Front leaders arrested, and party headquarters closed.

Another major confrontation between the Government and the opposition took place on 21 January 1962. University students clashed with police, the National Front called for a nation-wide strike, and hired thugs, in the pay of right-wing groups, took to the streets to incite violence. The Government moved ruthlessly against both the right and the left. On 26 January, Teymour Bakhtiar, the once powerful chief of the Security Organization (SAVAK) left the country on the Shah's orders, the monarch acceding to a request by the Prime Minister for his expulsion. The National Front later hotly denied charges that it had collaborated and conspired with right-wing groups. But the fact was that both the Front and Amini's reactionary opponents had been party to the violence in an effort to unseat the Government.

While Amini thus appeared to emerge victorious against his opponents, from January on the Government's attention and energies were increasingly sapped by the need to fight its political opposition. Amini also failed to resolve a budget deadlock which in 1962 further widened divisions within the Cabinet and between the army and the Prime Minister. Amini hoped to keep his development budget intact and to cut the deficit from the allocations for non-development spending, chiefly the army. The military failed to accept this decision and Amini, refusing to reduce development allocations, handed in his resignation in mid-July.

Reassertion of Royal Authority

The appointment of Asadollah Alam, a close personal friend of the Shah's, as Amini's successor marked the resumption by the Shah of direct control over governmental activities. Alam enjoyed a number of advantages over his predecessor. He was a more acceptable figure to the conservatives. His special relationship with the Shah precluded the tensions characteristic of the Amini period. Success in the foreign policy field relieved Alam from pressure from the Soviet Union at a time when domestic problems required all the Government's attention.

The Alam premiership presaged no radical departures. In fact Alam retained seven members of the Amini Cabinet, and based his programme on the Shah's 14 November *farman* issued to the Amini Cabinet. The retention of Arsanjani as Agriculture Minister was particularly significant, indicating a commitment to a continuation of the land distribution programme.

Land reform itself moved ahead with determination under the energetic direction of Hassan Arsanjani. Government counsels were divided, however, as to the necessary speed and scope of land distribution. Arsanjani made no secret of his conviction that land reform, up to then limited to the large estates, should be extended to cover middle-sized estates and the *waqf* (religious endowment) properties as well. Other Cabinet ministers urged a more cautious policy. On 11 December, the Shah announced a scheme under which *waqf* properties would be brought under the purview of land reform as well. Under the plan, the Government was to lease the *waqf* properties attached to the Shrine of Imam Reza in Meshed and to parcel them out on long-term sub-leases to the peasants.

To commemorate the first anniversary of land reform the Government convened a Farmers' Congress in Tehran in January 1963. It used this dramatic gathering of 4,000 peasants to mobilize public support behind land reform and other Government programmes and to still the voice of critics who charged that rule by Cabinet decree in the absence of parliament was unconstitutional. Inaugurating the Congress on 9 January, the Shah announced he was submitting land reform and five other bills approved by the Amini and Alam Cabinets to a national referendum. The five measures in addition to land reform submitted to public vote were a bill for the sale of State-owned factories to help finance land reform; nationalization of the nation's forests; a law which required up to 20 per cent of factory profits to be distributed among its workers; a revision of electoral laws to give more weight on the powerful supervisory councils to workers and farmers; and the Literacy Corps, a scheme under which young high-school graduates would be recruited into the army but would fulfil their military service requirements by teaching in village schools.

Shortly before the referendum, the land reform law was revised and given wider application. Its provisions were extended officially to cover the *waqf* properties, and the upper limit on landholding, previously set at one village per landlord, was drastically reduced. The practice of sharecropping was declared abolished.

Opposition to the referendum quickly materialized among a number of groups. Smaller landlords were discomfited by the extension of land reform to the middle-sized estates, while businessmen feared the consequences of the workers' profit-sharing law. But these two groups were anxious rather than actively obstructionist. More serious opposition came from the mullahs and the National Front. The mullahs, who had from the beginning opposed land reform because of its effect on their traditional allies among the great landlords, were further roused by its extension to *waqf* properties. The National Front declared themselves in favour of the reforms but opposed to the 'unconstitutional' method of carrying them out. This distinction, however, was lost on the mass of farmers and workers who favoured the reforms, while the Government managed through intelligent publicity to lump the Front with the mullahs and to brand both as reactionaries. Denied the right to assemble in public or openly to voice their views, the mullahs and the Front resorted to extra-legal means and once again on 22 January 1963 took to the streets. The demonstration was suppressed on 25 January and almost all 35 members of the National Front Central Committee as well as numerous religious leaders and theological students were put behind bars. Most of the Front leaders were later released. But Mehdi Bazargan and Mahmud Taleqani, the leaders of the Iran Freedom Movement, the most radical faction within the Front, were kept in prison and eventually brought to trial. A military court in January 1964 sentenced Bazargan and Taleqani to ten years each and seven other members of the movement to prison terms ranging between one and six years. These sentences were confirmed by an appeals court in March. The referendum itself was held on 26 January 1963 and, according to official returns, 5,598,391 (or 99.9 per cent) voted 'yes' against 4,115 voting 'no'.

An incidental by-product of the referendum was that it paved the way for female suffrage. Largely at the instance of Arsanjani, women were permitted to set up their own ballot boxes and to vote separately and unofficially during the referendum. The experiment was successful enough for the Shah to announce in February that women would no longer be barred from voting in future elections, and a measure to this effect was approved by the Majlis the following year, in February 1964. The extension of land reform did not solve intra-Cabinet differences about the speed with which land distribution should be carried out, the funds which should be allocated to this end, and the ultimate authority in the villages. These differences led to Arsanjani's resignation early in March. Although initially the pace of land distribution slowed down after his departure (the 'second phase' was not carried out until much later), the reform, once begun, could not be contained and was widely extended in subsequent years. The referendum had, however, greatly strengthened the Government's hand and had largely discredited those who had opposed it. While little more was heard of the National Front after January 1963, religious opposition of the Government, led by Ayatollah Khomeini, the most prominent of the Iranian

Ulema, continued. Khomeini, speaking from his pulpit in Qum, sharply intensified his attacks against the Government, whose measures he branded 'unconstitutional' and 'un-Islamic' during the mourning month of Moharram in May–June 1963. His arrest and that of 28 other religious leaders led on 4–5 June to riots in Tehran, which spread to Meshed, Tabriz, Qum, Shiraz, and Isfahan. The riots were quelled only after troops were sent into the streets with 'shoot-to-kill' orders and after many demonstrators had lost their lives. A national strike, called by the Ulema for 11 June, failed to materialize.

The Alam Government emerged victorious and the mullahs discredited from the June riots, and it was significant that the National Front had on this occasion not joined hands with the mullahs in seeking to unseat the Government. However, the cost of the collision was fearful, a lesson that was lost neither on the mullahs nor on the Government. Besides, it was clear that there were economic causes for working-class and middle-class unrest. The Alam Government's attempts to revive the economy had not borne fruit. Third Development Plan projects remained far behind schedule, unemployment soared, and investment by the private sector remained low. Businessmen's confidence had been sapped by land reform, by the workers' profit-sharing law, and the general atmosphere of uncertainty and disorder. The Government's own tendency towards budgetary indiscipline and unproductive spending aggravated the financial crisis. There was a continued clamour for an end to rule by Cabinet decree and a return to parliamentary government. Tribal disorder in Fars was not quelled until mid-1963.

On 17 September 1963, Alam finally held his long-promised general elections, this time under a revised set of procedures. Alam announced that the elections would be free, and that all would be permitted to participate. In fact, the candidates were carefully screened, participation limited, and the choice largely confined to the Government slate. The contacts were subsequently broken off. Thus in the September elections the major and practically only slate of candidates offered the electorate was the officially-blessed 'Union of National Forces', an organization of leading civil servants and officials, which included representatives of workers and farmers, put together with Government support. Official returns gave the bulk of seats to the Union and the new Majlis was inaugurated by the Shah on 6 October.

The largest group in the new parliament was the Progressive Centre, an élite club of high-ranking civil servants formed by Hassan Ali Mansur in 1961 with the stated purpose of carrying out scientific, económic, and social research. In June 1963 the Shah appointed the Centre his personal research bureau and a month later Mansur officially announced that his Centre would contest the forthcoming elections. In December Mansur redesigned the Centre as an exclusive, 500-man political party known as the Iran Novin (New Iran) party. These careful preparations bore fruit in March 1964 when Alam resigned and the Shah appointed Mansur to head the Government.

An account of the Alam premiership would be incomplete without reference to developments in the foreign field. In September 1962 the Government gave the Soviet Union written and verbal assurances that it would not permit foreign missile bases on Iranian soil nor allow Iran to become a base for aggression against the Soviet Union. The assurance ended an extended period of hostile feelings and laid the foundation for numerous bilateral agreements. Most immediately, a series of accords, negotiated in earlier years but never ratified, were brought to conclusion. These included a transit agreement in October 1962 and a frontier delineation agreement in December. In July 1963 the two countries concluded an agreement under which the Soviet Union extended to Iran a loan of $36 million to help finance a joint hydroelectric dam across the Aras River on the Iran-Soviet frontier, a string of silos in Iran, and the development, with Soviet assistance, of Iran's fisheries. In November 1963 Leonid Brezhnev became the first Soviet President to make a State visit to Iran. In the wake of improvement of relations with the Soviet Union, trade was also expanded with Hungary, Poland, Yugoslavia, and other Eastern European countries.

Experiment in Party Government: 1964–

Mansur's premiership marked the beginning of a long period in which the Government was free from serious opposition pressure, either in parliament or out of it. In the Majlis,

Mansur's Iran Novin party enjoyed a comfortable majority, and the Mardom party, nominally in the opposition, voted along with the Government on all bills. Outside Majlis, systematic arrests, prison sentences, and general controls weakened the ranks of organized political groups, while the Government's land distribution programme and other reforms undermined their appeal. Denied redress through normal channels, those opposed to the regime after 1964 tended increasingly to resort to underground activity and violence, although this was not of a scale to undermine governments. Ayatollah Khomeini, who had been released from house arrest in March 1964 and permitted to return to his base in Qum, once again took up the cudgels against the Government. He was arrested in November for 'instigations against the country's interests, security, independence, and territorial integrity' and sent into exile outside Iran. His arrest, unlike the previous year, did not on this occasion spark any unrest, an indication both of the Government's growing control and of the opposition's weakened position. On 6 October, six of the most powerful tribal leaders in Fars went before a firing squad after a military court found them guilty of fomenting and leading the 1962–3 tribal uprising in that province. Other Fars tribesmen were tried and imprisoned or executed in 1965–6.

These incidents aside, the Mansur Government was able to concentrate its full attention over the next few years on the twin pillars of its programme: administrative reform and economic development. On the administrative side, Mansur created four new ministries. He withdrew authority for drawing up the budget from the Ministry of Finance and established a separate Budget Bureau in the Plan Organization directly responsible to himself, a move which resulted in greater rationality in planning and budgeting.

On the economic side, the Mansur Government shortly after assuming office increased the size of the Third Development Plan from 145 to 200 billion rials, a step already contemplated by the outgoing Alam Government, and made possible by anticipated revenues from a number of new oil concessions about to be granted. Although there was a slight upturn in the economy in 1964, the constant diversion of development funds to non-development purposes, the expansion of the civil service, the reluctance of the private sector to invest, and drought all militated against full recovery.

Political violence once again became the order of the day when on 21 January 1965, a twenty-two year old youth shot Mansur. The Prime Minister died five days later from bullet wounds. The Government later charged thirteen men, some of whom had been members of the *Fadayan-i Islam*, with participation in the assassination plot. On 10 April there was an unsuccessful attempt on the life of the Shah by a conscript soldier of the Imperial Guards. The would-be assassin was killed by the Shah's bodyguards. But the Government subsequently brought to trial fourteen young men, most of whom had studied at British universities. Two were sentenced to death, one to life, and the others to various prison terms. Periodic trials of persons accused of plotting against the regime took place after this.

With the death of Mansur, the Shah appointed as Prime Minister Amir Abbas Hoveyda, a man who was Mansur's Minister of Finance and his deputy in the Iran Novin party. Under Hoveyda, the country experienced a remarkable economic boom. This was due to a number of factors. Hoveyda finally succeeded in winning the confidence of the business community, and private investment, after a long lull, began once again in earnest. Against the advice of some members of his Government, Hoveyda pursued an expansionist policy with good results. Industrialization was further spurred by the Ministry of Economy's policy of encouraging home industry and by an extensive programme of trade exchanges with the East European bloc, as well as with Western Europe and the United States. Timely oil revenues provided the funds with which to finance this ambitious programme.

Under an agreement concluded with the Consortium[13] in 1966, the members of the group agreed to relinquish within three months 25,000 square miles or one-fourth of their concession area and also to provide Iran, between 1967 and 1971, with 20 million tons of crude oil to market on its own. The relinquished area was subsequently exploited through new concessions while the crude that Iran acquired was by 1968

[13] See below, p. 286.

being marketed in East Europe. The June 1967 war, which interrupted Arab oil exports, permitted Iran considerably to boost its own production. Relations with the Consortium were, however, strained owing to Iran's conviction that the Consortium was lifting less oil from Iran than the Government had a right to expect. The protracted and sometimes acrimonious negotiations of 1967, during which Iran pressed for a guaranteed annual increase of 16.8 per cent in production in the 1968–73 period in order to finance the Fourth Development Plan, led early in 1968 to an understanding under which the Consortium agreed to increase production sufficiently to allow Iran to meet her financial requirements for the first year of the Fourth Plan.

In September 1967 elections for the twenty-second Majlis and the Senate were held. Once again, participation was limited to the approved parties and candidates. Some 80 per cent of the deputies to the twenty-first Majlis were returned, with the Iran Novin party taking 179 of 217 seats in Majlis, the Mardom party taking 31 seats, and the pan-Iranists taking five seats. In 1968 the Iran Novin party was able further to consolidate its position during the elections for municipal councils held in 136 towns throughout the country. Official returns gave the Iran Novin party control of a large majority of the councils and every single seat in 115 of them. But public apathy towards the elections was seen in the fact that only ten per cent of the entire eligible population in Tehran registered to vote, a ratio that was by no means untypical.

Although many administrative difficulties were encountered, the Hoveyda period witnessed a distinct improvement in the calibre and efficiency of the Government administration. There were also measures to settle the issue of the succession. According to the procedure laid down in the Fundamental Laws, if the Shah were to die while the Crown Prince was still a minor, Majlis was to meet to appoint the Regent. This meant there might be a delay of several days or even weeks (if, for example, parliament was not in session). After the attempt on his life in 1965, the Shah felt it essential that preparations be made for such an eventuality. A Constituent Assembly convened in September 1967 amended the laws and provided that the Queen should automatically be considered Regent unless the Shah in his lifetime designated someone else. In October 1967, in the twenty-sixth year of his reign, the Shah and the Queen were crowned.

The government succeeded in containing prolonged student agitation in Tehran in 1970 and 1971 without having to take drastic action. The regime was able to call upon the support of the workers' and peasants' organizations in denouncing the student troubles as inspired and encouraged from outside. In October 1971 a celebration of the 2,500th anniversary of the Persian monarchy was held in grand style at the capital of Persepolis. Many heads of state and representatives of foreign governments attended and doubts about the extravagant cost of the ceremonies were drowned in the general euphoria. When the Central Centenary Committee asked for money to build 2,500 new schools in rural villages the response was highly enthusiastic. Elections held at the end of 1971 resulted in an overwhelming victory for the Iran Novin party on which Prime Minister Hoveyda's government was based, with the party winning 230 of the 268 seats in the Majlis and 28 seats of the 30 that made up the elected half of the Senate. The extreme nationalist Pan-Iranian Party did not even attempt to contest the elections and appeared to make no headway with the public during 1972. However, the regime made use of severe repression through the SAVAK secret police to combat opposition. Early in 1972 at least 20 people accused of guerrilla activities, ranging from the murder of policemen to membership of Communist underground movements, were executed by firing squad and many more were imprisoned. International criticism of the procedure of the courts – the vagueness of the charges and the lack of witnesses – was growing. Suspicion of the Shah's regular use of torture was becoming widespread.

In July 1973, after lengthy negotiations, a new 20-year oil agreement was reached with the consortium of Western companies, to replace that of 1954. This had the effect of initiating a simple buyer-seller relationship between the oil companies and Iran and of giving Iran control over field operations. These operations, together with all facilities and installations previously worked by the Consortium, were vested in the National Iranian Oil Company while the Consortium agreed to provide technical staff and expert knowledge through a new service company.

The Middle East war of October 1973 had dramatic consequences for Iran. Although not taking part in the cut-back in oil exports to the West initiated by the Arab states, Iran did not hesitate to take advantage of the resulting energy crisis. The meeting of Persian Gulf oil ministers at which it was decided to double the posted price of oil was held in Tehran. The Shah warned the industrialized world at a press conference that it would have to realize that 'the era of their terrific progress and even more terrific income and wealth based on cheap oil is finished'. During 1974, with an expected balance of payments surplus of $10 billion in 1974/75 Iran immensely increased the scope and ambition of its development programmes, signing major agreements with several Western countries for nuclear power stations, petrochemical plants, and additional oil refineries, as well as for greatly increased imports of industrial goods. Plans for rural reconstruction and road-building were also stepped up. Iran's extended ambitions also applied to its armed forces. The West was ready to supply Iran with the most sophisticated weaponry to back the Shah's aim of making Iran the dominant military power throughout the Persian Gulf region.

With the declared aim of enlisting the mass of the population in support of his far-reaching plans, the Shah announced in March 1975 that the two-party system should be abolished and that a new party – the Rastakhiz or 'National Resurrection' party – would be formed which all men of good will should join. Prime Minister Hoveyda became Secretary-General of the new party which included among its aims a great extension in both public and private industrial enterprises. In the elections to the Majlis and Senate in May the electorate was invited to choose between three candidates selected by the Rastakhiz for each sect. In 1976 the break-up of the great landed estates and the distribution of land to the farmers were accelerated. The government launched a drive to improve departmental efficiency and to combat corruption, with mixed success. In August 1977, after Hoveyda who had been Prime Minister for twelve years had come under criticism for shortcomings in the electrical and other services, the Shah appointed Jamshid Amouzegar, Iran's representative with OPEC, to replace him. Amouzegar formed a cabinet of highly qualified technocrats in which the portfolios concerned with the country's basic sectors – agriculture, industry, and housing – all changed hands and the Shah called for urgent action to tackle immediate social and economic problems. Some measure of liberalization was encouraged and an unprecedented degree of criticism of the regime was allowed. This coincided with strong pressure from US President Carter on the Shah when the latter visited Washington in November 1977 to take steps to improve human rights. There were occasional assassinations of security police and, more rarely, of visiting foreign experts by underground elements. The stern reprisals taken by the SAVAK were strongly criticised in the report of a group of legal experts appointed by the International Commission of Jurists.

The regime identified the opposition as coming from an unnatural and opportunistic alliance between elements of the banned Tudeh Party and reactionary religious leaders. The term Islamic Marxists was coined to describe those who believed that the two types of opposition could be combined. But from the end of 1977, as the tide of unrest gathered momentum, it became apparent that popular discontent was massive and deep-seated. While foreign subversive elements were ready to exploit the growing hostility to the regime, its mainsprings were indigenous. With hindsight it was possible to regard 1973 as a watershed. The huge increase in spending which had followed the quadrupling of revenues had imposed intolerable strains on Iran's social and economic fabric. When over-expenditure led to entrenchment and recession combined with continuing inflation even the members of the new middle class who had benefited most from the Shah's policies became discontented while the mass of the population tended increasingly to see the hasty Westernization of the country as the source of evil. This soon developed into hostility towards the thousands of Western technicians, especially Americans, who were held to be the dominant influence in Iran. The *ayatollahs*, for so long denounced as reactionary and treated with some contempt by the Shah, became the natural leaders of this movement. Above all it was Ayatollah Khomeini, first from his exile in Iraq, and then, when forced to move on by the Iraqis, from his house near Paris, who emerged in 1978 as the main rival to the Shah for the loyalty of the mass of the Iranian people. The rumour that a leading article in the press denouncing Khomeini had been imposed on the newspaper by the Ministry of Information, set off a wave of rioting in Khomeini's home town of Qum. This triggered new violence in other cities which recurred at intervals of forty days – the traditional Islamic forty days. Banks, cinemas, and liquor shops were the main targets. There was violence in Yazd, Tabriz, Abadan (where on 19 August 400 were burned to death in a cinema in a fire which the enraged populace believed had been started deliberately by the SAVAK), and in Isfahan. At this point the Shah dismissed Amouzegar, who had had some success in curbing inflation but was out of control of the political situation, and appointed the elderly Jafar Sharif-Emami, the Senate President and a traditionalist with strong connections with the Moslem clergy. The new Prime Minister made several important concessions. He ordered the closure of Iran's casinos, promised free elections in June 1979, guaranteed the freedom of the press, and released some political prisoners. He restored the national calendar which had unwisely been changed in 1976 to an unpopular 'monarchical' system. In effect he allowed the Rastakhiz Party to collapse. The leaders of the two main wings of the Party resigned and a third wing emerged. The Shah had lost confidence in the one-party system he had created and as part of his hesitant moves towards liberalization he allowed the extreme nationalist Pan-Iranian Party and the National Front to operate overtly.

But these concessions were too small and too late. Prayer meetings and demonstrations against the regime continued in spite of a ban on public meetings and the imposition of martial law in Tehran and eleven other cities. In Tehran scores were killed when soldiers opened fire on the demonstrators. The Shah responded with a mixture of firmness and concession. He made strenuous efforts to form a coalition government with members of the moderate opposition and when these failed he appointed on 6 November a military government headed by General Gholam Reze Azhari, a trusted servant of the Shah and chief of staff of the armed forces.

The relaxation of authority at the centre in 1978 brought a flood of political factions as claimants to power. Of these the most important was the revived National Front led by Dr. Karim Sanjabi. In November 1978 he visited Khomeini in Paris but failed to reach an agreement with him which would have enabled Sanjabi to form a government with Khomeini's support.

Strikes by oil workers which began on 20 October in the Abadan Refinery and rapidly spread in the Khuzistan oil fields, drastically reduced oil production. By sending in troops and threatening the strikers with dismissal, the military government succeeded temporarily in restoring output to near normal by the end of November. However, in the country as a whole the situation remained deeply troubled. For the first time the Shah's own future was placed in doubt as Ayatollah Khomeini, with his uncompromising demand that the Shah should abdicate, gathered support throughout the country. When Komeini made a renewed call for a strike by oil workers on 4 December, an unrecognized body, the National Union of Iranian Oil Industry Workers responded and output was soon halved.

The Shiite holy month of Moharram which began on 2 December and reached a climax with the celebration of Ashura on 11 December, was a period of massive demonstrations in nearly all Iran's major cities, although these generally passed without bloodshed because of the policy of non-intervention by the military authorities. The oil situation rapidly worsened. Following the assassination of two senior American and Iranian officials of the Oil Service Company of Iran, production fell to about 5 per cent of normal by the end of December. Iran Air employees, followed by the customs and post office, came out on total strike and leading moderate politicians began to add their voices to those calling for the Shah to go.

The Shah's attempt to restore order with a military government having failed, on 1 January 1979 he appointed as Prime Minister Dr. Shahpur Bakhtiar, a veteran opposition politician and high-ranking official of the National Front. Dr. Bakhtiar was promptly expelled by the National Front. Dr. Bakhtiar, the least anti-monarchist of the opposition leaders, envisaged the retention of the Shah in a much reduced role and he suggested the Shah might depart on a prolonged vacation leaving the way open for the appointment of a Regency Council. Dr. Bakhtiar's dilemma was that for his government to acquire any popular legitimacy the Shah had to go, while the army, whose allegiance to the Shah appeared unshaken, refused to consider a civilian government with the Shah out of the country. There was a clear danger of a military coup. Finally, the Shah, who appeared to have lost the will to hold on to power, left for Egypt with his Queen on 16 January, ostensibly on holiday. Some two million supporters of Ayatollah Khomeini celebrated his departure in a demonstration in Tehran.

After some delay in which Dr. Bakhtiar tried to prevent Khomeini's return, the Ayatollah arrived from Paris in triumph on 1 February. As Dr. Bakhtiar continued to refuse the Ayatollah's demands for his resignation, on 5 February Khomeini appointed Dr. Mehdi Bazargan, a former leader of the National Front with a long record of opposition, to form and head a provisional government. After several days of fighting between the army and armed Khomeini supporters and, with a serious split developing within the armed forces, the army commanders declared their neutrality 'in the present political crisis' and ordered their troops back to barracks. Deprived of all political and military power, Dr. Bakhtiar announced his resignation the following day.

The Khomeini Regime

Dr. Bazargan failed to establish the authority of his administration. A system of parallel governments developed, with the main power retained by the Central Revolutionary Islamic Committee surrounding Khomeini, who retained his hold over the mass of the people even after he left the capital for his own city of Qum. A referendum held on 30 and 31 March resulted in an overwhelming vote in favour of an Islamic Republic. A series of trials by Islamic revolutionary courts led to the execution of scores of former Shah supporters but Dr. Bazargan was successful in securing an amnesty for all except those who had caused death under the Shah.

Opposition to Khomeini's authoritarianism developed during 1979 among secular and liberal middle-class elements as well as the left-wing guerrilla groups of which the most effective was the *Fadayan i-Khalq*. In addition to the National Front a new National Democratic Front was formed by Matin Daftari, a grandson of Musaddiq. But the opposition was uncoordinated and ineffective; the guerrillas were no match for the better-armed Islamic militia. The most serious potential opposition came from other leading Islamic figures such as Ayotallahs

Talaghani (until his death in September) and Shariat Madari, who established his own Muslim People's Republican Party. By September, Khomeini and his supporters had effectively muzzled the Iranian press and expelled the majority of foreign correspondents.

During 1979 a series of strong regional autonomy movements appeared which were partly among Sunni minorities against the assertion of Shiite nationalism. The most significant were in Kurdestan, the Turcoman Sahra and the Iranian Arabs of Khuzistan. The last was thought most serious because it threated oil installations but the heaviest fighting was in Kurdestan. However, this threat to Iranian unity helped to rally support for Khomeini among the Shiite leadership.

The Iranian Armed Forces were divided and demoralized after the Shah's overthrow but, in spite of political discontent in their ranks they were in no position to threaten a military take-over.

Foreign Policy: 1964–

In the field of foreign policy, major developments were centred on the expansion of ties with the Soviet Union and the East European bloc, on Iran's growing role in Persian Gulf affairs, and on the overall effect of these trends on relations with the United States and Britain. The *rapprochement* with the Soviet Union was initiated in 1962 and a trade and technical aid agreement was concluded in 1963. This was followed in 1965 by an accord under which the Russians agreed to extend to Iran a loan of about $300 million and to provide machinery and technical assistance for the construction of Iran's first steel mill. Iran agreed to repay the loan by exports of natural gas. A pipeline, running from the southern gas fields to the Iran-Soviet frontier at Astara, under construction for this purpose, was due for completion in 1971, and completed ahead of schedule. The expansion of Iran-Soviet trade has in these years been matched by considerable increase in trade with countries of the East European bloc, primarily Czechoslovakia and Rumania and to a lesser degree with Bulgaria, Hungary, and Yugoslavia

These deals marked a significant shift in Iranian foreign policy, reflecting partly the freedom of manoeuvre provided by the general thaw in East-West relations, partly the desire to secure capital goods through barter deals not entailing expenditure of precious foreign exchange, partly a disenchantment with Western arms policy towards Iran. Thus, in 1964, the Heads of State of Iran, Turkey, and Pakistan met in Istanbul to create 'outside the framework of the Central Treaty Organization' a body named Regional Co-operation for Development (RCD) to promote economic, social, and cultural co-operation amongst their three countries. Although RCD did not subsequently fulfil all that was expected of it, its creation was an early and concrete sign of the decline in the importance of CENTO. In 1966, American refusal to provide Iran with the arms it wanted and at the prices and terms it felt acceptable led to a flurry of reports that the Government would negotiate purchase of ground-to-air missiles from the Soviet Union. Eventually, however, the US Government was able to satisfy Iran's demands. In 1967 Iran did purchase $110 million worth of arms from the Soviet Union, but the deal was confined to light vehicles, half-tracks, and light weapons.

The desire to re-equip and strengthen the army arose from the Shah's concern over developments in the Gulf. Iran/Egyptian diplomatic relations were broken in 1960 and the Government did not welcome Nasser's ambitions on the Arab side of the Gulf, his involvement in the Yemen war, or Arab nationalist claims to Khuzistan as an integral part of the Arab 'homeland'. These concerns were heightened by the fact that Iran's oil fields were concentrated in Khuzistan; the Gulf itself was the outlet for oil exports and the bulk of the country's import-export trade passed through the waterway. Iran also claimed the Bahrain archipelago and other Gulf islands. Relations with Egypt and Syria remained strained. Relations with Iraq were not much better where disputes over navigation rights in the Gulf, the status of Iranians resident in Iraq, and frontier demarcation remained unsettled. The Government devoted its attention to building up relations with states whose policies were closer to its own. The friendship of Gulf shaikhs was cultivated and special efforts were made in the direction of Kuwait and Saudi Arabia.

King Faisal visited Iran in 1965, when an agreement delineating the continental shelf in the Persian Gulf between the two countries was signed and the two monarchs issued a call for a conference of Islamic Heads of State. Although the two countries increasingly felt the need to co-operate on joint defence of the Gulf following Britain's decision to withdraw from the area after 1971, complications arose as King Faisal felt he could not support Iran's claim to Bahrain. When, early in 1968, Faisal received the Shaikh of Bahrain as a guest in Saudi Arabia, the Shah cancelled a planned visit to Riyadh. The quarrel was patched up and the planned visit took place before the end of the year. In March 1970, on Iran's initiative, Britain and Iran submitted the question of Bahrain to the UN Secretary-General and agreed to abide by his findings. In April his representative reported that an overwhelming majority of Bahrainis wanted their island to be recognized as a sovereign State free to determine its own future. The UN Security Council accepted this verdict and the Majlis then formally renounced the Iranian claim to sovereignty.

The Bahraini settlement removed a major obstacle to improved relations with Iran's Arab neighbours but this was overshadowed by a fierce dispute with Iraq over navigation rights in the Shatt al-Arab. Iran, asserting that Iraq had consistently violated the treaty of 1937 which partitioned those rights, denounced it in April 1969 and claimed that the boundary with Iraq should follow a median line on the stream. Iraq then expelled large numbers of Iranians living in Iraqi territory and the two countries seemed on the brink of war. The situation further deteriorated in January 1970 when the Iraqi Government announced the discovery of a right-wing plot, accused Iran of financing and arming the conspirators and expelled the Iranian Ambassador in Baghdad and four of his staff. Iran massed troops near the frontier and announced a large increase in defence estimates. However, tension gradually fell and the general situation improved in March when Iraq reached agreement with leaders of its Kurdish minority whose nationalist insurrection the Iraqis had long accused Iran of aiding and abetting. In 1970 there was a marked improvement in Iran's relations with Egypt, and diplomatic relations were restored.

The improvement in relations with Iraq did not last long. On 30 November 1971, as British withdrawal from the Persian

Gulf approached, Iran occupied three small island at the mouth of the Gulf, the Greater and Lesser Tumbs and Abu Musa which belonged to local Arab rulers and were accordingly under British protection. Iraq immediately broke relations with Iran which retaliated on 4 December.

Iran's friendship with Pakistan was a means of promoting closer diplomatic relations between Iran and China. In August 1971 Iran took the step of recognizing the Peking regime as the sole legal government of China. Iran was further encouraged by the Nixon administration's pursuit of a policy of *détente* with both the Soviet Union and China during 1972. However, a new source of friction with both Iraq and the Soviet Union emerged in 1973 when Iraq, with Soviet support, began to give encouragement to secessionist movements in the western provinces of Pakistan. Iran saw that if this movement for a 'Free Baluchistan' were successful it would open the way to direct Soviet access to the Arabian Sea ports along Pakistan's southern coast and thereby strengthen the Soviet naval presence in the Persian Gulf region.

Although Iran was not directly involved in the October 1973 Arab-Israeli war and refused to take part in the Arab oil embargo on the West, the war and its consequences had a major impact on Iran's position in the area. The Shah declared that the era of cheap energy for the industrialized world had ended. Not only did Iran's oil revenues double, but it became one of the leading members of OPEC, demanding high increases in oil prices to compensate for the inflation in imported industrial goods from the West. The Shah greatly extended his already powerful ambitions for Iran, declaring in several press interviews that Iran would become one of the half dozen leading industrial powers in the world before the end of the century. Iran increased its allocations to the armed forces from their already high levels. As part of the country's determination to impose an Iranian Peace on the Gulf region and exclude pro-communist elements, some 3,000 Iranian troops were sent to Oman to help its Sultan against the left-wing rebels in Dhufar.

Iran's only combative opponent in the Gulf region was Iraq. There were more clashes on the frontiers in 1974 which brought the two countries close to war. Iran made use of a powerful weapon against Iraq's Baathist regime by supplying and providing artillery protection for Iraq's Kurdish rebels under Mustafa Barzani. However, in March 1975, after prolonged negotiations, the Shah of Iran and the Iraqi leader Saddam Hussein reached an agreement, through Algerian mediation, at the Algiers summit meeting of the OPEC countries. Both sides decided to settle all their border disputes, notably in the Shatt al-Arab waterway where the new boundary was fixed on the median line of maximum depth; under the 1937 agreement, which Iran had previously denounced, it had been on the Iranian bank. In return for this major Iraqi concession, Iran withdrew support for Barzani's rebellion, thereby causing its collapse.

A clear indication of Iran's increasing self-confidence was the conclusion of a far-reaching agreement with the Soviet Union in February 1975 under which, among other projects, Iran provided the financing for a new paper mill in the USSR and the Soviet Union undertook to pay an increase of 85 per cent in the price of natural gas supplied by Iran from the enormous new field at Kangan on the Gulf. Iran increased its aid to Pakistan and Turkey, its less affluent partners in the Regional Co-operation for Development scheme and offered large-scale assistance to Egypt with which relations had steadily improved since the death of President Nasser in 1970. In 1976 Iran continued to extend its influence in the West Asian and South Asia regions, mediating both between Afghanistan and Pakistan, and India and Pakistan. A conference of RCD ministers held in Lahore reached an agreement which pledged the three countries to reducing tariff barriers towards the establishment of a free-trade area within ten years. In March 1977 an important new treaty was signed between the three countries finalizing arrangements for the import from the West of technical skills and modern machinery. However, Iran's relations with Pakistan suffered in early 1978 from the development of an Iran-India axis. The Shah visited India and various schemes for increasing economic ties between the two countries were agreed.

In the 1970s Iran has been the main promoter of schemes for regional defence co-operation in the Persian Gulf area, but had little success in persuading its Arab neighbours in the

Gulf that without Iran any grouping for defence purposes would be useless. Although the Arab Gulf states and Saudi Arabia were aware of the dangers of a struggle between the superpowers for control of oil resources in the region, and also of the growth of dissident groups operating in the area, they were also suspicious of Iran's ambitions, and – with the exception of Oman – reluctant to regard Iran as a full ally in protecting regional security. However, when the Shah's own position was increasingly threatened by internal unrest in 1978 the Saudi leadership made it clear that they hoped he would survive because any likely alternative would be worse. Meanwhile the left-wing coup in Afghanistan, and the increase in Soviet influence in the region that this implied, greatly alarmed the Arab states as well as Iran.

The Shah's downfall had a major effect on all Iran's neighbours. Arab rulers and governments were apprehensive about the consequences although Ayotallah Khomeini was a hero to many of their people, both Sunnis and Shiites. The Iraqi government was especially apprehensive about the break-down of its 1975 agreement with the Shah and the potential effect on its own Kurds and Shiite Arabs. Khomeini's declarations of support for the Palestinians and his break with Israel were welcomed but Iran's relations with the Arabs did not prosper; in the case of Iraq they soon turned to bitter mutual recrimination.

The Khomeini regime remained primarily anti-American but the USSR had no cause for comfort. Khomeini declared Islam and Marxism incompatible and gave tacit support to the Muslim rebels fighting the hard-pressed Marxist regime in Afghanistan. Iran also cancelled the proposed second major natural gas pipeline to the USSR.

GOVERNMENT AND ADMINISTRATION

In theory Iran became a constitutional monarchy in 1906 when a constitution was granted. Shah Mohammed Reza succeeded his father in 1941. In 1939 he married Princess Fawzia, sister of Egypt's former King Farouk, divorced her in 1948, and married Soraya Esfandiari in 1951. The Shah had a daughter by his first wife, but Queen Soraya bore him no children. Moreover, Ali Reza, the only one of the Shah's brothers entitled to succeed him under the Constitution as amended in 1925 (which excluded from the succession anyone of Qajar blood) was killed in an aeroplane accident in 1954. There was thus no heir apparent.

In 1958, on the advice of the Imperial Council and as he was himself convinced that considerations of State required the country to have a Crown Prince, the Shah divorced Soraya and in 1959 married Farah Diba, the daughter of an army officer. She has since given birth to two sons (Reza in 1960 and Ali Reza in 1966) and one daughter (Farahnaz in 1963). The eldest, Reza, was designated Crown Prince by the Shah in November 1960. The Shah was crowned in October 1967, on his forty-eighth birthday, and on the same occasion placed a crown on the head of Queen Farah, making her the first Queen in Iranian history who is known to have been crowned.

The Shah was Commander in Chief of the armed forces, and had the power to declare peace and war, to confer military rank, and to appoint and dismiss ministers. In practice his *farman* was also required in confirmation of appointments to all the major posts in the country. Government was by Cabinet; ministers were not members of the National Assembly or the Senate but were jointly and severally responsible to both Houses. The Prime Minister was appointed by the Shah, but required a vote of confidence from Majlis. The Prime Minister and his ministers constituted the Council of Ministers which had general executive powers. If the Government was defeated on a vote of confidence in Majlis it resigned.

In practice the Shah, while theoretically respecting the constitution, wielded absolute power between 1954 and 1978. Following the Khomeini Revolution a draft Islamic constitution was published as a basis for debate by a 75-member Council of Examiners elected in April 1979. This gave a president similar powers to those held by the Shah, including supreme command of the Armed Forces and the right to appoint and dismiss ministers. The major difference was that he was to be elected by universal suffrage for a four-year term.

The country is today divided into fourteen provinces, or

ostans (Tehran, Gilan, Mazandaran, East Azarbaijan, West Azarbaijan, Kermanshah, Khuzistan, Fars, Kerman, Khorasan, Isfahan, Baluchistan and Sistan, Kurdestan, and the Persian Gulf and Sea of Oman Ports and Islands); and six independent governorates, or *farmandari-ye kol* (Bakhtiari and Chaharmahal, Boyr Ahmadi and Kohgiluye, Semnan, Hamadan, Luristan, and Ilam). These are further subdivided into governorates (*shahrestans*), which are in turn sub-divided into districts (*bakhsh*). The *bakhsh* normally comprises villages and small towns. The Governors-General (*ostandars*) of the provinces and the Governors (*farmandars*) of the independent governorates are nominated by the Ministry of Interior, approved by the Cabinet, and appointed by royal *farman*.

A law passed in 1949 and revised in 1967 provided for elected municipal councils in all major towns.

The Majlis

The Majlis, or Lower House (the term, *Majlis*, is also used to refer collectively to both Houses) is elected by universal adult suffrage, women having voted for the first time in the 1963 elections. The number of deputies was increased from 136 to 200 following the 1956 census and from 200 to 217 following the 1966 census. These numbers include one deputy elected by the Jewish community, one by the Zoroastrians, one by the Assyrians, and two by the Armenians. The term of each Majlis was extended from two to four years in 1957. By the Constitution, Majlis alone has the power to impose, reduce, or abolish taxes, make appropriations, approve loans, and grant concessions. All other bills have to be passed by both Houses. The groupings in Majlis are not normally along party lines.

In the early period of the Constitution there were a number of political parties. Under Reza Shah all parties ceased effective existence. After his abdication, various parties were formed. These represented personal groupings rather than political parties, their membership was never large, and their life was usually short. A notable exception was the Tudeh party, formed in 1941, which had a Communist nucleus but enjoyed the support of many non-Communists. It was proscribed in 1949, and again after the fall of Musaddiq in 1953.

Since then it has enjoyed a tenuous existence and in the 1960s split into pro-Peking and pro-Moscow factions. The National Front, actually a conglomeration of smaller parties which came together over the oil nationalization issue, went into demise after the fall of Musaddiq. The Melliyun and Mardom parties were formed with official support in 1957 to constitute a majority party and an official opposition. The Melliyun party disappeared from the scene after the abortive 1960 elections. The Mardom party continued to retain a few seats in parliament in subsequent elections. After 1963, parliamentary politics were dominated by the Iran Novin party, another officially sponsored organization. The pro-Government wing of the pan-Iranian party, an extreme nationalist grouping that was part of the National Front, was permitted to resume activities in 1964 and was able to send a few deputies to Majlis. In 1975 the Shah decreed the formation of a single National Resurrection (Rastakhiz Party) to replace the previous government-authorized political parties. Under the pressure of the events of 1978, the Rastakhiz Party fell into disarray. The National Front began overtly operating again. Only the Tudeh party remained underground.

Security

Under the rule of Shah Mohammed Reza, the Iranian armed forces were immensely expanded, especially in the 1970s. The number of men under arms rose from 161,000 in 1970 to 413,000 in 1978. Defence expenditure rose from $241 million in 1954 to $3.7 billion in 1974 and $9.7 billion in 1977. The United States, which was Iran's main source of arms, provided its most modern military equipment. By 1976 Iran had ordered or acquired 3,000 modern tanks. It had spent $11.8 billion on all types of aircraft and constructed a large network of operational bases. The biggest single area of expansion was in the navy as part of the Shah's aim of making Iran the main agent of regional security. Iran had the largest hovercraft fleet in the world and ordered four US destroyers for use in the Indian Ocean. Six naval bases had been built along the coast of the Gulf and a larger base was planned for Chah Bahar on the Indian Ocean.

SOCIAL SURVEY

Education

The rate of illiteracy in Iran has fallen from about 95 per cent in 1900 to about 75 per cent in 1956 and between 65 and 70 per cent in 1976. The rate is considerably higher among females than males, and in the countryside, where it is still 80 to 85 per cent, than in the towns, where it is as low as 25 per cent for children between the ages of 7 and 14. In spite of Adult Literacy Classes and the activities of the Education Corps – high-school graduates conscripted into the army to teach – the backlog of illiterate adults was still growing in the 1970s. At all levels there was a serious shortage of teachers and classes. The number of pupils in primary schools rose from 2,130,000 in 1965/66 to 4,119,000 in 1974/75 and the number in secondary schools rose from 480,000 to 1,818,000 in the same period. Between 1966 and 1977 some 15,000 primary schools covering 25,000 villages were established. Yet in 1973 the ILO reported that enrolment in primary education in the rural areas was still below 40 per cent compared with 90 per cent in the towns and the situation has hardly changed throughout the 1970s. The biggest expansion has been in university education, with the number of students increasing from 25,000 in 1965 to 170,000 in 1977 and a further 55,000 studying abroad, about half of them in the United States where in 1978 they formed the single largest group of foreign students.

Despite the expansion of educational services, the lack of qualified personnel remains the biggest single obstacle to Iran's development. The shortage has been made worse by the brain drain of skilled and educated manpower to Europe and North America, and by the reluctance of those Iranian doctors, engineers, and other qualified professional men who remained in Iran to work outside the major cities.

Health

Substantial improvements in health and nutrition standards have been achieved since the 1950s. Life expectancy has risen from 35 years to nearer 50 years; malaria and smallpox have been eradicated in many parts of the country by spraying or vaccination schemes; and the import or domestic production of pharmaceutical products has expanded rapidly. Nevertheless, most of the health and hygiene improvements have been directly related to higher real income levels throughout the country. Many endemic diseases, such as trachoma, dysentery, typhoid, and the venereal diseases remain untreated. Infant mortality remains high; at 139 per thousand it is the same as that of India.

Living Standards

The most striking feature about Iranian living standards is the gap between the urban and rural areas. This was already apparent before the drift to the cities became a flood with the industrial boom which followed the 1973 oil price rises. The Plan Organization estimated that the ratio of urban to rural income increased from 4.6:1 in 1959 to 5.6:1 in 1969 and a 1975 survey estimated that an urban family spent twice as much each month as a rural family. Some 90 per cent of rural Iranians live in mud-brick houses and only 30 per cent of the 65,000 villages have a population of more than 250. In 1966, 69 per cent of the dwellings in urban areas had electricity compared with 4 per cent in the villages. About 90 per cent of rural houses were without access to a piped water system either inside or outside the house.

The rush to the cities has also created serious social problems in the urban areas and especially in Tehran where the overcrowded and polluted southern half of the city contrasts vividly with the new commercial and residential areas of North Tehran.

ECONOMIC SURVEY

National Accounts

The economy of Iran started its upward climb in the 1930s. It was stymied by the onset of the Second World War but resumed an expansionary path in the late 1940s. The oil nationalization of 1951 brought the economy to a halt again, but a new turning-point was achieved in 1955. Basic statistics on the national income of Iran and its components were built up in the late 1950s so that from 1959 onwards fairly consistent series are available. Although these individual figures may be subject to a wide margin of error, the trend of these statistics shows that, with the exception of a slackening in the period 1961–3, the process of economic development which recommenced in 1955 continued at a rapid rate until 1975/76. GNP advanced at an average of 8.5 per cent annually at constant prices. During the years of the fourth plan, 1968/69 to 1972/73, a growth of 11.8 per cent a year was recorded compared with a plan target of 9.4 per cent.

The rate of growth for net national income in 1973/74 was 33.8 per cent, rising under the impact of the increase in oil prices to 42.0 per cent in 1974/75. In the wake of the fall in demand for oil and sharply declining oil revenues, growth fell back in 1975/76 to an estimated 2.7 per cent. After a recovery to some 13 per cent in 1976/77 the position deteriorated again to 2.4 per cent in 1977/78.

Although the benefits of the increase were not distributed evenly throughout the population there is some evidence that the great majority of Iranians at all levels of society were substantially better off in economic terms in the 1970s than in the 1950s. The proportion of Gross National Product taken by Private Consumption Expenditure declined from 75 per cent in 1959 to 66 per cent in 1968 and 39 per cent in 1977. This was due to increasing emphasis on Gross Domestic Fixed Capital Formation, which, though fluctuating, rose from 17 per cent to 20 per cent to 26.5 per cent, and Government Consumption Expenditure from 11 per cent to 15 per cent to 21 per cent in the same years. Net exports of goods and services increased from about 5 per cent in 1968 to 10.3 per cent in 1977. These trends imply that the Government was becoming associated to a greater extent with the development of the economy and that the development effort itself was increasing. Most Government expenditure on capital formation was made through the Plan Organization on large-scale infrastructure projects – roads, railways, ports, telecommunications, irrigation, and power networks. Capital formation by the private sector was mainly in small- and medium-scale industry and in residential building.

The share of agriculture in GNP declined steadily from 33 per cent in 1959 to 24 per cent in 1968 and 10 per cent in 1977. With the share of services (including transport and communications, finance, and distribution) remaining fairly constant the place of agriculture was taken by the oil sector whose share of GNP rose from 11 per cent in 1959 to 17 per cent in 1968 and 40 per cent in 1977.

Economic Policy and Development Plans

During the period following the Second World War the notion of national planning which originated in the 1930s with State control over the economy gained general support. A preliminary report was drawn up in 1947 by International Engineering Company Inc., an American organization, and after further studies and the publication of a plan document the First Seven-Year Plan began in 1949. Both in its original form and in a revised version the plan intended to spread the development effort fairly evenly throughout the economy. However, political instability and the cessation of oil revenues following nationalization meant that only about 15 per cent of the revised allocations was actually spent. For the most part these were directed towards the renovation of State-owned industrial projects and the transport network of the country.

A new start was made with the Second Seven-Year Plan which began in 1955. The transport sector was to receive the lion's share of funds, and in the event accounted for 40 per cent of total expenditure as the road, rail, and port facilities of the country were substantially extended. A number of large-scale hydro-electric schemes were also started and these accounted for most of the expenditure in the agriculture sector. Neither of the first two plans was comprehensive as the planners did not even possess the basic statistics to estimate population or Gross National Product. Nevertheless within the Plan Organization itself the Economic Bureau completed a series of valuable studies as well as a critical appraisal of the progress of the Second Plan.

With the aid of an American advisory team a move towards comprehensiveness was made. Because of the stabilization programme imposed by the International Monetary Fund the first two years of the Third (Five-Year) Plan was shrouded in a mist of confused estimates about the extent of foreign assistance and the absorptive capacity of the economy. In addition the land reform programme, which had not been considered by the planners, was pushed through its first stages, and various other social reforms were implemented. Then, suddenly, the economy started growing at 9–10 per cent each year, the price level was held stable, and private industry gained an impelling position as production increased at an annual 15 per cent. By the end of the plan (which in fact was extended to cover 5½ years), actual disbursements closely matched the revised estimates and the overall growth target of the plan, an increase in GNP by 6 per cent each year, had been achieved. The Government had continued its massive investment in infrastructure projects throughout the plan period and had produced an aura of stability and confidence which was complemented by the vigorous enterprise of private investors together with the solid support of an emancipated farming community.

In the fourth plan, for 1969–73, the bulk of public sector funds were directed towards water and power developments, while state participation in agricultural and industrial schemes was also set at high levels. Ample scope was left for the private sector, mainly in industry. Rapidly rising oil income in the plan period permitted the Plan Organization funds to be much augmented to a total of 577,000 million rials, 20.5 per cent above original allocations. The performance of the economy during the fourth plan was generally above expectations.

Adoption of a fifth five-year plan in 1973 brought important changes in the system of plan administration and implementation. The Plan Organization ceased to be responsible for financial disbursements by the executive ministries, which would themselves draw funds directly from the Ministry of Finance. The Plan Organization will undertake only long-term planning and advisory functions.

In a period of rapidly increasing state revenues on account of oil, the fifth plan was subject to revision. Original estimates of state investments in the plan period were set at 1,299 billion rials but this was increased in August 1974 to 2,847 billion rials, an increase of 119 per cent.

The major emphasis in the plan was on infrastructural development, especially electricity, transport, and communications, while industry, oil and agriculture also received large allocations. GNP was forecast to grow from 1,547 billion rials to 3,686 billion at an annual average rate of growth of 25.9 per cent.

Falling oil revenues, a trend that became apparent in mid-1975, led to a reappraisal of fifth plan prospects by the government. While the official forecasts of expenditure were not changed, it is on record that the plan expenditures are more likely to be spread over six rather than five years. In effect, a large number of individual projects within the plan have been postponed or slowed down and most projects adopted in the boom period 1974–5 have suffered a similar fate. It was announced in 1978 that for planning purposes the government would adopt a combination of two-year short-term plans with ten- or twenty-year long-term plans. In effect, a sixth plan, scheduled to begin in March 1978, was not announced and the traditional five-year plan appears to have been shelved for the time being.

Currency and Banking

The unit of currency is the Iranian rial with an exchange rate in August 1978 of \$1 = 70.48 rials and £1 = 135.40 rials. Ten rials equal one toman.

The Currency and Banking Act of 1960 requires a minimum gold and foreign exchange support for the note issue of not less than 40 per cent. The 1960 Act also created a Credit and Currency Board while parallel legislation authorized the establishment of a Central Bank which took over from the Bank Melli (National Bank) the functions of note issue and exchange control. In addition to the Central Bank there are seven other state banks including the Bank Melli, founded in 1927, the specialized Agricultural Bank of Iran which was also founded in the 1920s but only became a significant influence on the rural development of the country in the 1960s by helping to finance the land reform programme and the rural co-operative movement, the Mortgage Bank of Iran, and the Industrial Bank, financed by Plan Organization funds, which has been involved in hundreds of industrial projects in the five plans.

Bank Omran (Development Bank) and Bank Refah Kargaran (Workers' Welfare Bank) have been the most successful of the semi-specialized banks. The former, financed by the Pahlavi Charitable Foundation, directs its activities to farmers and co-operatives on distributed Crown Estates and also to alleviation of credit difficulties in the tribal areas. The latter, financed by the State Social Insurance Organization, has provided loans, especially for housing and new-year expenditures, to workers through industrial workers' co-operatives.

The Industrial and Mining Development Bank of Iran is a private joint-stock company partly funded by foreign capital. A clearing house for Irano-foreign banks was set up in March 1969.

The Central Bank's monetary policy retained a slightly deflationary flavour after 1963 in order to offset the expansionary spending of the general and development budgets. After 1973 this policy was much less successful.

1975 = 100

	End Year				
	1973	1974	1975	1976	1977
Wholesale Prices	79.2	92.6	100.0	109.0	127.7
Cost of Living	77.6	88.7	100.0	111.3	141.7

National Budget

In the period 1964–73, the state budget rigorously divided the current account from the development account and even within the development budget specific allocations were made for new development, recurrent development, and purely Plan Organization administrative expenses. Oil revenues retain great importance, not only in financing the budget as a whole but in providing the bulk of foreign exchange credits catered for in the budget. Rationalization of the taxation system since 1965 has enabled the government to mobilize greater domestic resources, and further tightening of the system of direct taxes was promised as a measure of social justice in 1978.

A new format for state budgets was adopted in 1973 whereby ordinary and development accounts were amalgamated, though the budgets of semi-autonomous government agencies were left separate. It is likely that all future budgets will become effective from mid-year so that budgets may take account of variations in weather conditions affecting agriculture. As from 1973, funds for the economic plan have been controlled by the Ministry of Economics and Finance and not as formerly by the Plan Organization.

Total revenues of the 1978/79 budget were set at $57.2 billion (4,003 billion rials) against expenditures of $59.2 billion (4,179 billion rials), the latter showing an increase of 17 per cent over 1977/78. A large borrowing requirement was built into the budget, and state agencies were expected to raise $4.3 billion on the domestic market and $4.4 billion from overseas sources. The ordinary budget was set at expenditures of 2,935.9 billion rials, a 23 per cent increase on the previous year. Allocations to development were forecast at 1,205.9 billion rials ($17,129.2 million) with the power sector dominating allotments and other infrastructural sectors similarly given priority. Industry and agriculture together account for only 10 per cent of all development outlays of the budget.

Trade and Balance of Payments

During the nine years 1960–68 the basic Balance of Payments was in deficit six times, and the foreign exchange reserves of the country were protected only by the receipt of substantial bonus payments from the expatriate oil companies. Moreover, the trade balance (including exports of oil) was favourable only twice. Since total receipts from the oil sector were expanding at about 14 per cent annually the causes of the generally adverse trade balance were the failure of non-oil exports to keep pace with the general expansion of the economy as well as an inability to stem the growing flow of imports owing mainly to the requirements of the development plans. On capital account the increased utilization of foreign long-term loans and credits more than offset the repayments of similar debts incurred in the past, and there was a net inflow of foreign private loans and capital.

The oil revenues played an increasingly important part in receipts on current account, representing 68 per cent of these receipts in 1960, 75 per cent in 1968, and 83 per cent in 1977. The large increases in oil revenues in the 1970s meant that the Balance of Payments was no longer in deficit, except in 1976/77, and foreign exchange reserves in the summer of 1978 stood at $12 billion. But the inflow of foreign funds continued and it was estimated that the foreign debts accrued by the Iranian banks amounted to $3.5 billion.

The growing inflow of foreign exchange on account of oil exports after 1973 permitted considerable relaxations in import controls. Most tariffs and commercial taxes on foodstuffs and basic raw material imports were reduced or eliminated. However, the policy continued to be to protect infant industries while encouraging the flow of capital goods into the country. Imports in 1975/76 rose by 77 per cent over 1974/75 with capital goods imports accounting for some 30 per cent of the total. West Germany, the USA and the UK are traditionally the main suppliers although Japan and France have lately increased their shares. Barter agreements with the communist bloc countries are tending to play a greater role in the pattern of trade.

Agriculture, Forestry, and Fishing

Iran has a surface area of some 165 million hectares, but only 79 million hectares are used or are classified as utilizable, while about 19 million hectares of this total are used each year for field and orchard crops and their associated fallow lands. It is estimated that approximately 4.8 million hectares of agricultural land are under perennial irrigation water supplies, mainly from the ancient Persian system of qanats (underground water channels) and modern water storage systems. Rain-fed agriculture has its main importance in the western provinces of Kermanshah, Kurdestan and Azarbaijan.

Since 1949 much effort has been directed at improving the use of scanty water supplies. The total storage capacity of dams completed under the economic plans amounts to 9,500 million cubic metres, permitting irrigation of 800,000 hectares of land, in addition to providing generating capacity for 800 megawatts of electricity and urban water supply. The main structures so far completed include the Dez, Sefid Rud and Karaj dams, while small units – Golpaygan, Shahnaz, Latian, Sangavar, Zayanderud, Mahabad and Aras – are currently in use. Additional capacity of 4,915 million cubic metres was provided during the fourth plan period by the construction of dams on the Halirud (Jiroft), Shahrud (Taleghan), Karun, Marun and other smaller streams. A project financed by the IBRD in the Qazvin Plain has enabled the sinking of wells for the supply of irrigation water for 34,000 hectares. Dams at Lar, Minab and Qeshlaq were scheduled to be built in the fifth plan period, while desalination of sea-water is expected to increase in importance in the near future.

Yields on land under crops are only fair but improving rapidly. Grains are the principal crops, including wheat, barley, and rice, though the regional variations in climate permit the cultivation of a great range of field and orchard crops, of which cotton, sugar beet, and tea have commercial importance. Production of wheat rose from 5.5 million tons in 1975/76 to a 6 million tons in 1976/77, (compared with 4.6 million tons in 1967), of barley from 1.4 million tons to 1.5 million tons (0.9 million tons in 1967), of rice from 1.43 million tons to 1.576 million tons, and of sugar beet from 4.67 million tons to 5.25 million tons (2.9 million tons in 1967).

Livestock retains considerable importance in the rural economy. Although the nomadic community is expected to decline somewhat, large-scale government expenditure on range management, breed improvement and modernized marketing facilities should result in an increase in output.

In 1975/76 there were estimated to be 35 million sheep, 14.3 million goats and 6.65 million cattle in the country.

As part of the regeneration of agriculture, begun in 1963, a drive has been made to mechanize agriculture in suitable areas. Some 29,000 tractors were in use in 1975. A 10,000-unit tractor assembly plant came into production in 1975. Numbers of combine harvesters are increasing: over 2,150 were in use in 1975. New agro-industries in Khuzistan have led to rapid mechanization of 78,000 hectares in the south, while between 700,000 and 1.4 million hectares will be mechanized during the fifth plan period.

Forest resources were nationalized in 1963 and close control of all wooded areas has been implemented since then. No less than 11 per cent of the country is under forest or woodland, including the rich Caspian area and the slopes of the Zagros Mountains, the former being the main source of commercial timber. Total roundwood output in 1975 was estimated at 6.2 million cubic metres. A traditional occupation is the collecting of the saps and resins of wild plants and shrubs and a substantial, though declining, trade is carried on in gum tragacanth, gum arabic and liquorice. A vigorous reafforestation programme is under way, especially in the area around Tehran.

Iran has direct access to both the Caspian Sea and the Gulf but fishing remains poorly developed in both areas. The Ministry of Natural Resources has taken over management of the northern caviare industry, the output of which is calculated at some 200 tons a year. Iran has so far taken less interest in developing the Gulf fisheries than adjacent countries, though the Southern Fisheries Company has taken tentative steps towards building up a fleet. The total catch in the area is set at 5,000 tons a year, though the Ministry of Natural Resources estimated the 1973 catch at 20,000 tons plus 2,000 tons of shrimp.

Agrarian Reform

Whereas the land tenure system was decidedly feudal before 1960, major structural reforms have changed the farming scene in Iran. Beginning in 1963, the state pushed through the sequestration of large landed estates totalling 16,000 villages in which land was redistributed to 743,406 farmers. In a second phase of the reform, the ceiling on land holdings was further reduced for those areas cultivated under the traditional share-cropping system and landowners were compelled to dispose of their land or substantially improve tenancy conditions on their estates through four courses of action: lease of land under revised terms; division of their land with the cultivating peasants in ratio to the old crop-sharing arrangements; setting up of a joint-stock company with the peasants; or buying out of the peasants' rights where the peasants were willing to sell. At the same time, leases on religious endowment land were radically improved. It is reported that at 21 March 1970, 54,480 villages and 19,557 farms had been affected by the terms of the reform. Later provisions of the reform programme will result in the forfeiture of all leased lands and the establishment of peasants in full ownership. Some 64,203 farmers had received land in full title by the end of 1971/72.

Co-operative organization has been extended across the country to back up the reform, and by March 1977 some 2,886 (re-grouped) co-operatives were in operation, catering for 2.9 million members. New features of the programme include the formation of farming corporations through the amalgamation and reorganization of traditional villages: some 65 units were operating by 1975. The government has also set up machinery for encouraging foreign investors to undertake agricultural projects in the country associated with the land now irrigated from the major storage dams, including Khuzistan, Marv Dasht and Dashte Moghan.

Oil and Petrochemicals

In the period from 1954 to March 1973 Iran's major oil fields were operated by the Iranian Oil Exploration and Producing Company for the Iranian Oil Participants, a consortium made up of British Petroleum (40 per cent), Royal Dutch/Shell (14 per cent), Gulf, Mobil, Exxon, Standard of California, Texaco (each 7 per cent), Compagnie Francaise des Pétroles (6 per cent) and Iricon Agency, made up originally of nine but, later, following mergers, six American independent companies. The Consortium was the successor of the Anglo-Iranian Oil Company which operated in the area of Southern Iran until May 1951 when the oil industry was nationalized. The second member of the Consortium was the Iranian Oil Refining Company which supervised refining activity at the Abadan refinery. The National Iranian Oil Company (NIOC) was responsible for providing all non-basic facilities in the Consortium area and remained the sole owner of all fixed assets.

With effect from 20 March 1973 a new agreement came into force governing operations in the Consortium area. NIOC then took over all operations, including oil production and refining and the Consortium's role in production was reduced to that of technical adviser and contractor for a period of five years. The 1973 agreement was under negotiation during 1978.

The 1954 agreement which brought the Consortium into existence, confined its activities to a limited strip in Southern

Iran known as the agreement area. In 1966 some 65,000 square kilometres of this area was relinquished to the government and the agreement area is now made up of two sections, one taking in all major oilfields and the other, further east, currently under exploration. The main producing fields are the Agha – Jari/Karani/Maran – Paris complex, Gachsaran, Bibi Hakimeh and Ahwaz, accounting for some 95 per cent of production. Whereas the export outlets for crude and refined products were once channelled through Bandar Mah Shahr and Abadan, respectively, a massive realignment programme executed in recent years now permits the export of crude from Kharg Island terminal and of refined products through Bandar Mah Shahr. Kharg Island terminal has been under constant development since the early 1960s. A four-berth facility for the handling of tankers of up to 500,000 tons was completed in 1972 and storage capacity on Kharg Island amounts to 14 million barrels.

NIOC has developed its operations considerably since 1954 and in addition to running the Naft-e-Shah field and topping plant it operates refineries at Kermanshah and Tehran. In addition to operations within the agreement area and NIOC's activities on its own account, NIOC is permitted under the 1957 law to allocate blocks to joint-venture companies in which NIOC holds a minimum of 50 per cent of the shares. Of the eight joint-venture companies established by 1963, four – one Italian and three American companies – were producing oil by 1972. In 1966 a new series of agreements was introduced, the first of which was arranged between NIOC and Erap, the French state company, under which Erap acts as NIOC's agent in exploration and finances commercial operations by NIOC. Erap has struck oil in commercial quantities offshore and production began in 1978. Two further agreements of the kind have since been negotiated with a European consortium and a US company. In 1971 three more joint-venture companies were formed with Japanese, American, and European companies and in 1974 three exploration contracts were awarded.

Before the political troubles of 1978 Iran was the world's second largest oil exporter after Saudi Arabia. Iran has maintained a favourable ratio of production to reserves despite a rapid ratio of increase in output. At the end of 1977 reserves were estimated at 62 billion barrels and gas reserves at 600 trillion cubic feet. Production from the Consortium area in 1977 was 5,090,000 barrels per day, and from NIOC and the joint-structure companies 564,000 barrels per day.

The Abadan oil refinery is one of the largest in the world with a capacity that was increased in 1976/77 to 600,000 b.p.d. Major petrochemical developments are the Shahpur Chemical Company, inaugurated in November 1970, producing sulphur and fertilizers, the Abadan Chemical Company, for the production of plastics, detergent and caustic soda, and the Kharg Chemical Company designed to produce sulphur from the Darius gas field. A vast expansion of petrochemicals projects in 1973/74 involved agreements worth $8 billion. A natural gas refining and distribution system is being set up in northern Iran.

Mining, Fuel and Power

Non-oil mining contributed roughly 0.3 per cent of GNP during 1959–68 and was thus of little economic importance. However, mineral development has undergone spectacular expansion in recent years, aided by the establishment of a geological survey in 1962. Traditional mineral products include coal, chromite, iron ore, manganese, antimony, borax and barytes. The most recent development has concentrated on the iron and coal deposits needed to supply the Isfahan steel mill since 1971, and active exploration and development are under way. Exploration for copper has intensified considerably following the discovery of extensive deposits in the Sar Cheshmeh area which will be developed by a national Iranian company with technical assistance from US interests.

Electricity generation was estimated at 17.2 million kilowatt hours in 1976/77 – an increase of 9.8 per cent on 1975/76. A master plan for the construction of a national power grid has been established to link Tehran, Khuzistan and Gilan and the country's major hydro-electrical and other power stations. Electrification of the country is proceeding rapidly and installed capacity increased by 1,421 megawatts during the fourth plan period, including 28 small and medium town generator developments. The fifth plan called for rapid development of nuclear power and agreements for co-operation in this field have been signed with the USA, West Germany, France and the UK. Severe shortages of electric power in 1977 caused stoppages and electricity rationing throughout the country.

Manufacturing Industry

The handicraft industry in Iran continues to show remarkable resilience and carpet production, in particular, supports a large export trade, valued at $84 million in 1976/77, accounting for 14 per cent of non-oil exports. Total output of carpets is estimated at 1.75 million square metres each year.

Modern sector industry was developed in the period 1930–40 by Reza Shah based on textile and food processing factories. State intervention in promoting industry was again a feature of the period of the mid 1950s, when fertilizer, sugar refining, cement, textile and sugar milling plants were set up. Private sector interest in the industrial programme grew rapidly in the late 1950s, aided by the grant of generous credits by the Plan Organization. Most of the units built at that time were concerned with light consumer goods and were located mainly in Tehran and its environs.

From 1964 a second wave of industrialization was put in hand with the public sector taking a leading role and the Shah, in particular, offering strong support for the programme. A major stimulus in the process was the Irano-Soviet agreement for the establishment of a steel mill and machine tools plant in return for the export of Iranian gas through the Igat line. The steel mill, located close to Isfahan, has begun production (and a second mill is contemplated at the same site with Soviet help), while the machine tools plant at Arak produces some 25,000 tons of equipment each year. Other important industrial deals with Eastern bloc countries include the construction of a Czech machine tools plant at Tabriz and a Czech motorcycle plant. Massey-Ferguson is to take over the Tabriz tractor plant where 5,000 units per year will be produced, rising later to 20,000 units per year.

Western participation in the industrialization programme has been on a large scale. In addition to the investments in new petrochemical units noted above, major schemes have included the establishment of an aluminium smelter at Arak under a joint Iran/US/Pakistan agreement. The automobile sector has expanded with the creation of the Iran National/Rootes, Iran National/Benz, and General Motors Iran plants for passenger cars, light vans, buses, and trucks, together with the opening of the Irano-French Citroën and Renault plants, augmenting existing output. Leyland has a major truck assembly plant in Tehran and is constructing a diesel engine plant at Tabriz, as is Mercedes-Benz, while Landrover utility vehicles are produced in Tehran and Mazda pick-ups are now manufactured locally. New partners for automobile ventures are being sought. The Industrial and Mining Development Bank has played an important role in mobilizing foreign private and domestic industrial development in the modern sector. Important new developments in steel production have emerged in which West Germany will build gas-fired steel mills with a capacity of some 1.5 million tons per year. The British Steel Corporation is to participate in a large cold rolling mill project in the south; France will construct a steel mill in Khuzistan, and Italy will provide a 3 million tons per year steel mill for Bandar Abbas. Total investment in industrial and mining machinery in 1976/77 amounted to 310 billion rials, an increase of 11 per cent over 1975/76.

Transport and Communications

In 1973 Iran possessed some 15,000 miles of all-weather roads of which about 6,000 miles were asphalted and 9,000 were gravelled. Feeder and earth roads provided an additional 9,000 miles of maintained access in rural Iran. Including army, NIOC, and forestry roads, the total road system covers some 25,000 miles, although the construction of highways under recent plans is adding to this total. Among those recently completed are the CENTO Takestan-Tabriz-Bazargan highway, the Tehran-Karaj freeway and the Heraz route to the Caspian (Tehran-Amal). The Iranian section of the Asian highway is now complete and plans are at an advanced stage for the construction of a new highway between Bandar Abbas and the Afghan frontier. In 1974 it was estimated that there were

589,200 passenger cars and 111,200 trucks and buses, but the number of vehicles is believed to have tripled between 1973 and 1977.

The main trunk of the Iranian Railway network was completed by 1938. The Trans-Iranian line crosses the country from Bandar Shahpur in the south via Tehran to Bandar Shah, a distance of 875 miles, with spurs serving Khorramshahr and the Shahpur Chemical Company. A major link to the line has been laid via Qum to Isfahan and the steel mill, and it is likely that following the extension of the line from Kashan to Bafq and Kerman a further spur will be laid to link Bandar Abbas. The system from Tehran also serves Tabriz (460 miles) with a fender spur to the Soviet frontier at Julfa, and Meshed (500 miles). Zahedan is tied to the Pakistani rail system and plans are on hand to join this with the Iranian system at Kerman and to the Gulf coast at Bandar Abbas. Under CENTO auspices, an important link has been laid between Tabriz and the Turkish rail system via Mas on the western shore of Lake Van. A large programme of electrification of the rail system is being undertaken.

Although Khorramshahr remains the major international port serving the country the growth of Bandar Shahpur, Bandar Abbas and smaller ports at Bushire, Lingeh and Chah Bahar has reduced its relative importance to some extent. Khorramshahr still handles about half of the non-oil cargo passing through the country's ports. Modernization programmes are being implemented at Bandar Pahlevi and Bandar Shah on the Caspian to provide for the increased trade between Iran and the USSR, while an entirely new port for the Caspian at Farahabad is proposed.

In addition to major international airports at Tehran, Bandar Abbas and Abadan there are 21 smaller airports. The new Tehran Airport under construction is due for completion in 1980. Communications services have improved following the opening of CENTO microwave link between Ankara, Tehran and Karachi. New automatic telephone facilities under current plans will link all major towns. In 1977 there were 781,537 telephones.

Post-Shah Policies

The lack of strong centralized government exacerbated Iran's economic difficulties in 1979. Policy decisions were mainly negative – the cancellation of major projects begun under the Shah and the elimination of important elements of the entrepreneurial class. The government provided some relief for the increasing numbers of unemployed and launched a $850 million campaign to encourage young activists to move to the the countryside to help farmers improve production levels; the response was enthusiastic but not very effective. By the summer of 1979 production in most sectors was below 50 per cent of normal and large food imports were required. Inflation was a serious problem; only rents and land prices fell as the foreign community departed.

All private banks and insurance companies were nationalized in June; a new Islamic Bank was establised. In July all private industry owned by 51 major industrialists was taken over by the state. The exodus of skilled workers, professionals and factory owners made the recovery of the economy more difficult. All major foreign contracts come under close scrutiny. Some, such as those for nuclear power plants, were entirely scrapped. Others, such as those for the steel, copper and automobile industries, were scaled down or revised. Petrochemical industry projects, on the other hand, were maintained.

Oil production reached 4.1 million b.p.d. in May (compared with 5.2. million b.p.d. in 1978) but, owing to both technical and labour difficulties, output fell to 3 million b.p.d. in September – or 20 per cent below target. However, increased oil prices gave Iran an extra one billion dollars in 1979. Budget spending for 1978/79 was 20 per cent down on the previous year, partly because of cuts in defence expenditure, and in the summer of 1979 the country's foreign exchange reserves were reported to be rising.

In September 1979 Iran's leading economic experts and planners held their first discussion of long-term economic policy since the Revolution in Tehran. Their chief conclusions were that oil and gas reserves should be conserved as far as possible through the limitation of exports; that imports should be reduced and price subsidies used to encourage local industries; and that full support should be provided for Iranian agriculture to achieve self-sufficiency in food. The principle was laid down that Iran's main low-productivity industries should be phased out but that new local industries should be established to replace essential imports and reduce the country's dependence on the major industrial countries. As a means of stimulating home food production and reducing food imports running at between $2 billion and $3 billion a year it was proposed to cut subsidies on meat, wheat, sugar, and vegetable oil, and to provide incentives to people to move back from the towns to the countryside.

V

IRAQ

THE LAND AND THE PEOPLE

The area of Iraq within its present frontiers is approximately 175,000 square miles. It is most conveniently divided into three distinct geographical sections: the Mesopotamian plain, the Uplands, and the Folded Mountain Belt. The first of these is historically the most important for it was the plain which nursed great civilizations in the past, and its two great rivers which nourished them.

The plain. To the north-east the southern alluvial plain follows the foothills of the Iranian mountains up from the sea, turns south-east across the old river estuaries at Samarra and Hit, and returns parallel to and west of the Euphrates. Within these limits the soil is stoneless alluvium. The two rivers flow in channels somewhat above the rest of the plain, which is consequently liable to be flooded during the high-water period in the spring when the snows melt in Kurdistan; local rain has comparatively little effect on the rivers. The Tigris rises in late March or early April; the Euphrates rises two or three weeks later; both rivers are at their lowest in September–October. At no point is the plain higher than 150 feet above sea-level.

The annual rainfall in the plain averages about 6 inches only; this occurs usually between mid-November and mid-March, the wettest month being February; but it is impossible to generalize, as the whole season's rainfall may occur in a space of three weeks. Cultivation in the plain depends almost entirely on irrigation, the rainfall often being insufficient to mature a winter crop.

The rivers, which have frequently changed their courses throughout history, unite about sixty miles above the city of Basra in a single great channel, the Shatt al-Arab. Also above Basra is the marshland of the Muntafiq and Amara provinces, where a distinctive group of Arabs – the 'marsh Arabs' – live on fish and the produce of their mudbanks and swampy islands, or tend their buffaloes from shallow-draft canoes.

The uplands. This region, which corresponds approximately to ancient Assyria, is undulating gravel steppe and rich plough-land, with some stone. Here, in an average year, the rainfall of 13 inches is sufficient to yield a winter crop without irrigation. In the districts of Kirkuk and Arbil, however, the rainfall is supplemented by the *kahriz* system of underground water channels, which is widespread in Iran. Mosul, Arbil, and Kirkuk are respectively 703, 1,250, and 1,087 feet above sea-level.

Between the two rivers in this area and south of latitude 36°N. is a wedge of uncultivable gypsum desert called al-Jazira (the Island).

The mountain belt. The crescent of mountain country included in the north-east frontier compromises the basins of the rivers Diyala, Lesser Zab, Greater Zab, and Khabur. It is peopled by Kurds, a hardy mountain race, living a life differing widely from that of the Arabs of the plain and uplands. Villages are stone-built and shelved into the sides of the hills, with tall silver poplars and terraced cultivation, including vineyards and tobacco. Large areas of mountainside are covered with scrub oak; the summits provide summer pastures.

Between the Euphrates valley and the western frontiers is a large section of al Badia, the Syrian Desert, populated only by nomad tribes with their flocks and camels.

Climate. The climate of Iraq is extreme. In the plains the January mean temperature is 42–52° F. (5.5–11°C.); in July, 86–96°F. (30–35.5°C.). In the mountains altitude decreases temperature in both seasons and increases the rainfall to as much as 40 inches.

The People

Between the censuses of 1957 and 1965 the population was recorded as increasing from 6.3 million to 8.3 million but civil war was raging in the north and the 1965 census was incomplete. A more comprehensive census in 1977 gave a total population of 12.2 million of whom 142,000 were resident abroad. The rate of urbanization is very high and in 1977 the urban population totalled 7.6 million. The population of the capital Baghdad has increased from 1.3 million in 1957 to 2.1 million in 1965 and 3.2 million in 1977.

Religions

Islam. The Sunnis and Shiis are mutually distinguishing and to some extent mutually suspicious sections of the Moslem majority, as are also the Arab and Kurdish sections of the Sunni group. Statistics are lacking, but the Shiis outnumber the Sunni Arabs. The Sunnis were closer to the Ottoman ruling group and since Ottoman times have continued to occupy more leading positions than the Shiis in official and professional circles. But the advance of education has brought the latter into greater prominence than before.

The Sunnis live mainly in the north of Iraq and in the *liwas* of Baghdad, Diyala, and Dulaim. There is one notable Sunni shrine in the country, that of Shaikh Abdul Qadir al-Gailani, whose mosque and tomb in Baghdad are a centre of pilgrimage from regions as remote as Indonesia.

The Shiis form a majority in the central *liwas* of Kut, Diwaniya, Karbala, and Hilla and in the southern *liwas* of Basra, Amara, and Muntafiq. Their religious life has as its background the four Holy Cities of Karbala, Najaf, Kadhimain, and Samarra. Najaf is the burial place of Ali, the first Imam; Karbala of Hussein, the third Imam. Thousands of Shiis from Iran, Afghanistan, and India take part in the traditional pilgrimages to the Holy Cities, where, during the first ten days of the month of Moharram, is enacted the famous Passion Play commemorating the death of Hussein ibn Ali at the battle of Karbala in AD 680. The Shii Mujtahids exercise not only religious but at times also political influence, as was demonstrated in the insurrection of 1920 and on subsequent occasions.

Christian Churches. Christianity in Iraq dates from the second century AD. The main Christian sects are now the Nestorian, which seceded from the main body of Christendom at the Council of Ephesus (431), the Syrian 'Orthodox' (or Jacobite), and Armenian 'Orthodox' (or Gregorian), which seceded at the Council of Chalcedon (451), and minority sections of these three churches which from the seventeenth century onwards have acknowledged Papal supremacy and are known respectively as the Chaldean, Syrian Catholic, and Armenian Catholic Churches. At the end of the First World War some 25,000 members of the Nestorian Church, which had survived mainly in the mountains of Iran and Turkey, were settled by the British authorities in Iraq; these were the so-called 'Assyrians' who suffered in the events of 1933. Today the ancient theological differences which had distinguished the churches are almost forgotten by their ordinary members, among whom the difference is rather one of liturgy, ecclesiastical discipline, and hierarchy; this is, however, sufficient to constitute minute nations rather than congregations, recognized by the Government as possessing competence in matters of personal status.

Jews. Until the war in Palestine in 1948–9 Iraq contained a large community of Jews whose families had been settled in the country for hundreds or even thousands of years. A law of 1931 gave Jewish communities self-government in their own affairs, and there was a highly organized communal life, with schools, hospitals, and charitable institutions. In consequence of ill-feeling arising from events in Palestine the majority of Jews left Iraq in 1950–52, mostly for Israel.

Yazidis. These are vulgarly known as 'devil-worshippers'. They are divided between Jabal Sinjar and the Shaikhan district north of Mosul and speak a Kurdish dialect; their sacred books, however, are written in Arabic.

Sabaeans. Most of them are craftsmen – especially silversmiths – in the large riverain towns.

Shabak. Of Kurdish origin, who live in the area of the Yazidis and are not clearly distinguished from them; their religion contains Yazidi and extreme Shii elements.

HISTORY AND POLITICS

Written history began in Iraq at the end of the fourth millennium BC, but archaeological remains from much earlier periods, first in the north and later also in the south, give evidence of palaeolithic man, of agricultural neolithic man and, from the sixth and fifth millennia, of increasing human progress expressed successively in extensive agriculture, copper and bronze work, wheeled vehicles, the potter's wheel, the sailing ship, bricks, temples, writing, seals, and sculpture of considerable maturity. Fully evolved urban life and written records appear before 3000 BC, with the emergence in southern Iraqi city-states of the magnificent Sumerian civilization, the first highly developed culture in the world. It was absorbed and transformed by the first historical Semitic immigration, that of the Akkadians (*c.* 2400 BC), who united the country into a single kingdom and extended it by foreign conquest. The unity, destroyed by tribal incursions from the east, was re-established for two centuries under the hegemony of Ur of the Chaldees, to be disrupted again, at the beginning of the second millennium, by a further invasion, of Elamites and Semitic Amorites, from which, in the eighteenth century BC, arose the Babylon of Hammurabi. Babylon, under various dynasties, absorbed and was itself modified by incursions of Hittites and Hurrians from the north and west and Kassites from the east, and in 745 BC fell to the Semitic Power of Assyria, which, expanding during the ninth and eighth centuries from a local city-state in the north, came to dominate the whole riverland and for a time controlled most of the Middle East. Assyria itself fell in 612 BC to the combination of a revived Babylon and the new Power of Media; and the neo-Babylonian Empire – that of Nebuchadnezzar and 'Balthazar' – was overcome in 539 BC by Cyrus, the founder of the first of the three great Iranian dynasties, which, during the next thousand years, extended westward over Iraq. The first, the Achaemenian, was overthrown by Alexander the Great, whose Seleucid successors continued to dispute Iraq with the second great dynasty, the Parthian, after it had evicted them; these fell in turn to the Sasanians, who, like their predecessors, warred with Imperial Rome from their capital at Ctesiphon.

In the seventh century AD the campaigns of the newly established Moslem community overthrew the Sasanian Empire, whose territories were thereupon governed successively from Medina and Damascus. In AD 750 the Abbasid family, which drew its support from Iraq and farther east, supplanted the related dynasty of Damascus; and in 762 it founded a new capital at Baghdad. During the 500 years of their Caliphate the area of Arab conquest became a religious and cultural unity in which Baghdad held an eminent, at times pre-eminent position; the material authority of the Abbasids, however, despite increased centralization and standardization of government, rapidly dwindled, as province after province fell to invaders, adventurers, or local princes and the central power was sapped in dynastic quarrels and the disputes of the powerful palace guard. From the tenth century AD the Caliph was little more than a religious figurehead under the temporal protection of successive Turkish dynasties, holding insecurely only part of an economically declining Iraq. In 1258 Baghdad was destroyed in a Mongol invasion and the Abbasid dynasty, long shorn of imperial power, was overthrown. The Mongol ravages intensified the ruinous aftermath of centuries of invasion and internal strife, and the country was subsequently despoiled and fought over by Turkomans and Tatars, then disputed by the Iranian and Ottoman Empires, each exploiting the internal religious division between Sunni and Shii Moslems and the opportunism of frontier Kurds. In 1638 Iraq, although still open to Iranian invasion, fell finally to the Turks and remained a province, or provinces, of the Ottoman Empire until the First World War.

The Period 1914–45

In November 1914 the Allied Powers, provoked by a Turkish attack on Russian sea ports, declared war on Turkey, and an Indian Army Brigade landed in Iraq. By the end of 1918 virtually the whole of what is now Iraq was in British hands.

British official opinion was divided in its policy towards Iraq and the civil administration which succeeded the military occupation was for long embarrassed by uncertainty about the future. Delay in making a definite pronouncement of policy had brought nationalist emotions in Iraq to the boiling point. The assignment of the mandate – highly unwelcome to nationalist sentiment – in April 1920 was followed by disturbances which developed in July into an insurrection; this, while it left large areas of the country unaffected, required considerable forces to suppress it. Pacification was completed early in 1921; and already, by October 1920, Sir Percy Cox, the first High Commissioner, had terminated military rule and established an Arab Council of State advised by British officials. The British Government decided to support for the headship of the new Iraq state the Amir Faisal, son of King Hussein, who had led the Arab revolt of 1916–18 and in 1920 had been expelled from Damascus by the French. Faisal's nomination as king was approved by the Council of State and confirmed in a referendum, and he was enthroned on 23 August 1921. The Anglo-Iraqi Treaty, in which the mandatory Power had decided to embody its obligations towards the League of Nations, was ratified by the Iraq Government on 10 October 1922 against the determined opposition of nationalist elements, who insisted that the treaty should terminate the mandate and British influence, whereas it in fact incorporated the provisions of the mandate, gave guarantees on judicial matters to make up for the abolition of the Capitulations, and guaranteed Britain's special interests in Iraq. Its period of validity, twenty years, was reduced the following year to four years from the ratification of peace with Turkey, which followed in July 1923.

In December 1925 the Council of the League of Nations awarded the Mosul *vilayet* to Iraq. In July 1926 a treaty between Turkey, Britain, and Iraq accepted the new frontiers as definitive and inviolable, while Iraq agreed to pay to Turkey 10 per cent of oil royalties for twenty-five years. In September 1929 the British Government undertook to support Iraq's candidature for League membership in 1932, and in 1930 yet another treaty was signed, which provided for a close Anglo-Iraqi alliance, to last for twenty-five years from the admission of Iraq to the League. There was to be consultation between the parties in matters of foreign policy which might affect their common interest; mutual assistance in the event of war, including provision by Iraq of communications and all other facilities and assistance and the right of passage to British troops; and lease of sites for air bases near Basra and west of Euphrates. The treaty was badly received by the nationalists, but was ratified by the Assembly in November 1931. On 3 October 1932, on the strong recommendation of the British Government, Iraq was admitted to the League of Nations as an independent state.

From Independence to the Iraqi Revolution

The independent governments faced serious difficulties from the start. During the period of the mandate there had been much material progress and an administrative structure far ahead of the previous one had been created. But a sense of unity was still lacking. The division between a larger Shii and a smaller but more influential Sunni population was a constant source of political disunity and weakness, and of regional as well as sectarian antagonism. In the north a part of Kurdistan, where communications were poor and a different language was spoken, had been included in Iraq. In addition to these formal divisions the population lacked social cohesion. A small, comparatively rich class lived among a majority of extremely poor workers on the land and in the towns. In between lay increasing numbers of students, members of the professions, the more well-to-do shopkeepers and middlemen, and technicians. Representative institutions were in their infancy and it was difficult to establish political parties transcending the divisions within the population. The monarchy was new and the sense of legitimacy around it was not yet firmly established. Tribal divisions remained: not only did the tribes inherit turbulent traditions from the distant past, but their poverty was a temptation to urban political factions to make use of them in their rivalries. To complicate these divisions, an Assyrian minority which had been rescued by British troops after their flight from Iran and had been settled in Iraq in the First World War, when they supplied many of the troops used by Britain to keep order among the tribes, were demanding full settlement but were dissatisfied with the proposed arrangements. They attempted to cross into Syria but were sent back by the French authorities. An unjustifiable scare led to the cold-blooded massacre of some hundreds of them by the Iraqi army under Bakr Sidqi.

Tribal revolts were suppressed by the army and a temporary alliance was made between a civilian group of liberal reformers, a young officer group and Hikmat Sulaiman, who was inspired by the achievements of the Turkish nationalists under Atatürk. The alliance seized power by a *coup d'état* in 1936.

The liberal social democrats soon found that the young officers were determined to keep control, and a disastrous precedent was set for military domination in Iraqi politics. King Faisal I had died in 1933 and his son Ghazi was too immature to control the military influence in politics. Early in 1939 he met a premature death in a car accident. He was succeeded by his son Faisal II, then an infant, with the Amir Abdul Ilah, his uncle, as Regent. In the following twenty years the Regent played an important part in Iraqi politics. The Hikmat regime disintegrated. The reforming social democrat ministers, opposed both by the army and the extreme conservative civilians, resigned. General Bakr Sidqi was assassinated, and the ministry gave way to another under Jamil al-Midfai. The new ministry attempted to curb the army's dangerous role in politics, with only temporary and limited success, and as the Second World War was approaching increasing differences over foreign policy began to develop.

Since independence popular feeling against Britain remained, but governments in practice kept on fairly friendly terms with British ambassadors in Baghdad. The Royal Air Force retained a base at Habbaniya and Russia refused to recognize Iraq as an independent country on the ground that it was still under British control. A group of army officers shared increasing sympathies with the German Nazi regime. Developments in Palestine had further alienated public opinion from Britain. The White Paper on Palestine (Cmd. 6019 of 1939), issued about three months before the war, had created a position more favourable to the Arabs which the Iraqi Prime Minister, Nuri al-Said, in 1940 endeavoured to use as the basis for a settlement. But Winston Churchill, by this time in power, was not willing to negotiate on this basis.

When the Second World War began General Nuri al-Said was Prime Minister. His Government promptly broke off diplomatic relations with Germany. Nuri decided to go further and declare war on Germany but was held back by the army. Increasing dissension in the Cabinet and the murder of his Finance Minister led, after an unsuccessful attempt to reconstruct his Cabinet, to his resignation in favour of Rashid Ali al-Gailani. The new Government declared at first that it would continue to follow the Anglo-Iraqi Alliance. But the Arab nationalist inclination towards Germany was increasing, partly owing to an agitation organized in Iraq by the former Mufti of Jerusalem. The fall of France encouraged anti-British sentiment in these circles. When Britain asked for approval to land forces in Basra to cross to Haifa, disputes arose over the interpretation of the Treaty, and Iraqi opinion was divided. London was poorly informed on local conditions, and on ill-judged advice from the British Embassy prematurely issued a blunt demand for the removal of Rashid Ali from the premiership. The effects of the ultimatum were to create closer relations between Rashid Ali and the military group which favoured Germany and was plotting with Von Papen. Hostilities eventually resulted from a confused situation in which miscalculations were made on all sides. After another military *coup d'état* the Regent, followed by Nuri al-Said, left for Transjordan. They were subsequently restored by British military action, and the four colonels who had instigated the *coup d'état* were executed.[1]

During the rest of the war the Iraqi governments that were reconstituted under the Regent were formed mainly from moderate nationalists and co-operated with Britain in military matters. Iraq and Iran formed a main route for the supplies passing from the Western allies to Russia. In 1943 Iraq made a formal declaration of war against Germany and her allies. In 1945 diplomatic relations were established with Russia and the United Nations Charter was signed. But in nationalist circles reservations against close identification with British and allied policies remained, even though the extremist groups in the army and among those influenced by the Mufti of Jerusalem were discredited by the decline of Germany and Italy.

Difficulties developed after the middle of 1943 in Iraqi Kurdistan. Nuri al-Said toured the area in May 1944 and endeavoured to meet Kurdish grievances by special social and economic measures and by proposing the creation of a new *liwa* of Dohuk. But the Regent blocked the proposal, and other measures were sabotaged by narrow-minded army officers as well as by a number of civilian ministers. This sequence of events was to be repeated several times in the

[1] See above, p. 27.

post-war years by different groups of ministers and army officers, and it was not surprising that Kurdish leaders lost hope that governments in Baghdad would deal with them in good faith.

Following the war martial law was ended, the censorship of the press was abolished, and political parties could be legally formed again, except the Communist party. The latter, however, carried on underground activities. The parties ranged from the right-wing Independence Party, through the mildly reformist Liberal Party to the National Democratic Party which modelled itself on European social-democratic policies and included some leading educated middle-class personalities. But ministries remained transient and subject to frequent reshuffling and intense personal rivalries. The parties remained poorly organized and attracted no mass representation: their members comprised only a small proportion of the population. So far as organization was concerned the Communist party was an exception, but in the period 1948–52 it was handicapped locally by the instructions which, along with other Asian parties, it received from the Comintern, led by Zhdanov, and by the indirect effects of Stalin's attempts, just after the war, to delay the Russian evacuation of Iran and to use the Tudeh party there for his own purposes. This pushed most of the moderate Iraqi leaders, especially Nuri al-Said, further towards the Western powers than they might otherwise have gone. The hanging of four Communist leaders in 1949 was resented even by the non-Communist left, and it created martyrs for the movement. A militant student group, aided by the Communist and Baathist organizations, organized political demonstrations against the regime from time to time.

But the growth of revenues derived from the operations of the oil companies in the 1950s enabled the short-lived oligarchic governments to lay the foundations for considerable economic and social advances. Nuri al-Said, who headed a number of ministries in this period, took the lead in measures to use some 70 per cent of the oil revenues in economic development. His Government established a Development Board which was to allocate the revenues among different projects. The Board included several foreign experts. Nuri consciously based his policies on the theory that ten or more years of economic advance would reduce social and political discontent and remove the danger of revolution. He had no wish to be a dictator but from 1954 his suppression of political parties and manipulation of elections alienated important sections of the middle classes and his and Abdul Ilah's policies of close links with the 'Western' powers alienated not only the middle classes but also the growing student class, the 'intellectuals', and even conservative and traditional Islamic circles. He failed also to grasp the declining comparative importance of the tribal chiefs. In the hope of maintaining their political support he refrained from adopting the proposals for land reform that were drawn up by some of his ministers. The difficulties of reform without loss of productivity were serious, but the arbitrary actions of some of the large landlords, who were almost a law to themselves in some areas, aroused much popular resentment and stimulated the growth of a revolutionary spirit.

None the less the country was comparatively quiet for most of the 1950s preceding the revolution of 1958. There was much outspoken criticism in which sections of the press sometimes joined. The regime could not be described as a dictatorship but was in practice an oligarchy. A number of ministers were men of capacity and experience.

The Revolution of 1958

Rumours of a coming attempt to overthrow the regime had been circulating in Baghdad for some weeks before the blow came on 14 July 1958. The sudden creation of the United Arab Republic in February had been followed by the declaration of a formal union between Iraq and Jordan. In these moves and counter-moves the public had not been consulted in any of the countries concerned. In Iraq and Jordan the majority of people appeared indifferent and some sections of it disapproving. The conflict in the Lebanon had widened the gap between the Government and public opinion. The Prime Minister, sharply at odds with President Nasser, hoped for 'Western' intervention in Lebanon, and seems to have prepared to use Iraqi troops if it came. This would have run sharply counter to sentiment throughout the country. Violent radio propaganda was launched from Cairo against the Iraqi Government and particularly against the Prime Minister.

For some time groups of 'Free Officers' had been meeting in secret to devise means of overturning the regime. A central organization was formed with Brigadier Abdul Karim Kassem as its chairman. An order to a brigade situated north-east of Baghdad to move to Jordan on 14 July gave them their opportunity. The second in command of this brigade, Colonel Abdul Salam Aref, a fellow-conspirator with Brigadier Kassem, agreed to direct the brigade into instead of around Baghdad, and to take over the capital, Kassem following close behind with another brigade from a neighbouring camp. The plan was successful. The police made no effort to repel the vanguard of Colonel Aref's forces. Security measures proved to be wholly inadequate. A contributory factor was the widespread lack of support for the regime. In the take-over the King, the Crown Prince, and all but one member of the Royal Family were shot dead.

The military officers had formed no agreed programme on the policy to be followed after power had been seized. In the first few days they suppressed mob disorders and obtained a firm hold on the country. The establishment of a Republic was announced. A 'Council of Sovereignty' was to exercise the functions of the President until a president was appointed. Two of its three members were army officers. A Cabinet was set up in which Brigadier Kassem was both Prime Minister and Acting Minister of Defence. Although parties had been banned in 1954 they had continued underground and, although still without legal recognition, they began to appear above the surface again after the Revolution. The Communist party was the best organized though its membership was not large.

From an early stage, the new regime was faced with serious dangers within and from without. The various groups which rejoiced at the passing of the old regime held widely different views over the nature of the regime that should follow it, ranging from the Moslem Brotherhood and the most conservative Islamic groups at one extreme to the Communists at the other. A large majority held intermediate, but still diverse, views, and the extent of political freedom which some of the most active among them desired fell far short of that advocated by the National Democratic Party. Among them were the Baathists, whose inspiration came from Syria, and the Arab Nationalist

Movement, based largely on Beirut. The term 'Arab nationalist', however, was often given a wider and looser significance, at times almost synonymous with the term 'Nasserite'. The formation of the United Arab Republic only a few months earlier had created an expectation in some quarters that, following the Revolution, Iraq would be added to it. Radio and press in Cairo and Damascus had maintained a long and violent attack on the former Iraqi regime. Opposition groups in Iraq had applauded this campaign for their own ends, but their willingness to accept Egyptian intervention and leadership was greatly over-estimated. Brigadier Kassem and the majority of his associates soon showed that the new regime would pursue its own way and maintain the independence of Iraq. Colonel Abdul Salam Aref, Kassem's associate in the 'take-over', soon broke with Premier Kassem, partly over the issue of relations with Egypt.

Faced with verbal attacks from Cairo and Damascus which encouraged dissident groups at home to seek the overthrow of his regime, Kassem pursued a policy aiming at a balance of power among the contending groups in the country. Throughout the autumn and early winter his greatest danger came from the extreme groups on the right, together with the Baathists, who were not yet disillusioned with the UAR. In March 1959, a plot organized by Colonel Shawaf, a former 'Free Officer' stationed in Mosul, with the aid of Colonel Sarraj, the UAR Chief of Security in Damascus, led to an uprising in Mosul which was suppressed by military force aided by left-wing groups in Mosul. In the course of the affray excesses were committed by Mosul Communists retaliating after the murder of two of their leaders by extremists on the right. Numerous arrests were made and political tension heightened. Relations with the UAR, which had aided the plotters, deteriorated further.

This was a succession of plots, in some of which UAR agents gave indirect help to Baathists; extreme Arab nationalists and dissident army officers had impelled Premier Kassem to give more scope to Communists than he wished to do, in order to maintain a balance of political forces. But when the outrages committed by them in Mosul in March were followed in July by the Kirkuk affray in which they played a part, Kassem acted quietly and swiftly to remove them from positions of power and arrest many of their members. This was scarcely done, however, when a group of Baathist extremists, aided by Syrians, attempted to assassinate him in August. Kassem survived, however, and continued his personal rule until February 1963.

These political preoccupations hindered economic reforms. Land reform was the most urgent need and the greatest failure, not only for the Kassem regime but for those which followed. For political reasons the power of the landlords had to be and was reduced, but at the expense of productivity, which fell disastrously, with unfortunate results for other economic sectors. The Development Board, with its foreign advisers, was abolished and a Ministry of Planning set up. In practice the new industrial programme was little more than a continuation of the old.

Political and economic relations were widened by the establishment of diplomatic relations with the Eastern European countries and China. This was followed by the conclusion of a variety of trade agreements and cultural exchanges with them as well as arrangements for loans and aid in economic development. Among the schemes which were eventually carried through was the conversion of the railway between Baghdad and Basra from narrow to standard gauge.

Notwithstanding the use at times of left-wing phraseology, the general economic policies of the new regime differed less than had been expected from those of its predecessor and the way was left open for private enterprise in industry. In 1961–2, however, Kassem took two steps which encountered much opposition abroad. The first, which is discussed elsewhere,[2] concerned the oil companies operating in Iraq; the second was to lay claim to Kuwait as part of Iraq. This was not a new Iraqi claim but it was made in April 1961 on the eve of Kuwait independence when rumours had circulated that she might join the Commonwealth. It alarmed the Ruler of Kuwait – who called for British military assistance – and other Arab states, which denied Iraq's claim. British troops were succeeded by Arab League troops. It does not appear that Kassem intended to use force, but the incident was a blow to his prestige.

In the later part of his period of rule Kassem lost much of his earlier popularity, except among the economically poorer

[2] See p. 349.

classes. At the same time, however, the country became more settled and greater freedom prevailed. There was little or no sign of any widespread desire for further political upheaval. But the Premier's failure to mobilize political support and to share power with others among the politically active classes gave an opportunity for Baathist plotters in the army to organize a rising in February 1963. Kassem was summarily executed.

From an early stage the new regime was torn by internal dissensions that became more and more acute as time went on. Its leaders established a 'National Guard' which became a paramilitary organization in the hands of its extremists on the 'left'. The Prime Minister, General Bakr, was unable to control the contending groups within the Government. Baathist ranks were unable to provide all the skills and experience required in government and the moderate group wished to fill positions from non-Baathists where it seemed desirable on grounds of efficiency. But the extremist groups were opposed to this and, led by a Deputy Prime Minister, Ali Saleh al-Saadi, obtained control of the National Guard which engaged in terrorist activities against political opponents. The police were powerless to protect the public against political acts of violence, including torture and murder.

In external affairs the career of the regime was almost equally stormy. The coup in Iraq was followed in March by a similar coup in Syria which overthrew the parliamentary regime that had followed the collapse of the UAR in 1961. The Baathist regimes in Syria and Iraq joined forces in demanding a new Arab union between the two countries and Egypt. The initiative was embarrassing to Egypt. It was obvious that the Iraqi and Syrian conception of union was one in which President Nasser would have had to share power with them, and the negotiations were foredoomed from the start. As a result the relations of Iraq with Egypt again deteriorated and Arab nationalists in Iraq, within the army as well as the public, were alienated further.

In November the crisis came to a head. The challenge to the army and police by the National Guard forced a showdown. The moderate Baathist leaders were obliged to draw in non-Baathist officers as well as to co-operate with the President Abdul Salam Aref to suppress the National Guard in an armed clash on a large scale in Baghdad on 18 November.

The widespread relief felt at the downfall of the Baathist regime created a favourable atmosphere for the new Government which at first was composed of a mixture of moderate Baathist and of Arab nationalist officers, together with some civilian ministers chosen on technical grounds. It was not long before the Arab nationalist elements in the Government succeeded in eliminating, one by one, the Baathist ministers, with the exception of Tahir Yahya, who proved to be an opportunist ready to accommodate his views to the changed conditions. He became Prime Minister in what was now a non-Baathist Government.

Policy now seemed to be oriented externally towards friendship with Egypt – with unfavourable results for relations with Syria – and internally towards greater support for free enterprise and away from socialism. But this was to overlook competition in ideology. Egypt had turned to 'Arab socialism' in 1961–2 and began to apply it in Syria during the union. This was largely undone by the parliamentary regime which succeeded after the collapse of the union. But 'renationalization' of the banks followed the Baathist seizure of power in 1963. These examples, among other influences, led to the introduction of sweeping nationalization measures in the middle of 1964 by the Aref–Yahya Government in direct contradiction to its previous declarations of policy. Difficulties quickly arose over the administration of such a wide range of public industries. While the Government could hardly be as unpopular as that of 1963, it soon lost its early favour. Outwardly it moved towards closer relations with Egypt, and an agreement was reached to establish a 'Joint Presidential Council' with subsidiary committees to meet once a quarter to prepare for the establishment of a union between the two countries. This was followed by agreement to set up a 'unified Political Command' which was to aim at 'constitutional unity' within two years. A third step was taken by the establishment of an 'Arab Socialist Union' on the model of Egypt, which was to constitute the sole political party in the country.

These moves were ineffective. The conditions for a real union did not exist. President Nasser was never ready to share power and President Aref, even if he had wished to do so, could not have overcome the opposition in Iraq, especially among the Shii and the Kurds, to Egyptian domination or any other form of autocratic outside rule in the name of unity.

Premier Yahya remained in office until September 1965 in the face of growing discontent at the failure to achieve promised economic advances, and to create the confidence needed to stimulate investment. Meantime the conflict in the north continued. The ministry collapsed in September 1965 and shortly afterwards Dr. Abdul Rahman al-Bazzaz was installed as the first civilian premier since the Revolution.

A programme of reforms was promptly adopted. Nationalizations were to be limited in the future and private enterprise encouraged. Dr. Bazzaz boldly declared that the time had come to return to normal civilian life and steps were to be taken to adopt an electoral law. He aimed at ending the Kurdish war but was at first obstructed by his Minister of Defence, General Uqaily. By personal visits and judicious diplomacy he markedly improved Iraq's relations with neighbouring countries, including Turkey, Iran, and Saudi Arabia.

In April 1966 President Abdul Salam Aref was killed in a helicopter crash. He was succeeded by his brother, Abdul Rahman Aref, another army officer. Groups of officers led by retired generals began from an early stage to plot for the removal of Dr. Bazzaz. But the Premier held on to office long enough to bring the Kurdish war to an end on the basis of a twelve-point plan which recognized Kurdish nationalism and provided for autonomy in a wide range of domestic affairs. Before these measures could be carried through, Dr. Bazzaz was removed – immediately after a successful visit to Moscow.

The succeeding military Government failed to gain public confidence. It was dominated by army officers who, though giving some lip-service to the Twelve Points, were in reality opposed to them and did nothing to carry them out. Meanwhile the Kurdish leader had firmly established his position in the north.

The new Government faced an early loss of revenue as a result of a Syrian conflict with the Iraq Petroleum Company which blocked the outlet for Iraqi oil. This led to the fall of the ministry on the eve of the war with Israel which started on 5 June 1967. Iraqi troops were sent to Jordan and remained there after the war had ended. Although Iraq's role was negligible in practice, the Government supported the position of Egypt and Jordan. Yahya returned as Prime Minister, and as long as the Aref-Yahya regime lasted it followed broadly the policy of co-operation with Cairo. Meantime the displaced military Baathist leaders were plotting to regain the power which they had lost in November 1963. Their general unpopularity made it unlikely that they would have succeeded but for the unwilling aid given by two army officers, one of them Head of Security and the other Head of the Presidential Guard, Col. Abdul Razzaq al-Naif and Lt.-Gen. Ibrahim Abdul Rahman al-Daoud, who determined to oust the President and Premier. They represented the widespread middle-class discontent and were not among the left-wing opponents of the regime. The Baathist plotters seized the opportunity to join them, and they took power on 17 July 1968.

In the first fortnight after the coup al-Naif and al-Daoud formed a moderate ministry but Generals al-Bakr, Hardan Takriti, and Ammash staged a second internal coup and eliminated the two authors of the downfall of President Aref and his regime. Thus a military Baath regime returned five years after it had been displaced.

The Baathist Regime 1968–

For some months the restored Baathist regime gave the impression that it would be no more successful in governing Iraq than its predecessors. Some prominent figures, including the former premier Dr. Bazzaz, were arrested and imprisoned on trumped-up charges of spying for Israel. In January 1969 the regime caused an international uproar by hanging fourteen alleged spies, nine of them Jews, and publicly displaying their bodies. While strongly denouncing any move by other Arab states towards a political settlement of the Middle East conflict it declared its all-out support for the Palestinian guerrillas. Yet when the civil war broke out in Jordan in September 1970 the 12,000 Iraqi troops who had been stationed there since the 1967 war failed to come to their support and it was left to the rival Baathist regime to intervene. Since the radical Baathists took power in Syria in 1966 and the founder and ideologist of the Baath Michel Aflaq (see p. 71 above) left Syria in disgust, relations between the Iraqi and Syrian Baathists have been consistently bad. Aflaq spent much time in Iraq and was honoured by the regime.

Despite its setbacks, the stability and self-confidence of the regime slowly improved. This was largely due to the efforts of the vice-president of the Revolutionary Command Council Saddam Hussein (al-Takriti) who established gradual control over the internal security services and the military wing of the Baath to emerge as the strong man of the regime. A leader of some vision, he proved considerably more competent than his predecessors. In June 1972 he took the bold step of nationalizing the Iraq Petroleum Company (see p. 350 below). For a time oil output stagnated but when, after prolonged negotiations, a settlement agreement was reached with IPC in 1973, Iraq benefited from a major boost to the economy as the increase in exports and oil prices brought a massive increase in revenues. In 1973 the regime attempted to broaden its basis by forming a National Front with the communist party, the Kurdish Democratic Party (KDP) and other acceptable national and independent groups. However, although the communists accepted, the main body of the KDP led by the veteran Mullah Mustafa Barzani refused.

Experience has proved that no regime in Iraq can be stable as long as the Kurdish problem remains unsolved. In March 1970 an agreement was reached with Barzani which was more far-reaching than any previous attempts at a settlement. Its fifteen points declared an end to the fighting and an amnesty for all insurgents, gave the Kurdish language equal status with Arabic in Kurdish majority areas (which were to have Kurdish administrators) and provided for the appointment of a Kurdish vice-president in the Baghdad government. But although relations improved for a time, they deteriorated again during the four-year proposed transitional period and in March 1974 Barzani and his followers rejected the Baghdad government's formal offer of autonomy as hypocritical and inadequate and rose once again in rebellion. The war between Iraqi forces and the Kurdish irregulars or *Pesh Merga* was renewed with customary ferocity.

In March 1975 events took a decisive turn when Vice-President Saddam Hussein was publicly reconciled with the

Shah of Iran at an Algiers summit meeting of OPEC states. Relations between Iraq and Iran, with territorial disputes and mutual charges of subversion, had been bad for some years and at times on the brink of war. In 1975 Iran was providing invaluable aid and sanctuary to Barzani's forces. Under the new agreement, Iran cut off its crucial support; the revolt collapsed and Barzani went into exile. Iraq proceeded with the establishment of a Kurdish Autonomous Region and invested heavily in its economic recovery. This did not mean that the Kurdish problem in Iraq was fully 'solved'. Kurdish emigré leaders charged the Iraqi government with large-scale deportation of Kurds to the south to reduce their numbers in the Kurdish majority areas. Sporadic incidents continued but the Baghdad regime was no longer engaged in civil war.

Although Iraq has enjoyed a period of relative internal stability since 1958, this stability can never be taken for granted. Apart from the Kurdish problem, Iraq's Shii population is liable to disaffection. It is not enthusiastic about the Baath Party's Pan-Arab ideology which derives from a Sunni-dominated vision of the Arab past. In February 1977 there was serious trouble among the Shiis which led to dissension in the Baathist high command. In the summer of 1978 Iraq's Shiis were aroused by the anti-Shah disturbances among their fellow Shiis of Iran. Nevertheless, the Iraqi Baath Party could be said to have achieved more than any of its predecessors in the supremely difficult task of establishing effective government in Iraq. The price was the frequent use of dictatorial and ruthless methods.

In its Arab and foreign policies the Iraqi Baathist regime has followed a path that is independent and radical to the point of extremism but also on occasion pragmatic, as in the agreement with Iran. In the October 1973 war it sent some troops to fight alongside the Syrians but when they accepted the UN cease-fire it ignored Syrian protests and withdrew them. Since then it has repeatedly offered to revive the Arab northern front against Israel but only on condition that Syria repudiates all UN resolutions aimed at a political settlement with the 'Zionist entity' (as Israel is officially named in Iraq). It was on this basis that it refused to join the 'front of steadfastness' of Arab states opposed to President Sadat's peace initiative of 1977–8. In fact, although denouncing Egypt's policies, Iraq consistently refused to break relations with Cairo. On the basis of its Pan-Arab ideology Iraq invited several thousand Egyptian *fellahin* to immigrate while tens of thousands more Egyptians of various professions and trades, some of whom were political emigrés, found employment in Iraq. Iraq's extreme radicalism did not preclude an improvement in relations with Kuwait, after settlement of outstanding territorial differences in 1977, or regular consultations with Saudi Arabia. Relations with the Soviet Union, Iraq's main arms supplier, were close while its attitude to the USA was hostile, but a majority of the foreign companies contracted to take part in Iraq's development plans were from the non-communist industrialized countries, including the USA. The size of Iraq's oil revenues reinforced the country's independence of action. In 1978 there was a sharp deterioration in relations with the Soviet Union as a result of the execution of 21 Iraqi communists accused of political activities in the army, and of Soviet aid for Ethiopia against Somali and Eritrean nationalists, supported by Iraq. The view of the regime, as expressed by its political strategist Saddam Hussein, was that time was on the side of the Arabs provided they made full use of their natural advantages and the fact that new 'centres of power' were emerging (such as Japan and China) in addition to the American and Soviet superpowers. For this reason there should be no compromise on Arab claims to Palestine.

Iraq's totally uncompromising stand on Palestine led in 1978 to an open breach with the Palestine Liberation Organization which blamed Iraq for sponsoring the Baghdad-based extremist Abu Nidal group held responsible for the assassination of the PLO London and Kuwait representatives, regarded as moderates. A running warfare developed with a series of attacks on Iraqi diplomats abroad and reprisals against PLO representatives. In October 1978 President Assad of Syria visited Baghdad, and the two Baathist regimes agreed to bury their differences. However, further planned moves towards a union of Iraq and Syria failed to progress and in

August 1979, shortly after Saddam Hussein had replaced Ahmad Hassan al-Bakr in the presidential role, the discovery of an alleged conspiracy against his regime by some of its highest members placed the Iraqi/Syrian *rapprochement* in jeopardy because of suspected Syrian involvement.

GOVERNMENT AND CONSTITUTION

Before the Iraqi Revolution of 1958 legislative power was vested with the King in parliament which consisted of the Senate and Chamber of Deputies. Senators, who were appointed by the King, were not to exceed in number one fourth of the Chamber of Deputies. The deputies were elected on the basis of one to every 20,000 male Iraqi subjects. Every bill had to be submitted to each Assembly in turn and then approved by the King.

In the revolution led by the military in 1958 the existing regime was eliminated and a new provisional constitution was announced. But the history of the 1960s was marked by frequent military *coups d'état*, after each of which the previous constitutions (mostly 'provisional') were abolished and announcements made of the intention to draft new and 'permanent' constitutions. In September 1968 the new Baathist regime produced a new provisional constitution which remains in force. In reality the power of the regime rests on a triple basis of the Baath Party, the state apparatus and the army. The Regional (i.e. Iraqi) Command of the Arab Baath Socialist Party was elected in 1973 with Ahmed Hassan al-Bakr as President and Saddam Hussein as Secretary-General, by the VIIIth Regional Congress of the Party. The Political Report of this Congress is a key document which is referred to by all levels of the Party cadre. The ABSP is the leading party in the state and as such controls the majority of trade unions, the general federation of peasants' association, the Union of Youth, the General Union of Iraqi Women, etc.

However, the Baath is not the only party. On 17 July 1973 a National and Progressive Front was formed of the Baath, the Iraqi Communist Party, a section of the Kurdish Democratic Party opposed to Mustafa Barzani, the Kurdish Revolutionary Party, and other small nationalist groups and independents acceptable to the regime. Linked to the Baath by a Charter of National Action, these other groups are associated with the exercise of power by the regime. The National and Progressive Front has regional committees in each of Iraq's 16 governorates.

The higher executive organ of the state is the Revolutionary Command Council (RCC) of which al-Bakr and Saddam Hussein were respectively President and Vice-President, until al-Bakr resigned in July 1979 and was replaced by Saddam Hussein. The President of the RCC is *ex officio* President of the Republic with the right to appoint vice-presidents, ministers, and judges. The RCC exercises overriding executive and legislative powers including that of initially appointing members of the National Assembly provided for by a decree of 1970 but not yet formed in 1978.

The Kurdish Autonomous Region

The RCC also controls the institution of the Kurdish Autonomous Region created on 11 March 1974 out of the three north eastern governorates of Erbil, Dahouk and Soulaimaniyeh. The RCC nominated the 84 members of the Kurdish Legislative Council which exercises legislative powers in the Autonomous Region except for matters reserved to the central governate – foreign policy, defence and finance. The President of the Executive Council of the Autonomous Region is chosen by the RCC.

Since 1968 the civilian wing of the ABSP led by Saddam Hussein has undertaken to ensure both the 'Baathization' of the army, police, and intelligence services, and ultimate non-military dominance in the regime. The military bureau of the party is entirely composed of civilians, and serving officers rarely attend party congresses. The Baath Party's insistence on its monopoly of political activity in the army led to the execution of 21 communists in May 1978 on charges of forming secret groups within the army.

SOCIAL AND ECONOMIC SURVEY

Education

Since 1957 the number of students at all levels of education has continued to increase much more rapidly than the population. Pupils in primary schools rose from about 430,000 in 1957–8 to about 977,000 in 1966–7. The numbers in secondary schools increased even more rapidly. By 1966–7 there were nearly a quarter of a million students in intermediate and secondary education combined. In higher education in the same year there were some 35,000 students.

The Baathist regime, with the aid of rapidly increasing revenues, has added a new impulse to the expansion of education. By 1977–8 the number of students in primary education had more than doubled to reach 2,049,000 while those in intermediate and secondary education had increased 160 per cent to 664,000. The greatest increase of all has been in technical education – from 10,200 students in 1966–7 to 35,188 in 1977–8.

The number in higher education has more than doubled to reach 75,500 in 1977–8. Here also the emphasis has been on engineering and technical education. The numbers graduating from engineering colleges increased from 514 in 1968 to 2,300 in 1978 and those from technical institutes from 340 in 1969 to 5,200 in 1978.

Special attention has also been given to women's education and the number of female students at all stages has increased from 379,000 in 1968 to 915,000 in 1977. The proportion of women in the field of pure sciences in 1978 reached 39 per cent, in education 35 per cent, and in medicine 33 per cent.

The Baath Party attaches great importance to its influence on the educational system. It also plays the leading role in the field of youth organization.

Health facilities have been the subject of a continuous expansion programme over the last decade, and conditions in rural areas have been much improved as clinics have been set up in regions distant from the main urban centres. In 1976 there were 194 hospitals with 23,324 beds. By 1977 the ratio of doctors was one to 2,200 of the population compared with one to 4,200 in 1968.

Agriculture

In spite of a movement of population from rural to urban areas over some years, agriculture still occupies more people than any other sector. Apart from oil, agricultural exports comprise about three-quarters of the total, and recent difficulties in the agricultural sector have been one of the chief handicaps to economic development. Agricultural natural resources and possibilities for development differ widely throughout the country owing to variations in climate, soil, and transport conditions.

Much of Iraqi agriculture is still small-scale and primitive, with traditional tools and methods in use in most areas. Despite a slow rise in agricultural output, rising living standards and a rapidly increasing population have led to large-scale imports of foodstuffs, especially grains and meat.

The cultivable area has two main divisions: first the region to the north and east of a line running south of Mosul and Kirkuk to Khanaqin, where the rainfall is sufficient to permit the cultivation of winter crops without irrigation; and second, the alluvial plain of the centre and south, where agriculture depends on the water of the Tigris and Euphrates for irrigation (by pump, flow, or natural irrigation). In the first region rainfed winter cereals predominate, and millet, maize, sesame and other summer crops are grown as subsidiaries where irrigation is possible. In the mountain regions of Kurdistan tobacco, timber, and fruit are produced.

In the central canal zone (Falluja-Baghdad-Diyala) wheat and barley are the principal winter crops; summer crops include millet, maize, sesame, and the produce of market gardens near Baghdad. Baquba, east of Baghdad, is an important centre for oranges and other fruit. From here southwards barley and rice predominate with a great concentration of date palms in all the riverain land especially around Basra on the Shatt al-Arab.

Rice-growing has not been extended into all areas where it could be grown successfully because of the rival demands for water for other crops and uses.

Iraqi dates constitute about three-quarters of world production and it is estimated that there are altogether some 20 million date-palms of fruit-bearing age. Some 350 varieties of date are said to be grown in Iraq, of which only four (Zahdi, Sayer, Hillawi, and Khadrawi) are usually exported in quantity. Total average production in normal times averages about 400,000 tons of which between 200,000 and 250,000 tons are exported and the rest consumed in Iraq both as food – dates are a staple item of diet – in natural form or as date syrup, and as a raw material for the spirit industry.

Livestock

Raising livestock is of major importance both in the internal economy of the country, by providing food, transport, and raw materials for essential manufactures, and also in foreign trade. Livestock and their products – wool, hides, and intestines (casings) account for about one sixth of Iraq's exports excluding oil. The quality of much of the stock is poor, the selection of breeding animals is based on defective criteria, and veterinary services are inadequate and insufficiently supplied with materials to combat disease. Over-grazing has led to erosion in many of the pasture lands.

Total holdings of livestock in 1976 were reported to be 8.4 million sheep, 2.6 million goats, and 2.1 million cattle. The biggest increase in recent years has been in poultry, with egg production reaching 635 million a year compared with about 60 million in 1965, and poultry meat production also increasing tenfold. Fishing is poorly developed but the Government is making strong efforts to build up a fishing fleet, with Soviet assistance.

Forestry

The forests of Iraq are situated mainly in the mountainous regions of the extreme north and north-east of the country. Oaks predominate, but on the thin soil of the mountain slopes they rarely reach timber size. Walnut, oriental plane, mulberry, and poplar are found in the valleys – the last providing a valuable source of poles and small timber both for local use and for the treeless regions of the plains. The total area of indigenous forests, including patches of riverine scrub scattered along the banks of the twin rivers, has been estimated at 7,000 square miles, most of it state property.

Irrigation and Flood Control

The control of floods accompanied by the storage of water has been a major concern in Iraq since early in the century when Sir William Willcocks pointed out that the Tharthar depression, which lay between the Euphrates and the Tigris, and Lake Habbaniya were excellently situated for the diversion and storage of excess water. The project, after interruptions during the World Wars, was completed in 1956 and Iraq has benefited greatly from the elimination of the chronic recurrence of floods. The storage capacity of Wadi Tharthar was estimated at the time as adequate for ten to fifteen years.

Developments during recent years include the Himrim dam, and the Eski-Mosul and Bekhone dams, but the Euphrates dam project, for which Soviet aid has been promised, has not yet been launched. Total water storage capacity has increased from 13.3 billion cubic metres in 1966 to 86.8 billion cubic metres in 1976. In the current development plan irrigation schemes have been directed towards using existing storage dams to more effect through the provision of irrigation works and drainage systems. The problem of drainage and the danger of increased salinity is one of the most serious handicaps in Iraqi agriculture.

Agrarian Reform and Development

Before the Revolution governments had refused to undertake comprehensive land reform measures, mainly from a desire to maintain the political support of the landlords. Opposition groups had committed themselves to reform and their propaganda tended to minimize the practical difficulties and to exaggerate the capacity of the agricultural labourers to dispense with the services rendered by the landlords. It was not realized that the removal of the landlord would require four or five well-staffed agricultural agencies to take his place.

The Land Reform Act of 1958 fixed maximum holdings at 750 hectares of rain-fed land and 500 hectares of irrigated land. Lands in excess were to be taken over and redistributed within five years. Compensation was to be paid to displaced landlords and the new landowners were to pay for their holdings over a period of twenty years. They were all required to join co-operative societies.

The Act was essentially a political measure designed to remove the power which many landlords exercised in their localities, where a number of them were a law to themselves. In this the Act was successful; but on the economic side its consequences were disastrous. The ministry established to administer the Act was crippled by political struggles over its interpretation and the manner of its administration. Long delays followed expropriation before redistribution was carried out and in the intervening period none of the cultivators had any incentive to produce. A large area went out of cultivation and salinity increased. The elimination of the landlord meant the elimination of the managerial class and in most areas the peasants were unable to take over the functions the latter had performed. Many of them abandoned cultivation as they were unable to cope with the problem of salination, or to obtain credit, or to undertake the marketing of their produce.

The administration of the Act was subject to sharp fluctuations as unstable military governments succeeded one another during the 1960s. It is only since 1975 that the government has made a concerted attempt to restore the agricultural sector through the creation of modern farm units based on three forms – state farms, collective farms and co-operatives. The provision of fertilizers, pesticides and technical advice to farmers has been greatly increased. The number of tractors and ploughs employed in the agricultural sector has more than doubled between 1967 and 1977.

Until 1975, war in the generally productive and fertile area of Kurdistan continually disrupted agricultural output. Peace provides the opportunity for this to be restored.

The Oil Industry

Oil concessions covering most of Iraq and lasting for 75 years were secured by the Iraq Petroleum Company (IPC) in 1925 and the associated Mosul and Basrah Petroleum Companies (MPC and BPC) in 1932 and 1938 respectively. They initially provided for royalties at the rate of 4*s*. gold per ton of crude oil exported. A new agreement, of 3 February 1952, made retroactive to 1 January 1951, provided that the Government should receive 50 per cent of the companies' profits from their operations in Iraq before deduction for foreign taxes, part of the half share consisting of oil in kind (12½ per cent of the net production of each of the companies).

As a result of this agreement and the increase in crude oil production, Iraq's oil revenues rose from £13.9 million in 1951 to £32.6 million in 1952 and £73.7 million in 1955.

Oil was struck for the first time in the IPC concession in 1927, near Kirkuk, and by the end of 1934 the company exported crude oil through two 12-inch pipelines, each of 2 million tons annual capacity, to Tripoli and Haifa on the Mediterranean coast. In 1949 a 16-inch pipeline of 4 million tons capacity was opened in Tripoli. A 30/32-inch pipeline was opened to Banias in Syria in 1952.

In the MPC concessionary area exploration and drilling were carried out before 1931, and in 1939 oil of some commercial value was discovered at Ain Zalah, north-west of Mosul, though production had to wait until after the war. In 1952 the field was linked by a 12-inch pipeline to the IPC pipeline system, to permit the export of its crude oil to the Mediterranean coast.

In the BPC concession area two fields were developed after the war at Zubair and Rumaila, west of Basra. A new terminal was opened in 1951 at Fao on the Gulf coast.

Iraqi oil was developed with moderate speed, exports rising from around 18 million tons in 1952 to over 47 million in 1960, with payments to the government exceeding £95 million. For some time, however, the Iraqi Government had been pressing for a variety of modifications in the agreement, and one of the first acts of Abdul Karim Kassem was to open new negotiations with the IPC. These negotiations were prolonged, and terminated in October 1961 without agreement on either side being reached. On 11 December 1961 the state, by Law No. 80, restricted the companies' area of operations to about 0.5 per cent of the previous area, declaring the rest of their concessions withdrawn. The company did not accept Law No. 80 and demanded international arbitration. Intermittent negotiation continued but the two sides remained deadlocked for several years and the rate of Iraq's oil exports fell. In February 1964 Iraq established its own national oil company (INOC) with the intention of taking an active part in the exploitation of the country's resources. In August 1967 the Government passed a law which assigned to the INOC most of the territory of Iraq for exploration and development. This was virtually a 'no concessions' law, but it did provide for joint ventures between the INOC and foreign companies. The owners of the IPC, however, had threatened legal action against any company undertaking to operate in territory to which they still considered they had legal rights. This deterrent was ignored by ERAP, a French state-owned company, with whom the Iraqi Government made a contract to explore and develop part of the expropriated areas, but excluding North Rumaila. The financial terms of this agreement were less favourable than those that had been offered by the IPC, but the Government preferred the more novel agreement (which was similar to an earlier ERAP/Iran agreement) with a newcomer to oil in Iraq.

The INOC turned its own attention to the development of the rich plum – North Rumaila. For help it turned to the USSR, negotiating the first of a series of loans at 2½ per cent interest, repayable in crude oil valued at international prices. The Russians were to develop North Rumaila, as well as some minor fields, build a pipeline, and reactivate the Fao port for export. The flow of oil from North Rumaila began in April 1972. The Russians supply equipment and technical assistance, selling the equipment outright to Iraq.

In 1972 Iraq decided on the full nationalization of IPC and MPC, and after prolonged negotiations final agreement was reached with IPC on compensation. In retaliation for the US and Dutch stands during the October 1973 war, US and Dutch interests in BPC were taken over. BPC was fully taken over in December 1975 when the residual British and French holdings were acquired against compensation. The assets and rights of the companies were vested in the Iraq Company for Oil Operations which in turn was replaced in 1976 by the INOC, attached to the Ministry of Petroleum.

As a measure to enable Kirkuk oil to be exported via Gulf terminals, a strategic pipeline was built to link Kirkuk with the south and opened in 1976. A pipeline between Kirkuk and a Turkish Mediterranean port was opened in 1977. Production exceeded 2.2 million b.p.d. in 1977, with a target of 3 million b.p.d. by 1979 and 3.5 million b.p.d. by 1980. With proved oil reserves estimated at 34 billion barrels, Iraq ranks fourth among Middle East producers behind Saudi Arabia, Kuwait and Iran although Iraq's position may be understated in view of important new discoveries in the Basra region and elsewhere.

As a result of the settlement of the nationalization issue and the steep rise in oil prices, Iraq's oil revenues rose from $584 million in 1972 to $1,650 million in 1973, $7,500 million in 1974, and $8.6 million in 1977.

Refining for general distribution is carried out by the General Organization for Oil Refining and Gas Processing. Iraq's refining capacity is rapidly being increased. The Daurah and Basra refineries have been expanded. A new refinery at Sammawa was opened in February 1978. A new $400 million refinery is to be built at Beiji by the Italian Sham Projetti, and plans are at an advanced stage for the construction of two 15 million tons a year export refineries.

Snam Projetti will also participate in the Iraqi southern gas-gathering scheme, a major project costing up to $1 billion to be spread over a number of years, involving the establishment of pipelines, compressor systems and storage capacity. A similar gas-gathering system is projected for the north. Hitherto the unusually high proportion of 85 per cent of Iraq's natural gas has been flared.

Iraq has been slow to develop petrochemicals and the first contract for a 120,000 tons a year ethylene plant at Basra was only placed in mid-1973. At Kirkuk a 120,000 tons sulphur recovery plant has been built to process gas from nearby oil fields. A nitrogenous fertilizer plant is to be built near Basra. Heavy emphasis is now being given to the development of petrochemicals industries to provide the raw materials of a plastics industry.

Other Minerals

These are still unimportant. Salt, low-grade coal, and gypsum exist, and iron and copper ore have been located by geological surveys. The major sulphur deposits have been developed by state ventures with Polish technical assistance. The development of rich phosphate deposits as the basis for a chemical industry began in 1976.

Manufacturing Industry

Most manufacturing establishments remain small despite government efforts to create major industries in recent years. Apart from oil-associated industries, a steel works, two sponge iron plants and an aluminium smelter are either planned or under construction. The iron ore and alumina will be imported. Of the rest, the larger produce construction materials or process agricultural products for import-substitution. Plans to quadruple cement output should produce a substantial surplus for export in 1980. A number of brickworks and plants for the manufacture of asbestos and pre-cast items, tiles, steel windows and furniture have been established. There are also cotton, wool, and silk spinning and weaving, jute and tanning, plants and others for the manufacture of vegetable oils, beer, soft drinks, cigarettes, and sugar. Altogether these accounted for about 5 per cent of GDP and this share is expected to double by 1980.

Transport and Communications

Railways. The railways built by the British forces in the First World War formed the basis of the Iraq State Railways, which became the property of the Iraqi Government in 1936. There were two gauges. Today the system consists of the Baghdad-Mosul-Yurubiyah standard line, which links up with the Turkish system, and the Baghdad-Maqal-Umm Qasr standard line, which was built in the 1960s with Soviet assistance. About half the 250-mile line to the Syrian border has been completed while a 75-mile line is being built to link Hsaiba with Akkasha for the transport of phosphates. The ultimate aim of the Railways Administration is the elimination of all the old metric gauge system.

Ports. One of the most serious limits to the process of development has been the congestion in Iraq's two ports of Basra and Umm Qasr. However, by 1977 this had largely been eliminated. Port improvement is concentrated on Umm Qasr which is due to replace Basra as Iraq's main port by 1980.

Economic Policy and Development

In the earlier years of statehood it was necessary above all to lay the foundations of economic advance by creating a network of transport and communications, a pure water supply, and various public services including an educational system and the beginnings of a health service, as well as, later, a number of welfare services. The Government took the initiative over a wide field but its financial resources were very limited until the great increase in oil revenues began in 1952.

A Development Board was established in 1950 in the hope of ensuring that oil revenues would not be dissipated by unstable governments but would be used for economic advance. However, the initial autonomy was removed three years later when it was brought under a new Ministry of Development, although a considerable proportion of its members remained non-political and, until the 1958 Revolution, some were foreigners.

Before 1958 the Development Board drew up three investment programmes. 70 per cent of the oil revenues were placed under the Board's control. Expenditures generally fell short of estimates owing to the difficulties in giving practical effect to development plans, but from 1956 the machinery was working more effectively. The Board achieved its best results in the early stages in irrigation and flood controls which involved the building of dams and other construction activities and the improvement of communications.

A number of reports and recommendations were made by outside bodies and individuals – notably Lord Salter in 1955, His report pointed out the need to bring demonstrable direct benefits to a wide public rather than to concentrate on schemes the benefit of which would be obvious only in the long term. Housing, pure water, and direct help to farmers were given as examples. Most of his recommendations were adopted but in 1958 the Revolution interrupted the machinery and organization of development programmes. The Development Board was replaced by a Planning Board composed mainly of ministers. The allocation of oil revenues was reduced from 70 per cent to 50 per cent. A new Ministry of Industry was created in 1959, but the Ministry of Finance was placed in a position of control over the departments concerned with carrying out the plans. The plans and projects of the Development Board's final plan were largely continued in the 1960s but for most of the decade the emphasis was shifted from agriculture to industry. It was not until the new plan starting in 1971 was drawn up that renewed emphasis was placed on the need for recovery and progress in the agricultural sector.

The 1971–5 five-year plan originally envisaged total expenditure of 973 million Iraqi dinars, of which the major share was allocated to agricultural development. Large increases in oil revenues permitted increased allocations in the past two years of the plan. But it was in the new five-year plan for 1976–80 that the great leap forward took place. Total investment is expected to be about $34 billion. Allocations for the 1978 annual plan alone amounted to ID 2,800 million or 48 per cent more than total investments allocated to all development plans before the 1968 Baathist revolution. In this plan the heaviest emphasis is placed on the oil industry, petrochemicals, and manufacturing industry, and a declining role for agriculture is forecast. (In April 1979 $1 = ID 0.310).

As its name implies, the ABSP is a socialist party but there is little socialist theory in its ideology. Baath socialism is achieved through the continuous expansion of the public sector (always referred to as the 'socialist sector'), socially egalitarian policies, and economic independence to reinforce the country's political independence. The regime's own estimate is that the share of the 'socialist' sector in total domestic production rose from 31 per cent in 1968 to 75 per cent in 1976, while the proportion of total investments in this sector rose from 53 per cent to 76 per cent. In agriculture the socialist share rose from one per cent to 29 per cent during the 1967–76 period, in the oil sector from zero to 100 per cent, in manufacturing industry from 41 per cent to 51 per cent, and in commerce from 11 per cent to 53 per cent.

However the private sector plays a more important role than these figures imply as it has been able to gain some advantages from the rapid increase in per capita incomes in the 1970s, estimated at an average of 9.6 per cent a year at fixed prices between 1969 and 1976. The Government encourages private sector investment in import-substitution industries by offering soft loans or capital participation through an industrial investment bank. Even when the Government acquires a majority share, the firms are still run by the private shareholders but are classed as part of the public sector.

The most serious limitation to economic growth is the shortage of manpower – especially skilled workers, technicians, and engineers. In October 1974 a law was passed offering a variety of financial and tax privileges to attract home the many thousands of trained expatriate Iraqis. In keeping with Iraq's Pan-Arab ideology the same privileges are offered to non-Iraqi Arabs.

VI

ISRAEL

THE LAND AND THE PEOPLE

Israel today comprises an area of approximately 7,900 sq. miles or roughly 77 per cent of the territory of British mandated Palestine. The boundaries up to the June 1967 war were fixed in 1949 in accordance with the armistice agreements signed with Lebanon, Syria, Egypt, and Jordan and, as such, are provisional.

In the north and west these boundaries were similar to those of mandated Palestine; to the north with Lebanon, to the north-east with Syria and to the west with the natural frontier of the Mediterranean. In the south, apart from the Gaza coastal strip, the frontier followed the old international boundary from the north-west corner of Egypt's Sinai Peninsula south-eastwards to Eilat on the Gulf of Aqaba. In the east the frontier is with Jordan which was created by Transjordan's annexation in 1949 of the West Bank – the 23 per cent of Palestine which remained in Arab hands. Until 1967 Jerusalem was divided into two cities: the old city within the walls and the suburbs in the east and north-east which were in Jordan, while the greater part of the new city was controlled by Israel. The Jordan river and the Dead Sea were under the part control of both Israel and Jordan. Only the northern section of the Jordan and the south-western part of the Dead Sea were within Israel's 1949 frontiers.

As a result of the 1967 war Israel's military frontiers were extended to include the West Bank of the Jordan, the Gaza Strip and the Sinai Peninsula, and the Golan Heights of Syria. All these territories were under Israeli military occupation in 1978 but only the old city of Jerusalem had been formally annexed by Israel.

The country is divided into strikingly varied geographical regions. The altitude varies from 3,963 ft. above sea-level – the height of Mt. Azmon near Safad – to 1,286 ft. below sea-level where the south-east boundary lies on the shore of the Dead Sea. Going inland from the Mediterranean the first region is the coastal plain, which varies in width from about four miles at Acre to about twenty miles at Ascalon. The northern section of this plain is known as the Plain of Sharon; and an extension of it running inland south-east from Acre is the Vale of Esdraelon (the ancient Armageddon or valley of Jezreel), a former swamp-land which, with the Huleh valley, is now one of the most fertile parts of the country and one of the main agricultural centres of Israel. Farther inland are the hill regions of Galilee in the north dipping down to the sub-tropical valley of Beisan south of Lake Tiberias and the hills of Samaria and Judea. To the south lies the arid Negev, which forms 60 per cent of the total land area, stretching from the southern edge of the Judean plateau to the Gulf of Aqaba at Eilat. Although in Byzantine times it supported a considerable population, the Negev was until the foundation of the State of Israel largely desert, small parts being intermittently cultivated. Within the last twenty years, however, the northern part has been extensively settled and put under the plough. The central part remains desert but contains mineral deposits which are being worked. In the far south of the Negev lies Eilat, Israel's outlet to the Red Sea, which is also of considerable strategic importance.

The climate is as varied as the topography. The coastal plain has a Mediterranean climate; the winters are warm and wet and the summers hot and dry. The amount of rainfall increases towards the north, being greatest in the Carmel range above Haifa. Inland both summer and winter are cooler, snow being not uncommon in Jerusalem during the winter. In the Negev, desert or semi-desert conditions prevail. Rainfall is scarce and irregular and the summers are hotter than on the coast.

The chief river is the Jordan. The Yarkon (Auja) which flowed into the Mediterranean north of Tel Aviv, has been largely diverted to the Negev. The mouth of the Kishon which flows into the bay north of Haifa has been widened to enable ships arriving at Haifa to unload near warehouses which are built on the river banks.

Population

The population has quadrupled in the thirty years since the state was founded. At the end of 1948 the estimated total population was 880,000 of whom 760,000 were Jewish and 120,000 non-Jewish. By January 1977 the estimated total had risen to 3,570,900 of whom 3,017,500 were Jews and 553,400 were non-Jews. Of approximately 1,200,000 who lived in Palestine in 1947, only about 100,000 remained when the census was held in the winter of 1948 for the election of the Constituent Assembly. Although there has been no general return of those who were driven out or fled during the Palestine War, a steady infiltration took place, both officially and unofficially, until by July 1956 the number of non-Jews reached over 202,000. As they also have one of the highest natural rates of increase in the world (3 per cent) their number reached 553,400 in 1977. Despite large-scale immigration the Arab proportion of the population has remained steady at about 15 per cent.

Immigration

During the years of British administration, 1919–48, about 452,000 entered, bringing the total, with natural increase, to some 650,000.

When the State of Israel was established, it immediately opened its gates wide, and up to the end of 1951 684,000 Jews came in. These came mainly from Eastern and Central Europe and from Eastern Arab countries such as Iraq and Yemen. There was a second major influx in 1955–7, mainly from North Africa.

Since then the tide has ebbed and flowed. Until 1960 it averaged 32,000 a year. During the next four years there was a large increase, almost 230,000 coming in, followed by a drop to about 81,000 in the period 1965–8. Following the 1967 war immigration increased again and reached almost 33,000 in 1969, about 45,000 in 1970, and 54,900 in 1973.

Much of this increase was among Soviet Jews of whom 33,500 immigrated in 1973. But after the October 1973 war there was a steep decline to about 20,000 (including 8,200 Soviet Jews) in 1975. Although precise figures were not available, emigration and immigration were probably about equally balanced in the late 1970s. From the founding of the State until the end of 1976, Israel received 1,589,629 immigrants.

This vast influx has raised serious problems, both economic and social. But the Government and people of Israel, at whatever cost, have stood by the 'Law of the Return', under which any Jew has the right to emigrate to Israel and settle there, unless he has been proved guilty of a criminal offence. The 'Ingathering of the Exiles' is a primary factor in Government policy and is embodied in the Declaration of Independence.

Since 1954, when the stream of immigrants declined, the Government abandoned the policy of transit camps and transported the immigrants straight to new settlements in development areas, sending with them experts on agriculture, education, and hygiene.

The Government recognizes the difficulty of absorbing a large and varied mass of people, in particular Oriental Jews unversed in Western ways and often economically backward. The Messianic hope and the sense of brotherhood are, however, great factors in integrating the new population. At present the pattern of Israel is set by those who arrived before the creation of the State, and the proportion of Oriental Jews in high office is small; but the Government and the early-comers spare no effort to weld the diverse elements into a single nation. In 1977 Israeli Jews constituted an estimated 20.9 per cent of the world's Jewish population.

The Arabs in Israel

The Declaration of Independence offers complete equality to all Arabs, and Government policy, as outlined in October 1951, stated that 'the Arab minority . . . will be guaranteed full and complete equality of rights and obligations in the civic, political, economic, social, cultural, and every other sphere'. In practice, however, Israeli policy towards the Arabs is ambivalent. There is a sincere desire to make the Arab population a contented and prosperous section of the community; at the same time there are fears of the threat to security which it represents as long as a peace settlement with the neighbouring Arab countries remains unattainable.

At the beginning of 1976 the Arab population was 548,000.

Of these 336,000 lived in Haifa and the northern region. There was also a large concentration of about 100,000 in Jerusalem (92,000 residents of East Jerusalem). These are permanent residents of Israel, rather than citizens of Israel, although they are able to opt for Israeli citizenship. Another important group of non-Jews are the 23 bedouin tribes of the Negev numbering about 40,000.

About 411,400 or 77 per cent of the non-Jews in Israel are Sunni Moslems, 42,000 are Druze, living in 18 villages throughout Galilee and on Mount Carmel, and 80,200 are Christians of 30 different denominations. The Christian proportion of 15 per cent of the Arab population is falling because of their low rate of increase (1.9 per cent annually compared with 4.1 per cent for the Moslems).

In 1948, the non-Jewish sector was mainly agrarian, using traditional methods. Over the years the area cultivated by Arab farmers has nearly tripled, while the irrigated area has increased over ninefold. The Government has regularly granted loans to Arab farmers to assist them in cultivating their land more intensively. On the other hand, the number of people employed in agriculture has decreased and today amounts to 16 per cent of the total work-force compared with about 60 per cent in 1948. About 110,000 Israeli Arabs are employed in all sectors of the civilian work force. The average income of an Arab urban wage-earning family in 1975 was £I 29,300 – similar to the average income of a Jewish wage-earning family. In 1978 there were about 15,000 wage-earning Arab women, of whom over 4,000 were married. The participation of Arabs in the state administration is not yet proportional to their numbers but is increasing steadily.

In 1978 there were 50 local councils in the Israeli Arab sector, with another 29 villages represented in regional councils. Moslems and Druzes have their own religious courts. The military administration which affected the vast majority of the Arab population living along the border was abolished on 1 December 1966. The provision of the law of 1950, concerning the property of absentee owners, deprived of their property many Arabs who are now resident in Israel but who were not in the country when the law was passed. Israeli

Arabs are served by 79 village clinics and 64 mother-and-child units. Infant mortality has dropped from 20.8 per cent in 1948 to 3.32 per cent in 1976 (compared with 1.62 per cent among Israeli Jews). The most revolutionary change has been in education. In 1948 only 32.5 per cent of the 5–15 age group attended school; in 1975 this had reached 95 per cent. In the same period the number of pupils rose from 11,129 to 153,280. In 1975/76 there were 261 kindergartens, 302 elementary schools, and 96 secondary schools, including agricultural and vocational schools, and two teacher training colleges. The number of teachers in the Arabic educational system has reached 7,000. Arabic is the language of instruction but Hebrew is taught in the higher classes. In 1976 there were 2,000 Israeli Arabs with degrees from Israeli universities; an equal number were studying in Israeli higher academic institutions as well as over 1,000 students in other institutes of higher education.

Integration of Immigrants

A primary aim of the State is to transform the heterogeneous mass of immigrants into a conscious national society, to substitute modern Hebrew for the babel of tongues which they bring from their native lands, and to raise the economic and educational level. Three instruments have specially served that policy. The first is the school: free compulsory elementary education was introduced in 1950 for all inhabitants, male and female.

The second instrument of integration – applicable only to the Jewish population, since the Arabs of Israel are liable but not called for military service – is the national service of three years for men between the ages of 18 and 55, and two years for women between the ages of 18 and 34. Only a part of the time is devoted to military training, the rest of the service being educational. The third instrument is the residential college for intellectuals, known as the Ulpan. There men and women who were engaged in the professions have intensive training in Hebrew for a period of half a year to a year to enable them to carry on their profession in Israel. About 30,000 attend these colleges at any one time. Adult education is intensively pursued. Specially trained lecturers, Hebrew teachers, and advisers on agriculture and sanitation travel to the remote settlements. It is a less welcome result that the younger generation tend to regard themselves as the true Israelis, superior to the immigrants of the older generation.

HISTORY AND POLITICS

While the conception of an independent Jewish state and the struggle to realize it, which culminated in the creation of Israel in 1948, emerged only with the foundation of the Zionist movement in the late nineteenth century, the events of the last fifty years can be fully understood only against the background of Jewish history from the time of the dispersion.

The subjection of the ancient kingdom of the Jews to the Roman Empire in 63 BC was followed by a period marked by a series of bloody nationalist uprisings. Attempts to regain Jewish independence continued until AD 135 when the revolt of Bar Kochba in Palestine was suppressed with great violence and the Roman religion was established in the Temple area in Jerusalem. Inside and outside Palestine Jewish political influence was in eclipse.

From that time until the beginning of the Zionist movement the Jews were scattered throughout the world, experiencing in varying degrees persecution and prosperity, discrimination and tolerance, but from the eighteenth century they shared in the general emancipation of Western Europe and in its economic expansion. During the nineteenth century liberalism and assimilation appeared to be steadily gaining ground in Western Europe, but persecutions continued in Eastern Europe, particularly in Russia and Russian Poland where the concentration of Jewish population was greatest. Just as anti-Jewish movements, influenced by the nationalist temper of the nineteenth century, began to emphasize race rather than religion, so the Jews themselves began, under the influence of their environment and pressure of persecution, to think in terms of a new Jewish nationalism. It was Theodor Herzl, an Austrian Jewish man of letters, who in 1897 founded Zionism as a political movement. Meanwhile there had been during the latter half of the nineteenth century a steady movement of Jews from Eastern Europe to settle in Palestine, many of them working on the land. As a result of this colonization movement, which was largely non-political and philanthropic, there were 80,000 Jews in Palestine by 1914. In 1903, when settlement by Jews in Palestine was difficult, the British Government offered the Zionist Congress a territory in East Africa for Jewish settlement, but the offer was rejected because the majority of the Zionists would not consider any other home than Zion. The aims of Zionism were given great encouragement when, on 2 November 1917, the British Government declared its 'sympathy with Jewish Zionist aspirations' in the Balfour Declaration.[1]

The Mandate

For nearly two years after the armistice with Turkey, Palestine was under British military authority, which was superseded by a civil administration in July 1920, after the Supreme Allied Council (sitting at San Remo) had allocated the mandate for Palestine to Britain on 24 April 1920. The mandate came into force on 29 September 1923. Under Article 2 Britain was made responsible for: 'the establishment of the Jewish National Home . . . and the development of self-governing institutions, and also for safeguarding the civil and religious rights of all the inhabitants of Palestine, irrespective of race and religion.'

While the Balfour Declaration and the terms of the mandate pledged help in founding a Jewish National Home, Britain as the mandatory Power found herself in an equivocal position, for in both cases the promise was not unqualified. Fulfilment was almost from the start rendered difficult by the promise of independence made to the Arabs during the war and by the provision in the mandate that the administration of Palestine should facilitate Jewish emancipation 'while ensuring that the rights and position of other sections of the population are not prejudiced'.

Britain's task became increasingly complicated in the decade before the Second World War. Arab hostility to a Jewish National Home in Palestine was aggravated, on the one hand

[1] See above, pp. 16–23.

by the rising nationalist aspirations and achievements of other Arab States, and on the other by the increasing pressure to find a refuge in Palestine for the Jews of Central Europe who were the victims of Nazi persecution from 1933.

Although during the Second World War Jews everywhere rallied to the Allied cause, anti-British feeling remained among the Jews in Palestine. In May 1939 the British Government had issued in a White Paper a fresh statement of policy, restricting Jewish immigration in the next five years to 75,000, after which period it would be subject to Arab approval, and limiting narrowly the right of Jews to purchase land from Arabs. The strict implementation of the White Paper policy, especially of the immigration provisions, seemed inhuman to the Jews in Palestine, who were deeply concerned about the Jews in Hitler's power. Still more, the rejection during the war of several boatloads of refugees who had contrived to escape from Europe and reach the borders of Palestine, their transfer to Mauritius, and the total loss in the Black Sea of a ship with nearly 1,000 refugees after it had been refused permission to land its passengers in Palestine, inflamed and embittered Jewish opinion.

By the end of the war anti-British feeling among the Jews of Palestine and elsewhere, strengthened by ill-informed and sometimes irresponsible support in the United States, had finally convinced Britain that compromise between Jews and Arabs was impossible. Outbreaks of terrorism in Palestine became frequent, and there was increasing Zionist pressure on the United States Government to use its influence with Britain to secure free entry of Jews into Palestine. After a series of unsuccessful attempts to find a solution to the Palestine problem acceptable to both Jews and Arabs, and after an Anglo-American commission had recommended measures which the British Government was unwilling to consider unless the United States was prepared to share the financial and military consequences, the British Government decided in February 1947 to refer the question to the United Nations. On 29 November 1947 a modified scheme of partition was adopted by the General Assembly; Britain abstained from voting, making it clear that she would accept no solution which would have to be imposed by force. At the same time she maintained her intention to withdraw from Palestine and end the mandate by 15 May 1948. The General Assembly had neglected to provide any means of enforcing its recommendations, while the mandatory Power would do nothing that could be construed as implementing the United Nations resolution. The decisions of the United Nations brought to a head the barely concealed civil war in Palestine, and as the mandate drew to a chaotic close, guerrilla fighting between Jews and Arabs increased in bitterness until it reached a state of open warfare.

The State of Israel and the Palestine War

The mandate ended at midnight 14 May 1948, and the State of Israel was officially proclaimed that evening. The next day regular forces of Egypt, Jordan, and Iraq began moving into Palestine. By that time there was a well-defined area of Jewish control, which included the most important parts of the area assigned to the Jewish state by the partition resolution. The Arab armies succeeded in occupying those Arab areas which were not yet under Jewish control, but in spite of their initial superiority in heavier armaments and the almost indefensible location of many Jewish settlements, their only other military success was the occupation of the Old City and part of northern Jerusalem and the reduction of the fanatically defended Jewish quarter of the Old City. The Arab armies, although vastly superior in numbers, were fighting in a strange environment, without a united High Command and with long lines of communication from Egypt and Iraq, whereas the Jews were fighting not only for their Promised Land but for their very existence. The success of their efforts roused Messianic hopes and enabled them to endure years of hardship in the period of armistices.

The Palestine War left Israel in possession of a share of the former mandated territory larger by more than a quarter than that recommended by the United Nations; it also left four cardinal problems: how to attain a peace settlement, an impracticable zigzag frontier, the Arab refugees, and the controversy as to the status of the Holy City.

The efforts of the Conciliation Commission, set up by the Security Council in December 1948, to negotiate a permanent peace treaty, proved unsuccessful. The Arab States refused to consider a peace treaty unless the Israel Government agreed to accept all Arab refugees who wished to return to Israel, in accordance with the resolution of the General Assembly of December 1948, while the Israel Government maintained that the future of the refugees could be discussed only as part of a general peace settlement. Israel, however, offered at one time to accept on certain conditions up to 100,000 Arab refugees (including 25,000 already in Israel) and affirmed to the United Nations her willingness to help resettlement by paying compensation for the immovable Arab property which she had taken over. In July 1957 Ben-Gurion said that the Arab refugees could not return as their lands had been settled by Jewish survivors of Nazi persecution.

The United Nations plan for the internationalization of Jerusalem has not been carried into effect. In 1950 Jerusalem was declared the capital of Israel and the seat of Parliament, and most Government departments were transferred there. In 1967 the Jordan sector of Jerusalem was officially incorporated into Israel, and negotiations with various envoys as well as with the representatives of other churches, were started in order to achieve a solution, guaranteed by international law, for the safeguard of the Holy Places.

The Arab-Israeli Conflict

From 1953 Arab-Israeli tension grew more and more acute. Incidents resulting in loss of life multiplied on the Jordan frontier. The most serious occurred in October 1953, when Israeli forces, in a reprisal raid on the village of Qibya, killed some fifty persons. Strenuous efforts on both sides to prevent incidents, and to settle on the spot such incidents as did occur before they could be exaggerated by press and politicians, maintained something like tranquillity for a considerable time. In 1955 frontier trouble broke out in the south, the Gaza strip, and a demilitarized area along the Sinai Peninsula, and in the north in the demilitarized area of the Huleh region and along the shores of Lake Galilee. In that area the Syrians resisted Israeli attempts to carry out works for diverting the waters of the Jordan for a comprehensive irrigation project. At the same time they and the other Arab States rejected the project of American engineers (the Johnston plan) for the use of the waters of the Jordan and the Yarmuk for the benefit of Jordan as well as Israel.

The news of the large-scale purchase of modern Czechoslovak heavy armament and aircraft by Egypt and perhaps by other Arab States caused the greatest apprehension in Israel. Britain and the United States were unwilling to sell equivalent modern arms to Israel, but France supplied her with jet aircraft and other weapons.

An aggravation of the trouble was that Egypt maintained a strict blockade, both in the Suez Canal and in the Gulf of Aqaba, not only against Israeli vessels but against those of any state which were carrying cargo to or from any Israeli port. She claimed this as a belligerent right, on the ground that she was still at war with Israel, though the Security Council in 1951 had resolved that her action was contrary to the terms of the armistice agreement.

The Sinai Campaign and its Consequences

The elections for the Jordan Parliament in October 1956 resulted in a victory for the pan-Arab parties. A unified command was established for Egypt, Syria, and Jordan, and the Arab States united in abuse of Israel and in announcements of an impending attack on her. Suddenly, on 29 October, Israeli forces began the invasion of Sinai. Within five days they were masters of Gaza, Rafa, and El Arish, and had also occupied the greater part of the Sinai Peninsula east of the Suez Canal, taken prisoner the Egyptian garrison of Sharm al-Shaikh, at the south-eastern tip, and occupied the island of Tiran which commands the eastern entrance to the Gulf of Aqaba. The declared objectives of the Sinai campaign were to wipe out the Egyptian outposts and *fedayeen*[2] bases in the Sinai Desert; to open sea communications with Eilat through the Gulf of Aqaba; to eliminate the Egyptian salient known as the Gaza strip; and, lastly, to put pressure on Egypt to negotiate a peace treaty.

On 7 November David Ben-Gurion declared that Israel would hold on to her conquests until Egypt made a settlement. The next day, however, after strong representations

[2] 'Devotees' (of Islam).

from Eisenhower and a severe warning from Bulganin, he announced that Israel would withdraw from Egyptian territory when satisfactory arrangements had been made in connection with the international force which the General Assembly had decided to send to Egypt. Israel took immediate steps to establish her hold in the Gulf of Aqaba and sent two frigates to Eilat. The evacuation of most of the Sinai Desert was carried out in December and January, but on 23 January the Knesset decided to maintain Israeli administration of the Gaza strip and forces at Sharm al-Shaikh. On 2 February the United Nations called on Israel to withdraw behind the armistice demarcation lines. After intensive negotiations and a further appeal by the President of the United States, backed by Britain and France, on 1 March the Israel Foreign Minister explained to the General Assembly that Israel was prepared to withdraw on the assumption that UNEF would take over exclusive responsibility for the Gaza strip and that Israel would be entitled to exercise the right of self-defence in the case of interference with her ships in the Gulf of Aqaba. The United States delegate did not support the Gaza strip assumption, but certain American assurances about freedom of navigation in the Gulf of Aqaba were given. The withdrawal was completed by 8 March and UNEF moved into both areas, but the Egyptian administration also returned to Gaza.

The three main consequences of the campaign had been, for Israel, the opening of a direct sea connection with East Africa and South-east Asia through the straits of Aqaba; the new close collaboration with France and the end of Arab infiltrations from Sinai and Gaza. The new security and freedom of movement for the State spurred Israeli diplomacy to work for the creation of a network of relations with both Europe and the Afro-Asian world.

The following years saw a strong reorientation of Israeli foreign policy from the USA towards Europe. Such a trend was mainly inspired by the new close military, scientific, and cultural relations with France, which neither the arrival to power of General de Gaulle in 1958 nor the end of the Algerian war altered significantly. But although no fundamental change was visible in the French attitude, in June 1964, when Premier Levi Eshkol visited Paris, a reappraisal of mutual positions was progressively taking place, with French diplomacy increasingly returning to a more pro-Arab line and Israel once more seeking military equipment outside France, mainly in the USA. Quite independently of France Israel continued to work for its association with the European Common Market and for closer relations with European countries. Ben-Gurion visited the Scandinavian countries in August 1962. But it was with Germany that the most radical change of relations took place. After a long period of tension, diplomatic relations between Jerusalem and Bonn were established in May 1965 on the basis of a 1961 secret agreement. These were followed by an economic agreement in May 1966 on the conclusion of German Reparations. Pope Paul VI's visit to the Holy Places in 1964, the subsequent ratification by the Vatican's second Ecumenical Council of the 'Document on the Jews' helped to strengthen the position of the Jewish State in the Catholic world. At the same time the new Israeli Foreign Minister Abba Eban tried consistently, from 1966 onwards, to reach a better understanding with the Communist world. His efforts brought tangible results only with Rumania which considerably improved its political and economic relations with Israel.

Greater results were achieved by Israel in Africa and Asia as well as in Latin America. All the new African states, with the exception of Somaliland and Mauretania, recognized Israel. An important system of economic, political, and technical aid relationships developed between Israel and the Third World. In spite of substantial African and Latin American support, Israel was unable to muster the necessary majority for a United Nations resolution calling for direct talks with the Arabs.

The hostility of the Arabs gained strength once more after 1964, following Syria's demand that Israel be deprived of the use of the waters of Lake Tiberias for irrigation purposes. Tension began to rise along the Syrian-Israeli Armistice Line and was heightened by the renewed infiltration of Arab commandos who received uneven backing from the Arab states. Serious fighting took place in July 1966 along the Syrian-Israeli border during which Israel destroyed most of the Syrians' diversion operations on the sources of the River Jordan. By the end of 1966 the Palestinian commandos also became active along the Jordan border and the Israeli raid on the village of Samua in October 1966 created considerable internal unrest in Jordan. Following a serious clash with the Syrians in April 1967 and Russian warnings to Egypt of an impending Israeli attack on Syria, Egypt mobilized its army in the Sinai Desert in May 1967, expelled the UN Force from the Gaza area and Sharm al-Shaikh, and closed the Tiran Straits. Conflict once more became inevitable and the Six Day War brought the Israelis along the Suez Canal, the River Jordan, and the Golan Heights.

During this period, Israel's political life underwent considerable strain. Most of this was the direct result of the social and economic adjustment of a State rapidly moving from the agricultural era to an industrial, or even post-industrial, era. But the new conditions of peace and economic prosperity made the country and the Government more attentive to the internal problems of the State and even to the fundamental question of the role of a Jewish State in modern times. The 1959 general election was fought against a background of growing social unrest owing to the demands of immigrants from oriental countries and some of the Arab minority for greater social and economic equality and better educational opportunities. Religious controversy increased sharply. The question of defining 'Who is a Jew?' caused a Government crisis in 1961 and precipitated a general election. It was followed by considerable tension between religious and secular Jews over such matters as work and travel on the Sabbath, the use of non-kosher food on national shipping lines, and medical autopsy. In July 1960 Israel celebrated the arrival of its one millionth immigrant. Between 1961 and 1965 about 250,000 new immigrants entered the country – many of them from Eastern Europe. The problem of the integration of these generally highly skilled and educated immigrants deeply influenced the debates of the 25th and 26th Zionist Congresses which took place in Jerusalem in 1960 and 1964. The definition of 'Zionist', the ways of attracting Jewish immigrants from developed countries, and the relations between Israel and the Diaspora became the central themes of discussions on the work and future of the Zionist organizations. In this context it is worth noting the tremendous psychological impact, both on the Diaspora and on Israel, of the trial of Adolph Eichmann, captured in May 1960 in the Argentine and executed in May 1962.

Of no less importance was the 'Lavon Affair' -- a clash between Ben-Gurion and Pinhas Lavon which originated in a security 'mishap' in 1954. At the time Israeli agents were arrested, tried, and some of them executed for allegedly attempting to blow up American installations so as to prevent a *rapprochement* between Washington and Cairo. Lavon, who was then Minister of Defence, was forced to hand in his resignation but in 1958 he made a partial political recovery when he became Secretary General of the Histadrut.

New evidence came to light in 1960 and induced Lavon to ask for a full rehabilitation which he obtained through a Cabinet Committee against the will of Ben-Gurion who pressed for a judicial enquiry. Ben-Gurion failed to have the affair discussed in court but he succeeded in obtaining Lavon's dismissal from his post in the Histadrut. In doing so Ben-Gurion provoked considerable public and party animosity against himself which resulted in reduced votes for his party in the 1962 elections and his consequent decision to withdraw from the Government in June 1963, and to create a new party, Rafi.

1967 and After

After the June 1967 war Israel soon abandoned any hope of an early peace settlement with the Arab states. The Government did not oppose the passing of the British-sponsored compromise Resolution 242 on 22 November 1967 which the Foreign Minister, Mr. Eban, interpreted as meaning that Israel should not move from the 1967 cease-fire lines except as a result of properly negotiated peace treaties with its neighbours. However, it soon became apparent that this interpretation was not shared by many countries including the Soviet Union, France, and many Afro-Asian countries which believed that Israel should first withdraw from all the occupied territories.

Israel continued to insist on direct negotiations with the Arabs although, as time went on, it placed more emphasis on the need for secure and recognized frontiers. Meanwhile the Defence Minister, Moshe Dayan, who exercised virtually complete control over the occupied territories, adopted a policy of consolidating Israel's economic and political hold over them while awaiting a time when the Arabs would be ready to make peace on something closer to Israel's terms. His method was to deal firmly with opposition and unrest while making the occupation as inconspicuous as possible. The 'open bridges' policy which allowed Arabs of the occupied territories to travel in Jordan and other Arab states, was maintained. Palestinian guerrilla activity did not cause Israel any serious security concern; casualties were heavier on the Suez Canal front. Some prominent Israelis (but not members of the Government) were in favour of negotiating with leading Palestinians for the establishment of an autonomous Palestinian state on the West Bank.

Tension increased after the attack on an Israeli El Al plane at Athens Airport by members of the Popular Front for the Liberation of Palestine (PFLP) in December 1968, Israel's retaliation against Beirut Airport, and the second PFLP attack on an Israeli plane at Zürich Airport on 18 February 1969. Mrs. Golda Meir's assumption of the premiership following the death of Levi Eshkol on 26 February was reflected in the sharper tone of Israel's policy declarations. On 17 March she rejected the concept of Great Power mediation embodied in the four-power (UK, USA, USSR, and France) discussions on the Middle East which had been launched on French initiative. She also dismissed the six-point peace proposal of King Hussein of Jordan on the ground that it was not genuine.

At the end of June 1972 Israeli official figures for all military and civilian casualties caused by all types of action by Arab regular forces and guerrillas since the end of June 1967 were: 817 killed and 3,119 wounded compared with 778 killed and 2,558 wounded in the June war itself. The majority of casualties were on the Suez Canal although there was continued sporadic action by Palestinian guerrillas of al-Fatah and other organizations. The PFLP claimed responsibility for most of the bomb explosions in Israeli cities, and the sabotage of Haifa and Tel Aviv ports indicated that the *fedayeen* were receiving some support from Israeli Arabs. Strikes and demonstrations on the West Bank – especially by schoolchildren – were frequent during 1969 but they did not present any serious security problem for Israel. The most serious trouble and the most bitter opposition to Israeli occupation were in Gaza, where guerrilla activities were not contained until 1971.

Israel pursued its policy of saturation bombing of Egyptian positions in the Canal Zone and of occasional deep penetration raids into Egyptian territory but it stopped the latter after April, almost certainly because of the danger of a direct clash with the Russians who were stepping up their aid to Egypt. Israel succeeded in reducing its rate of casualties in the Canal Zone but in June and July the installation of new Soviet SAM-3 missiles caused the loss of five Israeli Phantom planes. The Israeli Government was constantly aware of the possibility of an erosion of its relationship with the US on which it now depended almost exclusively for supplies of arms and financial aid. In March 1970 Secretary of State Rogers said that Israel's request for more Phantoms and Skyhawks would 'remain in abeyance' for a time. Meanwhile Israel's defence costs were rising rapidly to nearly 50 per cent of an increased budget. At this time it was apparent that the US did not fully accept the Israeli Government's estimate of the threat to Israel's security caused by the increased Soviet presence in Egypt.

When, in June 1970, the US Secretary of State formally launched his peace initiative based on the UN Security Council Resolution 242 Israel followed Egypt and Jordan in accepting his proposals, and a ninety-day cease-fire came into effect on 7 August. After some initial doubts the US accepted the Israeli charge that Egypt and the Russians had used the military standstill agreement to install new missile sites in the Canal Zone. The US then agreed to fulfil Israel's request for Phantoms and financial aid.

The new era of quasi-peace which followed the ending of the 'war of attrition' on the Suez Canal saw Israel in an unusually confident and relaxed mood. The Defence Minister Moshe Dayan returned from a visit to Washington with the conviction that the US still treated the Suez Canal as part of the front line of the cold war. The final expulsion of Palestinian guerrillas from Jordan in the summer of 1971 gave Israel an increased feeling of security. As the US peace initiative lost its momentum there was some alarm among the public that US support for Israel was being eroded. On 26 September 1971 Israel rejected a Security Council resolution calling on Israel not to change the character of Jerusalem and to rescind all steps already taken in that direction. However, the Government remained confident that the US-Israeli crisis was largely artificial. When Mrs. Meir visited Washington in October she received assurances of the kind of US military aid that Israel had requested.

The Government's confident feeling that Israel could resist any attempt to impose a Middle East peace settlement of which it did not approve continued through 1972. Even the progress of US-Soviet *détente* was not seen as a threat because it was apparent that the two superpowers preferred the status quo in the Middle East to any possible confrontation between them which might result from renewed hostilities in the region. A series of attacks on Israeli targets in Israel and abroad by Palestinian terrorist groups or their supporters (including the massacre of Israeli Olympic athletes in May) profoundly affected Israeli public opinion. Although Israel's overall security was not affected, they did raise doubts about the Government's complacency represented by the confident assertion of the Foreign Minister Abba Eban in the same month that 'the Middle East is no longer one of the world's trouble centres'. General Dayan's policy in the Occupied Territories was producing results. The Territories were experiencing an enormous boom in many sectors: 50,000 Arabs from Gaza and the West Bank travelled daily across the so-called Green Line to work in Israel. Guerrilla attacks and sabotage inside the Occupied Territories had virtually come to an end; 153,000 Arabs from outside Israel visited friends and relatives there in 1972 and stayed as long as three months. Even the special problems of Gaza were being treated and acts of sabotage in the Strip were becoming comparatively rare. Yet the sensational acts of international terrorism by Palestinian guerrillas raised the question of how far Israel's self-confident military superiority in the region was sufficient. The possibility of the establishment of a Palestinian state or entity in the West Bank was only advocated by a few prominent Israelis, such as the former Secretary General of the Labour Party Liova Eliav, but there was a growing realization that the

Palestinian problem would not disappear of its own accord and would have to be tackled.

Of more immediate concern to the Government was the domestic economic and political climate. The Government's relations with the trade unions grew progressively worse. There was a widespread feeling that the gap between rich and poor was growing, and a series of economic scandals involved cabinet ministers and officials.

On the international level Mrs. Meir's Government saw no reason to do more than hold fast to its previous position in the face of President Sadat's diplomatic offensive which was based on a demand for a complete Israeli withdrawal from all occupied territories. Continued assurances of American support gave the Government confidence, which percolated to all sectors of Israeli society, that time was on Israel's side. While international acts of Palestinian terrorism increased in the early months of 1973 Mrs. Meir authorized a counter-attack and on 10 April Israeli Army commando units raided Beirut, killed three Palestinian leaders, and destroyed a head-quarters of the Popular Democratic Front.

The possibility that a desperate President Sadat, faced with the failure of his diplomatic offensive, would launch an offensive across the Suez Canal was not discounted. In the spring Israel's armed forces were placed on full alert when Israeli intelligence reported a massive Egyptian build-up. The fact that the Egyptian preparations, which were almost certainly a bluff, did not lead to an attack greatly influenced Israel's political leaders who did not believe, when they received similar reports reinforced from US forces, that Egypt and Syria were jointly planning an offensive in early October.

The 1973 War and Aftermath

The Egyptian and Syrian attack at 2.00 p.m. on 6 October – Yom Kippur, the Day of Atonement, the most sacred occasion in the Jewish calendar – took Israel by surprise. Militarily the recovery was rapid. After initial reverses in which the Egyptian forces destroyed the Bar Lev line on the Suez Canal and secured a bridgehead in Sinai while Syrian forces threatened Northern Galilee, the hastily mobilized Israeli forces, reinforced by a massive airlift of American arms, succeeded in throwing back the Syrians to within 30 miles of Damascus and in crossing to the west bank of the Suez Canal in force. The psychological effects of the war went much deeper. Losses in tanks and planes were much heavier than in previous wars; 2,521 Israelis were killed and 7,056 wounded – about half of them permanently. Despite the Israeli victories in the latter part of the war, the performance of the Arab armies had been sufficient to destroy the myth of Israeli military invincibility. The reaction of the Israeli public, led by the press, was to launch a type of witch-hunt to apportion the blame for the blunders which had allowed Israel to be taken by surprise. The principal target of these attacks was Moshe Dayan, and to a lesser extent the Prime Minister, Mrs. Meir. In the general elections on 31 December the Labour Party lost ground to the right-wing opposition, the Likud. Labour remained the largest party but without an overall majority in the Knesset. Mrs. Meir with difficulty succeeded in forming a minority coalition government, which she persuaded Moshe Dayan to join, but in the face of unreduced political attacks she resigned on 10 April 1974. The chief of staff and ambassador to the US Yitzhak Rabin was elected as head of the Labour Party to succeed her, and in June he succeeded in forming a new cabinet based on a somewhat different coalition from that of Mrs. Meir and without either Moshe Dayan or Abba Eban.

The October 1973 War resulted in a marked deterioration in Israel's international position. Although the US remained a firm ally, it had re-established relations with several Arab states, notably Egypt, and henceforth adopted a more even-handed approach to the Middle East as between Israelis and Arabs. Largely as a consequence of the Arab oil embargo imposed during the war, West European states inclined much more strongly towards the Arabs while Cuba and 27 African states, several of which had been friends of Israel, severed relations before the end of 1973. Another consequence of the war was the greatly increased international recognition and support for the PLO. At their summit meeting in Rabat in October 1974 the Arab states recognized the PLO as the sole legitimate representative of the Palestinian people and in November the PLO leader Yasir Arafat was invited to address the UN General Assembly.

Because of US aid and support, however, Israel was not militarily weaker. By the end of 1974 its forces were proportionately larger than in October 1973 and qualitatively much improved. Moreover, US support enabled Israel to maintain an unrelenting refusal to have any dealings with the PLO. American assistance also helped to alleviate what would have been a disastrous economic situation, with a record $3.5 billion balance of payments deficit at the end of 1974 and 40 per cent inflation, requiring a drastic 30 per cent devaluation.

Relations with the US were now more central to Israeli affairs than they had ever been. These passed through a period of difficulty in the summer of 1975 when US Secretary of State Henry Kissinger declared that his mission to secure a second Egyptian-Israeli disengagement agreement in Sinai had broken down, making clear that Israel was mainly responsible for the failure. The US suspended the supply of arms for some weeks. However, when the agreement was finally signed on 1 September, it was not unsatisfactory to Israel. In return for handing back some 10 per cent of Sinai, including some important oil fields, Israel had virtually secured Egypt's removal from the Arab front, through the joint renunciation of the use of force.

Israel's international isolation was further demonstrated at the end of 1975 in the UN General Assembly, which supported the claims of the PLO to be represented at all negotiations with Israel and branded Zionism and, by implication, Israel as 'racist'. Yet these moves tended to unite the Israelis behind an unyielding policy towards the Palestinians and strengthened the hand of the Rabin government at a time when the country was suffering from acute economic and labour problems.

The strengthening of Israel's forces and the divisions among the Arab states, exacerbated by the Sinai 2 Disengagement Agreement, gave the country confidence in its own strength; but the defence burden, estimated at one third of the national product, was becoming increasingly intolerable. Although exports were buoyant and unemployment below 3 per cent in 1976, inflation remained at a high level and both direct and indirect taxation more than tripled between 1972 and 1976.

In December 1976 internal disputes in the Rabin Cabinet culminated in the resignation of the National Religious Party members of the coalition who accused the Prime Minister of having violated the Sabbath in a welcoming ceremony for some US fighter aircraft. Mr. Rabin resigned and called for general elections in May rather than November as originally scheduled.[3]

The Begin Government

The elections held on 18 March ushered in a new era in Israeli political life. The Labour Party coalition (Alignment) which had held power since the foundation of the State received only 24.6 per cent of the vote (compared with 40 per cent at the previous elections), while the right-wing Likud won 33.4 per cent. The head of Likud, Menahem Begin, former Irgun leader, became Prime Minister after years in the political wilderness. Moshe Dayan abandoned the Labour Party to become Minister of Foreign Affairs, and in October Yigal Yadin's newly-formed Democratic Movement for Change (DMC) joined the Cabinet with four ministers.

The Labour Party, divided and beset by scandals, lost the elections because after 30 years in power it no longer enjoyed the confidence of the mass of voters. The middle class and the better educated remained loyal to Labour although some defected to the DMC.

If the election was largely fought and won on domestic issues, it was certain to have a profound effect on Israel's external relations. The country's leader was now a man who had long been regarded outside Israel, as well as by some inside Israel, as a dangerous extremist with irrelevant mystical ideals about restoring the whole Land of Israel to the Jews. On his first visit to the US in July 1977, Mr. Begin went some way towards disarming American opinion and was almost wholly successful in allaying the doubts of American Zionists. President Carter and Mr. Begin agreed in general terms on a common approach to a resumption of the Geneva Middle East conference. However, a new US-Israeli rift arose when, within twenty-four hours of his return to Israel, Mr. Begin authori-

[3]An echo of events in 1961. See p. 370 above.

zed the legalization of three Jewish settlements on the West Bank of the River Jordan.

Israeli-US relations were now to suffer many vicissitudes but the overall trend was a gradual but significant erosion of US support for Israel of the kind that had for so long been discussed in the Israeli press. The US remained fully committed to the survival of Israel and continued to supply it with massive quantities of military and economic aid. But it was now clear that the US was tending increasingly to balance its interests in the Arab world against those in Israel. Moreover, Egypt's President Sadat was making strong headway in convincing American public opinion that the leader of the major Arab country wanted peace at least as much as Israel. Henceforth the US Government did not shrink from sharp public criticism of Israeli actions – especially over the question of Jewish settlements in the Occupied Territories – or from making clear that it regarded Israel as the main obstacle to peace.

When President Sadat invited himself to Jerusalem in November 1977 and the Knesset responded with a formal invitation, the Israeli public reacted with astonished jubilation. But in the extended and intermittent Israeli-Egyptian negotiations which followed, it soon became apparent that although a historic change had been achieved in Israel's relations with its most important Arab neighbour, the two sides had different objectives which would be difficult to reconcile. Israel wanted a full and lasting peace agreement with Egypt and was prepared to give up Sinai to this end. Egypt also wanted peace and the return of Sinai but it wished to avoid a separate peace which would isolate it from the rest of the Arab world. This remained the central problem even when the deadlock in Egyptian-Israeli negotiations which lasted throughout the spring and summer of 1978 was broken by President Carter's invitation to Mr. Begin and President Sadat to attend a joint summit meeting at Camp David in the USA in September. Although this resulted in two 'frameworks of agreement' for peace in the Middle East and for Israeli-Egyptian peace, and although further detailed Egyptian-Israeli negotiations produced a draft treaty, Egyptian insistence that there should be a clear linkage between an Israeli-Egyptian peace and a settlement of the Palestinian problem was resisted by Israel. At Camp David Mr. Begin had gone some way towards improving the terms of his proposals for autonomy in the West Bank and Gaza, but this was not enough for even the moderate Arab states to regard them as adequate, or for the PLO to consider co-operating in the election of an autonomous Arab council. Mr. Begin continued to insist that Israel would never allow the establishment of an independent Palestinian state in the West Bank.

At home Mr. Begin faced criticism from opposing quarters. On the one hand the feeling that he was sacrificing the chance of peace for the sake of his mystical belief in Greater Israel gave rise to a Peace Now movement which cut across party affiliations and held several successful mass rallies in the spring and summer of 1978. On the other hand, extremists of the Gush Emunim (Block of the Faithful) settlers launched a movement against the abandonment of Sinai and the granting of autonomy to the West Bank. Members of the Labour opposition also expressed the view that autonomy in the West Bank and Gaza would inevitably lead to an independent Palestinian state. However, this was not enough to persuade any of the elected Arab leaders in the Occupied Territories to co-operate with the autonomy plan.

The conclusion of the Treaty of Washington with Egypt in March 1979, through which Israel could look forward to the normalization of its relations with its main Arab opponent in return for a phased withdrawal from Sinai over three years, was a great achievement for the Begin Government. However, it did not lead to a general Middle East Settlement. The ensueing negotiations on Palestinian atuonomy were boycotted by all the other Arabs concerned, including the Palestinian Leadership. Mr. Begin's own definition of autonomy both narrowed and hardened and his government continued to establish Jewish settlements in the Occupied Territories. As a consequence Israel's relations with the US deteriorated and its international isolation increased.

Party, successor to the General Zionists founded in 1931 (in 1965 Herut and the Liberal Party formed the Gahad – Gush Herut Liberalism – bloc, which became the nucleus of Likud; (3) La'am, consisting of parts of the Free Centre Party, the State List, and the Greater Land of Israel Movement; (4) Shlomzion (General 'Arik' Sharon's party) which ran independently in the 1977 elections but shortly afterwards became a full member of the Likud; and (5) Ahdut (Unity), a splinter of the Independent Liberal Party which joined the Likud in the spring of 1977.

Labour Party – Mapam Alignment (Ma'arach) which gained 32 seats in the 1977 elections, is an electoral alliance formed after the 1969 elections between two separate parties: (1) the Israel Labour Party, formed out of Mapai (Israel Workers' Party, founded in 1930), Achdut Avoda/Poalei Zion (a group which split off from Mapai in 1954), and Rafi (another Mapai splinter group created in 1965); and (2) Mapam (United Workers' Party) – a left-wing Zionist Socialist Party.

National Religious Party, with 12 seats in the Knesset, was formed in 1965 by a merger of Mizrahi (founded in 1901) and its socialist component Ettapoel Hamizrahi.

Democratic Movement for Change (DASH), founded in 1976, holds 15 seats. It includes components of Shinui (Change), a protest movement founded in the wake of the 1973 war, and the Democratic Movement, headed by archaeologist Professor Yigal Yadin. In August 1978 the party split and eight of its members left the coalition with Likud.

Other parties represented in the Ninth Knesset are: (1) Agudat Israel (founded in 1912) which represents orthodox elements centred in Jerusalem's religious quarters; (2) Poalei Agudat Israel (Orthodox Labour, founded in 1923); (3) Democratic Front for Peace and Equality (founded in 1977), dominated by Rakah (communist), and including a group of the Israel Black Panthers and independent Arab groups (5 seats); (4) Shelli (founded in 1977), a combination of independent socialists, the former Moked Party, and the former Ha'olam Haze Party of Uri Avneri (2 seats); (5) Independent Liberal Party, successor of the Progressive Party of 1948; and (6) Citizens Rights Movement (founded in 1973), headed by Knesset Member Shulamit Aloni (one seat).

Political Developments and Policy

The main domestic issues in Israel's politics have centred on the controversy over education, religion, and economic policy. Although in all general elections Mapai was returned to power as the principal party, it had no clear majority and in each case had to form a Coalition Government. In 1949 and 1951 it had the support of the religious parties, and in 1952 it brought into the Government the second largest party, the General Zionists. The uneasy alliance between the moderate socialists and the religious groups on the one hand, and the bourgeois General Zionists on the other has led to frequent rifts and complicated the issues, involving the basic questions of church and state in Israel, a unified system of state education, conscription of women, and the formulation of a written Constitution. The inclusion of the General Zionists in 1952 enabled the Government to carry out the measures for a unified system of education. The formulation of an organic law setting out the rights of men and of a written Constitution was contemplated when the first Knesset was elected in 1949 to a Constituent Assembly. The plan, however, has been indefinitely postponed, partly because of the fundamental divergences on the religious issues. In the autumn of 1954, Ben-Gurion, who had been Prime Minister and Minister of Defence since 1948, announced that he would retire to a collective settlement in the Negev, and the Foreign Minister, Moshe Sharett, became Premier and maintained the existing coalition. Ben-Gurion was out of office, but not out of politics, for fourteen months. His retirement was part of an active campaign to inspire young Israelis to pioneer in the Negev and on the frontiers. In February 1955 he was recalled as Minister of Defence, and at once made it clear that he was prepared to be Prime Minister again if Mapai were successful in the general election. The results of the election disappointed Mapai, who lost 5 of the 45 seats they had held and 5 per cent of the votes, while the extreme Herut won 15 and became the second largest party.

Ben-Gurion, unable to form a coalition of the centre parties and implacably opposed to Herut, turned to the three Left parties and the religious socialists and the small Progressive group. His new coalition commanded 80 out of the 120 seats and relied less than its predecessors on the religious middle-class sections.

In October 1958 the members of the National Religious Party withdrew from the coalition over the question of the administrative definition of 'who is a Jew' in the State of Israel. The question was not solved by the time of the general elections of November 1959 which were fought against the background of social unrest among immigrants from Oriental countries. The Mapai Party strengthened its position in the Knesset but its unity was shaken by the Lavon affair and Premier Ben-Gurion's refusal to accept a ministerial enquiry to exonerate him. Ben-Gurion's resignation on 31 January 1960 was followed by long and unsuccessful negotiations to create a new Coalition Government which ended with a decision to hold fresh general elections in August 1961. The result was a disappointment for Mapai not only because it lost 5 seats (from 47 to 42) but because the new Liberal Party increased its representation to 17 seats which was equal to that of the Herut Party. The tenth and last Government to be led by Ben-Gurion took office in November 1961. It was a weak coalition of Mapai, Achdut Avoda, Poalei Agudat Israel, and the small Arab parties affiliated to Mapai and commanding 69 seats in the Knesset. It came to an end in June 1963 following Ben-Gurion's final resignation.

The succeeding Government headed by the former Finance Minister Levi Eshkol had the same composition as its predecessor and was officially described as a 'Government of continuation'. It soon faced internal difficulties because of the Lavon affair and the division of opinion among its members as to whether or not to reopen the enquiry and transfer it to the judicial commission Ben-Gurion was demanding. Another serious subject of controversy was the planned electoral union between Mapai and Achdut Avoda which many Ben-Gurion followers regarded as a move by the 'old guard' to block the access to power of the younger generation by a show of personal authority. Premier Eshkol resigned on 15 December 1964 but was asked by the President to re-form his Government a week later. The rift with Ben-Gurion continued and a month later his leading supporters in the Government – Moshe Dayan, Joseph Almogi, and Shimon Peres all resigned. These formed a new party named Rafi under Ben-Gurion's leadership, fought the next elections in November 1965, and won 10 seats. Eshkol formed a new coalition of Mapai, Mapam, the Independent Liberals, plus some smaller parties, and controlled 75 seats in the Knesset until the crisis preceding the June 1967 war when the opposition Rafi and Gahal parties joined the Cabinet of National Unity controlling 107 of the 120 parliamentary seats.

Rafi decided to rejoin Mapai and was shortly followed by Achdut Avoda. The new powerful Labour Party thus created found itself with an absolute majority for the first time in the history of the State, and Mapam decided to align itself with it in preparation for the 1969 elections.

In these elections the Labour Party won 56 seats, the conservative Gahal Party 26 and the religious bloc 18. Eight other small parties held the remaining 20 seats. The results indicated a slight shift to the right in the national elections, and there was a greater emphasis on independents in the municipal voting.

Following the death of Levi Eshkol from a heart attack on 26 February 1969, Mrs. Meir had quickly emerged as his natural successor and had been sworn in on 17 March. The coalition government which she formed after the 1969 elections included six ministers of the Gahal Party, but these withdrew from the Government in August 1970 in protest against Israel's acceptance of the Rogers peace initiative which they said would require Israel to hand back almost all the Arab territory occupied in 1967.

The new territorial position brought about by the 1967 conflict and the changed power relationship between Israel and its Arab neighbours, now directly supported by the military might of the Soviet Union, changed the traditional basis of Israel's political life. The ideological issue was no longer between the various forms of social and religious life within the Jewish State but whether Israel should exist as a Jewish national entity or as a mixed Arab-Jewish State. The political struggle was now not so much between parties as between personalities and groups within the new Labour Party. This tendency increased as a result of the October 1973 war. The Labour leadership, especially Moshe Dayan, was blamed by the public for the blunders in the early part of the war. In the December 1973 elections the Labour Party lost a number of seats to the combined right-wing coalition; it remained the largest single party but was no longer able to command a majority. Mrs. Meir succeeded in forming a weak coalition which she persuaded Moshe Dayan to join, but in April 1974 she resigned. Her successor, the former chief of staff and ambassador to the US, Yitzhak Rabin, had to face even greater difficulties within his Party as several of its leading figures refused to serve under him. However, with the support as Defence Minister of his chief rival for the leadership, Shimon Peres, Rabin succeeded in forming a government which gave the country for a time a sense of purpose and direction despite the fragile nature of the coalition on which the government was based. Rabin's experience as ambassador in the USA was of special value in this difficult period. However, internal differences intensified during 1976 and in December the expulsion by Mr. Rabin of the National Religious Party from the government resulted in his resignation and the bringing forward of the elections from November to May 1977. In April Mr. Rabin announced he was standing down from the leadership of the Labour Party and the premiership of the caretaker government because he and his wife were guilty of a technical irregularity in having a bank account in Washington.

The May 1977 elections caused a political upheaval in that they broke the 29-year hegemony over Israel's political life of the Labour Party and brought Menahem Begin to power as leader of the Likud. They also marked the emergence of the new party of Yigal Yadin – the Democratic Movement for Change (DASH), which won 15 seats at Labour's expense. This joined Mr. Begin's coalition in October to give it 78 certain votes in the 120-seat chamber.

Radical changes were to follow in view of the Likud's declared aim of liberalizing the economy and of settling the Occupied Territories. However, circumstances prevented Mr. Begin's government from going as far in either direction as they might have wished. The New Economic Policy announced in October introduced some important liberalization measures but the Labour Party continued to dominate the Histadrut in the June elections and the government drew back from a full-scale confrontation with organized labour. Similarly, President Sadat's peace initiative and the subsequent Israeli-Egyptian negotiations caused the Begin government to delay the full implementation of its settlement policy. But when a treaty with Egypt was successfully concluded in March 1979 the Settlement policy was vigorously pursued.

SOCIAL SURVEY

The influx of vast numbers of immigrants into Israel has brought with it profound changes in the social structure of the pre-state Jewish community. As has been noted, the fusing of the numerous strands of culture, language, and customs into a single nation is one of the most vital tasks facing Israel. The European ideal of economic aid and social progress on which Israeli life is based is strange to the Oriental Jews. Many immigrants have spent years in concentration and displaced persons' camps and must be trained to enter normal productive life, while others uprooted from their old professions and traditions must be helped to find new skills and attitudes of mind. Israel's immigration policy has, in addition, brought an increased, if willingly accepted, burden of old people, the sick, and parentless children, who must be cared for.

Education

Under the compulsory education law passed in 1949, free compulsory education is provided for all children between five and fourteen, Arabs as well as Jews. Secondary education is provided for children over thirteen. Half of the pupils, including all those who have passed examinations in development areas, are exempt from payment. Children in the 14–18 age group who have not completed elementary education must attend classes (free) till they reach the required standard. Primary education was complicated by the system of four 'trends' which was carried over from the mandatory period. Until 1953 there were within the state system four parallel types of school: general, Labour, Mizrahi (orthodox), and Agudat Israel (ultra-orthodox), corresponding in the main to shades of social, religious, and political opinion. By the state education law of 1953 all the administrative powers hitherto enjoyed by the bodies representing the trends were abolished, and the supervision and organization of all state schools was vested in the Ministry of Education. Private schools may be established provided the curriculum, teaching, and buildings meet the standards of the Ministry of Education. They are mainly religious schools.

In 1974/75 the Jewish network included 6,620 schools and 60,000 teachers. The Arab network had 355 educational institutions of various kinds.

In the year 1974/75 some 51,000 students attended Israel's seven institutions of higher learning, of whom 40 per cent were specializing in the natural sciences, the remainder in social sciences and the humanities.

The Hebrew University of Jerusalem has played a cardinal role in the training of the country's intellectual and academic leadership. Opened in 1925 on Mount Scopus (where the original buildings have been reopened since the 1967 war) it had 15,500 students in 1975/76. The University is responsible for the Beersheba Institute of Higher Education (500 students).

The Technion or Israel Institute of Technology in Haifa had 8,550 students and 1,500 teaching staff in 1974/75. It also provided extension courses for 7,600 students.

The Tel Aviv University had a teaching staff of 2,000 and a student body of 12,900 in 1974/75.

The University of Haifa is the new university of northern Israel. It has over 5,000 students, about one third of them Arab.

The Bar-Ilan University is a religious institution with a teaching staff of 680 and a student body of 7,000 in Arts and Science Faculties.

Ben-Gurion University of the Negev was established in Beersheba in 1965 to serve the needs of the country's south. In 1975/76 it had 3,650 students.

The most prestigious scientific institute in the country is the Weizmann Institute of Science devoted to fundamental research in the natural sciences. In 1974/75 it had 200 graduates and 350 post-graduate students. A non-profit-making subsidiary – Yeda Research and Development Company – deals with the commercial promotion of the Institute's industrial research.

The annual expenditure on scientific research of the Academic Institutes had reached £I 450 million in 1970/71, of which 60 per cent was provided by the Government. The research work is promoted and co-ordinated by: (1) the Israel Academy of Science and Humanities; (2) the National Council for Research and Development in the Prime Minister's Office, which is responsible in particular for the National Physics Laboratory and the Negev Institute for Arid Zone Research at Beersheba; and (3) the Atomic Energy Commission supervising the work of the Sorek Nuclear Research Centre and the Negev Nuclear Research Centre.

Cultural Development

It is a remarkable achievement that within so short a time Hebrew has become the living language of a nation composed of so many linguistic elements. Thirteen Hebrew and ten non-Hebrew newspapers are published daily; the two foremost morning papers have a circulation of about 50,000 and the evening papers over 225,000. There are 400 other periodicals including 50 weeklies and 150 fortnightlies or monthlies. The per capita theatre attendance is the highest in the world. Habimah, the Israel National Theatre, was founded in Russia in 1917. Of equal intensity is the musical life centred on the Israel Philharmonic Orchestra which was founded in 1936, and on the 29 Conservatoires.

Kol Israel, the Voice of Israel, broadcasts 55 hours daily in Hebrew and nine other languages including 14 hours in Arabic. Television began operating in 1969. There are 270 cinemas in the country and 113 films have been made locally since 1969.

European traditions dominate the plastic arts in Israel but this is not the case with music and folklore which have developed a distinctive local character. However, it is probably in the field of literature, crowned by the Nobel Prize awarded in 1966 to S. J. Agnon and Nelly Sachs of Sweden, that Israel has found its most original national expression. In 1978 Israeli letters were again honoured by the Nobel Prize for Literature, awarded to Isaac Bashevis Singer.

Health Services

In spite of mass immigration which brought to Israel a million immigrants of whom about 13 per cent suffered from chronic diseases, health standards compare well with those of Europe. In 1976 life expectancy was 70.9 years for males and 74.5 for females; infant mortality was 16.0 per thousand among Jews and 33.2 per thousand among non-Jews. In 1976 there was a total of 23,438 beds in 129 hospitals of all types of which the Government was responsible for 34 hospitals and 8,000 beds. Apart from the missions and private hospitals most of the health services of the country were provided by the Trade Union Health Organization and the Hadassah Medical Organization sponsored by Zionist sources in the USA.

The National Insurance scheme, started in 1954, covers 900,000 persons. This provides for pensions for men over 65 and women over 60, maternity benefits, and family allowances for children under 18 after the first child. The Ministry of Social Welfare provides most of the social workers, with special attention to youth.

Labour and Trade Unions

The economic and industrial organization of Israel is dominated, and complicated, by the peculiar position of the Histadrut, which is a confederation of most of the trade unions in the country and of the growing numbers of co-operatives and collective societies engaged in agriculture and industry, and conducts medical and welfare services for its members. Its membership grew to 1,124,000 in the spring of 1971 and includes half of all adults, including 62,000 Arabs and Druzes.

The Histadrut is the owner or part-owner on a co-operative basis of a number of large industrial concerns and financial institutions. The most important of these are: Hamashbir Hamerkazi (Co-operative Wholesale Society), which acts as supplier for the agricultural settlements and urban consumers' co-operatives, which in turn control a series of industrial enterprises including soap, flour, chemical, shoe-making, and rubber factories; Tnuva (Central Agricultural Marketing Co-operative), which markets the greater proportion of Israel's agricultural produce; Solel Boneh, which is the largest contracting enterprise, carries out public works both in Israel and abroad, and directly or indirectly exercises control over a large variety of industrial firms. The main financial institutions controlled wholly or in part by the Histadrut are the Workers' Bank, Hassneh Insurance Company, and two credit institutions. It also has interests in the Mekorot Water-Supply Company, two shipping companies, and Ampal (the American Palestine Trading Company), which extends dollar loans to the Government and to Histadrut-controlled enterprises and makes direct investments to the national air and shipping companies. It has entered into partnership with many private investors in Israel and abroad. All economic activities are controlled by the General Co-operative Association (Hevrat Ovdim) whose membership is the same as that of the Histadrut.

Apart from the social services, the Histadrut is responsible for many cultural and sports organizations, including three daily newspapers and hundreds of popular art circles. The Histadrut is affiliated to the ICFTU and through its Afro-Asian Institute provides courses for thousands of foreign students from developing countries.

There are three other trade union organizations formed on party lines, but associated for some purposes with the Histadrut: (1) the Mizrahi Workers' Organization (Histadrut Hapoel Hamizrahi) which maintains communal and co-operative settlements and has central organizations for the absorption of new immigrants; (2) the Agudat Israel Workers' Organization (Histadrut Poalei Agudat Israel), which also maintains settlements; and (3) the National Labour Federation (Histadrut Haovdim Haleumit), which was founded by the Revisionist Organization and has its own sick fund.

The Israel Labour League, which was an Arab trade union organization, and the Arab Workers' Congress, which was a near-Communist body, were dissolved in 1953. The Arab workers are now members of bodies affiliated to the Histadrut.

ECONOMIC SURVEY

The economic development of Israel since 1948 has been largely determined by her special political and social conditions. Some of these are a legacy from the mandatory period and the troubled events which preceded and accompanied the foundations of the State; some result from the struggle to maintain Zionist social ideals; and some from the absence of settled and peaceful relations with neighbouring states.

The last has been the most important single factor and it has compelled Israel to support an extremely heavy defence burden. It has been estimated at $65 million in 1954, $270 million in 1963, $1,000 million in 1969, about $1,500 million in 1971 and about $2,000 million in 1976, i.e. 35 per cent of GNP.

These political difficulties have also had an indirect effect. The blockade of Israel by the Arab States and particularly by Egypt, with her hold over the Suez Canal, handicapped foreign trade. It has shut Israel off from natural markets in the Middle East and from natural sources of grain in neighbouring countries; it has obliged her to import refined oil products which could otherwise have been produced by the IPC refinery from Iraqi crude oil; and it exposes commerce to constant interference.

Despite all these economic difficulties the Government has endeavoured to maintain a European standard of living and a high level in the social services in accordance with Zionist ideals of social justice. But all these factors have placed a great strain on Israel's balance of payments. Shortage of foreign currency has been a constant threat to essential investment on the one hand and to the level of consumption on the other, in spite of great capital transfers amounting to $6 billion from 1949 to 1965, 59 per cent of which were supplied by world Jewry, $1.73 billion by West Germany, and the rest mainly by the United States. Since 1973, US aid (grants and loans) has totalled between $1 billion and $2.5 billion a year. Israel's total foreign debt in 1976 stood at some $9 billion, and repayments of $1.2 billion were equivalent to half the added value of exports. By 1978 the international debt was estimated at $12.2 billion and in 1979 at $14 billion.

Pattern of the Economy

The Israeli economy has continued to expand although not at the same rate as the population. Between 1949 and 1970 the GNP increased annually by 9–10 per cent to reach £I 72 billion in 1975. In 1974, however, the rate decreased to 5 per cent and in 1975 it dropped to zero. A policy of planned economic restraint kept the rate down to one per cent through 1976 and most of 1977, but the last quarter of 1977 saw a sudden increase of 11.6 per cent.

The structure of the economy is similar to that of industrialized countries of Western Europe. Agriculture accounts for 6.8 per cent of the domestic product; industry 28.3 per cent; government and public services 20.2 per cent. A more detailed breakdown of these figures would show that the active population engaged in services of all kinds nears 50 per cent – much higher than in Europe. This is one of the main negative trends which successive Israeli governments have tried to change with relatively little success.

Economic Policy

For the first 29 years of the State of Israel, governments dominated by the Labour Party pursued a variety of socialist policies in a mixed economy adapted to meet Israel's special circumstances. The Histadrut trade union federation has always played a major role in the economy. The right-wing Likud government which took office in May 1977 announced a New Economic Programme of liberalization in October 1977 (owing considerable inspiration to the ideas of the American economist Milton Friedman), with the declared intention of making Israel a world financial centre and the Switzerland of the Middle East. Major elements in the NEP were the floating of the Israeli pound, the removal of most foreign exchange controls, the abolition of export subsidies, the import levy and the travel tax, and the raising of VAT to 12 per cent.

Inflation and Wages

The chief obstacle to the success of the NEP has been the continuing rise in prices. From a 23.5 per cent increase in 1975, 38 per cent in 1976, 42.5 per cent in 1977, it reached over 50 per cent in 1978, over 60 per cent in mid-1979, and was expected to exceed 100 per cent by the end of the year.

Wages comprise a basic rate together with a cost of living allowance, supplemented by family and seniority allowances and fringe benefits. As unemployment rose during the 1965–7 recession, the unions co-operated with the Government's wages policy and the Histadrut again reached an agreement with the Likud government in 1977 to hold down wages in an effort to fight inflation. But with average earnings in industry increasing by much less than prices, the Government was faced in 1978 by stiffening opposition from the unions to any extension of the agreement.

Currency

Israel's currency is the Israeli pound (£I), which is divided into 100 *agorot* (plural of *agora*). It was at first linked with sterling but has since been successively devalued. A system of creeping devaluation of 2 per cent a month was introduced in June 1975, and in 1976 linkage to the dollar was abandoned in favour of linkage to a basket of international currencies. When this linkage was abandoned entirely in the Likud government's NEP of October 1977 the Israeli pound at once devalued by some 45 per cent. Since then the Israeli pound has continued to devalue slowly to reach in mid-1979 £I 54.9 to the pound sterling, or £I 25.3 to the US dollar.

Agriculture

Jewish settlement in Palestine from Herzl to the end of the mandate laid stress on agriculture as a means of reclaiming land and as a way of life demonstrating *Haluziut*, the pioneering spirit which was so important to Zionists. This remains as important as ever. The Government has consistently encouraged immigrants to go on the land and considers agricultural training in the frontier villages as equivalent to army service. Moreover, since the creation of the State the economic grounds for developing agriculture have become more pressing, namely, to provide food for a rapidly increasing population and to conserve foreign currency by making the country as self-sufficient as possible.

Before 1948 three-quarters of the Arabs were cultivators, and they produced most of the grain, meal, fodder, and vegetable oil (olives). The Jewish settlements concentrated on mixed farming and citrus fruits. After 1948 and the departure of three-quarters of the Arab population, Arab cultivation had to be supplemented by imports until such a time as Jewish agriculture could be expanded and diversified to meet domestic requirements. In this the Government has been highly successful. Israel is now self-supporting in dairy produce, vegetables, and fodder; meat and wheat are the main items imported.

In the first half of 1978 agricultural exports reached $304 million – a 20.8 per cent increase on the first half of 1977. In 1975 the value of all farm produce was £I 8.5 billion, 6 per cent more than in 1974. Citrus fruit is easily the most important crop, representing 15 per cent of the total value of agricultural output: about half a million tons a year exported, mainly to Western Europe, earning about $170 million.

Emphasis is now being placed on the production of other cash crops such as cotton and grain, which will save foreign exchange on imports, and on sub-tropical fruits and vegetables for export, especially avocado pears. Since the 1960s increasing quantities of vegetables have been grown in hot-houses and under plastic.

About 22 per cent of Israel's land is at present cultivated; an increase in this proportion can only be brought about by more irrigation, as almost all usable land is either already cultivated or under pasture. Some 43 per cent of the land is already irrigated. It is estimated that total water resources would be sufficient to irrigate 300,000 hectares but this estimate takes account of water from the Jordan irrigation project. Plans for large-scale desalination of sea water, using nuclear energy, have been temporarily postponed because of their cost.

By the end of 1976 there were on Jewish farms 315,600 cattle (of which 100,050 were beef cattle), 103,000 sheep, 14,500 goats and 8.2 million poultry. On Arab farms there were 19,600 cattle, 115,000 sheep, 127,500 goats and 250,000 poultry. About 80 per cent of the demand for meat and 73 per cent of the demand for fish are now met locally.

The proportion of farm workers in the labour force has declined steadily from 15.7 per cent in 1958 to 9.7 per cent in 1969 and 6.4 per cent in 1975 (excluding transient Arab workers from the Occupied Territories).

Forestry

For centuries Palestine was gradually despoiled of its woods and forests which were famous in Biblical and Roman times. The conservation and reclamation of the soil, which has consequently been eroded, is one of the most important tasks facing the Government. During the mandate about 12,000 acres were planted with forest trees. By 1971/72 some 160,000 acres had been planted in addition to 100,000 acres of natural forest. A further 70,000 acres are capable of afforestation. Most of the trees are conifers. Some 60 million trees have been planted – 6 million to commemorate the Jews destroyed by Nazism in Europe.

Agricultural Settlements

The settlements are of various types, distinctive in their social structure and organization. The principle of the collective settlement or Kibbutz is that the village is a unit commonly owned; all property is held in common, and no person has any private possessions. Members pool their labour in accordance with the needs of the settlement and receive their requirements within the means of the community. Each Kibbutz usually has a communal dining-room and kitchen, kindergarten and children's quarters, social and cultural centre, library, and central stores. In most Kibbutzim there has been a tendency in recent years to provide living quarters for married couples and for their infant children. The Kibbutzim are mainly agricultural, but many are developing industrial workshops such as canneries, foundries, and plywood factories. Some specialize in lake fishing or breeding carp in artificial ponds. The products are sold through a co-operative marketing organization.

The co-operative settlements can be subdivided into three types, each based on co-operative principles but with distinctive features. The Moshav Ovdim, or workers' smallholding settlement, is founded on the principle of mutual aid between members. Each farm is worked by a family individually but all the produce is sold through a co-operative and all purchases for the settlement are undertaken on the same basis. Hired labour is prohibited. The Moshav is similar in type but is worked on less rigid principles. The Moshav Shitufi is a compromise between a collective and a co-operative settlement. It is based on private smallholdings combined with communal farming but each family has its own house. In all cases the land belongs to the community. It is acquired by the Keren Keyemet le-Israel (Jewish National Fund) which receives contributions from the Jews of the world, and it is leased to the collective or co-operative society. The Moshava is a rural village based on private ownership, and was the principal form of Jewish agricultural settlement in the period before the mandate. The land and house are owned by the individual. In 1976 there were 227 Kibbutzim and 378 Moshavim in addition to private Jewish and Arab farms.

Industry

Israel is poor in mineral resources but the mining of phosphates in the Negev and the extraction of potash from the Dead Sea are of increasing importance. Israel is also a minor producer of crude oil but output is only equivalent to a small proportion of domestic needs. After 1967 Israel exploited the oil resources in occupied Sinai. The Abu Rudeis oilfield was returned to Egypt in 1975 but oil has since been found in commercial quantities at the Alma oilfield in the Gulf of Suez off the Sinai coast. Exploration has continued in other parts of the region and also in offshore coastal areas of the Mediterranean.

Israel derives nearly one third of its national income from industry. The index of industrial production rose from 165.4 in 1973 to 184.7 in 1976 (1968 = 100). Industrial growth in recent years has been heavily directed towards exports. Exports rose by 25 per cent in 1976 while supply to the local market remained static. Industrial exports rose by 11 per cent in 1977 and local sales by 2 per cent. In the first half of 1978 industrial exports rose by 30 per cent. The most important industrial export is gem diamonds with sales reaching $641.6 million in the first half of 1978 (compared with

$890.3 million for all other industrial exports). The largest industry is the processing of foodstuffs, beverages and tobacco, followed by textiles, leather and clothing.

Since the wars of 1967 and 1973 there has been a very rapid growth in metal-using industries and electronics, especially in the field of military equipment (both for export and for local consumption). At the end of 1978 a huge expansion programme for the petrochemical sector and that based on the minerals of the Dead Sea was in its final stages. The output of chemicals, plastics, and rubber products was expected to double in seven years, raising their 1977 share of 20 per cent of industrial output to 24 per cent.

Ownership of industry is divided between the government, the Histadrut and the private sector. Most of the big industrial concerns, such as the Nesher cement and Shamen vegetable oil plants, are owned either solely by the Histadrut through its holding company Hevrat Ovdim or in partnership with private investors. The mining concerns are owned by the government or jointly by the government and Histadrut, while the private sector owns most of the textile industry. Mergers are encouraged between firms with a view to improving competitiveness overseas. Many firms are seeking special links with foreign companies, especially in north-west Europe and the USA.

Tourism has become a major industry for Israel. In 1977 there were 1,006,500 visitors, bringing earnings of $500 million.

Trade and Balance of Payments

Israeli exports have increased steadily from $41 million in 1949, to $1.56 billion in 1973 and $2.68 billion in 1976. But imports have continually outpaced exports, rising from $263 million in 1949, to $4.0 billion in 1973 and $5.42 billion in 1976. The large flow of aid in grants and loans has enabled the country to finance the growing visible trade deficit but this has placed a great strain on the balance of payments.

The deficit in the balance of payments was $1.7 billion in 1976, $1.4 billion in 1977 and approximately $1.8 billion in 1978. The Bank of Israel's gold and foreign exchange reserves reached a low point of $412 million in 1969 but since then they have been shored up by foreign loans and by December 1978 they stood at $2.242 billion.

The bulk of Israel's trade is with the industrialized world, led by the EEC and the US. Negotiations with the EEC on tariffs and quota concessions started in 1962 and resulted in a limited agreement in 1964 (excluding citrus fruit). This was replaced in 1970 by a five-year preferential trade agreement, and further negotiations for a closer association were concluded in 1974. According to this agreement tariffs on Israeli products entering the EEC were progressively lowered over a three to four year period, while duties on Israel's imports from the EEC were to be eliminated by the mid-1980s. As from 1 July 1977 Israeli industrial products entered the EEC duty free.

Communications

The rapid increase in the population and the accelerated economic development of the country have caused a vast increase in the volume of traffic, and the diversification and expansion of the economy have to a large extent depended upon an efficient transport system. In consequence the extension of the road and rail network has been made a high priority.

In 1976 Israel had just over 6,000 miles of highway, mostly first class. In 1948 the Israeli segments of the Middle East railway system were cut off from the system which connected Damascus and Baghdad with Egypt. Israel has not considered it profitable to operate more than a few lines, chiefly for freight. There were some 16,000 trucks in 1975 with a capacity of 2.2 billion tons.

There are three modern deep-water harbours: Haifa and Ashdod on the Mediterranean, Eilat on the Red Sea. Ashkalon has an oil port on the Mediterranean and Eilat is an outlet to the Red Sea and Asia. In 1975, 3,000 ships called at Israeli harbours, one third of them flying the Israeli flag.

El Al, the national airline, which ranks twelfth in terms of operational scope among the 102 members of the International Air Transport Association, flies half the passenger traffic into and out of Israel. The international airport is Ben-Gurion at Lod, south of Tel Aviv. In 1976 more than two million people passed through there compared with 117,000 in 1950. There are smaller airports at Atarot near Jerusalem, and at Eilat which is being developed for regular international traffic.

THE OCCUPIED AND ADMINISTERED TERRITORIES

The Arab territories occupied and administered by the Israeli military authorities since June 1967 include the West Bank of Jordan (now referred to officially in Israel as Judaea and Samaria), the Golan Heights, the Gaza Strip, and Sinai. In 1976 the population of the West Bank was estimated at 689,700, and of Gaza and Sinai 444,400. Nearly 60 per cent of the population was under 18 and their natural rate of increase one of the highest in the world. However, the rate of emigration from the Occupied Territories was also increasing. An estimated 17,000 left the West Bank in 1976 and 1977.

Municipal elections were held in the Occupied Territories in 1972 and 1975. In 1975 a number of mayors and councillors of major West Bank towns who were elected were known to have links with the PLO, but the Israeli Military Government firmly restricted overt political activities. Economically, there was substantial progress in the Occupied Territories after 1968 especially in the agricultural sector where increased irrigation and mechanization and improved methods as well as the new market outlets in Israel helped to raise the real value of agricultural output by some 10 per cent a year. Also a large number of workers from these territories found employment in Israel. In September 1978 they were estimated at 64,000, constituting about 30 per cent of all building workers in Israel, about 25 per cent of all agricultural workers, about 20 per cent of workers in various services, and 7 per cent of industrial workers. Altogether they formed 5.4 per cent of Israel's total labour force.

In 1976 there were 229,000 pupils in school in the West Bank and 140,000 in Gaza and Sinai. There were three institutions of higher education in the West Bank – Birzeit University near Ramallah which became a university in 1972, the Catholic University at Bethlehem, established in 1972, and Al-Najah University in Nablus.

Jewish Settlements

From 1967 onwards Jewish settlements have been established in all the Occupied Territories. In April 1978 there were 5 in the Gaza Strip, 11 in the Rafah Approaches, 2 on the northern Sinai coast and 8 in the rest of the Sinai Peninsula. These had a total population of some 3,200. On the Golan Heights there were 26 with a total population of about 2,500. In the West Bank there were 62, including 9 in the suburbs of Jerusalem. Their total population was an estimated 4,500.

VII

THE HASHIMITE KINGDOM OF JORDAN

THE LAND AND THE PEOPLE

The Hashimite Kingdom of Jordan lies on either side of the river Jordan. To the east is the whole of what was formerly the Amirate of Transjordan. To the west is the region of central Palestine that was taken over after the Palestine War (1948–9). Commonly known as the East Bank and the West Bank, the combined territories are about 36,715 square miles in area, 2,165 square miles constituting the West Bank and 30,700 the wide desert that encloses from the east the settled areas of the East Bank. The country is bounded on the north by the river Yarmuk and Syria, on the east by Iraq, on the south by Saudi Arabia, and on the west by Israel and the upper reaches of the river Jordan.

From east to west the desert gives place to the Transjordanian Highlands extending from north to south. Within their broad northern and central slopes is a fertile strip, thirty miles wide on the Syrian frontier and tapering into arid steppe near Maan and Petra. Westwards the hills rise sharply to a maximum of over 5,000 feet, forming a great escarpment above the Jordan-Araba gorge. The gorge cleaves the land from end to end and, within Jordanian territory, consists of: (1) the middle and lower reaches of the river Jordan twisting through its valley (10 miles broad on the south) to pass its waters into the Dead Sea (1,290 ft. below sea-level); (2) the northern end and eastern side of the Dead Sea and surrounding wilderness; (3) the wide sandy trench of the Wadi Araba running from the southern end of the Dead Sea to Aqaba on the Red Sea Gulf, which is Jordan's only port.

West of the Jordan valley the land rises again to the Palestinian Hills. This West Bank block contains the towns of Hebron, Bethlehem, East Jerusalem, Ramallah, Nablus, Tulkarm, and Jenin. Until the Six Day War of June 1967 Bethlehem and East Jerusalem remained Jordanian in spite of the UN

Partition Resolution which had designated Jerusalem as a *corpus separatum* and the General Assembly's restatement at the Fourth Session of its intention that Jerusalem and the surrounding villages and towns would be placed under a permanent international regime. At the time of writing, the whole of the West Bank is under Israeli military occupation and Israel has unilaterally incorporated the whole of Jerusalem into Israel.

In the hill country the climate follows a Mediterranean pattern except that the summers are fresher and the winters cooler. There is less rainfall on the East Bank than on the West. Snow often occurs in winter. In the Jordan valley rainfall is slight, summer intensely hot, and winter mild and pleasant.

At the census of 1961 Jordan's population numbered 1,706,226. It is growing at about three per cent per annum and was estimated to have exceeded two million by the end of 1965. In 1975 the estimate was 2.7 million of whom 0.9 million live on the West Bank. About two-thirds of all Jordanians were originally Palestinians.

In addition to the inhabitants of the West Bank which was incorporated into Jordan in 1950, many Jordanians lived until 1948 in what is now Israel. Some 800,000 left their homes during the Palestine War and more than half of these came to Jordan.

The East Jordanians were a homogeneous people largely descended from Arabian bedouin tribes of desert origin. The Palestinians derive from all the races that invaded or settled in Palestine before the Arab conquest and have been blended together by thirteen centuries of Islamic influence. Most of the Jordanian people are Sunni Moslems, but there is an important Christian minority. There are still a few nomads and semi-nomads. Tent dwellers made up a little more than 5 per cent of the population in 1961. The settled population live in towns and villages, more than one in three live in towns of over 10,000 inhabitants, and more than one in four live in Amman where the population has increased in thirty years from about 30,000 to about one million.

Other main towns on the East Bank are Irbid (491,000), Zerqa (110,000) and Kerak (90,000). The Arab population of East Jerusalem is about 400,000, and of other West Bank towns Nablus had a population of 427,000 in 1967 and Hebron 169,000.

The social pattern was distorted by the refugee influx from Israeli-held Palestine in 1948. Some 200,000 more fled across the Jordan in June and July 1967 and only about 14,000 were allowed to return.

About one third of the population is classified as Palestinian refugees, maintained by the United Nations Relief and Works Agency (UNRWA). Of these about 10 per cent are self-supporting.

The remainder all receive rations, but since the standard ration (costing $1.20 per month) is insufficient to keep body and soul together, they cannot be regarded as living in idleness on international charity, but rather, in the words of the Agency's 1965/66 Report, as receiving a modest subvention from the international community in their struggle to support themselves. Some 150,000 Jordanians were living abroad in 1978. Most of these were originally Palestine refugees. Many of them have made good in other Arab countries. The oil-producing countries in particular have been able to make use of their abilities, and their remittances have made a substantial contribution to Jordan's balance of payments.

Religious and Racial Minorities

There were 108,838 Jordanian Christians in 1961. Most of them live in Jerusalem and Amman, though other towns like Madeba and Salt on the East Bank, and Bethlehem and Ramallah on the West Bank, have substantial Christian populations. They are mostly Arabs of the Orthodox Church but there are many Catholics (both of the Roman and Byzantine rites) and Armenians, and a small community of Arab Anglicans.

A valuable element in the community is the Caucasian minority of some 10,000 persons. The greater proportion are Cherkasis (Circassians) and Sunni Moslems. The remainder (about 1,000) are known as Chechens and Shiis. These are all descended from Moslem immigrants from the Caucasus, who fled before the Russian advance in the nineteenth century.

HISTORY AND POLITICS

Southern Jordan was the scene of the wanderings of the Children of Israel before they crossed the river into Canaan. The histories of the riverside people overlap. The northern part of the cultivated strip on the East Bank was known as Gilead and attached to Solomon's kingdom, much of which is in contemporary Jordan. Ancient Ammon was situated on the East Bank, and Moab and Edom in the southern part of Jordan. In the Hellenistic period the Nabataeans, an Arabian tribe, established themselves in the south and gained control of the west Arabian caravan routes from their fortress capital at the 'rose-red city' of Petra: still one of the country's finest ancient monuments. To the north the country was Hellenized by the Seleucids, and the Greek cities of Philadelphia (now Amman) and Gerasa (now Jerash) came into being. Philadelphia and Gerasa were among the ten cities (the Dekapolis) which formed themselves into a defensive league against the nomad Arabs and Jews. The Nabataeans made formal submission to Rome and retained their autonomy, but then the kingdom was annexed by Trajan in AD 105 and became part of the Roman province of Arabia Petraea. Under Roman rule the country for five centuries enjoyed a high level of prosperity; many towns sprang up and Christianity spread. In the sixth century the control of the eastern areas passed to the Ghassanid Arabs, a tribal confederation which received an imperial subsidy; but just before the coming of the Moslems, the Ghassanids were overwhelmed by the Iranians, who sacked Jerusalem. A brief renaissance followed the Arab conquest when, under the Umayyad Caliphs, Islamic discipline was welded with Byzantine culture. Later, with the shift of the Moslem centre of gravity to Iraq and Egypt, the East Bank largely reverted to nomadism and during the Crusades was disputed for a time between Crusaders and Moslems. This period saw the last of the northward caravan trade, which thereafter passed either from the Euphrates to northern Syria or by the Red Sea to Alexandria, and Jordan's prosperity gradually crumbled away.

The Mandate

In Ottoman times the Damascus *vilayet*, with its western boundary on the Jordan, extended from Hama to Aqaba, while the country west of the Jordan – Palestine – was divided between the independent *sanjaq* of Jerusalem in the south and the *vilayet* of Beirut in the north. After the defeat of Turkey in 1918, in place of the large, independent Syria desired by Arab nationalists a French mandate was imposed upon Syria and Lebanon and a British mandate over Palestine, including Transjordan.[1] After Faisal had been driven out of Syria by the French, the British High Commissioner called a meeting of East Bank shaikhs and notables at Salt in August 1920 and declared that the British Government favoured self-government for them with the assistance of a few British officers; local administrations in Amman, Ajlun, and Kerak were then set up. Three months later Faisal's elder brother, the Amir Abdullah, appeared on the southern frontier with a small force from the Hejaz and was credited with the intention of raising the tribes against the French. On entering the country he was asked by the local administrations to form a national Government. This he proceeded to do and in March his position was acknowledged by the British Government, with whom he subsequently agreed to abandon anti-French activities and to accept the Amirate of Transjordan under a British mandate with a grant-in-aid. Under Article 25 of the mandate for Palestine the Mandatory was able, with the consent of the Council of the League of Nations, to exempt Transjordan from the operation of the Balfour Declaration. Jews were never allowed to acquire land or to settle in Transjordan.

On 25 May 1923 Transjordan was proclaimed an independent state, subject to British obligations under the mandate, and on 20 February 1928 an agreement was concluded under which the Amir Abdullah was to be guided by British advice (through a British Resident appointed by the High Commissioner for Palestine, who was also High Commissioner for Transjordan) in such matters as foreign relations, finance and fiscal policy, jurisdiction over foreigners, and freedom of conscience. The 1928 treaty was supplemented on 2 June

[1] See above, pp. 15–18.

1934 by an agreement enabling the Amir to appoint consular representatives in other Arab States. In 1939 the British Government agreed to the formation (in place of the existing Legislative Council) of a Council of Ministers (or Cabinet), each member of which was in charge of a department of the Government and responsible to the Amir. Finally, by treaties and agreements with Britain between 1939 and 1948, Transjordan attained independence (1946), and in 1948 the Amir was proclaimed King of the 'Hashimite Kingdom of Jordan', though it was not until 1949, after the Palestine War had left Transjordan in control of parts of 'Cis-Jordan', that the title was internationally recognized. The kingdom was recognized by the United States on 31 January 1949.

The Treaties with Britain

By an agreement concluded on 19 July 1941 the Amir allowed Britain to maintain armed forces in Jordan, and to raise, organize, and control sufficient armed forces in the country for its defence and for the preservation of peace and order. A treaty more in keeping with existing conditions in the country was signed in London on 22 March 1946, but it too was soon felt to be too vulnerable to Arab nationalist criticisms of King Abdullah's dependence on Britain. It was therefore replaced by another, signed in Amman on 15 March 1948. This treaty was for twenty years with provision for revision after fifteen, and provided that either party would come to the aid of the other if engaged in war. The Annex provided *inter alia* for the maintenance of RAF units at Amman and Mafraq until the parties agreed that 'the state of world security renders such measures unnecessary'. An accompanying Exchange of Letters provided for British help in economic and social development as well as for financial assistance. The Treaty was ended by an Exchange of Notes on 13 March 1957 and the last British troops stationed in Jordan under this Treaty left Aqaba on 6 July of that year.

The Palestine War and its Aftermath

On 15 May 1948, the date of the expiry of the mandate, Jordan's army (the Arab Legion) took part, with Egyptian and other forces of the Arab League, in the occupation of the Arab areas of Palestine.[2] The Legion did not intervene in Jerusalem until it became apparent that no steps were being taken by the United Nations to install an international regime in the city, which was in danger of being overrun by the Jews. With its Iraqi allies it held the central sector of Palestine and maintained the siege of the Jewish population in Jerusalem until both sides accepted the first United Nations truce in the summer of 1948. Desultory fighting continued until an armistice agreement between Transjordan and Israel was signed in Rhodes on 3 April 1949. By this agreement Transjordan was left in control of the part of Palestine that was not in the possession of Israel. The act of union took place on 24 April 1950, after general elections had been held on both sides of the river. Four leading Palestinians had already joined the Jordan Cabinet and, with the extension of the franchise to the West Bank, membership of the House of Representatives was doubled in order to give equal representation to Palestinians. The first act of its duly elected members was to vote for union.

The Palestine War had changed Transjordan into Jordan. With the accession of what remained of Palestinian territory allotted to the Arabs by the General Assembly Resolution of November 1947 Jordan acquired a Palestinian population more than twice as numerous as King Abdullah's former Transjordanian subjects. Nearly half a million of this new population were destitute refugees from the area allotted to the Jewish State and its extensions won by the Jews in the fighting. The new frontiers were mere Armistice lines which often separated villages from their lands or from their water supplies, divided Jerusalem into two unequal sectors, and cut off Jordan from any access to the Mediterranean Sea. The newly proclaimed Hashimite Kingdom of Jordan had to be built from the ground up under almost impossible economic and extremely adverse political conditions. It had been proclaimed without the prior agreement of the other Arab Governments whose war aims had not included the enlargement of Transjordan. The Palestinians were consulted and by majority welcomed this solution, but some were irreconcilably opposed

[2] i.e. those areas not already occupied by the Zionist forces before the end of the mandate. The aim of the intervention was, however, stated more ambitiously to be the elimination of the Zionist state.

to it and almost all harboured reservations about rule from Transjordan whose inhabitants they thought of as less advanced than themselves.

King Abdullah correctly perceived that peace with Israel presented the main hope for a viable Jordan. His realism however did not extend to a recognition of the state of mind produced in growing numbers of Arabs by years of impotence against European domination ending in humiliating defeat at the hands of a people they had been accustomed mildly to despise. This would in all likelihood have prevented a successful outcome of his discussions at Shuneh in 1949 and 1950 with Ben-Gurion's special envoy Moshe Dayan. In the event these failed because of Israeli intransigence but they could not be kept completely secret and their main effect was to strengthen distrust of King Abdullah which other Arab Governments did little to dispel and too often allowed themselves to encourage.

On 20 July 1951, when the King was entering the mosque al-Aqsa in Jerusalem, he was shot and killed by a Palestinian youth. At the trial a former Arab Legion officer who was nursing a grievance and had gone to live in Cairo was named as the instigator. Of the five others found guilty, the most prominent was Musa Husseini, a member of the Jerusalem clan whose leader, Hajj Amin Husseini, had been the most determined and uncompromising opponent of Zionism and the Mandate between the wars. He had thrown in his lot with the Axis Powers during the Second World War, but had returned to the Middle East in June 1946 and had become the leading figure in the so-called 'All Palestine Government' set up in the small area of Palestine around Gaza which was occupied by Egypt under her Armistice with Israel. Though it was possibly not unwelcome to Hajj Amin there is no evidence to connect the crime with the 'Gaza Government'.

Abdullah's elder son, Tallal, was mentally ill when he came to the throne. His reign opened with popular ovations, but by 11 August 1952 he had become so ill that his Government felt obliged to declare him unfit to rule. The succession passed smoothly to his eldest son, Hussein, who was only seventeen years old and was at school in England. Until his coming of age at eighteen and his enthronement on 2 May 1953 the duties of the Crown were vested in a Regency Council consisting of three elder statesmen, two from the East Bank and one from the West.

The long slow revolution in the Arab world – hitherto mainly directed against British or French domination began to take on a more radical complexion after the Second World War. The shock of defeat in the Palestine War powerfully reinforced disenchantment with the regimes responsible for its conduct and political violence increased in most Arabic speaking countries. King Abdullah fell a victim to these emotions but his death was not immediately followed by further political upheaval in Jordan. His long tradition of paternal rule had prevented the emergence of strong political antagonisms, while the strength of the British-officered Arab Legion provided an effective restraint on popular agitation.

The move away from paternalism under King Tallal was continued in the new reign by a new Prime Minister Fawzi al-Mulki, but the strength of the nationalist attack on the British connection and the fears and suspicions aroused by the Israeli policy of punishing individual forays of frontier villages into their lost lands, by organized military operations against their villages, led King Hussein to replace al-Mulki by the more conservative Tawfiq Abdul Huda in May 1954. His success in getting a more reliable parliament elected was dimmed by demonstrations of protest in the larger towns and this led him to seek popularity by demanding a revision of the Anglo-Jordan Treaty. The efforts of the Western Powers to organize the defence of the Middle East against a possible Soviet attack had had a partial success early in 1954 in the Baghdad Pact. This had enabled Great Britain to replace the Anglo-Iraqi Treaty of 1930 with an arrangement for reactivation of bases in time of war. The visit in December 1955 of the Chief of the Imperial General Staff, General Templer, to explore the possibility of a similar solution in Jordan caused the resignation of the four West Bank Ministers and serious rioting throughout the country.

The 1956–7 crisis

King Hussein bowed to the storm. His dismissal of General Glubb and most of the British officers in March was followed by an election in October 1956 which brought in a parliament of nationalists and a Prime Minister, Sulaiman Nabulsi, pledged to terminate the Anglo-Jordan Treaty. The Suez attack on Egypt by the forces of Britain, France, and Israel inflamed nationalist opinion further and the Anglo-Jordan Treaty was brought to an end by an Exchange of Notes in March 1957. The financial obligations it imposed on Britain were to be assumed by Saudi Arabia, Egypt, and Syria. In the same month the Jordan Government rejected American Aid under the Eisenhower Doctrine and moved towards diplomatic relations with the Soviet Union.

The King counter-attacked in April; with the aid of the bedouin regiments he foiled an army coup and strengthened by declarations of support from Washington and London, he imposed martial law, dissolved political parties, prorogued parliament, and purged the army and the civil service. The attempt to carry Jordan into the ranks of what were later called the 'progressive' Arab States had miscarried.

The only change brought about by the struggle between the King and the nationalists in 1957 was to transfer the main financial burden of keeping Jordan afloat from Great Britain to the United States of America; no more was heard of the Egyptian, Saudi Arabian, and Syrian commitments to replace the British subsidy. The basic predicament of Jordan's rulers remained unaltered. Jordan stayed in the front line facing Israel and was still the major target for Zionist punitive raids while her economy remained almost totally dependent on a major power committed to Israel's future. The ruler of Jordan still had every logical incentive to seek a settlement with Israel, as King Abdullah had tried to do seven years before. He could not do so because his subjects, two thirds of them Palestinians and a third of them destitute refugees from that part of Palestine now controlled by Israel, had strong emotional reasons for rejecting any settlement.

The ten years following 1957 were therefore perilous for Jordan and her King who was alternately engaged in fierce propaganda polemic with his Arab allies or warily joined with them in expressions of Arab solidarity. Because Jordan still contained a traditionally minded minority unequivocally loyal to the throne, an exceptionally resolute monarch was able to maintain and until 1967 even to strengthen his position. The crucial factor was that although she no longer had treaty relations with any Western power Jordan was able to count on their support because her independent existence seemed to them to be a necessary condition for preserving the precarious *status quo* on the borders of Israel.

The Arab Union

In February 1958 the two Arab countries in which Great Britain still retained some influence, Jordan and Iraq, tried to offset the emotional appeal which the union of Egypt and Syria exercised on their citizens by proclaiming a counter union of their own. This was killed six months later when the fall of the Hashimite monarchy in Baghdad moved Iraq decisively into the radical Arab camp. In this crisis King Hussein appealed for British military help but this could not be permanent and arrangements were made for a United Nations 'presence' which enabled the British troops to leave before the end of the year. Although Jordan's diplomatic relations with the UAR, broken in July 1958, were restored in the autumn of 1959, they remained strained through most of the period of Egyptian/Syrian union and the threat to Jordan's internal security was formidable. In 1960 the Prime Minister, Hazza al-Majali, and eleven others were murdered by a bomb explosion; in 1961 an attempt to blow up the Amman radio station was foiled. In the spring of 1961 King Hussein tried to start a serious dialogue with President Nasser, but relations with the UAR were again broken when Jordan immediately recognized the Syrian Government which broke away from Egypt in September of that year.

Jordan's relations with Saudi Arabia had tended to improve as Saudi relations with Egypt had deteriorated, and in September 1962 Jordan joined with the Saudis in supporting the traditional side in the struggle in Yemen which began after the death of the Imam Ahmad.

1963 was a difficult year for Jordan with severe internal disturbances in support of the Cairo Manifesto providing for union between Egypt and the newly installed Baathist regimes in Iraq and Syria. But the union movement proved abortive and in December 1963 King Hussein responded to President Nasser's invitation to the first Arab summit meeting called to restore Arab unity.

The Palestine Liberation Organization

For several years the Arab governments had been threatening war if Israel should carry out her plans to take water out of the Jordan Valley for irrigation in the Negev. When this event became imminent it was necessary to adopt some public attitude. President Nasser at least was aware that the Arab armies were in no state to challenge Israel, and he called the Arab Summit meeting in January 1964 to halt the drift to war resulting from the competition among the Arab States in the unreal bellicosity of their public statements about the problem of Israel. Among the issues which called forth this kind of competition was the question of the so-called Palestine entity.

The quarrel between those Arabs who accepted and those who rejected the Jordanian annexation of the rump of Palestine had never been settled. Although Jordan steadfastly asserted her sole right to speak for the Palestinians – in February 1960 she had offered Jordanian nationality to any Palestinian, wherever resident, who asked for it – she was unable to prevail. Egypt, although at one with Jordan in not wanting an immediate war with Israel, could not accept the total Jordan claim. In the event it was agreed that Ahmad Shuqairy, a Palestinian lawyer who had for years represented Saudi Arabia at the United Nations was commissioned to consult with his countrymen and draft a Palestinian National Charter for presentation to a conference in Jerusalem in May 1964. This conference duly endorsed Shuqairy's draft which established a Palestine Liberation Organization. The Charter stated *inter alia* that the PLO would not exercise any political sovereignty on the West Bank of the Jordan nor in the Gaza strip, but it also asserted that the Arab Palestinian people alone had the right to Palestine territory.

The Amman/Cairo *rapprochement* brought about by the Arab Summit meetings was never quite whole-hearted, and although Jordan accepted the Egyptian whip in breaking relations with West Germany in May 1965 she had already begun to move back to relations with Saudi Arabia as was shown by a frontier adjustment in her favour near Aqaba in August.

The Moslem Summit Movement

In the course of a State visit to Iran in December 1965, King Faisal joined with the Shah in calling for a Moslem summit. This was taken as a challenge to Egypt and was fiercely denounced in Cairo and Damascus. It received varying degrees of welcome from Tunisia, Jordan, Sudan, and Kuwait. Both sides were obliged by Arab public opinion to justify their policies in terms of Arab defence against Zionism and imperialism, and to claim to be better Moslems than each other. In this situation Shuqairy was able to make the maximum mischief. His Voice of Palestine had already started broadcasting from Cairo in March 1965, and although considerable effort was expended to bring about a *modus vivendi* between his PLO and the Jordan Government – in March 1966 an agreement between them was announced after talks with Shuqairy in Cairo – their objectives were fundamentally irreconcilable. As King Hussein put it in a letter to President Nasser dated 14 July 1966 – 'these saboteurs [the PLO] are seeking to push the Arabs into a war for which they are not yet ready.' In the same letter King Hussein defended his attitude to King Faisal's Moslem Front and this may have contributed to Nasser's decision announced a week later, not to attend a fourth Arab Summit meeting. The Summit agreement to refrain from inter-Arab attacks had finally broken down.

The Way to War

King Hussein's complaints about PLO activities were amply justified – Israeli reprisal raids for guerrilla actions mainly mounted from Syria, fell mainly on Jordan. There was a heavy raid on Qalqilya in September 1965, others on Irbid and Hebron districts in April 1966, and one on Samua supported by tanks and aircraft in November 1966 which led to sustained disorders in a number of West Bank towns. By the end of 1966 King Hussein had joined King Faisal and President Bourguiba as a target for the scurrility of broadcasts from Cairo, Damascus, and Baghdad and in the spring of 1967 was hitting back with suggestions that Egyptian troops should leave the Yemen for the Egyptian-Israeli border instead of leaving its defence to the UNEF. Taunts of this kind were one of the pressures which brought about the Six Day War.

Since the breakdown of the attempts at Arab unity in 1963 Syria had been governed by the Baath. The revolutionary Marxist wing of this party took control in a *coup d'état* in February 1966. In response to Israeli threats of reprisals for guerrilla raids the Syrian leaders made a joint defence agreement with Egypt in November. Tension on the Israel-Syria border increased in the early months of 1967 and the familiar pattern of Syrian shelling of Israel cultivation in the demilitarized zone recurred in April. This time however Israeli aircraft took a hand, penetrated deep into Syrian territory and shot down several Syrian fighters, two of which came down in Jordan. The Syrians believed Israeli menaces, and the pressure on Egypt to react grew heavy. Accused of sheltering behind the UNEF Nasser asked the Secretary-General for its withdrawal. Its departure entailed Egyptian occupation of Sharm al-Shaikh and two days later on 23 May he declared the Gulf of Aqaba closed to Israeli shipping.

Up to this point the Arab world had remained divided. Egyptian and Syrian broadcasts were still demanding the overthrow of King Hussein and the Jordan radio was saying out loud what the Syrians were saying more quietly, that Egypt was a paper tiger. The state of Jordan/Syrian relations was shown on 23 May when explosives intended for sabotage in Amman exploded prematurely in a Syrian car at the Jordan frontier post of Ramtha and killed fifteen Jordanians. However, once Nasser had risked war by closing the Straits of Tiran, the Arab States fell in behind him. King Hussein, who had been assured that Israel would not attack if he remained passive, hesitated for a week longer. Then on 30 May he flew to Cairo and signed a defence pact with Egypt which was immediately joined by Iraq. Hussein's position had become impossible as the war parties on either side gained the ascendancy. If war came, he was lost if the Israelis won, and equally lost if the Arabs won without Jordan. Six more days of tension were ended when the Israeli airforce attacked Egyptian airfields on 5 June.

For Jordan the result of the Six Day War was disastrous. It ended with the whole of the West Bank under Israeli occupation, the refugee population of the East Bank increased by about 200,000 and the economy practically non-existent.

Throughout 1968 there were almost daily artillery duels with Israel across the cease-fire lines in the Jordan Valley and on several occasions Israel launched heavy air and rocket attacks on Jordanian territory in reprisal for Palestinian commando raids. Jordan's internal stability was increasingly threatened by the rising power and prestige of the Palestinian guerrilla organizations. The Jordanian civilian and military authorities were divided in their attitude towards these organizations. Some were in favour of compromise while others wished to restrict and control their actions severely. In March the Jordanian Army and Palestinian commandos co-operated in a major engagement against an Israeli raiding force at Kerameh which inflicted heavier losses on the Israelis than on any previous occasion.

It was part of King Hussein's foreign policy to press continuously for the holding of a new Arab summit but for a long time he was unsuccessful, mainly owing to the opposition of King Faisal. When the summit was finally held in December 1969 Jordan derived little satisfaction as it only served to accentuate Arab divisions. Jordan was anxious to establish a co-ordinated Arab military policy but although the Iraqis had some 12,000 troops stationed in north Jordan, some Syrian units were moved into the same area in August 1969, and the Saudis maintained about 5,000 men near Kerak, no semblance of a cohesive Arab front against Israel was created.

Relations between the Jordanian authorities and the Palestinian guerrillas rapidly deteriorated during 1970. After each serious clash, which became increasingly frequent, an arrangement intended to avoid further clashes was made but it consistently broke down. The King still wavered between a policy of compromise with the Palestinians and accepting at least some of their demands, and listening to the advice of his 'hard-line' officers and advisers. The Palestinians were also divided in their attitude towards the Jordanian regime although the leading organization al-Fatah still aimed to avoid a direct confrontation with the authorities. The guerrillas as a whole were acting more and more like a 'state within a state' in Jordan and this increased the resentment of loyalist Jordanian Army elements and especially those of bedouin origin.

The situation deteriorated further after the King's endorsement on 26 July of the US Middle East peace initiative (or Rogers Plan) which the Palestinians regarded as a betrayal of their cause. The hijacking on 6–9 September of three Western airliners to a deserted air strip in east Jordan by the left-wing extremist Popular Front for the Liberation of Palestine led almost inevitably to the civil war which followed. The King appointed General Habis al-Majali as military Governor-General with sweeping powers and the Palestinians responded by calling a general strike.

By 17 September the fighting was general. It was heaviest in Amman and north Jordan – where the guerrillas, reinforced by Syrian armoured units that crossed the border on 19 September, held the towns of Irbid and Ramtha. Formal hostilities ended on 25 September when an inter-Arab mission representing Arab Heads of State who had hastily met in Cairo, arranged a cease-fire. This left the guerrillas in control of their two northern strongholds and some districts of Amman. Total casualties were variously estimated at 1,500 to 5,000 killed, and up to 10,000 injured. A high proportion were civilians.

Meeting in Cairo on 27 September, King Hussein and al-Fatah leader Yasir Arafat signed a 14-point truce agreement calling for the restoration of civilian rule and a series of further agreements were negotiated during the autumn. But the guerrillas were gravely weakened by the war and in the ensuing months they found themselves gradually expelled from the towns and confined to a few strongholds in the north. On 28 October King Hussein brought back one of his closest advisers Wasfi al-Tel as Prime Minister who adopted an uncompromising attitude towards the guerillas. The inter-Arab civilian and military commission which was set up after the civil war under the chairmanship of the Tunisian Premier Bahi Ladgham to mediate between the Palestinians and Jordanians withdrew in April 1971. Various Arab Heads of State expressed concern with the internal situation in Jordan but they were unable to exert much influence. In July 1971 the guerrilla military bases in Jordan were finally liquidated.

Jordan's position was still both isolated and dangerous. The anti-Palestinian campaign caused considerable emnity among other Arab regimes, especially in Libya, Iraq and Syria. Libya cancelled its aid to Jordan and Kuwait suspended it. In September 1971 the self-styled Palestinian Black September group assassinated the Prime Minister Wasfi al-Tel in revenge for the 1970 civil war.

As hopes of the US peace initiative behind the Rogers Plan fizzled out, Egyptians and Syrians talked of the inevitability of a new war with Israel. King Hussein declared that Jordan would not fight again because another conflict would only mean total disaster for the Arabs. But if the US could not or would not force an Israeli withdrawal from the River Jordan there was no other way in which Jordan could recover its lost territory. There were some of the king's Transjordanian supporters who favoured cutting the country's losses by letting the West Bank go and returning to the pre-1948 borders. But this was not acceptable to the king himself who has never abandoned his belief in the heritage of the Hashimites as the leaders of the Arab Revolt. He still regarded it as his responsibility to speak for the Palestinians and to regain the Old City of Jerusalem for the Arabs.

As had happened so often before, Jordan slowly mended its relations with the other Arab states. In September 1973 King Hussein amnestied all the Palestinian guerrillas still held in Jordanian prisons. About 1,000 were freed but they were not allowed to resume guerrilla operations from Jordanian territory.

When Egypt and Syria launched the October 1973 war to recover their lost territory, Jordan compromised. With no air cover to match Israel's Skyhawks and Phantoms, and no Soviet missile system, an all-out confrontation with Israel in the Jordan Valley meant certain disaster. But it would have been virtually impossible for Jordan to remain entirely aloof. Its solution was to send two armoured brigades to fight alongside Syria.

The move was diplomatically skilful. While the Jordanian army and territory were preserved, Jordan had played a role in the battle. Diplomatic relations and financial aid were restored by most Arab states. At the same time, Jordan's position vis-à-vis Israel was weakened in the aftermath of the war which ended with a stalemate but brought tangible political advantages to the Arabs. When, for the first time since 1957, American pressure was brought to bear on Israel to give up some of its conquest, Jordan was ignored. In 1974 it was the PLO which was gaining international recognition as the representative of the Palestinian people.

Even Jordan's ally Saudi Arabia, the only one of the three major oil states which had continued to provide a subsidy to Jordan after 1970, came round to this view. At the Arab summit meeting in Rabat in October all the other Arab states combined to place pressure on Jordan to accept their decision that the PLO was the sole legitimate representative of all the Palestinians with the right to set up an administration on any territory that might be liberated.

King Hussein gave way and from then on continued to declare that he felt bound by the Rabat resolution. However, he made no secret of his belief that the PLO would not be able to recover any lost territory without Jordan's help. Jordan continued to pay the salaries of West Bank government officials and provide funds to educational and religious institutions. West Bank mayors were regularly invited to Amman including some who publicly avowed support for the PLO.

One consequence of the second Egyptian–Israeli Disengagement agreement of September 1975 (Sinai 2) was to promote a Syrian–Jordanian entente, as President Assad of Syria and King Hussein shared the view that Egypt's virtual withdrawal from the Arab front with Israel presented a common danger to their two countries. In 1975 and 1976 a series of agreements provided for moves towards political, economic, and military 'integration and co-operation' between the two countries; but although these had positive results in many areas, and the two governments held regular consultations, they stopped well short of political federation or a merger of the two military commands which have to overcome both the obstacle of the different political nature of the two regimes and the fact that while the Syrian armed forces are Soviet-equipped Jordan's arms come from Western sources.

Jordan's reaction to President Sadat's peace initiative of 1977–8 was cautious and qualified. Although King Hussein was gratified by Egyptian proposals that the West Bank should be returned to Jordanian administration as a step towards a peace settlement, he refused to attend the Israeli–Egyptian–US summit at Camp David in September 1978 and expressed his disappointment over the results because they did not provide for an Israeli withdrawal from all the Occupied Territories or the restoration of Arab sovereignty over the West Bank and Gaza. When Egypt went on to conclude a treaty with Israel in March 1979, Jordan expressed its outright opposition and refused to join Egyptian – Israel negotiations on Palestinian autonomy in the Occupied Territories.

GOVERNMENT AND CONSTITUTION

The agreement with Winston Churchill in 1921 had stipulated that the Amir should rule constitutionally; an Organic Law was adopted in 1928 and a Constitution for the new Kingdom was passed in 1946. In practice, however, King Abdullah's powers were pervasive and the main check upon them was advice from the British Resident. On 1 January 1952 King Tallal signed a Constitution. It vested the Legislative Authority in the King and the National Assembly, made up of an appointed Senate and a Chamber of Deputies elected by adult male suffrage for a four-year term. The Executive Authority was vested in the King acting through his Ministers. By Article 51 the Prime Minister and the Ministers were individually and collectively responsible to the Chamber of Deputies.

The Assembly only met infrequently. Political parties were banned from 1957 onwards and when elections were held a high proportion of the candidates were returned unopposed.

The Assembly elected in fairly liberal conditions in 1962 was dissolved by the King when it refused a vote of confidence to the Prime Minister.

After the Rabat summit of October 1974 when the King accepted the PLO as the representative of the Palestinians the King reduced the number of Palestinians in the Cabinet from ten to four. The National Assembly was suspended pending the drawing up of a new Constitution recognizing the changed situation. In 1976 the King reconvened the Assembly but almost immediately dissolved it again in the wake of protests from the other Arab states that it violated the Rabat decision.

In April 1978 the King asked the Prime Minister to form a National Consultative Council to perform a similar function to the suspended parliament. The 60-member Council, which was to serve for two years, represented all regions of Jordan but not the occupants of the West Bank and the proportion of Palestinians was significantly lower than in the suspended parliament.

The country is divided into seven administrative divisions (*liwas*) under a Governor, and a desert area. The *liwas* are subdivided into districts under Administrative Councils, and Municipal Councils serve the towns and larger villages.

Armed Forces

The Jordanian Army, known as the Arab Legion until 1956, was raised for internal security purposes in 1921. Its first commander was Peake Pasha. In the 1930s under General Glubb it became an effective desert patrol which ended inter-tribal raiding among the Transjordan nomads. During the Second World War it played a distinguished part in operations in Iraq and Syria in 1941. Serving British officers were attached to the Legion from 1945 and a rapid expansion in the first half of the 1950s was financed by a British subsidy under the 1948 Treaty. The Jordanian Army preceded the independence of the State and played a major role in its construction under King Abdullah. Its cost still makes up the largest item in the budget; in 1951 and 1957 it exceeded the whole of the rest of Government expenditure. Until 1956 it was commanded and partly led by British officers and until about 1950 it mainly relied on British Middle East Forces for logistic support and technical services. The rank and file were generally recruited from tribesmen whose personal loyalties were given unreservedly to the King. Their basic education as well as their military training was provided by the Legion. The demand for more educated men as a result of the rapid growth of administrative and technical units in the early 1950s could not be met from the Legion's internal education system. Townsmen therefore came to be increasingly recruited and the army was no longer completely insulated from the radical nationalist political ideas current in the Arab world. Nevertheless the core of bedouin regiments personally loyal to the King has so far prevented Jordan's Army from playing the revolutionary role of many other Arab armies. Defence estimates for 1978 amounted to about one quarter of the total budget of $1,200 million.

SOCIAL AND ECONOMIC SURVEY

From its inception as the Amirate of Transjordan after the Cairo Conference of 1921 the main reason for the existence of the Jordan State has been the political convenience of other states. Its economy has always been precarious and for the last twenty years its political and social balance has been unstable. Until 1948 its population was overwhelmingly agricultural and pastoral, and standards of living and political awareness were low. The Turkish Government did little to administer the country which was part of the *vilayet* of Damascus and the main problems facing the Amir's Government in 1922 were public security and the control of nomadic lawlessness. These were solved by the Arab Legion, though there was naturally some backsliding during the anti-Zionist rebellion in Palestine which began in 1936. Land settlement was speedy and efficient and by 1939 political stability and a rather modest measure of prosperity had been achieved. The Second World War brought no fighting and no particular hardships to Jordan.

The 1948 war led to the incorporation of the poorer parts of Palestine into the newly proclaimed Hashimite Kingdom of Jordan and completely upset the balance which had been achieved. With the acquisition of the small part of Palestine successfully defended against the Zionists it brought to Jordan a new population twice as numerous as the East Jordanians, as King Abdullah's former Transjordanian subjects were now to be known. The elite section of this influx was better educated and socially more advanced than the corresponding class of East Jordanians and therefore posed a formidable threat to the balance of political power, while the destitute refugees from the areas of Palestine occupied by the Israeli State provided strong competition for jobs and homes to the ordinary East Jordanian townsman. Since 1948 the major internal problem for Jordan has been to integrate East and West Jordanians, politically, socially, and economically.

This problem has been aggravated by the fact that the refugees look to the United Nations Relief and Works Agency for some part of their needs and, since Agency ration scales in the word of the Agency's report for 1965–6 'provide about two thirds of the normal food intake of a poor Middle Easterner', are yet obliged to press heavily on Jordan's economy.

Nevertheless, despite the extremely unfavourable social and economic factors and constant internal and external threats to the country's stability, there was real economic progress between 1948 and 1967. The government administration was generally efficient and while much of the Palestinian population was inevitably a burden on the economy, the enterprise and skill of some of the Palestinians acted as a stimulus.

The IBRD mission of 1955 had recommended a ten-year economic development plan, and the Jordan Government brought out a Five-Year Plan to run from 1962 to 1967. It was superseded in 1965 by a Seven-Year Plan (1964–70) which was designed to raise the Gross National Product by about 50 per cent to 149 million Jordanian Dinars, and to reduce dependence on foreign assistance to JD 14.9 million annually. The 1967 war dealt a shattering blow to the Jordanian economy. Although economic viability had been a distant goal before 1967 and the country was destined to remain heavily dependent on foreign aid, per capita income increased steadily in the 1960s and there had been substantial development of the economic infrastructure, agricultural and mineral exports, light manufacturing industry, and tourism. The consequences of the war affected all these sectors with varying degrees of severity but its most serious long-term effect was to wreck the 1964–70 Seven-Year Plan in which so many hopes had been placed. Since Jordan was far from resigned to the permanent loss of East Jerusalem or to the occupied West Bank it lacked the incentive to devise a new revised plan for the rest of the country. After some measure of recovery in 1968 and 1969 the situation deteriorated again as a result of the civil war in September 1970.

In the light of these circumstances, the development of the Jordanian economy since 1971 has been remarkable. The psychological effect of the Rabat summit decisions of 1974 was to cause the government to consider the country's future without the West Bank and the result was the highly ambitious but not unrealistic Five-Year Plan for 1976–80. The virtual destruction of Beirut as a Middle Eastern services and commercial centre during the Lebanese civil war of 1975–6 brought many foreign companies to Amman as an alternative while the remittances from some 150,000 Jordanians working abroad gave strong assistance to the balance of payments.

Education

In common with most newly independent countries Jordan's educational facilities were rapidly expanded after the end of the Mandate. Arab education had been one major success of the British Mandate in Palestine and the influx of Palestinians after 1948 both stimulated and assisted education in Jordan. Legislation bringing all schools under Government control bore hardly on some foreign, mainly Christian, schools but on the whole education has both expanded and improved.

In 1976 UNRWA provided education for some 20 per cent of the total school population and foreign and national private schools for a further 10 per cent. There were 386,012 pupils in primary schools, 157,745 in secondary schools, and 11,873 in institutions of higher education. There was a University of Jordan near Amman and a University of Yarmouk at Irbid was established in 1977.

Agriculture

Agriculture, which accounts for about 15 per cent of GDP and some 20 to 30 per cent of exports, and employs more than a quarter of the labour force, remains the most important sector of the economy, although its share has been steadily declining with the loss of the West Bank to Israel and the shift of population towards the urban centres.

About 900,000 hectares (under 10 per cent) of the land is cultivated; it has been estimated there are seven million hectares of uncultivated land. There is rainfall on the East Jordan hills but further east the land is arid. About 80 per cent of the fruit-growing area, 45 per cent of the vegetable area and 25 per cent of the cereal area are situated on the West Bank. The main crops are cereals, lentils, beans, peas, vetches, tobacco and sesame. Fruit and vegetables are grown in the Jordan Valley.

Production depends heavily on the weather and varies significantly from year to year. Food imports are increasing with a serious effect on the balance of trade and the cost of living.

About 18 per cent of investment under the Five-Year Plan (1976–80) is allocated to agriculture with the aim of boosting valuable fruit and vegetable production from 30,000 hectares in 1975 to 62,000 hectares in 1980. However, agricultural development is obstructed by political considerations. The construction of the Maqarin dam on the River Yarmouk in the north is opposed by Israel because it will draw off water from the River Jordan.

Mining and Industry

Phosphates are mined at al-Hasa and Ruseifa and are Jordan's most consistent export although affected by the strong fluctuation in world prices. Output varied between 1.4 million tons and 1.7 million tons in 1974 and 1976 but revenues from phosphates rose from JD 4 million in 1973 to JD 19.2 million in 1976. Prospects for the industry improved with a series of long-term sales contracts to Eastern Europe in 1978, and the Jordan Phosphates Mine Company has forecast the quadrupling of exports to six million tons by 1980.

The long-delayed plan to extract potash from the Dead Sea was finally under way with sufficient funds by 1978 and the Arab Potash Company estimates that by the time the plant is fully operational the 1.2 million tons extracted annually should earn about $84 million in exports, Japan is seen as the main export target.

No oil has been discovered in Jordan despite considerable exploration efforts. The US Filon Exploration is the only company with an exploration concession at present.

Manufacturing industry, largely concentrated in Amman and Zerqa, is almost entirely of recent origin and accounts for less than 10 per cent of GNP. Food-processing, clothing, and construction materials form the bulk of the industries. New fertilizer factories, cement plants and a textile factory are included in the 1976–80 Plan.

Until the 1967 war, the tourist industry was one of Jordan's main foreign currency receipts but the loss of the main tourist attraction on the West Bank leaving Jordan with only Petra and Jerash caused receipts to fall from JD 12.3 million in 1966 to JD 3.1 million in 1973 and the number of visitors fell from 617,000 in 1966 to 268,200 in 1973. However, since tourists have been allowed to cross into Israeli-occupied territory in the Holy Land, the industry has recovered steadily with 887,500 visitors and receipts of JD 68.9 million in 1976. The surplus on travel in the current account was JD 12 million in the first quarter of 1978.

Transport and Communications

Since the establishment of Israel, Jordanians could only reach the Mediterranean through Syria and Lebanon, a roundabout and expensive route which was, moreover, quite often interrupted by political disagreements between Jordan and Syria. Jordan's only direct access to the sea is through Aqaba on the Red Sea. In 1948 this was merely a fishing harbour without any modern communications linking it with the centres of population. The port had been successfully developed first with British financial help and later with a loan from West Germany. Special phosphate and oil handling facilities have been installed and the tonnage of cargo handled by the port increased from 147,000 in 1957 to 829,870 in 1964.

The closure of the Suez Canal between 1967 and 1975 obliged Jordan to redirect much of its trade through Beirut but the development of Aqaba is now proceeding again. JD 29 million is to be spent to raise phosphate capacity to 1.2 million tons and general cargo handling capacity to 1.2 million tons by 1980.

The railway system consists of the section of the Ottoman-built Hejaz Railway from Deraa on the Syrian border through Amman to Maan and Ras Naqab in the south which was put back into use after World War I. A line has been built to carry phosphate rock from Hasa through Hittiya to Aqaba and its capacity is to be raised from 1.6 million tons to 7.5 million tons by 1980.

The state-owned national airline Alia has benefited from Amman's increasing importance as a regional centre. In 1978 it recorded a profit for the sixth successive year and announced plans to extend its flight network in America, Asia, and Africa.

Currency and Banking

The currency is the Jordanian dinar ($ 1 = JD 0.293 and £1 = JD 0.655 – August 1978). There has been a rapid expansion in the banking sector, stimulated by the difficulties of Beirut. There are a large number of Arab and Western commercial banks whose total deposits increased from JD 158 million to JD 227 million between the end of 1975 and the end of 1976. On 1 January 1978 a stock exchange opened in Amman and in April the country's first merchant bank.

Development and Economic Policy

The ambitious Five-Year Plan of 1976–80 calls for an investment of JD 765 million and an annual growth rate of 11.9 per cent. Domestic revenues are planned to increase by 16.5 per cent annually over the period with the aim of reducing Jordan's chronic budget deficits. The central purpose of the plan is to shift resources from the social services to the productive sectors to increase its share of GDP from 35 per cent to 44 per cent. Thus 29.9 per cent of investments are allocated to industry and mining, 18 per cent to agriculture and water, and 15.7 per cent to transport. Increases in defence spending are supposed to be kept down to five per cent a year.

Jordan is certain to remain heavily dependent on aid from the Arab oil states and Western countries (USA, UK, and West Germany). Prospects improved during 1978 because in addition to continuing budgetary and military aid from Jordan's traditional sources, good relations were restored with Libya and new economic ties were established with several East European countries. The Baghdad summit meeting in November 1978 brought a further inflow of Arab funds pledged to the front-line states.

Despite Jordan's chronic deficit in external trade, with visible exports and re-exports covering no more than 20 per cent of imports, the balance of payments situation has been remarkably healthy with the help of foreign aid, remittances from Jordanians working abroad and tourist receipts. In the summer of 1978 the buoyant foreign exchange situation allowed a certain liberalization of controls. Commercial banks no longer had to obtain Central Bank permission to provide foreign exchange, personal allowances for travel, education, and medical treatment were substantially increased, and Jordanians working abroad for more than three years were allowed to keep foreign currency accounts in Jordanian banks.

Inflation has been a serious problem for Jordan in the 1970s. It has been caused by inflationary wage settlements (due to the shortage of skilled labour), high import costs, and a sharp increase in the domestic money supply due to the large government deficit and the big expansion in credit granted to the private sector. The explosive growth of Amman (about 11 per cent a year), partly due to the decline of Beirut, provoked land speculation and investment in trade and business with a short turnover. Government measures to check inflation were partially successful in 1976 and 1977 but most of the causes remained.

VIII

LEBANON[1]

THE PEOPLE

The Lebanese are of very mixed ancestry with a great variety of racial types especially on the coastal lowlands. The great majority are Arabic-speaking; about 5 per cent speak Armenion; and in some middle-class Christian families French is spoken equally with Arabic. Both French and English are widely spoken in official and commercial circles.

From the end of the nineteenth century there has been considerable emigration from Lebanon although the rate declined from about 15,000 a year to 4,000 a year after World War II with increasing prosperity at home and reduced opportunities abroad. Between half a million and a million Lebanese live abroad in North and South America, Australia, and West Africa.

The civil war of 1975–6 and subsequent disturbances caused a further emigration of some 700,000 which showed signs of creating a semi-permanent Lebanese diaspora in the Arab world and Western countries, as only about half had returned by the end of 1978.

There has been no census since 1932 but a mid-1976 estimate gave a population of 2.96 million compared with 2.58 million in 1968 and 1.41 million in 1953. A private survey in 1975 stated there were about 1.5 million non-Lebanese resident in Lebanon of whom about 400,000 are Palestinians. The authorities have made the acquisition of Lebanese nationality increasingly difficult. The natural annual increase is estimated at three per cent.

A 1975 estimate of the population of Beirut, the capital, was 1.5 million. Other main towns are Tripoli, 200,000 (1970 estimate); Zahle, 40,000; Sidon, 36,000.

[1] For geographical description and history see pp. 504–12, where Syria and Lebanon are treated as a single entity.

Religious divisions are of greater political importance in Lebanon than in any other Arab state. The largest single community is the Maronite Catholics with about 30 per cent of the population. Among the Christians there are also substantial communities of Greek Orthodox, Greek Catholics, Armenian Orthodox, Armenian Catholics, and Protestants. Among the Moslems there is a small majority of Sunnis over Shiis while about 6 per cent of the population are Druzes. There are about 7,000 Jews.

As a political compromise governments have refrained from holding a census since 1932. The 1932 census showed the Christians to be in a small majority of six to five over non-Christians and political positions were allocated accordingly. It is quite possible that the Christians have now lost their majority owing to the higher birth rate among Moslems and the greater tendency for Christians to emigrate. However, there is no prospect of a census being held to establish the true position.

POST-INDEPENDENCE HISTORY

During 1944 the French Government gradually handed over its mandatory prerogatives to Lebanon to give the country control over customs, concessionary companies, press censorship, and public security until by 1945 Lebanon possessed almost all the powers of a sovereign government. The French retained only the locally recruited *troupes spéciales*, which remained attached to their own local command. However, the French Government had not abandoned the idea of replacing the lost mandate with a special treaty and on 17 May 1945 landed a contingent of Senegalese troops in Beirut to reinforce the French army in Syria and Lebanon. The Lebanese assumed that the French were planning to force a treaty on Lebanon which would limit the country's sovereignty. The strong public reaction reinforced by support from France's Allies obliged the French to give way. On 1 August 1945 the *troupes spéciales* were handed over to Lebanon and Colonel Fuad Chehab was appointed commanding officer of the new Lebanese Army.

The 1943 elections had resulted in an overwhelming victory for the Constitutional Bloc led by the Maronite Bishara al-Khoury and his principal Moslem allies led by Riyadh al-Sulh. The new Chamber of Deputies elected Bishara al-Khoury President of the Republic and he called upon al-Sulh to form a Government. As the joint authors of the National Pact al-Khoury and al-Sulh were regarded as the founders of Lebanon's independence in the form in which it was finally achieved two years later.

As soon as the last French troops had left Lebanon President al-Khoury took the initiative in restoring good relations with the former mandatory power. Lebanon was one of the five signatory states of the Protocol of Alexandria of September 1944 which led to the foundation of the League of Arab States in March 1945. Lebanon was also a founder member of the United Nations.

The task of creating a viable political system was not easy for the Lebanese Republic with the heterogeneous and often conflicting elements among its people. President al-Khoury achieved it through the creation of a machine consisting of political 'bosses' who could control the country through traditional affiliations. For a time he was remarkably successful and it may be said that his methods prevented Lebanon's disintegration and ensured its survival as an independent state. But they also encouraged factionalism and corruption which subsequently became the hallmarks of Lebanese political life. The increasing authoritarianism which President Khoury needed to maintain himself in power produced a counter-reaction which ultimately led to his downfall.

From 1943 onwards there were numerous defections by regional political leaders from his coalition. However, he was still able to ensure an overwhelming victory for his allies in the 1947 elections and had no difficulty in persuading Parliament to amend the constitution in order to vote him a second term of office in 1949.

In the 1951 elections President Khoury still succeeded in having some 60 of his supporters elected among the 77 members of the Chamber of Deputies. But the regime was increasingly unpopular in the country as a whole.

In the elections opposition crystallized around a group in the Chouf area of Mount Lebanon led by the Druze socialist

Kamal Jumblat, head of one of the principal Druze clans, and the Maronite Camille Chamoun.

Opposition to President Khoury did not run on sectarian lines. His mildly Arab nationalist foreign policy was satisfactory to most Lebanese Moslems and although all the key posts in the state, such as the command of the army and security services, were still reserved for Christians the proportion of Moslems and Druzes in the Government service was significantly increased. Finally as long as Riyadh al-Sulh headed the Government (he was Prime Minister continuously from 1943 to 1951 except for January 1945 to December 1946) the Moslem community as a whole could feel that their interests were strongly represented.

In the summer of 1951 Riyadh al-Sulh was assassinated in Jordan. This gravely weakened President Khoury's position and in 1952 the Jumblat/Chamoun group spearheaded the movement which forced him to resign on 18 September, two years before the end of his term. Five days later the Chamber of Deputies elected Camille Chamoun.

President Chamoun 1952–8

Camille Chamoun was elected with high hopes that he would institute a reformist and progressive regime. If these hopes were not realized it was largely because the influence of external events aroused sectarian differences which had lain dormant under President Khoury. However, in the initial stages of his presidential term Chamoun's problems were chiefly domestic. He had come to power at the head of a loose and temporary coalition of traditional political leaders, who had been excluded from power by President Khoury, and middle-class reformers outside the establishment. Inevitably this coalition soon fell apart and many of its leading members such as Kamal Jumblat himself, turned against him. However, Chamoun showed considerable skill in consolidating his position and in undermining the power of the traditional leaders.

Under Chamoun the liberal and laissez-faire economic policies inaugurated by President Khoury were maintained. These were undoubtedly suited to the mercantile characteristics of the Lebanese. Moreover there was no Government machine capable of administering socialist or *dirigiste* policies. The lack of State controls in Lebanon, in contrast to the increasingly centralized economies of most of its neighbours, attracted a flow of Arab and foreign capital to Beirut which was largely responsible for the country's marked prosperity in the 1950s. Similarly the freedom of the written and spoken word in Lebanon contrasted with the growing authoritarianism in most other independent Arab states. Beirut became the one Arab capital where all types of political ideas found expression and where Arab political exiles of various shades found refuge.

Nevertheless a Swiss type of neutrality was not possible for Lebanon; it could not have insulated itself from the emotional currents sweeping the Arab world even if it had tried. This became apparent from 1954 when the Arab world began to polarize between a radical 'neutralist' camp led by Abdul Nasser and Egypt and a pro-Western camp led by Nuri Said's Iraq and the Baghdad Pact. Although Chamoun accepted the impracticality of Lebanon joining the Baghdad Pact he made no secret of his pro-Western inclination. Lebanese Moslems, on the other hand, who had felt the weakness of their position in Lebanon since the death of Riyadh Sulh were strongly attracted to Abdul Nasser as the rising star of Arab nationalism. In effect this meant the breakdown of the 'National Pact' and the division of Lebanese opinion between Arab nationalists (mostly, but not exclusively, Moslems) and Lebanese nationalists (mostly, but not exclusively, Christians).

The crisis sharpened suddenly with the nationalization of the Suez Canal Company and the subsequent Suez crisis which raised Abdul Nasser to a new peak of popularity. As an Arab state, Lebanon officially sympathized with Egypt, but President Chamoun refused to break off diplomatic relations with Britain and France as Abdullah Yafi the Prime Minister and Saib Salam, the two leading Moslems in the Government, were urging. Yafi and Salam resigned and Chamoun formed a new Government led by the veteran Sami al-Sulh and with Dr. Charles Malik as Foreign Minister. This amounted to a declaration of war against neutralist and Nasserist influences in Lebanon. Sami al-Sulh had little following among Lebanese Moslems and Dr. Malik, who had for many years been Ambassador to the US and delegate to the UN, was known as strongly pro-Western.

In 1957 Lebanon, against strong Moslem opposition, accepted the Eisenhower Doctrine which purported to guarantee Middle Eastern states against foreign (i.e. Communist) subversion. Chamoun's opponents, Christian and Moslem, formed a united opposition which fought the parliamentary elections as a National Front. In the elections Chamoun exerted all his influence to see that an overwhelming majority of his supporters were elected and Salam, Yafi, and Jumblat were all defeated. The National Front was convinced that Chamoun's intention was to use his majority in Parliament to amend the constitution to enable him to have a second consecutive term of office. With its leaders excluded from the Chamber the Front was forced into unconstitutional opposition. Bomb incidents became increasingly frequent in Beirut and Jumblat's Chouf area of Mount Lebanon. Chamounists were alarmed and Arab nationalists aroused by the declaration of the Syrian/Egyptian union in February 1958 which brought Nasserism to Lebanon's borders.

The assassination on 8 May 1958 of an opposition (Christian) newspaper editor was the signal for the National Front to begin an armed insurrection. There was serious fighting in Tripoli and virtually all the Moslem and Druze majority areas in the country, including the Basta quarter of Beirut, turned themselves into rebel strongholds receiving arms and support from Syria. General Chehab, the army commander, rejected Chamoun's orders to suppress the rebellion and confined the role of the Lebanese Army to holding the ring for the disputants and preventing the rebellion from spreading. Although a large majority of army officers were Christians the proportion of Moslems was higher among NCOs and privates and General Chehab was uncertain of the loyalty of his troops if the situation should deteriorate into open civil war.

The Lebanese Government accused the UAR before the UN Security Council of aiding and instigating the rebellion. The UN sent observers to report on the situation but the results were inconclusive. The situation worsened even if open civil war was avoided; Beirut was under dusk-to-dawn curfew for five months. Elation of the opposition when Nuri Said was overthrown in an apparently pro-Egyptian coup on 14 July 1958 turned to anger when the US Government, fearing that all pro-Western forces in the Arab world might be swept away, answered President Chamoun's urgent request for help by landing 10,000 US Marines in Lebanon who were deployed in and near the capital.

If Chamoun and his supporters had expected the US to help him suppress the rebellion and ensure his second term of office they were disappointed. US Secretary of State Robert Murphy arrived in Beirut on 16 July as President Eisenhower's special representative and at once set about mediating between the two sides to reach the compromise that was essential if the Lebanese Republic was to survive. The consensus soon settled on General Chehab as Chamoun's successor. Although Chehab had only grudging support from many Christians and was bitterly accused of treachery by the more extreme Chamounists he was the only prominent Maronite who enjoyed some measure of confidence from all communities. He was elected President by Parliament on 31 July. However, Chamoun refused to step down until the last day of his term, 22 September, and the emergency continued.

The country came closest to civil war when President Chehab took office. When he appointed a Government with a majority of National Front sympathizers and led by Rashid Karami the leader of the insurrection in Tripoli, the Christians reacted with a general strike supported by armed action of the paramilitary Katayib party. When the situation deteriorated Chehab formed a new emergency four-man cabinet headed by Karami but including also the leader Pierre Jemayel. Under the slogan 'no victor, no vanquished' the Karami Government succeeded in restoring normality.

President Chehab 1958–64

With his shrewd and relatively objective understanding of the problem of governing Lebanon, President Chehab set about restoring the National Pact and adapting it to new circumstances following the state of near civil war. In foreign relations he restored the neutrality of Lebanon's attitude between the radical non-aligned and conservative pro-Western camps in the Arab world. In essence he revived President Khoury's policy, in a form suitable for the 1960s, by supporting Arab nationalist causes while safeguarding Lebanon's sovereignty and abstaining from projects for Arab political union.

Domestically Chehab's first task was to restore and strengthen national unity. His first instinct was to attempt to destroy the sectarian factionalism which was the basis of Lebanese political life but he soon realized that this would only leave a vacuum. Instead he chose to bypass the traditional system while allowing it free play.

In the 1960 elections for a parliament expanded from 77 to 99 members, almost all the political leaders with army following, Chamounist, anti-Chamounist, or neutral, were elected. But increasingly Chehab relied upon his own cadre of loyal technocrats to govern the country. Since he retained the loyal support of the army this opened him to the charge of ignoring the democratically elected parliament to govern through a concealed military dictatorship. But Chehabism gained the support of most progressive and moderate reformers in the country. Chehab reduced his official contacts with politicians to a minimum and moved his personal office to his private residence outside Beirut where for the first time in the history of the Lebanese Republic it was properly staffed by competent civil servants.

Aware that the key to unity and stability in Lebanon was that the Moslem and Druze communities should feel that the country belonged as much to them as to the Christians President Chehab took steps to see that more Moslems and Druzes were appointed to Government posts. The fifty-fifty principle for the allocation of posts between the two communities was applied even at the expense, in certain cases, of a decline in standards.

Chehab also favoured the principle of greater equality of treatment for the various regions of Lebanon. The public works policy of the Chehab regime was to devote attention to the previously neglected (and principally Moslem) areas outside Beirut and Mount Lebanon. The declared aim which was on its way to being achieved by 1964 was to bring roads, running water, and electricity to every Lebanese village. Although there was no serious question of abandoning Lebanon's basically laissez-faire principles the need to introduce some degree of planning was obvious. President Chehab called upon a French organization, the Institut de Recherches et de Formation en vue de Développement (IRFED), to prepare a comprehensive report on Lebanon's social and economic conditions which was published during his last term of office.

Corruption and inefficiency in the administration and factionalism in political life were not eliminated during President Chehab's term of office. Six years were too short for such fundamental changes. But Chehab's achievements were considerable. Taking office in a supreme crisis he restored national unity and went far towards assisting all the communities to feel they had a stake in the country. He left office with dignity after refusing repeated efforts to allow an amendment of the constitution to enable him to serve a second term.

President Helou 1964–70

In August 1964 a new parliament met to elect Charles Helou, a lawyer and former Minister, to succeed President Chehab. As President-elect, Helou attended the second Arab summit meeting in Alexandria in September to discuss Israeli plans to divert the Jordan waters. Lebanon's position was crucial because on the one hand it felt its defences were inadequate to hold a possible Israeli attack if the River Hasbani, a tributary of the Jordan, was diverted inside its territory while on the other it was not prepared to have other Arab forces stationed on its soil for additional protection. Most of the Arab states showed understanding of Lebanon's position.

President Helou pledged himself to continue President Chehab's reform policies but he lacked Chehab's power and authority. The attempt to bypass parliament by appointing a Government in July 1965 under Rashid Karami with all its members from outside the Chamber of Deputies aroused strong opposition from Lebanese political leaders and had to be abandoned a year later. However, the Karami Government did institute a sweeping reform of the civil service which involved the enforced retirement of a number of senior judges and diplomats.

In October 1966 the country's mercantile economy was seriously shaken by the failure of Intra, the country's biggest bank. Foreign investors' and depositors' confidence was affected and the dangers of the total lack of Government supervision of Lebanon's economic system became apparent. The Government undertook the reform of the banking system and set up a special body to guarantee small deposits.

Except for a brief air engagement Lebanon was not directly involved in the June 1967 war but the whole country was aroused and there was a serious danger of Christian/Moslem differences being sharpened as in 1956. Anti-British and anti-US feeling reached a high pitch, especially among the Moslems, and there was serious rioting and damage to Anglo-US property on 10 June. The British and US ambassadors were asked to leave but they returned in September.

The war and its outcome did further damage to business confidence. Tourism, construction, and other important sectors all suffered. But the most serious consequence of the war for Lebanon was the growth in political and military power of the Palestinian guerrilla organizations. Unlike Syria and Egypt, Lebanon lacked the means to control their activities. In Beirut they had virtually complete freedom to publicize their cause which had strong emotional support from many sectors of the Lebanese public. While most Lebanese had some sympathy with the Palestinian struggle, opinion ranged from those such as the Maronite political leaders Camille Chamoun, Raymond Eddé, and Pierre Jemayel who believed that the Palestinians should not infringe Lebanon's sovereignty and that their guerrillas should be excluded from Lebanese territory, to those such as the Socialist Party leader Kamal Jumblat who felt that it was Lebanon's duty to lend them all possible support. All Lebanese were sharply aware of the danger of Israeli reprisals and of Lebanon's relative defencelessness. However, Lebanon managed fairly well to stay apart from the Arab–Israeli conflict until 28 December 1968 when an Israeli helicopter-borne commando raid on Beirut destroyed thirteen civil aircraft. The raid was a reprisal for an earlier attack on an Israeli air-liner at Athens by two Palestinians who, the Israelis said, had come from Beirut. Lebanon at once appealed to the UN Security Council and disclaimed responsibility for commando activities on its territory.

The raid was followed by violent demonstrations led by students demanding that Lebanon improve its defences and adopt a more anti-Israeli line. In January 1969 the Cabinet of Abdullah Yafi resigned and was replaced by one led by Rashid Karami.

The issue of the Palestinian guerrilla presence in Lebanon had become of the utmost seriousness for the country, threatening to provoke civil war. In April, after a clash between the Lebanese Army and al-Saiqa, the commando group supported by the Syrian Baathists, there was serious rioting in Beirut and other towns.

As Israel continued to launch reprisal raids against guerrilla bases in Lebanon there were frequent clashes between the guerrillas and the Lebanese army in which the Palestinians suffered severe losses. In late October negotiations to end the dispute began in Cairo and on 2 November 1969 a ceasefire was arranged followed by an agreement between the Lebanese army and the Palestinian leadership whereby Lebanon endorsed the presence of guerrillas on its territory in return for a pledge by the guerrillas to co-operate with the Lebanese army. The Palestinians were also given the right to administer their own refugee camps in Lebanon.

At the end of March 1970 there was renewed threat of civil war after clashes between Palestinian guerrillas and the right-wing Christian Katayib in which forty Palestinians died. The crisis was surmounted with the help of Salah Buwaisir, the Libyan Foreign Minister, and the Cairo Agreement was again affirmed by both sides. In June the Government served notice that the guerrillas would be banned from firing rockets across the frontier and from carrying arms in the cities. The ban had little effect, but its announcement coincided with a particularly heavy flow of refugees from the southern border areas which provoked a threat by Imam Moussa al-Sadr, leader of the predominantly Shii southern Moslems, to paralyse the country's vital services failing adequate defence measures. The Government then voted £l 30 million to help an estimated 22,000 southerners driven from their homes by Israeli incursions. On 17 August the National Assembly elected (on the third ballot and by a majority of one) Sulaiman Franjieh, the Economics Minister, to succeed President Helou in September. The result caused some surprise as it had been widely expected that General Chehab would be re-elected or, when he refused to accept nomination, a 'Chehabist' candidate. The Chehabist camp was weakened by the last minute defection of Kamal Jumblat, Interior Minister and Progressive Socialist leader.

President Franjieh 1970–76

President Franjieh was the dark horse candidate of the anti-Chehabist Centre Bloc in parliament. But he soon showed his own independence of mind and toughness of character (a well-known feature of the North Lebanese). He chose the veteran Moslem politician Saib Salam to head the new Government and gave him his full support when, after ten days of vain attempts to satisfy all the factional interests inside parliament, Salam formed a cabinet entirely from outside it consisting mainly of young and highly educated 'technocrats'. The Lebanese public who had become increasingly exasperated by the sterile activities of the elected politicians, generally welcomed the new Government.

At first it seemed that Lebanon's internal stability had been helped by several factors. The Jordanian civil war and its aftermath had left the Palestinian resistance organizations in a weakened condition and therefore less of a threat to Lebanon's security. Also, the assumption of power by General Assad in Syria resulted in an immediate improvement in Syrian/Lebanese relations. A number of outstanding economic and administrative disputes were settled and in March 1971 President Franjieh made the first visit of a Lebanese Head of State in Damascus since independence.

Yet the 'technocrat' government had to cope with a different type of disorder as a series of strikes and disturbances swept the country, with students, teachers, peasants, and bank employees demanding improved conditions and social reforms. In 1972 the Palestinian guerrilla organizations recovered sufficiently to mount attacks on Israel from southern Lebanon, causing increasingly severe Israeli reprisals. Following the Munich Olympics massacre in September, Israel bombarded refugee camps in southern Lebanon which it claimed were sheltering guerrilla bases.

Parliamentary elections in April led to the re-election of many traditional political leaders and in May the 'technocrat' government was replaced by one almost entirely from inside parliament, but still headed by Saib Salam.

A new threat to Lebanon's fragile unity came with an Israeli commando raid on Beirut on 10 April 1973 and the killing of three Palestinian leaders. Tension rose as Palestinians accused the Lebanese authorities of offering no resistance to Israel. Saib Salam resigned when his demand for the resignation of the army commander in chief was refused. As Amin Hafez formed a government, violence erupted between the army and Palestinians and President Franjieh declared a state of emergency. Hafez reached an agreement with the guerrilla leadership that allowed the emergency regulations to be removed but his own leadership proved ineffective and he was soon replaced by a more traditional politician Takieddin al-Solh. Lebanon was largely successful in remaining out of the October 1973 Arab-Israeli war. The Lebanese Army did not interfere with the estimated 400 Palestinian guerrillas operating in southern Lebanon but these only played a minor role in the war.

In 1974 Lebanon benefited indirectly from the rising incomes of the Middle Eastern oil states and most sectors of the economy were flourishing but the twin threats remained of internal social discontent, resulting in widespread strikes, and hostility between much of the Lebanese Christian population and the Palestinians, which led to frequent clashes between the Christian militia and the guerrillas. Israeli reprisal raids caused unrest among the predominantly Shii Moslem southern population. Their spokesman and leader exonerated the Palestinians and blamed the regime for failing to provide protection. Ominously, the Takieddin al-Solh government fell in September after the resignation of ministers supporting the socialist leader Kamal Jumblat on the issue of the disarmament of the population. He was replaced by his cousin Rashid al-Solh.

Civil War

In 1975 the Israeli reprisal raids on southern Lebanon were overshadowed by the civil strife in the country which developed increasingly along Moslem-Christian lines. The sources of the conflict did not lie only in the Palestinian problem and the presence of some 400,000 stateless Palestinian Arabs in the country, although this was one of the principal factors. Severe social and political tensions had long existed. The laissez-faire system on which the country's commercial prosperity was based left much of the population poor and deprived. Secondly the Moslems, aware that they were almost certainly a majority, increasingly resented the Christians' domination of the country. Thirdly, the post-1967 war period saw the rise of the Palestinian guerrilla movements and their continuation in the Palestinian Liberation Organization which concentrated most of its military action on Lebanon following the expulsion of the guerrillas from Jordan in 1970–71.

The first signs of sectarian trouble began appearing in principally Moslem Tripoli in March and then spread to the capital Beirut.

The incident that may be said to have sparked off the war was the massacre of the Palestinian occupants of a bus by Christian militia on 13 April 1975 but the conflict was almost certainly inevitable. The Palestinian leaders declared their intention to keep out of the conflict but increasingly allowed themselves to be drawn into it.

On 15 May Prime Minister Rashid al-Solh resigned after placing full responsibility on the Christian Falangist militia. President Franjieh then announced the formation of an emergency cabinet of seven army officers and one civilian, but lacking any support from the main political groups it resigned immediately. Franjieh then called on Rashid Karami to form his eighth cabinet but he faced difficulties in forming a government because of the refusal of Kamal Jumblat's Progressive Socialist Party to serve with the Falangists. Finally Karami formed on 30 June a six-man cabinet without Falangists or PSP but introducing former President Camille Chamoun as Minister of the Interior to represent right-wing Christian interests.

Despite numerous local cease-fire arrangements which brought periods of relative calm, fighting spread to all parts of the country as the ordinary security forces were too weak to cope with the warring armed gangs. Scores of buildings were bombed or burned and numerous kidnappings and other atrocities occurred. Diplomatic efforts by Syria and other Arab states to resolve the crisis failed as the two sides became increasingly polarized. Lebanese Moslems were demanding a total restructuring of Lebanon's political system to give them more power, while the Christians held fiercely to the concept of a Lebanon with its own separate identity from the neighbouring Arab states. The concept of partition began to gain ground among the Christians. The conflict was greatly exacerbated by outside intervention in support of the different parties. Iraq supported the Palestinian leftists with arms and volunteers while Israel increasingly sided with the Christians. Syria initially gave support to the Palestinians but feared that an outright Palestinian victory would provoke Israeli intervention. Egypt, on hostile terms with Syria because of Syrian opposition to its second Sinai disengagement agreement with Israel of September 1975, opposed Syrian intervention in Lebanon.

In January 1976 the Christian Falangists blockaded the Palestinian refugee camps and leftist Palestinian forces responded by attacking Christian villages on the coast. Syria, which had sworn to prevent partition, if necessary by force, intervened by allowing Palestine Liberation Army forces (of the PLO) under its control to enter the country and this led to a Syrian-sponsored cease-fire on 22 January and the formation of a Syrian/Lebanese/Palestinian Higher Military Committee to supervise it.

An uneasy calm prevailed for several weeks but it was broken by political kidnappings, and a group of army deserters broke away to form a Lebanese Arab Army under Lieutenant Ahmed al-Khatib. The Palestinian/leftist forces made gains during March and April until they controlled some 70 per cent of the country. President Franjieh refused the leftist call for his resignation and barricaded himself in the presidential palace at Baabda. At this point Syrian forces intervened to halt the leftist advance, first revealing the split between Syria and the leftist Palestinian forces that was eventually to develop into an open alliance between Syria and the Lebanese right.

Parliament met and 90 deputies voted on 10 April to amend the Constitution to enable a new President to be elected six months before the expiration of the incumbent's term of office. On 24 April Franjieh reluctantly signed the amendment and on 8 May Elias Sarkis, a supporter of the former President Fuad Chehab, and strongly favoured by the Syrians, was elected. Fighting was general throughout the country in May and the leftists made further gains. On 1 June Syrian forces intervened on a large scale, advancing to occupy the Bekaa Valley and over Mount Lebanon where they met fierce resistance from the Palestinian/leftist forces.

The dispatch of a small Arab peace-keeping force in July succeeded in separating the two sides in Beirut. But President Franjieh refused to give way to President-elect Sarkis and appointed the hard-line Camille Chamoun as his Foreign Minister. Christian forces besieged Palestinian refugee camps in their territory and one of them, Tel al-Zaatar in eastern Beirut, became a symbol of Palestinian resistance. This fell on 12–13 August after seven weeks of siege and heavy loss of life.

On 23 September President Sarkis was sworn in at the Syrian-held town of Shtaurah. Offensives by Syrian forces in the centre and south of the country in September and October forced the hard-pressed Palestinians to retreat but a series of meetings by Syrian, Lebanese, Palestinian, and Arab League representatives failed to find a solution to the conflict. This had to await the outcome of the Arab summit meetings arranged through Saudi mediation in Riyadh and later in Cairo. These effectively endorsed Syria's role in Lebanon and enabled the Syrian forces to form the bulk of a more effective 30,000-strong Arab Deterrent Force. During November the ADF advanced gradually into Beirut to separate the combatants and reopen key roads. On 9 December President Sarkis appointed a new Cabinet of technocrats headed by Selim al-Hoss, a banker.

The civil war had killed some 45,000, injured 100,000 and caused more than half a million to flee the country. Much of the commercial heart of Beirut was destroyed and the country's service-based economy was brought to a standstill. Moreover, the end of the war had not brought any resolution of Lebanon's political problem. The already weak security forces had disintegrated and President Sarkis, with his country occupied by a large Syrian army, had no instrument with which to enforce the authority of the Lebanese state.

President Sarkis 1976–

In 1977 Lebanon made a low and partial recovery from the effects of the civil war but the conflict between Christian rightist forces and Palestinians near the southern borders remained unresolved. Syrian forces remained north of the Litani River to avoid provoking Lebanese intervention.

The Lebanese Front, comprising Maronite political and religious leaders, insisted that all Lebanese territory must be 'liberated from Palestinian occupation' but there was a division with the Maronite leadership. The Falangist leader Pierre Jemayel, showed greater willingness to compromise than the National Liberal Party leader, former President Camille Chamoun. In March Jemayel refused to support a general strike called by Chamoun to protest against President Sarkis's replacement of the army commander by a moderate more acceptable to Lebanese Moslems.

The danger of a revival of sectarian violence constantly threatened the regime. The task of rebuilding an effective Lebanese security force was slow and difficult. A series of explosions in the rightist Christian areas of Beirut in January was followed by retaliations against Moslems. The murder by unidentified assassins of the Druze leftist leader Kamal Jumblat on 16 March was followed by Druze attacks on Christian villagers and counter reprisals.

A cease-fire in the south in September involving Lebanese rightists, Palestinians, and Israel, arranged through US mediation, failed to hold and in December President Sadat of Egypt's peace initiative brought demonstrations and strikes from both Christians and Palestinians who feared a separate Egyptian/Israeli peace without a settlement of the Palestine problem.

In January 1978 the situation improved to some degree with signs of a political entente developing between the various factions. A declaration by President Sarkis that a solution to the Middle East problem could not be achieved by the permanent settlement of Palestinians in Lebanon was supported by Lebanese Christians and also the PLO. But there was a sharp setback in February with a serious clash between Syrian forces of the ADF and right-wing militia backed by some senior right-wing Lebanese officers. The former somewhat unnatural alliance between the Syrians and the Lebanese rightists was destroyed in 1978 and the latter received increasingly open backing from the Israelis.

On the night of 14/15 March Israel launched a full-scale invasion of southern Lebanon using tanks and air cover. Although the immediate cause of the invasion was the Palestinian guerrilla attack near Tel Aviv on 11 March, the Israeli objective was the destruction of the Palestinian guerrilla bases in southern Lebanon. The Israelis advanced to the River Litani. Syrian troops were not involved because they remained north of the river. Some 1,000 Palestinians and Lebanese were killed and 80 per cent of the villages in the south were damaged. About 200,000 Lebanese fled northwards, creating a serious refugee problem in Sidon and Beirut.

According to UN Security Council Resolution 425 of 19 March, troops of a UN International Force in Lebanon (UNIFIL) began to arrive immediately and the Israelis withdrew in stages until they had left Lebanese territory by mid-June. However, they continued to provide strong backing to the Lebanese Christian enclaves along the southern border.

In the summer of 1978 the Maronite camp was weakened by the deep split, reflecting an ancient rivalry, which took place between the Falangists, mainly of Mount Lebanon, and supporters of ex-President Franjieh in the north. On 13 June the ex-President's son Tony and his family were massacred by Falangists and Franjieh vowed revenge. The Syrians were close to Franjieh and the event contributed to a further deterioration in the relations between the ADF and the Lebanese rightists. In July and again in September-October, Syrian forces of the ADF surrounding Christian East Beirut bombarded the area heavily. As Israel threatened to come to the aid of the Christians, Arab foreign ministers met urgently in Lebanon and agreed that Syrian forces on the perimeter of East Beirut should be replaced by non-Syrians of the ADF. A measure of calm was restored but the situation remained highly explosive as the Maronite leadership defiantly called for the liberation of Lebanon from the Syrian occupation and vaunted their alliance with Israel which Syria and the other Arab states deplored. President Sarkis told his people that only they, and no outside agency, could save Lebanon from disintegration.

GOVERNMENT AND ADMINISTRATION

The Lebanese Constitution dates from 1926 with amendments in 1943 and 1947. Lebanon is a Republic with a President who is Head of State and of the Executive. It has a single Chamber of Deputies and a Council of Ministers. The President is elected by a two-thirds majority of the Chamber for a period of six years and may not immediately be re-elected. He appoints the Prime Minister and the members of the Cabinet. All Lebanese adults are electors; women were given the vote in 1952.

The normal term of the Chamber is four years. It has 99 members (increased from 77 in 1960) and the proportion of six Christian to five non-Christian representatives is maintained. By a very strong tradition the President of the Republic is a Maronite, the Prime Minister a Sunni Moslem, and the President of the Chamber of Deputies a Shii Moslem. All the other principal religious communities are normally represented in the Chamber and the Cabinet. The Foreign Minister is always a Christian, the Interior Minister is usually a Sunni, and the Defence Minister usually a Druze. Positions in the Government service are also allocated on a sectarian basis.

Political organizations range from cliques or caucuses centred on one political family or regional leader (such as Raymond Eddé's National Bloc or Camille Chamoun's National Liberal Party – NLP) to proper political parties such as the Katayib (Christian), Najjadeh (Moslem), or Tashnaq (Armenian) although these are narrowly based and sectarian in outlook.

Other parties such as the Baath Socialists, the Communists and the SSNP were active throughout the 1950s and 1960s but were officially illegal until 1970 because of their connections outside Lebanon.

The People's Socialist Party (PSP) created by the late Kamal Jumblat who was succeeded on his death in 1977 by his son Walid, draws much of its support from the Druze community.

The civil war of 1975–6 caused the development of two broad groupings: the Lebanese Front comprising the main right-wing Christian parties and bodies (NLP, Katayib, and others) and the National Movement including left-wing parties and organizations – the PSP, the Lebanese Communist Party and the Organization of Communist Action in Lebanon (OCL), and the Independent Nasserite Movement (with its militia the 'Marabitoun'). The Lebanese Front suffered internal divisions while the National Movement was frequently at odds with the pro-Syrian Lebanese Baathists, although the PSP and the Baath concluded a pact in September 1977. A third group, the Islamic Assembly, comprised conservative Moslem leaders.

SOCIAL SURVEY

As a result of the great expansion and development of Lebanon's mercantile economy since the Second World War, commercial interests have supplanted the former political power of the semi-feudal landed families. Beirut now has a large, expanding, and socially mobile middle class.

In the Druze community, however, feudal loyalties to a few leading families remain. Because there has been no agrarian reform and no socialistic legislation the distribution of wealth and property is highly uneven. There are many small proprietors in the mountain regions but in the plain of Tripoli and the Beqaa large estates take up most of the cultivated area. Over half the cultivated land is owned by 200 landlords.

General health and living standards have risen substantially over the past two decades but the rise has been uneven. Successive governments have done little to assist or protect the poorer sections of the community. Popular housing and welfare services have depended on private or religious organizations. Labour unions have been too small and fragmented to exert any general influence towards social reform although there were signs of change in 1970 when the Government agreed to introduce a comprehensive national health insurance scheme under pressure from the General Confederation of Labour. The IRFED report of 1960/61 estimated that half the population with family incomes of below $830 could be classified as 'destitute' or 'poor' and accounted for only 18 per cent of GNP.

The civil war caused widespread disruption of Lebanese society which in many respects has continued in the disturbed aftermath of the war. Damage to housing in Beirut was extensive. While hundreds of thousands left the country, others became internal refugees. Maronite families have fled from East Beirut to the Christian enclave around Jounieh; Shiite villagers who were driven from their homes by the Israeli invasion of March 1978 returned to find their villages in ruins. Public services of all kinds have deteriorated throughout the country.

The educational system has been constantly and seriously interrupted since 1975, with effects that have yet to be measured. Before the war educational standards were the highest of any Arab state, and literacy was estimated at about 90 per cent of those over fourteen years of age.

Although the state education system has been developed since independence, private institutions are still the mainstay of the system, especially at the secondary and university levels. In 1972/73 there were 497,723 pupils in primary schools, 167,578 in secondary schools and 4,603 in vocational schools. There were about 1,000 state schools and 1,200 private schools in the country. There were four universities with 50,803 students in 1971/72 including the American University of Beirut (with teaching in English), the Jesuit University of St. Joseph (with teaching in French), and the Lebanese University founded by the Government in 1953.

ECONOMIC SURVEY

From independence to the civil war, the Lebanese economy was remarkably prosperous. Lebanon has acted as a link between the rapidly developing countries of the Middle East and the Western world. The 1948 Arab–Israeli war and the consequent Arab boycott of Israel helped to make Beirut the principal entrepôt, traffic, and banking centre of the area by eliminating Palestine as a competitor. Transit trade benefited further from the closure of the Suez Canal in 1967. Foreign companies doing business in the Middle East almost invariably established their regional offices in Beirut while the investment of funds from other Arab states (including some political flight capital) helped to create an extraordinary real estate boom. Tourism and the entertainment industry flourished. However, an economy so heavily based on services is inevitably sensitive to political developments in the area. Business confidence was severely shaken by the 1958 crisis and the 1967 war and its aftermath, but the Lebanese have shown a remarkable adaptability. In the early 1970s, national income was estimated to be growing at between 4 and 5 per cent per annum. Per capita income was second only to those of the oil shaikhdoms in the Arab world, and was estimated at $500 in 1966.

In 1948, following the Arab–Israeli war, President Khoury's Government established a free foreign exchange and trade system which has since become synonymous with Lebanon in a Middle East where controlled economies are the general rule. In 1952 the exchange system became completely free and with a gold coverage of between 85 per cent and 95 per cent, the Lebanese pound acquired a reputation for stability. The liberal laissez-faire system and lack of controls helped to encourage foreign investment. Few Lebanese economists and fewer politicians question the basic assumption that Lebanon should maintain a predominantly private enterprise system. However in recent years the opinion has been gaining ground among the younger intelligentsia that complete laissez-faire is incompatible with the modern world and that the Government should play a bigger role in planning overall development and ensuring a fairer distribution of wealth.

The civil war was an unprecedented catastrophe for the Lebanese economy. No sector was spared. According to the 1977 estimate of the Beirut Chamber of Commerce total private sector losses amounted to £L 6,175 million and public sector losses £L 1,335 million. Real and potential losses to the year 1980 were estimated at £L 21 billion.

Because of the continuing political and economic uncertainty since 1976 few statistics are available, and pre-1975 figures bear little relation to the present.

Currency

The Lebanese pound is divided into 100 piastres. The exchange rate in July 1979 was $1 = £L 3.2475; and £1 = £L 7.1456.

Agriculture

About one quarter of Lebanon is uninhabited mountain country; only 11 per cent of the land is cultivable and much of this is marginal. However there are some highly productive areas on the coastal plain and in the Beqaa Valley. Farming is much more intensive than in Syria and about 25 per cent of the 270,000 hectares that are cultivated are irrigated.

About 20 per cent of the working population is engaged in agriculture. The war and subsequent outbreaks of fighting have seriously disrupted agricultural production, especially in the south where whole plantations have been destroyed.

Agricultural production in 1973 totalled £L805 million; fruit production was £L352 million; vegetables £L117.4 million and cereals £L23.1 million. The annual wheat crop (grown on about 60,000 hectares) varies between 50,000 and 70,000 tons, and about 200,000 tons has to be imported to cover local needs.

Fruit and vegetables are Lebanon's principal visible export. Production of citrus fruit, apples, and bananas doubled between 1948 and 1958 mainly through investment in terracing and irrigation. Total fruit exports were 370,029 tons in 1973 of which 204,000 tons were citrus fruits. Other crops include olives, grapes, sugar cane, sugar beet, and tobacco, mainly for local consumption. Before the civil war, Lebanon was the principal producer of wine and arak in the Middle East.

In 1974 there were an estimated 84,000 cattle and 229,000 sheep in the country and in 1972 the poultry population was estimated at 19.4 million. However, much of the livestock has been lost in the civil war.

Mining, Fuel, and Power

No mineral deposits of importance have been discovered. A little iron ore is smelted in Beirut and salt is produced from sea water. Attempts to find oil have been abandoned although there were once reports that Rompetrol of Rumania had found large reserves in the west of the country. The Government has awarded a concession for offshore exploration to the US company Tripco.

The government-owned refinery at Tripoli has a capacity of 30,000 b.p.d. and normally draws its oil from the Iraqi pipeline. The Sidon refinery which is owned by Medreco (Mobil Oil 50 per cent, Caltex 50 per cent) has a capacity of 16,500 b.p.d. and obtains its fuel from Tapline. Both refineries were damaged during the war which also led to the withdrawal of most of the foreign marketing companies. Throughput in the two refineries in 1977 was 34,000 b.p.d. A financial dispute with Tapline caused the temporary closure of the Sidon refinery in 1975 but in August 1978, with the aid of Saudi Arabia, an agreement was reached on past debts and future payments.

Total electricity production in 1975 amounted to 1,850 kilowatt hours. The Litani River scheme could eventually generate some 300 million kilowatt hours per year. The first phase of this work was completed in 1965. In 1975 the government ordered a review of this long delayed £L 600 million project but the civil war halted any further progress.

Manufacturing Industry

Lebanon is relatively highly industrialized compared with other Middle Eastern countries. In 1972 £L1,270 million were estimated to be invested in industry, and in 1974 industry's share in national income was £L1,040 million or 16 per cent.

Cement, textiles and foodstuffs are the largest industries, followed by the processing or manufacturing of beverages, leather, soap, cigarettes, furniture, and metal items. Cement output in 1975 was 1.4 million tons compared with 1.25 million tons in 1969. Plants have been opened in recent years for milk pasteurization, paper and cardboard, cosmetics and pharmaceuticals, steel products, aluminium articles, superphosphates, detergents, cans, car batteries, and sugar refining.

Although agricultural products remain the most important item of export, industrial exports – mainly to Saudi Arabia, the Gulf states, Iraq, and Syria – have been increasing rapidly from £L87.4 million in 1967 to £L456.6 million in 1973. The industrial sector was severely damaged by the civil war. Some 150 factories valued at £L1.5 billion were destroyed and losses were estimated at 35–40 per cent of total investment. The Syrian bombardment of Christian districts in 1978 caused further damage to industry both in immediate physical terms and in potential production.

Transport, Communications, and Tourism

Until the civil war Beirut Port, with its free port area and lack of currency or other restrictions, was the principal entrepôt centre for the Middle East. Transit traffic declined from 574,000 tons in 1954 to 317,000 tons in 1965 as Syria increasingly imported directly through Latakia, and Jordan through Aqaba, but it recovered after the 1967 war and the closure of the Suez Canal to reach 642,750 tons in 1967 and 832,000 tons in 1968.

Traffic in Beirut Port increased from 2.57 million tons in 1968 to 2.7 million tons in 1969 and 3.5 million tons in 1974.

The port was almost totally destroyed during the civil war and its rebuilding and development became a priority for the government when the war ended. However, further fighting closed the port for several periods in 1978 and even when open it remained at 15–20 per cent of normal activity. Many companies had moved to Cyprus or elsewhere for safer accommodation and the 6,000 port workers were reluctant to return. Reconstruction of the port was postponed indefinitely.

Beirut International Airport is one of the most important airports in the world and its expansion has continued despite intermittent fighting. In 1974 Beirut handled over 2.8 million passengers and 145,897 tons of cargo, a 33 per cent increase over 1973. Lebanon's Middle East Airlines (MEA) is one of the most successful and resourceful airlines in the world. Its profits in 1974 of £L35.5 million marked a 27 per cent increase on 1973. Even in the difficult year of 1977 its profits were £L20 million. Some 24 international airlines use the airport. In 1977 Christian separatists built their own airport at Haimat in Central Lebanon and named it Pierre Jemayal Airport.

The inauguration of an earth satellite station and of the Beirut–Marseilles submarine cable, both in 1969, greatly enhanced Lebanon's position as an international telecommunications centre for the Middle East. The laying of a Beirut–Alexandria submarine cable as part of a new Damascus–Cairo telephone service was completed in 1972.

Because of its relatively liberal atmosphere, Beirut was the principal centre of journalism and publishing in the Arab world before the civil war. Most newspapers continued publishing after the war but were thereafter hampered by censorship.

Tourism played a major role in the economy before the war. In the first three-quarters of 1974 there were 2.19 million visitors, representing a 50 per cent increase over 1973; and in 1974 foreign exchange earned from tourism was £L880 million compared with £L573 million in 1973. The civil war brought disaster to the industry. Most of Beirut's hotels were destroyed and the number of visitors dropped to zero. Since then recovery has been sporadic and constantly hampered by renewed violence.

Foreign Trade

The direction of Lebanese trade tends to fluctuate according to the state of political relations with the other Arab states. Probably some 70 per cent of Lebanon's exports (mainly industrial goods) go to Middle Eastern countries. The Lebanese have come to accept a large visible trade deficit as a permanent feature of the economy. However, there is little cause for alarm as gold and currency reserves continue to rise. The Lebanese pound only depreciated 9.8 per cent in the first year of the civil war, but sank to its lowest level in five years in June 1976. After that it almost entirely recovered. The gold backing to the currency has been maintained at around 80 per cent.

Few reliable statistics are available for Lebanese trade. Currency conversions are made at different rates and there are large amounts of contraband and unrecorded transactions. In 1977 total imports were estimated at £L4,636 million and exports at £L1,940 million.

Money and Banking

Before the civil war Lebanon had become an important banking centre which was rapidly expanding its activities as the massive increase in oil revenues in the area attracted foreign banks and other ancillary services. A Central Bank responsible for the fiduciary issue was established in 1964. A new banking law in 1967 was designed to encourage the merger of the weaker banks. Since then 10 of Lebanon's

85 registered banks have been taken over by the state but only two have merged. There is a semi-state Agricultural and Industrial Bank, a Popular Housing Bank and a National Bank for Industrial and Touristic Development.

Beirut became one of the world centres of the free money market in the 1970s. During 1972 and 1973 Beirut also established itself as an international financial centre when loans were arranged through Beirut banks to the IBRD, Renault, India, Iran and Algeria. Total deposits in 1974 were £L10.1 billion.

The banking sector was badly hit by the war. Apart from the loss of international confidence, many banks were burned to the ground and looted. A new banking free zone law, designed to attract the return of foreign firms, came into effect on 1 April 1977 and the moratorium on the licensing of new banks was lifted. Before the renewed fighting in the autumn of 1978 there were some hopeful signs of recovery. The problem of surplus liquidity was being met by the issue of short-term and medium-term Treasury bonds to which the banking sector reacted favourably.

Development

Development planning hardly existed in Lebanon until 1962. A £L800 million five-year plan was prepared in 1958 but was held up by the political crisis of that year.

A new five-year plan came into effect early in 1962, under the influence of President Chehab, providing for a total expenditure of £L450 million of which £L124 million was for roads, £L76 million for drinking water, and £L72 million for electrification schemes. Some progress was achieved although the Government was constantly held up by political crises, shortage of finance, and later by the need to increase defence expenditure to meet the Israeli threat to south Lebanon.

Several large projects recommended in the plans were undertaken including the construction of a third basin at Beirut Port, motorways, airport improvement, and rural electrification and water supply schemes. The new coastal highway from Beirut to Tripoli was being helped before the war with an IBRD loan of $25 million. The extensive works planned in the Litani River project have been delayed. The government launched a 'Green Plan' to bring 100,000 hectares of arid land under cultivation at a cost of £L27 million but little has been accomplished. Development projects were generally on a small scale, with many small grants being made to municipalities and villages.

In response to the civil unrest in 1975, caused partly by social disparities, the government announced a programme to aid agriculture in the south and to build schools and low-cost housing both in rural and urban areas. A national health plan was also under consideration. But all such projects were abandoned as the fighting gathered momentum.

Future Prospects

Lebanon's chances of recovering all or part of its former position as the principal commercial centre of the Middle East depend on the restoration of a minimum of security. This in return requires a measure of *détente* between the warring factions, the extension of the authority of the Lebanese government and the building up of Lebanese security forces to enforce it. As long as only the presence of 30,000 Syrian troops prevents the resumption of full-scale civil war, Lebanon cannot recover its former economic role.

In 1977/78 the government's hopes of large-scale aid from the Arab oil-producing states to carry out its reconstruction programme were not fulfilled. However in 1977 and the first half of 1978 there were some encouraging signs of recovery in various sectors, such as banking and industry. Although some business was permanently lost during the civil war to other centres of the region such as Amman, Bahrain, Cairo, Nicosia, and Athens experience showed none of them could fulfil all the roles that were formerly performed by Beirut. The principal reason was that only the Lebanese could provide the trained and specialized labour force. Most foreign companies preferred if possible to make Beirut their regional headquarters.

The renewed fighting in September-October 1978 was a further severe setback to hopes of recovery. Beirut Port came to a standstill and the population's chief concern became once again the search for the daily necessities of life. All economic sectors were affected as employees were afraid to go to work. While the possibility of recovery remained, because of Lebanon's special advantages, there were increasing doubts as to whether it could ever be achieved.

IX

THE SUDAN

THE LAND AND THE PEOPLE

Stretching across North Africa between parallels 22 and 4 of north latitude from the Red Sea coast to the borders of the Central African Republic, the Sudan has been for many centuries a corridor between West Africa and Arabia, and at the same time a 'vestibule' of swamp and desert between negroid Central Africa and the Mediterranean civilization of Egypt. The country is an immense plain covering 967,500 square miles with drainage entirely through the Nile, bounded on the east by the Red Sea hills and the Eritrean and Ethiopian foothills, and on the south by Kenya, Uganda, and the Congo.

The Climate

The determining factor of the climate is the rainfall which gradually increases from north to south, dividing the country into three fairly distinct zones. The northern zone is mainly arid desert inhabited by camel-grazing nomads and by the sedentary owners of the narrow strip of cultivation and date-palms on the fringes of the Nile; the centre has clay plains, which extend just north of Khartoum and as far east as Kassala, with 'goz' country of undulating sand to the west of them. The centre is the most thickly populated and most highly developed part of the country, with irrigation schemes, extensive rain cultivation, gum forests, and grazing for cattle. Towards the south of the clay plains are found steep-sided hills of which the largest group is the Nuba mountains in Kordofan Province, and at the western boundary of this great plain there is the Jabal Marra range of mountains in Darfur Province, rising to nearly 10,000 feet above sea-level and forming the Nile-Chad watershed.

South of the 12th parallel heavy tropical rains occur and the country consists partly of vast treeless plains and partly of savannah forests; much of it is the *sudd* or swamp area of the

Upper Nile Province. Still farther south tropical forests are found along the banks of rivers, and to the east of the Bahr al-Jabal is a series of massive mountain ranges with peaks rising to 10,000 feet; to the west in the Bahr al-Ghazal Province the country is an elevated plateau which forms the catchment area of that province.

The People

The first population census, held in 1955/56, gave a figure of 10.3 million. In mid-1970 it was estimated at 15.5 million and in mid-1975 at 17.8 million, an annual growth rate of 2.8 per cent. However, a different estimate by the World Bank gave a total population of 15.55 million in 1975, rising to 15.88 million in 1976, an annual growth rate of 2.1 per cent. About 55 per cent of the population is thought to be under 20 years and about 87 per cent live in rural areas, although the trend towards urbanization is increasing. About half the people live in 14 per cent of the country. The conurbation of Khartoum, the capital, with the adjoining towns of Omdurman and Khartoum North, was estimated to have a population of 246,000 in 1956, 350,000 in mid-1966, 800,000 in mid-1973 and 1.1 million in mid-1975. Mid-1973 estimates for the population of other main towns include El-Obeid 74,000, Wad Medani 82,000, Port Sudan 123,000 and Atbara 62,400. The population of Juba, the capital of the Southern Region, has increased rapidly in recent years to over 100,000.

There is a substantial resident population of West Africans in the Sudan. Many of them are staying temporarily in the country to earn money for the next stage of their journey to Mecca while others settle permanently. In 1971 the Government estimated that their number exceeded one million.

The division of the Sudan into two distinct areas – North (including centre and west) and South – springs from differences in historical origins, geographical factors, and the character of the population. The North, corresponding more or less to the Ethiopia of the ancients and to medieval Nubia, is largely arabized and Moslem in religion, and thus culturally belongs to the Middle East. It contains the two chief towns: Khartoum the capital, and Omdurman. The South, first penetrated by Arab slave-raiders and occupied by the Turco-

Egyptian Government after 1860, is inhabited by a variety of negroid pagan tribes who speak Sudanic languages and whose material culture and social organization are African. Three of the nine provinces, Equatoria, Bahr al-Ghazal, and Upper Nile, are entirely southern in character; one of the northern provinces, Kordofan, includes a large area inhabited by Nubas of southern type. It may be assumed that nearly three-quarters of the total population are Moslem northerners, mostly Arabic-speaking.

The Northern Sudan

The vast majority of the northern Sudanese are Arabic-speaking. Arab infiltration began soon after the Arab conquest of Egypt, but the mass migration of Arab tribes dates from the thirteenth and fourteenth centuries, and the process of arabization and islamization was completed about AD 1500, when the last remnant of independent Christian Nubia disappeared. But the Sudan Arabs differ from the other members of the Arab family owing to the presence of negroid and Hamitic substrata which have modified their physical character, and because the centuries-long separation from the rest of the Arab-Moslem world enforced by the desert has produced a distinctive national type. The spoken Arabic of the Sudanese also occupies an independent position among the Arabic dialects. But the northern Sudanese have maintained their essential Arab character in social organization and customs, and, in the sociological and political sense, they must be classed as Arabs.

The northernmost inhabitants of the Nile valley are Nubians, and have close affinities with the people of Upper Egypt, speaking Nubian languages of Hamitic origin. Apart from this narrow fertile river strip which crosses its centre from south to north, the dry steppe lands between the 15th and 13th parallels are the home of cattle-breeding nomadic tribesmen, with the Beja and Beni Amer in the east, the Shukriya and Lahawiyin of Kassala, and, west of the Nile, the Kababish, Dar Hamid, and Hamar of Kordofan. The first two speak Hamitic languages, but all follow a way of life and observe tribal customs still having a strong affinity with those of the bedouin of Arabia.

South of them, in regions where a higher rainfall provides suitable pasture and until the tsetse-fly areas are reached about the 10th parallel, there are nomadic and semi-nomadic cattle-owning Arab tribes whose territories extend across the Sudan in a vast strip from Ethiopia in the east to Chad in the west. Here and there, especially west of the Nile in Kordofan and Darfur, are substantial non-Arab communities generally in the more mountainous parts where they, the earlier inhabitants of the area, were driven by the invading Arabs. Of these the most numerous are the now flourishing cotton-growing Nuba tribes in the hills of south and east Kordofan, and the more backward Fur people of the Jabal Marra range in western Darfur.

The Southern Sudan

A few miles south of Juba the whole character of the Sudan changes from the Middle East to Africa, with the Dinka on the east bank and the Shilluk on the west. Farther south are more Dinka, and then Nuer. All these are designated Nilotes, but their languages and customs differ, and a century of contact with the Moslem and Western world has effected little change in their beliefs or mode of life. Their wealth consists in their cattle, which are also the medium through which they maintain relations with the spirits of their ancestors. The largest group is the Dinka, who number over half a million and are divided into several independent tribes which are, in the main, culturally homogeneous. The Nuer also have a homogeneous culture, but, like the Dinka, they are split up into a number of independent tribes.

The Nilo-Hamites of Equatoria Province differ greatly from the Nilotes in languages and culture. They are shorter in stature and are now more agricultural than pastoral. They were greatly reduced in numbers by the slave-raids of the nineteenth century.

The most important of the tribes inhabiting the Ironstone Plateau to the west of the Bahr al-Jabal are the Zande, who are also found in greater numbers in the Congo. They differ widely from the Nilotes and Nilo-Hamites in physical appearance, temperament, and culture, and, possessing no cattle, cultivate extensively and show themselves readily adaptable to settlement and economic development. Under the Zande Scheme, based at Nzara, they are learning to grow cotton, sugar, and oil-palms.

HISTORY AND POLITICS

The present-day Sudan, as a political entity, is a creation of the Turco-Egyptian period (1820–85). Knowledge of the early history of the Sudan is restricted to the northern part of the country (Biblical Kush and classical Ethiopia), where the remains of a distinct civilization, ante-dating Egyptian penetration, represent the presumed origins of later Meroitic culture. Powerful Egyptian frontier fortresses dating to about 2000 BC have been excavated somewhat to the south of the present frontier. After a withdrawal from about 1700 BC, probably caused by the Hyksos invasions of Egypt itself, the Egyptian presence was renewed under the New Kingdom (1580–1100 BC) and an Egyptian administration penetrated as far as Jabal Barkal (near modern Merowe), perhaps only for a short period, but leaving behind a strong cultural influence, especially in certain religious centres, on the temple architecture, and on the cult itself. In return the local dynasty (the best known rulers were Piankhy and Taharqa) invaded Egypt in the eighth century BC, where it established its rule for a time. In 23 BC the Prefect of Egypt, Publius Petronius, provoked by a raid on Upper Egypt by the Queen Candace, or Queen Mother, in the previous year, retaliated in force, but it is now thought less effectively than Roman claims at the time made out. Two principal (but so far as our present knowledge goes, not necessarily separate) areas of civilization are known in the north (modern Merowe) associated with the name of Napata, and further south (modern Shendi area) associated with the Isle of Meroe. The history and even the full geographical extent of the kingdom are still obscure; the kingdom was at its zenith at about the beginning of the Christian era, but little is known about the causes of its decline. It is uncertain what the situation was at the time of the Axumite invasion (from modern Ethiopia) of the fourth century AD.

During the reign of Justinian, in the sixth century AD, the conversion of the Sudan to Monophysite Christianity began, and the Christian kingdoms of al-Maris, extending north to Aswan (capital Faras, where a remarkable series of frescoes was discovered), al-Muqurra (capital Dongola), and Alwa (capital Soba) were the successors to Napata and Merowe. Al-Maris and al-Muqurra, united perhaps in the early seventh century, formed the Kingdom of Nubia; Alwa extended southwards in the direction of Sinnar. The Mameluke defeat of the Nubian Christian King Dawud in 1276 is only one among many episodes that mark the gradual process of the arabization of al-Muqurra and its conversion to Islam by conquest, infiltration, and inter-marriage, especially by nomadic tribes who themselves were moving south under Mameluke pressure. The conversion of Dongola Cathedral into a mosque by the first Moslem king of the old royal house in 1317 marks the end of Christianity as the religion of the state, though it is now known that the Christian hierarchy lingered on much later than was formerly supposed. The kingdom disintegrated under Arab rule, the essential defect of which, according to Ibn Khaldun, was that it 'denied the subordination of one man to another'. In Alwa the Christian hierarchy suffered from its increasing isolation, but Christian rule of a kind survived until Soba fell to the attack of the Arab tribes towards the end of the fifteenth century. The Arabs in their turn were defeated by the rising kingdom of the Funj (a people of uncertain origin) in 1504 and Funj rule from Sinnar dominated this central area of the Sudan until the Egyptian invasion in 1820. It was during this period that the real conversion of the Sudan to Islam took place under the influence of a series of Ulema and Sufi leaders who came from all parts of the Arab world, but particularly from Egypt and from the Hejaz. The later years of the Funj kingdom were described for European readers by the Scottish traveller, James Bruce.

The Turco-Egyptian Period[1]

During the later Middle Ages Egypt shared in the outside cultural influences on the Sudan and there was a regular trade. Two caravans, from Sinnar and from Darfur, annually

[1] R. Hill, *Egypt in the Sudan, 1820–1881* (Oxford, 1958).

brought ivory, gum, ostrich feathers, gold dust, and slaves to Assiut in Upper Egypt, and returned with manufactured goods. About 1810 most of this trade was diverted to Red Sea ports, and at about the same time the survivors of the Mamelukes established themselves in Dongola. Political and economic reasons combined to motivate the invasion of the Sudan by the armies of Mohammed Ali Pasha (later Viceroy) of Egypt; the search for mineral wealth, and for slaves to conscript as soldiers, was prominent among them. The first few years of Turco-Egyptian rule in the Nile Valley were unhappy; heavy and unaccustomed taxation stimulated revolt, which the murder of Ismail (son of the Viceroy) by Nimr, *mak* of the Jaliyin of Shendi, sparked off, and which was brutally suppressed. The capital of Sinnar was transferred from the eponymous site near the present city to Wad Medani, and again in 1824 to Khartoum, then an insignificant village. The long rule of Ali Khurshid from 1826 to 1838 saw the introduction of the whole machinery of modern government; in 1833 he became Governor of the united Sudan, joining Kordofan to Sinnar. It is to the fifty-five years of Egyptian rule, gradually extending east, west, and south, that the Sudan owes its present boundaries, the basic organization of its government, and even a tradition of administrative method which shows continuity through Mahdist and British rule into modern times.

The Mahdiya

In 1881 occurred a widespread revolt led by Mohammed Ahmad al-Mahdi, which ended in the capture of Khartoum in 1885. The causes of this revolt have been much debated. A common opinion is that the Turco-Egyptian regime deteriorated, inflicting on the Sudan misgovernment, financial oppression, and the slave trade, and that the proclamations of the Viceroy Said abolishing slavery remained a dead letter; and the reports of the explorer Sir Samuel Baker, who returned to the southern Sudan as Governor of Equatoria in 1870, and of his successor General Gordon, can be cited in support of this point of view. Egyptian opinion, on the other hand,[2] holds that the Mahdiya was caused by European (and specifically British)

[2] M.F. Shukry, *The Khedive Ismail and Slavery in the Sudan* (Cairo, 1938).

interference to suppress slavery and the slave trade; by the Khedive Ismail's injudicious appointment of European (particularly British) officials to implement this policy; and by the paralysis, through British action, of Egyptian attempts to retain hold of the Sudan after the British occupation of Egypt.

After the destruction of the Egyptian force under Hicks Pasha in November 1883 the British Government advised that the Sudan should be evacuated. The major problem was the withdrawal of the Egyptian garrisons and their families, and General Gordon was sent to advise on this. The failure of his mission, and his tragic death in Khartoum in January 1885, stirred the imagination of the British people and contributed to the revulsion from the Mahdiya which coloured contemporary accounts.[3] These works, also written or greatly modified by Wingate, created a body of emotional opinion and can best be characterized as war propaganda. The Mahdi died in June 1885, by which time most of the former Egyptian Sudan had come under the control of his agents. In his last months he founded the city of Omdurman, across the junction of the two Niles from Khartoum. He had sought to restore the pristine purity of Islam and to supersede the tangle of Sufi sects. Unfortunately the unity he had begun to create did not survive the test of time, and ended by dividing the Sudanese people into two opposing camps. The Sufi sects, deeply implanted in Sudanese history, would always resent the attempt of the Mahdist revolution to obliterate their contribution to the national consciousness. His successor, the Khalifa Abdullahi, developed the rudimentary fiscal and administrative system into an elaborate bureaucracy which owed much to the traditions and personnel of the Egyptian regime. The governorships were increasingly confined to the Khalifa's own kinsmen, the Ta'aisha, who with other western tribes were brought to Omdurman. This great population movement, following on the anarchy of the revolutionary war, contributed to a severe famine, while epidemics were frequent. A diminution of agri-

[3] F.R. Wingate, *Mahdism and the Egyptian Sudan* (London, 1891) and R.C. Slatin, *Fire and Sword in the Sudan* (London, 1896). Cf. P.M. Holt, 'The Source-materials of the Sudanese Mahdia' in St. Antony's Papers, 4 (London, 1958), and N. Daniel, 'The Sudanese Mahdiya' in *Islam Europe and Empire* (Edinburgh, 1966).

culture and a decline of population ensued, but there is no statistical basis for the traditional estimate of a fall from 8 to 2 millions. The riverain tribes, who had been influential under the Mahdi, were hostile to the Khalifa personally, though they gave indispensable co-operation to his administration. At first he attempted to realize the Mahdi's policy of the *jihad* against neighbouring states. The invasion of Egypt was tacitly abandoned after the Mahdist defeat at Tushki (Toski) in 1889, but frontier raiding was subsequently resumed. Intermittent warfare against Abyssinia culminated in the Mahdist victory of Gallabat in 1889: later, however, diplomatic relations were established between Abdullahi and Menelik. In 1886 and 1891 Abdullahi was threatened by armed risings of the riverain element, whose head was the Mahdi's relative, the Khalif Mohammed Sharif. These however failed, as did a widespread revolt in western Darfur in 1881–9. Other and less serious disturbances resulted essentially from Abdullahi's attempt to establish a strong personal monarchy over tribal communities scattered over a vast territory where communications were difficult. When the reconquest began in 1896 the Khalifa's rule was firmly established in most parts of the northern Sudan, but it was virtually ineffective in the South.

The rule of Abdullahi had done much to strengthen the unity of the Sudanese state, and not least by bringing to Omdurman at once the supporters he trusted and the opponents he feared, and so creating a capital city which was more than an administrative centre. On the other hand he had profoundly alienated the tribes of the North, whose influence was destined to grow, and to intensify the division between the friends and enemies of the Mahdiya.

The reconquest of the Sudan in 1898 by British and Egyptian forces under Sir Herbert Kitchener was welcomed enthusiastically by the British people. The motives underlying the campaign, which was undertaken as soon as the rehabilitation of Egyptian finances permitted, have not yet been elucidated with certainty. A widely accepted opinion is that the object was to avert a threat to Egypt which the policy of the Mahdi was believed to constitute; on the other hand it is held that the aim was, by extending Anglo-Egyptian influence southwards, to forestall any French attempt to establish a footing on the

Upper Nile. The expansion of European colonization in Africa during the rule of the Khalifa had brought Italy, France, and Belgium to the borders of the Sudan. The Italians in their new colony of Eritrea were threatened by the Ansar[4] and asked for British support. The French occupied parts of former Egyptian territory in the Bahr al-Ghazal, and an expedition under Major Marchand was sent to the White Nile in 1896 to extend French influence to that region, or, possibly, to provoke an incident which would enable France to reopen the question of the British occupation of Egypt. After negotiations between the British and French governments the Marchand expedition was withdrawn. The victory over the Ansar at Omdurman established Anglo-Egyptian authority in their place, but at first over a relatively small area. It spread slowly, and many years were to pass before it was firmly established in the Southern Sudan. Darfur was added to the Sudan by conquest in 1916.

The Anglo-Egyptian Convention and the Condominium

On 4 September 1898, two days after the battle of Omdurman, the British and Turkish flags were hoisted on the ruins of Gordon's palace in Khartoum; and on 19 January 1899 there was concluded the Anglo-Egyptian Convention; a working compromise which recognized that the reconquest had been effected by the joint financial and military efforts of Britain and Egypt. The Sudan became a condominium which its author, Lord Cromer, described as a 'hybrid form of government hitherto unknown to international law'. Supreme military and civil command were vested in a Governor-General appointed by the Khedive of Egypt on the recommendation of the British Government; the Governor-General was invested with full legislative powers; the two flags were to fly throughout the Sudan. Two very important provisions, adopted in the interests of the Sudanese, were that future Egyptian laws, and the privileges enjoyed by foreigners in Egypt under the Capitulations, should not apply to the Sudan. No foreign consuls were to be allowed to reside in the Sudan without the consent

[4] This word, meaning 'helpers', was originally applied to the supporters of the Prophet Mohammed at Medina. The Mahdi ordered it to be used for his followers, who at first had been generally known as Dervishes. During the Condominium the word came to be applied to the followers of Sayyid Abd al-Rahman, the Mahdi's posthumous son.

of the British Government. Thus the new regime in the Sudan made a start unfettered by the disabilities suffered by Egypt and other parts of the Ottoman Empire at the hands of their foreign creditors.

The New Administration

In the early years of the Sudan administration the senior posts were filled by recruitment in Britain and by the secondment of British and Egyptian officers from the Egyptian army; the great bulk of the medical, technical, and clerical staff came from Egypt and Syria. The original administration, as was natural in a newly-occupied area, was direct. The District Commissioner and his assistant, the *mamur*, were judges, policemen, tax-collectors, builders, road engineers, and sometimes doctors and veterinary surgeons of a rough-and-ready description. This system, efficient enough from the purely administrative point of view, contained no germ of future development and was little more than a military occupation.

Anglo-Egyptian Differences over the Sudan

The Condominium Convention presupposed that Egypt would continue to acquiesce in British predominance and that the Sudanese should continue to accept a status about which they had not been consulted. So long, however, as Britain held authority in Egypt the Sudan Government could continue to administer the Sudan without outside interference. This was in fact the case until after the First World War, when there was intense Egyptian agitation against the British Protectorate which had been declared in 1914, and for the restoration of the Sudan to Egypt. Egyptian demands were partially met by the Declaration of 1922, which recognized Egypt as an independent sovereign state but included the status of the Sudan in a list of four reserved points.

For over twenty years Egypt shared in the administration of the Sudan, the garrisons throughout the country consisting of Egyptian troops and the great majority of the junior officials in charge of districts (*mamurs*) being officers seconded from the Egyptian army. In 1924, however, Egyptian officials and military units were withdrawn. For twelve years after 1924 all that remained for Egypt in the Sudan was in fact the Egyptian flag.

Lengthy negotiations followed, and it was only in 1936 that Egypt and Britain signed their 'treaty of friendship and alliance'. This provided for the continuance of the Sudan administration in accordance with the Condominium Agreement of 1899, specifying the welfare of the Sudanese as the primary aim of the two governments, and leaving the question of sovereignty over the Sudan open.

The Egyptian case for the indivisibility of the Nile valley was continually restated and was submitted to the Security Council in 1947 without result, except that the Council unanimously recognized the right of the Sudanese people to self-determination. Subsequent negotiations in Cairo led only to the abrogation of the 1936 treaty and the 1899 agreement by the Government of Nahas Pasha in October 1951. Neither the British nor the Sudan Government recognized this unilateral action and the administration continued as before.

The revolutionary Egyptian Government of 1952 adopted a new attitude towards the Sudan which resulted in direct talks in Cairo between the leaders of Sudanese political parties and Egyptian representatives. Under an agreement reached in February 1953 Egypt recognized the right of the Sudanese to self-government and to the exercise of self-determination within three years.

The Early Development of the National Movement

British negotiations with Egypt provided only a background to Sudanese opinion, but Egyptian attitudes naturally affected the growth of political opposition in the Sudan. The first twenty years of the Condominium saw the establishment of a stable system of administration and justice based on an exiguous Political Service. (There were never more than 150 officers in the Sudan at one time.) The 1920s and 1930s were a period of formation of Sudanese opinion and of the search by the British for a secure basis of rule under changing conditions. The support of the Ansar during the war very greatly modified British hostility to Mahdism. Meanwhile, Sudanese educated opinion had been developing faster than their rulers realized. The Sudanese Union Society was formed early in 1920. The founders came of good family; they were mostly Gordon College graduates and were active in literary as well as political discussion. Their movement was based on the cell system; they distributed leaflet attacks on British imperialism and published articles supporting the unity of the Nile Valley in Egypt, but not in the Sudan. In 1922 a junior subaltern of Dinka origin, 2nd Lt. Ali Abd al-Latif, endeavoured to publish a paper demanding greater opportunities for Sudanese, and was imprisoned. On his release in 1927 he joined forces with Ubaid Hajj al-Amin and others of the Sudan Union Society to form the White Flag League. It is uncertain how far the League defined its pro-Egyptian objectives, or whether Egypt was rather a source of inspiration and tactics. It appears that there was an alliance with a Communist organization. From this perhaps derives a certain revolutionary phraseology common to Communism and nationalism. In 1924 public demonstrations had some success, reaching a climax in an Egyptian mutiny in Atbara. The murder of Sir Lee Stack in Egypt was followed by Allenby's demand for the withdrawal of Egyptian troops and officials from the Sudan. The Sudanese troops mutinied in loyalty to the Egyptian King but the mutiny was suppressed with considerable loss of life and the Egyptian withdrawal was completed. The White Flag League, now defeated by an effective show of force, had achieved considerable success among the educated people in the towns, but little in the country.

British Reaction and Indirect Rule

Already in the summer of 1924 Sayyid Abd al-Rahman al-Mahdi had organized the 'loyal petition' of the older and wealthier Sudanese, which asserted their traditional right to govern, and the independent nationality of the Sudanese. Ostensibly an attack on the Egyptian influence, it also seemed to the British at that date a dangerous claim to 'ultimate independence'. Nevertheless, during the later 1920s Sayyid Abd al-Rahman was allowed to build up both wealth and authority, becoming a major landlord in the new cotton schemes and also in the capital itself, and receiving Government contracts and loans.

The style of Sayyid Ali al-Mirghani, leader of the Khatmiyya, was different; he preferred to remain always in the background, and throughout his long life he would never commit himself to a political party or solution as closely or as publicly as the descendants of the Mahdi came to do. At this time both the Sayyids encouraged the now rather subdued educated class in a moderate nationalism which was often more a sentiment than a policy. The British, though suspicious of the older leaders, were much more so of the small group that they themselves had educated.

Sir John Maffey (Governor-General 1926–33) explicitly wished to build up the tribal leaders as a shield between the 'agitator' and the Government, to 'sterilize and localize the political germs'. Sir Harold MacMichael, his Civil Secretary, was sympathetic to this in principle, but he was also reluctant to trust the tribal leaders, either too far or too soon. In practice little was done because of shortage of funds.

The approach of Sir Stewart Symes (Governor-General 1933–40) was radically different. He reversed his predecessor's policy, building up revenue for a modest development programme, encouraging the expansion of education and the health service, and trying to make friends with the intellectuals. To him were due the beginnings of an Anglo-Sudanese political service, better opportunities for promotion of Sudanese in the police, the development of professional agricultural and veterinary services, and fuller utilization of Sudanese who were qualified in medicine and the law. Even so, the progress of the Sudanese in the administration, whether in the capital or the provinces, was not fast enough to satisfy educated people, and in the end Symes was a disappointment to them. He had lacked the money to implement his own policy, a policy which could only tend to the termination of British rule.

One element in his thinking was a fear of the resurgence of the influence of the sects; Sayyid Abd al-Rahman was almost ostentatiously powerful, and Sayyid Ali al-Mirghani was pressing for equality of treatment. Some British administrators were for playing them off against each other, but Symes preferred to try to isolate the intellectuals from sectarian influences. In fact Mahdist influence was strong in the early days of the Graduates Congress, and it was the qualified Mahdist support of the Government during the war which allayed British suspicions, while arousing those of the nationalists.

Nationalist Pressure and Self-determination

From 1939 to 1955 the political intentions of the British rulers limped painfully after Sudanese opinion, which exerted a not immoderate but a continuous pressure. Government tolerated rather than encouraged the formation in 1938 of the Graduates' General Congress by more than a thousand school graduates. British acceptance was the last product of the Symes policy of co-operating with the intelligentisa, and in 1939 both sides were already disenchanted. The nationalist movement, perceiving insufficient advantage from British liberalism, turned again to Egypt for alliance and support; the British were increasingly preoccupied by the war effort; the Italians invaded the Sudan and held Kassala, and the threat did not disappear until the battle of Keren in 1941, in which Sudanese troops played an important part; the Sudan remained an important link in African communications as long as the fighting in North Africa continued. The Congress leadership supported the war effort at least until 1942, but in return expected to be treated as representative of the nation, and Sir Douglas Newbold (Civil Secretary 1939–44) maintained his predecessor's refusal to regard the Congress in that light. The members of Congress, in view of the Government's attitude, could most easily find nation-wide support through an alliance with one or other of the major sects. From this period dates the definitive translation of sectarian rivalry into national politics, but also an increasing gap between educated and tribal groups, and between urban and rural interests.

In April 1942, Newbold rejected a Memorandum, presented by Congress, which demanded self-determination after the war, nationalization of the Gezira Cotton Scheme and full Sudanization of the civil service; he did so on the now familiar ground that Congress was unrepresentative. Realizing that it was necessary to create some organ for maintaining touch with public opinion, Government now devised an Advisory Council to represent such opinion as it was itself willing to listen to.

The Ansar co-operated with reservations within the framework of the Council, and in 1945 formed the Umma party to express the secular policies of the sect, independence from both Egyptian and British influence, and a dominant position in the country. The Ashigga ('full brothers'), formed in 1943 under the leadership of Ismail al-Azhari, at first represented the Khatmiyya sect (with which it and its successor groupings maintained changeable relations) and also all those interests which opposed a neo-Mahdist hegemony. The term 'Unionist' applied to this group and to related groups up to 1969; in the 1940s the term related to the Union of the Nile Valley. The Ashigga worked indefatigably to build up political support, allowing no occasion to pass which might be used to help create a wide personal network of alliances in the capital and larger towns, and employing in addition all the usual devices of party propaganda.

The Sudan Administration Conference of 1946 (boycotted by Congress) led to the creation in 1948 of a Legislative Assembly. It compared favourably with the Advisory Council in that it was mostly elected, was more representative, and had more powers, but it continued to lag behind the accelerating public demand. Congress also boycotted the Assembly and the boycott was largely effective, but in consequence the Umma party naturally gained most of the seats. The leadership of the Assembly and of the new Executive Council was held by Abdalla Khalil, Secretary-General of the Umma party, and effectively advisory Prime Minister during the whole life of the Assembly. He was dependent on rural support of a rather poor quality. The British preferred the Umma party because it was anti-Egyptian but the Mahdists themselves had little confidence that the British would not surrender to Egyptian demands, and from 1950 pressed hard for an end to the Condominium. The Ashigga and related Unionist groups preached the union of the Nile Valley, but this seems to have represented recognition of a common cause with Egypt against Britain, and of a common cultural inheritance, rather than any planned constitutional policy, or consideration of what union might actually involve. The progressives now called, not for 'independence', like the Umma, but for self-determination; they seem to have argued that it would be time enough when the principle had been achieved to decide what to do.

In 1951 Egypt (arguing that Britain, in establishing the Legislative Assembly, had acted unilaterally and not as one of two co-domini) had declared Farouk King of Egypt and the Sudan, and so brought about a deadlock of which it was difficult to see an easy solution; but it was in fact quickly resolved by the new revolutionary Government which came to power in Egypt in July 1952. The new regime was capable of more flexible action that the old. The Umma party signed an agreement with the Egyptian Government in October, and in January 1953 an Agreement, known as the Agreement of the Parties, was signed between the Egyptian Government and all the Sudanese political parties. It specified immediate full self-government, self-determination within three years, and elections to be held under an international commission. It was now Britain that had no room to manoeuvre, and an Anglo-Egyptian Agreement in February, incorporating the points included in the January Agreement of the Parties, was given effect in a Self-Government Statute of 31 March.

A general election, the first in the country's history in which all parties took part, was held in the same year, under international supervision. The result was an overwhelming victory for the National Unionist Party, which won 51 seats. Although the Mahdists amount to about half the nation, the Umma party gained only 22 seats, and Ismail al-Azhari became the first Prime Minister of the Sudan, with a clear mandate. It was incontrovertibly demonstrated that he had correctly interpreted the wishes of the country, at least so far as the end of the colonial regime was concerned.

In two years of Unionist rule before independence, Sudanese opinion also turned decisively away from union with Egypt. The Governor-General and his staff dealt honestly and constitutionally with the new Government, and earned the confidence of men who after so many years of frustrated opposition had come to expect hostility. The programme of Sudanization proceeded quickly and efficiently, and a scheme of generous compensation hastened or facilitated both forced and voluntary retirements of British officials. It was now clear to all that the British were handing over power. Meanwhile, in a serious riot in March 1954, the Ansar demonstrated the strength of the threat underlying their objection to a formal link with Egypt; Sayyid Abd al-Rahman, moreover, went out of his way to renounce any monarchical ambition. Sudanese opinion, finally, tended to disapprove of a number of developments in Egypt itself. For all these reasons it became clear that self-determination would after all mean independence.

The work of Sudanization was complete by August 1955. It was proposed to hold a plebiscite on the question of independence, and on 3 December Britain and Egypt reached agreement about its conditions. On the same day the two Sayyids announced a common programme of general aims; a joint announcement was quite unprecedented. On 19 December, parliament declared the country independent from 1 January immediately following, without plebiscite. Sovereignty was vested in a Commission of Five, and a transitional constitution was completed and approved only on 31 December. The Prime Minister was able to declare the Sudan independent on 1 January 1956.

The First Parliamentary Regime

Economic and foreign policy and the constitutional issue were the main topics of political interest in the years 1956–8. Not only did the country need development; successive governments also needed to show that they had promoted it, despite their unsuccessful financial control. The beginning of the Manaqil extension of the Gezira scheme and the extension of the railway to Darfur were planning achievements of the period. A Foreign Ministry and diplomatic service were created, and the general lines of foreign policy, from which the Sudan has not yet seriously deviated, were given expression: neutralism, Arabism, and Africanism, all dictated by the country's geographical position. The maintenance of efficient government was in part the achievement of an able body of civil servants. Little progress was made towards agreement on a permanent constitution. The Unionists wanted an executive presidency, the Umma a Head of State with formal powers and elected by parliament; and those who were not Mahdists wanted a non-Mahdist Head of State.

During the period preceding independence, Azhari had quarrelled with and dismissed the most distinguished of his colleagues. Independence was not generally seen to be his personal achievement, and his Government carried the responsibility for the serious mutiny of Southern troops in August

1955, and was under pressure from Southern politicians to establish the federal State they believed they had been promised. Once independence, on which alone all were agreed, had been achieved, a number of dissensions were brought out of cold store. In July, Abdalla Khalil of the Umma Party was elected Prime Minister and a new coalition was formed, within the existing parliament which excluded Azhari from office; he now led the loyal NUP in opposition. This Government was considered to be the fruit of the agreement between the Sayyids, but the differences between the sects and the parties were unresolved, not only in respect of the Presidency, but also within the agreed foreign policy. The neutralism of the People's Democratic Party (allied to the Khatmiyya) leant towards Egypt, and that of the Umma party was biased to the West. However, the coalition was returned to power in a general election held early in 1958 on a revised electorate. The Government was weakened by the causes of dissension outlined above, and a poor cotton crop brought financial weakness to crisis proportions. The size of the NUP vote was significant in representing the loyalty of the progressive and urban vote to a secular policy based upon neither sect.

In July an American Aid Agreement was ratified only after difficulty, and parliament was adjourned till November. The autumn was a period of conflicting rumour in which the sense of instability increased. On the morning of 17 November the army was found to have seized power, and ministers were under house arrest. The Umma party was divided; the Prime Minister, Abdalla Khalil, was convinced that an Egyptian takeover was imminent, and he was generally believed to have been privy to the army coup; on the other hand Sayyid al-Siddiq, who succeeded his father as Imam in 1959, always remained hostile to the new regime. The PDP and the Khatmiyya for a considerable period supported it.

The First Military Regime

The Commander-in-Chief, Major-General Ibrahim Abbud, now held power delegated to him by a Supreme Council of the Armed Forces; he was constitutionally President of the Council, not of the Republic, and also Prime Minister and Minister of Defence. A somewhat neutral and even gentle figure, he never seemed to dominate either the country or his own regime. This was not altogether a true impression; he worked closely with the Chief Justice, Mohammed Mustafa Abu Ranat, an internationally distinguished lawyer. Civilian ministers, notably Ahmad Khair (Foreign Minister) preserved a link with the revolutionary politics of the Condominium past.

The new regime concentrated on a restoration of the country's finances by orthodox measures which at least at first were successful. In many ways the greatest success of the regime (though one that brought many difficulties with it) was the Nile Waters Agreement with Egypt which the parliamentary regime had failed to negotiate and which had been increasingly urgent ever since the decision to erect the High Dam at Aswan. The new Government also left the matter in suspense for nearly a year but then came quickly to an agreement in Cairo in November 1959. The Sudan increased its share of the waters to 18,500,000 cubic metres, a quantity in excess of its immediate requirements, even taking into account the major irrigation works which could now be undertaken at Khashm al-Qirba and al-Rusayris. Egypt paid £E15m. compensation to the inhabitants of Wadi Halfa, who were to be flooded. They were to be resettled at 'New Halfa' at Khashm al-Qirba; the amount of the compensation was far too little for the cost of resettlement. Nevertheless, an intractable and inescapable problem had been solved, however imperfectly.

The regime lasted six years, in the course of which a number of its activities were acceptable to most shades of opinion, notably the exercise of a genuinely neutralist foreign policy. The ten-year development plan was a careful and reasonable scheme for the period 1960–71.

There seemed to be little serious opposition to the regime at first. The Communist party, already illegal, was suppressed with greater severity than is usual in the Sudan. On the whole, the Government was only gently repressive, making the public aware of surveillance without making itself feared. People of this high calibre and academics of the University of Khartoum were accustomed to voice their criticisms of the Government in public and with impunity. Teachers in the schools were largely left-wing in sympathy, and were very critical; the

Gezira tenants were prosperous, but illustrated Tocqueville's thesis that revolutionary discontent flourishes most among those who wish to prosper faster. The university students in particular, divided more or less equally between the Communist party (and its sympathizers) and the Moslem Brothers, felt it their duty to express the political opposition with particular force. In the meantime a form of 'pyramidal democracy' had been introduced, with local councils elected on a wide suffrage and a Central Council (or legislature) partly nominated and partly elected indirectly by Provincial Councils. This did nothing to meet the criticism.

The Southern Sudan to 1964

It is convenient to deal separately with the earlier history of the Southern Sudan, although it is intricately and inextricably tied to the history of the North. The Anglo-Egyptian reconquest of the Sudan in 1898 had the strong support of the churches. They do not seem to have expected the ban on proselytization in the North which both Kitchener and Wingate imposed. It was natural that the Government should wish to divert Christian interest to the largely pagan South. As late as 1910 Wingate doubted the wisdom of replacing Arabic by English as the Southern lingua franca, or transferring the weekly holiday to Sunday in the area. The missionaries continued throughout their history to fear Islamic advance; the Government tended to be unenthusiastic about conversion, even when it turned decisively against Arab influence in the South. In any case, the Southern provinces were divided between the missionary societies; the use of English and the Sunday holiday were conceded; and their position was strengthened by the failure to introduce a Government school system.

A policy of excluding Arabs from the North, their trade as well as their language and religion began through (*a*) provision of non-Arabic speaking administrators and clerical and technical staff; (*b*) control of immigrant traders from the North; (*c*) necessity for British staff to be familiar with 'the beliefs and customs and languages of the tribes'; (*d*) 'use of English where communication in the local vernacular was impossible'. This policy, which may be associated with the policy of indirect rule in the North, was effectively implemented in some respects only. The ultimate tendency of policy seemed to be to integrate the Southern provinces into East Africa, but, though this was often discussed, nothing was done to put it into effect.

The Civil Secretary (Sir James Robertson) in 1946 reversed the previous policy. It was at last recognized that, though the Southerners were a distinct people, 'geography and economics combine . . . to render them inextricably bound for future development to . . . the arabicized Northern Sudan'. He also realized that they must be 'equipped to stand up for themselves in the future as socially and economically the equals of their partners' in the North.

The complaint of Southerners is that not nearly enough was done to equip them to deal as equal partners; to the Northern objection that the South was isolated they add that they feel that it was at the same time retarded. As independence approached there was an increasing lack of confidence in the South; the Sudanization programme gave them far fewer posts than they had hoped for, and there was a series of conflicts and misunderstandings with some Northern administrators. On 18 August the Southern Corps at Torit mutinied, shot their officers, and massacred Northern civilians. During the rest of the month the 'disturbances' spread across Equatoria, affecting primarily the non-Nilotic peoples. Order was restored by the army during the first week of September; there were some conciliatory measures, some mutineers were executed and many were taken to prisons in the North; the Torit garrison, which had apparently for a time believed it would receive British support, retired into the bush, and formed the nucleus of a guerrilla force which was to continue its struggle with the North for sixteen years. The mutiny had a traumatic effect on both Northerners and Southerners. The problem of independence was an immediate one; no Southerner had taken part in the Cairo Agreement of the Parties, and the Southern members of parliament agreed to independence on condition that a federal constitution would be granted.

In 1954 an International Commission on Secondary Education had recommended the re-adoption of Arabic in the South, as the medium of instruction in the schools; but it was only in 1957, when the effects of the mutiny seemed past, that policies previously determined were resumed. The Minister of Education now announced the immediate take-over of elementary schools, and an early take-over of other schools by the Government.

The situation deteriorated rapidly during the military regime. In establishing a number of Moslem religious schools and institutes, the Government considered that it was only reversing the Condominium policy, and attaching education to religious conversion. Southern intellectuals, however, considering that this policy and that of taking over the Christian schools consorted unequally, decided that the policy was a device for retarding development. In 1961 religious meetings for prayer or catechism, other than in church, were forbidden, and in 1962 a Missionary Societies Act was passed which forbade proselytization except under licence. The Government saw its actions as an attack, not on the Christian religion, but on foreign interference in religious affairs. Early in 1964, believing that they had collected incontrovertible evidence of missionary interference in politics, all the foreign missionaries in the South (272 Catholics and 28 Protestants) were expelled. This was put into effect abruptly and arbitrarily, and lost the Sudan considerable European and American goodwill; yet it may not have been entirely to the disadvantage of the Churches that the future of Sudanese Christianity in the South, however great the difficulties, would henceforth be solely in the hands of Sudanese Christians.

The 1955 Commission of Enquiry had rightly judged that 'the real trouble in the south is political, not religious'. That the military regime superimposed a religious problem over the political one was one of many errors; but its political repression was of itself sufficient to create large-scale emigration of villagers over the borders of Ethiopia, Kenya, Uganda, the Central African Republic, and the Congo from 1960 onwards. A number of active politicians fled, and were given political asylum in Uganda, where they were allowed to carry on political activities. With them was William Deng, an outstanding personality, and an able administrator whose defection caused the Government more concern than that of the politicians. The exiles, accusing the North of colonization, began to demand separation, instead of that federation which they believed they had been first promised and then refused.

In 1961 a large number of former mutineers were amnestied without being offered employment, and not unnaturally they joined their fellow-mutineers already in the bush. The earlier part of 1963 was quiet, but in the autumn the guerrillas reappeared under the name of Anya-Nya; they were now a highly organized group comparable to the Mau-Mau, independent of the exiled politicians in Uganda, and determined to wage war seriously, and under no leadership but their own. From this time forward unhappy villagers were punished by both sides for help rendered to the other. Their attempt, early in 1964, to capture Wau, capital of Bahr al-Ghazal Province, showed them to be a genuine military danger, and in any case the climate and vegetation make the Southern Sudan at certain seasons ideal for guerrilla operations. The military Government began to pour men and money into an attempt to regain military control, for which the army had not sufficient experience. From this date onward it will be more convenient to discuss the history of North and South together.

The October Revolution of 1964

The failure of policies of repression in the South, and much more mildly against the students, combined to bring about a crisis of confidence. After students were shot by police in the course of suppressing a meeting at the university, rioting by the crowd, and non-co-operation by officials, began to gain momentum. On 30 October a caretaker Government was announced, under the premiership of Sirr al-Khatem al-Khalifa, an educationalist with long experience in the South. For the first time the Communist party and its sympathizers were included in a Government composed of all who considered themselves progressives. A 'Night of the Counter-Revolution' when it was erroneously believed, as the result of an unauthorized Communist broadcast, that the army was about to attempt a counter-coup, brought thousands of ordinary citizens into the streets to defend their freedom, and demonstrated the substantial unity of the nation at this date.

It was after this that Abbud himself resigned, and that a five-man Council of Sovereignty was reinstated.

For the first time a sensitive ministry was given to a Southerner. Clement Mboro, then Deputy Governor of Darfur, became Minister of the Interior, and a leading member of the new Southern Front. But rumours that he had been betrayed caused Southerners to run amok in central Khartoum, provoking counter-violence against them in North Khartoum. Many returned to the South, some joined the Anya-Nya and others took to robbery and murder on their own account. In spite of these events it was obvious that for the first time there were men in authority who really wanted a solution to the problems of the South, and it was this that made it possible to convene the Round Table Conference which met in March after some complex negotiation.

The Sudanese African National Union (SANU), the organization of the Uganda exiles, split on the question of attendance, and the section that came was headed by William Deng. Aggrey Jaden, himself an exile, and not strictly a member of the Khartoum Southern Front, nevertheless voiced the views of the Front. SANU demanded federation, and the Front demanded total independence; the Northern parties, which were well represented by their best known leaders, could agree to neither. Yet if the Conference achieved nothing else, it did achieve a good deal of plain speaking, and the strength of Southern points of view was now perhaps for the first time widely understood in Khartoum. Revolution gave foreign policy a new orientation in favour of other revolutionary African movements, even to the extent of helping Congolese insurgents believed to be allied with the Anya-Nya. By February, the political parties, confident of their support in the country as a whole, were pressing very hard for elections. Elections were held in April and May and gave the Umma party 74 seats against the NUP's 51, sufficient to enable a coalition of the two to have an overwhelming majority. Mohammed Ahmad Mahjub became Prime Minister as senior Umma politician, and lost no time in amending the provisional constitution to allow Ismail al-Azhari to become perpetual President of the Supreme Council. Conditions were far too unsettled in the South to allow elections there, and these seats were put into cold storage. Most progressives disliked the election because it brought the revolution to an end; indeed, the country now stood exactly where it had stood on the eve of the military coup, when an Umma/NUP coalition had just been announced.

The Second Parliamentary Regime

The leaders of the late regime were released in July; the Government resumed a foreign policy based on support for the Accra principle of African non-intervention, and, in reaction against the spirit of revolution, a period of mild repression set in in the North. This culminated in the banning of the Communist party which was not seriously enforced. In the South the situation deteriorated rapidly. The Anya-Nya had never suspended their operations, and these were stepped up in July and August; the Government, disillusioned about the prospect of conciliation, ordered the restoration of law and order; and the shooting of considerable numbers of civilians occurred in Juba and Wau. A real Southern opposition now existed, however, in Khartoum: the section of SANU headed by William Deng and the Southern Front, which included most of the intellectuals.

The Imam al-Siddiq al-Mahdi had been succeeded by his brother al-Hadi, but the political charisma descended to his son al-Sadiq, who emerged after the Revolution, though then barely thirty, as the leader of the reconstituted Umma party. In two respects he was genuinely in accord with the aims of the late Revolution, now already in abeyance; he wanted to root out corruption, and he wanted a real settlement in the South. He had published a pamphlet on the South in 1964 in which he advocated the integration of an Arabic-speaking Moslem South into a united country on a basis of real equality; he believed that Islam would quickly succeed, if it were allowed to compete with Christianity on equal terms. His uncle the Imam remained firmly sectarian and bitterly resented his nephew's political leadership. It was in an atmosphere of bitter party and family division that al-Sadiq was elected Prime Minister at the end of July 1966, and that the outgoing premier, Mohammed Ahmad Mahjub, led a section of the Umma party into opposition.

The new Government paid particular attention to the rural water problem, though the ultimate effect of some of the action now got under way was the creation of new areas of erosion. In the South, the Anya-Nya again stepped up activity in October and November during the Prime Minister's tour of the disturbed areas. Nevertheless pacification had had some success. A greater emphasis on ordinary civil government was one factor in restoring stability.

Parliament was slow to fulfil its function as a Constituent Assembly. The constitutional committee came to agreement on a Presidency of executive type, and it was clear that the Umma and the National Unionists would have to compete for this single major office. The Imam announced his candidacy; relations between al-Sadiq and al-Azhari deteriorated, and even more between al-Sadiq and the Imam. Al-Sadiq was neatly eliminated in a parliamentary manoeuvre in May, and the former coalition under Mahjub was resumed. Shortly after the new Government took office the Israeli war occurred; the country necessarily rallied to the Government, which, by the time the crisis was past, was firmly established. For reasons generally attributed to the weakness of his position in the coalition and to his lack of experience, al-Sadiq had lost the confidence both of favourable observers outside his party and, of course, of those within it who supported the Imam.

At the general election in May 1968 the two factions of the Umma party put up rival candidates and the whole influence of the Imam was concentrated against al-Sadiq and his chief followers, all of whom lost their seats. Al-Sadiq proposed that the opposition should be led by William Deng, who retained his seat, but who was found after the election murdered in an ambush near Rumbeck (a crime which occurred, it was publicly alleged, with the connivance of the Government).

The coalition, formed of the Imam's Umma and the Democratic Unionist Party (a merger of the NUP and PDP), remained in power for a further year. There was no real improvement in the South (and in April 1969 a provisional Government of 'The Nile' on Sudanese soil was announced by the rebels, apparently the result of the impatience of Anya-Nya fighting men with the politicians in exile; a similar provisional Government had been announced the year before and apparently 'elected' in 1967.) The Khartoum Government tended, at least formally, to follow the traditions of its immediate predecessors. Foreign policy was based on four points: neighbourliness, neutralism, Arab League membership, and OAU membership. Economic aid continued to be sought more widely, though US aid ended in June 1967; it was official policy to promote Sudanese control of commercial and financial interests. Corruption was generally said to be rife, and there was a general mood of disillusion. On the morning of 25 May Radio Omdurman announced that the army under Colonel (later Major-General) Jaafar Mohammed al-Nimairi had taken over the country and put all ministers and the Sovereignty Council under arrest.

The Second Military Regime

In the previous months the idea of a new military coup had been widely and sympathetically discussed, and doubtless considered, by most politicians, but the form that it took and the date on which it happened were universally a surprise. The initial public reaction was favourable, although there was dismay in some quarters at the inclusion of members and friends of the Communist party.

The Prime Minister, Babikr Awadalla, the former Chief Justice who had been living in retirement for rather more than a year, announced a programme of Arab unity (subsequently endorsed by al-Nimairi's personal meetings with President Nasser), of support for liberation movements everywhere and of replacing foreign capital, if necessary by self-help. It now became known (what had been known to the IMF for some months) that the country was on the verge of bankruptcy, and the new Government met this situation with orthodox financial measures. In October 1969 al-Nimairi replaced Babikr Awadalla as Prime Minister, while Babikr remained Foreign Minister and became Deputy Chairman on the Revolutionary Council (which had replaced the Sovereignty Council). Other changes in the Government during 1969 were all designed to reassure a public suspicious of Communist influence. All political parties were dissolved in May 1969, and the effective continuation in being of the Communist party led to the events of July 1971. The new Government was conscious that it was renewing the revolution of 1964; al-Nimairi said (October 1969) that its allies were those who had fought for independence against British rule and those who had struggled for a new society against the reactionary military dictatorship; its enemies the leaders of the defunct reactionary political parties. These categories were not altogether mutually exclusive; al-Azhari, who undoubtedly belonged in the first as well as the third, had died (under arrest but in his own house) in August.

In June 1969 the Government announced a programme of 'regional autonomy within a united Sudan' for the South, and of amnesty, development, and training for Southerners. this would have been wholly acceptable in 1956, but in February 1970 the attitude of the Anya-Nya was an intransigent as ever, and their position rather stronger than before. A Ministry for Southern Affairs was created, and the Minister appointed was Joseph Garang, a member of the Communist party, one of the ablest of Southern politicians, well-known in the North and familiar with Northern society, but relatively unknown (and suspected by some of being a Communist) in the South.

The other great problem over the years has been the sectarian division of the nation. The new Government early showed itself sensitive to counter-plots; the revolution in May 1969 was followed by immediate opposition from the Moslem Brothers, many of whom were arrested. Progressives were divided, and many at this time inclined to the centre, partly from fear of provoking an ultimate right-wing reaction. Sayyid Ali al-Mirghani, the leader of the Khatmiyya who had come to Sudan at the Reconquest, died in 1968 and was succeeded by a young son, Sayyid Uthman. The sect had no real quarrel with the new revolution, unless on the Communist issue, and Sayyid Uthman gave it his support. The real danger to the regime came from al-Sadiq, who could now offer the only alternative government, and from the Imam, who was totally irreconcilable. Al-Sadiq was early placed under arrest, while the Imam took refuge in Gezira Aba, an island in the White Nile which had once been a base of the Mahdi, and where Sayyid Abd al-Rahman had acquired extensive interests. In March 1970 General al-Nimairi judged that the attitude of the Mahdists constituted a threat to his Government, and landed troops on the island. Fighting inevitably resulted in the destruction of the Ansar as an organized force capable of bearing arms. On 31 March it was announced that the Imam al-Hadi had been shot dead while trying to cross the Ethiopian border. Al-Sadiq was transferred to the hospitality of the Egyptian Government.

During the following year, the Government was seeking substantial and reliable support, without wholly satisfying any group. Significant opposition developed in the university, where a number of distinguished members of staff, including the previous Vice-Chancellor, were dismissed, and where dissatisfaction reached a peak in a narrowly-averted massacre of students by the armed forces and the closure of the university in the spring of 1971. This period was marked by constant rumours of impending political changes. The seizure of power by Major Hashim al-Atta on 19 July 1971, was quickly recognized as a bid for domination by the Communist party, and a military government was in course of formation when, three days later, the revolutionary process was reversed by the spontaneous action of army elements under junior leadership, who restored the authority of al-Nimairi. Within a week, and after trial *in camera*, a number of soldiers involved in the temporarily successfuly coup were shot; some civilians were hanged, and others associated with the Communist party received severe sentences of imprisonment. Among those executed were Abd al-Khaliq Mahjub, Secretary of the Communist party, but widely respected in more moderate circles, and Joseph Garang. Southerners were now appointed to the three Southern Governorates, without, however, solving the problems of the South. Al-Nimairi felt the need of more widely-based support, began to move in the direction of civilian rule, and showed a new sympathy with moderate and even conservative elements. The Revolutionary Command Council was dissolved in August, and from elections conducted in September al-Nimairi emerged the first President of the Sudan, and was sworn in on 12 October.

Jaafar al-Nimairi's Presidency

The occasion was marked by the release of a very large number of political prisoners, and those who remained in prison were treated more leniently. The Sudan Socialist Union, which had been set up in May, was retained, and developed along lines comparable to those followed by the parallel organizations in Egypt. Its Political Bureau was formed in January 1972. In September 1972 elections were held by a 207-member People's Assembly charged with drawing up the country's first permanent constitution.

President al-Nimairi held the firm belief that no Government of the Sudan can finally remain in power that does not solve the problem of the South. It was for this reason that during 1971 and 1972 he gradually disengaged Sudan from its political commitments to the Arab world. By opting out of the proposed federation with Egypt and Libya he incurred the special emnity of Libya's Colonel Qaddafi, who accused Sudan of betraying the Arab nationalist cause. But al-Nimairi realized that a settlement with Sudan's non-Arab southerners was incompatible with its Arab neighbours.

Al-Nimairi continued a military drive against the southern insurgents with a vigorous diplomatic campaign to come to terms with the rebel leaders through British and Ethiopian mediation. Finally in February 1972, after months of painstaking negotiations, the representatives of the Sudan Liberation Movement, who felt the tide of war was turning against them but had become convinced of the sincerity of the al-Nimairi regime, accepted an agreement in Addis Ababa providing for an immediate cease-fire, autonomy for the three southern provinces within the Sudanese republic, an amnesty for all who took part in the fighting, and the reintegration of 6,000 Anya-Nya fighters into the Sudanese army. The agreement stipulated that Arabic was to be the official language of the state, although it was agreed that English would be a working language in the south along with other local languages. Former Anya-Nya leader Joseph Lagu was appointed a major-general, later becoming the first southerner to reach the rank of military commander-in-chief.

The southern settlement was incorporated into the new constitution signed by al-Nimairi on May 8 1973; elections for the 60-seat Regional Assembly were held in November 1973 throughout the south; and Abel Alier was installed as Chairman of a 13-man Southern Region Executive as well as Vice-President of the Republic.

The restoration of the South after 17 years of conflict has inevitably been slow and difficult. Funds have been inadequate to meet the high cost of reintegrating the displaced population and of development. However, there were only infrequent and small-scale manifestations of unrest: student riots in July and October 1974, mutinies in Wan and Akoba in early 1975, the desertion of some former members of Anya-Nya in February 1976 and a quickly suppressed attempt by an airforce unit to seize control of Juba airport in February 1977. Potentially more serious discontent caused by southern fears of an upsurge of Islamic revivalism in Sudan, added to the chronic shortage of basic commodities in the south, was apparently contained by the regional elections held in March 1978 which led to radical changes in the Regional Higher Executive and the replacement of Abel Alier by Joseph Lagu. In July the one remaining opposition group in exile, the United Sudanese National Liberation Front, formed mainly of certain members of the Nuba tribes in Western Sudan who had not accepted the 1972 Addis Ababa agreement, announced that it was dissolving itself because it no longer had doubts about President al-Nimairi's good intentions towards the country.

From 1972 onwards it was no longer the South which was the main threat to the al-Nimairi regime's stability. Between then and 1978 there were three attempted coups which were officially admitted and at least ten more which were unofficially reported.

In 1973 the non-communist opposition of the Umma Party amalgamated under the leadership of Sadiq al-Mahdi. However 1974 saw a liberalization in political attitudes towards the right and many Umma Party political detainees were released. The main threat came from the left. In September 1975 a small group of army officers attempted a coup but were quickly suppressed.

The Umma Party leaders were far from reconciled; they still sought revenge for the suppression of the Ansar in 1970. A far more serious attempted coup took place in July 1976 which was masterminded by Sadiq al-Mahdi with Libyan support. Al-Nimairi's supporters regained control of Khartoum from 1,000 alleged 'mercenary invaders' after three days of fierce fighting which left some 600 dead. About 100 executions followed the failure of the insurrection. President al-Nimairi then gave up the posts of Prime Minister (to a civilian), Defence Minister, and Secretary-General of the Sudanese Socialist Union, and took various steps both to try to strengthen his regime and to make it more popular.

In July 1977 he made the surprising but most effective move in this direction by jointly deciding with Sadiq al-Mahdi, who had been condemned to death *in absentia*, on reconciliation to build a 'new Sudan'. Al-Mahdi gave up his opposition to a one-party state and returned to his home in Omdurman. In March 1978 President at Nimairi carried the process of national reconciliation a stage further by appointing Sadiq al-Mahdi, Ahmad al-Mirghani (the leader of the Khatmiyya sect), and the former leader of the Moslem Brotherhood members of the SSU Political Bureau. In April 1978, many of the al-Mahdi's followers who had remained in exile, decided to follow his example and return home. The National Front was dissolved and its guerrilla bases closed down. In February 1978 President al-Nimairi allowed elections to take place with relatively little government interference.

There was a close relationship between Sudanese internal affairs and foreign policy. Sudan's relations with the Soviet Union which had been moving closer in the 1969–71 period, were embittered by the events of 1971 and the subsequent suppression of the Sudanese Communist Party. They continued to deteriorate until in mid-1977 Soviet military experts were expelled from the country and Moscow was asked to reduce its military representation in Khartoum. The reconciliation with Sadiq al-Mahdi and the Moslem Brotherhood was encouraged by Saudi Arabia which helped as a mediator. Yet it was not a simple matter of confirming Sudan's membership of the conservative anti-communist camp in the Arab world. The opposition National Front had been supported by Libya and the left-wing regime in Ethiopia as well as Saudi Arabia. After the return of al-Mahdi, Sudan's support for Egypt was moderated and diplomatic relations with Libya and Ethiopia were resumed. On 29 May 1978 Sudanese communists were released from detention and in the same month the Soviet ambassador returned to Khartoum after a year's absence since the expulsion of Soviet advisers. On African affairs in general, President al-Nimairi began to take a more neutral and less pro-Western and anti-Soviet stand than in the previous year, to the extent that the USA began to reconsider its promise to supply the Sudan with fighter aircraft. In avoiding too close a conformity with Egyptian policies, President al-Nimairi was upholding a common principle in Sudanese attitudes. Sudan's relationship with Egypt, although inevitably close and ultimately inextricable, is also highly sensitive. The Sudanese are watchful of anything which might give the impression of Egyptian attempts at domination.

However, President al-Nimairi was one of the very few Arab heads of state who supported President Sadat's Middle East peace initiative of 1977–8. In March 1978 a meeting of the Arab League Council, which was boycotted by the anti-Sadat Arab states, decided to form a committee to achieve Arab solidarity under the chairmanship of President al-Nimairi who later toured Arab capitals in an unsuccessful attempt to heal the split between the Arabs.

In the summer of 1978 Sudan took several steps to normalize its relations with all its African neighbours in preparation for the 15th summit conference of the Organization of African Unity held in Khartoum in July. President al-Nimairi took over as Chairman of the OAU. In his address he strongly condemned intervention of Africa by both West and East.

In 1979 President al-Nimairi had to face strong internal discontent which was due both to rising prices and deflationary policies aimed to reduce the large payments deficit, and to opposition to his pro-Egyptian line. The greatest potential danger to the regime was a *de facto* alliance between Islamic forces and the left.

GOVERNMENT AND ADMINISTRATION

From independence on 1 January 1956 until the first military coup in November 1958 Sudan was governed according to a Provisional Constitution. This was revived after General Abbud's overthrow in 1964 and amended, but in the following four and a half years of parliamentary government successive governments failed to push a permanent constitution through the Constituent Assembly. After the second military coup in May 1969 led by Colonel al-Nimairi real power lay in the hands of the Revolutionary Command Council. Political parties were banned although the Communist party, whose leadership at first co-operated with the new regime, continued to function. In 1971 it took steps to establish a political organization along the lines of Egypt's Arab Socialist Union, with a Political Bureau and Central Committee. This system was codified in the permanent constitution of 1973 which also provided for a parliament, the People's Assembly. The new constitution incorporated the terms of the 1972 Addis Ababa agreement on regional autonomy for the three southern provinces.

The Sudan is divided into nine provinces which have powers of taxation and responsibilities in the spheres of health, education, and veterinary services. Provincial governors are responsible to the Minister of the Interior.

SOCIAL SURVEY

Education

The 1955/56 census showed that over 85 per cent of the population aged five years and above had never attended school of any kind. In 1975 there were about 1.6 million pupils of whom about one third were girls. During 1970/71–1974/75 Five-Year Plan the primary school period was extended from four to six years and the numbers in primary school doubled to reach 1,257,000 in 1975. Apart from some 4,000 government schools there are about 200 non-government schools run by the National Schools Board, missionary societies and foreign communities. In recent years there has been a rapid increase in the proportion of non-government secondary schools (45 per cent in 1973). In 1952 there were over 500 mission schools in the South but most of them have been taken over by the State.

In 1975 there were 22,200 students in various forms of higher education. In 1978 there were five universities: the State Khartoum University (formerly the Gordon Memorial College) with faculties of agriculture, arts, science, engineering, law, medicine, and veterinary science; the Khartoum Branch of Cairo University; the Islamic University at Omdurman; the University of Juba, established in 1977; and the University of the Gezira established in 1978. English is the language of instruction at Khartoum University.

Health

In the early years, backwardness of communications and popular suspicion of Western medicine complicated the task of dealing with an ill-nourished and disease-ridden people. The Sudan had the reputation for being extremely unhealthy, and epidemics of sleeping sickness, meningitis, and yellow fever were frequent. Today there are about 70 Government hospitals and in mid-1967 the ratio of hospital beds to population was 0.79 per 100. Rural areas are served by dispensaries, dressing stations, and health centres which numbered about 1,250 in 1965/66. The major task of preventive medicine in the Sudan is the control of malaria, meningitis, and bilharzia and other parasitic diseases.

Labour

During the Second World War, and especially after it, the rising cost of living and the enhanced political and social consciousness of the workers caused some unrest and minor strikes. The railway workers took the lead in forming an association and the Sudan Government responded by securing the services of a British trade union expert to advise both workers and Government on the most suitable lines of development. The result was a series of enactments in 1948 which constituted an advanced scheme for the improvement of working conditions, the development of trade unionism, and the regulation of industrial relations. At independence, 130 trade unions were registered although some were very small and the general level of union administration was low owing to the lack of full-time unionists.

Under an amending ordinance of the 1948 law in 1960, provision was made for closer control by the labour commissioner and it was prescribed that labour disputes should be compulsorily arbitrated when negotiation and conciliation failed. Sudanese trade unions, which are generally highly political in character, remain among the most developed in the Arab world.

ECONOMIC SURVEY

The Sudan is a predominantly agricultural country dependent largely on cotton. Successive governments have attempted to diversify the economy and a number of pilot schemes for the cultivation of alternative crops have been carried out. Industrialization is still in its early stages and the lack of sources of fuel and power is a serious handicap. The rivers are generally unsuitable for generating hydro-electric power. The South has been a particularly difficult region to develop because of its remoteness and the backwardness of its tribes on the one hand and the many years of civil strife on the other.

Nevertheless, the industrial sector has grown since independence. In 1956 the share of industry in GDP was 4.3 per cent and of manufacturing only one per cent. In 1977 it was about 15 per cent.

The Sudan is recognized as having one of the greatest potentials of any Arab state with its vast area of cultivable but uncultivated land, it is seen as the future 'bread-basket' of the Arab world. The discovery of oil in 1978 held out the possibility that Sudan might become an important producer.

Agriculture

It is estimated that about one third of the country's land surface could be used but that only one eighth or 75 million feddans is in any way productive at present. Of this total, about 18.5 million feddans were being used for arable farming and the rest was grazing land.

In the 1960s and 1970s there have been big increases in output but these have been achieved by bringing more areas under cultivation rather than by the introduction of improved methods. In 1978 the total irrigated area was about 4 million feddans of which about one third has been added since 1960, but the Sudan is still only using about two-thirds of the Nile water allocated to it under the 1959 agreement with Egypt.

Cotton

Cotton is much the most valuable cash crop and brings in about 50 per cent of total export earnings. The Sudan is a major producer of long-staple cotton which still accounts for 80–85 per cent of the total crop although weakened world demand for long staples since 1960 has prompted some increase in the production of medium and short-staple (mainly American) varieties.

Cotton exports have suffered from wild fluctuations in the international market. From 1.2 million bales worth £S 84.3 million in 1973 they fell to 0.5 million bales worth £S 43.3 million in 1974. However, a world cutback in cotton production raised prices and in 1977 864,200 bales worth a record £S 112.2 million were exported, rising to £S 116.7 million in 1978.

As part of the 1970 measures a State Corporation for Cotton Marketing was established. Four state-owned companies, incorporating fourteen former private firms, operate as exporting agencies and so contribute an element of competition in both buying and selling within the nationalized system.

The Gezira Scheme

The Gezira Scheme was initiated with the completion of the Sinnar Dam in 1925 which made cotton the mainstay of the Sudanese economy. The area between the Blue and White Niles south of Khartoum was transformed into good arable land, especially suitable for cotton but also for grain and fodder. The original gross area of 300,000 acres has been steadily increased and in 1970 reached 1.8 million acres, including the Manaqil extension.

Wheat now occupies in the Gezira an equal area to cotton, and substantial crops of maize, groundnuts, rice, and vegetables are also grown.

The scheme is worked as a three-cornered partnership between the Sudanese tenant-farmers, the Government, and the Sudan Gezira Board (which in 1950 replaced two private commercial companies – the Sudan Plantations Syndicate and Kassala Cotton Company). The net proceeds from cotton are divided 42 per cent to the Government, 42 per cent to the tenants, and 10 per cent to the Sudan Gezira Board; the remaining 6 per cent is distributed between the social services, a tenants' reserve fund, and local government councils. The Government provides the land and is responsible for dam construction and maintenance; the Sudan Gezira Board is a public corporation which administers the scheme, makes loans to tenants, and markets the produce.

Besides constituting the backbone of the Sudan's economy, the Gezira Scheme has been widely acclaimed as a model of a pioneering effort on a partnership basis.

Other Schemes

The project using the waters from the Roseires Dam was inaugurated in December 1977 and the land is being planted with an assortment of cotton, groundnuts, fruit, vegetables, and timber. Under Stage I, 300,000 acres are being brought under irrigation in 1978–9 using the long-furrow method for the first time in the history of the Sudan. Stage II will add another 500,000 acres. A third project is planned for Setait, exploiting the waters of the Atbara to irrigate 600,000 acres. A fourth, and eventually much bigger, scheme is that of the Jonglei Canal in the South. First conceived in 1974, implementation of this project was finally made possible by a 1974 co-operation agreement between Egypt and Sudan. A 175-mile canal will cross an enormous bend in the White Nile between Jonglei and Malakai. It will partially drain the Sudd marshes, recovering 4 billion cubic metres of the 32 billion cubic metres of Nile water that is lost every year through either seepage or evaporation. About 300,000 acres will be reclaimed on the west bank of the canal in the first stage but the long-term potential approaches 4 million acres. Work on the giant scheme finally began in June 1978.

Other Crops and Livestock

In the west and south of Sudan both crops and livestock are produced mainly for subsistence and little is sold. In the north and east surpluses are available and are moved to the towns or exported. Sudan is virtually self-sufficient in basic foods, the only large imports being sugar, wheat flour, coffee, and tea. The chief food crops are the common millet (*durra*) and bulrush millet (*dukhn*), the cultivation of which has been steadily extended during the twentieth century to meet the needs of the growing population. Wheat and maize are also grown, and sugar is becoming increasingly important. Sudan has one of the world's largest sugar plantation and refining complexes in the world in the shape of the Kenana sugar estate between the Blue and White Niles being developed by Sudanese, Arab, and foreign interests. When completed this scheme should produce 350,000 tons a year which, together with four other factories already in production, would make a total output of 600,000 tons a year, leaving a large surplus for export. However, delays in the Kenana scheme and escalating costs meant that Sudan was still importing sugar in 1978.

At present the most important export crops after cotton are groundnuts, sesame, and gum arabic, which is tapped from hashat trees. Gum arabic has declined in importance compared with groundnuts although Sudan remains the world's biggest supplier. The prospects for soya bean, rice, tea, coffee, and sisal are all encouraging. The area under wheat increased from 420,000 acres in 1973/74 to 714,000 in 1975/76 but yields remain low and production only rose from 236,000 tons to 264,000 tons in those years.

Pastoral farming extends throughout the country except in the desert of the north and north-west, and on the south-western plateau which is infested with tsetse fly.

Estimates of livestock in 1973/74 were 14.15 million head of cattle, 13.37 million sheep, 16.5 million goats and 2.7 million camels but livestock numbers are hard to estimate because about 60 per cent of the cattle and 80 per cent of sheep and goats are owned by nomads. For the nomads the animals are usually more valuable to keep than to sell. About 5,000 tons of hides and skins are exported annually and live animals and chilled meat are also exported to the other Arab states. Several projects are on hand to control disease, raise fodder output, and improve marketing.

Investment and the Future

With the aim in view of making Sudan the main food supplier of the Arab world by the end of the century, two development plans are envisaged for 1975–85 and for 1985–2000 on the basis of feasibility studies carried out in 1974/75 by the Arab Fund for Economic and Social Development (AFESD). Over one hundred projects costing a total of £S2,287 million are planned for Phase I with the aim of meeting 42 per cent of Arab vegetable oil requirements, 20 per cent of Arab sugar import requirements, 15 per cent of wheat, and 58 per cent of animal foodstuffs. During this phase 1.5 million acres of land would be irrigated and another 5 million acres of rain-fed land cultivated. An Arab Authority for Investment and Agricultural Development has been established with headquarters in Khartoum and an authorized capital of $1.4 billion to be subscribed by 20 Arab centres. An Agricultural Investment Act of 1976 provides a wide range of tax concessions and guarantees against nationalization and confiscation.

Oil and Minerals

Hopes of the discovery of oil in Sudan's vast area since independence were given a sudden boost in May 1978 when the US Chevron Overseas Petroleum, one of several international companies drilling in the Sudan, struck oil in commercial quantities in the Upper Nile province of west-central Sudan. This gave rise to rumours – which could not be confirmed by the company and had to be damped down by the authorities – of the discovery of a vast 'oil lake'. Despite the technical difficulties of exporting crude oil from remote areas, the rise in oil prices could make it commercially feasible and any reduction in Sudan's high fuel import bill would greatly benefit the balance of payments. Sudan has only one refinery, at Port Sudan. An oil products pipeline from Port Sudan to Khartoum was opened at the end of 1977. Some natural gas has been found in the Red Sea which may eventually be used for desalination. President al-Nimairi claimed in June 1978 that the world's biggest natural gas fields had been discovered in Fasher province.

Until recently little has been done to exploit the country's mineral potential, although there are deposits of iron ore, manganese, chromite, copper, gold, lead, asbestos, mica, and talc. Chrome mining, which had declined, is now being developed with Japanese assistance.

Manufacturing Industry

The industrial sector as it developed after independence was generally confined to the production of very simple consumer goods and the primary processing of local raw materials. Factories were concentrated in and around Khartoum North and industrial development was generally left to the private sector which received generous incentives through the Industrial Development Act of 1968. However, the public sector also began to enter the field in the 1960s and already at the time of the sweeping nationalizations of 1970 it owned most of the largest and most modern enterprises in the country – two sugar factories, a tannery, a dozen cotton ginneries, and various food-processing plants. In 1970 several important foreign-owned concerns were nationalized, including a cement company, a shoe factory, a brewery, and a truck assembly plant. Since then, however, policy has again been reversed and, while the public sector retains a leading role, private investment, both Sudanese and foreign, is encouraged.

Many confiscated businesses were returned to their owners and compensation paid for assets that remained nationalized. The Development and Promotion of Industrial Investment Act of 1972 was designed to restore confidence through a wide range of tax concessions and other incentives. Among the results of this policy in 1978 was a Canadian company's agreement to build a urea plant, a South Korean company's to build a tyre factory, and Bata Shoe Company's decision to take back a 51 per cent interest in the factory and chain of shoe shops it owned before nationalization. The public sector has come increasingly to concentrate on sugar (see above, p. 498), textiles, and leather. Despite the country's cotton output, textile imports still represent a substantial share of imports although this is rapidly declining as many new textile factories are being opened.

The 1972 Act also provided extensive tariff protection for

local industries, at the discretion of the Ministry of Industry. This is probably the cause of declining productivity and under-used capacity.

Transport and Communications

The lack of an adequate transport network is the most important single cause of the delay in exploiting the Sudan's great economic potential. The import of capital equipment, and exports, especially perishable agricultural produce, both suffer. In 1969 there were only 250 miles of paved roads in the country and by 1973 this had increased to 310 miles and 1,100 miles of gravel tracks. The rest are merely cleared tracks which are impassable after rains. A massive road-building programme is now under way and absorbing about half the total spending on communications. The biggest single project is the 750-mile road from Khartoum to Port Sudan, the country's only port, via Wad Medani and Kassala, which was nearing completion in 1979. The addition of a further 1300 miles of roads is envisaged under the development plan to 1982/83.

Sudan Railways currently operates some 3,262 miles of track, most of it single and narrow gauge. The Khartoum-Port Sudan track suffers severe strain during the cotton-exporting season, and modernization had to await the opening of the oil products pipeline in December 1977 because 40 per cent of the rolling-stock was previously devoted to the transport of oil products. In early 1978 $146 million was pledged to a three-year railway improvement programme which will have French and Japanese technical assistance.

Currency and Banking

The currency is the Sudanese Pound, divided into 100 piastres, which in mid-1978 was giving an official exchange rate of £S1 = $2.50. However, in addition there is a 10 piastres per dollar subsidy on incoming foreign exchanges, and equivalent tax on foreign exchange leaving the country, so the new rate represented a 20 per cent devaluation of the pre-June 1978 exchange rate. This devaluation was the product of three years' intensive negotiations with the IMF, and although the IMF had wanted a 30 per cent devaluation it cleared the way for the provision of credits and other benefits to the Sudan. Exceptions to the new rate will be remittances from Sudanese workers abroad which will continue to be at the rate of £S1 = $1.76, and cotton exports which continue as before to be priced in dollars and do not receive the 10 piastre premium.

In 1969 the government passed a law stipulating that not less than 75 per cent of the shareholdings in each bank should be locally owned. In 1970 banks were nationalized, leaving the Bank of Sudan (the central bank) and three development banks handling specific sectors of the economy. A new law of 1973 brought the banks into a policy-formulating government council. However, as part of the general move towards liberalization, foreign banks were encouraged to come in to finance foreign trade and development. Since then a number of Western and Arab banks have opened branches in Khartoum.

Development and Economic Policy

A ten-year development plan for 1961–70 had effectively been abandoned by 1967. A new five-year plan was launched in 1970 but in order to incorporate some additional sources of revenue this was later extended to 1977 by a two-year interim action programme. The current six-year plan launched in July 1977 envisages total investment of £S2,670 million of which £S1,570 million will be spent by the public sector. Of total public sector investment, £S425 million is allocated to agriculture, £S335 million to industry, power, and tourism, and £S 320 million to transport and communications. The rest will cover general regional developments including the special requirements of the south. The target is an annual average growth rate of 7.5 per cent with an increase in per capita income from £S110 in 1976/77 to £S307 by 1982.

Before 1956 Sudanese foreign trade was principally with Western countries but in that year the Soviet Union began to buy Sudanese cotton in large quantities. The shift towards economic links with the Eastern bloc increased after the 1967 Middle East war, which led to a major arms deal with the USSR in 1968. By 1970 the Soviet Union had become the Sudan's most important trading partner, buying about 20 per cent of exports and providing about 7 per cent of its imports, although the UK remained the most important supplier (followed by India).

The 1969 coup meant a further shift to the left in economic policy as the sweeping nationalization measures of May and June 1970 were promoted by the left-wing members of the regime. However, some of these measures were hasty and ill-considered and led to serious economic consequences. Since 1972 there has been a swing back towards more liberal economic policies, although the public sector retains the major share in the economy, and to trade with non-communist countries. In 1976/77 Italy was the main destination for Sudanese exports and the Soviet share had fallen to below 4 per cent. The UK remained the main supplier, followed by West Germany.

X

SYRIA

1. Syria and Lebanon

For purposes of geographical description and historical narrative it will be convenient to treat Syria and Lebanon together. They can be regarded as forming part of a single geographical and social entity, and until the most recent period it would be difficult wholly to separate the history of the one from that of the other.

THE LAND

The following rough geographical divisions may be made:

1. *The coastal strip.* A strip of low and fertile land runs along the Mediterranean coast of Syria and Lebanon. Near Latakia it is about twenty miles wide, and rather less north of Tripoli; but in some places it practically disappears, and the mountains meet the sea. Olives, vegetables, citrus, and bananas are cultivated, particularly round Beirut.

2. *The mountain ranges.* These stretch mostly from north to south. Just behind the coastal strip in the north is the Jabal Ansariya, which averages 4,000 feet; vines, olives, tobacco, and cotton are grown in places, and the population is comparatively large. South of it lies a gap of low land leading from Tripoli to Homs, and south of this again lie the ranges of Lebanon, with peaks of over 10,000 feet, which drop (to the south) into the hills of Galilee in Palestine. Here too water is plentiful, vines, olives, tobacco, and (in recent times) apples are cultivated on the seaward slopes, and the villages are prosperous – particularly those near Beirut which have become summer resorts for the city folk as well as for visitors from other Middle Eastern countries. Parallel to Lebanon, and east of it across the plain of the Beqaa, lie the ranges of Anti-Lebanon (over 7,000 ft.) and Hermon (9,200 ft.). Here water and cultivation are less plentiful, although they are found in

patches. Farther inland still, lying east of Hermon across the plain of Hauran, is the Jabal Druze (5,000–6,000 ft.), where also patches of vines and olives lie around the springs and streams.

3. *Plains and plateaux.* East of the mountain ranges, the land consists of a plateau, high above sea-level, but sloping generally in a south-easterly direction. Those parts of it which lie nearer the south, and within the area of heavy rainfall, and also those through which rivers flow, are capable of rich agricultural development. The countryside of Aleppo, Homs, and Hama; the valley of the Beqaa, with the Orontes and Litani flowing through it; the Ghab depression through which the Orontes flows farther north; the Jazira district lying south of the foothills of Asia Minor; the valleys of the Euphrates and its tributaries, the Balikh and Khabur – all these districts contain good land where cereals and cotton can be cultivated, and where possibilities of irrigation and hydro-electric power exist. The Jazira has seen particularly rapid development in the last thirty years. Around Damascus too there is a fertile region, the Ghouta, where an ancient system of canals makes use of every drop of water in the rivers which fall eastwards from Anti-Lebanon, and fruits of many kinds are grown. Elsewhere, however – in the plain from Homs to Damascus, and in Hauran south of Damascus – water is not sufficient to provide a good crop every year, although cereals are grown in parts, and livestock are pastured.

4. *The steppe and desert.* To the south and east of the fertile area stretches the Syrian Desert, the northern extension of the great deserts of Arabia. Covering more than one-third of the total area of Syria, it is rock and gravel steppe, not sandy desert, and has hills rising more than 3,000 feet both north and south of Palmyra.

Temperature and rainfall vary from one region to another. In the mountains about 40 inches of rain fall every year, in the desert almost none. In general, rain is heaviest in the west and north. On the coast winters are not severe, but in summer humidity is great and diurnal winters are not severe, but in summer humidity is great and diurnal variation small. In the mountains snow lies on the topmost peaks for most of the year, and even main roads are sometimes blocked in winter; summer days are hot but the nights are cool. Farther inland, plateaux and steppes have low humidity and great extremes of heat and cold.

HISTORY

The History of Syria and Lebanon has been moulded by three processes: the movements of tribes and smaller groups from the Arabian Peninsula, and their mingling with peoples of earlier settlement to form a rural population whose languages and folk-ways have been Semitic for thousands of years; the movement of armies as well as goods along the great trade routes, and the establishment (at least in the towns and river valleys) of alien governments, and often alien languages and cultures; and the resistance of the mountain communities to the incursions of governments, peoples, and ideas from outside.

Egyptians, Babylonians and Hittites, Greeks, and Romans in turn established their rule and made Syria part of their empires. In AD 636 Damascus fell to the Moslem armies; from that time Syria formed part of the Caliphate, and gradually the Arabic language replaced the older Semitic speech, and the religion of Islam conquered the majority, although the Christian sects maintained themselves, and Moslem heterodoxies found refuge in the mountains. Under the Umayyads (661–750) Damascus was the capital of the Caliphate, but with the Abbasids the centre of gravity shifted to Iraq. As the unity of the Caliphate broke up, parts of Syria fell under other domination. The Crusaders held the coast for a time, and first the Ayyubids and then the Mamelukes incorporated Syria and Egypt in a single state. Then in 1516 the Ottoman Turks occupied the country, which remained part of their Empire until 1918.

Under the Ottomans, Syria was divided into a number of provinces administered by governors sent from Istanbul. In its great days Ottoman rule was reasonably just and efficient. Agriculture and trade were protected and regulated, and the great towns flourished: Aleppo, the centre of foreign trade, Sidon (Saida), a port much frequented by the French, and

Damascus, the point of departure of the Pilgrimage and a home of Islamic culture. In the seventeenth and eighteenth centuries the strength of Ottoman rule decayed, security declined, the nomads began to penetrate the settled land, rural production diminished and many peasants left their villages. But the great cities still flourished, and the semi-autonomous life of the mountains went on. Even when Ottoman rule had been strong it had scarcely extended to Lebanon, whose local ruling families controlled the mountain community, subject to collection of taxes for the Ottoman Government, and to some control by the governors of Tripoli and Sidon.

No government of Egypt can be indifferent to what happens on its eastern frontier. The Mameluke Ali Bey, and later Bonaparte, tried to conquer Syria from Egypt; and thirty years after Bonaparte Mohammed Ali succeeded in doing so. The ten years of Egyptian rule under his son Ibrahim Pasha (1831–40) were important for Syria. The Egyptians centralized and improved administration, reformed the tax system, increased international trade, extended the area of cultivation, allowed missions to open schools, and established equality of Moslems and Christians. But they also brought heavy taxation, conscription, and disarmament, and when British and Ottoman forces drove Ibrahim out in 1840 they were supported by a popular rising. The Turks returned, but their rule was not so effective as that of the Egyptians, and in Lebanon they began a policy of destroying the traditional autonomy by undermining its basis, the entente of Druzes and Maronites. They were aided in this by the growth of social tension. For 100 years the Maronites had been growing in numbers and strength. Missions and closer contacts with Europe had revived their intellectual life, and their peasantry was moving southwards into lands controlled by Druze lords. Social tension gave rise, for the first time in the history of the mountain, to religious hostility, which led to the civil war of 1860; Druze victories in Lebanon touched off a massacre of Christians by Moslems in Damascus, and the Powers intervened. Napoleon III sent an army, and a conference of Powers resulted in the creation of an autonomous province of Lebanon, with a Christian majority and a Christian governor; it included the mountain range, but neither the Beqaa valley nor the coastal towns of Tripoli, Beirut, and Sidon with their mainly Moslem populations. For the next half-century autonomous Lebanon flourished, under the protection of France and the other Powers. Emigration and silk brought prosperity to her villages, and the mission schools produced an educated class; the rest of Syria prospered too. Turkish administration and rural security improved. Railways were built: the French network linking Beirut, Damascus, and Aleppo was constructed from 1895 onwards, and the Pilgrims' Railway linking Damascus and Medina was opened in 1908. Thanks to security and railways, the area of settled agriculture expanded, and at the same time economic links with the outside world grew stronger. Beirut became the main centre of foreign trade and influence: one of the largest ports in the eastern Mediterranean, the home of the Jesuit University of St. Joseph (1875) and the Syrian Protestant College (1866 – later to become the American University of Beirut), and, largely through them, second only to Cairo as a centre of modern Arabic literature and thought. The Lebanese journalists and writers, alike in Cairo and in Beirut, played an essential part in the transformation of the Arab mind. Beirut, and Lebanon behind it, were centres of radiation of French influence; the French Government subsidized the missions, and French investments in public utilities were considerable. By 1914 Lebanon and the Syrian coast were generally regarded by the other Powers as being in the French sphere of influence.

As prosperity and culture grew, there grew also a more articulate sense of community, which was given form by the Western idea of nationalism, and impetus by the attempts of the Young Turks (1908–18) to impose Turkish domination on the multi-national Empire. There emerged both a Lebanese nationalism, mainly among the Maronites, and a more general Syrian or Arab nationalism, which organized itself in political societies, both open and secret. When war broke out in 1914 Lebanese sentiment was on the side of France, and some of the Arab nationalists were willing to make an agreement with Britain, and use her help to obtain their independence. When the Sharif Hussein revolted in 1916 after negotiations with Britain, he had behind him the Syrian nationalist societies.

Syrian Arabs helped in the Arab revolt, many nationalists both in Syria and Lebanon were executed by the Turks, and Lebanon had her autonomy suppressed and was ravaged by famine.

The French Mandate

When the war ended in 1918, Syria and Lebanon were controlled by Allied troops, mainly British. Under British supreme control there was a French military administration on the coast, and an Arab administration, under Hussein's son Faisal, in the interior with its centre at Damascus. The views of French and Arabs on the future of the country were opposed. The French wanted to control it, both for the sake of their Christian protégés and for reasons of strategy; the Maronites and some of the other Christians wanted an enlarged Lebanon under French tutelage; most of the other groups wanted Syrian independence, and would have preferred American or British to French tutelage. French and Arabs alike looked for support to Britain, which possessed real control and had made commitments to both sides.[1] The Peace Conference discussed the subject and made no decision, except the general decision to apply the new idea of the mandate to the Arab provinces of the Ottoman Empire. At the end of 1919 British troops were withdrawn, and matters moved rapidly to a crisis. In March 1920 a Congress at Damascus proclaimed Faisal King of a united Syria; in April the inter-Allied conference at San Remo refused to accept this, and allotted the mandate for the whole of Syria to France; in June France sent an ultimatum to Faisal and occupied Damascus and the interior. The text of the mandate was approved by the League of Nations in 1923, but before that France had started organizing the territory. In 1920 the state of Greater Lebanon was set up, including the Beqaa and the coastal towns; in 1926 it became the Lebanese Republic. In the rest of the mandated region, after some experiments, separate Governments of Jabal Druze and the Alawis (or Latakia) were set up, and the remainder was formed into the State of Syria; within it the district of Alexandretta was given a special administrative regime, in view of the mixed nature of its population (Turkish, Arab, and Armenian).

[1] See above, p. 16.

A French High Commissariat exercised general supervision and control over the Governments, through a network of 'advisers', and also administered certain services, such as the customs, in which they had a common interest.

During the twenty or so years in which France had the full exercise of her mandate, there was much economic and social progress in both countries. Trade and agriculture increased; the decay of the silk industry in Lebanon was offset by the development of the Jazira; modern textile factories were started; education was expanded, and the amenities of urban life improved. Partly this was a natural process, but partly it was due to the mandatory Government, which built roads, improved internal security, began land survey and settlement, and founded state schools (although more in Syria than in Lebanon, where religious bodies still had almost a monopoly of education). But on the other side, the standard of the French administration was not uniformly high; economic life suffered from the fluctuations of the franc; little was done to train the peoples in the exercise of authority; and the French never established a harmonious relationship with those whom they were supposed, by the terms of the mandate, to prepare for self-government.

In Lebanon, the main political difficulty was that the State in its enlarged form included groups which did not want to belong to it – some non-Catholic Christians as well as most Sunnis and Shiis. An attempt was made to appease them by the system of distributing offices according to the relative strength of the sects, while effective power was kept in French and Maronite hands. But a large part of the population remained unwilling to accept the existence of Lebanon, the domination of Maronites in it, and French control; this, and the universal rule of sectarian considerations, made it difficult for Lebanon to develop unity or a stable national life.

In Syria the Sunni Arab majority was even more unwilling to accept French domination, because of the separation of Syria from the other Arab countries, its internal subdivisions, the denial of the promised independence, and the fear that France would wish to make it a permanent part of her Empire. In 1936 Franco-Syrian and Franco-Lebanese treaties were signed by the Popular Front Government. They provided for the transfer of power, the entry of the two states into the League of Nations, the incorporation of the Druze and Alawi districts into Syria, and the retention by France of two air bases in Syria, and of unlimited military rights in Lebanon. The treaties, however, were never ratified by the French Government. Their main results were to increase the resentment of the nationalists, and to lead to the loss of Alexandretta.[2]

The Syrian Constitution was suspended in 1939, just before the outbreak of war, the Lebanese just after. The collapse of France and the German advance through the Balkans brought both countries within the zone of war. In 1941 the use, contrary to the terms of the Franco-German Armistice Agreement, of air bases in Syria by German and Italian aircraft on their way to support Rashid Ali in Iraq, the use of the French-controlled railway for that purpose, and German infiltration and the danger of an attack across Turkey, led Britain to occupy both countries, with Free French collaboration, after a short campaign. Before the entry of the British and French troops the Free French issued a proclamation of Syrian and Lebanese independence which was confirmed by the British Government, and in an exchange of letters between them and Britain the latter recognized that France should have a predominant position over other European Powers, once the promises of independence had been carried out. The Free French, however, hesitated to carry out their promises while the war was undecided; they did not wish to appear to France to be liberating French territories only to give them up, and they feared that Britain wanted Syria and Lebanon to be independent in order to draw them into her own sphere of influence. If forced to carry out their promises they wished to secure a treaty in return. The Syrians were unwilling to sign a treaty, not only because of memories but also because there was no advantage to be gained in linking themselves with a France which could no longer help or protect them. They wished to bring matters to a crisis while Britain was still there. Their attitude was shared by a large proportion of the Lebanese; many Lebanese now felt strong enough to stand by themselves without French protection, and the mercantile interests of Beirut, which played an increasing part in the life of the Republic, wanted more scope for their activities than the

[2] See above, p. 20.

mandate gave them. In 1943 a 'national pact' was reached between certain Moslem and Christian leaders, to the effect that Lebanon should remain independent within its existing frontiers, but should follow an Arab foreign policy. The British were insistent that the promises of independence should be carried out, for reasons of general Middle Eastern policy; they wished this to happen, if possible, without disorders which might affect other Arab countries, but equally without harm to Anglo-French relations.

Elections were held in 1943, and in both countries opponents of the mandate were in the majority. The new Lebanese Government proposed to remove from the Constitution those clauses which safeguarded French control; the French replied by arresting the President of the Republic and almost the whole Government. Faced with a popular rising, world-wide protests, and a British ultimatum, the French gave in. From that time they gradually transferred power to the two Governments. Syria and Lebanon were allowed to establish their own foreign representation, and they joined the United Nations. But the French still retained control of the local armed forces, and tried to use this as a bargaining counter to compel the Governments to make treaties. In May 1945 a new contingent of French Senegalese troops landed at Beirut. The Syrian Government and people took this as a first step in an attempt to do what had been done in 1920: to build up French strength and crush Syrian nationalism as soon as the British withdrew. Tension grew, local fighting broke out, and the French bombarded Damascus. The British Government now intervened and asked the Free French authorities to order their troops to cease fire and withdraw to their barracks. This was virtually the end of French rule, but French and British troops still remained. After some delay, the matter was brought before the Security Council of the United Nations in February 1946, and in March agreement was reached on the simultaneous withdrawal of British and French troops from Syria by the end of April, and from Lebanon by the end of December. From this time the history of the two States diverges, and it will be more convenient to deal with each of them separately.[3]

[3]For Lebanon see p. 430.

2. Syria

POST-WAR HISTORY AND POLITICS

When foreign troops withdrew in 1946, Syria had already been ruled for three years by a nationalist Government, whose adherents were soon to organize themselves in the National Party. Shukri Quwatli, one of the leaders of the party, had been President since 1943, and two others, Saadullah Jabri and Jamil Mardam, became Prime Minister in succession. Until 1949 the main struggle for power was between them and other politicians of the same type, although mainly of a slightly younger generation, organized in the People's Party (Shaab). But beneath the surface both of them were losing their hold on the country. The men who had led the struggle against the French did not prove adept at the task of ruling. They had to try to impose the authority of the Government in a country where local, tribal, and religious leaders were strong, and where the transfer of power had taken place suddenly, without the co-operation of those who had previously possessed it; to build up an administration; and to face the economic difficulties involved in the change from war to peace, and from dependence to independence. Something, it is true, was done. New elements were drawn into the administration; Syria left the franc bloc and became financially independent; agreement was reached with the American Tapline Company for the building of a pipeline from the Persian Gulf across Syria to Sidon (ratified in May 1949). The President obtained an extension of his term of office in April 1948, but his influence and that of the regime were waning. To the rising cost of living and the knowledge of corruption in high places was added public anger at the failure of the Arab governments in regard to Palestine. In December 1948 there were riots against the Government. Order was restored by the army, and a change of Government was made. The army had shown it was the only force which could maintain the authority of the Government, and from that it was only a short step to its taking upon itself to decide what government it was willing to maintain. On 30–31 March 1949 an army group under Colonel Husni Zaim carried out a bloodless *coup d'état*. The President and the Prime Minister resigned, and Zaim himself took the latter post, and later the Presidency. The Chamber was dissolved and all political parties abolished, and Zaim announced his intention of carrying out sweeping reforms. Among the measures planned or promulgated were the building up of the army, the political emancipation of women, the proclamation of a civil code, the reorganization of the Syrian University, and the building of an international port at Latakia. Some of these measures were later achieved; but Zaim himself soon lost what popularity he had at first possessed. In his foreign policy he alienated Iraq and Jordan, after at first inclining towards them, and leaned strongly towards Egypt and also towards France; he shocked a powerful group by first giving asylum to the Lebanese leader of the Syrian Social Nationalist Party, Antoun Saadeh, and then handing him over to the Lebanese Government to be executed. On 14 August 1949 another army coup took place under Colonel Sami Hinnawi; Zaim and his Prime Minister were executed, and Hashim Atassi became President; he was one of the most respected of the older nationalist leaders, and had already been President from 1936 to 1939. He took office with a Government drawn largely from the People's Party, and elections held in November (the first at which women had been allowed to vote) gave this party the largest number of seats. It had a leaning towards the Iraqi connection, and the question of union with Iraq under a Hashimite King was now raised. The National Party withdrew its objections, and union seemed near. Those who opposed it, inside and outside Syria, joined forces to prevent it, and on 19 December a third *coup d'état* took place, this time under Colonel Adib Shishakli. A new Government was formed, under an independent Prime Minister but with representatives of the People's Party, and constitutional life proceeded apparently undisturbed; on 5 September 1950, the Constitution now in force was promulgated. But there was a persistent and growing tension between the two seats of authority, parliament with the People's Party as its dominant group, and Shishakli and his collaborators in the army. Gradually the balance shifted in favour of the army. In 1951 the struggle between Government and army came to a head, and on 29 November Shishakli carried out a further coup, and arrested almost all the members of the Government. President Atassi resigned, and Shishakli dissolved parliament. From that time power was in his hands. He became Chief of Staff and Deputy Prime Minister, and one of his associates, Fawzi Silo, became Head of the State and Prime Minister. In April 1952 all political parties were dissolved, and later an official party, the Arab Liberation Movement, was set up. In the summer of 1953 a further change took place, when a new Constitution was issued, more on the American than the French model, and a referendum in July resulted in the Constitution being adopted and Shishakli elected as President and Prime Minister for five years; Silo withdrew from public life. But beneath the surface opposition to the dictator was growing. In February 1954 trouble broke out in Jabal Druze, and this gave the opportunity for an army rising, beginning in northern Syria. Shishakli resigned and left the country; part of the army still supported him, but after a confused period agreement was reached on the return of Atassi as President.

The four years during which Shishakli dominated Syria left their mark. However unpopular his rule, he imposed the authority of the Government on the whole country. He had leanings towards social reform, and for a time worked closely with Akram Hourani, who founded the Socialist Party in 1950; in October and November 1952 he issued two decrees limiting the amount of state domain any individual could hold, and providing for its distribution in smallholdings. In economic matters he initiated the policy which subsequent governments have carried on. The young industries of Damascus and Aleppo were protected by tariffs. This involved the dissolution, in March 1950, of the customs union which Syria and Lebanon had inherited from the French mandate; Lebanon's interest was as much in free trade as Syria's in protection. Some public works were started; work began on Latakia harbour in 1950, and preparations were made for land reclamation in the Ghab depression. In general economic development was left to private enterprise, with some official control. In foreign policy Shishakli's policy was pro-Egyptian and pro-Saudi in Arab affairs; he tended to lean towards

France and away from the other Western powers, but he was also opposed to Communism.

After the fall of Shishakli the Constitution of 1950 was restored and elections were held in September 1954. They resulted in the return of about 28 members of the People's Party, 13 of the National Party, and 16 of the Baath (Socialist) Party; the rest of the Chamber of 142 were Independents or belonged to smaller groups, and for the first time a Communist was elected. None of the organized parties could form a Government without the support of some of the Independents.

The year 1955 was one of comparative quiet. A fairly stable coalition governed the country, with only minor changes. In foreign affairs it continued to align itself with Egypt and Saudi Arabia. The election of Shukri Quwatli as President in August, when Atassi's term came to an end, was a sign of the movement of opinion in favour of the Egyptian and Saudi connection, of which he had long been a supporter.

In 1956 the main line of Syrian policy continued. On 5 July Syria announced her intention of negotiating a federal union with Egypt. In October a joint Syro-Jordanian-Egyptian military command was agreed on. Next month, the Anglo-French armed intervention in Egypt led to the breaking off of relations with Britain and France, and the blowing up of the IPC pipeline. At the same time efforts were made to establish closer connections with Jordan, which was now moving away from the British alliance. On 6 August a customs and economic union was agreed on; in October, when it was feared that Israel might attack Jordan, Iraqi troops at the request of the Jordan Government were concentrated on the Iraq–Jordan frontier, while Syrian troops with Jordanian agreement moved into Jordan. Under the Arab Solidarity Pact of January 1957 Syria undertook to contribute £E 2.5 million a year towards the £E 12.5 million required to replace the British subsidy.

Throughout the year, however, there were signs of a change both in the balance of Syrian policy and in the composition of the Government. The Soviet offer to supply arms (through Czechoslovakia) first to Egypt and later to Syria, dependent hitherto on supplies doled out by the Western Powers under the 1950 Declaration, created a sharp pro-Soviet feeling in Syrian military circles. This was due less to Communist sympathies than to the perennial distrust of Western policy in regard to Israel and gratitude to the Soviet Union for general support of the Arab cause against Israel and in particular for the supply of arms. In July Syria recognized Communist China.

This new policy of friendship with the Soviet Union was closely connected with the growth in power of the Baath Party. On 15 June 1956 Sabri Assali, Secretary of the National Party, formed a new coalition Government in which the Baath Socialists were represented, and in the next months they gained strength. They succeeded, better than any other group, in canalizing popular nationalist feeling, pro-Egyptian, vaguely reformist, neutralist with an anti-Western inclination; and they were on close terms with a group of officers, led by Abdul Hamid Sarraj and strongly neutralist in feeling, which was dominant in the army.

There was, however, still opposition, by certain members of the People's Party. In December 1956 the Government announced that they, as well as other opponents of the regime, had been discovered to be implicated in a plot, in agreement with Iraq and the Western Powers, to overturn the Government at the time of the attack on Egypt. Those of them who had not fled the country were arrested and brought to trial.

The beginning of 1957 was marked by the formation of a new parliamentary bloc with a neutralist and popular nationalist programme. As a result the Government was reconstructed, with Assali still as Prime Minister. The new Government rejected the Eisenhower Plan on 10 January, calling it superfluous, and declaring that the United States had no right to send troops to any Arab country without the previous approval of the United Nations.

Inside the Government there was a struggle between the influence of the Baath and that of Khalid al-Azm, an unsuccessful candidate for the Presidency of the Republic in 1955. It was perhaps with an eye to future elections and to outbid the Baath that he became the chief spokesman of the pro-Soviet group.

The close relations with the Soviet Union as well as internal tension and instability complicated Syria's relations with the West and with her neighbours. The United States Government made no secret of its anxiety about developments in Syria. On the other hand many Syrians suspected the United States of instigating the opposition in Syria, or her neighbours, to overturn the regime, while the neutralists fiercely opposed the Baghdad Pact, and then the Eisenhower Doctrine, as designed to draw Middle East states into the American sphere of influence. Above all the American attitude towards Israel, which remained unchanged, determined the attitude of the average Syrian towards the West, just as it was the main cause of any pro-Soviet feelings he might have.

The struggle between Right and Left continued. Sarraj remained in his post in spite of efforts to have him transferred abroad. The opposition felt growing pressure from the Government, and some of the most prominent left the country. A Shaabist, the President of the Chamber, was replaced by Akram Hourani, the most powerful of the leaders of the Baath.

The complicity of Syria in the troubles of the Nabulsi period in Jordan was shown on the occasion of the flight of Abu Nuwar and his successor as Chief of Staff to Syria. The intention of the Syrian Government to bring about the annexation of Jordan seemed sufficiently clear to Iraq and Saudi Arabia to prompt them to take military measures to forestall it. The Jordanian request for the withdrawal of Syrian troops, which were stated to have interfered in the internal affairs of Jordan, was complied with by Syria with an ill grace.

Only with Egypt did relations remain good. Nevertheless there were signs that Egypt feared lest Syria's policy should lead to a world conflict, and wished to bring her back to the path of strict neutrality.

A threat of aggression against Syria was alleged both by Syria and by the Soviet Union, which in September charged Turkey with massing troops on the frontier with the intention of attacking Syria. Egypt sent a small body of troops to Syria and announced that it was to assist her against the Turkish threat.

Although the Syrian Parliament and political life were still apparently dominated by oligarchs of the old school, real power from 1954 onwards was shifted steadily into the hands of the Baathists, the Communists, and their respective sympathizers especially in the army. In the summer of 1957 an officer with Communist affiliations, Colonel Afif al-Bizri, became Army Chief of Staff.

The Syrian/Egyptian Union 1958–61

The chief impulse behind the Syrian/Egyptian union was the Syrian Baath. President Nasser at first opposed the idea of union and when he agreed he insisted that it should not be heavily centralized and not a federal union as the Syrians wanted, and that political parties should be dissolved. The Syrian Prime Minister, Khalid al-Azm, the Deputy Premier, and the Communists all attempted to prevent the union but without success.

On 2 February 1958 Presidents Nasser and Quwatli jointly announced that a United Arab Republic of Egypt and Syria would be set up with legislative authority vested in an assembly in which Syria would have one quarter of the seats and Egypt three quarters. A plebiscite held in both countries on 21 February resulted in an almost unanimous vote in favour of the union and of Nasser as the first President. Shukri al-Quwatli retired with the honorific title of 'First Citizen of the UAR' and the Communists went undergound.

The Syrian Baathists were given high office in the Union. But the Baathists, after nominally dissolving their organization together with the other political parties, had hoped to control Syrian political life through the National Union organization and to this President Nasser was strongly opposed. Colonel Sarraj, the powerful Interior Minister for the Syrian region, co-operated with Cairo against the Baath who were consequently unable to screen the candidates for the National Union elections held in July 1959. The result was that an estimated 250 Baathists were elected out of a total of 9,445 seats. In August President Nasser dismissed Riyadh al-Malki, the Baathist Minister of National Guidance and the remaining Baathists in leading positions resigned *en bloc* in December 1959 and went into retirement or self-exile in Lebanon.

Colonel Sarraj succeeded Akram Hourani as Chairman of the Syrian Executive Council and President Nasser increasingly relied upon him and his police methods for governing Syria.

In 1960, however, Nasser sent his closest colleague, Field-Marshal Abdul Hakim Amer, as a quasi-proconsul to Syria with instructions to alleviate the causes of growing Syrian opposition to the union. These included army resentment against the appointment of senior Egyptian officers in the Syrian forces, middle-class antipathy for Egyptian socialist legislation, economic restrictions and bureaucratic methods, landowners' opposition to agrarian reform, and the intelligentsia's dislike of limitations to intellectual freedom. Since the departure of the Baath Syria appeared more than ever as the junior partner in the union. Finally, three years of consecutive drought in Syria's agrarian economy did nothing to increase the Government's popularity. President Nasser retained most of his personal popularity among the Syrian people and drew wildly enthusiastic crowds on his visits. But he had manifestly failed to discover a satisfactory method of governing Syria.

In August 1961 even Sarraj fell from favour and was moved to Cairo as Vice-President. A month later he resigned and returned to Damascus. But it was a group of other army officers who on 28 September arrested Field-Marshal Amer, put him on a plane to Cairo and announced Syria's secession from the UAR.

1961–1963

President Nasser decided not to resist the secession by force but at once began denouncing the 'reactionary secessionist' regime in Syria. The elections which were held under the pre-union electoral system in early 1962 resulted in a victory for the right-wing forces who watered down the UAR land reform and repealed most of the socialization measures.

The Syrians responded by strongly asserting their Arabism and continued devotion to the cause of Arab unity. They called their state the 'Syrian Arab Republic' and circulated Arab governments with a draft plan for federal union. In repealing the UAR socialist legislation they claimed to be replacing opportunist measures by 'constructive socialism'. But it was difficult for the Syrians to sustain a progressive socialist image and the Government was manifestly weak and unstable. The Syrian left-wing soon turned against the predominantly right-wing regime.

On 28 March 1962 the Syrian army high command moved against the civilian regime it had brought to power and arrested President Qudsi and most of his Government. But the army was divided in purpose; a pro-Nasser section in Aleppo which had declared for a new union with Egypt succumbed to a force sent from Damascus. Army officers of different tendencies either fled or were exiled and, after failing to find enough civilian politicians to form a new Government, the army command was obliged to release President Qudsi and his Cabinet. A Government was formed under Dr. Bashir al-Azma.

The Azma Government partially restored some of the UAR socialization measures and took some steps towards improving relations with Cairo. But these gestures did not suffice to placate Cairo. The radio war was soon resumed and the deterioation in Syrian/Egyptian relations culminated in a violent clash at an Arab League meeting in Lebanon in August 1962.

In an effort to strengthen its fragile position the Syrian Government cultivated its relations with the Iraqi leader Abdul Karim Kassem. But this proved fatal as Kassem and his regime were overthrown by a Baathist coup on 8 February 1963. Demoralized and weakened, the Syrian regime was easily swept away in a bloodless coup on 8 March.

1963–1966: The First Baathist Regime

As in Iraq, a National Revolutionary Command Council (NRCC) of anonymous officers and civilians assumed power and appointed a predominantly Baathist Cabinet headed by Salah Bitar.

The coup had not been led by the Baath but in the political vacuum created by the coup the Baathists were the only organized political group outside those associated with the deposed regime. The Nasserists may have been more numerous but they lacked cohesion. The NRCC chose as its president Colonel Louay al-Atassi a mild and moderate young army officer who, although not a Baathist, was known as a sympathizer. Brigadier Amin al-Hafez, a much stronger and more forceful character who was a Baathist became Minister of Interior in the new Government.

The Baathists held the key posts in the Government but it included members of other Arab unionist organizations. At this stage these other parties assumed that the Baath would be prepared to share power with them. They believed that they would be indispensable to the Baathists in the tripartite unity negotiations between Syria, Iraq, and Egypt which began in a mood of pan-Arabist euphoria immediately after the Syrian coup. In return the Syrian Baathists showed readiness to co-operate but only as a tactical manoeuvre.

The unity talks were held in three stages between 14 March and 14 April; some of the discussions included the Iraqis and some were bilateral Egyptian/Syrian negotiations. President Nasser did not conceal his dislike and suspicion of the Syrian Baathists whom he had not forgiven for their mass resignation from the UAR Government in 1959 and there were many sharp exchanges.

Friction between Damascus and Cairo had already become open, with strong mutual press criticism before the end of March. Nevertheless the differences were papered over sufficiently to enable a final agreement on the form of a tripartite federal state to be published on 17 April.

In view of the mutual mistrust between the parties and their different interpretations of this agreement its collapse was inevitable. The fundamental flaw in the agreement was that the Syrian Baathists wanted President Nasser's approval and support for their government of Syria but not his interference. President Nasser rejected this arrangement. Within two weeks of 17 April Syrian/Egyptian relations deteriorated sharply. The Syrian army expelled scores of Nasserist officers while the civilian Baathists foiled the efforts of the non-Baathist Arab unionist parties to obtain a larger share of power.

Syrian/Egyptian relations had deteriorated to such a point that General Louay Atassi headed a delegation to Alexandria on 18 July to discuss them with President Nasser. A few hours after the Syrians left Damascus Airport an ill-organized pro-Nasser coup was attempted and ruthlessly crushed and on 22 July Nasser, who had held his fire until then, made his long-awaited speech attacking the Baath in Syria as a 'secessionist, inhuman, and immoral regime'.

The Syrian Baathists were now on as bad terms with Egypt as the preceding regime had been. On the other hand, the Syrians drew closer to Iraq. On 8 October a Syrian/Iraqi military union was agreed upon and the Iraqi Defence Minister General Saleh Mahdi Ammash became Commander-in-Chief of the combined armies.

Just when it seemed that the Baath Party might succeed in creating a Syrian/Iraqi union where so many earlier attempts had failed, the Iraqi Baathists were swept from power by President Aref and other non-Baathist officers in a coup on 18 November. The Syrians bitterly condemned the coup.

At odds with both Iraq and Egypt, Syria was isolated within the Arab world. But General Hafez, who had quietly replaced General Louay Atassi as President of the Syrian NRCC, inaugurated a period of firm and authoritarian government. Syria's isolation was underlined at the meeting of Arab Kings and Presidents which convened in Cairo in January 1964 at President Nasser's invitation to discuss means of opposing Israel's plans to divert the waters of the River Jordan. Syria's demand for urgent military action against Israel was rejected by the other Arab states.

Relations with the Aref regime in Iraq worsened and on 28 April the Iraqi/Syrian military union was abrogated. At the second Arab summit meeting in Alexandria in September 1964 the Syrians were again somewhat isolated but General Hafez, formerly one of Egypt's strongest critics, adopted a policy in favour of a *rapprochement* with Cairo. He was bitterly opposed by anti-Egyptian Baathist officers led by Colonel Salah Jedid.

Despite frequent reports that the Baathists intended to enlarge the Government to share real power with non-Baathist unionist elements this was not done. During 1965 the Baathists tightened their control of the country.

In August 1965 an all-Baathist National Revolutionary Council was established with the task of drafting a permanent constitution. However, there was a clear division within the party between the radical extremists and the more moderate elements who favoured conciliating the middle classes. In January 1966 the radical Cabinet led by Dr. Yusuf Zuayen was replaced by one more Government led by the moderate Salah Bitar. However, on 23 February 1966 the extremists seized power in a violent coup led by Colonel Jedid. General Hafez was imprisoned and Salah Bitar and Michel Aflaq went into exile. Dr. Zuayen formed the new Government and Dr. Nureddin Atassi became Head of State. The Cabinet included two Communist sympathizers, and restrictions were lifted on the activities of the Syrian Communist party.

The Second Baathist Regime

The new regime moved closer to the Soviet Union which in April 1966 concluded, in place of West Germany, a deal for the construction of a Euphrates Dam. Although the Government was cool and mistrustful in its general attitude towards President Nasser and Egypt, circumstances brought the two countries closer together. The Syrians were anxious to end their isolation while Nasser hoped to be able to exert some influence over the hot-headed young neo-Marxists in power in Damascus. The new Syrian regime was if possible even more anti-Israeli in its attitude than its predecessor. In July 1966 the Israelis successfully bombarded Syrian diversion operations on the River Banias from the air and the Syrians abandoned the work. Nasser could not ignore Syrian requests for a closer military alliance, especially when Egyptian spokesmen had so often claimed that Egyptian forces were the most formidable in the Arab world. In November 1966 Egypt signed a comprehensive defence pact with Syria providing for a full merger and a joint command for the two armies in the event of war. But the Syrians were still too distrustful of Egypt to accept the stationing of Egyptian troops and planes on their territory which alone would have made the pact effective.

The June War

The Syrians bear a measure of responsibility for the outbreak of the 1967 Six Day War. The Israelis had responded to Syria's open support for the Palestinian guerrillas with military reprisals and threats of heavier action. In the early months of 1967 there were frequent incidents on Syria's armistice line with Israel, and in April Syria lost six MiG fighters in an air clash during which Israeli aircraft flew over Damascus. On 12 May the Israeli Chief of Staff General Rabin declared that until the revolutionary regime in Syria had been overthrown no Government in the Middle East could feel safe.

Rumours were circulating in Syrian Government circles of an impending major Israeli offensive. When these reports reached President Nasser and were confirmed by his own intelligence services and Soviet sources he felt compelled to take action and asked for the UN Emergency Force in Sinai to be removed. Syrians and Jordanians had often criticized Nasser for hiding his forces behind the protection of UNEF. His subsequent closure of the Straits of Tiran led the Israelis to attack Egypt on 5 June.

When war came the Syrians did not attempt to invade Israel although they used their artillery from the Golan Heights against Israeli positions. After defeating Jordan, Israel turned against Syria, stormed the Golan Heights, and occupied the key town of Quneitra. The Syrians agreed to a ceasefire on 10 June, one day later than Egypt.

After the war the Syrians maintained the view that the Arabs should continue the struggle at all costs although they were widely criticized in the Arab world for having held back in the war. The Foreign Minister Ibrahim Makhous attended the Arab Foreign Ministers meeting at Khartoum in August but was not authorized by his Government to represent it at the summit conference that followed. Consequently Syria was excluded from the Arab oil states' aid to Egypt and Jordan to compensate them for their war losses.

Syria's total rejection of any political solution to the Arab-Israeli conflict was not backed up by any energetic military action and there were few incidents on the Golan Heights during 1968. Tension and uncertainty at home were increased by the July coup in Baghdad which brought to power in Iraq the orthodox Baathists of the kind that had been ousted in Syria in 1966. A division appeared between Colonel Jedid, assistant Secretary-General of the Baath Party in Syria, who wished to pursue Syria's independent radical line, and the Defence Minister, General Hafez Assad, who favoured a *rapprochement* with the Iraqi Baathists and disliked Syria's increasing dependence on the USSR. A widely noted feature of the regime was that many of its leaders including Jedid and Assad were of the minority sub-Shii Alawite sect which had not traditionally held political power in Syria and is not generally attracted to pan-Arabist ideas.

In the spring and early summer of 1970 the Syrians demonstrated their intention to reactivate their front with Israel which had been relatively dormant since the 1967 war. Their aim was to reduce the pressure on Egypt at the Suez Canal and to reassert their claim to the Golan Heights in the event of a Middle East settlement. In late March and early April Syrian forces made a series of raids on Israeli forces in the Golan Heights and there were more serious engagements in June.

As the Jordanian crisis deepened in August and September the Syrians expressed vigorous support for the Palestinian guerrillas. On 19 September, after the outbreak of the Jordanian civil war, Syrian armoured units entered northern Jordan. They withdrew a few days later, having suffered severe casualties.

This action helped to bring to a head the submerged conflict between the civilian wing of the Baath led by Salah Jedid and the military wing led by General Assad. When the civilian Baathists criticized General Assad who had opposed the intervention in Jordan he took counter-measures to ensure his position and the loyalty of the armed forces. He formed a new Syrian Regional Command of the Baath of his own supporters on 18 November. The relatively unknown Ahmad Khatib became Head of State, and General Assad himself as Prime Minister and Defence Minister headed a new Coalition Government of Baathists and Nasserists (with two Communists). He also took over control of al-Saiqa guerrilla organization.

In February 1971 Ahmad Khatib resigned and Hafez Assad assumed the Presidency for a seven-year term.

President Assad

President Assad's advent to power marked some relaxation in the political atmosphere and an improvement in relations with most Arab states. He released several hundred political prisoners and announced the restoration of public liberties. He broadened the base of the regime to give Communists, Nasserists and other left-wing Arab nationalist groups a genuine share of power for the first time since 1963. A People's Council – Syria's first legislative assembly since 1966 – was appointed by the Baathist Regional Command; of its 173 members, 87 were Baathists, 8 Communists, and 36 representatives of the

General Union of Farmers. One consequence of the change in regime was the 'personalization' of authority for the first time since Gamal Abdul Nasser lost power in Syria with the break-up of the Syrian/Egyptian union in 1961. Amendments to the constitution gave the President wide powers similar to those of the Egyptian President.

In March President Franjieh of Lebanon made the first official visit to Damascus of a Lebanese head of state since either country's independence, and in April President Assad signed the agreement for the Egyptian-Libyan-Syrian federation in Benghazi.

In March 1972 a further step was taken to loosen exclusive Baathist political control when a National Progressive Front was formed to comprise an 18-member central leadership including President Assad, nine other Baathists and two members from each of four non-Baathist parties. At the same time some mild but significant forms of liberalization were pursued. Import restrictions were relaxed, private enterprise and foreign investment encouraged, and steps taken to attract expatriate Syrian and Arab capital.

In March also President Assad gave evidence of Syria's new flexibility when he said for the first time that Syria accepted UN Security Council Resolution 242 as a basis for a political settlement in the Middle East provided it meant a complete Israeli withdrawal from territories occupied in 1967 and full restitution of Palestinian rights. This contributed to a further improvement in relations with President Sadat's regime in Egypt although Syria did not follow Egypt's example in expelling its Soviet military advisers. In fact it was announced in September that Syria and the Soviet Union had agreed on a military build-up in Syria. President Assad was anxious to avoid a complete break between Egypt and the Soviet Union. He made a secret visit to Moscow at the end of September which prepared the ground for the partial Egyptian-Soviet *rapprochement* that followed.

While Syria was taking steps to improve its relations with Saudi Arabia and the conservative Arab Gulf states, its relationship with the rival Baathist regions in Iraq underwent strains and difficulties. The atmosphere improved when Syria nationalized the Iraq Petroleum Company's installations in

Syria in the wake of Iraq's nationalization of IPC in June. But in October a new dispute arose over the level of Syria's transit dues for Iraqi oil. The Iraqi government continually condemned Syria for having accepted the principle of a political settlement of the Arab-Israeli dispute.

Co-operation with Egypt became steadily closer during the year and relations with Jordan also improved for the first time in several years. Diplomatic relations between Amman and Damascus were restored in October.

The October War

On 6 October 1973 Syria launched a massive offensive, in collaboration with Egypt, to try to recover territory in the Golan Heights occupied by Israel following the 1967 war. After initial advances the Syrian forces were thrown back in fierce fighting until the front was stabilized some thirty miles from Damascus. Syria suffered severe losses in men and equipment and from Israeli air attacks on the Homs refinery, oil terminals at Banias and Tartus, power stations, and other installations. The Government later estimated its material losses at one billion pounds sterling. However, the military engagements with the Israelis were much more evenly matched than in 1967, and Syrian morale remained fairly high even when the fighting ended. Syria delayed more than twenty-four hours before accepting UN Security Council Resolution 338 calling for a cease-fire on 22 October, and a week later President Assad said that Syria was ready to resume fighting unless Israel withdrew from Arab territory. Syria refused to submit lists of prisoners and instead stipulated a series of conditions and accusations. Israel meanwhile accused Syria of torturing and murdering Israeli prisoners. At least partly because of this dispute, Syria refused to participate in the Middle East peace conference that opened in Geneva on 21 December.

Iraq sent 18,000 troops with tanks and aircraft to fight alongside the Syrians but these were withdrawn, against Syrian protests, as soon as Syria accepted the cease-fire. Jordan sent two battalions of troops and this further cemented Jordanian-Syrian relations.

In the winter and spring of 1974 there was a danger of a renewed outbreak between Syria and Israel as Syria conducted a war of attrition against Israel on the Golan Heights. Despite the vigorous diplomacy of the US Secretary of State Dr. Kissinger, no progress was made towards a disengagement of forces similar to the one agreed between Israel and Egypt in January. Syria received strong support from the Soviet Union which was displeased at being kept out of the Israeli-Egyptian disengagement negotiations. But Dr. Kissinger persisted and Syria, recognizing that the US remained the key to any Israeli withdrawal, continued to negotiate with strong Egyptian encouragement. Finally Dr. Kissinger's shuttle diplomacy between Damascus and Jerusalem was successful in reaching an agreement on 29 May. This provided for Israel to withdraw to the pre-1973 boundaries and to relinquish an additional band of territory including the former Golan Heights capital Quneitra. When the Israeli forces left, Syrian civilians were allowed to return but they found the city had been razed to the ground. The Syrians maintained that it could not be restored to life unless the agricultural areas surrounding it were handed back to Syria.

As a consequence of the agreement with Israel there was a limited *rapprochement* with the US. President Nixon visited Damascus in June 1974; the Syrian welcome was friendly but much more restrained than the Egyptian. Agreement was reached on the full restoration of relations which had been broken off since 1967. Relations were also restored with West Germany in August, and Syrian attitudes to the West in general became more friendly. However, in 1975 Syria became increasingly critical of US diplomatic initiatives aimed to achieve a second disengagement agreement between Israel and Egypt, and embittered by the failure to secure any further withdrawal of Israeli forces from Syrian territory. When Israel and Egypt finally signed the agreement on 1 September, President Assad angrily attacked it as a breach of Arab solidarity. Syria's feeling of isolation in the face of Israel, following Egypt's virtual withdrawal from the front, caused it to move even closer to Jordan. Joint Syrian and Jordanian political and economic committees were formed, customs barriers were removed at the frontier and the leaders of the two countries exchanged frequent visits. In contrast, relations with Iraq showed no signs of improvement with the Iraqis continuing to denounce the Syrians as capitulationists for having accepted UN Resolutions which implied a political solution to the Arab-Israeli conflict.

In addition to its anxiety about the Arab-Israeli position, Syria was closely concerned with the civil war that developed in Lebanon during 1975.

Intervention in Lebanon

Throughout 1975 and the early part of 1976 the Syrian government tried to mediate between the warring factions in Lebanon, although its balance of sympathy lay with the Lebanese leftists and their Palestinian allies. Syrian mediation actually led to a cease-fire in January and the Constitutional Declaration of 14 February which seemed to provide the basis for a permanent settlement. However, the situation began to deteriorate again in March and the Syrian-backed Saiqa guerrilla forces prevented the Palestinian/leftist forces from pressing the advantage they had gained in most of the country and driving President Franjieh from office. Syria was anxious to avoid the partition of Lebanon into a majority area dominated by the Palestinians and leftists, which would be likely to involve Syria in a war with Israel, and a Christian enclave which would most probably be in alliance with the Zionist state. In April some 4,000 Syrian troops crossed into Lebanese territory to back up Saiqa. Although the Syrian-supported candidate for the Lebanese presidency, Elias Sarkis, was elected on 8 May, the civil war continued to escalate and on 31 May the Syrian army intervened on a massive scale, occupying the Beqaa Valley and advancing along the road to Beirut against Palestinian/leftist opposition. The Syrians had surprisingly become the allies of the Lebanese right-wing Christians. Iraq and Egypt, (stung by Syrian attacks on Sinai 2), and of course the PLO, were highly critical of Syrian intervention; but Syria insisted it would only withdraw its troops if replaced by an adequate Arab League force capable of restoring peace. It was not until mid-October that Saudi-Kuwaiti mediation succeeded in arranging a summit meeting of Syria, Egypt,

Lebanon, Kuwait, and the PLO in Riyadh, which agreed on an increase in the token Arab League force already in Lebanon to 30,000 with the addition of Syrian troops. These decisions were endorsed by a general Arab summit a week later. The cease-fire came into force on 21 October, and by mid-November the Arab Deterrent Force, as it was called, had entered Beirut.

The ending of the Lebanese civil war and the acceptance of Syria's peace-keeping role enhanced the prestige of President Assad's regime. Syria's dominance of Lebanon and its close relationship with Jordan raised the possibility of revived Greater Syria in the region under Syrian leadership. However, the intervention in Lebanon created some besetting problems for Syria. It tied down a substantial proportion of its armed forces at an estimated cost of about £1 million a day. Although Saudi Arabia and other Arab oil states were helping to finance the Arab Deterrent Force they were not anxious to promote the Greater Syria concept. Syria now had the responsibility for bolstering President Sarkis and his regime and supporting his efforts to restore some authority to the Lebanese government as a means of re-uniting the country. In the pacification of Lebanon, Syria was faced by a clear dilemma: because it was unable to deploy its forces south of the River Litani for fear of provoking a direct clash with Israel, it was unable to restore peace in Southern Lebanon, where severe clashes continued throughout 1977 between Palestinians and leftists on the one hand, and Christian militia in their border enclaves, closely supported by the Israelis on the other. This dilemma became more acute in March 1978 when Israel invaded Southern Lebanon in an attempt to clear the area of Palestinian guerrillas and Syria was unable to risk intervention.

During 1977 Syria joined Egypt in attempting to resume the Geneva peace conference. President Assad had a friendly meeting with US President Carter in Geneva on 9 May. However, differences of emphasis and approach from Egypt became apparent, and Syrian spokesmen grew increasingly critical of what they regarded as excessive Egyptian deference to US wishes. In November President Assad tried to dissuade President Sadat from launching his peace initiative to Jerusalem and, when this failed, he declared it to be a betrayal of the Arab cause. Syria joined Algeria, Libya, the PDRY and PLO in the anti-Egyptian Front of Steadfastness. For some months this did not mean any reconciliation with Baathist Iraq which continued to insist that Syria should repudiate all UN resolutions calling for a political settlement in the Middle East; but when in October 1978 President Assad visited Baghdad, Syria and Iraq agreed to bury their differences. This prepared the ground for the Baghdad summit meeting of Arab states opposed to the Camp David agreements between Egypt, Israel, and the US. It was apparent that if the Syrian-Iraqi alliance could be maintained and strengthened it would mean a major realignment of forces in the Arab World. But a fundamental difference remained between Syria's acceptance of the principle of a political settlement and Iraq's opposition which had only been toned down for tactical reasons.

In 1978, Syria returned to a more natural alliance with the PLO in common opposition to Egypt, although considerable mutual suspicion remained. Similarly, this implied a break between Syria and the majority of its former temporary allies along with the Lebanese Maronites who now openly vaunted their close relationship with Israel which they believed would come to their support. In the summer and autumn of 1978 the Syrian forces in Lebanon clashed with the Lebanese Christian militia in the fiercest fighting since the civil war.

A plebiscite held in March 1978 confirmed Hafez Assad's second seven-year term as President by a huge majority. His figure still dominated the regime which seemed secure despite the country's difficulties. However, there were signs of unrest which was partly directed against President Assad's own Alawite minority, several of whom were assassinated in 1978. Corruption in the administration was also an issue and the government attempted various counter-measures. Nevertheless the major problem confronting the regime remained that of extricating itself from the involvement in Lebanon without the consequences of partition or a resumption of the civil war.

The *rapprochement* with the rival Baathist regime in Baghdad in the autumn of 1978 temporarily strengthened Syria's position but planned moves towards an Iraqi/Syrian union held fire and in August 1979 the new relationship was endangered by Iraqi suspicions of Syrian involvement in an attempted coup in Baghdad. At home the opposition to the Alawite-dominated regime by Sunni Moslems, led by the Moslem Brothers, intensified and in September 1979 there was severe sectarian rioting in Latakia.

THE PEOPLE

The September 1970 census gave the population as 6.3 million. The mid-1977 estimate was 7.84 million. The 1976 estimates of the population of the main towns were Damascus 1,842,000; Aleppo 1,571,000; Homs 684,000; Hama 617,000; Hasakeh 548,000; Latakia 453,000.

The nomadic bedouin population has declined steadily since the war and the greatest population density is in the Hauran, Jabal Druze, and Hama regions. Arabic is the standard language, with English and French widely spoken. Most Syrians are of Semitic stock (primarily Arab); the principal minorities are Armenians (about 150,000) who live mainly in Aleppo and Damascus, and Kurds (about 50,000) who live mostly in the Turkish border areas and in Damascus. The Assyrians, estimated at 20,000, often speaking the Syriac language, live in villages along the Nahr al-Khabur in the north-east and on the western slopes of the Anti-Lebanon Mountains.

Religious differences are of considerable although declining political importance. Christians, mainly Orthodox, form about 8 per cent of the population and are largely an urban middle-class community. The main Moslem sects are orthodox Sunni (the majority), Alawis, Shiis, Ismailis and Druzes. The Druzes (about 200,000) and Alawis (about 600,000) both exert a disproportionate amount of political influence. There are about 5,000 Jews.

GOVERNMENT

Syria has a written Constitution dating from 1950 establishing it as a democratic parliamentary regime. After the Baath Socialist Party seized power in 1963 the country was ruled by the coalition of army officers and civilians who formed the

National Revolutionary Council. In February 1971 the Provisional Constitution was amended to give the President wide powers similar to those of the Egyptian President, and these were further extended in June 1972.

Administratively, the country is divided into 11 *Muhafazat* (provinces) which are subdivided into 37 *mantiqat* (districts) and 99 *nahiyat* (sub-districts). The Ministry of the Interior appoints the *Muhafiz* (Governor) of the province and other district officers.

Political Organizations

Political parties in Syria are banned except for the Baath but though dormant they are not extinct. The Communists remain a 'petit bourgeois' group drawn mainly from the professional classes and the religious minorities with little support from the peasantry although there are signs of Communist influence in the new industrial proletariat. Relations between the Communists and the Baath fluctuate but the Baath does not accept a Communist challenge to its authority. The Moslem Brotherhood still has a following – especially in Damascus and Hama – but it was never a paramilitary terrorist organization as in Egypt.

SOCIAL SURVEY

The political power of the landowners who were formerly the most coherent social group in Syria has been steadily eroded during the 1950s and 1960s. In the cities the older bourgeoisie of merchants (largely Christian and Jewish) had been replaced by a new middle class of lawyers, teachers, and Government officials.

Since 1958 various measures have aimed to improve conditions for industrial and agricultural workers. Decrees of March 1964 declared that farm labourers were to receive 40 per cent of the crop (10 per cent more than the traditional share) depending on the services supplied; they could also negotiate an agreement (usually 35 per cent) with the consent of both parties. The 1961 law passed under the UAR providing for 25 per cent of all industrial and business profits to be distributed to the workers remains in force.

There has been steady improvement in health standards in the 1950s and 1960s. Malaria is now almost eliminated and diseases such as trachoma, tuberculosis, and dysentery are on the decline because of improved water facilities and rural medical treatment through clinics built by the villagers and staffed by Government employees.

The Government's aim is to make primary education free and compulsory for a period of six years. Many new schools have been opened in recent years and by the mid-1970s there were more than 1,184,000 pupils in primary schools and 34,000 teachers. There are about 424,000 pupils in secondary schools with 20,000 teachers, 22,000 pupils in vocational schools, and 9 teachers' training colleges. In 1972/73, there were 51,000 students at Damascus University and Aleppo University.

ECONOMIC SURVEY

Syria has one of the greatest economic potentials of any of the Arab states. Political instability in the 1950s and 1960s was the main factor which prevented this from being realized. In the early 1960s, successive governments reversed many of the socialist policies of the Syrian/Egyptian union period, including the nationalization of banks and businesses. After 1963 the Baathist government renationalized the banks and reimposed exchange controls. Since 1964 it has nationalized most of the industrial sector and foreign trade. The latter is handled by the state-owned trading corporation SIMEX. Since President Assad's take-over, however, the Government has taken some steps to revitalize private enterprise and to form closer links with the West European and US economies, a policy which was reinforced in early 1974. Damage from the 1973 war was estimated at $1 billion but in 1974–6 Syria received large amounts of aid as well as favourable loans and grants to help development. Exchange controls and the repatriation of funds were also liberalized to encourage Arab and foreign investment. Foreign companies may either take up an equity participation in state-controlled industries or invest directly in one of the various free zones. Although the Syrian government is unable to give any absolute guarantee that particular enterprises will not be nationalized, West German, Japanese and US investors have all signed major contracts in recent years. Closer economic relations with Jordan have also helped to open up the Syrian economy.

Agriculture

Agriculture employs about half the working population and contributes about a fifth of GDP but its share is declining in relation to industry.

The decade following independence at the end of the Second World War was a period of fast growth under a laissez-faire capitalist system. Reinvested war profits were used to develop the dry farming areas of Jazira in the north-east and to irrigate lands adjoining the Euphrates and Khabur rivers. Cotton and grain production both expanded rapidly but capital investment in agriculture began to fall off in the mid-1950s with the growth of socialist influences on the Government. There was a further decline during the Syrian/Egyptian union (1958–61) when land reform was introduced and which coincided with three consecutive failures in rainfall.

In 1976 some 94 per cent of the total cultivable area of 5.9 million hectares was under cultivation although this represents only 30 per cent of Syria's total land area. The irrigated area has increased from 284,000 hectares in 1946 to 538,000 hectares in 1967 and 547,000 hectares in 1976. Sugar beet cultivation and areas under wheat and barley have risen sharply. Areas under cotton increased from 135,200 hectares in 1953/54 to 250,400 hectares in 1971 but in recent years the proportion of cultivated land devoted to cotton has been decreasing, largely because of the increased cost of production and unfavourable weather conditions. The area dropped to 206,000 hectares in 1974 and 181,800 hectares in 1976.

Agricultural performance depends heavily on rainfall. 1972 was a record year but the 1973 October War caused dislocation to the agricultural sector and production was further aggravated by labour shortages and transportation difficulties. Output of most products fell drastically. In 1974 the economy recovered fully, with cereals production almost reaching 1972's record output. Two more good years followed with new records reached in 1976.

The Euphrates Dam at Tabqa, completed in 1978, will make possible the doubling of the present irrigated area. By the year 2000 projected land reclamation schemes should bring some 1.6 million acres of new land into use. Agreements have already been concluded with the USSR, Japan, Rumania and other countries for schemes involving irrigation, drainage and reclamation. All such land will be exploited on the basis of co-operatives and state farms.

Apart from cotton, wheat, and barley important crops are maize, sugar beet, millet, pulses, vegetables, oil seeds, and tobacco. Olives and fruit are also important and there are estimated to be 89 million fruit and olive trees, about 70 million vines and about 457,000 hectares of forests. Livestock rearing is primarily pastoral. In 1976 there were 574,000 cattle, 956,000 goats, and 6.5 million sheep, and the value of livestock production constituted about 30 per cent of agricultural output.

In 1973 all agricultural products accounted for approximately 45 per cent of total exports. In 1974, however, oil took over from cotton as Syria's largest export item, accounting for over 30 per cent.

Cotton is still the main cash crop, although output of ginned cotton has fallen from 200,000–250,000 tons in 1968–73 to 140,000–150,000 in 1977–9. The share of cotton in exports has fallen from 43 per cent in 1965 to 33 per cent in 1973 and 15.4 per cent in 1976.

Agrarian Reform

Agrarian reform was implemented in September 1969 by a decree which limited land holdings to 80 hectares of irrigated land or 300 hectares of rain-fed land per person.

Early in 1969 the Government announced the completion of the first stage of land reform in Syria whereby 708,000 hectares in 1,413 villages had been redistributed to 40,000 families. The sizes of lots distributed to new owners have been chiefly conditioned by the size of the family but limited to a maximum of 30 hectares of non-irrigated or 8 hectares of irrigated or tree-planted land. Confiscated but non-allocated land that would otherwise remain idle was rented to anyone who would farm it, and liberal credit was granted by the nationalized banks to finance the purchases of farm materials. The second stage of agrarian reform will be the development of agricultural co-operatives. In 1976 over 30 per cent of all cultivated land and 48 per cent of all cultivable land was managed by co-operatives.

Mining, Fuel, and Power

In 1974 oil exports worth about $450 million became the single largest export item. Production reached 11.2 million tons in 1976 but dropped back to 10.1 million tons in 1977. The country's proved oil reserves are estimated at 250 million tons but the true amount could be as high as 1,000 million tons.

The three main fields are at Suweidiya, Rumaila and Karachuk in north-eastern Syria, and production is under the overall control of the Syrian General Petroleum Authority. In 1975 it was decided that of the promising oil acreage 25,000 square kilometres should be set aside for exploration by the state-owned Syrian Oil Company and 50,000 square kilometres opened up to offers for service contract agreements from foreign companies. Agreements have since been made with Rumanian, Yugoslav, French, Hungarian, and UK companies. In 1968 a pipeline was opened from these fields to a terminal at Tartous on the Mediterranean.

The Homs oil refinery was opened in 1959 and has since been expanded to 100,000 b.p.d. capacity. A second refinery, with 120,000 b.p.d. capacity, is being built at Banias, and a third refinery is under consideration for the Syrian/Jordanian free zone. All distributing companies, including three foreign firms, were nationalized in March 1965. Consumption is estimated at 7.8 million tons in 1980 and 12.8 million tons by 1985.

Production at the Homs refinery was halted at the end of 1973 owing to the Israeli bombing, and capital loss was estimated at $630 million. The refinery was designed to process Iraqi crude, supplied through the pipeline from Northern Iraq but in 1976, after the breakdown of negotiations with

Iraq over oil transit dues, Iraq cancelled the transit arrangements and cut off the oil supplies, causing Syria an annual loss of some $140 million. Since then, Saudi Arabia has acted as the main supplier.

There is renewed interest in investigating the possibility that the country contains many more mineral deposits than was at one time imagined. The Ministry of Oil and Mineral Resources appointed Hunting Geology and Geophysics of the UK as consultant on the development of Syria's minerals including phosphates, uranium, chromite, and salt, and a wide range of industrial materials.

Syria's first phosphate plant was opened near Homs in September 1971 and two more phosphate mines began operations in 1974. Phosphate output amounted to 700,000 tons in 1976 and is being expanded by Rumanian, Polish and Bulgarian firms.

Total production of electric power rose from 116 million kilowatt hours in 1950 to 1,732 million kilowatt hours in 1976. Expansion is in progress at Damascus, Aleppo, and Homs, and the electrification of all villages with more than 100 inhabitants is to be completed by 1987. The biggest single project, the Euphrates Dam, which was completed in 1978, is capable of producing 800 megawatts from its eight turbines.

Manufacturing Industry

Light industry has expanded as a result of heavy protective tariffs and the availability of cotton and food products which require processing. Nationalization measures during the union with Egypt and again in 1964–5 caused a certain amount of stagnation but expansion has now been resumed with Government support.

Production trebled over the period 1970–75. Until now the most developed have been the textile industries, including spinning and weaving, knitting, dyeing, and finishing.

Production of cotton and silk yarn was 34,000 tons in 1976, compared with 20,900 tons in 1964, and of cotton and silk fabrics was 36,700 tons in 1976 compared with 25,300 tons in 1964. Now, however, industries such as cement production are gaining in importance. There are cement plants at Damascus, Aleppo, and Homs, with an estimated capacity of 2.5

million tons a year, and four more are being built by East Germany. Other industries include sugar refining, tanning, vegetable oil extraction, and canning, and the manufacture of soap, matches, glass, beer, aluminium, cables, plastic items, washing-machines, and refrigerators. Over 75 per cent of the capital investment in industry is now in the public sector; in 1975 the manufacturing sector employed 211,000 people.

Tourism

With its climate, beautiful and varied natural scenery, and exceptional range of Roman, Byzantine, and Islamic monuments, Syria has a great tourist potential which is only now being developed. The number of foreigners visiting Syria in 1976 was 1.38 million – an increase of 30 per cent on 1974. The government is aiming at a target of two million tourists and the creation of 75,000 hotel beds by 1980.

Transport and Communications

There were 14,076 kilometres of surfaced roads in 1976. Until recently the railway system, of varying gauge and built during the Ottoman empire, was of little economic use.

However, the new Latakia-Aleppo-Kamishli line linking the coast with the north and east of the country was completed in 1975, the Tartous-Akkari-Homs-Aleppo line is being reconstructed, and a line from Damascus to Homs via Mehine, and from Mehine to Palmyra, is being built. The completion of these lines will mean that Syria's main towns and the centres of phosphate mining, oil industries, and cereal and cotton production will be linked with the ports by a fast rail network. A project is also under way to link the Syrian and Iraqi rail system, which will provide the first direct Arab rail route between the Mediterranean and the Gulf but this has been held up by political difficulties. In 1977 railway freight traffic was 905 million tons-kilometres compared with 150 million in 1975.

The port of Latakia handled 1.92 million tons of cargo and Tartous 1.83 million tons in 1976. Plans for port expansion over the next few years include the doubling of Latakia's present capacity to 3.5 million tons a year and increasing that of Tartous to an annual 5 million tons. Tartous harbour will be deepened to accommodate ships of up to 50,000 tons.

There are two major airports, at Damascus and Aleppo. Over a million passengers used Damascus Airport in 1976 compared with 754,800 in 1975.

Currency and Banking

The currency is the Syrian pound, divided into 100 piastres. Exchange rates in August 1979: \$1 = £S 3.962; £1 = £S 8.72. Syria used to operate two exchange rates: the official market rate which applied to major export and import items and remittance for study abroad, and the parallel market rate which covered other trade, current invisibles and capital transactions by the public and private sectors. As a result of currency upheavals and floating rates the official rate was allowed to move in line with the parallel market rate as of August 1973.

Currency management is in the hands of the Central Bank, and policy of foreign exchange rests with the Ministry of Economics. In May 1963 all Syrian banks and Syrian branches of Arab banks were re-nationalized, having been de-nationalized a year earlier. Foreign banks have been in state hands since the first nationalization measures of 1961 during the union with Egypt. In August 1963 Syria's sixteen banks were amalgamated, and all commercial banks were merged into the newly created Commercial Bank of Syria. There is also a State Agricultural Bank, an Industrial Bank, a Real Estate Bank and a Popular Credit Bank. Since 1971 measures have been taken to encourage the repatriation of Syrian emigrant funds and the investment of Arab capital, by guaranteeing investors security against nationalization or confiscation. In March 1974 decrees were issued to end strict state control over the economy and encourage private investment. The provisions include the lifting of controls on hard currencies, the repatriation of frozen assets, tax exemptions and other ancillary benefits to foreign investors. Import restrictions were relaxed but in the latter part of 1976 some restrictions were reintroduced.

Development and the Future

In 1957 an aid agreement was signed with the USSR, under which separate agreements are still being concluded for individual projects. The USSR carries out studies and provides technical help and rouble credits for materials repayable with 2.5 per cent interest in Syrian goods or freely convertible currencies. The first ten-year plan for 1958/59 to 1967/68, launched during the union with Egypt, was superseded by a larger and more specific five-year plan running from 1960/61 to 1964/65, but by the end of 1964 only about 60 or 70 per cent of public investments had been made or considerably less in the private sector. A second five-year plan for 1965–69 aimed to double the national income level of 1960. Railways, the oil pipeline to Tartous, and the Euphrates Dam were the main features in the capital investment programmes. The third five-year plan for 1970–74, with a total investment of £S 8 billion, aimed at an annual increase in national income of 8.2 per cent with a doubling of national income in nine years. During the 1970–74 period GNP is estimated to have risen from £S 9,624 million to £S 24,942 million at current prices – a rise of 159 per cent. Even taking into account a high rate of inflation (estimated at 30 per cent in 1974) and the fact that the figures include military spending, the economy sustained a considerable rate of expansion – especially in the development of light industry. This growth was possible because of the massive injections of capital provided by Arab countries after the 1973 war.

The cost of Syria's military intervention in Lebanon in 1976 and the reduction of Saudi and other Gulf aid in addition to the loss of Iraqi oil transit dues has placed the fourth five-year plan for 1976–80 in doubt. Much will continue to depend on external political factors.

The boom years following the 1973 war saw a sharp growth in the private sector, as many middlemen, traders, and land speculators made sudden fortunes. Damascus developed for the first time what has been described as a 'boutique' economy, with luxury shops and restaurants (many of them managed by Lebanese). With the onset of a severe crisis in 1976 and 1977, as inflation raged and essential foodstuffs and housing were in short supply, the Government was obliged to take urgent measures to crack down on conspicuous consumption and corruption. But these measures were only half-heartedly pursued, partly because they affected too many individuals close to the centre of power. At the end of 1978 the debate was resumed over public versus private investment and the extent to which the 'open door' policy should be pursued. No clear stand has been adopted on economic liberalization. The country has opened itself to the West, but mainly in terms of goods and services trade. The regime is still devoted to the concept of public ownership and by 1978 only two joint ventures – one with Spain and the other with France – had been undertaken. Despite government support for the principle of private investment in such fields as tourism this has so far been minimal.

STATISTICAL APPENDICES

APPENDIX I
GENERAL DATA

1. Population Growth (estimated)
(thousands)

	1937	*1950*	*1955*	*1960*	*1965*	*1970*	*1976*
Bahrain	82	110	128	147	185	198	266
Egypt	16,008	20,393	23,063	25,948	29,600	33,330	38,228
Iran	16,200	16,276	18,325	20,182	23,428	29,260	33,592
Iraq	3,940	5,278	6,152	7,085	7,160	9,440	11,505
Israel	386[1]	1,258	1,748	2,114	2,563	2,910	3,591
Jordan	442[2]	1,269	1,437	1,695	1,976	2,320	2,779
Kuwait	n.a.	n.a.	n.a.	223	475	710	1,066
Lebanon	925	1,257	1,466	1,646	2,330	2,790	2,961
Oman	500	550	550	565	565	750	1,500
Qatar	16	20[3]	35	45	70	80	190
Saudi Arabia	6,130	n.a.	6,036	n.a.	6,750	7,740	7,013[4]
Sudan	6,880	n.a.	10,263[5]	11,770	13,540	15,700	16,126
Syria	2,628	3,215	3,681	4,555	5,300	6,250	7,595
United Arab Emirates	76	80	80	86	111	200	656[6]
Yemen (Aden)	650	100[7]	139[7]	1,155	1,240	1,440	1,749
Yemen (Sanaa)	3,990	4,500	n.a.	5,000	5,000	5,700	6,400

[1] Jewish population of Palestine only. Palestine 1,383,000.

[2] Excluding West Jordan.

[3] 1949.

[4] 1974 census.

[5] 1950.

[6] 1975 census.

[7] Aden Colony only.

Sources: United Nations (FAO, UNESCO); International Monetary Fund; World Bank.

2. Basic Economic Indicators

	Population (millions) 1976	*Area (thousands of square kilometers)*	*Per capita GNP (US dollars) 1976*	*Per capita Average Annual Growth (per cent) 1960–76*	*Index of Per capita Food Production: 1965–7 = 100 (Av. 1974–6)*
Bahrain	0.3	0.6	1,880	n.a.	n.a.
Egypt	38.2	1,001	280	1.9	104
Iran	33.6	1,648	1,930	8.2	109
Iraq	11.5	435	1,390	3.6	89
Israel	3.6	21	3,920	4.3	126
Jordan	2.8	98	610	1.6	47
Kuwait	1.1	18	15,480	–3.0	n.a.
Lebanon	3.0	10	726	3.1	95
Oman	1.5	310	530	n.a.	n.a.
Qatar	0.2	22	10,552	n.a.	n.a.
Saudi Arabia	7.5	2,150	4,480	7.0	102
Sudan	16.1	2,506	290	0.4	117
Syria	7.6	185	780	2.2	113
United Arab Emirates	0.7	84	7,500	n.a.	n.a.
Yemen (Aden)	1.7	333	280	–6.3	97
Yemen (Sanaa)	6.4	195	250	n.a.	101

3. Total Exports

($ US million f.o.b.)	*1960*	*1970*	*1971*	*1972*	*1973*	*1974*	*1975*	*1976*	*1977*
Bahrain	23	49	290	347	484	1,270	1,203	1,517	1,847
Egypt	568	762	851	813	1,000	1,672	1,567	1,609	1,993
Iran	845	2,354	3,724	3,966	6,122	21,356	20,432	23,959	24,356
Iraq	654	1,099	1,594	1,364	2,204	6,980	8,301	n.a.	n.a.
Israel	217	776	1,003	1,219	1,563	2,005	2,180	2,671	3,389
Jordan	38	116	109	164	256	529	522	706	850
Kuwait	960	1,580	2,912	3,368	5,987	10,326	9,015	10,141	10,304
Lebanon	42	184	252	382	827	1,472	n.a.	n.a.	n.a.
Oman	n.a.	136	214	218	333	1,215	1,418	1,580	1,586
Qatar	n.a.	121	337	397	624	2,013	1,805	2,206	2,050
Saudi Arabia	820	2,361	3,505	4,328	7,531	30,091	27,150	35,467	40,084
Sudan	182	298	355	347	435	480	527	555	n.a.
Syria	120	203	196	299	356	783	930	1,066	1,064
United Arab Emirates	n.a.	458	905	1,081	6,357	6,896	8,485	8,485	9,508
Yemen (Aden)	168	146	100	106	107	234	187	177	n.a.
Yemen (Sanaa)[1]	n.a.	10	7	4	8	13	11	8	11

[1] Estimates

Main Source: International Monetary Fund.

4. Total Imports

($ US million f.o.b.)	*1960*	*1970*	*1971*	*1972*	*1973*	*1974*	*1975*	*1976*	*1977*
Bahrain	27	167	301	347	466	1,005	1,070	1,490	1,813
Egypt	668	787	1,131	1,170	1,429	2,914	3,941	3,842	4,121
Iran	559	1,658	2,069	2,591	3,985	7,257	12,898	15,973	15,823
Iraq	389	508	634	667	850	2,754	4,162	3,463	n.a.
Israel	503	1,451	2,206	2,305	4,014	5,088	5,650	5,320	5,424
Jordan	410	628	650	810	1,001	1,475	2,215	3,098	4,181
Kuwait	242	625	780	809	1,119	1,770	2,510	3,797	4,703
Lebanon	311	559	690	867	1,238	2,246	n.a.	n.a.	n.a.
Oman	n.a.	64	104	160	234	712	1,084	1,080	1,296
Qatar	28	64	105	125	176	242	363	743	1,095
Saudi Arabia	235	693	866	1,275	2,103	3,713	5,998	10,396	14,355
Sudan	183	288	399	403	391	508	908	979	n.a.
Syria	120	203	381	445	569	1,039	1,425	2,102	2,592
United Arab Emirates	n.a.	276	305	439	745	1,542	2,408	3,010	4,095
Yemen (Aden)	214	201	428	423	505	1,050	n.a.	n.a.	n.a.
Yemen (Sanaa)	n.a.	52	n.a.	n.a.	n.a.	423	538	1,042	1,580

Main Source: International Monetary Fund.

APPENDIX II
OIL

1. World 'Published Proved' Reserves at End 1977

	Oil Billion Tonnes	Oil Share of Total	Oil Billion Barrels	Natural Gas Trillion[1] Cubic Feet	Natural Gas Share of Total	Natural Gas Trillion[1] Cubic Metres
USA	4.6	5.4%	35.5	208.8	8.3%	5.9
Canada	1.0	1.2%	7.9	59.5	2.4%	1.7
Total North America	**5.6**	**6.6%**	**43.4**	**268.3**	**10.7%**	**7.6**
Latin America	5.7	6.2%	40.4	108.6	4.3%	3.1
Total Western Hemisphere	**11.3**	**12.8%**	**83.8**	**376.9**	**15.0%**	**10.7**
Western Europe	3.7	4.2%	27.2	138.7	5.5%	3.9
Middle East	49.7	55.9%	365.8	719.1	28.5%	20.4
Africa	7.9	9.0%	59.2	207.5	8.2%	5.9
USSR	10.2	11.5%	75.0	920.0	36.5%	26.0
Eastern Europe	0.4	0.5%	3.0	10.0	0.4%	0.3
China	2.7	3.1%	20.0	25.0	1.0%	0.7
Other Eastern Hemisphere	2.7	3.0%	19.7	122.7	4.9%	3.5
Total Eastern Hemisphere	**77.3**	**87.2%**	**569.9**	**2143.0**	**85.0%**	**60.7**
World (Excl. USSR, E. Europe, and China)	**75.3**	**84.9%**	**555.7**	**1564.9**	**62.1%**	**44.4**
World	**88.6**	**100.0%**	**653.7**	**2519.9**	**100.0%**	**71.4**

[1] Trillion = 10^{12}; one million million.

Sources: USA – American Petroleum Institute and American Gas Association; Canada – Canadian Petroleum Association; All other areas – Estimates published by the *'Oil & Gas Journal'* (Worldwide Oil issue, 26 December, 1977).

Notes:

a. Proved crude oil reserves are generally taken to be the volume of oil remaining in the ground which geological and engineering information indicate with reasonable certainty to be recoverable in the future from known reservoirs under existing economic and operating conditions.

b. The recovery factor, i.e. the relationship between proved reserves and total oil in place, varies according to local conditions and can vary in time with economic and technological changes.

c. For the USA and Canada the crude-oil data include oil which it is estimated can be recovered from proved natural gas reserves.

d. The data exclude the oil content of shales and tar sands.

e. Percentages are based on volume.

2. World Oil Consumption 1977 and 1976

	(Million Tonnes)		*1977 Share of*	*1977 over*	*Annual Average Change*	*(Thousands of Barrels Daily)*	
	1977	*1976*	*Total*	*1976*	*1972–7*	*1977*	*1976*
USA	867.3	822.4	29.2%	+ 5.5%	+ 2.3%	17,945 [1]	16,980 [1]
Canada	85.4	85.9	2.9%	- 0.6%	+ 1.5%	1,795	1,790
Total North America	**952.7**	**908.3**	**32.1%**	**+ 4.9%**	**+ 2.2%**	**19,740**	**18,770**
Latin America	192.1	186.5	6.5%	+ 3.0%	+ 4.9%	3,990	3,850
Total Western Hemisphere	**1,144.8**	**1,094.8**	**38.6%**	**+ 4.6%**	**+ 2.6%**	**23,730**	**22,620**
Austria	11.0	11.5	0.4%	- 4.4%	+ 0.3%	220	280
Belgium and Luxembourg	28.0	28.0	0.9%	+ 0.1%	- 2.0%	565	560
Denmark	16.6	16.7	0.6%	- 1.0%	- 3.2%	330	335
Finland	12.5	12.8	0.4%	- 2.5%	+ 1.1%	250	255
France	114.6	119.5	3.9%	- 4.1%	+ 0.1%	2,350	2,430
Greece	10.6	10.6	0.4%	+ 0.6%	+ 4.3%	210	210
Iceland	0.6	0.6	—	+ 1.0%	+ 1.3%	10	10
Republic of Ireland	5.6	5.3	0.2%	+ 6.0%	+ 2.4%	115	105
Italy	95.9	98.8	3.2%	- 2.9%	- 0.5%	1,940	2,065
Netherlands	37.6	39.2	1.3%	- 4.0%	- 1.3%	770	795
Norway	8.8	8.6	0.3%	+ 2.7%	+ 0.6%	175	175
Portugal	7.1	7.1	0.2%	—	+ 4.1%	150	145
Spain	44.9	48.3	1.5%	- 7.2%	+ 6.6%	920	970
Sweden	28.2	29.6	0.9%	- 5.0%	- 0.3%	565	590

1. US processing gain has been deducted from total domestic product demand.

2. World Oil Consumption 1977 and 1977 continued

Switzerland	13.1	13.0	0.4%	+ 0.5%	- 0.8%	270	270
Turkey	16.8	15.4	0.6%	+ 9.0%	+10.9%	340	310
United Kingdom	92.3	91.5	3.1%	+ 0.9%	- 3.4%	1,895	1,865
West Germany	137.1	138.9	4.6%	- 1.3%	- 0.5%	2,855	2,855
Yugoslavia	13.9	13.2	0.5%	+ 4.7%	+ 6.5%	280	265
Cyprus/Gibraltar/Malta	1.4	1.3	–	+ 9.2%	+ 1.9%	25	25
Total Western Europe	**696.6**	709.9	**23.4%**	**- 1.9%**	- 0.1%	**14,235**	**14,465**
Middle East	79.2	74.7	2.7%	- 6.0%	+ 5.8%	1,570	1,475
Africa	57.0	55.2	1.9%	+ 3.2%	+ 5.1%	1,165	1,135
South Asia	34.5	32.6	1.2%	+ 5.7%	+ 2.3%	705	665
South East Asia	94.3	88.7	3.2%	+ 6.3%	+ 5.8%	1,885	1,770
Japan	260.1	253.5	8.8%	+ 2.6%	+ 2.1%	5,345	5,190
Australasia	37.9	36.6	1.3%	+ 3.4%	+ 3.3%	795	770
USSR	395.0	380.0	13.0%	+ 3.9%	+ 5.9%	8,025	7,670
Eastern Europe	100.0	90.0	3.4%	+11.1%	+ 8.3%	2,060	1,845
China	73.0	66.0	2.5%	+10.6%	+ 20.6%	1,465	1,320
Total Eastern Hemisphere	**1,827.6**	**1,787.2**	**61.4%**	**+ 2.3%**	**+ 3.1%**	**37,250**	**36,305**
World (excluding USSR, E. Europe, and China)	**2,404.4**	**2,346.0**	81.1%	**+ 2.5%**	**+ 2.0%**	**49,430**	48,090
World	**2,972.4**	**2,882.0**	**100.0%**	**+ 3.1%**	**+ 2.9%**	**60,980**	**58,925**

1 U.S. processing gain has been deducted from total domestic product demand.

3. Middle East Proved Oil Reserves, End 1978
(million barrels)

Saudi Arabia	165,700	Qatar	4,000
Kuwait	66,200	Oman	2,500
Iran	59,000	Syria	2,080
Iraq	32,100	Egypt	3,200
Abu Dhabi	30,000	Dubai	1,300
Libya	24,300	Bahrain	250
Neutral Zone	6,480	Sharja	16
	Israel	1	
	Total	397,127	

Source: *Oil & Gas Journal*

4. Production of Crude Oil
(thousands of b.p.d.)

	First commercial production	*1973*	*1974*	*1975*	*1976*	*1977*	*1978*
Saudi Arabia	1938	7,344	8,212	6,827	8,344	9,017	8,066
Iran	1912	5,897	6,057	5,386	5,881	5,663	5,234
Iraq	1934	1,932	1,849	2,262	2,415	2,493	2,629
Libya	1961	2,182	1,521	1,510	1,933	2,078	1,977
Kuwait	1946	2,753	2,276	1,838	1,915	1,783	1,880
Abu Dhabi	1962	1,307	1,411	1,397	1,596	1,655	1,447
Qatar	1949	570	521	439	497	435	482
Egypt	1909	255	227	300	327	415	482
Neutral Zone	1954	527	543	495	466	350	434
Oman	1967	293	291	340	366	339	314
Dubai	1969	220	242	254	317	320	362
Syria	1968	110	123	183	192	174	171
Bahrain	1934	68	67	61	58	58	55
Sharja	1974	–	28	38	37	28	22
Israel	1955	1	1	1	1	1	1
Total		23,439	23,369	21,331	24,345	24,576	23,556

Sources: BP Statistical Review; companies' annual reports and production announcements; *Petroleum Economist.*

5. Revenues from Oil of Main Producing Countries
($ US million)

	1973	*1974*	*1975*	*1976*	*1977*	*1978*[2]
Saudi Arabia	4,340	22,574	25,676	30,748	42,384	35,800
Iran[1]	4,399	17,155	18,440	19,020	21,020	19,300
Iraq	1,843	5,700	7,500	8,200	9,630	10,150
Kuwait[1]	1,780	6,545	6,420	6,860	8,900	9,750
United Arab Emirates	900	5,536	6,000	7,200	9,030	8,200
Libya	2,223	6,000	5,100	7,500	8,850	8,420
Qatar	409	1,600	1,690	2,020	1,994	2,200
Oman	177	857	1,100	1,340	1,390	1,270
Bahrain	50	178	287	396	400	400
Total	16,121	66,145	72,213	83,284	103,598	95,490

[1] Calculated from official figures for fiscal years.

[2] Estimated.

READING LIST

1. GENERAL

A. Historical

Cambridge History of Islam (2 vols., Cambridge, 1971).

Coulson, N.J., *History of Islamic Law* (Edinburgh, 1964).

Gibb, H.A.R., *Mohammedanism* (2nd rev. edn., London, 1969).

Goitein, S.D.F., *Jews and Arabs: Their Contacts through the Ages* (New York, 1955).

Hitti, P.K., *History of the Arabs* (London, 1964).

Hurewitz, J. C., *Diplomacy in the New and Middle East: a Documentary Record*, vol. 1: *1535–1914*; vol. 2: *1914–56* (Princeton, 1956).

Levy, R., *The Social Structure of Islam* (Cambridge, 1957).

Lewis, B., *The Arabs in History* (4th edn., London, 1968).

MacDonald, D.B., *Development of Muslim Theology, Jurisprudence and Constitutional Theory* (Lahore, 1960).

Mez, A., *The Renaissance of Islam*, tr. by S.K. Bakhsh and D.S. Margoliouth (London, 1937).

Schacht, J., and Botsworth, C.E., eds., *The Legacy of Islam* (Oxford, 1974).

Shaban, M.A., *Islamic History A.D. 600–750: a New Interpretation* (Cambridge, 1971).

Toynbee, A.J., *A Study of History: Abridgement of vols. 1–6*, by D.C. Somervell (London, 1946).

Von Grunebaum, G.E., *Mediaeval Islam* (2nd edn., Chicago, 1953).

B. Modern Times

Allen, R., *Imperialism and Nationalism in the Fertile Crescent* (New York and London, 1974).

Antonius, G., *The Arab Awakening: the Story of the Arab National Movement* (Beirut, 1962).

Arberry, A.J., ed., *Religion in the Middle East* (2 vols., Cambridge, 1969).

Baer, G., *Population and Society in the Arab East* (London, 1964).

Be'eri, E., *Army Officers in Arab Politics and Society* (London, 1970).

Berger, M., *The Arab World Today* (London, 1962).

Blaisdell, D.C., *European Financial Control in the Ottoman Empire* (New York, 1966).

Berque, J., *The Arabs: their History and Future* (London, 1964).

Bonne, A., *State and Economics in the Middle East* (2nd edn., London, 1960).

Busch, B.C., *Britain, India and the Arabs* (Berkeley, 1971).

Davis, H.M., *Constitutions, Electoral Laws, Treaties of States in the Near and Middle East* (Cambridge, 1947).
Europa Publications, *The Middle East and North Africa* (London, annually 1948-).
Fernea, E.W. and Berzigan, B.Q., *Middle Eastern Women Speak* (Austin, 1977).
Fisher, S.N., ed., *Social Forces in the Middle East* (New York, 1968).
Fisher, W.B., *The Middle East: a Physical, Social and Regional Geography* (6th edn., London, 1971).
Haim, S.G., ed., *Arab Nationalism, an Anthology* (Berkeley, 1974).
Halpern, M., *The Politics of Social Change in the Middle East* (Princeton, 1963).
Heikal, M., *Sphinx and Commissar* (London, 1978).
Hershlag, Z.Y., *Contemporary Economic Structure of the Middle East* (Leiden, 1971).
Hirst, D., *The Gun and the Olive Branch: The Roots of Violence in the Middle East* (London, 1977).
History of the Second World War: the Mediterranean and the Middle East (vol. 1. London, 1954).
Hoskins, H.L., *British Routes to India* (London, 1966).
Hourani, A.H., *Minorities in the Arab World* (London, 1979).
– *Arabic Thought in the Liberal Age 1798–1939* (London, 1970).
Howard, H.N., *The Partition of Turkey: a Diplomatic History 1913–23* (Oklahoma, 1931).
Kedourie, E., *England and the Middle East: the Destruction of the Ottoman Empire, 1914–21* (London, 1956).
– *In the Anglo-Arab Labyrinth: the McMahon-Husayn Correspondence and its Interpretations* (Cambridge, 1976).
Kerr, M.H., *The Arab Cold War* (3rd edn., New York, 1971).
Laqueur, W.Z., *Communism and Nationalism in the Middle East* (London, 1956).
– *The Road to War, 1967* (London, 1967).
– *Confrontation, The Middle East War and World Politics* (London, 1974).
Lawrence, T. E., *The Seven Pillars of Wisdom* (London, 1935).
Legum, C., ed., *Middle East Contemporary Survey, Vol. 1: 1976–77* (London and New York, 1978).
Lenczowski, G., *The Middle East in World Affairs* (2nd edn., Ithaca, NY, 1956).
Longrigg, S. H., *Oil in the Middle East* (3rd edn., London, 1968).
Mansfield, P., *The Arabs* (London, 1976).
Monroe, E., *Britain's Moment in the Middle East* (London, 1963).
Nutting, A., *The Arabs* (London, 1974).
Polk, W. R., *The United States and the Arab World* (Cambridge, Mass., 1965).
– and Chambers, R. L., eds., *Beginnings of Modernization in the Middle East; the Nineteenth Century* (Chicago, 1968).
Rahman, F., *Islam* (London, 1966).
Rodinson, M., *Islam and Capitalism* (London, 1974).

Rosenthal, E. I. J., *Islam in the National State* (Cambridge, 1965).
Smith, W. C., *Islam in Modern History* (Princeton, 1957).
Stocking, G. W., *Middle East Oil* (London, 1971).
Tibawi, A. L., *Anglo-Arab Relations and the Question of Palestine* (London, 1977).
Von Grunebaum, G. E., ed., *Unity and Variety in Muslim Civilization* (Chicago, 1956).
Warriner, D., *Land Reform and Development in the Middle East: a Study of Egypt, Syria and Iraq* (2nd edn., London, 1962).
– *Land Reform in Principle and Practice* (Oxford, 1968).
Zeine, Z. N., *The Emergence of Arab Nationalism* (Beirut, 1966).

2. ARABIA

Al-Farsy, F., *Saudi Arabia: a Case Study in Development* (London, 1978).
Busch, B. C., *Britain and the Persian Gulf, 1894–1914* (Berkeley, 1967).
De Gaury, G., *Rulers of Mecca* (London, 1951).
Dickson, H. R. P., *The Arab of the Desert: a Glimpse into Badawin Life in Kuwait and Sa'udi Arabia* (London, 1949).
– *Kuwait and her Neighbours*, ed. by C. Witting (London, 1956).
Doughty, C. M., *Travels in Arabia Deserta* (2 vols., London, 1936).
Graham, H., *Arabian Time Machine* (London, 1978).
Habib, J. S., *Ibn Sa'ud's Warriors of Islam: the Ikhwan of Najd and their Role in the Creation of the Sa'udi Kingdom 1910–1930* (Leiden, 1978).
Halliday, F., *Arabia Without Sultans* (Harmondsworth, 1974).
Hawley, D., *The Trucial States* (London, 1970).
– *Oman and its Renaissance* (London, 1977).
Hobday, P., *Saudi Arabia Today: an Introduction to the Richest Oil Power* (London, 1978).
Holden, D., *Farewell to Arabia* (London, 1966).
Hopwood, D., ed., *The Arabian Peninsula* (London, 1972).
Ingrams, D., *A Time in Arabia* (London, 1970).
Ingrams, H., *Arabia and the Isles* (3rd edn., London, 1966).
Little, T., *South Arabia: Area of Conflict* (London, 1968).
Marlowe, J., *The Persian Gulf in the Twentieth Century* (London, 1962).
Meulen, D. van der, *Aden to the Hadhramaut* (London, 1947).
Monroe, E., *Philby of Arabia* (London, 1973).
Morris, J., *Sultan in Oman* (London, 1957).
Philby, H. St. J. B., *Arabian Jubilee* (London, 1952).
– *Forty Years In the Wilderness* (London, 1957).
– *Saudi Arabia* (London, 1968).
Rumaihi, M. G., *Bahrain: Social and Political Change Since the First World War* (London, 1976).
Sanger, R., *The Arabian Peninsula* (Ithaca, NY, 1971).
Scott, H., *In the High Yemen* (London, 1942).
Stephens, R., *The Arabs' New Frontier* (London, 1973).
Trevaskis, Sir K., *Shades of Amber* (London, 1968).

Twitchell, K. S., *Saudi Arabia* (3rd edn, Princeton, 1958).
Wenner, M. W., *Modern Yemen, 1918–66* (Baltimore, 1967).
Winstone, H. V. F. and Freeth, Z., *Kuwait: Prospect and Reality* (London, 1979).

3. EGYPT

Abdel-Malek, A., *Egypt: Military Society* (New York, 1968).
Baring, E., 1st Earl of Cromer, *Modern Egypt* (2 vols., London, 1908).
Berque, J., *Egypt, Imperialism and Revolution* (London, 1972).
Hansen, B. and Marzouk, G. A., *Development and Economic Policy in the UAR* (Amsterdam, 1968).
Heikal, M., *The Road to Ramadan* (London, 1975).
Hurst, H. E., *The Nile* (London, 1952).
Issawi, C., *Egypt in Revolution* (London, 1963).
– *Egypt in Revolution* (London, 1963).
Lacouture, J., *Nasser* trs. from the French by D. Hofstadter (London, 1973).
Lloyd, Lord, *Egypt since Cromer* (2 vols., London, 1934).
Little, T., *Modern Egypt* (London, 1967).
Love, K., *Suez, the Twice-Fought War* (London, 1969).
Lutfi al-Sayyid, A., *Egypt's Liberal Experiment* (Berkeley, 1977).
Mabro, R., *The Egyptian Economy 1952–1972* (Oxford, 1974).
Mansfield, P., *Nasser's Egypt* (2nd edn., London, 1969).
– *The British in Egypt* (London, 1971).
Marlowe, J., *Anglo-Egyptian Relations, 1800–1953* (London, 1953).
Mitchell, R. P., *The Society of Muslim Brothers* (London, 1969).
Nasser, Gamal Abdul, *Egypt's Liberation: the Philosophy of the Revolution* (Buffalo, 1959).
O'Brien, P. K., *The Revolution in Egypt's Economic System: from Private Enterprise to Socialism, 1952–1963* (London, 1966).
Richmond, J. C. B., *Egypt 1798–1952: her advance towards a modern identity* (London, 1977).
Sadat, A., *Revolt on the Nile* (London, 1957).
– *In Search of Identity: an autobiography* (London, 1978).
Stephens, R., *Nasser* (London, 1971).
Vatikiotis, P. J., *The Modern History of Egypt* (London, 1969).
– *Nasser and his Generation* (London, 1978).

4. IRAN

Avery, P. W., *Modern Iran* (2nd edn., London, 1967).
Banani, A., *The Modernization of Iran, 1921–1941* (Stanford, 1961).
Bharier, J., *Economic Development in Iran, 1900–1970* (London, 1971).
Binder, L., *Iran: Political Development in a Changing Society* (Berkeley, 1962).

Cambridge History of Iran, vols. 1–5 (8 to be published) (Cambridge, 1968–).
Curzon, G. N., 1st Earl of Kedleston, *Persia and the Persian Question* (2 vols., London, 1891, repr. 1966).
Cottam, R. W., *Nationalism in Iran* (Pittsburgh, 1964).
Elwell-Sutton, L. P., *Persian Oil–a Study in Power Politics* (London, 1955).
Graham, R., *Iran: the Illusion of Power* (London, 1978).
Halliday, F., *Iran: Dictatorship and Development* (Harmondsworth, 1979).
Lambton, A. K. S., *Landlord and Peasant in Persia* (London, 1953).
– *The Persian Land Reform, 1962–1966* (Oxford, 1969).
Millspaugh, A. C., *Americans in Persia* (Washington, 1946).
Pahlavi, M. R. Shah, *Mission for My Country* (London, 1960).
Sykes, Sir P. M., *History of Persia* (3rd edn., 2 vols., London, 1930).

5. IRAQ

Bell, G., *Letters* (2 vols., London, 1927).
Birdwood, Lord, *Nuri as-Said* (London, 1970).
Dann, U., *Iraq under Qassem, a Political History, 1958–1963* (London, 1969).
Edmonds, C. J., *Kurds, Turks and Arabs* (London, 1957).
Foster, H. A., *The Making of Modern Iraq* (London, 1936).
Haseeb, K., *The National Income of Iraq, 1953–1961* (Oxford, 1964).
IBRD, *The Economic Development of Iraq* (Baltimore, 1952).
Khadduri, M., *Independent Iraq, 1932–1958* (2nd edn., London, 1960).
– *Republican Iraq; a Study in Iraqi Politics since the Revolution of 1958* (London, 1969).
– *Socialist Iraq: a Study in Iraqi Politics since 1968* (Washington D.C., 1978).
Longrigg, S. H., *Iraq, 1900 to 1950* (London, 1953).
Main, E., *Iraq from Mandate to Independence* (London, 1935).
Penrose, E. and E. F., *Iraq: International Relations and National Development* (London, 1978).
Sluglett, P., *Britain and Iraq, 1914–1932* (London, 1976).
Wilson, Sir A. T., *Loyalties: Mesopotamia, 1914–17* (London, 1930).
– *Mesopotamia 1917–30: a Clash of Loyalties* (London, 1931).

6. ISRAEL

Agress, E., *Golda Meir* (London, 1969).
Barbour, N., *Nisi Dominus, a Survey of the Palestine Controversy* (Beirut, 1969).
Bar-Zohar, M., *The Armed Prophet: a Biography of Ben-Gurion* (London, 1967).
Bentwich, N., *Israel: Two Fateful Years, 1967–69* (London, 1969).

Brecher, M., *Decisions in Israel's Foreign Policy* (London, 1974).
Burns, E. L. M., *Between Arab and Israeli* (London, 1962).
Davis, J. H., *The Evasive Peace. A Study of the Zionist–Arab Problem* (London, 1968).
Eisenstadt, S. N., *Israeli Society* (London, 1969).
Horowitz, D., *The Economics of Israel* (Oxford, 1967).
Laqueur, W. Z., *A History of Zionism* (London, 1972).
Lucas, N., *The Modern History of Israel* (London, 1974; New York, 1977).
O'Ballance, E., *The Arab–Israeli War, 1948* (London, 1956).
Perlmutter, A., *Military and Politics in Israel: Nation-building and Role Expansion* (London, 1969).
Sachar, M., *A History of Israel from the rise of Zionism to our time* (Oxford, 1977).
Stein, L., *The Balfour Declaration* (London, 1961).
Sykes, C., *Crossroads to Israel* (London, 1965).
Weizmann, C., *Trial and Error* (London, 1949).

7. JORDAN

Abdullah Ibn al-Hussein, *The Memoirs of King Abdullah of Transjordan*, ed. by P. P. Graves (London, 1950).
– *My Memoirs Completed* (*al Takmilah*), trs. by H. W. Glidden (London, 1978).
Dearden, A., *Jordan* (London, 1958).
Glubb, J. B., *The Story of the Arab Legion* (London, 1948).
– *A Soldier with the Arabs* (London, 1957).
Harris, G. L., *Jordan: its People, its Society, its Culture* (New Haven, 1958).
Hussein, (King of Jordan), *Uneasy Lies the Head* (London, 1962).
Kirkbride, Sir A., *A Crackle of Thorns* (London, 1956).
Sinai, A. and Pollack, A., eds., *The Hashemite Kingdom of Jordan and the West Bank: Handbook* (New York, 1977).
Vatikiotis, P. J., *Politics and the Military in Jordan; a Study of the Arab Legion, 1921–1957* (London, 1967).

8. LEBANON (See 10. Syria and Lebanon)

9. SUDAN

Abbas, M., *The Sudan Question: the Dispute over the Anglo-Egyptian Condominium, 1884–1951* (London, 1952).
Abd al-Rahim, M., *Imperialism and Nationalism in the Sudan* (Oxford, 1969).
Albino, Oliver, *The Sudan, a Southern Viewpoint* (London, 1970).

Beshai, A. A., *Export Performance and Economic Development in the Sudan* (London, 1976).
Beshir, M. O., *The Southern Sudan* (London, 1968).
– *Revolution and Nationalism in the Sudan* (London, 1977).

10. SYRIA AND LEBANON

Binder, L., ed., *Politics in Lebanon* (New York, 1966).
Hitti, P. K., *History of Syria, including Lebanon and Palestine* (London, 1951).
Hourani, A. H., *Syria and Lebanon* (Beirut, 1968).
Hudson, M. C., *The Precarious Republic: Political Modernization in Lebanon* (New York, 1968).
Lammens, H., *La Syrie* (2 vols., Beirut, 1921).
Longrigg, S. H., *Syria and Lebanon under French Mandate* (Beirut, 1968).
Rabinovich, I., *Syria under the Ba'th 1963–1966: the Army-Party Symbiosis* (Jerusalem, 1972).
Salibi, K. S., *A Modern History of Lebanon* (London, 1965).
– *Crossroads to Civil War: Lebanon 1958–1978* (Delmar, 1976).
Seale, P., *The Struggle for Syria: a Study of Post-War Arab Politics, 1945–1958* (London, 1965).
Tibawi, A. L., *A Modern History of Syria including Lebanon and Palestine* (London, 1969).
Van Dam, N., *The Struggle for Power in Syria,* London, 1979).
Ziadeh, N. A., *Syria and Lebanon* (London, 1956).

JOURNALS WHICH DEAL WHOLLY OR PARTLY WITH THE MIDDLE EAST

Asian Affairs. London.
International Affairs (quarterly) and *The World Today* (monthly).
International Journal of Middle East Studies (quarterly). London, from 1970.
Journal of Palestine Studies (quarterly). Beirut, from 1971.
Middle East International (fortnightly). from 1971.
Middle East Journal (quarterly). Washington, from 1947.
Middle East Studies (three yearly). London, from 1964.
L'Orient (quarterly). Paris, from 1957.
Oriente Moderno (quarterly). Rome, from 1921.
also
Palestine Monographs of the Palestine Research Centre, Beirut.

INDEX